Handbook of Psychotherapy for
Anorexia Nervosa and Bulimia

Edited by

David M. Garner / Paul E. Garfinkel

Toronto General Hospital and the University of Toronto

Foreword by Gerald Russell

THE GUILFORD PRESS
New York • London

© 1985 The Guilford Press
A Division of Guilford Publications, Inc.
200 Park Avenue South, New York, N.Y. 10003

Printed in the United States of America

LIBRARY OF CONGRESS CATALOGING IN PUBLICATION DATA
Main entry under title:

Handbook of psychotherapy for anorexia nervosa and bulimia.

  Includes bibliographies and index.
  1. Anorexia nervosa. 2. Bulimarexia. I. Garner,
David M., 1947–   II. Garfinkel, Paul E., 1946–
[DNLM: 1. Anorexia Nervosa—therapy. 2. Appetite
Disorders—therapy. 3. Psychotherapy—methods. WM 175
H236]
RC552.A5H36   1985   616.85′2   84-19332
ISBN 0-89862-642-0

Although we recognize that it is not customary to dedicate the works of others in an edited volume we would like to beg this indulgence in dedicating this volume to Professor Hilde Bruch.

Contributors

Arnold E. Andersen, MD, Henry Phipps Psychiatric Service, The Johns Hopkins Medical Institutions, Baltimore, Maryland

Mary Jo Barrett, MSW, Midwest Family Resources, Chicago, Illinois

Kelly M. Bemis, BA, Department of Psychology, University of Minnesota, Minneapolis, Minnesota

Belinda Berkowitz, PhD, The Bridge Counseling Center; Center for the Treatment of Eating Disorders; and The National Anorexic Aid Society, Columbus, Ohio

Hilde Bruch, MD, Department of Psychiatry, Baylor College of Medicine, Houston, Texas

Paula Butterfield, PhD, The Bridge Counseling Center; Center for the Treatment of Eating Disorders; and The National Anorexic Aid Society, Columbus, Ohio

Donald V. Coscina, PhD, Section of Biopsychology, Clarke Institute of Psychiatry; and Departments of Psychiatry and Psychology, University of Toronto, Toronto, Ontario, Canada

Laurene E. Davis, RN, Department of Psychiatry, University Hospitals, Minneapolis, Minnesota

Elke D. Eckert, MD, Department of Psychiatry, University Hospitals, Minneapolis, Minnesota

Amy Baker Enright, MA, The Bridge Counseling Center; Center for the Treatment of Eating Disorders; and The National Anorexic Aid Society, Columbus, Ohio

Christopher G. Fairburn, MA, MPhil, MRCPsych, Department of Psychiatry, University of Oxford, Warneford Hospital, Oxford, England

Paul E. Garfinkel, MD, Department of Psychiatry, Toronto General Hospital; and the University of Toronto, Toronto, Ontario, Canada

David M. Garner, PhD, Department of Psychiatry, Toronto General Hospital; and the University of Toronto, Toronto, Ontario, Canada

Peter N. Gilchrist, MB, BS, MRANZCP, DipPsychother, Flinders Medical Centre, Bedford Park, South Australia

Gretchen Goff, MPH, Department of Psychiatry, University Hospitals, Minneapolis, Minnesota

Alan Goodsitt, MD, Department of Psychiatry and Behavioral Sciences, Northwestern University Medical School; Institute of Psychiatry, Northwestern Memorial Hospital; and Psychosomatic and Psychiatric Institute, Michael Reese Hospital and Medical Center, Chicago, Illinois

Alyson Hall, MB, BS, MRCPsych, Consultant in Child and Adolescent Psychiatry, The London Hospital, London, England

Katherine A. Halmi, MD, Department of Psychiatry and Eating Disorder Program, Cornell University Medical College; and The New York Hospital — Westchester Division, White Plains, New York

Dorothy Hatsukami, PhD, Department of Psychiatry, University Hospitals, Minneapolis, Minnesota

Craig Johnson, PhD, Institute of Psychiatry, Eating Disorders Program, Northwestern University Medical School, Northwestern Memorial Hospital, Chicago, Illinois

Ross S. Kalucy, MRCPsych, FRACP, FRANZCP, MANZAGP, FACRM, Department of Psychiatry, The Flinders University of South Australia, Bedford Park, South Australia

Sidney Kennedy, MB, BCh, Department of Psychiatry, Toronto General Hospital; and the University of Toronto, Toronto, Ontario, Canada

J. Hubert Lacey, MB, ChB, MPhil, MRCPsych, Academic Department of Psychiatry, St. George's Hospital Medical School, London, England

Harold Leitenberg, PhD, Department of Psychology, University of Vermont, Burlington, Vermont

Ronald Liebman, MD, Philadelphia Child Guidance Clinic, Children's Hospital of Philadelphia; and Departments of Child Psychiatry and Pediatrics, University of Pennsylvania School of Medicine, Philadelphia, Pennsylvania

Alexander C. McFarlane, MB, BS, MRANZCP, DipPsychother, The Flinders University of South Australia, Bedford Park, South Australia

Catherine M. McFarlane, MB, BS, MRANZCP, Flinders Medical Centre, Bedford Park, South Australia

James E. Mitchell, MD, Department of Psychiatry, University Hospitals, Minneapolis, Minnesota

Cathy L. Morse, RN, BSN, Henry Phipps Psychiatric Service, The Johns Hopkins Medical Institutions, Baltimore, Maryland

Marion P. Olmsted, MA, Department of Psychiatry, Toronto General Hospital, Toronto, Ontario, Canada

Susie Orbach, The Women's Therapy Centre Institute, New York, New York; and The Women's Therapy Centre, London, England

Richard L. Pyle, MD, Department of Psychiatry, University Hospitals, Minneapolis, Minnesota

Wendi Rockert, BA, Department of Psychiatry, Toronto General Hospital, Toronto, Ontario, Canada

James C. Rosen, PhD, Department of Psychology, University of Vermont, Burlington, Vermont

George Saba, PhD, Behavior Sciences Program, Division of Family and Community Medicine, University of California School of Medicine, San Francisco, California

Karen S. Santmyer, RN, BSN, Henry Phipps Psychiatric Service, The Johns Hopkins Medical Institutions, Baltimore, Maryland

John Sargent, MD, Philadelphia Child Guidance Clinic, Children's Hospital of Philadelphia; and Departments of Child Psychiatry and Pediatrics, University of Pennsylvania School of Medicine, Philadelphia, Pennsylvania

Richard C. Schwartz, PhD, Family Systems Program, Institute for Juvenile Research; and Department of Psychiatry, University of Illinois College of Medicine, Chicago, Illinois

Michael Silver, MD, Philadelphia Child Guidance Clinic, Children's Hospital of Philadelphia; and Department of Psychiatry, University of Pennsylvania School of Medicine, Philadelphia, Pennsylvania

Michael Strober, PhD, Teenage Eating Disorders Program, Neuropsychiatric Institute, School of Medicine, University of California at Los Angeles, Los Angeles, California

O. Wayne Wooley, PhD, Eating Disorders Clinic, Psychiatry Department, University of Cincinnati Medical Center, Cincinnati, Ohio

Susan C. Wooley, PhD, Eating Disorders Clinic, Psychiatry Department, University of Cincinnati Medical Center, Cincinnati, Ohio

Joel Yager, MD, Adult Outpatient Eating Disorders Program, Neuropsychiatric Institute, School of Medicine, University of California at Los Angeles, Los Angeles, California

Foreword

The title of this book indicates that it is a handbook, a word that should not be taken too literally in view of the volume's size and weight. Instead, the reader should expect to meet a series of exhaustive and comprehensive reviews on the chosen subject — the psychotherapy of patients with anorexia nervosa and bulimia. It is noteworthy that the treatment of these patients is restricted in this *Handbook* to their psychotherapy. Thus the nutritional, endocrine, and pharmacological methods of treatment are excluded, and it is as well to explain this exclusion. First, it is true that the place of these "physical" methods of treatment is more readily defined and is generally accepted as limited, at least for the time being. Moreover, the psychotherapy of patients with eating disorders has hitherto been neglected and requires a careful exposition of its underlying principles and its different methods. The increased incidence of these eating disorders during recent decades has stimulated the interest of professional workers from a wide range of nonmedical disciplines, for whom psychotherapeutic methods have a greater appeal. There has been a tendency to treat these patients more often as outpatients, perhaps of necessity in view of limited resources, and this setting is more suited to the use of the psychotherapies. Yet the ward setting for the treatment of anorexic patients is covered thoroughly in the *Handbook*, with an appropriate emphasis on the setting's psychotherapeutic components.

The authors have presented their material in different ways. Some have given a full account of their theoretical bases; others have preferred to adopt a more empirical approach. All, however, have endeavored to provide practical guidance on the strategies and methods employed when engaging their patients in their chosen form of psychotherapy. Certain methods of treatment have been covered by more than one set of authors, thus enabling the reader to exercise some selection in the methods he or she wishes to use. Every contributor gives the benefit of his or her personal experience. The handbook thus covers the full range of the psychotherapies — individual, group, and family therapy; cognitive and behavioral methods of psychological treatment; and methods more specifically adapted to the special needs of patients suffering from anorexia nervosa and bulimic disorders, including self-help and support groups.

What is the present status of these various psychotherapies? The aim of the editors has been to compile a thorough exposition of what is currently available, and thus to delineate more clearly specific treatment strategies relying on the psychotherapeutic approach. A perceptive reader of the *Handbook* may detect a relative lack of objective evidence in support of the efficacy of these various methods, but he or she should refrain from a harsh judgment, in view of the embryonic nature of the subject. It is true that some aspects of the treatment of patients with anorexia nervosa do not require controlled trials to establish their efficacy. For example, the restoration of an emaciated patient to a healthy nutritional state as a result of skilled nursing in a psychiatric ward is so dramatic that a simple weight chart is all the proof that is needed. The problem is much greater when assessing the benefits of psychotherapy, since the aims of this treatment are likely to be more ambitious. They often consist of achieving more fundamental changes in the patient (and possibly the patient's family) so as to improve radically the outcome of the illness. Thus the most important first step in assessing the psychotherapies has been achieved in this book — namely, a clear and detailed description of the methods used, so that they can be replicated in future research.

It is appropriate to return to the name of this book as a handbook. If the German tradition of the *Handbuch* is to be followed, it can be expected that a whole series of further volumes will be added to this one. Indeed, it would be reasonable to expect Volume 2 of the *Handbook* to appear within 5 years, and to contain the results of controlled trials of different psychotherapies as they are used in the treatment of the eating disorders.

In the meantime, I wish to congratulate the editors for assembling a team of authoritative experts who have provided the reader with the fruits of their labors, and also to acknowledge the quality of the contributions written by the editors themselves.

Gerald Russell, MD
Institute of Psychiatry, London

Preface

In recent years, a variety of psychotherapeutic modalities have been developed for anorexia nervosa and bulimia that complement the valuable insights provided by pioneers in the treatment of these disorders. Despite the extensive literature on both disorders, there has been a need voiced by clinicians for more detailed descriptions of what is actually done in psychotherapy. The primary aim of the current volume has been to address this need through the efforts of a distinguished group of clinical theorists who have made notable contributions to the treatment of eating disorders. By articulating the specific details of their respective approaches, the authors have provided a sound base for further revision of our present knowledge and ability to treat anorexia nervosa and bulimia.

The editing of this volume has been assisted by the efforts of a number of people. We are grateful for the support and encouragement from Professor Vivian Rakoff, Chairman of the Department of Psychiatry, University of Toronto; Mr. Vickory Stoughton, President, Toronto General Hospital; and Dr. Don Layne, Vice President of Research, Toronto General Hospital. We appreciate the continual stimulation of our interest in psychotherapy through discussions among the clinical staff in the Department of Psychiatry at the Toronto General Hospital. Victoria Mitchell and Vanessa Boratto provided many hours of valuable technical assistance in the preparation of this volume. We are grateful to Marie Sprayberry for her very helpful comments and suggestions as copy editor. We wish to thank Seymour Weingarten and the others at The Guilford Press for thoughtful advice and for making the *Handbook* a high-priority project. Finally, we are indebted to the Medical Research Council of Canada, Health and Welfare, Canada, and the Ontario Mental Health Foundation for support during the completion of this volume.

Contents

PART ONE

The Context for Psychotherapy

CHAPTER ONE

Introduction

DAVID M. GARNER / PAUL E. GARFINKEL

Only a decade ago, patients with anorexia nervosa were apparently not being treated in great numbers outside of centers specializing in the management of the disorder. Bulimia occurring in nonemaciated individuals was not widely recognized. In the past 10 years, however, a growing public and professional awareness of these disorders has paralleled their increased prevalence. On the positive side, the increased interest has led to an explosion of research and clinical writing in the past several years. The quality of scientific research has increased, and much has been clarified about mechanisms that play a role in these disorders. Specialized treatment facilities with experienced staffs have become increasingly available, and the quality of patient care has undoubtedly improved. There have also been some negative elements in the burgeoning interest. In some instances, both anorexia nervosa and bulimia have been glamorized through certain novels, television dramas, films, and popularized accounts of media stars' battles with these disorders. The disorders have been embued occasionally with a social connotation that is not altogether unfavorable (Branch & Eurman, 1980; Garner, Garfinkel, & Olmsted, 1983). This situation clearly must be rectified, since it may be partially responsible for the development or perpetuation of some cases of these conditions, which are anything but benign.

With the proliferation of literature about these eating disorders, it is reasonable to question the need for another book about them. However, we believe that there is a gap in the emergent literature, which can be filled by a comprehensive volume that delineates in greater detail the treatment approaches currently being advocated for anorexia nervosa and bulimia. In particular, there is a need for one reference that allows the reader to compare and contrast these methods. We have been very fortunate to be able to assemble a group of distinguished clinicians and researchers who have been at the forefront of recent treatment innovations.

The *Handbook* is intended primarily for the practicing clinician who wants to understand and implement the various psychotherapeutic modalities that are currently being recommended for anorexia nervosa and bulimia. At the same time, the scientific orientation of most contributors has resulted in scholarly presentations that should make the *Handbook* of particular interest to the academically oriented clinician. Theories of pathogenesis have been described, but the emphasis is on the details of the practice of each approach. Most chapters have been heavily punctuated with clinical vignettes and case examples, which promise to be valuable to the practitioner

David M. Garner and Paul E. Garfinkel. Department of Psychiatry, Toronto General Hospital; and the University of Toronto, Toronto, Ontario, Canada.

faced with patients suffering from these troubling disorders. One of the major obstacles in evaluative research has been that the descriptions of treatment methods has not been elaborated in sufficient detail to allow critical examination or replication in clinical trials. The contributors to the *Handbook* have been courageous in their willingness to define their methods explicitly and then to defend them. This type of openness has yielded an abundance of fresh insights, which are essential to continued progress in the field.

Nevertheless, bringing together authors operating from diverse theoretical perspectives has highlighted a number of unanswered questions and issues for future debate. One of the most fundamental questions pertains to the overlap between anorexia nervosa and bulimia. The disorders have been dealt with for the most part in separate chapters, by editorial request. However, the theoretical relationship between the disorders, as well as the degree to which they benefit from similar or unique therapies, is unsettled. The third edition of the *Diagnostic and Statistical Manual of Mental Disorders* (DSM-III) (American Psychiatric Association, 1980) and other sources have considered bulimia in nonemaciated patients as a separate syndrome from bulimia in anorexia nervosa. Others have emphasized the resemblance between these conditions and have offered similar treatment recommendations for both. However, there have been few direct comparisons between these disorders to determine the justification of the diagnostic distinction. It has been our impression and that of others that the symptom of bulimia, whether it occurs in anorexia nervosa or without substantial weight loss, is associated with similar clinical features, and that generally bulimic patients may be distinguished from restricting anorexia nervosa patients. However, there is considerable heterogeneity within these groups of patients. Subtyping of patients based exclusively upon these behavioral or weight-related distinctions may be of limited value. Perhaps a more elegant solution might involve extending these dimensions to take into account different psychobiological typologies, which could be matched for optimal outcome to specific therapeutic strategies.

The chapters in the *Handbook* reflect a wide range of variations in orientations and treatment philosophies. As might be expected, this results in divergent points of emphasis and occasionally in conflicting recommendations on fundamental issues. For example, some of the behaviorally oriented approaches to bulimia focus on interrupting episodes of binge eating, while others emphasize controlling self-induced vomiting. Discrepant views on bulimia stem from different models of etiology. Mitchell and his colleagues (see Chapter 11) view bulimia as analogous to an addictive behavior, and they base some elements of their abstinence model on the Alcoholics Anonymous philosophy. Except for the occasional "slip," involvement in the program is contingent upon not vomiting. Lacey (see Chapter 18) prefers "contracting" for a gradual reduction of symptoms. Some authors emphasize interpersonal or psychological precipitants of binge eating (e.g., Lacey, Chapter 18; Fairburn, Chapter 8; Orbach, Chapter 5; Schwartz, Barrett, & Saba, Chapter 13), while others stress the interaction between cultural forces and the biological response to dietary restriction (e.g., Garner, Rockert, Olmsted, Johnson, & Coscina, Chapter 21; Wooley & Wooley, Chapter 17).

Recommendations for determining an appropriate body weight also differ. Lacey argues against setting a target weight for bulimics, since "the patient's weight is within a normal range." Most advise setting a target weight based upon average weight or 90% of average weight as derived from population norms; others argue, based upon the concept of "set point," that target weights must be highly individualized, reflecting personal and family weight histories. These and other contrasts between various aspects of treatment represented in the *Handbook* underscore the fact that many questions remain and that further research in these areas is necessary.

Despite these points of controversy, the overwhelming impression one receives from reviewing the chapters of the *Handbook* is the remarkable agreement on many aspects of treatment. The treatment approaches described in this volume are the product of many years of clinical and research experience. While these approaches have evolved from very different vantage points, there is an extraordinary accord in many areas. Most authors recognize the multidimensional and heterogeneous nature of eating disorders. There is an acceptance that not all therapies will suit all patients. Family therapists (e.g., Sargent, Liebman, & Silver, Chapter 12; Schwartz *et al.*, Chapter 13) recognize the need for individual therapy, and individual therapists are convinced of the merits of the family approach. The multicomponent treatment programs represented in the *Handbook* (i.e., Strober & Yager, Chapter 16; Wooley & Wooley, Chapter 17; Andersen, Morse, & Santmyer, Chapter 14; Kalucy, Gilchrist, McFarlane, & McFarlane, Chapter 19) exemplify this trend by integrating group, family, and individual methods. Depending upon the symptom area addressed, they employ behavioral, cognitive, and psychodynamic principles. With regard to the treatment of bulimia, there is a consensus on the value of normalizing food intake through structured eating, meal plans, and diaries.

Perhaps more impressive is the trend on the part of those from traditionally opposite ideological poles to describe similar phenomena and offer congruent advice, perhaps using slightly different terminology. Psychodynamic theorists appreciate the importance of focusing directly on issues of food, weight, and renutrition. Cognitive-behavioral approaches have begun to address self-concept deficits and the therapeutic relationship. Therapists from different schools emphasize the recognition and expression of affect; the value of exploring family interactional patterns; and the relevance of such developmental issues as separation, autonomy, sexual fears, and identity formation. These accommodations are reassuring, since they imply that we are attending to what our patients are telling us and are adapting our procedures to address these recurring themes. This parallels a more general move toward integration among clinicians and psychotherapy researchers. The systematic application of several strategies may be preferable to operating from a unitary theoretical model. Goldfried (1980) has commented on this trend and has also argued that a more powerful psychotherapy results from drawing on empirically derived clinical strategies without swearing exclusive allegiance to one theoretical position. According to Goldfried, this is accomplished by finding meaningful "points of commonality among different orientations" (1980, p. 994).

There has been virtual unanimity among contributors to the *Handbook* regarding the need to understand both the psychological and the physical aspects of anorexia nervosa and bulimia. In particular, there has been a growing recognition of the profound effects of starvation on behavior, emotions, and thoughts. These observations do not apply only to emaciated anorexic patients; they may also pertain to many bulimics, who may be at a statistically normal weight but have dieted well below their own natural or healthy weight. The interaction between primary psychopathology and secondary features of starvation is one of the most fascinating aspects of these conditions. In this sense, they may be thought of as prototypical examples of psychosomatic disorders. The reverberation between the various elements of the patients' inner and outer worlds, and their later battle against their own symptoms, are important considerations in the treatment of anorexia nervosa and bulimia. Primary deficits must be separated from the secondary elaboration of symptoms. It requires the therapist to be able to bridge several complex fields within psychology and medicine. Virtually all of the contributors to the *Handbook* demonstrate this awareness of the interaction among predisposing, precipitating, and perpetuating factors. Moreover, they provide the practicing clinician with helpful suggestions for dealing with these interdependent processes.

Finally, although the chapters of the *Handbook* are aimed at treatment, our efforts must increasingly be applied toward prevention. One of the major obstacles in prevention is that it is predicated on a clear understanding of variables that predispose individuals toward or precipitate these disorders. While many of these remain obscure, research over the last decade has led to the identification of likely risk factors. Health scientists may be able to alter these or to offer counseling to those who are vulnerable. For example, it is possible that education will result in an increased awareness of the negative social, psychological, and physical consequences of excessive dieting that is related to unrealistic standards for shape. If social contagion plays even a small role in the increased prevalence of anorexia nervosa, the media may be discouraged from subtly glamorizing the disorder.

Growing awareness of risk factors and of early warning signs allows active intervention to reduce the incidence or morbidity. Already, some training schools for high-risk activities, such as ballet, gymnastics, and figure skating, have changed policies that may have exacerbated the problem. Weekly "weigh-ins" have been discontinued, and teachers have been cautioned not to employ negative sanctions against those whose weight falls above the standards. Moreover, students who are beginning to display symptoms are provided with counseling and occasionally with assistance in choosing pursuits or careers that do not stress a thin image. Obviously, these are modest achievements, but they serve as examples that prevention can be effective in some cases.

In summary, the chapters of the current volume represent an array of approaches to anorexia nervosa and bulimia. The clinician may draw upon the range of expertise in selecting the appropriate strategy for a particular setting or patient.

REFERENCES

American Psychiatric Association. (1980). *Diagnostic and statistical manual of mental disorders* (3rd ed.). Washington, DC: Author.
Branch, C. H., & Eurman, L. J. (1980). Social attitudes toward patients with anorexia nervosa. *American Journal of Psychiatry, 137*, 631–632.
Garner, D. M., Garfinkel, P. E., & Olmsted, M. P. (1983). An overview of sociocultural factors in the development of anorexia nervosa. In P. L. Darby, P. E. Garfinkel, D. M. Garner, & D. V. Coscina (Eds.), *Anorexia nervosa: Recent developments* (pp. 65–82). New York: Alan R. Liss.
Goldfried, M. R. (1980). Toward the delineation of therapeutic change principles. *American Psychologist, 35*, 991–999.

CHAPTER TWO

Four Decades of Eating Disorders

HILDE BRUCH

BACKGROUND

This chapter was prepared as the annual Daniel Prager Lecture of the Department of Psychiatry of George Washington University. Preparing it brought back to my mind the stimulating time I spent in the Washington area in the early 1940s as a candidate at what was then the Washington–Baltimore Psychoanalytic Institute, while I was a resident at the Phipps Psychiatric Clinic in Baltimore. The invitation to prepare the lecture was a stimulus to review the changes in our approach to eating disorders and to psychoanalysis itself during these four decades.

Psychoanalysis in the Washington area was at a remarkable stage in the early 1940s, with a brilliant array of stimulating and challenging teachers. The work of Frieda Fromm-Reichmann and Harry Stack Sullivan is probably best known. It would be difficult to reconstruct today the heat of the controversy—whether their emphasis on interpersonal process was still "analysis," or whether only pure libido theory deserved that title.

I had come to Johns Hopkins and the Phipps Clinic in the hope of learning something that would be useful in the treatment of fat children and adolescents, in whose development I had become interested after I, a refugee pediatrician, had found a position at Babies Hospital in New York. It was also the motivation for my studying psychoanalysis; becoming an analyst was incidental to this main purpose—and has remained so to some extent. This was during the war years, and everything was different and somewhat odd. Even under those circumstances I must have impressed teachers and fellow students as a maverick who considered fat children more interesting and special than theory or becoming a training analyst. The fat children and their successors proved themselves stronger than Institute policies, but not than my interest in theoretical formulations.

Remarkable changes have taken place in medicine in general, including psychoanalysis and psychosomatic medicine. In early discussions, the interaction of organic and psychological factors was viewed as an either–or proposition. Modern thinking reflects a tendency toward integration of the various factors. It is generally recognized that the characteristics of each particular person have a basis in his or her genetic biological endowment, but that early life experiences are essential for the differentiation and organization of the innate potential. Recent explorations of the neurochemical processes of the brain have revealed the close association of psychological experiences

Hilde Bruch. Department of Psychiatry, Baylor College of Medicine, Houston, Texas.

with alterations in brain metabolism, rendering the old dichotomy between physiological and psychological events untenable.

When I focus here on psychological issues in eating disorders, then there is need
to emphasize the complexity of these conditions. They reflect the interaction of biological, psychological, and sociological factors. It is not always possible to keep the
various factors, which work in close interaction, separate.

Though fat children represented my entrance ticket to psychiatry, their appeal
was superseded, as time went on, by their clinical counterparts—those who starve
themselves, the sufferers from anorexia nervosa. It was so rare in the early 1940s that
it was practically an unknown disease, though physicians had heard about it in medical school. It has become so common that now it commands great medical interest
and is responsible for an endless stream of made-to-order research and publications.
Even more amazingly, it has become an object of media interest and has aroused great
popular curiosity. Another condition, bulimia, has been practically invented by the
media, and popular attention to it is steadily increasing.

As to anorexia nervosa, my own education appears to have been somewhat more
complete than that of most: Early in the 1930s, during my internship, I actually saw
one case, for whom the professor claimed that the pituitary origin was recognizable by
the O-shape of the thighs. Don't ask me why and how, but that stuck in my memory.
It may also serve as an illustration of the superficial way in which at that time an endocrine label was attached to a poorly understood condition.

During my residency at the Phipps Clinic, an anorexic girl was assigned to me.
I did my up-to-date reading and was impressed by the definiteness with which mere
assumptions were presented as scientific facts. There were two fields of knowledge
that existed side by side. When anorexia nervosa was described, a little more than 100
years ago, the emphasis was on "nervous" factors, which were presented in the terms
of the psychology of their time. In 1914 the autopsy findings on certain cases of cachexia prompted the theory of a pituitary origin, and this opinion dominated the field
for the next three or four decades. During the 1930s the diagnostic criteria of a psychogenic form of anorexia nervosa were recognized as different from those of cachexia of pituitary origin.

Psychoanalysis played an important role in bringing about the new understanding of psychological factors, but it presented its principal theoretical assumptions as
fixed knowledge, the way many topics were presented as definite at that time. Investigative focus was on the disturbed eating function, the "oral" component. Anorexia
nervosa was viewed as a form of conversion hysteria that symbolically expressed repudiation of sexuality, specifically of "oral impregnation" fantasies. This view dominated the field during the 1940s and 1950s, and has not yet completely departed. I
looked eagerly for such fantasies in my patient. When I did not find them, I reassured
myself that she had not stayed long enough at the Clinic for them to be discovered.
I was sure that they were there somewhere. The literature reveals that experienced analysts too would offer similar explanations if they failed to expose these specific psychodynamics, so firmly established was their "factual" existence.

Classical psychoanalysis was considered the treatment of choice, though some
analysts acknowledged quite early that traditional psychoanalysis was rather ineffective and that the mental disturbances from which these patients suffered were more
severe than those observed in neurosis.

It was not until the early 1950s, while I practiced psychoanalysis in New York

City, that I began to see anorexic patients with any degree of regularity. It was assumed that my experience with the psychotherapy of fat adolescents had prepared me for treating anorexics. By 1960 I had studied a sufficient number to be considered a specialist in anorexia nervosa. I began to publish independent and in many ways unconventional observations and deductions. The first paper, in 1961, was based on observations of 12 anorexic patients, then a relatively large number. Search of the records of Presbyterian Hospital in New York revealed that during the preceding 30 years only 30 patients had been recorded under that diagnosis, not more than one patient per year. It is more than likely that others were recorded under an endocrine label, but the condition was rare. Since the late 1950s, the incidence has rapidly increased. No reliable figures are available about the actual frequency. One might speak of an epidemie, though the contagion does not appear to be of an organic nature, but seems to be related to psychosociological factors.

The explanations for this increase are only speculative. The common argument points to the cultural emphasis on increasing slenderness as the determining factor. In my opinion, this does not do justice to the psychological complexity of the disorder, which reflects a much more severe disturbance than dieting out of control. Normal weight control is distinctly different from the frantic preoccupation with excessive slenderness of the anorexic. My own observations suggest that the changing status of (and expectations for) women plays a role. Girls whose early upbringing has prepared them to become "clinging-vine" wives suddenly are expected at adolescence to prove themselves as women of achievement. This seems to create severe personal self-doubt and basic uncertainty. In their submissive way, they "choose" the fashionable dictum to be slim as a way of proving themselves as deserving respect.

PRIMARY ANOREXIA NERVOSA

With increasing incidence of anorexia nervosa, diagnostic clarification became possible. My own observations suggested that what clinically was called anorexia nervosa did not represent a uniform condition. A specific syndrome, "primary anorexia nervosa," could be differentiated from unspecific forms of psychologically determined weight loss that were secondary to some other psychiatric illness, such as hysteria, schizophrenia, or depression. Many cases in the older literature represent such atypical forms. They still occur, though not more often than before, and in some of them the psychoanalytic explanation that was traditional at that time may apply, in contrast to its absence in the primary form. It is the primary form that has increased in recent years. Characteristic factors, in addition to the severe weight loss, are severe body image disturbances, inaccuracy in identifying bodily and emotional states, and an all-pervasive sense of ineffectiveness.

Primary anorexia nervosa affects mainly adolescent girls and young women from educated and prosperous homes; it occurs only rarely in the male, usually in prepuberty.[1] An important new finding was that patients with primary anorexia nervosa do not suffer from loss of appetite; on the contrary, they are frantically preoccupied with food and eating. In this they resemble other starving people. Relentless pursuit of thinness seems to be the outstanding symptom, and in this pursuit they deliberately —

---

1. Throughout this chapter, anorexic patients are referred to as female.

seemingly willfully—restrict their food intake, and overexercise. It is of interest that the German name for the condition is *Pubertaets Magersucht*, or addiction to thinness. These girls are panicky with fear that they might lose control over their eating; when they do, they will gorge themselves on often unbelievably large amounts, which they vomit afterward. Anorexics have also been found to be uncertain in identifying hunger or satiety, and they use eating, or refusal to eat, for the pseudosolution of personality difficulties and problems of living. It was also recognized that the basic illness is not a disturbance of the eating function, though the physical and psychological consequences of the severe malnutrition dominate the manifest clinical picture; the deeper psychological disorder is related to underlying disturbances in the development of the personality, with deficits in the sense of self, identity, and autonomy. Needless to say, there are numerous disturbances in sexual maturation and gender identity; these are part of the larger maldevelopment and are not of any specific etiological significance.

With increasing psychotherapeutic investigation, it was possible to reconstruct the antecedents of the anorexic illness, and new concepts emerged about the nature of the underlying developmental disturbances. Long before the illness becomes manifest, these girls have felt helpless and ineffective in conducting their own lives, and the severe discipline over their bodies represents a desperate effort to ward off panic about being completely powerless. Psychiatrically, the condition appears to be more akin to borderline states—narcissism or schizophrenia—than to neurosis. Anorexia nervosa represents an illness in its own right, in which psychological and somatic factors closely interact.

One of the puzzling aspects of this serious illness is that it occurs in individuals who, according to their families and also to school reports, have been unusually good, successful, and gratifying as children and who have been well cared for in stable, even privileged homes. The onset of the disorder is accompanied by marked changes in behavior, and previously compliant girls become negativistic, angry, and distrustful. They stubbornly reject the help and care that is constantly offered to them, claiming not to need them and insisting on their right to be as thin as they want to be.

In therapy, they reveal that underneath this self-assertive facade they experience themselves as acting only in response to demands coming from others, and not doing anything because they want to. Perceptions of their bodily and emotional sensations are often inaccurate, and they do not trust themselves to identify their own needs and feelings accurately. They claim not to "see" the severe emaciation and do not consider it abnormal or ugly; on the contrary, they take pride in their skeleton-like appearance. They also fail to experience their bodies as being their own, but look upon them as something extraneous, separate from their psychological selves, or as being the possessions of their parents. This split between body and self is a basic issue and yields only slowly to therapeutic efforts.

The rigid discipline over their eating, with the visible weight loss, gives them the experience of being effective and in control in at least one area. The displayed defiance is not an expression of strength and independence, but a defense against the feeling of not having a core personality of their own, of being powerless and ineffective when they "give in."

The illness usually becomes manifest at or around puberty, or at other times when the patients are faced with new experiences and expectations for which they feel unprepared. Until then they have been vaguely aware of something missing in their development, and they suffer from a deep fear of being incompetent—a "nothing"—

and of not getting or even deserving respect. They are *de facto* deficient in the awareness of their core identity, in their sense of autonomy, and in their ability to make
decisions about their future.

*They continue to function with the morality and style of thinking of early child-
hood that Piaget has called the period of egocentricity, of preconceptual and concrete operations. They cling rigidly to early childhood concepts and interpret human
relationships this way.*The next step in conceptual development — that of formal operations, with the new ability to perform abstract thinking and evaluation, which is
characteristic of adolescence — is deficient or completely absent in them. Dissatisfaction about feeling incomplete, enslaved, and exploited emerges with puberty. In their
concrete way of thinking, they expect that through discipline over the body they can
establish interpersonal effectiveness. One may conceive of the illness as an attempt
at self-cure, which, however, fails and thus leads to further isolation and helplessness.

The patients who were seen during the 1950s and 1960s had in common that each
one was an original inventor of this effort at self-assertion. It was amazing that the
manifest clinical picture and the psychological reaction showed so many similarities.
Each one had developed the style of reacting completely on her own; they had never
heard about such a condition, nor had their parents or even their physicians. Yet they
shared certain reactions — particularly the conviction that they were not sick, but, on
the contrary, were doing something positive about their lives. Body sensations, hunger
experience, eating behavior, and hyperactivity were described with great similarities.
Similar also was their resentment about their parents' or professionals' interference
with something they considered a positive achievement. At no time did I have reason
to doubt the genuineness of their symptoms and reactions.

This originality gave to the behavior of each individual patient an aura of special
power and superhuman discipline. Some changes seem to have occurred when anorexia nervosa became more frequent. Those who developed the illness during the 1970s
often had "known" about the illness, or even knew someone who had it. During the
past few years several patients deliberately "tried it out" after having watched a TV
program or having assembled a science project. There is no doubt in my mind that
this "me-too" picture is associated with changes in the clinical — in particular, the psychological — picture; I am not yet able to define them, except that something like "passion" has gone out of the picture. Instead of the fierce search for independence, these
new "me-too" anorexics compete with or cling to each other. That they seek support
in self-help groups or respond to the various "programs" that have sprung up all over
the country may be an illustration of this development. The desire to be special,
unique, or extraordinary is expressed with less vigor and urgency, and I cannot suppress the suspicion that in some the symptoms are imitative or faked. It is my feeling
that ultimately the condition will lose its specific psychodynamic meaning. As it becomes more commonplace, the picture will become blurred and gradually disappear
until the conditions are right again for genuine primary anorexia nervosa.

BULIMIA

It may well be that the sudden, nearly explosive interest in bulimia is a sign of a beginning dissolution. Not all anorexics are able to maintain rigid control over their eating. When they give in to their desire for food and gorge themselves, they will devour
huge amounts of food. Subsequently they will vomit and thus maintain the low weight.

About 25% of the group on which I reported in 1973 in *Eating Disorders* showed this symptom. The anorexics who would binge did not look too different from the abstainers, though they appeared to be less rigid and emotionally somewhat more alert, but also more disturbed. During the last 5 or 10 years, binge eating has occurred more often — in more than 50% of the recent cases. There is agreement that it makes treatment more difficult and represents a dangerous complication.

During the past few years, bulimia has made its appearance as the great new eating disorder. It appears in the *Diagnostic and Statistical Manual of Mental Disorders*, third edition (DSM-III), but is mainly discussed in the media and popular press. It is presented as closely related to anorexia nervosa; someone has even invented a semantic atrocity, "bulimarexia," as if to indicate that the two conditions are nearly identical, which they are not, or as if they occur in the same person. I have grave doubts that bulimia is a clinical entity. Compulsive overeating may occur in different conditions and with different severity.

The patients with bulimia whom I have studied bear little resemblance to those with genuine anorexia nervosa, though they too are inaccurate in hunger awareness and show poor control over food intake. They make an exhibitionistic display of their lack of control or discipline, in contrast to the adherence to discipline of the true anorexics, even those with eating binges.

Many bulimics will vomit after overeating to avoid weight gain as a consequence. The modern bulimic is impressive by what looks like a deficit in the sense of responsibility. Bulimics blame their symptoms on others; they may name the persons from whom they "learned" to binge, in particular those who introduced them to vomiting. Often this has occurred in a single episode, but from then on they act like completely helpless victims. Though relatively uninvolved, they expect to share in the prestige of anorexia nervosa. Some complain about the expense of their consumption and will take food without paying for it. They explain this as due to "kleptomania," which indicates, like "bulimia," an irresistible compulsion that determines their behavior. To consider them part of the anorexia nervosa picture confuses instead of clarifying the issues.

THE ROLE OF THE FAMILY

Psychotherapy and direct study of the families have helped to shed light on the puzzle of why seemingly well-functioning homes raise children who mistrust their ability to face the future and who shy away from adult living. On one level, child care appears to be excellent: Everything is provided for, materially, psychologically, and culturally. However, little attention is paid to the child's expression of needs, wants, and feelings.

A decided shift has taken place in our conceptions of infants and their abilities. Emphasis is increasingly placed on infants' own individual contribution to their development from birth on. Though immature, infants give the clues and signals to their unfulfilled needs. How these needs are responded to, gratified, or disregarded appears to be the crucial point for infants' becoming aware of their different needs, or failing to achieve this. Two basic forms of behavior, relating to the biological and social–emotional field, need to be differentiated from birth on: namely, behavior that an infant *initiates* and behavior that occurs *in response* to stimuli. The mother's behavior is either *responsive* or *stimulating*, and the interaction can be rated as *appropriate* or *inappropriate*, depending on whether it fulfills the expressed needs or disregards or distorts them. Absence of regular and consistently appropriate responses to the infant's needs, particularly to the need for food, deprives the developing child of the essential groundwork for "body identity," with accurate perceptual and conceptual awareness of his or her own functions. Instead, the child will grow up perplexed when trying to differentiate between disturbances in his or her biological field and emotional and interpersonal experiences.

Anorexics are deficient not only in their hunger awareness and control over the eating function, but also in their sense of separateness. With puberty, they feel helpless under the impact of new bodily urges, including increased hunger, and in a counterphobic effort they overcontrol their needs. The effect is self-starvation, which represents the most conspicuous expression of this.

They also feel incomplete in their sense of separateness. With too little or no encouragement, or even prohibition of independence, children will remain tied to their parents, deprived of developing their own autonomy and decision-making ability. Obedience and overconformity characterize the behavior of anorexics during childhood.

Expression of feelings is also not encouraged, and anorexics can identify only a narrow range of emotional reactions. There may be some awareness of primitive, helpless rage and anger, which they keep in check until they become sick or treatment begins. Having feelings of their own or learning that these feelings count is for many a surprising discovery. A response like "My mother always knew how I felt; I never thought that it mattered what I said I felt" is not uncommon.

In this model, the development of personality and the sense of self is conceived of as the outcome of a continuous stream of circular and reciprocal transactions between parent and child. This concept is in good agreement with other recent studies of infancy. There is much evidence for the fact that a seemingly innate function, such as regulation of food intake, requires organizing learning experiences early in life, as well as continuous and ongoing interaction with an appropriately responding environment.

APPLICATION TO TREATMENT

Anorexia nervosa has the reputation of offering unusually difficult treatment problems. On principle, these patients resist treatment: They feel that in their extreme thinness they have found the perfect solution to their deep-seated unhappiness — that thinness makes them feel better. They do not complain about their skeleton-like appearance; on the contrary, they glory in it and actively maintain it.

For effective treatment, changes and corrections must be accomplished in several areas. The deficient nutrition must be improved, but enforcing it carries the danger of doing damage to the patient's shaky sense of autonomy. Refeeding must be integrated with various other factors: A certain nutritional restitution is a prerequisite for psychotherapy to be effective. But weight gain alone is not a cure. Psychotherapists not uncommonly commit the error of not correcting the dangerously low weight, in the unrealistic hope that it will correct itself once the underlying problems have been identified and solved. There is hope that eventually metabolic or pharmacological substances will become available to interrupt the self-perpetuating cycle of secondary changes due to the starvation.

Nutritional improvement and resolution of psychological problems should occur in close interaction, and lasting recovery requires a change of the inner image a patient has of herself. Ideally, the active involvement of a patient permits her to relax her overrigid discipline and to gain weight on her own over an extended period.

The stagnating patterns of family interaction need to be clarified and unlocked. But family therapy alone is not enough. Regardless of what the family contribution to the illness has been in the past, the patient has integrated these abnormal concepts about herself and others into her own personality. Individual intensive psychotherapy is necessary for correction of the underlying faulty assumptions—for correction of the self-deceptive pseudosolution that anorexia nervosa represents.

Direct work with the family and individual psychotherapy complement each other. Parents need help with their own anxieties to permit the young person more freedom and to prevent premature interruption of treatment when the patient shows true signs of developing independence. Parents often comment, "If only she could be again the girl she was," overlooking the fact that "the girl she was" was unable to face growing up and adult living. The knowledge and understanding gained through work with the family give the therapist important guidelines on what problems and issues to pursue in individual therapy.

PSYCHOTHERAPY

The psychotherapeutic approach is derived from psychoanalysis, but its application to the needs of primary anorexia nervosa has demanded marked modification of the classical model. It was recognized quite early that the classical analysis was associated with unfavorable results. To these patients, "receiving interpretations" in the traditional setting represents in a painful way a re-experience of being told what to feel and think, confirming their sense of inadequacy and thus interfering with the development of a true self-awareness and trust in their own psychological abilities. The therapeutic task is to encourage anorexics in their search for autonomy and self-directed identity in the setting of a new intimate interpersonal relationship, where what they have to say is listened to and made the object of exploration.

It is useful to give anorexics at the beginning of treatment a simple explanation of the dynamic meaning of the illness: that the preoccupation with eating and weight is a cover-up for underlying personality problems—namely, their doubt about their own worth and value. They need help to discover their positive qualities and assets, but also need to be told that at this stage the severe starvation interferes with their psychological functioning. It is important to clarify from the outset that the goal of therapy is to accomplish something for a patient's benefit, not to appease the parents. A patient needs to become an active participant in the treatment process, so that she can reach the point of differentiating herself from others, of discriminating bodily sensations and emotional states, and of growing beyond the helpless passivity, hateful submissiveness, and indiscriminate negativism.

Patients need to experience that close and alert attention is paid to what they have to say and contribute. This is essential in order for the individuation process, which has miscarried early in their lives, to take place. The therapist's task is not to give insight about the symbolic significance of symptoms and behavior, but to help patients to face the realities of their lives in the past and present.

It is important to reconstruct the emotional interactions and involvements during the preillness period. If this is made the focus of inquiry, patients will gradually recognize the extent to which they have always done what they had thought they were supposed to do, repressing their genuine development. As a matter of fact, the encouraged "good" behavior can be recognized as an important source of the maldevelopment. Faked and make-believe expressions and reactions are praised as if they were genuine, with the result that the ability to differentiate between genuine and pretended feelings does not develop. The task of therapy is to help patients discover their genuine selves, and what is valid about themselves. They need to face the problems of living in the present and also to reconstruct what has gone on during the preillness period. Deficits in encouragement and validation of expression of their needs have interfered with their developing a sense of self and competence.

In a way, each anorexic patient has to build up a new personality after all the years of faked existence. Patients are eternally preoccupied with the image they create in the eyes of others, always questioning whether they are worthy of respect. An attitude of basic mistrust permeates their self-concept and all relationships. Every anorexic fears that basically she is inadequate, low, mediocre, inferior and despised by others. All her efforts to be outstanding or perfect are directed toward hiding the fatal flaw of her inadequacy. Anorexics are convinced that all people look down on them with scorn and criticism, and that they have to protect themselves against this. This mistrust is usually hidden from the therapist under the facade of pleasing cooperation.

Therapy represents an attempt to acknowledge the conceptual defects and distortions and to create a climate in which these developmental delays can be identified — a necessary first step toward their correction. An important step in this process is the re-evaluation of the family interactional experiences, so that the forces that have interfered with normal development can be recognized and the overly close ties to the parents can be loosened. Patients are reluctant to engage in this process. They not only deny their own illness and need for treatment; they also deny that there has been anything troublesome in their relationship to their parents. Everything is perfect; their parents are superior and provide privileges and opportunities; and they consider efforts to look at what really has taken place and how they have experienced it as being forced to "blame" the parents. They will, however, complain about the parents' interference with eating behavior, and also about their having made arrangements for treatment. Others are tireless in expressing blind and indiscriminate hostility toward one parent or the other.

By paying minute attention to the way in which a patient talks about her experiences, one may find an entry into this rigid denial. An 18-year-old severely anorexic girl had accepted treatment only because she "detested" arguing with her mother. She felt happy because she weighed so little; as a matter of fact, she considered it a sign of superiority. She had grown up abroad and had been raised by governesses who changed every 2 years. When I inquired about the emotional hardship of having to adjust to so many different people, she said reassuringly, "I knew they all loved me. I made sure they would." She became upset when her "*making* sure" of their love was discussed as implying doubt about being loved if she just behaved naturally. This led to her talking, at first tentatively and with much resistance, about her great efforts to be always beyond blame and criticism and deserving of admiration. All her activities — at home, in school and in sports — were dominated by an extraordinary ambition to be recognized as outstanding, and she would drive herself to exhaustion: "Only then [when exhausted] can you be at peace that you have done enough. If you have not given the last drop of strength, you do not deserve to sleep or to eat." As treatment progressed and as she became more relaxed about her obligations, she reviewed with much emotion the hardship of being the youngest child in a successful, wealthy home where everybody else had been considered "brilliant"; she had felt that nothing she ever did was good enough and that she would never live up to what she felt "they" expected of her.

Clarification of the patients' justified reasons for feeling that approval is coming their way only on condition of superior performance is slow work. It involves re-examination of patients' erroneous assumptions about life and relationships. They must come to recognize that there have been factual situations that have interfered with their developing a sense of inner rightness — that from the beginning the scales have been weighted against their becoming distinct, self-reliant individuals. They also need to learn that children will interpret such experiences as proving that they themselves are in some way undeserving, not good enough, even defective. The frantic demand for acknowledgement and praise that is finally acted out in the anorexic illness reflects true deprivation, not only during the early years but continuing into the present.

The unrealistic aspects of the patients' feeling that "Mother always knew what I felt" need to be re-examined. In fact, the opposite has been true: Their mothers have often disregarded their feelings, and it is the task of therapy to help them discover their own needs and values. Thus they can come to the point of trusting their own decisions and respecting their own opinions, instead of being overpowered by the judgment of others. By being tuned in to the slightest distortion in the patients' sense of reality, the therapist can instigate, without being judgmental, necessary re-evaluations. They may agree with what has been worked through in one session, but they have a tendency to undo what has been clarified because the old convictions come back. The difficulty is that they have lived so long with their self-belittling assumptive reality that they have become convinced that they cannot change, particularly when they have been exposed to ineffective or mechanical treatment efforts in the past. They may politely agree with what has been clarified, and at the same time maintain the secret conviction, "I know better — I know for me things are different."

These patients compensate with grandiose aspirations for the self-belittling attitude, and it requires a real sacrifice of pride to reduce their ambitious dreams of glory to human proportions. The need to be superspecial is so compelling that any conclusion that seems to be based on common human experience, or on observations of other anorexic patients, is rejected; it cannot apply to them. They want to be human in a way that is different from the rest of mankind, to the point of their feeling inhuman in their demands.

One patient expressed the despair of being completely isolated from people as feeling like being on an island in a river, unable to cross to the mainland. In a way, therapy that emphasized the validity and worthwhileness of her core personality gave her the courage to cross the bridge.

COMMENT

Dissatisfaction with the results of traditional interpretative psychoanalysis in the treatment of anorexia, and also of obesity, prompted a change in my approach. Instead of searching for definite underlying unconscious conflicts, the focus became reconstruction of what had really happened during patients' early development or on how they recalled the past. This fact-finding approach, which I have called "the constructive use of ignorance," implies that the therapist does not know and can find out only with the patient's active participation in the inquiry. The use of the approach was accompanied by better treatment results. With increasing experience, it could be shown that the active involvement served as a stimulus for the development of something that had been deficient in the patients' early interactional patterns — namely, reliance on their own thinking.

For many, therapy is the first consistent experience that what they have to say is listened to as important. These patients experience emotions and bodily sensations in a bewildering way and often cannot describe them; they need help and encouragement with learning to identify their feelings, and also to control them. If, instead, they are given interpretations of the "real" meaning of what they express, the basic deficiency may be reinforced. For an understanding of these findings and their developmental significance, a new model of child development was constructed. The emphasis was on some essential qualities of the intimate interaction between mother and child: Paucity or absence of continuing responses to child-initiated clues appeared to be related to the patients' deficits in self-concept and in hunger awareness. This generalized formulation served as a guide for the inquiry into family interactions and attitudes. It also supported the focus on initiative and autonomy as a basic function of the treatment process.

These formulations and their application to therapy were independently arrived at during the last 20 years. They do not stand in isolation, but show many parallels to other re-evaluations of psychoanalytic therapy, particularly in its application to narcissism, borderline states, and schizophrenia. Most sweeping were the reformulations, during the 1930s and 1940s, of Harry Stack Sullivan in his interpersonal theory. I consider him my most influential teacher. Traditional psychoanalysis, too, has undergone many changes and modifications, from the classical biologically determined approach to those of ego psychology, of object relationship theory, and recently of self psychology.

The considerations I have presented here show a fairly close resemblance to those expressed by Kohut in his psychology of the self. He considers favorable interaction with the environment as necessary for the healthy development of the self and calls the positive responses to a child's expressions of his or her needs "mirroring." He stresses "empathic" tuning in on a patient's bewilderment and distress, as well as reconstruction of early experiences, with examination of the factors that have interfered with the development of an adequate self-concept.

These modern developments in psychoanalysis have broadened the range of conditions that can be favorably influenced. This is of particular importance in the treatment of anorexia nervosa and other eating disorders, where the clinical picture is complicated by the distorting influence of the abnormal nutrition on psychological processes. A clear theoretical formulation represents an indispensable guide through the maze of seemingly contradictory psychological responses.

CONCLUSION

In conclusion, I should like to state that reviewing my work in a four-decade perspective, against the background of psychiatry and psychoanalysis in general, has been stimulating and satisfying. Probably the happiest discovery was that psychoanalysis has revealed itself as more flexible, less rigid and dogmatic, than I had feared during the early 1940s. Since I went my own way, I have often felt like an outsider; I now feel that I again have a home.

An unexpected finding was that the illnesses on which my work is based have shown changes and developmental trends of their own. Adolescent obesity continues to occur in a steady stream, but its study has suffered in comparison to the disproportionate amount of attention anorexia nervosa receives, even at times when it is rare. Its increased frequency during the past 20 years appears to be related to psychosociological factors, chiefly to those of the women's movement.

Observing that the rise is on the point of being followed by a fall, or at least the beginning of a disintegration, was unexpected. I probably will not be around to learn whether my prediction is correct, though I should like to be kept informed!

Working with these youngsters in their desperate search for selfhood and value is difficult and often frustrating. I have found it also deeply rewarding. Basically, it amounts to helping youngsters to discover their creative and human potential, and to give up the hateful, unlovable, empty, and defective self-image that underlies the illness.

CHAPTER THREE

Initial Consultation for Patients with Bulimia and Anorexia Nervosa

CRAIG JOHNSON

INTRODUCTION

The recent increase in the incidence of anorexia nervosa and bulimia has created a significant demand for clinical services for patients who present with these eating disorders. There is also a growing awareness among therapists that the psychological, biological, and sociocultural aspects of these two disorders, as well as the heterogeneity of patients affected, require multidimensional and specialized treatment programs. An underattended, yet critical component of constructing a specialized treatment program is the development of a sophisticated initial diagnostic interview.

The current chapter on the initial consultation is written with three goals in mind. First, it introduces a standardized interview format (Diagnostic Survey for Eating Disorders, or DSED) for obtaining intake information that has both clinical and research utility. Second, it presents various clinical observations that will help therapists identify the bio/psycho/social factors that have contributed to the onset and perpetuation of a patient's eating behavior. Finally, it offers preliminary observations regarding various subtypes of eating-disordered patients and what treatment strategies are useful with the subgroups.

Description of the Instrument

The DSED (see Appendix) is a multi-item survey that focuses on various aspects of anorexia nervosa and bulimia. The questionnaire is divided into 12 sections, which provide information on demographic factors, weight history and body image, dieting behavior, binge eating behavior, purging behavior, exercise, related behaviors, sexual functioning, menstruation, medical and psychiatric history, life adjustment, and family history.

The survey can be used as a self-report instrument, or as a semi-structured interview guide. Our clinic makes use of the instrument in both forms. Following the initial phone contact, we request that patients complete and return the questionnaire prior to their actual first visit. During the consultation, the interviewer then reviews the self-reported information in the various sections for validation of the self-report, to elicit

Craig Johnson. Institute of Psychiatry, Eating Disorders Program, Northwestern University Medical School, Northwestern Memorial Hospital, Chicago, Illinois.

more details, and to assess the affective responses to the various topics covered in the survey.

The DSED was not constructed with the intention of developing a scaled instrument. Instead, the purpose was to provide a standardized format for collecting relevant information that would enhance communication between various treatment centers regarding descriptions of different patient groups.

Overall Philosophy of the Clinic

We attempt to establish an overall frame of reference in our clinic, which we refer to as the "adaptive context." Essentially, we emphasize to staff and patients that anorexia nervosa and bulimia are multidetermined disorders that affect a wide range of patients, and that the symptoms are adaptations to a variety of biological, intrapsychic, familial, and sociocultural issues. We further stress that anorexia nervosa and bulimia are desperate behaviors that usually reflect desperate attempts to adapt to desperate circumstances. We emphasize the adaptive context, because patients with bulimia and anorexia nervosa are often difficult and frustrating individuals whose resistance to change can provoke significant countertransference as early as the initial interview. Establishing the adaptive context as a frame of reference often helps staff "maintain perspective" as resistance heightens and provocative behavior ensues.

The First 5 Minutes of the Consultation

It has been our experience with eating-disordered patients that the first several minutes of the consultation are extremely important. The interview is usually initiated by inquiring how the person is feeling about coming for the consultation. The objective in asking the question is to assess whether the person is seeking help voluntarily or through various degrees of coercion from friends, family, or the community. Although there are always exceptions, bulimic patients are usually at the consultation on a much more voluntary basis than anorexia nervosa patients.

Shortly after the initial inquiry, we ask if the patient has ever talked with anyone specifically about her difficulties with food.[1] Our purpose with the question is to assess how ego-syntonic the symptoms are and to attempt to be sensitive to the fact that many individuals have never acknowledged their difficulties with food and feel very ashamed and humiliated in doing so. This is particularly true for patients who present with bulimic symptoms.

After the two initial questions, the agenda for the consultation is presented to the patient. We mention to her that we have many questions to ask, some of which may seem intrusive. We acknowledge that our reason for asking so many questions in such a short space of time is to assess, as quickly as possible, where she is in the course of the eating disorder so that we can make treatment recommendations.

Overall, the most important task of the first 5 minutes is to communicate to the patient, either directly through words or through the spirit of the interview, that we are interested in a collaborative inquiry, rather than an inquisition into the events that may have resulted in the onset of her symptoms.

1. Throughout the chapter, the feminine pronoun is used to refer to anorexic and bulimic patients.

Structured versus Unstructured Interview

While there may be some important advantages to conducting an unstructured interview, we believe that the costs outweigh the benefits. While waiting patiently and quietly for the patient to disclose her difficulties can yield important information about her capacity for tension regulation in an unstructured situation, the level of her social skills, and her capacity to articulate internal states without assistance, it may also be viewed by the patient as sadistic withholding or as evidence that the therapist does not have specific knowledge regarding her particular problems. The structured interview allows the therapist to demonstrate an awareness of some of the unique aspects of eating problems through knowledgeable inquiry. It also establishes a common language at the outset. Most of the eating-disordered patients' lives revolve around food-related thoughts and behavior; consequently, their language reflects this preoccupation. While the task of the treatment is to provide different ways to organize their lives (or a different language), in the initial stages of contact, we have found it helpful to inquire directly about food-related attitudes and behaviors. We have found this to be particularly important with patients who, in previous treatments, have been discouraged from talking specifically about these matters.

WEIGHT HISTORY AND BODY IMAGE

The structured interview begins with questions regarding the patient's weight history and feelings toward her body. The overall objective in this section is to investigate how much weight preoccupations and fluctuations have affected the patient's self-esteem and life adjustment.

After obtaining the patient's current height, weight, and ideal weight, we investigate whether there are occupational considerations that affect the patient's attitudes toward her weight. Individuals in the entertainment and fashion industries are high-risk groups because of rigorous and often unrealistic criteria for weight regulation (Druss & Silverman, 1979; Garner & Garfinkel, 1980). These groups are often special treatment problems because their self-esteem and livelihood are unalterably tied to industries that demand a weight maintenance that is debilitatingly subnormal.

After gathering information regarding current weight and occupational considerations, an inquiry is made about the patient's highest and lowest past weights since the age of 13. If periods of significant weight fluctuations are mentioned, potential correlations with specific life events, such as major transitions, separations or losses, family problems, recurring illness, and the like, are investigated. This early process of inquiry regarding possible psychological correlates of weight fluctuations can help the patient begin to think psychologically about the relationship of her food, weight, and body-related behavior to events in her life.

During the initial consultation, patients will often, for the first time, see patterns and repetitions between their weight-related behaviors and life events. For example, many of our patients realize that when they are rejected in a romantic relationship, they attempt to "start over" or restore a sense of control by dieting or losing weight. It is interesting to note that if this process is repeatedly successful at restoring control and self-esteem following some rejection (and it is often successful because our culture responds favorably to weight loss, particularly among women), then initiating weight loss or dieting can eventually become a generalized response to a wide range of traumatic situations.

Information about weight during childhood and early adolescent years is often unreliable. Consequently, we focus on how much emphasis the family and peer milieu have placed on such factors as thinness, dieting, and appearance—and what influences this emphasis has had on the patient's self-concept and beliefs about such issues as self-control, social acceptance, and the like. We also inquire very specifically whether the patient has been teased about her weight. It is important to establish the extent of the teasing, the context, the content, who specifically was doing the teasing, and its impact on the patient.

Periods of significant weight decrease are important to determine—with particular attention paid to the speed and method of weight loss. Recent research indicates important personality and outcome distinctions between patients who lose weight by restricting their food intake and patients who lose weight as a result of purging behavior accompanied by episodes of binge eating (Casper, Eckert, Halmi, Goldberg, & Davis, 1980; Garfinkel, Moldofsky, & Garner, 1980). We also inquire whether amenorrhea developed during the weight loss, and, if so, within what range it occurred.

Body Image

Body image perception among eating-disordered patients ranges from mild distortion/dissatisfaction to severely delusional thoughts regarding body size. Likewise, the degree to which body image perception affects life adjustment falls along a continuum from mild to severely debilitating. Consequently, the primary task of this phase of the interview is to assess the level of body image distortion, what psychological adaptation it may be serving, and investigate to what extent it is interfering with life adjustment.

While most women do report that they are dissatisfied with the size and shape of their bodies, their dissatisfaction does not necessarily interfere with life functioning. We attempt to investigate how much the patient's self-consciousness about her body affects her life adjustment by inquiring whether the dissatisfaction prevents her from doing certain things, such as dating, becoming sexually involved, exercising, or participating in activities that require some bodily exposure. While investigating this interface, we also attempt to assess the discrepancy between the patient's perception of her body size and her actual body size. If the body perception is quite distorted, we often ask the patient if others disagree with her perception of her body size. Patients with more delusional body image distortion are threatened by this inquiry, and often react with hostile resistance.

Assessing the degree of body image distortion is most important because outcome research with anorexic patients indicates that those individuals who persistently maintain the cognitive distortion that they are terribly fat despite their emaciated condition show the poorest improvement with treatment (Garfinkel, Moldofsky, & Garner, 1977). We have found this finding to have particular clinical relevance because of the psychological adaptation that the more delusional distortion serves for the anorexic patient.

It is our opinion that the anorexic's distorted belief about her body is a necessary distortion that allows her to develop a psychological organization that gives her life meaning and purpose (Casper, 1982; Garner & Bemis, 1982; Chapter 6, this volume;

Garner & Garfinkel, 1982; Garner, Garfinkel, & Bemis, 1982). It can be viewed as similar to the paranoid-state patient who suddenly and without apparent evidence decides that the next-door neighbor is trying to kill him or her. The paranoid-state patient will then develop an extensive psychological organization to protect himself or herself against the perceived threat. The defense of the self against the perceived threat then provides a mechanism for structuring his or her life. Obviously, the patient has to cling to the one central distorted belief, because if the one belief is not true, then all the subsequent behavior does not make sense.

The distorted body image allows the anorexic patient to develop a cognitive system organized around a perceived threat (fat); this gives her a sense of *purpose*, and the fear associated with the perceived threat (fat) provides *motivation* to avoid the perceived threat. If she acknowledges her thinness (no fat), then purpose and motivation are lost. Essentially, she must believe she is fat in order to preserve the psychological system she has created.

It follows, then, that those patients who cling most tenaciously to the distorted body image are most susceptible to experiencing a psychological collapse as a result of relinquishing the delusional organization. Consequently, these patients also have the poorest outcome because of the brittleness of their intrapsychic structure.

To reiterate, the important assessment to make in this section is to determine the extent of the delusional *distortion*, as opposed to *dissatisfaction*, and to identify what impact the distortion is having upon life adjustment.

DIETING BEHAVIOR

The primary purpose of this section is to assess the length of time the patient has been involved in dieting behavior, how much psychological and physiological deprivation is being experienced, and the cognitive–emotional system that has evolved around the behavior. We attempt to learn when dieting first began, why, and whether there was a particular source of encouragement.

Of particular interest is how preoccupied other members of the family are with food and weight. As one would suspect, we find that many of our patients have parents who are food and weight preoccupied (Kalucy, Crisp, & Harding, 1977). We are also beginning, like others (Crisp, 1980; Garfinkel & Garner, 1982), to see families that have several children who have had, or are currently having, difficulty with anorexia nervosa or bulimia.

It is also important to assess how much of a psychological system has developed around the concept of dieting. We inquire whether the patient thinks of food as "good" or "bad," and how it affects her to eat either "good" or "bad" foods. We also try to assess how much magical or superstitious thinking is associated with the food-related behavior (Garner & Bemis, 1982) by asking the patient to explain her understanding of what calories are, how food is digested, what the function of fat is, and how most fad diets work.

Finally, we attempt to assess to what extent either psychological or physiological deprivation may be triggering such behavior as binge eating or specific food cravings (Garner, Rockert, Olmsted, Johnson, & Coscina, Chapter 21, this volume; Wardle, 1980; Wardle & Beinart, 1981). We are particularly interested in determining whether the patient is avoiding any specific food groups, such as complex carbohydrates (Wurtman, Wurtman, Growdon, Henry, Lipscomb, & Zeisel, 1981).

SCALE BEHAVIOR AND EXERCISE

Ritualized behavior around body measurement and exercise are common side effects of a chronic preoccupation with dieting. It is important to assess how frequently the patient weighs or measures herself, how ritualized the behavior is, and how minor fluctuations in weight affect self-concept and daily activities.

We also investigate the longest period of time during the past 6 months that the patient has gone without weighing or measuring herself, and what events correlate with this period of time. We will often ask whether the patient would be willing to temporarily delegate the monitoring of her body to the clinic staff to assess how integral the measurement process is to her psychological homeostasis.

Exercise, like scale behavior, can become highly ritualized and quite debilitating. We find it most important to investigate what adaptive function the exercise serves in the patient's psychological system. Inquiry regarding how the patient experiences the absence of exercise often offers clues regarding the adaptive context. We have found that the exercise can serve a variety of purposes, including a hypomanic defense against a fear of paralyzing depression, a form of masochistic self-punishment, a goal-oriented pursuit of achievement serving narcissistic/exhibitionistic concerns, or as a general mechanism for regulating such tension states as anxiety, anger, and the like.

BINGE EATING

Our objective during this phase of the interview is to investigate, at both a micro level and a macro level, the adaptive significance of the binge-eating behavior. At the macro level, we are interested in determining when the problem eating began, the precipitating circumstances, and whether fluctuations in the eating behavior correlate with recurring life events.

Information about the absence of binge-eating behavior is also critical. We inquire about the longest period the patient has gone without binge eating and investigate the circumstances that facilitated the binge-free period. Vacations away from home, entering relationships, and escaping bad relationships or bad work situations are times when patients will often have symptom-free periods. Patients' affective responses to symptom-free periods often vary, and we inquire whether the patients experience a greater or lesser degree of disorganization, sense of loss, anxiety, or depression.

We usually begin the micro-level inquiry by asking the patient to describe her daily eating pattern. We have her describe in detail the previous day's activities, including meals, binge episodes, and routine events. Initially, we are particularly interested in learning when and to what extent she is eating meals. We also want to know what she regards as a reasonable meal and a binge, because many bulimic and anorexic patients have come to interpret any consumption of food as a loss of control.

After describing her daily eating patterns, we have the patient focus more specifically on her binge-eating episodes. We attempt to assess whether there are particular foods, events, times, or emotional states that recurrently trigger binge-eating episodes. Research has indicated that most patients have difficulty with food when they are alone in unstructured situations. This is usually during evening hours when they are at home alone (Larson & Johnson, in press; Pyle, Mitchell, & Eckert, 1981).

They generally binge on foods they normally deprive themselves of, such as sweets or carbohydrates, which they regard as bad foods. We have learned that, unfortunately, most of our patients will not eat during the day, the period of time that is most structured, and will attempt to eat at night, which is their most unstructured time. These high-risk evening hours are thus made more difficult because the patients are usually calorie-deprived at their most vulnerable period during the day.

At this point in the interview, we also investigate the patients' phenomenological experience of binge eating. We are specifically trying to discover what type of tension states they are attempting to regulate, or what type of affective release they are seeking through the binge eating.

Boredom, loneliness, anger, and depression are the affective states that appear to be the most troublesome (Johnson, Stuckey, Lewis, & Schwartz, 1982). There are, however, any number of adaptations the binge eating can serve. These may include eroticized impulse expression, aggressive impulse expression, pleasurable discontrol, oppositional acting out, self-soothing, disassociation, self-punishment, and so on (Johnson, Lewis, & Hagman, 1984). It is clear that the act of binge eating carries a unique significance for each patient, and it is incumbent upon the interviewer to try to understand what specific function or functions the behavior serves.

PURGING BEHAVIOR

Overall, in this part of the interview, we want to determine the onset, precipitants, duration, frequency, and method of purging behavior. Early research has indicated that most bulimic patients use self-induced vomiting as a preferred evacuation technique, and that they begin purging approximately 1 year after the onset of binge eating (Johnson *et al.*, 1982; Pyle *et al.*, 1981).

The act of purging, like binge eating, can serve several adaptive purposes. The purging behavior can serve as a release of a dysphoric affect, such as anger, or as a means to return to a sense of self-control after feeling out of control with the binge eating. It can also serve as a self-punishment or an undoing behavior that expiates guilt. As a masochistic act it can serve a function similar to self-mutilation, in that it reorganizes or reorients a patient who may be fragmenting under the impact of an intense feeling state. It is unquestionably a powerful reinforcer, simply by the fact that it protects the patient from the dreaded weight gain, and frees them from the constraints of chronic restrained eating. Since abstinence from purging can be a crucial tool for recovery, it is important to understand how *primary* the purging behavior has become in the binge–purge sequence. Some of our initial research has suggested that, for many bulimic patients, the act of purging is more tension regulating than binge eating (Johnson & Larson, 1982). Our clinical experiences have confirmed the early research, in that for some patients a transformation occurs over time whereby they begin to binge eat so that they can purge, rather than purge so that they can binge eat.

As with the binge eating, it is important to inquire about the longest period of time the patient has gone without purging since the onset of the behavior. It is important to know what precipitated the abstinence, what effect it had on the binge eating, and how uncomfortable the patient was during this time.

Recent research has indicated that laxative abuse is very predictive of life impairment (Johnson & Love, 1984). Consequently, we make a particular effort to explore how laxative abusing patients think about their laxative abuse. Our experience has been that the laxative abusers are usually misguided about the effectiveness of laxatives as a mechanism for controlling fat. They often have rather peculiar notions about the laxatives, which indicate more serious cognitive disturbances. We explain to these patients the ineffectiveness of laxatives to control calorie absorption, as demonstrated by a recent study (Bo-Lynn, Santa-Ana, Morawski, & Fordtran, 1983). One of our objectives in providing this information is to assess to what degree the patients can take advantage of didactic information to correct their distorted beliefs.

After exploring the adaptive context of the binge eating and purging behavior, we find it useful to learn what strategies the patient has attempted to use to manage the symptomatic behavior. Questions about efforts to stop or prevent the behaviors often shed light on how ego-syntonic the symptoms are and allow the interviewer to assess the degree to which the patient feels helpless or hopeless.

Recent studies have indicated that most eating-disordered patients (particularly bulimics who purge) experience a depressive phenomenon that has been referred to as "learned helplessness" (Seligman, 1975). Learned helplessness is a construct that has emerged from work with laboratory animals exposed to repeated shocks without opportunity for escape. Observers noted that after a prolonged period of time these animals would not even use an escape if it were provided. Essentially, they had developed a type of amotivational syndrome as a result of feeling trapped by their circumstances.

Like these animals, many bulimic patients experience a type of "learned helplessness," and feel hopelessly trapped by the binge–purge cycle. For these patients the symptoms are ego-syntonic; they have come to feel that there is little or no chance for escape. One important function the initial consultation can serve is to provide the hope that the symptomatic behavior can be managed, so that it does not seriously disrupt the patient's life. There is preliminary evidence that simply restoring hopefulness to these patients in an initial meeting provides sufficient motivation to reduce binge-eating episodes by up to 50% (Connors, Johnson, & Stuckey, in press).

RELATED BEHAVIORS

Affective Illness

During this phase of the interview, we want to investigate the nature of the depressive experience. We are particularly interested in determining whether the patient has a primary affective disorder, as opposed to a more psychological depression.

Recent research has indicated that bulimic patients in particular may be at significant risk for primary affective disorder (Strober, Salkin, Burroughs, & Morrell, 1982). Primary affective disorder is a depressive state characterized by vegetative symptoms, such as mood variability, persistent fatigue, sleep difficulty, frequent crying episodes, irritability, listlessness, and appetite disorders. Preliminary work has suggested that tricyclic medication and monoamine oxidase (MAO) inhibitors have been helpful with bulimic patients who present with this type of mood disorder (Pope, Hudson, Jonas, & Yurgelun-Todd, 1983).

Even in the absence of a biologically based affective disorder, most eating-disordered patients report significant psychological depression (Johnson *et al.*, 1982;

Pyle *et al.*, 1981). We attempt to identify whether the patient has a more anaclitic depression (Lidz, 1976; Sugarman, Quinlan, & DeVenis, 1981) or a more introjective depression (Blatt, 1974), and to what extent she has become amotivational as a result of learned helplessness.

Patients with anaclitic depressions are highly dependent and have an intense need to be directly connected to a need-satisfying object. They feel disorganized and lost when alone, because they lack the internal resources to direct themselves when others are not present. They generally have very fragile boundaries and are quite vulnerable to loss of impulse control and enmeshment in interpersonal relationships. These patients are usually frightened of being abandoned and present as quite weak and helpless.

In contrast, patients with more introjective depressions present with a more obsessive preoccupation with performance, achievement, and perfectionistic strivings. They critically judge all their efforts and report a persistent sense of guilt and shame. They generally feel they have failed to meet expectations and standards, and there is usually a desperate attempt to gain approval and acceptance through their achievements.

Essentially, these distinctions are helpful in making treatment recommendations, which are discussed more fully in a subsequent section.

Multiple Substance Abuse and Impulse Problems

In this part of the interview, we attempt to assess whether the symptomatic eating behavior is only one aspect of a generalized borderline personality organization. Recent research has indicated that bulimic patients in particular often present with positive histories of multiple substance abuse and various impulse-dominated behaviors, such as shoplifting, promiscuity, and self-mutilation (Casper *et al.*, 1980; Garfinkel *et al.*, 1980). These individuals have poor outcomes, have significant structural and characterological deficits, and represent a more disturbed subgroup among the spectrum of eating-disordered patients.

SEXUAL AND MENSTRUAL HISTORY

Traditionally, anorexia nervosa has been regarded as based in a fear of sexuality and the self-starvation, with its concomitant loss of secondary sexual characteristics, has been viewed as an attempt to achieve a prepubescent state (Crisp, 1980). However, research has shown that sexual drive, sexual behavior, and feelings about sexuality vary greatly among anorexics and bulimics (Abraham & Beumont, 1982; Beumont, Abraham, & Simpson, 1981). More recent conceptualization suggests that for eating-disordered women, problems with sexuality may simply be a reflection of more basic difficulties with autonomy and self-regulation (Bruch, 1973). Thus, the main objective in this part of the interview is to strive to understand the individual's specific sexual feelings and experience as part of her overall adjustment.

It is well known that libido usually decreases dramatically in individuals with anorexic weight levels and sexual behavior also usually decreases (Keys, Brozek, Henschel, Mickelsen, & Taylor, 1950). Nonetheless, we find it useful to inquire about the individual's thoughts, feelings, and interest in sex as well as her actual behavior.

Research indicates that some anorexic women who are married or in a steady relationship continue to engage in sex despite little pleasure or interest (Beumont *et al.*, 1981).

Eating-disordered women have reported a full range of sexual interest and behavior up to frank promiscuity. Women who binge or who binge and purge tend to report more frequent sexual activity and interest. This is often interpreted as part of a larger problem with impulse control. Women who merely restrict their food intake seem to be on the whole less interested in sex (Abraham & Beumont, 1982).

The major reason we obtain a menstrual history is to determine if amenorrhea has occurred. Cessation of menses usually accompanies anorexic body weights and it is useful to inquire within what weight range it occurred. We try to use the menstrual weight as the target weight if weight restoration is necessary. However, amenorrhea can also occur in normal-weight women, in women who frequently binge and purge, and in women whose weight fluctuates markedly (Beumont *et al.*, 1981). We find it helpful to inquire about the premorbid menstrual history to evaluate the current impact of the disordered eating on the menstrual cycle. We also inquire whether the eating problems vary according to the menstrual cycle. Clinical evidence is beginning to suggest that these may be related in some women, especially those prone to premenstrual syndrome. These women sometimes report that their appetite, especially for sweets and carbohydrates, increases just prior to menstruation. An understanding of the possible impact of the menstrual cycle on appetite and eating may be helpful in planning treatment.

FAMILY HISTORY

When taking the family history, we are particularly interested in assessing the patient's biological vulnerability to illness (psychiatric and medical) and in investigating the nature of the family environment.

Research has indicated that affective disorders and alcoholism are highly prevalent among first-degree relatives of bulimic patients. A positive family history and positive vegetative symptoms of depression among patients are usually indications that a trial of antidepressant medication may be beneficial.

When investigating the family environment, we generally try to assess several parameters. Following the observations of Minuchin, Rosman, and Baker (1978), we try to determine whether the family is enmeshed, disengaged, overcontrolled, or undercontrolled. We also try to assess how much free expression of affect exists, the extent of achievement orientation or perfectionism, and how much stability and flexibility exists in the system. We also attempt to explore the quality of the parent–child relationship and the extent to which the child's symptomatic behavior may be serving an adaptive function within the family system.

While data-based studies of eating-disordered families are scarce in the literature, preliminary reports have indicated significant family disturbance. Johnson and Flack (1984) found that when compared to a control sample screened for eating disorders, normal-weight bulimic women reported higher levels of conflict and negativity, and lower expressiveness and emphasis on independence in their families.

Anorexic families have been characterized as enmeshed, overprotective, rigid, and lacking in capacity for conflict resolution (Minuchin *et al.*, 1978). In a series of data-based studies, Strober *et al.* (1982) found important family differences between bulimic anorexics and restricting anorexics. Bulimic anorexics' families were characterized by high levels of conflict, marital discord, and negativity among family members. Bulimic anorexics also reported feeling more distant from both parents, but particularly from their fathers.

Several personality attributes were also found to differentiate parents of bulimic anorexics from parents of restricting anorexics. Fathers of bulimic anorexics were more impulsive, were more hostile, and reported lower frustration tolerance. In contrast, fathers of restricting anorexics appeared more withdrawn and submissive. Mothers of bulimic anorexics were more psychosomatically preoccupied and depressed, compared to mothers of restricting anorexics, who were more introverted and phobic. Both mothers and fathers of bulimic anorexics reported more family problems, higher hostility, and less inner control than parents of restricting anorexics.

Although more research is needed, preliminary reports suggest that, overall, bulimic families appear to be openly conflicted, with more parental impulse disturbance and depression. In contrast, families of restricting anorexics appear to be more rigidly enmeshed, with more introverted and phobic parents.

LIFE ADJUSTMENT

In this section of the interview, we want to assess the overall quality of the patient's life and to determine how much the symptomatic behavior has affected her work, daily activities, interpersonal relationships, and sexual activity. Outcome studies with anorexia nervosa patients indicate that the syndrome is quite debilitating. Reviewing 700 cases across 12 outcome studies of anorexia nervosa patients, Schwartz and Thompson (1981) found that 49% were cured of their weight difficulties, 26% continued to have fluctuating weight problems or became obese, 18% remained chronically anorexic, and 7% died of anorexia or suicide. The original outcome studies reported very little about the quality of the patients' lives or the extent of continued food-related thoughts and behavior. Overall, the studies indicated that 90% of the anorexics worked, but that only 47% had married or were maintaining active heterosexual lives.

Although extensive outcome studies with bulimics are not available, a preliminary report by Johnson and Berndt (1983) indicated that bulimic patients, when compared to a community sample, had significantly more impaired life adjustment in the areas of work, social and leisure activities, family life, marital adjustment, and overall adjustment.

It is also important in this section to investigate the extent to which the patient is capable of engaging in self-enhancing activities. What is the breadth and quality of her involvement in hobbies or activities that give her pleasure? It has been our experience that eating-disordered patients are self-sacrificing, achievement-oriented individuals who take much better care of others than of themselves, and who are often too goal oriented to simply enjoy activities.

MEDICAL ISSUES

The task of this section of the interview is to investigate whether the patient has ever experienced a major illness, whether she is currently on medication, and the date of the most recent medical evaluation. All eating-disordered patients should be medically evaluated and followed accordingly during the course of treatment.

The most common physical symptoms observed with anorexics and bulimics include electrolyte abnormalities, tooth decay, enlarged parotid glands, edema, hypothermia, fatigue, dizziness, sleep difficulties, gastrointestinal problems, and menstrual difficulties (Fairburn, 1982; Garner *et al.*, Chapter 21, this volume; Mitchell & Pyle, 1982; Russell, 1979). These symptoms should be noted and monitored throughout treatment.

THE FINAL FEW MINUTES

Before making treatment recommendations, we usually pose the following question to normal-weight patients who are purging: "Would you be willing to gain ten pounds in exchange for not having any more difficulty with binge eating, purging, or food preoccupation?" We explain to the patient that the question reflects our experience that if the purging behavior is curtailed, then binge eating often dramatically decreases in quantity and frequency. Interrupting the purging behavior restores some restraint, because the biological and psychological consequences of unrestrained eating (nausea, painful fullness, weight gain) cannot be avoided.

One group of patients often assures us that they would rather be dead than gain 10 pounds. This is the group of patients who have experienced a Cinderella-like transformation as a result of losing weight. These women have either become socioeconomically upwardly mobile, or their romantic–social life has improved significantly as they have achieved thinness. Their weight loss is usually accomplished *vis-à-vis* highly restrictive dieting, which cannot be maintained over a long period of time. Rather than return to what they experience as a "social isolation," which they feel would occur with weight gain, they begin to use various purging techniques so they can abandon the restrictive diets and yet maintain thinness. They are frightened of change, because they have actually experienced the social discrimination and alienation of overweight individuals, particularly toward females, in our current culture. Their severe dread of gaining 10 pounds reflects an entrenched yet fragile psychological integration, and is not a favorable prognostic indicator.

TREATMENT RECOMMENDATIONS

Throughout this chapter, we suggest that anorexia nervosa and bulimia are multi-determined eating disorders and are affecting an increasingly heterogeneous group of patients. Given the multidetermined and heterogeneous nature of the disorders, comprehensive outpatient clinics should have access to a variety of treatment modalities that include individual, group, family and marital psychotherapy, pharmacotherapy, and medical consultation. Assigning a patient to a particular mode of treatment depends upon the unique needs of the patient.

Certain eating-disordered patients may require hospitalization. The criteria we use to make this decision after the initial consultation include the following: significant medical difficulties resulting from low body weight or persistent self-induced vomiting, laxative, or diuretic abuse; significant suicide risk or demonstrated inability to provide self-care; inability of family or current living arrangement to provide an adequate psychological environment for improvement to occur; the need to facilitate

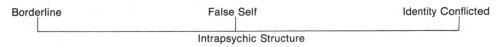

Figure 3-1. Continuum of intrapsychic structure.

a complex differential diagnosis; and, on occasion, the need to interrupt the binge–purge cycle.

While it is difficult to subclassify anorexic and bulimic patients because of the heterogeneity of the group, we have found one method helpful in making outpatient treatment recommendations. Swift and Stern (1982) have suggested that eating-disordered patients can be broadly characterized as falling along a continuum of intrapsychic structure ranging from borderline personality organization to identity conflicted (see Figure 3-1). The following paragraphs outline major characteristics of these different groups, as well as the treatment modalities we have found most helpful.

Borderline Personality Organization

Patients who fall into this category (Masterson, 1977) are usually polysymptomatic; their eating disorder is secondary to a more serious problem of understructured internal resources. They present generally chaotic and impulse-dominated life histories. Their affect is quite labile, fluctuating between rageful agitation and an anaclitic, empty depression. Intrapsychically, they are diffuse and undifferentiated, and have fragile self–other and inner–outer boundaries. Interpersonally, they intensely seek need-gratifying relationships and are very dependent upon external sources for tension regulation and self-management. Their cognitive style is concrete and dichotomous. They generally think in black-and-white, all-or-none terms, and can be quite superstitious and magical (Garner & Bemis, 1982). Their primary defenses are primitive denial, splitting, and projective identification. Among the bulimic patients, binge eating is often experienced more as depersonalization than as disassociation, and purging is often very masochistic (similar to self-cutting) — an attempt to ward off self-fragmentation (Goodsitt, 1977).

Our experience has been that these patients respond most favorably to highly structured, directive, supportive interventions that are aimed at life management. Abstract, insight-oriented therapy is often difficult because of the concrete and impulse-dominated cognitive milieu. We find that "more is better" with these patients. A team approach, consisting of individual, group, family, and medical treatment, is important because of the intense demands that these patients' needs place on a treatment setting. Food-related symptoms will usually remit only after the patients feel securely "held" by the treatment setting.

False Self

The group of patients with "false self" organizations (Winnicott, 1965) is loosely grouped together by some common dynamics. They are not as seriously disturbed as the borderline patients, and yet they seem to have more psychological difficulty than the identity-conflicted group. In our opinion, this group is distinguished more by what we do not know about them than what we do know. They generally present with life histories that appear uneventful, and their current life adjustments appear quite adequate.

During the initial consultation, one often feels that the interview questions are painfully and threateningly intrusive to these patients, to a degree that one feels reluctant to pursue the inquiry. They are also reluctant to talk about food-related behavior, because to do so is to expose a less-than-adequate aspect of self. They are generally very compliant and nondemanding patients, who seem very careful about becoming too involved in treatment.

The nature of the relationship these patients develop with a therapist seems to reflect the overall nature of their interpersonal world. They superficially accommodate to treatment demands without becoming involved in intimate disclosure. They continue in treatment without complaint, but the therapist feels that he or she is not quite connecting with such patients in a significant way. Their compliance and avoidance of controversial issues seem to be efforts to avoid actually relating to the therapist. There is usually a prevailing feeling in the therapist that he or she has a fragile alliance with patients who want to be in treatment, but are very frightened about the potential development of the therapeutic relationship. It has been our experience that this ambivalence represents a basic wish–fear dilemma that is a central dynamic.

Essentially, we have found that there is often a common developmental theme among "false self" patients that has resulted in the wish–fear dilemma. We have learned that for one reason or another (physical or psychological illness of the mother during a patient's infancy, or a situation in the family that has resulted in early physical or psychological separation), the patients were forced to separate prematurely and develop psychological autonomy. A successful pseudomature adaptation was an enormous relief to such a child's mother or the system, with the result that the child received positive reinforcement and a sense of self-esteem for compliant, nondemanding behavior.

The prefix "pseudo-" is appropriate, because while the child had adequate structure to make the superficial adaptation, she did not have adequate structure to accommodate all of her infantile needs. Since the mother, or the system, could not respond to the infantile needs, the needs became split off, isolated, and interpreted by the patient as troublesome, perhaps destructive, or even as a sign of being out of control. Progressively, the patient feels that she is two people: one who appears to be competently in control of things, and another who feels needy and out of control. The wish–fear dilemma revolves around the patient's wish for someone to identify and respond to her needs, which is juxtaposed against her fear that allowing someone to see the needy and dependent side will collapse the self-esteem and self-organization that has evolved as a result of the pseudomature behavior.

Food, for these patients, is their safest and most trusted ally. Essentially, they will allow themselves to behave in the presence of food in ways they would not allow any other person to observe. They will also invest food with the ability to regulate different tension states. Allowing a person to help with these feelings would mean risking too much exposure.

The treatment recommendation for these patients is long-term, relationship-oriented, individual psychotherapy. We have found that a nondirective, nonintrusive approach is most helpful. Directive interventions aimed at the food-related behavior are usually met with resistance until a consistent and stable relationship has developed with the therapist. Group therapy is usually refused by these patients because of their fear of exposure.

Identity Conflicted

Identity conflicted patients primarily represent those who have adequate intrapsychic structure and have become involved in food-related behavior for more neurotic reasons. There are often clear precipitants for the onset of the behavior, or the behavior can be conceptualized as a developmental adjustment reaction. The pursuit of thinness among this group often revolves around identity and achievement issues; for bulimics, the eating behavior may be a compensatory alternative to conflictual drives, such as aggression or sexuality. If depression is observed, it is usually the introjective type of depression described earlier.

Cognitively, this group of patients is very capable of functioning abstractly, and their behavior can be understood and interpreted in a symbolic manner. Their interpersonal relationships are differentiated and developmentally appropriate. These patients often respond quite well to short-term, symptom-focused interventions. Both individual and group interventions that challenge their beliefs about dieting behavior, the pursuit of thinness, achievement, guilt, failure, rejection, assertiveness, approval, and sexuality can interrupt the symptomatic behavior rather quickly.

SUMMARY AND COMMENTS

The initial consultation serves a vital function in most comprehensive treatment programs. It is a delicate task with multiple demands. The clinician must obtain sufficient information to render a diagnosis; must make treatment recommendations according to observed distinctions among patients; and must quickly establish a therapeutic relationship with the patient that simultaneously challenges, supports, and offers hope.

As our ability to accomplish these tasks in the initial consultation improves, so will our treatment effectiveness. The clinical observations, as well as the DSED (see Appendix), are offered in the hope that they will contribute to an increasing sophistication in conducting initial consultations.

APPENDIX

D.S.E.D.

DIAGNOSTIC SURVEY FOR EATING DISORDERS

INSTRUCTIONS: This questionnaire covers several eating problems that may or may not apply to you. You ma find it difficult to answer some questions if your eating pattern is irregular or has changed recently. Please read each question carefully and choose the answer that **best** describes your situation **most of the time.** Also, please feel free to write remarks in the margins if this will clarify your answer. Thank you.

Name

Date

Current Address

Permanent Address

Current Telephone

Permanent Telephone

Social Security Number

I would like to thank the following people for their suggestions during the construction of the DSED: Arnold Andersen, MD; Elke Eckert, MD; David Garner, PhD; James Mitchell, MD; Richard Pyle, MD; and Michael Strober, PhD. Parts of the DSED were adapted from the Social and Psychiatric History Form for Eating Disorders used at the University of Minnesota Medical School.

Identifying and Demographic Information

Sex   Male ☐1   Female ☐2

Age _____   (17-18)

Race (Check one)

White ☐1   Black ☐2   ·Other (Specify) ☐3   (19)

Your present religious affiliation (Check one)   (20)

Protestant ☐1 Catholic ☐2   Jewish ☐3   No Affiliation ☐4

Other (Specify) ☐5

Religious affiliation of your family of origin (Check one)

Protestant ☐1   Catholic ☐2   Jewish ☐3   No Affiliation ☐4   (21)

Other (Specify) ☐5

Marital Status (Check one)   (22)

Presently in first marriage   ☐1
Divorced and presently remarried   ☐2
Divorced or separated and not presently remarried ☐3
Widowed and presently remarried   ☐4
Widowed and not presently remarried   ☐5
Never married   ☐6

What is your present primary role? (Check one)   (23)

Wage earner ☐1   Housewife ☐2 Student ☐3 Other (Specify) ☐4

Highest Occupational level attained   Check one for each person   (24-31)

		Self	Father	Mother	Spouse
Higher executive, proprietor of large concern, Major professional	1	☐	☐	☐	☐
Business manager of large concern, proprietor of medium sized business, lesser professional	2	☐	☐	☐	☐
Administrative personnel, owner of small independent business, minor professional, owner of large farm	3	☐	☐	☐	☐
Clerical or sales worker, technician, owner of little business, owner of medium sized farm	4	☐	☐	☐	☐
Skilled manual employee, owner of small business	5	☐	☐	☐	☐
Machine operator, semiskilled employee, tenant farmer who owns little equipment	6	☐	☐	☐	☐
Unskilled employee, sharcropper	7	☐	☐	☐	☐
Does not apply (Never worked in paid employment)	8	☐	☐	☐	☐
Does not apply (No spouse)	9	☐	☐	☐	☐
Information not available	10	☐	☐	☐	☐

Current living arrangement (Check one)   (32)

With Parents or relatives ☐ 1

Dorm or
Shared apartment with Friend ☐ 2

Conjugal (intimate relationship with one other
person, including spouse, boyfriend, etc.) ☐ 3

Alone ☐ 4

Highest level of education   Check one for each person   (33-40)

		Self	Father	Mother	Spouse
Completed post-graduate training	1	☐	☐	☐	☐
Some post-graduate training	2	☐	☐	☐	☐
Completed college, received four year academic degree	3	☐	☐	☐	☐
Attended college, but didn't receive four year academic degree	4	☐	☐	☐	☐
Completed high school; may have attended or completed trade school or other non-academic training requiring high school completion	5	☐	☐	☐	☐
Attended high school	6	☐	☐	☐	☐
Completed grammar school (8th grade)	7	☐	☐	☐	☐
Attended grammar school	8	☐	☐	☐	☐
No schooling	9	☐	☐	☐	☐
Does not apply (No spouse)	10	☐	☐	☐	☐
Information not available (Specify why)	11	☐	☐	☐	☐

Please describe your current occupation: _____

Weight History

Current weight	_____ lbs.	(41-43)
Current height	_____ inches	(44-45)
Desired weight	_____ lbs.	(46-48)

Adult Years

Highest adult weight since age 18   _____ lbs.   at age _____   (49-53)

Lowest adult weight since age 18   _____ lbs.   at age _____   (54-58)

How long did you remain at your lowest adult weight? ____ days ____ months ____ years   (59-61)

Adolescent Years

Highest weight between ages 12-18   _____ lbs.   at age _____   (62-66)

Lowest weight between ages 12-18   _____ lbs.   at age _____   (67-71)

Childhood

How did you perceive your weight as a child between the ages 6-12 years old?

Extremely Thin	Somewhat Thin	Normal Weight	Somewhat Overweight	Extremely Overweight	
1	2	3	4	5	(72)

As a child were you teased about your weight?

    Yes about being underweight ☐1   (73)

    Yes about being overweight ☐2

To what extent were you teased?

Extremely	Very Much	Moderately	Slightly	Not at All (74)
1	2	3	4	5

At your current weight do you feel that you are (Circle one)

Extremely Thin	Somewhat Thin	Normal Weight	Moderately Overweight	Extremely Overweight
1	2	3	4	5 (75)

Are you involved in an occupation that requires you to maintain a certain weight?   (76)

    Yes ☐1   No ☐2

    Please explain:

How much does a two-pound weight **gain** affect your feelings about yourself?   (77)

Extremely	Very Much	Moderately	Slightly	Not at All
1	2	3	4	5

How much does a two-pound weight **loss** affect your feelings about your self?   (78)

Extremely	Very Much	Moderately	Slightly	Not at All
1	2	3	4	5

Has there ever been a time when your feelings about yourself or your social life have changed substantially as a result of losing weight?   (79)

Yes ☐1 No ☐2

Please explain: (80) = 1

How dissatisfied are you with the way your body is proportioned?   (10)

Extremely Dissatisfied	Very Dissatisfied	Moderately Dissatisfied	Slightly Dissatisfied	Not at All Dissatisfied
1	2	3	4	5

(11-17)

Please indicate on the scales below how you feel about the different areas of your body.

	Strongly Positive	Moderately Positive	Neutral	Moderately Negative	Strongly Negative
Face	1	2	3	4	5
Arms	1	2	3	4	5
Shoulders	1	2	3	4	5
Breasts	1	2	3	4	5
Stomach	1	2	3	4	5
Buttocks	1	2	3	4	5
Thighs	1	2	3	4	5

How fat do you feel? (18)

Extremely Fat	Very Fat	Fat	Somewhat Fat	Not at all Fat
1	2	3	4	5

How often do you weigh or measure your body size? (19)

More than daily ☐ 1   Daily ☐ 2   More than weekly ☐ 3   Weekly ☐ 4

Monthly ☐ 5   Less than monthly ☐ 6

Dieting Behavior

Have you ever been on a diet? (20)

Yes ☐ 1   No ☐ 2

At what age did you begin to restrict your food intake due to concern over your body size? (21-22)

_____ years old

In your first year of dieting how many times did you start a diet? (23-25)

_____ No. of times

Over the last year how often have you begun a diet? (26-28)

_____ No. of times

Please rank from 1-9 your preferred way of dieting (1 = most preferred, 9 = least preferred) (29-37)

Skip meals	_____	Reduce portions	_____
Completely fast	_____	Go on fad diets	_____
Restrict carbohydrates	_____	Reduce calories	_____
Restrict sweets	_____	Other (specify)	_____
Restrict fats	_____		

If you have ever been encouraged to diet, please rank from 1-10 the people that encouraged you to diet the most (1 = most encoraged, 10 = least encouraged) (38-47)

Boyfriends	_____	Sister	_____
Girlfriends	_____	Employer	_____
Mother	_____	Teacher/Coach	_____
Father	_____	Other relative	_____
Brother	_____	Other (Please specify) _____	

Binge Eating Behavior

Have you ever had an episode of eating a large amount of food in a short space of time (an eating binge) (48)

Yes ☐ 1   No ☐ 2

Please circle on the scales below, how characteristic the following symptoms are of your binge eating

	Never	Rarely	Sometimes	Often	Always	
I consume a large amount of food during a binge	1	2	3	4	5	(49)
I eat very rapidly	1	2	3	4	5	(50)
I feel out of control when I eat	1	2	3	4	5	(51)
I feel miserable or annoyed after a binge	1	2	3	4	5	(52)
I get uncontrollable urges to eat and eat until I feel physically ill	1	2	3	4	5	(53)
I binge eat in private	1	2	3	4	5 _	(54)

How long does a binge usually last   (55)

Less than one hour ☐ 1
1 - 2 hours ☐ 2
More than 2 hours ☐ 3

Please rank 1-9 the times of day that you are most likely to binge (1 = most likely, 9 = least likely)   (56-64)

8 am - 10 am _____   6 pm 8 pm _____
10 am - 12 pm _____   8 pm - 10 pm _____
12 pm - 2 pm _____   10 pm - 12 am _____
2 pm - 4 pm _____   After midnight _____
4 pm - 6 pm _____

Please rank from 1-6 the places where you are most likely to binge (1 = most likely, 6 = least likely)   (65-70)

Home _____
Work _____
Restaurant _____
Car _____
Party _____
Other: Please specify _____

Please rank from 1-5 how likely you are to binge eat in the presence of the following people   (71-75)
(1 = most likely, 5 = least likely)

Friends _____
Parents _____
Alone _____
Spouse/Significant Other _____
Children _____

How old were you when you began binge eating   (76-77)
_____years old   80=2

How long have you had a problem with binge eating?   (10-12)

_____ Days   _____ Months   _____ Years

Within the last month, what has been your average number of binge episodes per week?   (13-15)

_____ Binges

What is the longest period you have had without binge eating since the onset of the problem? (16-18)

_____ Days   _____ Months   _____ Years

What were the circumstances that helped you to **not** binge eat for that period of time (If more   (19-31)
  than one event is applicable please rank order the importance of the event with 1 = most important)

Began dieting	_____
Started exercising	_____
Sought professional help	_____
Began romantic relationship	_____
Left romantic relationship	_____
Developed illness	_____
Left home	_____
Divorce	_____
Marriage	_____
Pregnancy	_____
Work	_____
Vacation	_____
Other: Please specify	_____

Please rank from 1-7 the foods that you are most likely to binge on: (1 = most likely, 7 = least likely)   (32-38)

Bread/cereal/pasta	_____
Cheese/milk/yogurt	_____
Fruit	_____
Meat/fish/poultry/eggs	_____
Salty snack foods	_____
Sweets	_____
Vegetables	_____

Please rank from 1-7 the foods that you are most likely to eat when you are not bingeing: (1 = most likely,   (39-45)
  7 = least likely)

Bread/cereal/pasta	_____
Cheese/milk/yogurt	_____
Fruit	_____
Meat/fish/poultry/eggs	_____
Salty snack foods	_____
Sweets	_____
Vegetables	_____

Were there any particular events in your life, either positive or negative, which preceded or coincided   (46-59)
with the onset of your eating problems? (Check as many as applicable)

Death of significant other   ☐
Leaving home   ☐
Illness or injury to self   ☐
Failure at school or work   ☐
Difficult sexual experience   ☐
Illness or injury to family member or   ☐
    significant other
Problems in romantic relationship   ☐
Family problems   ☐
Teasing about appearance   ☐
Prolonged period of dieting   ☐
Marriage   ☐
Pregnancy   ☐
Work transition   ☐
Other: Please specify   ☐

Using the scale below, please select the number which indicates the intensity of each of the following   (60-76)
feelings **before** a binge   (80) = 3

Extremely Intense	Very Intense		Moderately Intense		Slightly Intense	Not at all Intense
1	2		3		4	5

Calm	___	Bored	___
Empty	___	Frustrated	___
Confused	___	Panicked	___
Excited	___	Relieved	___
Angry	___	Guilty	___
Spaced out	___	Depressed	___
Inadequate	___	Nervous	___
Disgusted	___	Other: Please specify	___
Lonely	___		

Using the scale below, please select the number which indicates the intensity of each of the following
feelings **after** a binge

Extremely Intense	Very Intense		Moderately Intense		Slightly Intense	Not at all Intense
1	2		3		4	5

Calm	___	Bored	___
Empty	___	Frustrated	___
Confused	___	Panicked	___
Excited	___	Relieved	___
Angry	___	Guilty	___
Spaced out	___	Depressed	___
Inadequate	___	Nervous	___
Disgusted	___	Other: Please specify	___
Lonely	___		

Have you noticed a relationship between the frequency of your binge eating and your menstrual cycle?   (27)

Yes ☐ 1   No ☐ 2

Card 4
Column

If yes, please indicate when during your cycle you feel most vulnerable to binge eating.   (28)

During Menstruation   ☐1
11-14 days prior to menstruation   ☐2
7-10 days prior to menstruation   ☐3
3-6 days prior to menstruation   ☐4
1-2 days prior to menstruation   ☐5
After menstruation   ☐6

How uncomfortable are you with your binge eating behavior?   (29)

Extremely uncomfortable	Very uncomfortable	Uncomfortable	Somewhat uncomfortable	Not at all uncomfortable
1	2	3	4	5

How willing would you be to gain 10 pounds in exchange for not binge eating any more?   (30)

Extremely willing	Very willing	Willing	Somewhat willing	Not at all willing
1	2	3	4	5

Purging Behavior

Have you ever vomited or spit out food after eating in order to get rid of the food eaten?   (31)

Yes ☐1   No ☐2

How old were you when you induced vomiting for the first time?   (32-3
___ years old

How long have you been using self-induced vomiting?   (34-3

___ Days   ___ Months   ___Years

Have you ever used laxatives to control your weight or "get rid of food" ?   (37)

Yes ☐1 No ☐2

How old were you when you first took laxatives for weight control?   (38-4

___ years

How long have you been using laxatives for weight control?   (41-4

___ Days   ___Months   ___Years

How often are you now able to eat a "normal" meal without "binge eating" and without vomiting?   (44)

Never   ☐1   Several meals a week   ☐4
Less than one meal a week   ☐2   One meal a day   ☐5
About one meal a week   ☐3   More than one meal a day ☐6

How soon after eating do you induce vomiting?   (45

0 - 15 minutes   ☐1
16 - 30 minutes   ☐2
31 - 45 minutes   ☐3
46 - 60 minutes   ☐4
One hour or longer   ☐5

Which of the behaviors, "binge eating" or vomiting after meals came first?   (46

"Binge eating" came first   ☐1   Vomiting came first   ☐5
They both occured at the same time   ☐2   Neither came first, I have never had   ☐6
Neither came first. I have only "Binge eating" episodes ☐3   "binge eating" or vomiting episodes
Neither came first. I have only vomiting episodes   ☐4

Card 4

Column

During the entire **last month**, what is the average frequency that you have engaged in the following behaviors? (Check one for each behavior)

	Never	Once a month or less	Several times a month	Once a week	Several times a week	Once a day	More than once a day	
Binge eating	☐1	☐2	☐3	☐4	☐5	☐6	☐7	(47)
Vomiting	☐	☐	☐	☐	☐	☐	☐	(48)
Laxative use	☐	☐	☐	☐	☐	☐	☐	(49)
Use of diet pills	☐	☐	☐	☐	☐	☐	☐	(50)
Use of water pills	☐	☐	☐	☐	☐	☐	☐	(51)
Use of enemas	☐	☐	☐	☐	☐	☐	☐	(52)
Exercise to control weight	☐	☐	☐	☐	☐	☐	☐	(53)
Fasting (Skipping meals for entire day)	☐	☐	☐	☐	☐	☐	☐	(54)

Using the scale below, please select the number which indicates the intensity of each of the following feelings state **before** a purge.　(55-71)

Extremely Intense	Very Intense	Intense	Slightly Intense	Not at all Intense
1	2	3	4	5

Calm	_____	Bored	_____
Empty	_____	Frustrated	_____
Confused	_____	Panicked	_____
Excited	_____	Relieved	_____
Angry	_____	Guilty	_____
Spaced out	_____	Depressed	_____
Inadequate	_____	Nervous	_____
Disgusted	_____	Other: Please specify	_____
Lonely	_____		

80 = 4

Card 5

Column

Using the scale below, please select the number which indicates the intensity of each of the following feelings state **after** a purge　(10-26)

Extremely Intense	Very Intense	Intense	Slightly Intense	Not at all Intense
1	2	3	4	5

Calm	_____	Bored	_____
Empty	_____	Frustrated	_____
Confused	_____	Panicked	_____
Excited	_____	Relieved	_____
Angry	_____	Guilty	_____
Spaced out	_____	Depressed	_____
Inadequate	_____	Nervous	_____
Disgusted	_____	Other: Please specify	_____
Lonely	_____		

Exercise

How many minutes a day do you currently exercise (including going on walks, riding bicycle, etc.)?　(27-29)

___ Minutes

Have you ever competed in any of the following physical activities? (Check as many as are applicable)

Distance running ☐
Weight lifting ☐
Dancing ☐
Gymnastics ☐
Wrestling ☐
Tennis ☐
Swimming ☐
Other: Please specify ☐

Other Behavior

Do you feel that you have ever had an alcohol or drug abuse problem? (Circle one)   (38)

Extreme	Very Much	Moderate	Slight	Not at All
1	2	3	4	5

When did the drug or alcohol problem start in relationship to the eating problem?   (39)

I never had a drug or alcohol problem ☐1
Before the eating problem began ☐2
After the eating problem began ☐3
At the same time the eating problem began ☐4

Please indicate how frequently you have used the following substances since the onset of your   (40-4⁻)
eating problem.

Alcohol (specify type)	Amount	Daily 1	Weekly 2	Monthly 3	Less than Month
_____	_____	☐	☐	☐	☐
Amphetamines (Uppers)	_____	☐	☐	☐	☐
Barbiturates (Downers)	_____	☐	☐	☐	☐
Hallucinogens	_____	☐	☐	☐	☐
Marijuana	_____	☐	☐	☐	☐
Tranquilizers	_____	☐	☐	☐	☐
Cocaine	_____	☐	☐	☐	☐

Cigarettes: None ☐1   0 to ½ pack/day ☐2   1 pack/day ☐3   More than 1 pack/day ☐4

Have you ever made a suicide attempt?   Yes ☐1   No ☐2   (48)
Describe:
_____
_____

Have you ever tried to physically hurt yourself (i.e., cut yourself, hit yourself with intent to hurt, burn   (49)
yourself with cigarettes)?
Yes ☐1   No ☐2
Describe:
_____
_____

Since the onset of your eating problem, have you been involved in stealing? (50)

Yes ☐ 1 No ☐ 2

If yes, please describe types of items stolen: _____

_____

Sexual History

Have you ever engaged in sexual intercourse? (51)

Yes ☐ 1 No ☐ 2

If your answer is **yes**, at what age did you first engage in sexual intercourse? (52-53)

Age _____

Have you ever engaged in masturbation? (54)

Yes ☐ 1 No ☐ 2

If your answer is **yes**, at what age did you first engage in masturbation? (55-56)

Age _____

Please indicate on the line below your interest in sex **before the onset** of your eating problem: (57)

No Interest	Somewhat Interested	Interested	Very Interested	Extremely Interested
1	2	3	4	5

Please indicate on the scale below whether there has been a change in your sexual interest **since the onset** of your eating problem: (58)

Much Less Interested	Somewhat Less Interested	Equally Interested	Somewhat More Interested	Much More Interested
1	2	3	4	5

Please check your sexual preference: (59)

Exclusively heterosexual ☐ 1
Primarily heterosexual, some homosexual ☐ 2
Bisexual ☐ 3
Primarily homosexual, some heterosexual ☐ 4
Exclusively homosexual ☐ 5
Asexual (no sexual preference) ☐ 6
Autosexual (prefer masturbation to sexual ☐ 7
    relations with others)

Marriage and pregnancy (Check as many as applicable) (60-64)

	Yes 1	No 2
Was married before onset of the eating disorder	☐	☐
Was married after the onset of the eating disorder	☐	☐
Was pregnant before onset of the eating disorder	☐	☐
Was pregnant after onset of the eating disorder	☐	☐
Have one or more children	☐	☐

How satisfied are you with the quality of your sexual activity? (65)

Extremely Satisfied	Very Satisfied	Satisfied	Somewhat Satisfied	Not At All Satisfied
1	2	3	4	5

Menstrual History

Age at onset of menses (if you have never gotten your period please mark O)   (66-67)

_____ Years

Since the onset of your eating problems, how many times have you stopped menstruating for three   (68-69)
months or more (which were unrelated to pregnancy)

_____ Number of times

Before the onset of your eating problems, how many times had you stopped menstruating for three   (70-71)
months or more (which was not related to pregnancy)

_____ Number of times

Since the onset of your eating problems, what is the total number of months that you have not   (72-74)
menstruated (months unrelated to pregnancy)

_____ Months

Before the onset of your eating problems, what was the total number of months that you did not   (75-77)
menstruate (months unrelated to pregnancy)

_____ Months

Approximate regularity of cycles **before** onset of eating difficulties (Check one)   (78)

Fairly regular (Same number of days +3)   ☐1
Somewhat irregular (Variation 4-10 days)   ☐2
Very irregular (Variation greater than   ☐3
   10 days)
Never menstruated   ☐4

Approximate regularity of cycles **since** the onset of eating difficulties (Check one)   (79)

Fairly regular (Same number days +3)   ☐1
Somewhat irregular (Variation 4-10 days)   ☐2
Very irregular (Variation greater than   ☐3
   10 days)
Never menstruated   ☐4

How many times in the past have you had episodes of loss of menstrual periods lasting 3 months or more
associated with significant weight loss when you were not "binge eating" or pregnant?

_____ Number of times

Medical and Psychiatric History

Have you ever had any serious medical difficulties?   (12)
Yes ☐ 1   No ☐ 2
Please explain:

Please indicate any prior hospitalization for eating or emotional problems.

	Most Recent	Second Prior	Third Prior	Fourth Prior	
Date Admitted	_____	_____	_____	_____	
Date discharged	_____	_____	_____	_____	
Duration	_____	_____	_____	_____	(13-20)
Age	_____	_____	_____	_____	(21-28)
Primary reason for admission*	_____	_____	_____	_____	(29-32)

*Use number code: 1=bulimia; 2=anorexia nervosa; 3=chemical dependency; 4=depression; 5=psychiatric other than depression; 6=other)

Prior outpatient treatment for eating or emotional problems (i.e., a logically continuous series of treatments)

	Most Recent	Second Prior	Third Prior	Fourth Prior	
Date begun	_____	_____	_____	_____	
Date last visit of series	_____	_____	_____	_____	
Duration (weeks)	_____	_____	_____	_____	(33-40)
Age	_____	_____	_____	_____	(41-48)
Primary reason for treatment	_____	_____	_____	_____	(49-52)

*Use number code: 1=bulimia, 2=anorexia nervosa; 3=chemical dependency; 4=depression; 5=psychiatric disorder other than depression; 6=other)

	Most Recent	Second Prior	Third Prior	Fourth Prior	
Please indicate the types of treatment you have been involved with	_____	_____	_____	_____	(53-64)

*Use number code: 1=individual psychotherapy; 2=group psychotherapy; 3=psychiatric medication)

Are you currently on any medication? (65)

Yes ☐ 1   No ☐ 2

Please identify: _____

What physical problems have you had since the onset of your eating problems? (If more than one response is (66-73)
applicable please rank order your answers with 1 = most troublesome, 8 = least troublesome)

Sore Throat	_____	Sores or calluses on fingers due to induction of vomiting	_____
Weakness or tiredness	_____	Dental problems	_____
Seizures	_____	Other	_____
Feeling "bloated"	_____		
Stomach pains	_____		

Have you ever taken psychiatric medication? (74)

Yes ☐1   No ☐ 2   (80) = 6

Please identify: _____

Card 7

Column

Please circle on the scale below how frequently you experience the following symptoms:

	Never	Rarely	Sometimes	Often	Always	
Depression	1	2	3	4	5	(10)
Anxiety	1	2	3	4	5	(11)
Difficulty getting up in the morning	1	2	3	4	5	(12)
Crying episodes	1	2	3	4	5	(13)
Irritability	1	2	3	4	5	(14)
Fatigue	1	2	3	4	5	(15)
Difficulty falling asleep	1	2	3	4	5	(16)

Life Adjustment

Please circle on the scale below the quality of your relationship with each of the following:

	Terrible	Poor	Fair	Good	Excellent	
Mother	1	2	3	4	5	(17)
Father	1	2	3	4	5	(18)
Husband/Other	1	2	3	4	5	(19)
Male Friends	1	2	3	4	5	(20)
Female Friends	1	2	3	4	5	(21)
Children	1	2	3	4	5	(22)

Please circle on the scale below how much your eating problems interfere with the following:

	Never	Rarely	Sometimes	Often	Always	
Work	1	2	3	4	5	(23)
Daily activities (other than work)	1	2	3	4	5	(24)
Thoughts	1	2	3	4	5	(25)
Feelings about myself	1	2	3	4	5	(26)
Personal relationships	1	2	3	4	5	(27)

Family History

Have any of your first degree relatives had any of the following problems?
(First degree relatives include children, brothers, sisters, parents)

	Number of persons	Relationship to you(e.g. sister)	Require Outpatient Care? (If yes check below)	Require Hospitalization? (If yes, check below)	
Ulcers	28-29	30-34	35	36	Card 7 Column
Colitis	37-38	39-43	44	45	
Asthma	46-47	48-52	53	54	
Depression	55-56	57-61	62	63	
Manic-Depressive	64-65	66-70	71	72	80 = 7
Schizophrenia	10-11	12-16	17	18	Card 8 Column
Paranoid Thinking	19-20	21-25	26	27	
Hallucinations	28-29	30-34	35	36	
Obesity	37-38	39-43	44	45	
Alcohol	46-47	48-52	53	54	
Drug Abuse	55-56	57-61	62	63	
Severe Anxiety	64-65	66-70	71	72	80 = 8
Phobias	10-11	12-16	17	18	Card 9 Column
Bulimia	19-20	21-25	26	27	
Anorexia Nervosa	28-29	30-34	35	36	
Suicide Attempts	37-38	39-43	44	45	
Other	46-47	48-52	53	54	
_____	55-56	57-61	62	63	
_____	64-65	66-70	71	72	80 = 9

REFERENCES

Abraham, S. F., & Beumont, P. J. V. (1982). Varieties of psychosexual experience in patients with anorexia nervosa. *International Journal of Eating Disorders, 1*(3), 10–19.

Beumont, P. J. V., Abraham, S. F., & Simpson, K. G. (1981). The psychosexual histories of adolescent girls and young women with anorexia nervosa. *Psychological Medicine, 11*, 131–140.

Blatt, S. (1974). Levels of object representation in anaclitic and introjective depression. *Psychoanalytic Study of the Child, 29*, 107–157.

Bo-Lynn, G., Santa-Ana, C. A., Morawski, S. G., & Fordtran, J. S. (1983). Purging and calorie absorption in bulimic patients and normal women. *Annals of Internal Medicine, 99*, 14–17.

Bruch, H. (1973). *Eating disorders*. New York: Basic Books.

Casper, R. C. (1982). Treatment principles in anorexia nervosa. In S. C. Feinstein, J. G. Looney, A. Z. Schwartzberg, & A. D. Sorosky (Eds.), *Adolescent psychiatry* (Vol. 7, pp. 431–454). Chicago: University of Chicago Press.

Casper, R. C., Eckert, E. D., Halmi, K. A., Goldberg, S. C., & Davis, J. M. (1980). Bulimia. *Archives of General Psychiatry, 37*, 1030–1035.

Connors, M., Johnson, C., & Stuckey, M. (in press). Brief psychoeducational group treatment of bulimia. *American Journal of Psychiatry*.

Crisp, A. H. (1980). *Anorexia nervosa: Let me be*. London: Academic Press.

Druss, R. G., & Silverman, J. A. (1979). Body image and perfectionism of ballerinas: Comparison and contrast with anorexia nervosa. *General Hospital Psychiatry, 2*, 115–121.

Fairburn, C. (1982). *Binge-eating and bulimia nervosa*. London: Smith, Kline & French.

Garfinkel, P. E., & Garner, D. M. (1982). *Anorexia nervosa: A multidimensional perspective*. New York: Brunner/Mazel.

Garfinkel, P. E., Moldofsky, H., & Garner, D. M. (1977). Prognosis in anorexia nervosa as influenced by clinical features, treatment and self-perception. *Canadian Medical Journal, 177*, 1041–1045.

Garfinkel, P. E., Moldofsky, H., & Garner, D. M. (1980). The heterogeneity of anorexia nervosa. *Archives of General Psychiatry, 37*, 1036–1040.

Garner, D. M., & Bemis, K. M. (1982). A cognitive–behavioral approach to anorexia nervosa. *Cognitive Therapy and Research, 6*, 123–150.

Garner, D. M., & Garfinkel, P. E. (1980). Socio-cultural factors in the development of anorexia nervosa. *Psychological Medicine, 10*, 647–656.

Garner, D. M., & Garfinkel, P. E. (1982). Body-image in anorexia nervosa: Measurement, theory and clinical implications. *International Journal of Psychiatry in Medicine, 11*, 263–284.

Garner, D. M., Garfinkel, P. E., & Bemis, K. M. (1982). A multidimensional psychotherapy for anorexia nervosa. *International Journal of Eating Disorders, 1*, 3–46.

Goodsitt, A. (1977). Narcissistic disturbances in anorexia nervosa. In S. C. Feinstein & P. Giovacchini (Eds.), *Adolescent psychiatry*, (Vol. 5, pp. 304–312). New York: Jason Aronson.

Johnson, C., & Berndt, D. (1983). Bulimia and life adjustment: A preliminary investigation. *American Journal of Psychiatry, 140*, 774–777.

Johnson, C., & Flack, R. A. (1984). *Family characteristics of bulimic and normal women: A comparative study*. Manuscript submitted for publication.

Johnson, C., & Larson, R. (1982). Bulimia: An analysis of moods and behavior. *Psychosomatic Medicine, 44*, 341–353.

Johnson, C., Lewis, C., & Hagman, J. (1984). Bulimia: Review and synthesis. *Psychiatric Clinics of North America, 7*(2), 247–273.

Johnson, C., & Love, S. (1984). *Bulimia: Multivariate predictors of life impairment*. Manuscript submitted for publication.

Johnson, C., Stuckey, M., Lewis, L. D., & Schwartz, D. (1982). Bulimia: A descriptive study of 316 patients. *International Journal of Eating Disorders, 2*, 1–15.

Kalucy, R. S., Crisp, A. H., & Harding, B. (1977). A study of 56 families with anorexia nervosa. *British Journal of Medical Psychology, 50*, 381–395.

Keys, A., Brozek, J., Henschel, A., Mickelsen, O., & Taylor, H. L. (1950). *The biology of human starvation*. Minneapolis: University of Minneapolis Press.

Larson, R., & Johnson, C. (1981). Anorexia nervosa in the context of daily living. *Journal of Youth and Adolescence, 10*, 439–456.

Larson, R., & Johnson, C. (in press). Disturbed patterns of solitude among bulimic patients. *Addictive Behaviors*.

Lidz, T. (1976). *The person: His and her development through the lifecycle*. New York: Basic Books.

Masterson, J. F. (1977). Primary anorexia nervosa in the borderline adolescent: An object relations view. In P. Hartocollis (Ed.), *Borderline personality disorders* (pp. 475–494). New York: International Universities Press.

Minuchin, S., Rosman, B. L., & Baker, L. (1978). *Psychosomatic families: Anorexia nervosa in context*. Cambridge, MA: Harvard University Press.

Mitchell, J. E., & Pyle, R. L. (1982). The bulimia syndrome in normal weight individuals: A review. *International Journal of Eating Disorders, 1*, 61–73.

Pope, H. G., Hudson, J. I., Jonas, J. M., & Yurgelun-Todd, D. (1983). Bulimia treated with imipramine: A placebo controlled double blind study. *American Journal of Psychiatry, 140*, 554–558.

Pyle, R. L., Mitchell, J. E., & Eckert, E. (1981). Bulimia: A report of 34 cases. *Journal of Clinical Psychiatry, 42*, 60–64.

Russell, G. F. M. (1979). Bulimia nervosa: An ominous variant of anorexia nervosa. *Psychological Medicine, 9*, 429–448.

Schwartz, D., & Thompson, M. (1981). Do anorectics get well?: Current research and future needs. *American Journal of Psychiatry, 138*, 319–323.

Seligman, M. E. P. (1975). *Helplessness*. San Francisco: W. H. Freeman.

Strober, M., Salkin, B., Burroughs, J., & Morrell, W. (1982). Validity of the bulimia–restricter distinction in anorexia nervosa: Parental personality characteristics and family psychiatric morbidity. *Journal of Nervous and Mental Disease, 170*, 345–351.

Sugarman, A., Quinlan, D., & DeVenis, L. (1981). Anorexia nervosa as a defence against anaclitic depression. *International Journal of Eating Disorders, 1*, 44–61.

Swift, W. J., & Stern, S. (1982). The psychodynamic diversity of anorexia nervosa. *International Journal of Eating Disorders, 2*, 17–35.

Wardle, J. (1980). Dietary restraint and binge eating. *Behavior Analysis and Modification, 4*, 201–209.

Wardle, J., & Beinart, H. (1981). Binge-eating: A theoretical review. *British Journal of Clinical Psychology, 20*, 97–109.

Winnicott, D. W. (1965). *The maturational processes and the facilitating environment*. London: Hogarth Press.

Wurtman, J. J., Wurtman, R. J., Growdon, J. H., Henry, P., Lipscomb, A., & Zeisel, S. H. (1981). Carbohydrate craving in obese people: Suppression by treatments affecting serotoninergic transmission. *International Journal of Eating Disorders, 1*, 2–15.

Psychoanalytic Approaches

CHAPTER FOUR

Self Psychology and the Treatment of Anorexia Nervosa

ALAN GOODSITT

THEORY

Anorexia nervosa is a baffling, disturbing, and intriguing syndrome. Comprehending its meaning requires knowledge of biology, sociology, and psychology. Each of these frames of reference contributes different and at times conflicting perspectives. Psychoanalysis alone offers three divergent theories: the drive–conflict, object relations, and self-psychological points of view.

Which theory is applied in the treatment of a specific patient is not an academic issue. Theory influences what the therapist perceives and ultimately what he does. Gedo and Goldberg (1973) have written cogently on the importance of a correct fit among a specific clinical phenomenon, a psychological model, and a treatment modality.

In this chapter, I examine anorexia nervosa from a self-psychological perspective. I propose that anorexia nervosa is a disorder in the organization of the self. The symptoms of anorexia nervosa represent both a disruption of the self and the defensive adaptive measures against further disruption. I review what I consider to be the limitations of the drive–conflict and object relations models in explicating anorexia nervosa. Specifically, neither of these adequately lends itself to or facilitates the comprehension of the deficits in the self that are characteristic of anorexic patients.

A full description of the syndrome is not needed here. It suffices to state that the particular manifestations of anorexia nervosa state something about the times we live in. Garner, Garfinkel, Schwartz, and Thompson (1980), Garner and Garfinkel (1980), and Schwartz, Thompson, and Johnson (1982) have demonstrated the sociocultural pressures that lead increasing numbers of vulnerable young girls into the pursuit of thinness.

It is unfortunate that this era is also noteworthy for increasing numbers of individuals who suffer from a sense of emptiness, depletion, and aimlessness. These individuals complain of not feeling alive, of a sense of deadness, or of life seeming boring, routine, and mechanical. They cannot fully enjoy themselves, muster enthusiasm, or feel a sense of purpose and direction. They are passive creatures who

Alan Goodsitt. Department of Psychiatry and Behavioral Sciences, Northwestern University Medical School; Institute of Psychiatry, Northwestern Memorial Hospital; and Psychosomatic and Psychiatric Institute, Michael Reese Hospital and Medical Center, Chicago, Illinois.

react and respond, but rarely initiate. They rely on external influences to tell themselves what to do and how to feel. Their fragile self-regard needs repeated booster shots from sources outside of themselves. Without external support and structure, they are liable to feel in pieces or incomplete. They have been described as suffering from identity confusion and diffusion (Erikson, 1959). They seem to be out of touch with or alienated from themselves and their core feelings and values. Instead, they tune in to others and devote themselves to taking care of others. Some of these individuals develop anorexia nervosa.

Most anorexics or future anorexics fit this description. It is these kinds of symptoms and behavior that the drive–conflict model and the object relations theory fail to comprehend as well as self psychology does. The symptoms of alienation from the self, depletion, and disruption are signs of our times. These manifestations are quite different from what Freud observed in the well-defined and well-structured, but sexually oppressive, society of late 19th- and early 20th-century Vienna. His patients were conflicted about sexuality, and his drive–conflict theory accurately explained the data. For the most part, our anorexic patients could not care less about sexuality. Their drives seem diminished, not conflicted. A theory of deficit phenomena is more applicable.

Self theory, as systematized by Kohut (1971), provides a better framework for understanding deficit phenomena. Once the therapist accepts he is dealing with a deficit in the self, he is encouraged to go beyond confrontive and interpretive interventions. Long ago, Hilde Bruch (1962) realized the futility of interpretation in working with anorexics. I propose that what is effective is the therapist's actively filling in the deficits in the patient's self. The main thrust of therapeutic activity is to manage the transference rather than to interpret it. The therapist allows himself to be utilized as a "transitional object," in Winnicott's (1953) terms, or a "selfobject," in Kohut's (1971) language.

Later in this chapter, I address in detail the implications of the self-psychological viewpoint for the psychotherapy of anorexic patients and the management of specific symptoms. In a final section, I explore psychological dynamics in depth. Before proceeding with a comparison of the three analytic theories here, I offer some definitions.

When I speak of the "self," or "self organization," I am referring to three things. First there is the person's hierarchy of unconscious and conscious goals, aims, values, and priorities (Gedo, 1979). The self contains affects and cognitions. It includes biological needs and acquired wishes. It replaces the structural model of id drives, ego interests, and superego values.

Second, there is an experiencing aspect of the self organization. When Kohut refers to the "fragmentation of the self" or the "loss of cohesiveness," he is referring to the experiencing self, which feels disrupted or disorganized. This disruption may also be experienced as a depletion, an emptiness, an enfeeblement, and a loss of self-esteem.

Third, there is the self-regulatory structure. The psyche's capacity to maintain self-esteem, cohesiveness, and vitalization, and to regulate tensions and moods, are functions of the self-regulatory apparatus.

By "anorexia nervosa," I refer to a symptom complex or syndrome that may occur within a variety of ego or self pathologies. I am discussing here that core group of anorexics that is most typical and that Bruch (1973) calls "primary anorectics." Besides the drive for thinness, these anorexics manifest a severe disturbance both in their sense of effectiveness, and in their awareness of inner feelings, experiences, and sensations. They also manifest body image distortions or delusions. These disturbances in interoceptive experience and body image reflect defects in the ego or self organization. It is the explication and treatment of these defects that self psychology facilitates.

Drive–Conflict Model

Freud's (1923/1961) final model of the mind consisted of three agencies: the id, the ego, and the superego. Symptom formation was said to occur as a result of conflict between these agencies.

This model of the mind works best for the neurotic patient whose psyche is well structured. To be more specific, when an individual has a strong sense of morality (a well-developed superego), he or she is more prone to be in conflict with his or her drive impulses.

The early theories about anorexia nervosa were of the drive–conflict type. Moulton (1942), Rowland (1970), and Waller, Kaufman, and Deutsch (1940) all postulated that self-starvation was a defense against sexual fantasies of oral impregnation. Berlin, Boatman, Scheimo, and Szurek (1951) and Masserman (1941) thought that the refusal of food was a defense against ambivalent oral sadistic and cannibalistic fantasies. Blitzer, Rollins, and Blackwell (1961), Grimshaw (1959), Margolis and Jernberg (1960), Masserman (1941), and Tustin (1958) all emphasized either ambivalent oral impregnation or oral sadistic fantasies.

These types of conflicts are confined to the focal area of drive impulses and fantasies and are typically dealt with by neurotic symptom formation, social inhibition, and/or sexual inhibition. They do not require the formation of body image distortions and delusions that are characteristic of anorexic sufferers. Considerable anorexic symptomology is left unexplained by this drive–conflict model. Disavowal of emaciation, delusions of fatness, misperception, and alienation from inner feelings and sensations all reflect more profound and pervasive disturbances in the mental structure of the anorexic patient. Frequently what seems to be a simple sexual conflict will, upon careful exploration, prove to be more complex. The following case report illustrates this.

Mary was 13 years old when hospitalized for anorexia nervosa.[1] She presented during sessions as a passive, empty shell. She said little unless asked. When I would open the door to the interview room, the door would hit the doorstop and invariably bounce back and hit her unless I stopped it. In her transference to me, I was expected to protect her and magically cure her without her exerting any effort to participate in the treatment. In fact, I was to understand her magically, without her having to communicate verbally to me. She related to me as if I were an omnipotent, omniscient symbiotic object. When I pressed for her feelings, she would sometimes refer me to her parents — thus placing the ownership of her attitudes outside herself.

She responded well to benign, supportive, and exploratory therapy, and to the implicit hope that she would eat and gain weight. Early in treatment I took a week's vacation, which coincided with the wedding of her brother. It was at this point that she resumed menstruation. On the wedding night, she psychologically fragmented and delusionally proclaimed that her father was dead. Associative material revealed a pregnancy fantasy and a feeling of being too close to her father. She believed her father would die if he knew how wild (in her own fantasy) she was.

---

1. For the full case report, see Goodsitt (1969).

We were then able to reconstruct what initiated her self-starvation in the first place. Her father had previously had a heart attack. It was her fantasy that her developing sexuality had so disturbed him that it brought on the heart attack. We learned that she had an idealized symbiotic relationship with her father (as opposed to her mother), which is the usual case. She had experienced symbiotic merger with him, just as she did now with me in the transference. As one cuts off a gangrenous arm to save the body, she sacrificed her sexuality to save her father and their symbiosis.

Sexuality was feared not because it was taboo or a transgression against superego precepts, as in a typical neurosis, but rather because it disrupted the symbiotic bond that she felt was vital for both herself and her father. We learned that she was a symbiotic character whose central anxieties were those of fragmentation, annihilation, separation anxiety, and loss of object and self, and not guilt related to superego transgression. Seemingly, sexual anxiety and conflict was secondary to and functioned to deal with these more primary pre-Oedipal issues. A simple drive-conflict theory fails to explain the data in this case adequately.

Object Relations Theories

The object relations theorists attempt to fill in the holes in the drive–conflict model by grafting onto it yet another developmental theory. Mahler's (1968) theory, derived from infant observation, postulates several stages of object relations. The child moves from infantile autism to symbiosis to separation–individuation, and then on to object constancy.

Selvini-Palazzoli (1978) adds the language of Mahler to the language of drive-conflict theory. The future anorexic has unresolved problems in the oral incorporative stage, which impede separation–individuation. The anorexic fantasizes an oral incorporation of a maternal, bad, and overcontrolling object. This maternal introject is then equated with the anorexic's body; the anorexic experiences an identity of her body as her mother. Self-starvation is thus the adolescent's attempt to end the feminization of her body and thus to minimize the confused ambivalent identification with mother. Selvini-Palazzoli explains anorexic behavior as resulting from these distorted mental representations of body, self, and object.

The problem I find with Selvini-Palazzoli's theory is that although it makes theoretical sense, there are few clinical data to support it. Anorexic patients do not reveal confusion of their bodies with their mothers, based upon oral incorporative fantasies. Anorexics to a certain degree starve themselves to prevent feminization of their bodies and to minimize identification with their mothers, but I do not find oral incorporative fantasies as the basis for this. Furthermore, this explanation is much too limited.

Anorexics actually view their bodies in multiple ways. Many see their bodies as the battleground of the separation–individuation war. Who owns her body is a matter of contention (Goodsitt, 1977), but this is different from saying that the anorexic equates her body with the maternal bad object via an incorporative fantasy.

Adolescent anorexics perceive their bodies to be the last vestige of their infantile, archaic grandiosity. Grandiose individuals need to be the center of all things around which the word revolves, to feel they are in total control of everything, and to experience themselves as perfect. They focus all of these needs on their bodies. Now their bodies must be perfect and unchanging, and they must be in total and absolute control of them. The changes of puberty in a child, then, threaten this grandiosity and thereby threaten the adolescent's fragile psychic equilibrium. None of this has anything to do with oral incorporative fantasies.

Furthermore, the problem with the body seems to be its lack of integration into the self organization. Anorexics are often strangely indifferent to their bodily needs. They fail to take adequate care of their bodies. They ignore nutritional needs. They are strangely unconcerned about dangerous changes in the heart and other organs. They are out of touch with their inner bodily experiences and feelings. They seem not to cathect or to invest in their bodies in a wholesome manner.

In this regard, it should be noted that the self is at core a body-self. The nucleus of the self is bodily sensations. Freud (1923/1961) stated, "The ego is first and foremost a bodily ego" (p. 26). This applies to the self, which is first and foremost a body-self. As Kohut (1971) has pointed out, when the cohesive self becomes unstable, bodily symptoms (hypochondriasis) result. The anorexic's failure to invest appropriately in the body, and the resulting bodily distortions and delusions, are all symptomatic of a lack of cohesiveness of the self organization. The body is poorly integrated into the self organization.

When the integrity or cohesion of the self is threatened, anorexics experience this threat concretely in terms of loss of control of the body. In an attempt to stave off further disruption of the self, the anorexic typically hypercathects, stimulates, and obsessively focuses on the body (Goodsitt, 1983). The anorexic's constant activity and exercise are her attempts to feel herself within her body. They are attempts at feeling whole and cohesive (Goodsitt, 1977).

The therapeutic implications for this different perspective are profound. Rather than interpret to the anorexic that she equates her body with her mother, or interpret the oral incorporative fantasy, the therapist should attempt to heal the disintegrated body-self. How this is done is taken up later.

Masterson (1978) is another object relations theorist who adds Mahlerian thinking to the libido theory of the drive–conflict model. For Masterson, the anorexic is plagued by an array of introjects. There is a hostile, rejecting, withdrawing, maternal introject in response to the anorexic's attempt at separation. There is a supportive, rewarding, maternal introject in response to the anorexic's regressive, clinging behavior. There are thus two corresponding self representations that are inadequate, bad, guilty, and empty, and passive, compliant, and good, respectively. Although Masterson speaks of arrested development at symbiosis and separation–individuation, with corresponding ego defects, the main thrust of his theory is to point to the distorted self and object representations as the cause of anorexic behavior. Masterson, like Sours (see below), is burdened in his theoretical writing by abstruse and unwieldy object relations language, with its multiple self and object representations.

Sours (1980) takes the object relations theory a step further in stressing defects in the ego and the self, as well as symbolic, dynamic conflicts and distortions. He refers to defects in the ego, sense of self, poor self–object differentiation, and the failure to develop self and object constancy. Yet his theory of his treatment for these patients hardly differs from that for an analyzable neurotic who does not have structural defects.

Sours notes that the starving anorexic, prior to the restoration of nutrition, is not inclined to report affects, memories, or fantasies, and is, furthermore, not inclined to participate in a therapeutic alliance. For Sours, the therapeutic thrust is toward developing a therapeutic alliance by *understanding* the nature of the fixated, deviational, and atypical development of ego functions, self representations, and object representations. The main barrier to the development of the alliance — primitive defenses of denial, negation, disavowal, splitting, and omnipotence—must be dealt with, apparently by confrontation and interpretation.

In contrast to Sours's experience, I have found that primitive defenses in these severely disturbed, starving patients are better managed than interpreted (Goodsitt, 1982). These patients are not ready or equipped for analytic work. Neither the analysis of defenses nor the restoration of normal nutrition becomes the pivotal point that turns a frightened, negativistic patient into one who participates cooperatively. Rather, for the out-of-control, starving anorexic, the turning point is the therapist's taking over (i.e., stepping in and taking whatever measures are necessary to prevent the destructive starvation from continuing). The therapist takes over responsibility for feeding the patient. The patient protests, but is relieved, and *then* engages in the treatment process.

How is this to be understood? The patient is unable to manage her eating behavior. The therapist recognizes this and takes over. He thereby fills in for the deficits in the self and the ego. It is not simply distortions and defenses that are analyzed, but deficits in the ego and the self, which are filled by the therapist acting as external ego, "selfobject," or transitional object. Filling the defects unburdens and frees up the patient's ego and/or self, and an alliance is forged. The alliance is the result of therapeutic action, and not a prerequisite for it. The alliance takes shape when the therapist decides to take over, take a firm stand, and restore nutrition, and long before nutrition is actually restored. Levenkron (1983) provides an excellent example of a therapist effectively utilizing these principles.

Reliance on a theory that emphasizes early structuralization, conflict, and deviational self and object representations limits the object relations theorists from acknowledging the importance of deficit phenomena. If the problem is deviational self and object representations, then interpretations of these distortions should suffice. In my experience, much more is required.

Sours accurately notes that the difficulty these patients have in discussing their own affects, memories, and fantasies is, in part, secondary to starvation and lack of a therapeutic alliance. This explanation does not go far enough, however. For some time anorexics have been observed to be alexithymic and described as nonverbal (Eissler, 1943; Goodsitt, 1969; Jessner & Abse, 1960; Scott, 1948; Wall, 1959). I believe that their difficulty in relating inner experiences is yet another manifestation of defects in the self organization. These patients fail to relate inner experiences because they have an impaired capacity to live within the body-self. They are out of touch with their core experiences. There is a failure to integrate bodily, cognitive, and affective experiences into an organized core self.

Therapists like Garner, Garfinkel, and Bemis (Garfinkel & Garner, 1982; Garner & Bemis, 1982; Garner, Garfinkel, & Bemis, 1982) have called our attention to the cognitive defects that are one aspect of this phenomenon. Bruch (1962) has long emphasized the need to help these patients get in touch with their feelings. Levenkron (1983) points out that these patients do not have a language for talking about themselves. As therapist, he takes an active role in providing and teaching them a vocabulary for the self. To my mind, all of these therapists recognize the deficits in the self and the ego. They have all devised treatment techniques to deal with these defects. In contrast, the object relations theorists emphasize confrontation and interpretation, which are more effective for conflict resolution.

Selvini-Palazzoli (1978), Masterson (1978), and Sours (1980) emphasize distortions in body, self, or object representations. Sugarman and Kurash (1982) are object relations theorists who propose an ego defect as a central causative factor. Restricting themselves to a consideration of bulimic patients, Sugarman and Kurash assert that these patients lack the ego function of object constancy. Thus, when separated from the symbiotic mother, they are unable automatically to evoke a mental representation of the mother and become soothed. Since eating is a sensorimotor activity associated with the childhood feeding experience with the mother, bingeing becomes a means of evoking the sensorimotor object representation of the symbiosis.

Some years ago, working within an object relations framework, I proposed that anorexics manifest ego defects in synthetic and integrative functions (Goodsitt, 1969). Anorexics reveal impaired self–object differentiation, and they lack object constancy. I asserted that they have a symbiotic character disorder and are arrested at the developmental levels of symbiosis and separation–individuation. They require a symbiotic relationship to remain whole and to defend themselves against psychosis, annihilation, and separation anxiety.

At that time, I did not specifically address what the symbiotic partner provides that is so vital for ego integration and cohesion of the self. What is it that allows the individual to remain intact in the absence of the symbiotic object? Is it the capacity to evoke a mental representation of the symbiotic object, or is it the internalization of the functions of the object?

Theories of Deficits in the Self

For the self psychologist, the capacity to tolerate separation without some form of psychic decompensation depends upon the internalization of certain mental functions and structure. Important functions include the capacity to provide one's own cohesiveness, soothing, vitalization, narcissistic equilibrium (sense of well-being and security), tension regulation, and self-esteem regulation. These are regulatory functions that are initially provided by an external source, such as the mother. It is the mother who initially provides soothing, doses out stimuli, and protects the infant from stimulus overload. Later these functions are transferred to a transitional object, such as a blanket (Tolpin, 1971). It is then the transitional object, which the child totally controls, that provides a sense of well-being and security. The transitional object is cognitively perceived as external but is experienced as a part of the self (Goodsitt, 1983). If adequate mothering (Winnicott, 1965) occurs, these functions go inside (Tolpin, 1971) and become part of the child's mental structure. Thus the transitional object is a way station between external structure and internal structure (Tolpin, 1971). If the internalization process goes awry, the individual cannot separate successfully, because he or she cannot provide for his or her own sense of well-being, security, soothing, vitalization, cohesion, tension regulation, and self-esteem regulation. Without these functions, initiative is seriously impaired.

Kohut (1971) emphasizes the importance of empathic "selfobject" parenting that provides mirroring or confirming of the child's grandiosity and allows idealizing of the parental selfobject figures. By a "selfobject," Kohut is referring to an object, like a "transitional object" in Winnicott's words or a "symbiotic object" in Mahler's language, that is cognitively perceived as external to the self, but is experienced as a part of the self. One relates to a selfobject as one does to a part of oneself, such as one's arm. A person functioning as a selfobject for another is not perceived as having his or her own qualities, characteristics, needs, and wishes, and is not allowed to be a person in his or her own right.

Given appropriate selfobject responsiveness, the child's archaic grandiosity and idealization are converted into a cohesive self with good self-esteem and healthy goals and ideals. A disorder of the self or narcissistic personality disorder may result if the internalization process is aborted. Without available external selfobject support, this individual is liable to feel helpless, ineffective, overwhelmed, unworthy, unreal, incomplete, or empty. Activities are perceived as boring, mechanical, and routine. Life is passively experienced.

Some years ago, Bruch (1962) described anorexics in very much the same fashion. She asserted that helplessness, passivity, and ineffectiveness are cardinal features of anorexia nervosa. Many of the features of the disorder are illuminated by self-psychological understandings. Anorexics feel excessively influenced and exploited precisely because they are deficient in self-regulatory structure and are therefore dependent upon external contingencies (selfobjects) for their well-being (Goodsitt, 1977, 1983). It is a well-integrated self that enables one to feel in control, and not just an empty receptacle easily distorted (fattened) or invaded by external forces—whether that external force is food or people. The absence of reliable internal self-regulation results in the anorexic's feeling inadequate, ineffective, and out of control (fat)—one bite leads to a thousand; one pound leads to a hundred. Lacking reliable self-soothing, tension, and mood regulation, and feeling restlessly bored, empty, and aimless, the anorexic is driven to constant activity and strenuous physical exertion to drown out these painful internal conditions. She finds in being something special (i.e., an anorexic) some compensation and some contrived meaning to her existence. By focusing on food and weight, by turning off her need of others and turning inward to herself, by filling up her life with rituals that help her feel a sense of predictability and control, she narrows down her world to something she feels she can manage. She attempts to negate her reliance on the needed selfobjects that she unconsciously perceives have failed her. By devoting herself to the care, feeding, and well-being of others, she becomes a selfobject for them and thereby attempts to negate her own selfobject needs. By starving herself, she feels strengthened and temporarily superior to others. This is the antidote to her feelings of weakness and inadequacy related to her true need of selfobjects.

Anorexia nervosa is a disorder of the self. It is also very much a disorder of separation–individuation (selfhood). Anorexics are deficient in self-regulatory structure and are thus ill equipped to separate. The therapy of this disorder must address itself to the psychological deficit as well as the dynamic conflicts. The therapist, by functioning as a selfobject or transitional object, fills the deficit and enables an aborted maturational process to resume (Goodsitt, 1982, 1983).

THERAPY

In this section, I discuss the process of dynamic individual psychotherapy with anorexics. The treatment style and stages, as well as the therapist's role, are considered. I examine the importance of the therapist's flexibility and activity. I discuss how, functioning as a selfobject, the therapist provides and teaches tension regulation and integration. He utilizes the leverage of idealization. He explores, values, and confirms the patient's true self, thus facilitating the self's growth and maturation. He teaches the patient what her symbiotic needs are. He attempts to establish a narcissistic equilibrium.

Role of the Therapist

I first address the importance of the therapist's flexibility and activity. Since the syndrome of anorexia nervosa occurs along with all levels of object relationship and the whole range of ego and self strength and organization, the therapist must be flexible (Garner *et al.*, 1982). Any individual patient may be organized at more or less mature levels at any given point in time. The therapist needs to change his mode of therapy, depending upon the type of psychic organization presented (Gedo & Goldberg, 1973). For example, when the anorexic patient presents in a conflictual mode, utilizing repression as a major defense, then confrontation and interpretation are appropriate. When the patient is more disturbed or is arrested in psychic functioning, the therapist must be more active in helping the patient.

A general principle of therapy is that the therapist should allow the patient to do whatever the patient can reasonably accomplish without external assistance. The therapist will support the patient's independent functioning, but he must be ready to step in and actively take over at a moment's notice. This requires therapeutic judgment and flexibility.

Patients who are so out of control as to require hospitalization need the therapist to be more active in structuring than do office patients who are making progress. Gedo and Goldberg (1973) state that when the patient is in an overstimulated state, the patient needs soothing. If the patient is fragmented, the patient needs assistance with reintegration. The primary anorexic, with bodily delusions, interoceptive disturbances, and inadequate self-regulatory structure, generally requires these modes of active therapeutic intervention. When the therapist provides these functions, he is acting as external auxiliary ego and selfobject (i.e., as a part of the patient's mental structure). As such, the therapist's role is conceptualized as being a transitional object or selfobject (Goodsitt, 1983).

It is my impression, noted elsewhere (Goodsitt, 1982), that therapists tend to overestimate the capacities of anorexic patients. The typical therapist is not active enough. Taking half measures when full measures are required is both dangerous and disruptive to the therapeutic process. A common fault is the therapist's being fooled by the patient's apparent self-sufficiency (Modell, 1975). The patient often disavows the seriousness of her illness. The therapist may go along with the patient's pleas to "let me do it on my own" when she simply cannot do it.

The anorexic frequently needs the therapist to be her tension regulator. Patients with eating disorders, and in particular primary anorexics, suffer from intense chronic or recurrent tension states (Goodsitt, 1977, 1983). Bereft of internalized psychic mechanisms to sooth or regulate tensions, they are driven to drown out their tensions by intense external self-stimulatory activity. Thus these patients are driven to starve, binge, vomit, and engage in strenuous and constant physical exertion.

Swift and Letven (1984), discussing bulimics, state that the "conveying of insight may be therapeutically less important than the intuiting of unmet developmental needs and emphatically responding to them" (Marohn, 1982). They continue,

[It is] most important for the therapist to be attuned to the impairment in tension regulation and to empathically respond to mirroring and idealizing needs (Kohut, 1971); for example, by confirming the patient's nascent, often halting attempts to develop self soothing capacities, to erect a protective stimulus barrier, and to discover new outlets. (p. 496)

I fully agree; furthermore, I submit that all of this quotation applies to anorexic patients. Anorexics require the therapist, acting as a selfobject, to provide internal tension regulation.

The therapist actively reassures or calms the patient. If the patient is panicked about her stomach ballooning up when she eats or drinks, the therapist provides reassuring knowledge about the digestive process (Levenkron, 1983). The therapist should not wait until the patient is panicked. He should empathically anticipate the panic and dose out the preventive medicine of reassuring information. If the patient is hospitalized, he must be sure to provide for supportive reassurance just before, during, and after meals, when the patient is most anxious.

As a tension regulator, the therapist not only soothes the patient, but anticipates her distress and teaches her how to manage it herself. When asking a patient to eat more, he explains that he knows he is asking her to do something that is most difficult. He explains that he is asking her to give up a major adaptive defense that has served important protective functions for her. He expects her to feel anxious. He asks her to sit with her anxiety (while he sits with her). He explains that asking her to give up an adaptive defense is like asking a person who cannot swim to let go of the life preserver and try swimming. The danger is drowning.

The therapist insists on the patient's sharing her distress with him about eating when she does eat. He wants her to try eating, but he also wants to hear about her distress. She will not be left alone to sink or swim. The therapist may point out that it is really a choice she must make. She may continue to desperately hold on to what seems a life preserver to her (i.e., her illness), and continue to feel some temporary relief in not eating. She can also expect to continue her lonely, miserable, suffering life unchanged. On the other hand, he continues, she can choose to let go and take a chance on eating — and life. Clearly, by doing so, she is entering a forbidding unknown. He knows she has little faith in her capacity to relate to others or to really live an enjoyable or satisfying life of her own. She may indeed have good reason, based on past experience, not to be optimistic about her future. If this is the case, the therapist should acknowledge that. But the therapist tells the patient that he is committed to seeing that she learn the skills (ego and self functions) she needs to make her life better. Until now, she has been trying to learn to swim with one hand tied behind her back. No wonder it is difficult!

This approach is quite different from analyzing the unconscious symbolic meanings of eating and gaining weight. It is not that analysis is not needed: It is needed, but it is not enough.

The anorexic often needs the therapist to provide integration of the disparate parts of her personality. She may act as if the left hand does not know what the right hand is doing. Desperate for appreciation and longing to be listened to, the anorexic devotes herself to taking care of and listening to others. She ignores, dismisses, and devalues her own inner values and needs. These inner experiences have a low priority.

Garner, Garfinkel, and Bemis (Garfinkel & Garner, 1982; Garner & Bemis, 1982) have emphasized the importance of recognizing and clarifying underlying cognitive assumptions. Some anorexics, for example, assume that if they are thin, life will be perfect. In their hierarchy of values, goals, and ideals, thinness is a higher priority than health. Perfection may be more valued than happiness or well-being.

Certain cognitions are not balanced by the emotional price paid for having them. Wanting cognitively to be perfect, the anorexic wreaks havoc on a perfectly normal body and feels miserable. This failure to integrate various parts of the personality is abetted by the anorexic's inclination to use the defense mechanisms of splitting or disavowal. Some anorexics may cognitively acknowledge their emaciation, but the significance of this fact is dismissed (disavowal). They act as if the information is irrelevant. One anorexic, when told of dangerous abnormal findings on her cardiogram, asserted, "That is my doctor's problem," and continued her strenuous physical activity.

It is the therapist's job to point out that choices have been made and what the alternatives are. The therapist needs to provide the missing integration and to teach the patient how to integrate reasonably. For the more disturbed starving patient, the therapist must step in and take over this function relatively completely. A decision to restore weight within a controlled hospital environment, despite the patient's disavowal of nutritional need, is often necessary.

For the somewhat less disturbed patient, integrative work is reduced. Instead, the therapist may use the leverage of an idealizing transference to direct the patient to eat. The patient may not be able to provide self-caring (Khantzian, 1978; Krystal, 1978) and take the responsibility of organizing her caloric intake, but she may follow a prescription from the therapist. This can involve detailed meal planning. The therapist may, still using his authority, delegate this function to a nutritionist. Furthermore, the therapist may utilize behavioral techniques for symptom control or delegate this aspect of the work to a colleague familiar with this technique.

For the patient who is healthier still, the idealizing transference itself will prove sufficient. In certain rare cases, the patient seems to get better before the therapist can do something. In one such instance, the patient was the anorexic daughter of a physician who had read an article I published. This patient came to me expecting magical healing from an "expert." Almost before I could open my mouth, she had stopped starving herself. In these cases, it is important that the therapist tolerate the idealization and not disabuse the patient of her illusions prematurely (Kohut, 1971). Then the therapist has leverage to accomplish therapeutic ends. When the therapist allows idealization or provides mirroring of the patient's grandiosity, the well-being of the self organization is enhanced (narcissistic equilibrium). Symptomatic improvement often results from this healing of the self. Furthermore, it creates a more stable balance within the patient, so she is enabled to work better in therapy.

Growth of the self and enhancing the self organization also depend upon knowing oneself. When one is in touch with inner feelings—what feels good and is enjoyable, what feels bad or is boring, what is satisfying, and what is self-destructive— then one is in a good position to make wise life decisions. Anorexics are woefully alienated from core feelings and experiences. Not knowing one's feelings means that

one can be easily manipulated, which is a typical anorexic phenomenon. It also produces the inner experiences of feeling empty, bored, and aimless. The anorexic has
little to say partly because of her alienation from inner experience.

It is the therapist's job to help the patient to direct her attention to inner experience. He values and takes seriously her feelings. Often he knows, by close observation of facial expression and behavior, that the patient is depressed, angry, or
disturbed before the patient is aware of it. When the patient denies that anything is
wrong, he asks her to look inward to find out what she is feeling. When she explains
her bingeing or vomiting as simply habit, he asks her to examine more carefully what
was occurring and how she was feeling immediately prior to the binge–purge. When
the patient anxiously and urgently demands a hospital privilege, the therapist asks
the patient to examine her feelings. Often, when the privilege is denied and the therapist
actively inquires into what has precipitated such desperate pleas, the patient eventually
confesses that she was troubled by some disturbing feeling. One such patient, whose
demand for immediate discharge from the hospital to go home was denied, broke
down and confessed that she had found herself just then deeply hating her parents.
To deny this feeling, she wanted to demonstrate that she wanted to be home with
them.

Anorexics short-circuit getting in touch with their feelings by instead taking some
action. Starving, bingeing, vomiting, and hyperactivity are measures used to short-
circuit recognition of disturbing feelings and cognitions. I have observed that anorexic families as a rule short-circuit feelings by taking actions that cover over and cover
up inner experience. The family members of the patient mentioned above who
demanded immediate hospital discharge wanted to accommodate her wish, despite
their feeling that the patient and they were not ready for her to be home.

Anorexic families do not, as a rule, know how to encourage the exploration and
sharing of inner experience. When anxiety or depression occur, it is ignored, minimized, or smothered. The result, for the future anorexic, is a diminished sense of
self. When the distress of the child is not ignored, it is frequently dealt with by un-
empathic responses: for example, "You are too sensitive. That is nothing to be upset
about," or "You're okay. Don't worry about it." Such responses dismiss the child's
anxiety. Some parents are so overwrought with the child's distress that they have to
do something urgently to remove the anxiety before they themselves become infected
with it. The future anorexic then senses that what counts is not her own experience,
but rather not being a burden to others. In these cases, what actually bothers the child
in the first place and is causing the stress is never examined. The foundation of the
child's budding self, her inner experience, is not contacted, recognized, confirmed,
or taken seriously. Under these circumstances, the self becomes atrophied.

The therapist sees his role as building up and enhancing the self. He does this
by truly listening to and taking seriously the patient's feelings and thoughts. He may
disagree openly with the patient, but he is sure to affirm the legitimacy of the patient's
viewpoint. He must be prepared actively to help the patient find her own feelings and
to elicit the expression of them.

By helping the patient to get in touch with her inner experience, the therapist is
helping her to ground or center herself. He is helping her to integrate external behavior
with inner feelings and beliefs. The discrepancy that exists between her "true self" and
her "false self" adaptation (Winnicott, 1965) is reduced. This enriches the personality

and solidifies the self organization. When this is accomplished, the patient will no longer experience herself as empty, bored, passive, dead, indecisive, and aimless.

When this is not accomplished, the anorexic combats her sense of inner void by seeking external challenges. To be the thinnest person she knows is one such challenge. It provides the patient with a sense of direction and purpose. One patient reported she could not eat a piece of cake because she would then lose the chance to look forward to and anticipate eating the cake. She would not have a goal. The whole symptom complex of anorexia nervosa, with the goals and values it dictates, thus substitutes for a reasonably organized hierarchy of goals based on true inner needs and desires. The anorexia nervosa provides a substitute self organization. It is also maladaptive, self-defeating, and destructive. Maturation ceases.

Much anorexic behavior is compulsively determined by the urgent need to drown out tensions that exist because the anorexic is not aware of her needs and desires and therefore cannot fulfill them. Actions, then, are simply reactions to a disrupted self, rather than expressions of initiative from the depth of the self—its values and goals. It is the therapist's job to help the patient find her true self and her values and goals. Only then is fulfillment possible.

If the patient is unable to regulate her own tensions and self-esteem, the therapist must inform the patient of her symbiotic or selfobject requirements. She needs to know that she is easily shattered by slights, criticism, and disapproval, so that she can take preventive measures. She learns, in a nonjudgmental way, that she takes separations from selfobjects very hard. When the patient knows, accepts, and then fulfills her needs, she is no longer driven to disavow her needs through acts of self-denial and abstinence, such as self-starvation. In doing much of what is described above, the therapist is also attempting to establish a narcissistic equilibrium (i.e., a nondisrupted or balanced self organization). If the patient is constantly trying to put out internal emotional fires, she is in no condition to change, learn, or develop.

The therapist is many things. He is a parent, guide, teacher, and coach (Levenkron, 1983). He makes himself available as a committed, caring professional. He is involved. He relates. He encourages, cajoles, and exhorts. He provides his expert knowledge and experience. He empathically anticipates and cares about the patient's subjective experience. He patiently explains and clarifies her cognitions and the significant issues. Most important, he is the carrier of hope for a future for his patient, while at the same time truthfully acknowledging her present shortcomings. He does not criticize or belittle her defensive adaptation. There are good reasons for all her behavior, incapacities, and feelings. By doing all of this and more, the therapist is lending her his ego and self organization—his capacity to anticipate, to delay gratification, to use sound judgment, to relate to another, to regulate tension and moods, and to integrate feelings, cognitions, and behavior.

Stages of Therapy

Certain problems are more or less germane to specific stages of therapy. In the first stage of therapy, the main issue is the anorexic patient's reluctance to be a patient. The disavowal of illness must be addressed during the initial consultation. Frequently the patient appears to have been pushed into the consultation room. She looks as if the therapist and his office are, respectively, the last face and place on earth she would rather see and be! When a resistance appears, it should be addressed immediately, or the patient will be gone.

The therapist carefully explores the patient's motivation for therapy. If she presents with considerable disavowal of illness or a facade of self-sufficiency, it is important to find and make contact with that part of the patient that hurts or experiences psychic pain. The therapist will actively elicit how miserable, hopeless, and despairing the patient feels. The therapist needs to determine whether the patient believes she is entitled to help and whether it is permissible to seek help for her misery. He must surely advise her that it is precisely because people feel the way she is feeling that they seek and in fact do obtain relief within a psychotherapeutic process. The therapist should explore what myths the patient harbors about the process of therapy.

The therapist keeps in mind that, as a rule, these young women are withdrawn, distrusting, and frequently alexithymic. He understands that the anorexic is a private person who prides herself upon her independence. She is terrified of intimacy, closeness, and being in an office alone with another person. She is ashamed of her dependent longings. He also understands that she is performance-oriented and therefore panicked about the expectation that she be able to carry the conversation. The therapist must have minimal expectations that these alexithymic patients can verbalize their inner feelings. The responsibility for establishing meaningful contact and rapport rests with the therapist. He psychologically reaches out to the patient and tries to anticipate and allay her misperceptions and anxieties about therapy. He does not allow silences to continue so that both he and the patient feel terribly uncomfortable. These patients must eventually be taught how to explore their feelings and how to utilize therapy.

During the initial consultation, the therapist verbally anticipates that the patient may not feel comfortable with therapy and may wish to run from it. He tells the patient that when this happens, he wants her to bring this important feeling to him. If the patient is there under duress, he makes it clear that his mission is to help her feel better about herself. He is her agent—not anyone else's. He attempts to establish a verbal contract with the patient to help her with the specific problems that have been identified.

The middle stage of therapy is when the various transferences have been established. The relevant issues repeatedly arise and are worked on. Since I address later what some of the typical issues are, I now proceed to a discussion of the termination phase.

Throughout the middle and especially the later stages of therapy, a particular phenomenon occurs in many patients that is characteristic of anorexics—the negative therapeutic reaction. This refers to an impasse or regression that occurs when least expected. Solid therapeutic work and insight have been achieved, and the patient has made good progress. Then, without warning, the patient acts out self-destructively, falls apart psychologically, or relinquishes hard-earned previous gains. What has happened?

Both pre-Oedipal and Oedipal determinants have been observed to be the root cause of negative therapeutic reactions. Doing well, growing up, and being successful may precipitate guilt because it means surpassing, replacing, or defeating the Oedipal rival. In most anorexics, this is not the issue. Rather, for anorexics, growing up and being successful mean giving up the symbiotic object or selfobject that they feel is vital for their existence, cohension, or well-being (Goodsitt, 1969, 1977). Growing up means to the anorexic that, in a very concrete sense, she must be totally self-reliant and never depend or rely on anyone again. It means being sentenced to a life of isolation. This is illustrated in the following case report.

Ann, aged 18, was in the termination phase of a successful 10-month hospitalization. She had been hospitalized the day after her high school graduation, when she weighed 27.273 kg (60 lb) (she was 158.974 cm or 5 ft 2 in tall). With five-times-weekly psychotherapy, she gained to 90% of her ideal weight and made solid psychological progress.

While on a 24-hour pass at home, she was able to eat meals without conscious concern for calories. Feeling proud of her accomplishment, she contemplated discharge from the hospital. That night she dreamed that her parents took in a boarder at home. She consoled herself that since she was younger than the boarder, she might still obtain some small share of parental attention. We understood several things from this dream. Her progress and her growing up in general meant loss—loss of attention and loss of attachment to the pre-Oedipal nurturer and symbiotic object. Furthermore, Ann was also the boarder. She would return home and no longer have the only role she had known—the dependent, symbiotic child. Progress and adulthood meant becoming an isolated boarder or stranger in her own home.

Guilt does play an important role in negative therapeutic reactions in anorexic patients. However, this guilt differs in many ways from the guilt that has been classically described. I call the guilt anorexics manifest "self-guilt," and I will discuss this in detail later. For now, I wish to point out that rather than being guilty for an Oedipal victory, this guilt is more related to becoming a person, developing a selfhood, experiencing pleasure, and separating from parents.

Like Ann, Beth was in the termination phase of a successful hospitalization of 3 months' duration. She too had regained to 90% of her ideal weight after entering the hospital very ill, extremely dehydrated, and 35% under ideal weight. She responded immediately to our taking over the management of her eating and to five-times-weekly psychotherapy. Like Ann, she had an intensely symbiotic relationship with her mother.

Beth was feeling both pleasure and great pride about her recent accomplishments in the hospital. She was boldly and maturely addressing the differences between herself and her mother directly with her mother. After having essentially dropped out of life and living almost totally in her room at home prior to hospitalization, she was now planning to enter college and to live away from home for the first time.

At this point, while on a group excursion from the hospital, she very obviously attempted to steal pills at a drug store and was caught. In explaining her action to me, she stated she had been feeling "too happy" and felt she had to "kill the happiness. It didn't feel natural or right. I shouldn't be happy." She went on to explain that she was undeserving because of "all the bad things I did and the way I was"—referring to how sick and burdensome she had been for her mother. Beth felt guilty for her happiness while she was planning to establish a life of her own apart from her mother. Enjoying life apart from her mother was an act of disloyalty and betrayal. Beth stated that she had been the center of her mother's life and that her mother could never be happy without her.

These termination issues of symbiotic loss, separation anxiety, and self-guilt occur repeatedly and must be worked through by thorough analysis. Each new incident allows the patient and the therapist to view the issue from a slightly different perspective. It is then observed and analyzed in all its ramifications. To get the patient to confront these issues in real life, the therapist encourages, cajoles, prepares, rehearses, offers suggestions, or takes the patient by the hand and guides her through the task. Fortunately, Beth was able to take what she learned during sessions and immediately put it into action in her life. Patients who do not do this must be confronted with their resistance.

SYMPTOM MANAGEMENT

Food, Weight, and Body Image

In this section, I address the management of food, eating, exercise, weight, body image, family involvement, and hospitalization. As noted earlier, the approach one takes depends upon the psychic state of the patient. The more chronic the symptoms and the more disturbed the patient, the more important direct management of the symptoms becomes. For the less disturbed office patient, management of eating and weight may consist of setting appropriate diet and weight goals, examining the psychic issues, encouraging the patient to meet the goals, and providing support for the concomitant anxiety. Some patients need more direction from the therapist, such as being given a prescription to eat. Others benefit from behavioral contingencies.

It should be clear at this point that directly discussing the targeted symptoms is warranted. I used to believe that it would be counterproductive to allow a patient to become or remain obsessed with calories, food, and weight. Since these preoccupations were simply symptoms of underlying psychological conflicts or disruptions of the self organization, then the real work should consist of dealing with these latter problems. Analyze the conflicts, restore the equilibrium of the self organization, and the symptoms will diminish or disappear.

For some patients this is what happens, but for others, more is required. Certain patients will work well psychologically, but they are too ashamed of their eating, bingeing, and vomiting to focus on these in therapy. The place and function of the symptoms in the patient's life never get examined. What, how, when, and where does the patient eat, not eat, binge, or vomit? What precipitates these events? These patients need encouragement to discuss these activities.

On the other hand, certain patients will isolate the symptoms from the context of their lives by discussing *only* their weight, body, and food preoccupations. These patients need encouragement to look at the context of the symptoms in their lives. How one does this is crucial. The therapist must respect the importance of the symptoms for the patient. The patient's present, albeit misguided, mode of feeling in control, effective, and powerful is tied up in the symptoms. It is useful for the therapist to acknowledge from the start that the symptoms serve an important function and may be the best current solution to the patient's dilemma.

Carol is an 18-year-old girl who was hospitalized when she was 31% under ideal weight. Her parents were divorced. Her home environment was chaotic and destructive. She had nothing in her life to point to with pride and truly nothing to look forward to. She felt weak, ineffective, incapable, unlikable, and defeated. Her delusional obsessions and compulsions made her feel strange and freakish.

Unlike other anorexics, who attempt to burn off calories with exercise, she would rather sit in one place and hold or press her stomach in. She could not tolerate *any* expansion of her abdomen. She sat because she felt that if she stood up, she would more or less "hang out."

Any attempt to use reality testing by pointing out her thinness or the flatness of her abdomen resulted in her feeling crushed. Reality testing meant that people were telling her she was crazy, and she would then hold on to her stomach even more intensely. Her therapist reassured her that her symptoms were meaningful. She eventually was able to say that if she did not continue to hold her stomach in, she would be overwhelmed by intense despair and depression. She would feel empty and face the "nothingness" inside. The therapist acknowledged that to remove the symptoms meant, to her, taking away her life preserver and drowning in her depression. She needed to feel she had something else to hold on to, and she needed to learn how to swim. The therapist would let her hold on to him until he could teach her to swim, but she would have to take the risk of letting go of her current life preserver.

The therapist may approach the body image distortion by acknowledging that food and water do in fact expand the abdomen—especially noticeable to the patient, since her abdominal muscles are atrophied and she has no abdominal fat. Rather than argue with Carol that her stomach was not fat, her therapist explored why she could not tolerate any bodily or other imperfection. In patients with tenuous self-cohesion and self-esteem, defensive adaptations are often better managed as above than hammered by confrontive reality testing. When patients are preoccupied with food, weight, and their bodies, it is a mistake to tell them that those issues will not be discussed, since they are not the real problem. Rather, the therapist should acknowledge such patients' concern and listen for the underlying significance of the obsession.

Carol berated herself that all she talked about was food and her body. The therapist told her that when one has a toothache, all one can think about is the ache. The mind addresses itself to problems. They must find the *good* reason that she is so preoccupied. Carol continued to belabor the point that she was fat, her eating uncontrollable, her body distorted, and that she could not do anything about it. The therapist acknowledged her concerns and said, "I hear from what you say that you also have those feelings about yourself in life. You generally feel you are not in charge, unable to regulate, feel good, or like yourself. You feel weak, ineffective, and helpless." Thus the therapist takes what are tendered—the concrete bodily expressions of a damaged self—and translates them into understandable feelings and cognitions. If the therapist had insisted that Carol not talk about her food and bodily obsessions, she would have felt wrong or strange to be so obsessed, and she would have been hard put to find other words or concepts to convey her inner experience.

Hospitalization

Hospitalization is indicated when office psychotherapy proves insufficient in stopping or reversing an impasse or a deteriorating physical or psychological course. One can and should develop meaningful and specific criteria, but in the end, the therapist must make a sound judgment as to the need for hospitalization. Usually the patient has lost considerable weight and is physically weakened. Office psychotherapy has proved insufficient in mobilizing the patient's inner resources. It has become apparent that it is asking too much of the patient to change or improve without more structural assistance. The patient's deficits in self require active filling by the therapist and the hospital milieu.

Inpatient treatment differs considerably from office therapy. The therapist's activity consists much more of filling deficits by assuming responsibility for the care of the patient. His interventions can be characterized by the acts of stepping in, taking by the hand, and taking over. He establishes a weight restoration program in which the patient is expected to gain at least .454 kg (1 lb) per week, up to a target weight of 90% of ideal weight.

Programs that are strictly behavior modification tend to graft weight onto anorexics while the core pathology, an aborted development of the self organization, is ignored. The potential for self-enhancement and individuation is forced underground, as the anorexic must exclude her inner needs and conform to a totally controlling environment. The patient simply surrenders a part of herself, her body, to the therapist. The result is a "person who suffers as before, but looks normal — an anorectic [sic] clothed in weight" (Goodsitt, 1977, p. 311).

In contrast, hospital programs that do not fill the deficits expect too much of the starving patient, who is already overburdened and out of control. I learned this through experience. Initially, I had some success with patients who were stabilized and were eventually enabled to eat simply by being in a structured, supportive hospital milieu. I interfered as little as possible with the patients' autonomy. The patients controlled their own eating, with the stipulation that the treatment team would take over if and when their health was endangered. They would not be allowed to die. Weekly tests closely monitored their physical condition.

The problem that occurred with this treatment approach was that most patients were unable to take the responsibility for feeding themselves. Some patients would simply maintain a status quo and never get better. Others would lose weight, but not enough for us to intervene on the basis of keeping them alive. Furthermore, these patients lost confidence in the treatment program.

Debbie was typical of these patients. She was 158.974 (5 ft 2 in) tall and weighed 31.818 kg (70 lbs) when hospitalized. She then lost 5.455 kg (12 lb) slowly, and, amazingly, her lab tests showed no damage to her bodily functions. Nevertheless, she became more and more depressed, sullen, and negativistic. She was correct when she accused us of not helping her by letting her lose the additional 12 lb.

We decided not to wait any longer. We took over the management of her eating. She vehemently protested this abridgment of her freedom, but her affect and her outlook immediately brightened. For the first time, she engaged in the therapy process and worked cooperatively with her therapist.

When we proceeded on the basis that we would respect the patient's autonomy and not intervene prior to damage to the patient's body, we were overestimating and expecting too much of the patient. We did not fully understand the depth of the pathology — the structural deficits. Furthermore, we were actually neglecting, rather than respecting, the whole person and her needs — psychological as well as physical.

Thus it is important to find a middle ground between respect for autonomy and total dictatorial control. Psychotherapy combined with weight restoration through direct management of eating has proved successful. Bruch (1977), Casper (1982), Crisp (1980), Garner et al. (1982), and Garfinkel and Garner (1982) all stress the importance of nutritional or weight restoration. Starvation per se produces many reversible anorexic symptoms (Casper & Davis, 1977; Dally, 1969; Garner & Bemis, 1982; Garner et al., 1982; Keys, Brozek, Henschel, Mickelsen, & Taylor, 1950; Russell, 1970). From a psychological viewpoint, Crisp (1980) writes cogently that anorexics are able to avoid heterosexual maturational issues while maintaining prepubescent bodies. Issues related to separation, individuation, the right to a life of one's own, being an adult, assuming responsibility, making career and other decisions, competition with peers, and working through the loss of one's childhood are also avoided through anorexia nervosa. Allowing a patient to remain at an anorexic weight is not therapeutic.

It is useful, as Crisp (1980) states, to reach an agreement with the patient and her family prior to hospitalization on the necessity for weight restoration. The rationale for this program is fully explained and must be accepted if the patient is to be treated. A target weight of 90% of ideal weight is appropriate, since it approximates the weight of return of menstruation, thus signifying a normal physiology. The fact that only 90% of ideal weight is requested also assures the patient that the therapist does not need her to be fat — only healthy.

The patient may be allowed to acclimate to the hospital during the first week. The patient manages her own dietary intake, with the knowledge that if she does not gain weight, her treatment team will take over. An extensive laboratory workup is done. The pediatrician or internist closely monitors her physical condition. Weekly examinations and tests keep the internist abreast of the patient's electrolytes, protein, glucose, blood count, and hydration, as well as the condition of the heart, liver, kidneys, and endocrine system.

If after the first week it appears that the patient is continuing an anorexic course, then the treatment team takes over the management of eating and activity. The patient is informed that she will be expected to gain .454 kg (1 lb) a week up to her target weight. The dietician calculates the calories required. The patient is informed that she needs to learn how to eat normally and nutritiously. She will satisfy her caloric needs in three daily supervised, balanced meals. Selecting from a menu, she must satisfy so many exchanges of specific food types to meet the requirements for carbohydrates, fat, and protein. Rarely is it necessary to use nutrient drinks to satisfy caloric needs. Rather, the patient is expected to learn to eat normal foods.

Refeeding is started at a caloric amount calculated only to maintain weight. This is generally much more than what the patient is used to. The patient will gain .908 to 2.170 kg (2 to 5 lb) the first week due to rehydration and retention of fluid alone. The patient is warned of this and is informed that her weight will soon reach a plateau. At that point, she is started on a caloric amount calculated to have her gain .454 kg (1 lb) per week. Usually, this caloric amount also proves inadequate, and the calories are gradually increased to reach the goal. Typically, this takes 2000 to 3000 calories daily.

Eating is supervised by nursing personnel during each meal and for an hour after the meal to prevent purging. If the patient cannot eat as instructed, she is informed that tube feeding or intravenous feeding will be necessary. In almost all cases, this is not needed. It is understood that eating is stressful and that the patient requires extra support at mealtimes. When the supervisory personnel is nurturing, benign, patient, nonpunitive, willing to explain and encourage repeatedly, but able to be absolutely firm in the expectation that the patient will eat, more intrusive medical procedures are not required. Hyperalimentation, with all its medical complications, is unnecessary.

Firm limits combined with sympathetic listening go a long way. This combination of qualities is not easily maintained. It requires devoted and committed nursing personnel. They must be able to listen patiently without letting the patient talk obsessively and endlessly and thus avoid the task at hand. Meals should not last longer than 30 to 40 minutes. I believe that when one sets a limit on some behavior, the limit setter is obligated to listen to the feelings of the patient about the limit. One should not do the former without doing the latter.

Activities may be curtailed, but bed rest is not required. Strenuous physical exertion, exercise, and pacing are prohibited. These activities indicate disruption or disturbance of the self organization. As such, it is a signal to others that the patient needs immediate attention and support.

Given the deficits in self of these patients, it is important for the members of the hospital staff to extend themselves and go more than halfway to meet or connect with the patients. A nurturing, caring approach is indicated. When there is a conflict between a staff member and a patient, the patient cannot be expected to take the initiative to settle the difference. It is preferable for the staff person to take the patient by the hand (metaphorically) and teach the patient, step by step, how to settle differences. Often this will be the first time anyone has taken this approach with the patient.

Anorexic patients who are not comfortable with their enormous needs resort to primitive and maladaptive measures to fill their needs. These patients are known to be provocative, controlling, and manipulative. Those who work with them feel unappreciated, as well as provoked, controlled, and manipulated. It is crucial that the staff members understand these feelings within themselves as communications from a patient of precisely what the patient feels. It is also crucial to take the feeling of being manipulated a step further and to ask, "Manipulated toward what end? What is the patient missing, and what can't she ask for directly?" It is not enough for a staff member to label the patient as difficult, willful, manipulative, and divisive, and then walk away satisfied that the patient has not abused him or her.

Family Involvement

The question of family involvement is intimately related to the issue of separation–individuation. Anorexia nervosa develops within a family setting of arrested symbiosis and separation–individuation (Goodsitt, 1969). For both office and hospitalized patients, the therapist must consider what to do with the family and the symbiosis. Generally the goal is to achieve a disengagement from the entangled family relationship, coupled with individuation of the family members. The modes of achieving this vary from family therapy, separate individual therapy, and couples therapy, to total physical separation of a child from her parents.

Family therapy is most useful with the young high-school-age anorexic who lives at home with her family. Individual therapy may occur simultaneously. For the young adult or older anorexic who lives apart from her parents, individual therapy with a goal toward intrapsychic change is indicated. The same applies if she is hospitalized and plans to live apart. In these instances, supportive counseling for the parents is important. They will need help in allowing their daughter to individuate. They are also vulnerable to depression and psychic decompensation upon "losing" their daughter.

Both the patient and her parents need each other symbiotically. To sever the symbiosis, it may be necessary to bar all visiting and contact between the parents and the hospitalized anorexic. In less extreme cases, individual therapy is directed at the anorexic's gaining a more realistic perspective of her parents and the symbiotic nature of her relationship with them. Does the anorexic feel that it is her birthright to grow up and live her own life? She may clearly describe disturbed, enmeshed family relationships, but she may not have the capacity to formulate them as such. Much of the separation–individuation work consists of the therapist's helping the patient to gain perspective by formulating what she has already described.

PSYCHOLOGICAL ISSUES

In this section, I discuss some of the major psychodynamic issues underlying the symptom complex of anorexia nervosa. These dynamics involve both structural needs and unconscious fantasies. I discuss the structural deficits in the ego and the self organization that result in symbiotic, transitional, and selfobject needs. Apart from this may be unconscious or conscious desires to regress to an ideal childhood with ideal parents. Related to these regressive needs and fantasies are intense narcissistic needs and fantasies involving archaic grandiosity and idealization. I then discuss the deeply repressed and disavowed hostile, vindictive fantasies of anorexics. Finally, I propose the concept of self-guilt in anorexia nervosa. Successful psychotherapy involves working with and through these dynamic issues.

Regressive Needs and Fantasies

Anorexic patients who are developmentally arrested at the levels of symbiosis and separation–individuation, and have not yet achieved self-cohesion, self constancy, and object constancy, require external objects to supply the missing mental regulatory structure. This is the function of a selfobject or transitional object. The anorexic is not consciously aware of this, but she may be quite aware of the manifestations of this missing mental structure. She feels terribly ineffective, incapable, emotionally labile, tension-ridden, desperately needful of external approbation, unable to be alone with herself and her inner feelings, at odds with herself, and lacking togetherness or wholeness. She defends herself against the realization of her symbiotic needs by adopting a facade of pseudo self-sufficiency. Nevertheless, she is aware on some deeper level of her symbiotic needs and is afraid to grow up. Pubertal bodily changes panic her because they mean becoming a self-sufficient adult woman and doing without a symbiotic object. Growing up means loss, loneliness, utter helplessness, and coming apart. The prospect of doing well or gaining weight is dreaded.

Growing up also means giving up the fantasy of being able to return to early childhood and this time having it come out right. In her fantasy, the anorexic can "go home," start over, and this time around be a perfect child to perfect parents. To give up this fantasy is to reconcile herself to the fact that there is no going back and starting over. Any conscious inkling of this fills her with depression. Now she is frightened both of going forward and of the unnerving depression that she has always tried to avoid. The therapist not only deflates her regressive fantasy, but must help her to tolerate the ensuing depression.

The therapist must also address the patient's deficient mental structure. He does this by filling in the deficit by providing the missing mental functions. In addition, the therapist educates the patient about her need for external approbation and assistance so that she can structure her life accordingly. Further down the road, the anorexic will, via internalization, develop her own internal self-regulatory mechanisms.

Narcissistic Issues

There are many narcissistic features in the anorexic syndrome. The patient's incapacity to maintain a reasonable internal level of self-esteem has been highlighted. Here I focus on the anorexic's grandiosity, exhibitionism, and need for external mirroring, responsiveness, power, and control. The deficient self-regulatory capacities leave the anorexic feeling not only inadequate and helpless, but desperately out of control, powerless, and vulnerable to external influence. An example of this is the fear that if she takes one bite of food or gains an ounce, she will not be able to stop eating and will immediately gain a vast amount of weight. To restore her sense of control and self-esteem, she rigidly counts calories and regulates ingestion. Feeling her self organization to be out of control, she insists on meticulous control of her body-self. She furthermore attempts to take total control of her environment—her peers, family, and therapist, all of whom feel tyrannized.

This tyrannical behavior is often misconstrued as willful and manipulative. If the therapist and treatment team do not comprehend the underlying desperate sense of being out of control, they are liable to react with countertransference reactions. This may vary from withdrawal to a hostile, vindictive exercise of overcontrol of the patient. The overcontrol takes two basic forms. The first is a rigid behavioristic approach, which totally controls the patient's behavior and weight while denying the patient's unique individuality. A more subtle version of this occurs in any hospital program when institutional and staff needs take precedence over patients' needs. The second form of overcontrol is a type of psychological tyranny. The patient is instructed that since eating, food, and body obsessiveness are not the real problems but only the symptoms, the patient will not be allowed to discuss these concerns. The patient's feelings are prohibited rather than worked with.

Psychological tyranny can also express itself through psychologically sophisticated but inappropriate use of transference interpretations. For example, one patient reacted angrily to a questionable limit imposed on her. The therapist deflected the patient's anger directed at him and his real action by interpreting that she was really angry at her controlling mother and transferring her anger at the mother to him. The patient was made to feel that she had no right to be angry at the therapist. She then believed that her feelings were inappropriate and crazy. Transference interpretations should be reserved for situations in which the patient's feelings are truly inappropriate to the current situation, rather than actually provoked by it.

Coexisting with the terrible sense of ineffectiveness of these patients are grandiose fantasies of omnipotence and invulnerability. This is manifest in the failure of the anorexic to be alarmed about her condition when she is close to dying. The need to be perfectly thin, and perfect in everything else too, reflects primitive, unmodified grandiosity. "Life is not worth living unless one is perfect" is the grandiose position taken by anorexics.

The anorexic body and the patient's sickness in general make dramatic exhibitionistic statements to others: "Take notice. Don't ignore me. I'm here. Getting some attention and responsiveness, even if it is negative, is better than none and feeling like nobody." The implication of these demands for self-confirmation is that core needs for confirmation, mirroring, and responsiveness have not been met during early childhood. This may occur when a parent is unable to provide appropriate responsiveness because the parent is anxious, overwhelmed, depressed, or psychotic. Given these circumstances, the future anorexic frequently commits herself to never being a burden. Her goal is to maintain the parent's well-being or narcissistic balance. She becomes the compliant model child who has turned off her own needs. This is the typical picture of the young girl prior to the onset of the anorexic illness. Theoretically, she can be described as having a "false self" adaptation (Winnicott, 1965). She is devoted to being a selfobject rather than being a self. She cannot allow her wishes and needs to take precedence.

With the onset of the illness, these needs and wishes break through. The illness permits the expression of the wish to be the center of all things and in omnipotent control of at least a narrowly defined world. Nothing else matters except control, and especially control of her body as the concrete representation of her self organization. Her environment is made to dance to her tune. It cannot ignore or be indifferent to her demands.

The therapeutic task here is to make the anorexic aware of and understand the legitimacy of her true feelings, wishes, needs, values, and goals. Once this is accepted, she no longer requires the indirect, maladaptive, pathological means of self-confirmation that she obtains by being ill. Prior to the development of insight, the therapist provides mirroring, responsiveness, and empathy. If this goes well, the patient's narcissistic equilibrium is enhanced. The resulting stabilization of the self organization both allows the patient to be amenable to insight and may by itself produce symptomatic relief.

Hostile, Vindictive Fantasies

For the most part, anorexics find it difficult or impossible to be angry. Anger is disavowed. Nevertheless, an observer may see it written on the anorexic's face or expressed in her behavior. For example, an anorexic frequently stops eating when her mother or anyone else is pleased by her eating. In the anorexic's profound stubbornness, negativism, and oppositionalism, anger is apparent.

A central unconscious fantasy at play in the anorexic's self-starvation is for her to become a concentration camp victim, a vision of (impending) death, a walking cadaver. This can occur in response to a parent's having identified the future anorexic with an ambivalently loved relative who died. In the mind of this parent, the future anorexic is a replacement for the dead relative (Falstein, Feinstein, & Judas, 1956; Goodsitt, 1969). Fearing the realization of unconscious death wishes now directed at the child, this parent anxiously and phobically overprotects the child and fosters an overly controlling symbiosis. The parent acts as if death is always just around the corner. The anorexic's appearance is her cruel, vindictive parody of the parent's worst fears (Goodsitt, 1969).

A variation on this theme is illustrated by the patient Ann (described earlier). Ann had a fantasy of her parents grieving over her dead body. She could then gloat that her parents finally realized the wrong they had done her, but now it was too late. The patient Beth (also described earlier) went even further: She kept her bedroom darkened except for candlelight, and created an altar in front of which she prayed. She fantasized herself as her parents' human sacrifice upon the altar. This gloomy, sacrificial room, permeated with the sense of death, was meant to deliver a vindictive accusation to her parents: "You have killed me." Beth reveled in the knowledge that when her mother embraced her she would be aghast with horror in feeling only bones. Beth hoped her appearance evoked shock in others as well. She wanted to be sick, ugly, pitiful, and freakish.

This pursuit of ugliness is an often overlooked phenomenon. In contrast, much has been said about sociocultural standards equating thinness with beauty. On a conscious level, anorexics claim they are striving to be perfectly beautiful by becoming thin. On a less than conscious or unconscious level, just the opposite is found, as described above. The goal is rather to achieve a degree of emaciation that is repulsive, ugly, and shocking. This not only fulfills fantasies of revenge, but represents an attempt by the anorexic to awaken her parents to her dreadful plight.

Self-Guilt

The concept of separation anxiety as a significant impediment to separation–individuation has been thoroughly elucidated by Mahler (1968). Individuals who remain symbiotically bound experience annihilation anxiety, psychic disruption, or fragmentation during separation. Those individuals who have progressed to the level of separation–individuation are more able to remain structurally intact or cohesive. These individuals are more aware of their dependency and are thus more vulnerable to experiencing separation anxiety than to experiencing psychic disruption.

In working with anorexic patients, I have found another factor that I believe significantly impedes the separation–individuation process. Anorexics suffer profound guilt for the wish to separate and the act of separation and individuation. This guilt is manifested in different ways from the guilt expressed by neurotics who are conflicted over specific or focal taboo drives or impulses.

Self-guilt, in contrast to neurotic guilt, is experienced by an anorexic as a more ill-defined but pervasive sense of discomfort for simply being or existing. She generally cannot articulate this experience. Nevertheless, she feels guilty for occupying space. She is in constant fear of burdening others. She refrains from making demands and expressing wishes, desires, and needs. She allows others to use and abuse her. She does not confront those who do abuse her. She does not represent herself (her selfhood) well with others. She feels uneasy and guilty when given to. She turns away gifts and compliments. She acts as if she is undeserving. Nevertheless, she considers herself selfish.

The anorexic negates her selfhood. She extols the virtues of self-denial, discipline, and asceticism (Mogul, 1980), while abhorring anything that smacks of indulgence. Unlike the neurotic, who feels guilty for indulging specific taboo desires, the anorexic feels guilty for the act of indulgence itself. Pleasure *per se* is taboo. The emaciated body shape is an ideal that graphically portrays this moral value of self-negation.

Self-negation is evident in the anorexic's devotion to meeting the expectations of others. Duty, obedience, and obligation occupy high positions in the anorexic's hierarchy of values and ideals. By leading a highly regimented, ritualized life, regulated by rules, taken up by schedules and obligations, the anorexic precludes any chance to look inward and consider her own wishes and needs. She thereby negates her selfhood. Instead, she directs her attention to pleasing, accommodating, and being sensitive to others. The guiding rule for life is to serve others by meeting their needs. She strives to become a selfobject and not a self.

It is as if the future anorexic has a hard time justifying her existence. Modell (1965) first described a type of patient who suffers separation guilt. He notes that these patients are arrested in the phase of separation–individuation. They experience a vague yet pervasive and ill-defined type of guilt. He aptly states that these patients do not feel they have a right to a life (of their own). Anorexics are not only afraid to grow up (separation anxiety), but experience guilt for growing up and thereby abandoning the parent(s). Anorexics feel disloyal for having feelings, wishes, needs, interests, values, and goals that are different from those of their parents. They feel guilty for wanting or having a separate identity or selfhood.

Ann reported that she would feel herself "click off" in the presence of her mother and "click on" in the mother's absence. Debbie told her depressed mother that she would never leave her mother as her older brothers had; they had left home to marry and establish lives of their own. Another anorexic described how she had always felt she owed her mother her life. This patient struggled to feel that her life was her own to live. Beth, as noted earlier, spoke of her being the center of her mother's life; she felt that her mother could "never be happy without me." Any time Beth felt happy, she proceeded to "kill the happiness." She explained, "I am not supposed to be happy. I should give all that to mother."

These illustrations demonstrate both the anorexic's self-guilt and the belief that her role in life is to be a selfless selfobject. Often she feels she is a special or precious child, born to fill an emptiness or the needs of a parent. She sees herself as compensating her parent for a disappointing spouse or sibling. This goal would then intensify the anorexic's need to be perfect—to be a model child for the parent.

The need to be a selfobject may also be evident in the transference to the therapist. Ann would begin each session by scrutinizing the therapist's face for any sign of fatigue. She could not begin to talk about herself until she had been reassured that the therapist was okay or in a good mood.

Since it is the anorexic's obligation to be a selfobject, she experiences self-guilt when she does not fulfill this role. She cannot say "no," refuse to accommodate others' demands and needs, or obtain gratification for herself unless she does it in a disguised or unacknowledged fashion. The illness of anorexia nervosa serves this purpose well. It provides an excuse for being negativistic and for obtaining exhibitionistic, narcissistic gratification and self-confirming responsiveness.

A conceptualization of self-guilt makes meaningful some aspects of self-starvation. To eat means to give to oneself. It means that one responds to inner sources of need versus outer expectation, duty, or obligation. To eat means one has made a decision that one has a right to consider oneself a priority vis-à-vis others. Self-interest is legitimate. Thinking of oneself and giving to oneself are legitimate; they have their place—and, in fact, their priority—in the scheme of things.

For the anorexic, the act of eating is an unjustifiable self-indulgence. It is a betrayal of the function of being a selfobject. Any act that indicates or suggests self—self-indulgence, self-direction, self-caring, self-interest—is pejoratively labeled or experienced as selfish and is therefore considered illegitimate.

When presented with an anorexic's self-guilt, the therapist takes the position that it is the patient's birthright to have a life of her own. Self-interest is differentiated from selfishness. Clarification and insight are crucial in working through this issue.

CONCLUSIONS

In 1962, Bruch reported that standard psychoanalytic interpretations did not work for anorexic patients. Bruch found these patients to be out of touch with inner experience (rather than conflicted over drives). She described the anorexic's sense of ineffectiveness, interoceptive disturbance, and body image disturbance. She related these symptoms to early childhood experiences, which resulted in the child's failure to tune in to inner experience and learn about herself. Bruch's therapy aimed at eliciting and respecting her patients' feelings.

Bruch realized that she was dealing with something that had not been described in the psychoanalytic texts. Without theoretical aid from people like Winnicott, Kohut, Tolpin, Gedo, and Goldberg, she described patients whose actions were not centered in inner experience. Their selves failed to thrive and were stunted or atrophied. Bruch devised a therapy perfectly suited for her patients — a therapy aimed at centering, cultivating, and nurturing the self. To my mind, she pointed us in the right direction.

Self psychology has given us a theoretical language to describe what Bruch knew all along. Anorexics are arrested in self-development and deficient or incomplete in self-regulatory structure. I believe that the role of the therapist is to provide an opportunity for growth and healing of the self. The therapist fills in for the missing structure by offering himself as a selfobject or transitional object. Given the deficits in the patient, he actively reaches out, teaches, coaches, encourages, takes by the hand, and takes over if necessary.

Often even this is not enough. The patient cannot let herself grow and be. She acts as if she must be a selfobject and never a self. Self-guilt precludes selfhood. The therapist must help his patient to believe that it is her birthright to be a person. If all then goes well, he will have the distinct pleasure of watching the psychological birth of his patient.

REFERENCES

Berlin, I. N., Boatman, M. J., Scheimo, S. L., & Szurek, S. A. (1951). Adolescent alternation of anorexia and obesity. *American Journal of Orthopsychiatry, 21*, 387–419.
Blitzer, J. R., Rollins, N., & Blackwell, A. (1961). Children who starve themselves: Anorexia nervosa. *Psychosomatic Medicine, 23*, 369–383.
Bruch, H. (1962). Perceptual and conceptual disturbances in anorexia nervosa. *Psychosomatic Medicine, 24*, 187–194.
Bruch, H. (1973). *Eating disorders: Obesity, anorexia and the person within*. New York: Basic Books.
Bruch, H. (1977). Anorexia nervosa. In S. C. Feinstein & P. Giovacchini (Eds.), *Adolescent psychiatry* (Vol. 5, pp. 293–303). New York: Jason Aronson.
Casper, R. C. (1982). Treatment principles in anorexia nervosa. In S. C. Feinstein, J. G. Looney, A. Z. Schwartzberg, & A. D. Sorosky (Eds.), *Adolescent psychiatry* (Vol. 10, pp. 431–454). Chicago: University of Chicago Press.
Casper, R. C., & Davis, J. M. (1977). On the course of anorexia nervosa. *American Journal of Psychiatry, 134*, 174–178.
Crisp, A. H. (1980). *Anorexia nervosa: Let me be*. New York: Grune & Stratton.
Dally, P. J. (1969). *Anorexia nervosa*. New York: Grune & Stratton.
Eissler, K. R. (1943). Some psychiatric aspects of anorexia nervosa, demonstrated by a case report. *Psychoanalytic Review, 30*, 121–145.
Erikson, E. (1959). *Psychological issues: Identity and the life cycle* (Vol. 1). New York: International Universities Press.

Falstein, E. I., Feinstein, S. C., & Judas, I. (1956). Anorexia nervosa in the male child. *American Journal of Orthopsychiatry, 26*, 751–772.

Freud, S. (1961). The ego and the id. In J. Strachey (Ed. and Trans.), *The standard edition of the complete psychological works of Sigmund Freud* (Vol. 19, pp. 3–66). London: Hogarth Press. (Original work published 1923)

Garfinkel, P. E., & Garner, D. M. (1982). *Anorexia nervosa: A multidimensional perspective*. New York: Brunner/Mazel.

Garner, D. M., & Bemis, K. M. (1982). A cognitive–behavioral approach to anorexia nervosa. *Cognitive Therapy and Research, 6*, 123–150.

Garner, D. M., & Garfinkel, P. E. (1980). Socio-cultural factors in the development of anorexia nervosa. *Psychological Medicine, 10*, 647–656.

Garner, D. M., Garfinkel, P. E., & Bemis, K. M. (1982). A multidimensional psychotherapy for anorexia nervosa. *International Journal of Eating Disorders, 1*, 3–46.

Garner, D. M., Garfinkel, P. E., Schwartz, D., & Thompson, M. (1980). Cultural expectations of thinness in women. *Psychological Reports, 47*, 483–491.

Gedo, J. E. (1979). *Beyond interpretation*. New York: International Universities Press.

Gedo, J. E., & Goldberg, A. (1973). *Models of the mind*. Chicago: University of Chicago Press.

Goodsitt, A. (1969). Anorexia nervosa. *British Journal of Medical Psychology, 42*, 109–118.

Goodsitt, A. (1977). Narcissistic disturbances in anorexia nervosa. In S. C. Feinstein & P. Giovacchini (Eds.), *Adolescent psychiatry* (Vol. 5, pp. 304–312). New York: Jason Aronson.

Goodsitt, A. (1982). [Book review of *Starving to death in a sea of objects* by J. A. Sours.] *International Journal of Eating Disorders, 1*, 70–76.

Goodsitt, A. (1983). Self-regulatory disturbances in eating disorders. *International Journal of Eating Disorders, 2*, 51–60.

Grimshaw, L. (1959). Anorexia nervosa: A contribution to its psychogenesis. *British Journal of Medical Psychology, 32*, 44–49.

Jessner, L., & Abse, D. W. (1960). Regressive forces in anorexia nervosa. *British Journal of Medical Psychology, 33*, 301–312.

Keys, A., Brozek, J., Henschel, A., Mickelsen, O., & Taylor, H. L. (1950). *The biology of human starvation* (2 vols.). Minneapolis: University of Minnesota Press.

Khantzian, E. (1978). The ego, the self, and opiate addiction. *International Review of Psycho-Analysis, 5*, 189–198.

Kohut, H. (1971). *The analysis of the self*. New York: International Universities Press.

Krystal, H. (1978). Self representation and the capacity for self care. *The Annual Review of Psychoanalysis, 6*, 209–246.

Levenkron, S. (1983). *Treating and overcoming anorexia nervosa*. New York: Warner Books.

Mahler, M. (1968). *On human symbiosis and the vicissitudes of individuation*. New York: International Universities Press.

Margolis, P. M., & Jernberg, A. (1960). Anaclitic therapy in a case of extreme anorexia. *British Journal of Medical Psychology, 33*, 291–300.

Marohn, R. (1982). *The negative transference in the treatment of juvenile delinquents*. Paper presented at the Department of Psychiatry Grand Rounds, University of Wisconsin School of Medicine, Madison.

Masserman, J. H. (1941). Psychodynamics in anorexia nervosa and neurotic vomiting. *Psychoanalytic Quarterly, 10*, 211–242.

Masterson, J. F. (1978). The borderline adolescent: An object relations view. In S. C. Feinstein & P. L. Giovacchini (Eds.), *Adolescent psychiatry* (Vol. 6, pp. 344–359). Chicago: University of Chicago Press.

Modell, A. H. (1965). On having the right to a life: An aspect of the superego's development. *International Journal of Psycho-Analysis, 46*, 323–331.

Modell, A. H. (1975). A narcissistic defence against affects and the illusion of self-sufficiency. *International Journal of Psycho-Analysis, 56*, 275–282.

Mogul, S. L. (1980). Asceticism in adolescence and anorexia nervosa. *Psychoanalytic Study of the Child, 35*, 155–175.

Moulton, R. (1942). A psychosomatic study of anorexia nervosa including the use of vaginal smears. *Psychosomatic Medicine, 4*, 62–74.

Rowland, C. V., Jr. (1970). Anorexia nervosa: A survey of the literature and review of 30 cases. *International Psychiatric Clinics, 7*, 37–137.

Russell, G. F. M. (1970). Anorexia nervosa: Its identity as an illness and its treatment. In J. H. Price (Ed.), *Modern trends in psychological medicine* (Vol. 2, pp. 131–164). New York: Appleton-Century-Crofts.

Schwartz, D., Thompson, M., & Johnson, C. (1982). Anorexia nervosa and bulimia: The socio-cultural context. *International Journal of Eating Disorders, 1,* 20–36.

Scott, W. (1948). Notes on the psychopathology of anorexia nervosa. *British Journal of Medical Psychology, 21,* 241–247.

Selvini-Palazzoli, M. (1978). *Self-starvation.* New York: Jason Aronson.

Sours, J. A. (1980). *Starving to death in a sea of objects.* New York: Jason Aronson.

Sugarman, A., & Kurash, C. (1982). The body as a transitional object in bulimia. *International Journal of Eating Disorders, 1,* 57–67.

Swift, W. J., & Letven, R. (1984). Bulimia and the basic fault: A psychoanalytic interpretation of the binging–vomiting syndrome. *Journal of the American Academy of Child Psychiatry, 23,* 489–497.

Tolpin, M. (1971). On the beginnings of a cohesive self. *Psychoanalytic Study of the Child, 26,* 316–352.

Tustin, F. (1958). Anorexia nervosa in an adolescent girl. *British Journal of Medical Psychology, 31,* 184–200.

Wall, J. H. (1959). Diagnosis, treatment and results in anorexia nervosa. *American Journal of Psychiatry, 115,* 997–1001.

Waller, J. V., Kaufman, M. R., & Deutsch, F. (1940). Anorexia nervosa: Psychosomatic entity. *Psychosomatic Medicine, 2,* 3–16.

Winnicott, D. W. (1953). Transitional objects and transitional phenomena. *International Journal of Psycho-Analysis, 34,* 89–97.

Winnicott, D. W. (1965). *The maturational processes and the facilitating environment.* New York: International Universities Press.

CHAPTER FIVE

Accepting the Symptom: A Feminist Psychoanalytic Treatment of Anorexia Nervosa

SUSIE ORBACH

THEORETICAL CONSIDERATIONS

A critical entry point for the treatment of anorexia nervosa (and indeed for bulimia and compulsive eating as well) is the understanding of anorexia nervosa as a solution to a complex of socially constructed but clearly individually experienced set of psychological problems. The facts that anorexia nervosa is almost exclusively a distress symptom associated with girls and women, and that there has been a dramatic rise in the incidence of anorexia nervosa over the last 15 years (Crisp, Palmer, & Laccy, 1976), suggest that both an analysis of the disorder and the possible treatment avenues must take into account the psychological construction of femininity and the vicissitudes of the passage from girlhood to womanhood in contemporary society.

The Construction of Femininity

Feminist theorists (Gordon, 1970; Mitchell, 1973) have identified the family as the transmitter of a psychology of women. It is within the family structure, and in particular the mother–daughter relationship, that a girl learns her social role simultaneously with her developing sense of self (Eichenbaum & Orbach, 1983a). In our culture, mothers are responsible for the psychological and social development of infants from sexed categories to gendered ones (Money & Erhardt, 1973; Stoller, 1968). In other words, the mother directs her children's development in gender-appropriate ways, both at the level of socialization and in terms of the formation of psychic structure. The impact of this social demand on the mother–daughter relationship is profound. The mother–daughter relationship is inevitably an ambivalent one, for the mother, who herself lives a life circumscribed in patriarchy, has the unenviable task of directing her daughter to take up the very same position that she has occupied. Explicitly as well as unconsciously, she psychologically prepares her daughter to accept the strictures that await her in womanhood. She needs to do this so that her daughter is not a misfit. Of course, there are a broad range of behaviors and activi-

Susie Orbach. The Women's Therapy Centre Institute, New York, New York; and The Women's Therapy Centre, London, England.

ties that mothers indicate are acceptable, but the construction of femininity is bounded by fundamental social laws that delineate the parameters of a woman's life.

The psychological requirements of successful femininity for the adult women today include three basic demands. The first is that she must defer to others; the second is that she must anticipate and meet the needs of others; and the third is that she must seek self-definition through connection with another.[1] The consequences of these requirements are that by denying themselves, women are unable to develop an authentic sense of their needs or a feeling of entitlement for their desires. Women become dependent on the approval of those to whom they give, preoccupied with others' experience, and unfamiliar with their own needs. The imperative of affiliation means that many aspects of self are underdeveloped, producing insecurity and a shaky sense of self.[2] Under the competent care giver lives a hungry, deprived, and needy little girl who is unsure and ashamed of her desires and wants (Eichenbaum & Orbach, 1983a). Thus social requirements and their consequences create a particular psychology for women.

There exist in all women, to one degree or another, two deeply internalized taboos (which are socially reinforced). One is against the expression of dependency needs, and the other is the taboo against initiating (Eichenbaum & Orbach, 1983b). Most people are keenly aware of the existence of the taboo against female initiation and autonomy, but are unaware of how forcefully girls and women repress their needs for dependence and nurturance. The situation is complicated by the fact that simultaneous with the covert instruction to curtail one's needs are two seemingly paradoxical injunctions. First, girls are encouraged to display a range of dependent and deferential behavior, such as appearing "not to know" and requiring aid in such matters as changing a light bulb (in order to give life to the ideological dictum about men's superior strength and women's weakness); second, they are guided to convert their own wish to be attended to into caring and responding to others. Thus women's true dependency needs are deeply buried and are inevitably experienced with shame and distress. Their needs, thwarted and unmet, go underground. A psychological consequence of the suppression of women's desires for both dependency gratification and autonomy is that women do not feel worthwhile within themselves. They feel unentitled, they feel wrong. They constantly search to feel all right, and the approval of others temporarily quiets the uneasy feelings inside.

This is one aspect of the psychology that women bring to mothering. In relating to a baby girl whose needs are obvious and pressing, the mother's own life experience of containing her dependency needs and restricting her initiating desires is stimulated in particularly painful ways. The role of mothering includes directing a daughter in gender-appropriate ways. Just as a mother cannot set up false expectations for her daughter about adult life, so in their relationship, the mother knowingly as well as unconsciously distills the social laws. Thus the mother–daughter relationship itself becomes marked by a kind of rejection of the daughter's dependency needs as well as of her desires for autonomy. Because the daughter does not receive adequate grati-

---

1. For a more detailed discussion, see Eichenbaum and Orbach (1983a, pp. 36–67). Please note that although these values are changing for those raising children currently, these features are at present crucial to a woman's sense of self.

2. Many commentators have discussed the positive implications of women's affiliative capacities and permeable boundaries; for example, see Miller (1976), Gilligan (1982), and Chodorow (1978).

fication of early dependency needs, she has difficulty in the separation process, for she still needs an experience of consistent nurturance. According to Fairbairn (1952) and Guntrip (1969), the capacity to individuate rests on the gratification of early dependency needs. Thus the developmental phase of separation–individuation is impaired. The mother is reluctant to let her daughter go (for the mother herself may be merged with her daughter out of her own lack of a separated self), and the daughter herself has not yet embodied a sufficient sense of self to separate.

Femininity and Food

There is evidence to suggest that these taboos on female desire and the stricture "not to expect too much" are expressed in the feeding and holding aspects of the mother–daughter relationship. In a study of Italian infants, Brunet and Lezine (1966) report marked differences in feeding patterns and the feeding ambience, based on gender. Of the girls, 66% were breast-fed, as compared to 99% of the boys. Girls were weaned significantly earlier than boys, and in general, time allotted to feeding activities was distinctively less for girls than for boys. The same discrepancy was observed in relation to patterns of holding. Girl infants were held for shorter periods of time than boys. Informal reports[3] by child analysts and developmental psychologists confirm these kinds of differences (even where the issue is not bottle versus breast, but time and contact). These observations point to a continuity between the early feeding patterns of girls and accepted feeding patterns in adult women. The earlier behavior is in a sense preparatory. Just as adult women are counseled to curb their desires for food in the interest of current aesthetics, so girl children become accustomed early to getting less.

Thus the first relationship that a girl experiences is one in which she takes in a powerful message of denial—both of emotional nurturance and of the desire for autonomy—in relation to the restraint of physical appetite. These broad statements are not intended to hold exactly true for each mother–daughter relationship, but rather to delineate the parameters of that first most crucial relationship in the girl's life. There is a mismatch between the daughter's desires and the responses to them. In another distortion of infant feeding, many girl children are overfed from birth onward; many mothers, desperate to comfort their newborn, offer food—the breast and the bottle—when other strategies for soothing might be more appropriate (Orbach, 1978). Bruch (1973) and Selvini-Palazzoli (1974) have discussed how cues for comfort misinterpreted as hunger signals retard and distort the development of the physical–psychological mechanism of hunger (this will be the case when hunger is not adequately responded to, as well). Thus the early feeding relationship, an important and central aspect of the infant's development, is often one in which the infant's needs are not matched rhythmically. The feeding relationship may be fraught and become the site of struggles both mother and child must make in relation to developmental tasks.

Food is an extremely powerful cultural shaper in all societies. Cross-culturally, there is a broad range in the way infants are introduced to food and the subsequent socializing experiences surrounding food. In the Western world, a most striking feature

3. I have discussed this finding with several child analysts and developmental psychologists in seminars, and they have observed gender-based differences in the holding and feeding of infants.

is the almost exclusive involvement of women in food preparation in the home. For hundreds of years, women have obtained and transformed foodstuffs into daily meals for their families. Girls grow up knowing that an integral part of their role is to cook and provide nourishing meals for their families. An important dimension of woman's self-esteem derives from her capacity to fulfill this role. Since World War II, with the advent of mass refrigeration, freeze-drying, and other technological developments applied to food and food delivery (such as the supermarket), there has been a decrease in real time required for food preparation in the home. At the same time, the period following World War II — which is of interest to us, because the major rise in ano-rexia nervosa has occurred in the population whose mothers and fathers were parenting at this time — was characterized by an ideological thrust to get women back into their kitchens and away from the habits of working in the marketplace, which were developed out of the necessities of a wartime economy. Female ambition was to be replaced by the role of the professional mother and homemaker — a job requiring more skills, time, and input from other experts (Friedan, 1963; Spock, 1957; Ehrenreich & English, 1981). Women were induced to put their considerable energies into the household. Motherhood was elevated to almost saintly proportions,[4] and women were told that their satisfactions would come from the knowledge that they were good home-makers and mothers. Numerous experts materialized to guide women in this new (al-beit, according to the ideology, biologically destined and therefore almost holy) role. Women's magazines of the period attest to the importance of the mother in the well-being and the mental health of her children[5] and in the wife's role in the career development of her husband. (Needless to say, the latter depended on a wife's sensitivity to the husband's needs and the holding back of her own: "Don't nag.") The family became invested as the haven from the world of competition at work, the natural site for the care of preschool children, and the desired domain of women (Gordon, 1970).

Women's power was to be felt in every area of family life, but in none so poignantly as in the arena of food. The mother provided breakfast, take-away lunch, dinner, and snacks, according to a well-thought-out mix among children's desires, nutritional requirements, and the family's economic position.[6] At the same time that advances in food technology potentially reduced the time a person might need to spend preparing food, women were counseled to spend more time in the kitchen and at the stores, thinking about the food that would be the expression of their love and caring for their families. Families gathered around the breakfast and dinner table twice a day. A mother's work came to fruition in the meals that she prepared. They expressed her originality and her skill at balancing the budget. Food became her statement of love, power, and giving in the family. The children's receptivity to the mother's food became an area involving discipline, sometimes by the mother, sometimes by the father. Food personified the mother, and she was rejected or accepted through it. In this way, food became divorced from its biological function[7] and took on this highly

4. See Friedan (1963), as well as the popular movies and magazines of the late 1940s and 1950s.

5. This statement is based on unpublished research by Lela Zaphiropoulos.

6. This became institutionalized in the 1950s, when girls in all class backgrounds learned domestic science and home economics in school so as to be adequately prepared for married life.

7. This is, of course, true in all cultures; the point at issue here is that in the Western world during the past 30 to 40 years, women's centrality to the kitchen has surpassed any actual necessity and expresses our culture's relationship to food in its particular way.

reified meaning. It was the conveyor belt for all manner of feelings expressed among family members.

In addition to food delivery as a central aspect of a woman's existence, we must fold in another dimension of the social requirement of femininity. We must take into account that throughout history, women's feeding others has been coupled with the necessity for self-denial. In times of scarcity, the men and male children are fed the most prized foods,[8] and they receive the largest portions. In contemporary America, where food scarcity is less subject to natural causes than to current economic arrangements, we grow up with an expectation of food availability. And yet women still hold back on their desires for food, because food that a woman prepares in an expression of love and nurturance for others is a far more dangerous commodity for the woman herself. What do I mean by proposing this? At various stages in history and in different societies, woman's body has had to conform to the local culture's idea of what constitutes sexual attractiveness.

The Idealization of the Female Body

Since the Renaissance, the feminine ideal has swung between an emphasis on buxomness and its polar opposite, the Victorian 18-inch waist. Until recently (the last 15 years), these changes in body desirability extended over epochs and were of principal concern to women of the *haute bourgeoisie* and courtesans. What is striking about the last 60 years is the impact that the idealized feminine form has produced on the great mass of women (and, to a lesser extent, men). The advent of the movies and mass culture has created a population responsive to imitate and take up the received images of femininity. These images have projected a few limited body types for women, and the female beauties of an age have corresponded in their own unique way to the body type. The mass media have selected their models and photomontages to conform to the aesthetic ideals of the age, and in this way women who have been unable to match their own bodies or looks to those of the mannequin have had an ideal to strive for. What is particular about the last 15 years is the rate of acceleration in the changing aesthetics of the female body. As though they were hemlines that could be shortened or lengthened seasonally, the current aesthetic of women's bodies has been changing almost yearly. Since the late 1960s, women's bodies—as reflected in fashion magazines, glamorous serials on television, and so on—have been getting slimmer and slimmer and slimmer. Gone are the bosoms of the 1950s; spiraling angularity is *à la mode* today. Whereas 50 years ago a woman might bemoan the fact that her body did not "go out and in" as she desired, no woman today can rest assured in the knowledge that she has a good figure, for no woman today has the right body for more than a season or two. The aesthetic ideal is forever changing.

Body insecurity is almost bred into women, then, both at the level of mass culture and in the family dynamics. Few mothers of young adult and adult children today (those aged 15–35) have been able to feel secure in the natural shape of their bodies

8. This would seem to be a universal cultural phenomenon. I have uncovered no evidence of cultures in which women—unless gestating or lactating—were first in line for food.

9. See, for example, the vogue for sleek, long women in 1940s movies—Lauren Bacall, Joan Crawford, Greta Garbo.

and to convey this confidence to their daughters. The psychological sense of wrong-ness, discussed earlier, finds a vehicle for expression in a discomfort with one's body and a desire to have it reflect the contemporary norm. But before I discuss this point at some length, I should like to draw the reader's attention to another post-World War II cultural development, which, taken together with those already outlined, pro-vides an understanding for the specificity of eating disorders as a logical distress pat-tern of late 20th-century America. This is the development of a consumer society in which objects of the marketplace are reified and sexuality has become a commodity.

Women's bodies have come to be used as the hidden persuaders in the forging of a society whose economic rationale is consumption. Commodities from cars to Cokes to centrifuges[10] are displayed with young women close by, signaling availabil-ity and sexuality. The alienated commodity becomes more desirable, once washed with a human attribution. In other words, the sexuality of women's bodies has become split off and reattached to a whole host of commodities reflective of a consumer culture. Cars, Cokes, and centrifuges become a form of sexuality. At the same time, sexuali-ty itself is packaged in seemingly endless variety. As the alienation increases by arith-metic progression, the availability of sexual "fixes" appears to increase geometrical-ly. The physical link between objects as commodities and sexuality as a commodity is inevitably a woman's body.

The receptiveness of women in relating to their bodies as deficient, and their con-sequent desire to attempt to transform them must be explained. We need to make the links between those aspects of women's psychology, such as unentitledness, insecuri-ty, shaky boundaries, and outer-directedness, that make them susceptible to seeking validation and safety by acquiring the "correct" body. We need to situate this strug-gle in the complex of social forces that simultaneously creates the body insecurity and prohibits its adequate resolve. Amidst this, we need to understand the culture's fascination and fear of women as expressed through the desire to control women's bodies.

The Power of the Mother

To start with the last point first, current child-rearing arrangements, in which women mother (Chodorow, 1978), ensure that the power of the mother is deeply embedded in our psychologies. The mother is the person with whom the baby most closely re-lates. The mother's body provides nourishment and comfort for the baby, and the mother's physical presence provides a sense of containment for the developing child (Winnicott, 1965). In the process of psychological birth of the human infant, from utter dependence to separation–individuation, the mother's psychology is "taken in" by the developing person and forms the very core of his or her personality (Fairbairn, 1952; Guntrip, 1969). During the first year of life, the mother is a most powerful pres-ence in a number of ways. She is the mediator for the baby's experience; her actions organize the stimuli that flow back and forth between the baby and the world (Mahler, Pine, & Bergman, 1975; Spitz, 1965). She relates to the baby and its needs: Some-

10. I am grateful to Joseph Schwartz for pointing out to me that any instrumentation issue of *Science* or *Nature*, or the advertisements issued by manufacturers of scientific instruments, will show pretty young women standing alongside scintillation counters, ultracentrifuges, and the like in an effort to promote sales.

times she is able to meet them, and sometimes she is not. Her steady presence in the baby's life means that she comes to represent, in their most basic forms, both good and bad experiences. The baby is unable to control or comprehend the actions of the mother and is primarily the recipient of positive or negative experiences.

In the first year of life, although the baby is thought to be engaged in an enormous amount of internal mental activity, physical relating (i.e., being held, fed, changed, hugged, rocked) is the arena in which mother and child most obviously meet. The mother's physical presence or absence is constantly felt. The mother's body seems to provide or withhold comfort. But, as I have pointed out above, the baby is vulnerable in this relationship. He or she may influence the mother's actions, but, helpless and needy, is unable to control or direct them. Dinnerstein (1976) has argued that the child's inability to "control" the mother leads to a splitting mechanism in which the "good" and "bad" aspects of the mother's relating become both internalized and projected onto all women. Dinnerstein's bold conclusion is that a kind of mass internalized misogyny results. In identifying with their same-sex mothers, girls distrust their own power and their "good" and "bad" parts. Boys in the separation process attempt to repudiate their own femininity and primary identification with their mothers, and repress their own "good" and "bad" parts. In later life, they fear closeness with women, because it brings up their repressed feminine identity. In addition, they project onto women — their wives and lovers, as well as women in general — the "good" and the "bad." They attempt to control what they could not control earlier. They reject the power of the mother through the political and psychological subjugation of women.

Although I have some minor disagreements with Dinnerstein's analysis, I think that in broad strokes it provides a useful model, which I should like to extend for the purposes of this chapter to explain the cultural propensity to control women's bodies. Paradoxically, it is a woman's body that provides for her biological power, her capacity to reproduce. In our culture, this capacity is both denigrated and exploited. The patriarchial state's control over reproduction and sexuality, alongside the denial of women's natural body shape, suggests that the fear of a woman's body is immense. The existence of several hugely profitable industries in the "body insecurity business" attests to the experience of men and women today. To take Dinnerstein's thesis a step further, then, one can argue that the current child-rearing arrangements create in both boys and girls, men and women, conditions of fear and a desire for contact with women. The mother's body, once the symbol of comfort, is repudiated out of desperation, for the mother's body defies the control that the omnipotent infantile part of the personality so wishes. In turn, a collective attempt to control the female form is expressed in the objectified relations both sexes have toward women's bodies. The desire to control the mother is somewhat assuaged by the control exercised over female reproduction, sexuality, and aesthetics.

Developmental Tasks of Adolescence

The sequence of development in girls' personalities, described earlier, provides the psychic environment in which an insecurity toward oneself becomes easily transposed into an insecurity in relation to one's body. As girls enter adolescence, the issues that are still alive from the earlier developmental phase of separation–individuation re-emerge in a new and dramatic form. The struggle for an identity separate from the family is made on fairly shaky foundations. Detaching from the family and realigning oneself with peers involve tension and distress, because just as the earlier separation is desired at one level and feared at another, the wish to stay close and "protected" within the well-known psychic ambience is in conflict with the pull away from the family and toward the development of a preadult identity. Lambley (1983) discusses how parents of anorexic children interfere in the children's attempt to establish normal peer relations. The parents are inclined to criticize the daughters' choice of friends or groups, out of the need to keep the children close to home and exclusively involved in the emotional life of the families.

The insecurity felt by the adolescent — the fear and the wish for acceptance in the new, critical peer environment — produces in girls an overwhelming desire to conform. In addition, the dramatic physical changes that occur in puberty rock the young woman's already tenuous psychic foundations. Her body is changing, and the outcome of those changes are unpredictable.

During adolescence, the mother–daughter relationship loses none of its intensity or ambivalence. The mother's feelings about her daughter's sexual development are experienced within the mother–daughter relationship. Because the mother herself has lived with the pressure to have her body be attractive and conform to the standards of her time, she is unlikely to have had an experience of well-being, of feeling relaxed in her body. If she has battled with a "weight problem" for many years, she may impose this problem on her adolescent daughter by becoming watchful of what she eats and preoccupied with her changing body contours. She does this with the best of intentions, but her observations are frequently experienced as intrusive. Alternately, many mothers, threatened by their daughters' developing sexuality, are unable to authenticate the exciting body changes through which the young women are going. Therefore, the daughters seek confirmation and understanding outside of their families, from girlfriends and the magazines written explicitly for the teenage market. One thing that adolescent magazines uniformly preach as the solution to the crises of adolescence is dieting and weight control. Young women read that dieting is both the passport to the normal teenage life and the answer to a whole host of named and unnamed problems. The psychic insecurity is now addressed by the modern panacea — diet and control. Thus girls are initiated into the adult relationship they are to have with their bodies: Be vigilant; control your desires for food (and incidentally for sex); be frightened of your body, because it is always waiting to let you down.

The adolescent girl is learning to develop a split between her body and her self. Her body is rapidly being presented to her and being perceived by her as an artifact, albeit an essential one, both divorced from and yet reflective of the very essence of herself. What do I mean by this paradoxical statement? A woman tends to view her image in the mirror with a certain distance and the question of whether it (that is, she) is acceptable (Berger, 1972). The standard she applies reflects her internalization of cultural values. She measures how far from the norm she is; she fantasizes the benefits that arise from conforming. Her body is a statement about her, the world, and her position in the world. Since women live within prescribed boundaries, women's bodies become the vehicle for a whole range of expressions that have no other medium (Orbach, 1978, 1982). The body, offered as a woman's ticket into society (i.e., through it she meets a mate, and thus her sexuality and her role are legitimized), becomes her mouthpiece. In her attempts to conform or reject contemporary ideals of femininity, she uses the weapon so often used against her. She speaks with her body.

TREATMENT

Mode and General Description

Although I have worked with anorexic women in a variety of treatment modalities, including short-term groups (6 to 10 sessions), self-help groups (as an initiator or consultant), and short-term individual therapy, the method I find most useful and discuss here is individual open-ended psychotherapy. The course of treatment has varied from 2½ to 4 years. The treatment settings have been at The Women's Therapy Centre and in private practice.[11] On average, private practice patients have once-weekly sessions, whereas clinic patients meet with the therapist two times per week. It is my impression that the frequency of patient contact does not dramatically affect outcome, although twice-weekly contact may be preferable by virtue of creating and maintaining a holding environment.

Sessions are held on a formal basis for 50 minutes. Object constancy (i.e., the providing of a reliably good and consistent environment) is an essential part of the treatment. While rescheduling is sometimes necessary, based on a patient's occupation, regularity generally provides a symbolic continuity that may be put to good use by the patient. In those instances where the patient is young (i.e., 16 or under), the parents may be involved from time to time during the treatment process; however, in many instances I have not found it necessary to have contact with parents.

The Initial Consultation

The ground covered in the initial consultation, which may extend over two sessions, includes attention to a number of issues. The focus is an assessment as to whether or not I can be helpful to a particular woman. I anticipate that she will be wary of seeking treatment, because of her previous treatment history and/or because of a reluctance to expose feelings about herself, food, or her body. In anticipating her reticence, I try to address the part of her that is behind or buried in the defense, and thus to begin an evaluation and the development of a treatment alliance.

The ambience I wish to create in the initial consultation, and indeed in subsequent sessions, is a sense of openness so that the anorexic may begin to find words to express the painful circumstances she has found herself in. Thus my approach could be described as compassionate and, if you like, "on the patient's side." In other words, in trying to find out how the problem has developed and is being maintained, and how to enable the woman to change, I wish to engage in a partnership with the patient on the basis that if we understand her situation together, we may be able to help her sort through the particular solution she has chosen for herself. So I am concerned to find out the particulars of her daily experience — for example, what she is able to eat:

11. In addition, I supervise the work of therapists who see anorexic patients. In all cases the therapists are women, so all discussion relates to women patients working with women therapists. The institutional framework has not produced any visible treatment effect, either at the level of projections on to the person of the therapist or of unconscious fantasies. The financial arrangements at the Women's Therapy Centre in London provided for a treatment plan based on the therapists' and patients' optimum wishes. In other words, number of sessions per week were not contingent on direct payment of standard psychotherapy fees; thus, frequency of contact was more appropriate than is generally possible in private practice.

PATIENT: Well, I have a bagel in the morning.

THERAPIST: How much of that can you manage?

PATIENT: Well . . . a bagel, you know . . .

THERAPIST: Is a quarter about right, or is that too much for you?

PATIENT: Well, sometimes I can eat that much, but sometimes it's a half of a quarter.

THERAPIST: Can you manage the inside of the bagel as well?

PATIENT: It depends on how I'm feeling. See, I allow myself a bagel a day, well a half really, and I can divide it.

We begin to talk the same language. She knows I know just how little she manages to eat; she does not have to hide that from me. So we can proceed on the basis of trying to get a real picture together of what her actual eating behavior is like.

The second thing in which I am interested is how the patient feels when she approaches food, what her eating experiences are like, how often she binges and what quantity she consumes in a binge (if she is a bulimic anorexic), and how she handles food situations with others. Of course one can only get a smattering of such information in the initial session, but I am doing several things in this kind of inquiry. I am finding out whether she has words for feelings; I am discovering what kind of variation there is in her eating and her relationship to it; I am opening up the notion that it could be safe to talk about food; I want to know how her friends and parents react to her eating—whether she can sit and not eat with them, or whether she has to engage in elaborate plans to avoid eating or disposing of the food when she is at the table. In this connection, I am interested to know the eating habits of friends and family members. These usually have enormous meaning for the patient. I want to know about the circumstances of the onset of the symptoms—the ideas the patient attached to food deprivation, dieting, and getting slim. I am interested in the course of her day, the amount of time she spends bingeing or thinking obsessively about food, the existence of other rituals, and her level of social functioning. Of course all of these questions are the very content of the therapy for the weeks, months, and even years to come, but I am eager to raise them—both to assist me in making an assessment, and to demonstrate the breadth of topics the patient can feel free to talk about.

The Beginning of Therapy

Although I have offered treatment for as short a time as 6 months, I do not generally think it advisable to do time-limited psychotherapy with the anorexic. So many of the central issues affecting the patient require working through within the therapy relationship, and this is not possible with short-term work. In general, I do not see the course of psychotherapy with an anorexic as much different from the course of general psychotherapy. The beginning stage of therapy, in which we are establishing an initial way of being together and the therapist is creating an atmosphere that will allow for disclosure without the risk of rejection, can last from 1 to 6 months. The middle stage of therapy, in which a treatment alliance has been achieved and the patient is able both to regress and to take new stances toward herself, lasts from 2 to 4 years. The final stage of therapy lasts approximately 6 months to a year.[12]

---

12. For a discussion of stages of the therapy relationship, see Eichenbaum and Orbach (1983a, pp. 68–108).

Where the therapy differs markedly from general psychotherapy, or indeed from work with women who have other eating problems (such as compulsive eating or bulimia) without any anorexic features, is in the feeling in the room during the first stages of the therapy relationship. There is a kind of fright or fear that emanates from the anorexic patient. This arises from a real worry that by sharing and talking she will lose what little she has managed to create for herself. In other words, sharing can be experienced as a loss rather than a relief. It can be felt as an invasion of the fragile inner world into which the anorexic retreats most of the time. Thus the woman may be "difficult" or "distant" or "withholding," or there may be an atmosphere of coldness in the room that disinclines the therapist to intervene. The anorexic's defense pushes the therapist away in much the same way as it keeps others out and her locked in. The symptoms constitute a highly elaborated defense structure that has been developed to protect a pre-related (Orbach, in press) or severely underdeveloped self. It provides for a sometimes reassuring "false self" (Winnicott, 1965), which stands in for and shields an unintegrated ego.[13] Thus the woman is fearful of losing the self she has created and relied on.

In the beginning phase of therapy, I am inclined to make reference to the role of the defense — to demystify it, if you like — because I have found that it enables the patient to understand herself and her upsetting behaviors, thoughts, and practices better. There is no sense in doing away with the defense at this stage. Rather, it is a matter of explaining its function as it reveals itself.

The object of my interventions is to make contact with this pre-related self. This means offering interpretations that speak to the vulnerable and needy little-girl (Eichenbaum & Orbach, 1983a) behind the defense. There will be some resistance encountered throughout the therapy to interpretations. It is my observation that the therapist needs to be both precise as to content and careful as to timing when making interpretations. Otherwise they run the risk of being experienced as intrusive or simply wrong, and thus of being rejected. Of course, making a wrong or untimely interpretation is not a cardinal sin in therapy,[14] but it may be hard to talk with the anorexic about how she feels about an incorrect intervention. She may feel that the trust has been broken, or that the intervention "shows the therapist does not understand" or is "pushing too hard." In those instances when an interpretation is offered too early, it will be the therapist's responsibility to determine the impact on the patient in subsequent sessions and to provide opportunities for the patient to comment — several times if necessary — so as to repair the damage. It is not that the anorexic is so fragile that a "wrong" interpretation is a treatment disaster — rather, when such an incident occurs, it affords the therapist an opportunity to repair the psychic "mismatch" in the patient. The therapy relationship is much like the attempt of mother and child to become rhythmic. The patient has already experienced grievous mismatching, and therefore the relationship, rather than proceeding straightforwardly, is often studded with emotional uncertainties. The patient is not used to having another person make the effort to be in tune with her.

An important issue in the initial consultation is my assessment of whether the patient can meet certain conditions regarding eating. A key feature of the treatment

13. I am using "ego" in the Fairbairnian sense, to stand for the totality of the psyche.

14. In general psychotherapy, an untimely interpretation rarely produces the same kind of withdrawal or "shutdown" by the patient. It may hurt and thus needs to be discussed, but not usually with the same kind of vigilance on the part of the therapist for all traces.

program is the anorexic's being actively responsible for her food intake. This may seem like an alarming proposition to practitioners who are involved in food management, but the fact is that the anorexic *is* in charge of her food, and for several years she has tried to resist the intrusions of others (usually family, sometimes doctors) into this area. Out of their concern and worry, parents, educators, and friends have watched her and made suggestions about what and how she should be eating. Each one of the kindly made suggestions is experienced by the anorexic as a pressure she cannot meet. She is in a kind of despair about her food, but the interventions of others — focused as they are almost exclusively on nutritional considerations — lead her into further helplessness, which she deals with by tightening her control over food, acting more terrified of what it can do to her, and engaging in schemes to limit her intake further and rid herself of the little food she does consume. Thus her control over her food needs to be firmly recognized and acknowledged.

Provided there is no medical emergency (I do not consider a stable low weight a medical emergency), I make the following arrangement with the patient: I agree not to intervene regarding her actual food intake if she agrees not to go below the weight at which we initially meet. The joint assumption (which may not be initially accepted by the patient) must be that she ultimately should be at a healthier weight, but for the present, the crucial therapeutic work must start, and as little as possible should interfere with it. The patient as a whole person (i.e., including her anorexia nervosa) must be respected. I do not believe it is possible to cut out the offending behavior surgically. I endeavor to ease the symptom until its strength and tenacity dissolve through its not being needed any more. Of course, this dissolution is easier described than achieved, and I discuss shortly how the symptom continues to manifest itself through the middle stage of therapy. The main point I wish to emphasize here is the therapeutic advantage to be gained by the open acknowledgment that the patient is in control of her food. In making this arrangement, the therapist is proposing a relationship in which she is neither spying on the patient, undermining her, nor becoming a policewoman. The therapist is respecting the patient. As a result, therapist and patient are not engaged in a constant power struggle over who will determine what the food intake should be. The patient does not need to hide from the therapist and can begin to discuss openly, even if with difficulty, what the actual experience of eating, wanting, and fearing food is like. There is no threat that the therapist will judge, cajole, or threaten the patient. The therapy can proceed in a humanitarian fashion.

In addition to the therapeutic advantages of this arrangement, it also makes sense at a theoretical level. The development of anorexia nervosa is in part fueled by the need to provide some stability and control in a chaotic and unintegrated internal life. The control over food intake is an attempt to ameliorate the inability to control emotional incursions. The anorexic seeks to control her physical desires and needs — her appetites — and in so doing gains a measure of self-respect in a troublesome area of life. Her emotional appetites can perhaps be subjected (in fantasy only) to the same kind of treatment. As I discuss earlier in this chapter, emotional desire is an extremely fraught and complex area for a woman. Although, paradoxically, the culture has invested women with the responsibility for emotional matters, women's facility in recognizing and meeting their *own* needs is restricted by the developmental imperatives that create taboos on the expression of a whole range of desires, including the needs for dependency, nurturance, initiation, and autonomy. The anorexic woman has not experienced in her development an ease in recognizing her emotional needs. In case after case, I have observed a developmental pattern in which needs and initiations were ignored, disparaged, or thwarted in one way or another. This has enormous implications for the themes that will be worked through in the therapy, but a precondition for cutting into the notion that one's own desires are bad or wrong is the arrangement made with the new patient in relation to her control over food. If she can trust that her therapist can allow her to act on her own desires — however circumscribed they are — with regard to food, the therapist is slowly and gradually kindling the idea that desire and implementation themselves are not bad.

Beyond this theoretical point is the tremendously positive effect such an arrangement has in creating a therapeutic alliance. For vast periods of the therapy, the therapist will be relying on a treatment alliance in order to help the patient muddle her way out of the most persistent vicissitudes of the anorexic defense structure. The patient relies on her experience of the therapist as someone who is genuinely supportive and reasonable. The arrangement with food exemplifies this stance perfectly. At the same time, one cannot ignore food intake or the weight of the patient. The therapist needs to keep an awareness about these matters, and especially needs to make openings in the therapy to let the patient talk freely about food. But weight charts and food plans have no place in this treatment model.

In my experience, few anorexic patients are able to alter their eating behavior radically in the first phase of therapy. Of course, those practitioners who advocate food management may observe eating changes early in the treatment, but their patients are often still left with a fear of food and an inability to build a structure that can guide them from the inside. Many anorexics fear that they will not be able to limit their eating when they break away from the rigidity of the scheme that has been their survival mechanism. Although weight gain and menstrual functions are achieved, the fear of food and the fear of fatness continue to plague the woman. The goal of the treatment program described here is to enable the woman to have the best possible chance at living her life unafraid of food. We are aiming to help her develop the necessary skills to respond to her body's desires for an unlimited range of foodstuffs. We are helping her develop a comfort with hunger signals so that she can respond to them, and a confidence that she can stop eating when physically satisfied. Although this is an important goal of successful treatment, we cannot anticipate that the patient will be able to experiment freely enough with food to achieve such a goal until she is well into the treatment. In fact, except in atypical cases, the strategy I employ is to shift the emphasis away from food intake and focus on those areas that initially led to the onset of the symptom and those issues that are keeping the symptom going. Unless the conflicts, despairs, and myriad of themes enmeshed in the symptoms become disentangled and directly confronted, the defense will persist, or there will be a symptom switch.[15]

The Middle Stages of Therapy

A painful theme running through the psychology of each anorexic woman I have seen is what can only be described as a kind of self-hatred. This is usually discussed in terms of low self-esteem and little self-respect, but I think those terms are finally too mild

---

15. Examples of this I have encountered are switches from anorexia nervosa to bulimia and then to alcoholism, as well as from anorexia nervosa to heroin addiction.

to describe the strength of negative feelings that anorexics have shared with me. Furthermore, the term "low self-esteem" does not conjure up a sufficiently strong image of the brutality of the anorexic's internal life. Although the anorexic is engaged in a struggle to gain some self-respect and self-esteem, it is as a counterpoint to the internal warfare raging inside. The anorexic's inner world is chaotic and full of horror and anxiety. Ghastly thoughts attempt to mask the emotional turmoil. The institution of rules and regulations about food, exercise, and habits of work or study are meant to assuage the explosive inner life by containment. The ritualistic performance of tasks, physical exertion, and food practices provides a kind of comfort and certainty in a mass of emotional bonfires. This is illustrated by one patient's personal account:

I first started to control my food and do all those other kinds of things like walk 5 miles, just before my parents split up. I was so *disgusted* with them and the havoc at home, the constant yelling and the awful state they were both in, when I thought, "I don't have to be like them — all out of control. I can be responsible and in charge. I'll watch and control my eating." Pretty soon, I got results. I lost the weight I had thought was excess, and it wasn't so much that I was getting lots of positive attention at school, as much as I felt great, like I was better than my parents. I didn't need anything; I was above all that.

Sadly, that was only one side of the patient's experience, for as she came to understand in the course of her therapy, the feelings of disgust she had toward her parents were closely linked to her own feeling that needs of any sort were all wrong and needed to be immediately pushed down or done away with. In time, she came to understand that needs themselves terrified her, and for good reasons. Her family had been quite neglectful at an emotional level. They were not actively unresponsive, but her cues were frequently misinterpreted; her emotional initiatives of one sort or another were turned into something else — usually the family's projection of a need it could answer. She felt emotionally exploited and unsure of her physical or psychic boundaries. Her taking up the food and exercise regimens was an attempt to create a boundary where one did not exist. It was an adolescent form of the construction of false boundaries related to difficulties in separation–individuation. Having not received what she needed early in her development, her capacity to develop self–object relations was impaired. She still needed so much that she could not separate from a consolidated strength; rather, she needed to wrench herself away and create an illusion of differentiation. In this way, she could be distinguished from the need her parents expressed, and she could suppress her own needs at the same time.

If we look at this patient's words a little more closely, we cannot help noticing the positive feelings she was able to develop out of achieving her goal of controlling her food and gaining the capacity to transform her body. She was able to feel the pleasure of achievement in this particular sphere, and this then became transposed into a feeling she would like to achieve consistently: "At first I liked seeing the scales going down and down. I felt I'd really done something no one could interfere with or mess with." Later the pleasure that she experienced from this achievement paled, and she got satisfaction from knowing that she could control hunger pains, tiredness, and physical debility. Of course, these feelings could only temporarily quiet the various emotional and physical appetites she was bent on repressing.

Treatment proceeded on the basis of trying to uncover and work through the restrictions on recognizing or meeting needs of any sort. During the first year of therapy, this patient still found the notion of needs disagreeable and could rarely discover any needs in herself that did not bring up in her a feeling of guilt or a desire to engage in punishment. Slowly things shifted: She would come to sessions, report the week's events for the first 10 minutes or so, and then slump back in the chair, staring at the therapist. She was relaxing and using the therapy relationship as a place to sit and be—an unusual experience for her, and one she could tolerate first for 10 minutes, later for most of the session. It was as though a part of her had regressed to the state of "being" that Winnicott (1965, 1978) considers so crucial in the psychic development of self. These periods of being (feeling the therapist's presence and relying on her psyche to hold her own as yet unintegrated self) were punctuated by periods of severe depression and despair. She was initially fearful of experiencing the despair and would frantically try to get herself out of it, but gradually she was able to tolerate it.

Such a period in therapy is a difficult time for any therapist, who may feel discouraged by the patient's apparent lack of progress; however, the patient's capacity to contain the despair was actually an extremely positive development. She was taking in what she needed; she was simultaneously able to acknowledge a need and use the therapy relationship to satisfy it. The important thing about this example is that the therapist was able to sit with the patient and contain her despair. The fact that the therapist could convey an assurance that painful times could be tolerated gave the patient the confidence to believe that she too could live through them. They would destroy neither the patient nor the therapist. The anorexic patient tends to believe that the negative and frightening feelings that live inside of her are as frightening to the therapist as they are to her and obviously were to her parents. In many cases, negative feelings were barely tolerated in the family, particularly those feelings that were related to being unsure or needing things. The patient had always had to make sure that she projected a sense of being all right. The parental figures were unable to absorb and contain the normal range of distress that children express. Thus, the anorexic has an inordinate fear of negative feelings. She experiences them as calamitous, and a constant theme during the middle stage of therapy will be a question about whether it is really all right to "impose" these upset feelings on the therapist or to bring them in to the therapist. There is a fear that the therapist will withdraw from the patient—that the exposure of upset feelings will produce the same kind of response it did in parental figures. Alerted to this dynamic, the therapist can speak to the patient's concern during the course of therapy, so that gradually the refrain enters the patient's experience and she can begin to change a deeply held pattern of relating.

Obviously, not every patient is able to use the therapy situation in this way. I have worked with patients who were not able to contain the chaos that was lurking inside during the session time, and who felt and acted frantic or shared their distress at being suddenly overcome by eating binges. Again, the therapist may feel inclined to become discouraged at this point, but I would argue that this is an important developmental phase in the therapy. All that has been held back is now coming to the fore, and the content of the chaos can be examined. The anorexic can experience going through the chaos with someone on her side. She does not have to keep preempting its expression; it can come up and act as an emotional purgative.

While chaos or the containment of periods of despair are central aspects of the middle phase of the therapy relationship, the being "in tune" described earlier is the attempted form of relating. The therapist works hard to try to place herself in the patient's experience. To "know" what it is the patient is feeling may help her know that she is not alone. But this very being "in tune" may be distrusted by the patient, and so she may disparage the therapist's efforts or reject her comments. If this is anticipated by the therapist, then it need signal neither failure nor misunderstanding. It can be understood as an expression of the defense working within the therapy relationship, making sure (or, rather, checking out) how safe things really are. For someone who has experienced the kind of continual emotional rejection and mismatching felt by the patient, it is easy to understand that she continually has to test the reliability of what the therapist purports to be offering. To minimize the patient's agony during this process, the therapist may share this aspect of the process.

Outside of the actual vicissitudes of the therapy relationship, but forming an important part of the middle stage of the therapy, is the patient's gradual coming to terms with the fact that she does have needs — emotional ones, sexual ones, and physical ones pertaining to appetite and sleep. In my experience, this involves a slow, painful, and at times disbelieving grasp of the notion that needs exist and have a place in her life and psychology. The recognition of need stirs up great feelings of guilt, anger, and confusion: guilt as a reflexive response, anger as a reaction to the denial, and confusion about how to relate to needs in the present. Many of the needs will not be able to be met in the present, and so there will be much mourning to be done or loss to be faced for what can never happen or ever be given. It is important that the patient not confuse the denial of historic needs and the impossibility of those needs' ever being met with the denial of day-to-day needs. The anorexic finds it hard to accept that needs are something like speech, which gets newly produced as the situation stimulates it. The patient needs to learn how to negotiate these needs as an adult. This involves sustaining distress when needs are not met, without interpreting the distress as a reason for doing away with needs.

As the patient begins to develop facility in meeting emotional needs, both inside the therapy and outside the sessions, she begins to gain practice at following desires that arise from within her. She can translate this into the area of food and begin to take the risk of listening to her bodily needs for nutrition, thirst, and sleep. During this middle phase of therapy, if the patient's eating patterns are not chaotic, she is often able to relax her tight control over food and begin to experiment with food. This may be difficult, since the patient has neither eaten anything resembling a "normal" meal nor ingested food that her body has actually desired for many years. Many patients need extra contact and support at this time, including daily telephone calls. The fear of being out of control or of doing something very bad is very strong, and feeling the therapist's presence can be helpful.

It would be unwise to think that the first time the patient begins to break out of the rigid pattern of relating to food, she is likely to have a series of consistently positive eating experiences. The therapist would be well advised to anticipate the psychic difficulty such experiments can bring, and the anguish and worry they call up in the patient. It is also important to be wary of setting up expectations of what the patient should be able to achieve. Given the patient's history of pleasing others, a food experiment intended as a growth experience could become a transferential attempt to please the therapist. Of course, the patient will be nervous and may only half believe that she can eat. However, it is this part of the patient that the therapist needs to help, so that she can try to eat on the basis of hunger. Each eating experience is an opportunity for experimentation, rather than a signal of success or failure. Each eating experience can be evaluated for its emotional and physical resonances.

Certain foods may be particularly difficult for anorexics to try. However, this is a time to discuss food and what it is for, food habits of the family, and why certain foods have become taboo. I have found patients much reassured by the notion that no foods need be taboo. We can look at food groups or food items, one by one, to help a patient integrate them into her diet.

The obsession with food gets exploded and discussed. It no longer remains an area of disgust and self-humiliation for the patient. She has allowed the therapist to enter a very secret part of her world, because she has been ready to change it, and that is an exciting step forward in the therapy.

During the course of therapy, the theme of sexuality emerges. For those women who have never experienced their sexual feelings directly because of early onset of anorexic symptoms, the therapist may intermittently sense a curious and somewhat embarrassed preadolescent in the room (even if the woman is in her 20s). For women whose anorexia nervosa began after several sexual experiences, the sexual act may have become extremely problematic during the anorexic phase. Intercourse or closeness with another may be simultaneously desired and feared. The anorexic may feel shut off from intimacy and close contact; just as in other areas, the anorexic may have been trying to meet the sexual needs of her partners and unable to call up her own desires.

The therapy relationship provides a model relationship in which intimacy is experienced without being invasive, and in which the needs of the patient can arise and be legitimized. Clearly her first intimate relationships in the family may have been experienced as exploitative, unbalanced, and/or mismatched in fundamental ways. In the therapeutic relationship, the patient is experimenting with being close and learning that it is not necessarily dangerous. As she is able to open up in the safety of this relationship and feel a whole range of desires that emanate from herself, she gathers the confidence to take these desires outside the consultation room and into other relationships.

Since the patient may be isolated, a sexual relationship, even if desired, may not be immediately practical. The patient may fear that she will bring all the needs she is discovering for friendship, love, and connection to one person in an inappropriate way. While one goal of successful treatment of anorexia nervosa obviously is the capacity to relate fully with others, the actual symptoms may pass before the patient is able to find a satisfactory sexual relationship. More important criteria that I look for are the ability to connect with others at the level of friendship and the reshaping of mental images of parental figures. The ability to exist in the social world seems to me fundamental to being able to maintain a valid sense of self. Peers interact, give feedback and nurturance, and are engaged with each other. The anorexic has often suffered from an overinvolvement with the family or from a series of relationships that are structurally unequal. Having discovered a self that is solid in the therapy, the anorexic has less need to seek parental approval. She can take in the love and involvement offered by friendship with peers.

This does not mean that the issue of sexuality should be avoided. Sexual desire and sexual relationships obviously need to be discussed, as well as the allied issues of periods and reproduction. There is often a reticence to talk about periods because of mistaken beliefs, such as that the very having of them means the woman must conceive, or that periods are an expression of uncleanness. These kinds of issues surrounding sexuality are often expressions of the crudest views of female sexuality in this culture; the anorexic's beliefs become a caricature of the most extreme sexual stereotypes. Reassurance may help the anorexic experience a safety with a sexual self that she can bring to selected partners.

Body image is one of the most curious and thorniest of themes for the anorexic. When she enters treatment at a very low weight, she is inclined to have a distorted view of her body size, imagining herself to be all right or perhaps not even thin enough. Even if she recognizes that she is thin, she may be bent on holding to that weight. She is unable to see what we see when we look at her. Her cadaverous frame is a source of pleasure to her, for it represents the achievement to transform herself in a most dramatic and visible way.

I encourage the women I see to talk about themselves at various different weights, and to try to contact both the unconscious as well as conscious experiences of different sizes. For those women who have previously experienced themselves as chubby or overweight (and, indeed, where this is confirmed from the evidence of weight histories or photographs, which I encourage them to bring in), being large is often remembered as a period of enormous stress and self-disgust. The anorexia nervosa represents the visible achievement of having overcome being fat. When I probe further, I often discover that the chubbiness was felt as disgusting, but that more positive ideas attach to it also (Orbach, 1978). These are explored, as are all the weights at which the woman remembers herself before the onset of the symptoms. I am interested in determining what the most recent preanorexic and satisfactory or quasi-satisfactory size was felt to be; this may provide a hint of a size that the patient may ultimately be able to aim for. Usually it is a size that allowed menstruation but was still on the slim end of the weight continuum. Often women will bring in pictures of that time and will recall an emotional trauma or disappointment that triggered the onset of weight loss. Often the trauma was the loss of a relationship with a boyfriend or husband. Anorexia nervosa became a way for the patient to take hold of herself after the rejection — to do something to make it all come out all right. In the woman's mind, the loss itself was unacceptable. An idea was substituted that it was being that size that brought the rejection, and that she must lose weight. However, there is not always a correlation between a size an outsider considers appropriate and a particular emotional event for the patient.

One of the difficulties in working with a very low-weight anorexic is that because she is eating so little, she is subject to a tremendous amount of anxiety, which creates mental distortions. Often when a woman has been able to eat a little more steadily, she is able to see how plagued with these distortions she has been. When she is in the midst of the experience, however, there is little the therapist can do to help, although some women do respond and feel relieved to hear that their experience is distorted and that the distortions are exaggerated by having so few physical resources to call upon.

In addition, it may be very painful for the therapist to sit in the room session after session with an emaciated figure; the therapist may be tempted to "help" the patient with dietary advice or to tell her just how dreadful her body looks. I have not found that these kind of interventions enable the anorexic to see herself any more clearly. She may change her behavior superficially, but this will be done for the therapist's benefit and not experienced as a genuine change. In general, it is best to stay outside of the situation as much as possible, offering the view that the patient does have a distortion and trying to achieve a treatment alliance based on the idea that a part of her may know that. The more important thing to be available for is to work through the meanings of various sizes with the anorexic and to try to enable her to think and feel herself into the body that she has been at various times in her life.

The therapist's body may be a useful sort of role model in such instances. The therapist can project an ease with her body and in her size, and thus a confidence that life can be lived at a larger size than the anorexic imagines possible. Frequently I have noticed a change in my patients' clothing during therapy. They wear bright colors, such as I am inclined to wear. They may discuss what it means to be identifying with another woman's body, a body perceived of as different from their mother's and more desirable to them. They may go through a phase of wishing to imitate and I will provide permission to be like me until they tap into their own style and express their own uniqueness through their clothing.

As the anorexic gradually gains weight, it will be crucial to talk about how she feels about this, and it is wise for the therapist to anticipate that weight gain will be both a good and a bad experience for the woman. She will not feel as delighted as the therapist does that she has reached a certain weight. She may feel a loss of the control she had at her low weight. She may fear a careering up the scale, or she may re-experience the traumas she had when she was at a similar weight and on her way down.

Moving toward the End of Therapy

As with all themes that are important in the lives of anorexics, close attention to the nuances of feeling expressed in regard to body image and exploration of the disgust that so many women feel toward their bodies are of paramount importance. Toward the end of therapy, as the woman is able to eat more and her body is gradually changing, the therapist is available to work through the feelings that being more "normal" engender. The patient may fear that if she looks "normal," she may have to do whatever she thinks "normal" women do. An important component of the therapy will be for her to learn to express herself in ways other than through the dramatic transformation of her body. If she is feeling lousy, she needs to learn how to respond to a compliment about how well she looks with the phrase, "But actually I'm not feeling so good in myself today," or "Yes, it's curious—my food and body problems are mostly cleared up, but I can feel very blue." In other words, she needs a richer vocabulary for self-expression than a diminishing body and a diminishing food intake. She has to learn to speak to and about her insides more directly.

In every case of anorexia nervosa I have worked with, the woman has a great interest in having a life that is rich and meaningful. The retreat from a life that appeals to her results from a fear that she will not measure up, that she is not good enough, and that she will not be accepted in the world of work or social contacts. She carries around a deep sense that she has to be constantly "doing"; just being is not sufficient. Again we can see the internalized eyes of the disapproving parental figures. Their own lives were unhappy, and nothing their daughter did could make up for the misery. Her job was to provide happiness for them; the impossibility of achieving this task rendered the patient unable to judge that she had an intrinsic value to others. During the course of therapy, the patient begins to experience being valued in the therapy relationship. She is not required to perform impossible psychic gymnastics. She begins to feel accepted and to be able to comprehend internally that she is of value for herself.

This change in self-image characterizes the latter part of the middle phase of the therapy relationship. It is a signal that therapy may be nearing the end of its course and that the patient has "taken in" enough good experiences to develop confidence and a feeling of wholeness. She has accustomed herself to coping with a certain level of conflict and emotional upset, without these causing the kind of self-hating attacks that in turn used to lead to food deprivation. She has begun to feel safer around food and to develop the notion that she might be able to be "normal" in this area. A characteristic and positive shift in self-definition is the acceptance of the idea that she has needs for food and rest in the same way that others do. She need not be on hunger strike any more, for she has found a way to deal with her internal protest differently. She becomes used to paying attention to her bodily needs. Sometimes this will mean eating small amounts of food many times a day. Other women find that regular meals provide the experience of normality. In one of the most satisfying cases I have worked with, the patient was able to change her eating very early in the therapy and to increase the tiny amounts she ate to slightly bigger portions; she gained .454 kg (1 lb) a week at a steady rate. She was not frightened by the weight gain; she enjoyed feeling her effectiveness in this way, and even though she relapsed from time to time and "skipped" a small meal, she struggled hard to allow herself to eat manageable portions.

Changing one's food habits, feeling reasonably comfortable in one's body, and knowing that it will not explode or disappear are key features in the recovery from anorexia nervosa. But it would be a mistake to use only weight gain and good body image as the criteria for success. Equally important is the development of an integrated sense of self, with the accompanying attitude that one is entitled to what life has to offer, as well as the capacity to respond to internal cues related to either emotional or physical needs and hungers. The woman nearing the end of treatment now embodies the capacity to be responsive to herself (as well as others) without guilt. She has been responded to within the therapy relationship and has had a chance to develop an internal confidence and a language with which to express herself without shame. She has had a chance to repair the deficits in her upbringing that led her to take up an anorexic response.

As we unravel some of the themes that are characteristic of anorexia nervosa, we are bound to come in the middle stages of treatment to a deeper understanding of what on the surface appears as a compulsion to perform. We often discover that involvement in studies or high achievement on the job has been propelled by the desire to be accepted. Not having been able to take the success in, however, the anorexic patient has driven herself harder and harder. As the function of this defense is uncovered, there may be an initial fear that she will be unproductive, and indeed there may be a period of rebellion from the previous phase of intense performance. Often as we discuss what is occurring, we notice particular meaning in the intensity of a chosen profession or way of studying. For one woman, studying all night and achieving good grades was more complicated than just wanting to please her mother and father. It also contained an attack on parental values, for the mother especially was disparaging toward the girl's efforts in higher education, expressing the sentiment that such endeavors were really quite unnecessary. Another patient, a nurse in a terminal cancer ward, discovered that her need to look after others in a critical condition was partially motivated by an unconscious identification with the needs of the dying patients. She felt herself to be "dying inside," and, imagining how they felt, she could be responsive and empathic. She looked after others with much care and affection. She wished she could be the recipient of the same kind of caring attention.

A third patient, who wished to pursue a career in design, realized that constantly pushing herself to get her drawings better was in fact entirely unnecessary. She had been first in her class 2 years running and had received many positive responses from her teachers. When she was able to slow down somewhat, she was plagued with a fear that all might be taken away from her. She discovered voices inside of her that disapproved of her pursuing a career. She identified these as the injunctions of her mother. Slowly she was able to recognize that some of her ambition was an attempt to be different from her mother, not to have to follow in her footsteps, to be able to fulfill a desire that she had to express herself in the world. Such an insight was only arrived at with tremendous pain. She felt the loss of her mother's opportunities deeply. Her mother had been a seamstress before marriage and had always wished to be a dress designer. This activity was outside of the customary route for a woman of her class, generation, and ethnic background, so she devoted herself to becoming a good mother and raising the five daughters in the family. The mother had had to suppress her own ambitions quite brutally, and she had tried to save her daughters from this fate by bringing them up without any ambitions. She encouraged them not to think of themselves as people who would work outside the home, but to model their lives after hers. She wished to spare them the disappointment she had lived with for so many years. But things had changed since the mother had married, and opportunities for girls were growing. The eldest daughter (the one who became anorexic) developed a strong wish to design. She went back to college after working at a series of cooking jobs. When she could see the complex of themes that came to be expressed in her very compulsive attitude toward her design work, she was able to relax, feel pain for her mother, and realize their separateness. She went through a phase of feeling guilty about her success, but from there she was able to move on toward enjoying it and toward working less hard. She came to see that her talent and her experience were things she had developed, and that they could not be wrested away from her.

Ambition, a desire to make one's mark in the world, a wish not to be confined or easily labeled — these are the themes that are deeply felt by all the anorexic patients I work with. Their desire to express individuality has been thwarted, and they have felt that the only way to hold on to any kind of sense of self, however false, is in the construction of an elaborate and highly rigid defense that can protect them from others. The making of the individual is the whole *raison d'être* of the therapeutic work. The emphasis is always on discovery of who she is and who she wishes to be, both at the level of defense and at the level of what the defense conceals. The therapy process is one in which the developing person creates a "self" in front of one's eyes. The patient goes from being a highly defended, fearful mass of rules and regulations, through a very difficult period of feeling her chaos and lack of integration, to the discovery of the desire, need, and wish for relationship and self-actualization. While all these phases are studded with spectacularly difficult times, the work is ultimately extremely rewarding, for the practitioner has the opportunity to participate in the most intimate way in the development of a fuller human being.

REFERENCES

Berger, J. (1972). *Ways of seeing.* London: Pelican.

Bruch, H. (1973). *Eating disorders: Obesity, anorexia and the person within.* New York: Basic Books.

Brunet, O., & Lezine, I. (1966). *I primi anni del bambino.* Rome: Armando.

Chodorow, N. (1978). *The reproduction of mothering: Psychoanalysis and the sociology of gender.* Berkeley: University of California Press.

Crisp, A. H., Palmer, R. L., & Lacey, R. S. (1976). How common is anorexia nervosa? *British Journal of Psychiatry, 128,* 549–554.

Dinnerstein, D. (1976). *The mermaid and the minotaur: Sexual arrangements and human malaise.* New York: Harper & Row.

Ehrenreich, B., & English, D. (1981). *For her own good.* New York: Anchor/Doubleday.

Eichenbaum, L., & Orbach, S. (1983a). *Understanding women: A feminist and psychoanalytic approach.* New York: Basic Books.

Eichenbaum, L., & Orbach, S. (1983b). *What do women want?: Exploding the myth of dependency.* New York: Coward McCann.

Fairbairn, W. R. D. (1952). *Psychoanalytic studies of the personality.* London: Tavistock.

Friedan, B. (1963). *The feminine mystique.* New York: W. W. Norton.

Gilligan, C. (1982). *In a different voice.* Cambridge, MA: Harvard University Press.

Gordon, L. (1970). *Families.* Cambridge, MA: Bread & Roses.

Guntrip, H. (1969). *Schizoid phenomena and object relations theory.* New York: International Universities Press.

Lambley, P. (1983). *How to survive anorexia.* London: Muller.

Mahler, M., Pine, F., & Bergman, A. (1975). *The psychological birth of the human infant: Symbiosis and individuation.* New York: Basic Books.

Miller, J. B. (1976). *Towards a new psychology of women.* Boston: Beacon Press.

Mitchell, J. (1973). *Women's estate.* New York: Pantheon.

Money, J., & Erhardt, A. (1973). *Man and woman, boy and girl: The differentiation and dimorphism of gender identity from conception to maturity.* Baltimore: Johns Hopkins University Press.

Orbach, S. (1978). *Fat is a feminist issue.* New York: Paddington Press.

Orbach, S. (1982). *Fat is a feminist issue II.* New York: Berkeley Books.

Orbach, S. (in press). Visibility, invisibility: Social dimensions in anorexia nervosa. In S. Emmett (Ed.), *Anorexia.* Boston: Beacon Press.

Selvini-Palazzoli, M. (1974). *Self-starvation.* London: Chaucer.

Spitz, R. A. (1965). *The first year of life: A psychoanalytic study of normal and deviant development of object relations.* New York: Basic Books.

Spock, B. (1957). *The common sense book of baby and child care.* New York: Duell, Sloan and Pearce.

Stoller, R. J. (1968). *Sex and gender: On the development of masculinity and femininity.* New York: Jason Aronson.

Winnicott, D. W. (1965). *The maturational processes and the facilitating environment.* New York: International Universities Press.

Winnicott, D. W. (1978). *Primary maternal preoccupation: Collected papers.* London: Tavistock.

PART THREE

Cognitive and Behavioral Therapies

CHAPTER SIX

Cognitive Therapy for Anorexia Nervosa

DAVID M. GARNER / KELLY M. BEMIS

Treatment for anorexia nervosa may be broadly divided into two phases: initial weight restoration, usually conducted within an inpatient setting, and long-term psychotherapy aimed at preventing relapse. In a review of 16 outcome studies, Hsu (1980) has indicated a consensus among most authors that the initial in-hospital phase of treatment "is relatively simple and usually successful" but that "an initial gain in weight to a satisfactory level, whatever the treatment method adopted, does not necessarily ensure long-term improvement" (p. 1045). Hsu (1980) concludes that disturbed eating patterns are very common among treated anorexic patients, with most studies reporting a majority of patients engaging in some degree of dietary restriction, bulimia, vomiting, laxative abuse, and anxiety when eating with others. Moreover, pathological attitudes or beliefs about eating and weight frequently persist in clinically recovered as well as in symptomatic patients. Theander (1970) reported that virtually none of the patients in his follow-up study were free from "neurotic fixations" on body weight. Dally and Gomez (1979) have concluded that abnormal attitudes toward food and weight are among "the most distressing and long lasting features of anorexia nervosa . . . and are likely to continue or to recur in situations of crisis for many years" (pp. 134–135). These observations are consistent with those of others who have emphasized the importance of maladaptive thinking in the development of anorexia nervosa (Bruch, 1973, 1978; Galdstone, 1974; Ushakov, 1971). Our experience has confirmed the significance of distorted thinking patterns in the maintenance of the anorexic syndrome and has led to the proposal of a cognitive–behavioral approach to treatment (Garner & Bemis, 1982), as well as to the incorporation of cognitive methods into a somewhat broader "multidimensional" psychotherapy for anorexia nervosa (Garner, Garfinkel, & Bemis, 1982). The principles of this therapy are derived from the cognitive model delineated by Beck and his coworkers (cf. Beck, 1976; Beck, Rush, Shaw, & Emery, 1979) for the treatment of depression and neurotic disorders. While the general process and specific procedures conform closely to those outlined by Beck, we have found that strategies have had to be modified or created to deal with the particular thinking patterns presented by anorexic patients. The current chapter extends our previous reports by providing further details regarding cognitive intervention techniques. Cognitive mediating processes relevant to the development and maintenance of anorexia nervosa are elaborated upon, along with examples of

David M. Garner. Department of Psychiatry, Toronto General Hospital; and the University of Toronto, Toronto, Ontario, Canada.

Kelly M. Bemis. Department of Psychology, University of Minnesota, Minneapolis, Minnesota.

common irrational beliefs and faulty assumptions. Finally, specific strategies are described for modifying cognitive distortions underlying self-concept deficiencies in anorexia nervosa and bulimia.

THE COGNITIVE MODEL FOR THE DEVELOPMENT OF ANOREXIA NERVOSA

A Proximal Paradigm

Following different etiological postulations, many forms of psychotherapy have been recommended for anorexia nervosa. While some still conceptualize anorexia nervosa as having a unitary cause, there is a growing recognition that the disorder is multide-termined, in the sense that it may develop from the complex interaction of different predisposing factors within different individuals (Andersen, 1979; Casper, 1982; Garfinkel & Garner, 1982; Garner et al., 1982; Lucas, Duncan, & Piens, 1976; Strober, 1980, 1983). It has been argued that a particular advantage of a cognitive–behavioral understanding of anorexia nervosa is that it is not necessarily incompatible with other models that view the origin of the disorder as related to early developmental defects (Garner & Bemis, 1982; Garner et al., 1982). The cognitive model may be viewed as a proximal paradigm of causal and maintaining variables. Regardless of the theoretical orientation, most investigators would accept that at some point, causal factors converge at the patient's belief that "it is absolutely essential that I be thin." Thus, much of the apparently bizarre and irrational behavior observed in anorexia nervosa is the direct result of a set of beliefs, attitudes, and assumptions about the meaning of body weight. It is not necessary to rely upon distal and occasionally abstruse symbolic interpretations of behavior. The surplus meaning that anorexic patients attach to weight and eating not only accounts for current behavior, but also provides a window to understanding their broader system of self-evaluation.

Positive and Negative Contingencies Maintaining Behavior

A number of antecedent events have been linked to anorexia nervosa; however, during the active phase of the disorder, rigid dietary control may be determined by both positive and negative reinforcement contingencies. Recently, several authors have systematically examined the functional relationships among antecedent events, positive reinforcers, and negative reinforcers in the development as well as the maintenance of anorexia nervosa (Bemis, 1983; Garner & Bemis, 1982; Garner et al., 1982; Slade, 1982). Slade (1982) has observed that most theories have emphasized the impact of antecedent variables and have neglected the role of reinforcement in anorexia nervosa. The operation of cognitive or self-administered reinforcement has received even less attention.

Much of the speculation regarding the pathogenesis of anorexia nervosa conforms to the avoidance paradigm, which assumes that the probability of a behavior increases following negative reinforcement (i.e., the removal or offset of an aversive stimulus). This model accounts for much of the anorexic's stereotypical behavior, such as dieting, exercise, vomiting, and the use of purgatives to avoid the feared stimulus (i.e., fatness). It is also compatible with the conceptualization of anorexia nervosa as an adaptive disorder, where the "weight phobia" represents a retreat from feared circumstances associated with psychosexual maturity (Crisp, 1965, 1980b; Kalucy, 1978; Lacey, 1983; Palmer, 1979). According to this view, dieting becomes the mechanism by which the development of an adult shape and hormonal functioning is interrupted or reversed. These physical changes assist the patient in her efforts to avoid the developmental challenges for which she feels unprepared.[1] In some cases, the sources of apprehension (aversive stimuli) are not clearly articulated; in others, they are closely associated with specific themes, such as sexuality, high performance expectations, separation from the family, or family conflicts.

It is well recognized that avoidance behavior is resistant to extinction, because it insulates the individual from recognizing when aversive contingencies are no longer in operation. Cognitive variables may contribute to this process. Beck (1970, 1976) has observed that avoidance behavior may be perpetuated by "hyperactive" cognitive sets, which may eventually operate in an autonomous fashion. A belief system develops and acts as a Procrustean mold, to which incoming information is shaped to fit; data that are inconsistent with the system are either disregarded or distorted in the interest of the predominant belief. We have previously commented on an aspect of the anorexic's avoidance behavior that appears to be unique to the disorder (Garner & Bemis, 1982): The patient cannot really place much distance between herself and the "phobic object," since the feared stimulus is *herself* at higher weight levels. Since total escape from the aversive stimulus is impossible, it may be controlled only through constant vigilance. Moreover, unlike other disorders in which avoidance plays a major role, the anorexic may not want to be relieved of her anxiety about food and weight gain. For her, these aversive experiences are *functional* (Garner & Bemis, 1982), in that the threat they hold assists her in the difficult task of oral self-restraint, despite voracious hunger.

Finally, anorexia nervosa may be distinguished from a simple phobic disorder, since symptoms are maintained by *positive* as well as negative reinforcement. Weight loss provides not only a solution for avoiding the feared situation of "fatness," but also a sense of gratification in its own right. A higher weight is not simply avoided; a thinner weight is actively pursued through dieting. It is not difficult to understand why an adolescent who is struggling with extreme feelings of ineffectiveness might embrace the idea that a thinner shape could enhance her value. Within our affluent culture, women are continually bombarded with the media's message that the unisex body is a sign of sexuality, beauty, success, and social competence. All of these qualities are presumably within the grasp of the conscientious dieter. However, social reinforcement does not adequately account for the development of anorexia nervosa, since the emaciated state achieved by most patients is well beyond the societal standards for shape. Rather, the relentless dieting is maintained by potent *cognitive self-reinforcement* from the sense of mastery, self-control, and competence derived from successful dieting. For the anorexic, hunger is no longer simply an aversive stimulus. It acquires a new meaning, because it is associated with a higher-order accomplishment. The anorexic's extraordinary attempts to control her appetite provide a long-coveted sense of mastery within the context of lifelong feelings of incompetence.

---

1. Because of the disorder's preponderance of females, we have adopted the convention in this chapter of using feminine pronouns when referring to anorexia nervosa patients.

Weight control or weight loss becomes the preeminent barometer of achievement and a reliable referent for self-evaluation. Much like the religious ascetic, the anorexic attains virtue through resisting corporal needs. Selvini-Palazzoli (1978) has observed that, for the anorexic, "every victory over the flesh is a sign of greater control over ones biological impulses . . . [and a] magic key to power . . . [in search of] freedom, beauty, intelligence and morality" (pp. 72–74). Bemis (1983) has surveyed the literature and has noted that various authors have commented on the pride that the anorexic takes in weight loss; patients may characterize their weight status as an "accomplishment" (Bruch, 1977b; DuBois, 1949), an "achievement" (Casper & Davis, 1977), a "virtue" (Rahman, Richardson, & Ripley, 1939), and a "source of positive pleasure" and "sensuous delight" (King, 1963). Moreover, Bemis (1983) has noted that patients who are successful at weight loss have been described as "exhilarated" (Mogul, 1980; Stonehill & Crisp, 1977), "elated" (Crisp, 1977; Meyer & Weinroth, 1957), "delighted" (Vigersky, Loriaux, Andersen, Mecklenburg, & Vaitukaitis, 1976), "triumphant" (Bruch, 1975; Casper, Kirschner, Sandstead, Jacob, & Davis, 1980; Crisp, 1977; Mogul, 1980), "powerful" (Boskind-Lodahl, 1976; Bruch, 1978; Mogul, 1980), and "proud" (Bruch, 1977a, 1978, 1979; DuBois, 1949; Galdstone, 1974; Rahman *et al.*, 1939). The fact that most patients extol the virtues of their pathological state and prefer to maintain their "ego-syntonic" symptoms distinguishes anorexia nervosa from a simple weight "phobia," and may account for the recalcitrance of the disorder.

Several writers have emphasized that the positive self-reinforcement of weight loss has such a profound impact because it occurs within the context of feelings of inadequacy in most other areas of functioning (Bemis, 1983; Bruch, 1978; Casper, 1982; Casper, Offer, & Ostrov, 1981; Crisp, 1980b; Garner & Bemis, 1982; Selvini-Palazzoli, 1974; Slade, 1982). Understanding the cognitive process of positive and negative self-reinforcement, the cognitive aspects of self-concept deficits, and the cognitive distortions characteristic of anorexia nervosa provides both a conceptual model for the disorder and a framework for particular cognitive–behavioral interventions.

THE THERAPEUTIC RELATIONSHIP

The circumstances surrounding the initiation of treatment for anorexia nervosa differ from those of the more typical psychiatric patient who readily admits to psychological discomfort. The anorexic patient's behavior is often defined as a "problem" by relatives who have desperately tried to persuade or even coerce her to gain weight or stop vomiting, and who finally encourage or require her to seek professional help. By the time that she has arrived for treatment, she is poised to resist, since she anticipates the same pressure from the therapist. She usually perceives that the goal of therapy is to rob her of her low weight, which, as mentioned earlier, is an achievement that she values tremendously—both in its own right and because it may also provide safety from developmental concerns. Patients' reluctance to participate in psychotherapy may also be a reflection of a basic mistrust of relationships. In previous relationships, they have felt inferior, incompetent, and vulnerable to influence; although they have responded with compliance and passivity, this has not been done without resentment. Given these expectations, it is not difficult to understand the resistance, stubbornness, and defiance displayed by some patients in psychotherapy.

These negative attitudes and behaviors may produce "strong feelings of aggression in the therapist" (Selvini-Palazzoli, 1978) and "intense emotional reactions . . . perhaps the most intense encountered in a therapeutic relationship" (Cohler, 1977, p. 353), and have undoubtedly led to the malevolent and punitive forms of treatment occasionally reported (Blue, 1979; Quaeritur, 1971). Because mutual distress and distrust affect *both* participants in the therapeutic enterprise, the establishment of a strong alliance is unusually difficult.

Various systems of psychotherapy have acknowledged the crucial role of the therapeutic relationship (cf. Frank, 1973; Marmor, 1976), and recent elaborations of cognitive therapy are no exception (Beck *et al.*, 1979; Guidano & Liotti, 1983; Mahoney, 1974). In adapting the cognitive approach to anorexia nervosa, several authors have emphasized that establishing a strong therapeutic alliance is a prerequisite for effective psychotherapy (Garner & Bemis, 1982; Garner *et al.*, 1982; Guidano & Liotti, 1983). Warmth, genuineness, honesty, and an attitude of acceptance are qualities of all skilled therapists, and these facilitate the development of the bond between the clinician and the patient. These qualities and the strength of the relationship may be particularly important in the treatment of anorexia nervosa, for several reasons. First, it is obvious that the quality of the relationship will be one important determinant of the patient's initial willingness to consider confronting the terrifying prospects of eating and weight gain.

Secondly, assessment of cognition, affect, and behavior is largely dependent on self-report data, and therefore the accuracy of the information derived will be predicated upon the establishment of a trusting, cooperative relationship. In its absence, the patient is understandably reluctant to reveal vital aspects of thinking and may consciously falsify her experience.

Finally, the relationship provides a conduit for examining distortions and misperceptions that the patient applies to her interpersonal world. When the patient's reactions to the therapist are viewed within the context of other current or past relationships, they provide data that may illuminate beliefs, assumptions, and attitudes that are salient for the patient. The relationship becomes a key source of data for assessment of beliefs, since the patient repeatedly assumes that the therapist evaluates her by the same negative and harsh standards that she applies to herself (Bowlby, 1977a, 1977b). The patient frequently makes specific inferences about the therapist's feelings toward her, and these may constitute themes that re-emerge in therapy: for example, "You don't really care about me, it is a facade," "You can't wait for me to gain weight so that you can get on to a more deserving patient," "How could you accept me knowing that I failed?", or "I expect you to reject me because you can see my bad qualities." As we describe later, the therapist can correct these distortions and can help the patient become aware that they constitute patterns of expectations. In many instances, it is worthwhile to explore the nature of other present or past relationships to uncover experiences that could have led logically to particular expectations and feelings. The identification of such influences serves to place current distortions within an understandable historical context. Cognitive theorists have been reluctant to promote openly the idea that the patient's way of construing the therapeutic relationship may furnish valuable information, possibly because it sounds dangerously close to a traditional "transference" interpretation; however, there are substantial distinctions in theoretical frameworks and modes of conducting therapy that make the parallel between approaches very limited. It is the distortion and its logical historical derivatives, rather than unconscious, impulse-laden motives, that are of interest to the cognitive therapist.[2]

It must be noted that not all anorexic patients are intrinsically distrustful of the therapeutic relationship. Patients who have only had the disorder for a brief time, or those who, after years of struggling, are resolute in their conviction to give up the disorder, are remarkably open and trusting. If this initial genuineness is met by warmth from the therapist as well as *a clear knowledge of the disorder and its treatment*, the process may proceed with surprising ease. On the other hand, patients whose identity as "anorexics" has been crystallized, who approach therapy with deep ambivalence, or who are struggling with extremely potent maintaining variables are likely to display resistance.

We join the ranks of other recent cognitive theorists who adopt the position that a strong therapeutic relationship is not only a precondition for successful treatment, but also a valuable prototype for determining beliefs about meaningful past and present relationships in the patient's life (Guidano & Liotti, 1983).

THE INITIAL INTERVIEWS

The anorexic usually comes to therapy with the conviction that her experiences are idiosyncratic and that no one (especially someone without the disorder) could possibly appreciate life from her perspective. The therapist must have an understanding of the *phenomenology of the disorder* that involves an awareness of probable beliefs and attitudes dominating the anorexic's current experience. Several tasks are important to accomplish in the first one or two interviews:

1. *Begin to establish a trusting therapeutic alliance* by communicating warmth, concern, and empathy.

2. *Assess the circumstances surrounding the initiation of treatment.* Some patients will have sought therapy on their own, and others will have reluctantly acquiesced to the demands of parents after months of bitter struggle. Regardless of the antecedents, the therapist should clarify that the purpose of therapy is to address the patient's underlying unhappiness, which has been responsible for the weight loss. If "unhappiness" is denied, the point should not be pressed, and greater attention should be focused on the effects of starvation. It should be emphasized that low weight itself is aberrant and usually *produces* a predictable set of physical and psychological symptoms.

3. *Collect information regarding weight history, current eating patterns, and behaviors employed to lose weight.* Highest premorbid weight, highest stable weight maintained without dieting, weight at which the disorder began, lowest weight, and current weight all provide data that may be useful in establishing the optimal recovery

---

2. Even some psychodynamic therapists are becoming disenchanted with the somewhat esoteric inferences of traditional analytic theory. Bowlby (1977a, 1977b) questions the utility of ascribing "misattributions and misperceptions" to processes such as "projection, introjection or phantasy." According to Bowlby, the resulting formulations are apt to be ambiguous and "the fact that such misattributions and misperceptions are directly derived from previous real-life experiences is either only vaguely alluded to or else totally obscured." He concludes that framing the processes in terms of cognitive psychology provides much greater precision, since hypotheses regarding the causative role of various childhood experiences can be advanced in testable form (Bowlby, 1977a, p. 209).

weight (Garner, Rockert, Olmsted, Johnson, & Coscina, Chapter 21 this volume). Determination should be made of the presence of bulimia, vomiting, abuse of laxatives, diuretics, drugs, and other weight control strategies, in each instance noting amount, frequency, duration, and associated circumstances.

4. *Obtain information regarding family context, brief history, and living circumstances.* This information should be gathered slowly and with particular sensitivity to the way in which the patient sees herself, her goals, and her family relationships, and to the meaning she attributes to potentially frightening issues associated with adolescence.

5. *Provide information about anorexia nervosa.* Attention should be given to clarifying various myths that have resulted from inaccurate or conflicting reports appearing in the media. Some patients will want to talk about the disorder and will be uncertain as to whether or not they meet the diagnostic criteria. Belaboring the details of diagnosis is unnecessary, but a definitive "yes" or "no" will at least set the stage for establishing therapy goals. Occasionally we recommend books on anorexia nervosa, such as those by Bruch (1978), Crisp (1980a), or Palmer (1980). These may be helpful in diminishing guilt about the disorder and may allow patients to identify with others who have recovered. Bibliotherapy can be a useful clinical strategy for furnishing patients with information about their disorder and providing collateral support for specific topics. Moreover, sharing material may be seen as an indication of the therapist's openness and desire to let the patient evaluate the "evidence" for herself. After reading such material, patients are often more receptive to pursuing psychotherapy. However, one must be cautious about the possibility that reading material may become a means of avoiding psychological issues; it must be offered as an adjunct to, not a substitute for, discussion.

6. *Differentiation of the effects of starvation from anorexia nervosa.* If the patient has lost a substantial amount of weight, it is useful to describe in detail the effects of starvation derived from studies with normal volunteers (Keys, Brozek, Henschel, Mickelsen, & Taylor, 1950; cf. Garner *et al.*, Chapter 21, this volume). Many of these symptoms, including amenorrhea, food preoccupations, dry skin, hair loss, lanugo, fatigue, paresthesiae, hypothermia, poor concentration, and hypersensitivity to noise may have become quite distressing to the patient. Psychological disturbances, such as anxiety, depression, labile mood, feelings of inadequacy, irritability, and social withdrawal, are also heightened by starvation and are felt to be unpleasant to the patient. Patients usually do not associate these symptoms with a common cause, and the description of the "starvation state" helps them integrate their experiences. Moreover, describing these symptoms as, in part, physiologically determined may mitigate the guilt surrounding what are often seen as unacceptable "psychological" symptoms.

7. *Accept the patient's beliefs as genuine.* The patient arrives for treatment operating from the basic assumption that her self-worth is fundamentally dependent on achieving and maintaining a low weight. Direct confrontation of this set of beliefs may be construed as a personal attack and may provoke a defensive retreat. However, we have suggested lines of inquiry that may *begin to introduce doubt about the basic premise* that thinness is a valid and dependable criterion for inferring self-worth (Garner & Bemis, 1982). For example, the therapist may inquire: "Is it *functional* for you to conform to this idea?" or "Are you obtaining what you hoped to gain from your present state?" Having the patient attempt to enumerate the benefits of a particular belief or behavior rather than defend its correctness will minimize defensive-

ness; in contrast, a direct attack often hinders shameless re-examination of the belief, even when patients do recognize some flaws or disadvantages in their present
system. Individuals who are convinced of the factual or moral legitimacy of their position are often prepared to defend its logic tenaciously. However, they may recognize
that it is not always advantageous to permit a single idea to dictate the conduct of
one's life or the content of one's thoughts. Therapists may find the following lines
of questioning productive:

What other values are important to you? How does thinness relate to achieving them? If you
believe that there should be a connection between losing weight and attaining your other goals,
how does it seem to be working out in practice? What role will your present concerns about
weight play in your life five years from now? Ten years? Do you think that you will be able
to keep up this struggle until you are forty? (Garner & Bemis, 1982, p. 132)

    8. Describe the self-perpetuating cycle of bulimia and vomiting. Originally, vom-
iting or laxative abuse provided the patient with a method of establishing control after
eating. However, these practices soon led to a loss of control because they "legitimize"
bingeing. The patient assumes that the caloric consequences of overeating may be easily avoided, and is therefore more likely to succumb to the temptation in the future.
Explaining this vicious cycle (Garner *et al.*, 1982; Garner *et al.*, Chapter 21, this volume; Russell, 1979) and its metabolic sequelae to patients enables many of them to
begin to accept the idea that the cycle must be broken.
    9. Indicate that the disorder serves an adaptive function. After gathering some
background data, it may be useful to provide a simplified explanation of the "adaptive" nature of anorexia nervosa. This may be limited to an elaboration of the positive and negative reinforcement variables that maintain the disorder, or may extend
to a discussion of the *surplus meaning* that weight has acquired in regulating self-
esteem. For patients whose beliefs suggest that the disorder is a retreat from frightening issues associated with normal adolescence, it is valuable to follow Crisp's (1970)
recommendation by explaining how a subpubertal weight can appear to "resolve" these
developmental concerns. We often illustrate this process, as well as provide evidence
for the metabolic and homeostatic control of weight (cf., Garner *et al.*, Chapter 21,
this volume), with a modified version of Crisp's well-known weight graph (see Figure
6-1). The interpretation of this "phobic" response to perceived demands of adulthood
and its consequent reversal of the normal hormonal substrate is a concept that many
patients readily appreciate as having personal meaning. Some patients are able to recognize that the weight that they fear most is remarkably close to that which represents
the threshold for the return of menses and the normalization of their hypothalamic-
pituitary functioning. They frequently seize upon this opportunity to elaborate upon
fears of "growing up." It should be cautioned, however, that this theme is only relevant to a subset of patients and should not be generalized to all.
    From the foregoing discussion, it may appear that we have combined the dynamic
formulations of several theorists into an eclectic approach to anorexia nervosa. It must
be emphasized that while we share many of their observations and subscribe to similar rules for the conduct of psychotherapy, our approach specifically assumes that
it is the *belief structure* that requires modification, and that cognitive psychotherapy
offers various powerful clinical strategies for accessing and altering beliefs. The importance of belief structure is implicit in the writings on anorexia nervosa by many

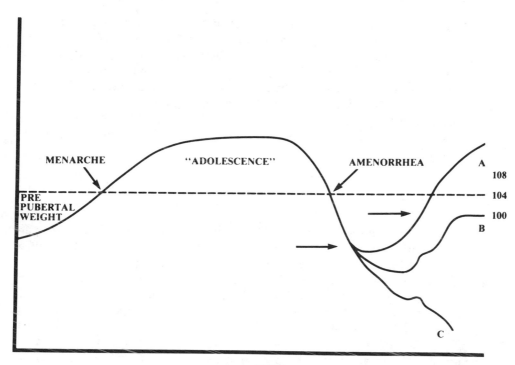

Figure 6-1. The weight course in anorexia nervosa. The dotted line represents the "menstrual weight threshold," which is approximately 47 kg (104 lb) for a woman 163 cm (5 ft 4 in) tall (Frisch, 1983). A represents the weight that must be achieved for recovery; B indicates the "suboptimal" weight that many patients would prefer to maintain, although it is inconsistent with recovery; and C indicates a chronic course ending in death. The two horizontal arrows represent weights at which anorexic patients typically express panic: at the initiation of weight gain, and when they approach the "menstrual threshold." (Adapted from *Anorexia Nervosa: Let Me Be* by A. H. Crisp, 1980, London: Academic Press.)

prominent theorists. For example, Crisp and his colleagues have emphasized the *meaning* of subpubertal weight and the importance of the patient's construing herself in terms of weight (Crisp, 1980b; Kalucy, 1978).

The cognitive approach to anorexia nervosa may be distinguished by its *explicit* concern with beliefs, values, and assumptions. Moreover, as long as the constructs are relevant to the patient's belief system, a cognitive model does not require adherence to a unitary theory and may retain conceptual integrity while borrowing from the valuable observations of various notable clinical theorists. A central aim of much of the information gathering in the initial interviews is to understand the patient's belief system, which is comprised of attitudes about weight, assumptions about self-worth, values related to performance, and developmental expectations, as well as attitudes about the family. These occasions also provide the opportunity to assess the preponderance of certain types of formal reasoning errors (Garner & Bemis, 1982; Garner *et al.*, 1982) and general cognitive style.

Finally, the style of the cognitive approach parallels others that avoid stiff formality, unnecessary jargon, and dynamic interpretations (Bruch, 1978, 1982; Groen & Feldman-Toledano, 1966; Russell, 1973; Selvini-Palazzoli, 1978). The "collaborative empiricism" characteristic of the cognitive approach (Beck, 1976) parallels Bruch's

(1973) recommendation of an "objective, fact finding attitude in which the patient and therapist are true collaborators in the search for unknown factors" (p. 338). Our experience conforms to the observations of others that the data-gathering, quasi-scientific approach of cognitive therapy reduces resistance to treatment, as the patient and therapist become allies in the attempt to overcome the disorder (Bedrosian & Beck, 1980; Guidano & Liotti, 1983). Emphasis should be placed on the validity of conscious thought and the "authentication of introspective data" (Beck *et al.*, 1979); this emphasis provides the first lesson in personal trust by "legitimizing" the patient's experience.

COGNITIVE METHODS

The cognitive procedures we recommend for the treatment of anorexia nervosa are largely adaptations of those described by Beck and his colleagues (Beck, 1970, 1976; Beck *et al.*, 1979); however, some methods have been adapted from other cognitive approaches (Ellis, 1962; Goldfried, 1971; Mahoney, 1974; Meichenbaum, 1974), and some have been created to deal with the self-concept deficits that are characteristic of anorexia nervosa. Central to these formulations is the assumption that maladaptive feelings and behaviors are mediated by distorted or maladaptive thinking and that the primary aim of clinical intervention is to alter these cognitive processes. It has been noted that there are remarkable parallels between Bruch's (1973, 1978, 1982) recommendations for the conduct of psychotherapy and the principles advocated by cognitive therapists (Garner & Bemis, 1982; Garner *et al.*, 1982; Guidano & Liotti, 1983). Bruch has repeatedly emphasized the gradual but deliberate relabeling of "misconceptions and errors in the patient's thinking" in a psychotherapy that

is a process during which erroneous assumptions and attitudes are recognized, defined and challenged so that they can be abandoned. It is important to proceed slowly and to use concrete small events as episodes for illustrating certain false assumptions or illogical deductions. (1978, pp. 143–144)

Despite the apparent resemblance between Bruch's suggestions and cognitive principles, there are significant differences in their theoretical derivation. Moreover, there is no indication that Bruch would confirm the correspondence we have observed between her methods and those proposed by cognitive theorists. Nevertheless, as Goldfried (1980) has argued, the existence of *common clinical strategies* across different therapeutic orientations should be reassuring, since they probably indicate the most durable methods for promoting behavior change. The major distinctions between cognitive and other approaches often relate more to philosophical and methodological points of emphasis than to procedural issues. For example, cognitive therapy advocates (1) a reliance on conscious and preconscious experience rather than unconscious motivation; (2) an explicit emphasis on cognitions as mediating variables accounting for maladaptive feelings and emotions; (3) the use of questioning as a major therapeutic device; (4) active and directive involvement on the part of the therapist; and (5) a methodological allegiance to behavioral and scientific psychology, in which theory is continually shaped by empirical findings. Moreover, there is a commitment to clear specification of treatment methods and objective assessment of changes in target behaviors.

It has been our experience that conventional cognitive strategies must be adapted to address the specific features of the anorexic patient. These include (1) the patient's reluctance to enter treatment, the ego-syntonic nature of some symptoms, and the overall recalcitrance of the disorder; (2) the interaction between physical and psychological elements; (3) the prominence of deficits in self-concept related to the patient's lack of awareness of and confidence in internal state; and (4) the idiosyncratic beliefs related to food and weight.

The first of these features may necessitate the more gradual introduction of structured cognitive procedures and exceptional emphasis on the slow development of a trusting relationship, with the expectation that the duration of therapy may be somewhat longer than for other disorders. The second feature requires a special recognition of the effects of starvation and the physical complications of the disorder. Direct education and clarification related to these issues occupy a substantial portion of time, particularly earlier in the treatment process. The third feature involves the somewhat delicate task of helping the patient alter misperceptions without undermining her already inadequate trust of internal experiences. It also involves identifying and changing "underlying assumptions" related to self-concept. Suggestions for accomplishing these tasks are made in a subsequent section on modification of self-concept deficiencies. The fourth feature is elaborated in a subsequent section on normalization of weight and eating.

Beck (1976) has suggested that various neurotic disorders may be characterized by common errors in thinking but may be distinguished in terms of ideational content. Based upon Beck's (1976) taxonomy of thinking errors, we (Garner & Bemis, 1982) have linked various types of cognitive distortions to faulty beliefs that are peculiar to anorexia nervosa.

One of the most prominent and persistent logical errors is dichotomous reasoning, which involves thinking in extreme and absolutistic terms. The tendency to divide food into "good" and "bad" categories, the fear that gaining a pound indicates the imminence of obesity, the oscillation between fasting and bingeing, and the inability to deviate from a rigidly prescribed dietary regimen without assuming complete failure are all based on dichotomous reasoning. This style of thinking is not restricted to food and weight issues, but permeates all aspects of the anorexic's evaluation of herself and others. Extreme attitudes are evident in the fanatical pursuit of sports, school, careers, and acceptance from others, as well as philosophies related to such concepts as happiness, morality, self-confidence, self-control, and success. Other people, particularly parents, are evaluated either as completely perfect beings or as intolerable monsters. Much of the dichotomous logic revolves around volitional issues related to self-control: "If I am not in complete control, I will lose all control," "If I learn to enjoy sweets, I will not be able to restrain myself," "If I stop exercising for one day, I will never exercise," "If I enjoy sexual contact, I will become promiscuous," "If I become angry, I will devastate others with my rage." A major therapeutic task is to teach the patient to recognize when she is using this style of thinking, to examine the maladaptive consequences that result, and to explore its validity through calculated experimentation with the "in-betweens."

The anorexic patient's thinking may be characterized by other reasoning errors, including personalization, superstitious thinking, magnification, selective abstraction, and overgeneralization (Garner & Bemis, 1982; Garner et al., 1982). Guidano and Liotti (1983) have identified other idiosyncratic thinking styles and faulty beliefs in anorexia nervosa. For example, they suggest, following Ellis's (1962) formulations, that the anorexic patient suffers from irrational beliefs related to the "dire need to be loved" and "the absolute unbearability of disappointment." Empirical confirmation will be required to verify the prominence and specificity of these and other erroneous thinking styles in anorexia nervosa.

From a clinical perspective, we have found it useful to make patients gradually aware of the cognitive model as proposed by Beck (1976). Accordingly, patients are taught that learning to do the following will be a vital aspect of therapy:

1. Monitor their thinking or heighten their awareness of their own thinking.
2. Recognize the connection between certain thoughts and maladaptive behaviors and emotions.
3. Examine the evidence for the validity of particular beliefs.
4. Substitute more realistic and appropriate interpretations.
5. Gradually modify the underlying assumptions that are fundamental determinants of more specific beliefs.

Particular care and sensitivity has to be taken to avoid allowing interventions to deteriorate into an inquisition or argument over points of logic. Anorexic patients come to therapy feeling inadequate and distrustful of their thinking; direct challenging of their thinking may only reinforce the opinion that they are inadequate. Probes and suggestions must occur in an atmosphere of acceptance. Specific interventions derived from Beck and others, but adapted to anorexia nervosa, are illustrated below. These are general guidelines that should be tailored to the individual needs of each patient.

Articulation of Beliefs

Regardless of orientation, most psychotherapists assist patients through synthesizing and condensing vast quantities of verbal material into more manageable phrases or ideas. Simplifying or consolidating a belief may make the distortion highly apparent and sometimes leads automatically to attitude change. For example, one patient rigidly adhered to a set of exercise rituals that required her to perform a specific number of calisthenics every time that she entered her room alone. On further query, she stated that she believed that a failure to engage in this superstitious routine would mysteriously thwart the development of a lasting friendship. The improbability of the association between these events became readily apparent upon verbalization, and the exercise was promptly terminated. With most patients the results are less spectacular; the simple articulation of a distorted belief may have a perceptible effect, but often requires repeated reinforcement and the accumulation of convergent evidence from other sources.

Decentering

This is a strategy for evaluating a particular belief from a different perspective in order to evaluate its validity more objectively. It is particularly useful in combating patients' egocentric conviction that either they or their behavior are central to other people's attention. For example, a patient may complain, "I cannot bear to go out in public because my stomach is so bloated," or "I am worried that other people will notice that I have gained 5 pounds." The therapist may respond with the following types of comments: "Do you really notice when other people gain or lose small amounts of weight? Do you remember whether my weight was up or down a week ago? Even if you did notice, would it have been a major event? It would be nice, in a way, to be the object of other people's preoccupation, but realistically most people are pretty busy with their own personal concerns."

One patient was experiencing difficulty in the residence cafeteria because she believed that others were scrutinizing her eating. The therapist employed decentering through the following line of questioning: "How much do you really think about others' eating? You may think about it quite a bit because it is a highly sensitized topic for you, but what about other behaviors? What is the extent of your awareness of the types of clothes others wear? Although you may notice, it is hardly something that you would ruminate about for hours at a time—true? This is probably the degree of concern that others have about your eating." Through the technique of decentering, the patient may be encouraged to develop a more realistic idea of the impact that most behavior has on others.

Decatastrophizing

This is a familiar technique, originally proposed by Ellis (1962), for combating anxiety resulting from magnification of the negative consequences of a particular event. It involves translating vague and implicit predictions of calamity into more realistic expectations by asking, "What if the feared situation did occur? Would it really be as devastating as imagined? Could strategies be generated to cope with such circumstances?" Finally, the "catastrophizing" in which patients engage often inadvertently results in the very condition that is most feared! In a desperate attempt to avoid social rejection and isolation, patients may withdraw from all social interactions and become isolated. Failure for some patients comes as the result of a scrupulous avoidance of any risk that could result in failure. "Catastrophizing" may be seen as involving the absolutistic *demand* that something *must* or *must not* happen, and this psychological stance virtually always leads to anxiety, regardless of the outcome. The patient who *demands* thinness in order to be happy is obviously anxious when she considers herself "fat." Unfortunately the anxiety does not disappear, even at a low weight, since she always knows that there is a risk of gaining.

Challenging the "Shoulds"

The extreme thinking reflected in "catastrophizing" and dichotomous reasoning is also indicated in the anorexic patient's excessive reliance on the words "should," "must," or "ought" in directing her actions. This tendency has been observed in many psychological disorders (Beck, 1976; Ellis, 1962), and its oppressive nature was captured by Horney's (1950) declaration that the "tyranny of the shoulds" is the cornerstone of neurotic disturbance. Many of the anorexic's internal imperatives about food and weight are framed by the words "should" or "must": "I should avoid fattening foods," "I should always diet," "I must eat the same foods every day," "I should exercise daily."

An analysis of the thinking behind the inordinate compliance observed in anorexia nervosa also reveals the operation of "should" statements: "I should always do what is expected," "One should never disappoint one's parents," "I should never deviate from the rules." The moralistic and arbitrary natue of such commands virtually always leaves the patient feeling inadequate because of her failure to live up to virtually unattainable standards.

It would be linguistically awkward to refrain from the use of the word "should" altogether; however, Vertes (1971) has suggested that its legitimate uses may be distinguished from inappropriate applications. "Should" may be used correctly in the suggestive sense ("You should read this novel"), or as a statement of contingencies ("You should study or else you will fail the exam"), but it is the moralistic, absolute, and arbitrary command "I should or must behave in a particular way" that produces chronic anxiety.

As Beck *et al.* (1979) have suggested, "response prevention" may be used to provide empirical evidence that "shoulds" can be ignored without dire consequences. A variation of response prevention may be effective in modifying the anorexic patient's compulsive behavior and attendant cognitions (e.g., "I must perform my exercise routine and eat the same 'safe' food every day or I will gain weight uncontrollably"). The rigid rules may be revised slowly as they are exposed to contradictory evidence. Since successful "response prevention" may elicit intense anxiety, the therapist must be sensitive to the conflict imposed by "should-resisting" experiments. Initial reports of the effectiveness of response prevention in the treatment of bulimia have been very encouraging (Leitenberg, Gross, Peterson, & Rosen, in press; Rosen & Leitenberg, Chapter 9, this volume). Considerable support may be required, and tasks may be graded to minimize the possibility of failure.

Challenging Beliefs through Behavioral Exercises

In addition to response prevention, other personal experiments may provide valuable corrective experiences that promote belief change. These may be targeted at idiosyncratic eating patterns or at the beliefs underlying social avoidance or excessive dependence on parents. By practicing self-initiated behavior, patients can gradually provide evidence to contradict their conviction that they are incompetent. These principles may be illustrated by one 24-year-old patient who was unable to use the telephone because all attempts at independence had been blocked by her intrusive and overprotective parents. After developing an awareness of the disadvantages inherent in having her parents make all of her telephone calls, she was gradually required to initiate calls on her own.

Prospective Hypothesis Testing

We (Garner & Bemis, 1982) have described elsewhere the application of this cognitive strategy to anorexic patients. It involves the translation of specific predictions and conclusions into formal hypotheses, which may be evaluated by collecting information from planned experiments. For example, a patient may express the opinion that "everyone believes that thinner people are more desirable and competent."

From this assumption, specific testable hypotheses may be generated, such as the following:

1. Do others really believe that thinner people are more desirable?
2. Is this a linear relationship — the thinner you are, the more desirable and the more competent you are?
3. Is this true of *all* people, or just a subset who may have uncritically accepted a current trend in fashion?
4. When most people think of the words "desirable" or "competent," do they also think of thinness?

The therapist may assist the patient in formulating experiments to test these hypotheses. However, since it may be argued that our current culture suffers from inadequate education regarding weight regulation (Garner et al., Chapter 21, this volume) and places an undue and unhealthy premium on thinness in women, the therapist must carefully distinguish the extreme nature of the anorexic's beliefs from the more moderate (although also unrealistic) cultural norms. If experiments involve obtaining feedback from others, the patient must be prepared in advance to interpret potential negative results as valuable information that may be used to shape beliefs (Garner & Bemis, 1982).

When applied to hypotheses that the patient generates regarding her own behavior, prospective hypothesis testing may not be as vulnerable to unpredictable peer responses. For example, the patient may postulate, "I cannot cope with eating in public." She may be able gradually to collect data to discredit this belief from a series of successively more "public" eating experiments.

Reattribution Techniques

Rather than directly modifying the body image misperception frequently observed in anorexia nervosa, we have recommended assisting patients in altering their *interpretation* of their self-perceptions (Garner & Bemis, 1982; Garner & Garfinkel, 1981; Garner et al., 1982). This approach is opposite to the general therapeutic goal of promoting trust in the validity and reliability of internal experiences. Since the anorexic patient's refractory perception of herself as too fat is instrumental in maintaining dieting efforts, she must begin to question the validity of her subjective experience of her body. This may be accomplished by interrupting or overriding self-perceptions of fatness with counterarguments, such as "I know that people with this disorder cannot trust their own size perception" or "I expect to feel fat during recovery, so I must consult the scale or my therapist to get an accurate reading of my size." Obviously, this strategy is dependent on a trusting relationship, since the patient is asked to respond to a specific set of counterarguments, rather than to intrusive thoughts that she repeatedly experiences regarding her body.

The reattribution technique may also be applied to other areas of bodily experience that provide feedback inconsistent with recovery. For example, in the emaciated patient, loss of hunger, postmeal bloating, and excessive energy must be attributed to "distortion" inherent in the starvation process, rather than interpreted as reliable experiences that may be used to dictate behavior.

Palliative Techniques

Patients are often uanble to employ more sophisticated cognitive techniques to challenge maladaptive thoughts for a variety of reasons, and palliative strategies such as "parroting" or "distraction" may avert destructive behaviors that could sabotage weeks of therapeutic progress. If overwhelming anxiety related to food or shape interferes with reasoning ability, the anorexic patient may be taught to parrot "coping phrases" to get her through the experience. In problem situations, she may be encouraged to say to herself: "I will finish each bite of my meal," "I will not get fat," "This is part of getting better," "My meal has been prescribed by the therapist; I must take my meal like medication," "I need food to keep me healthy," "Regardless of what I feel, I am at a thin–normal weight." Anxiety and maladaptive thoughts accompanying eating may be interrupted by distraction devices, such as watching television or listening to music while attempting to lock one's attention onto these stimuli. Going for a walk, making a telephone call, or meeting a friend immediately after eating may provide potent enough distraction to assist the patient in avoiding intrusive thoughts or strong urges to vomit. Essentially, these techniques involve forcefully "changing the cognitive channel," rather than attempting to modify beliefs through challenging, disputing, or examining evidence in a systematic way.

"Parroting" adaptive beliefs may be useful for patients who become ensnared in protracted debate and indecision about whether or not they are "fat" or whether they should adhere to their plan for weight gain. One patient spent hours in front of the mirror examining herself to determine whether she really could be considered to be at a "thin–normal" weight. Like many patients, she simultaneously held two apparently contradictory opinions about her shape: (1) "There is little objective evidence that I am fat," and (2) "I am fat because I *feel* fat." She explained that she believed the first intellectually and the second emotionally; however, as Beck *et al.* (1979) have pointed out, such an explanation is a semantic error, since, in this case, the terms "emotional" and "intellectual" simply reflect *degree of belief*. The patient was not convinced by the "evidence" and more *strongly* believed that she was fat; consequently, she had difficulty generating counterarguments. For her, it was useful not to insist that she completely believe her adaptive comments about her shape. She was simply encouraged to *say* them: "I *am* at a thin–normal weight," "My shape *is* attractive," "My perceptions of fat *are* all wet." This procedure enabled her to become "unstuck" from the obsessive decision-making process. Moreover, rehearsing the self-enhancing phrases may facilitate genuine belief change. After several months, she observed, "Sometimes I actually believe what I say about myself when I look in the mirror." This realization was frightening to her, because she concluded that she was losing her will to be emaciated, and this meant that she might become equally accepting of becoming obese. A detailed examination of this belief revealed the distorted reasoning.

The endorsement of an adaptive belief may be tied to a particular situation and break down under more anxiety-provoking conditions. For example, a patient may be able to entertain the belief that her weight is acceptable at all times except immediately after eating. In this case, parroting adaptive phrases and engaging in distraction may be viable methods of dealing with the transient but potentially overpowering thoughts and feelings that occur in particular situations. Finally, it has been our experience that "palliative" techniques are most useful in the early stages of therapy when the patient's thinking capacity may be diminished, or in later stages of therapy when the patient already subscribes to a more adaptive belief, but is temporarily overwhelmed by anxiety in particular problematic situations. With this in mind, it is often helpful to have the patient reach the adaptive conclusion herself through other cognitive techniques before requesting that she "parrot" it in moments in which she is overwhelmed by anxiety or the urge to engage in maladaptive behavior. The likelihood of success is remote if the patient is in complete disagreement with the parroted phrase.

Challenging Cultural Values Regarding Shape

It is obvious that our culture exerts a powerful influence in shaping our beliefs, values, and expectations. One of the major obstacles in encouraging the anorexic patient to relax her intense striving for thinness is that this therapeutic objective is in opposition to prevailing standards for physical attractiveness for women within Western society (Garner, Garfinkel, Schwartz, & Thompson, 1980). Her arduous struggle to recover from her disorder occurs amidst media messages glorifying the virtues of dieting and thinness. Furthermore, the anorexic's vulnerability to external influence increases the impact of these social pressures. In some cases, these values have been augmented by the family. The cultural obsession with slenderness is perhaps reflected by the recent evidence that anorexia nervosa itself has become a "culturally syntonic" disorder. Some have argued that it has acquired a not altogether unfavorable social connotation (Branch & Eurman, 1980; Garner, Garfinkel, & Olmsted, 1983), which may interfere with the motivation for recovery.

A fundamental component of therapy involves assisting the patient in developing more realistic attitudes about shape, despite the less than auspicious social medium. Several procedures have been useful in this regard; some involve the tactful progression of questions and hypothesis testing suggested by Beck (1976), while others parallel the persuasive methods advocated by Ellis (1962). Patients are encouraged to examine for themselves the evidence related to the conflict between the biological determinants of weight and the recent cultural preferences for thinness among women (Garner *et al.*, 1980; Garner *et al.*, Chapter 21, this volume). We occasionally show patients examples from magazine advertisements in which unrealistic shapes are being promoted, or in which women are being subtly devalued by equating female worth with physical attractiveness in general and thinness in particular. Other ads recommending ridiculous or dangerous cosmetic and dietetic practices may be offered in support of the argument that women are being exploited by the fashion and diet industries. Some patients feel a healthy sense of indignation at the definition of feminine attractiveness in terms of a prepubertal shape. However, most are in continual conflict over ideals related to shape and require sustained support in challenging pernicious social norms. In all circumstances, the therapist must scrupulously avoid assault on the patient's values. Through true collaboration and careful dialogue, the sources of erroneous convictions may be extirpated by understanding their heritage and disputing their validity.

Space limitations prohibit an exhaustive presentation of cognitive interventions for anorexia nervosa; other specific strategies have been presented elsewhere (Garner & Bemis, 1982; Garner *et al.*, 1982; Guidano & Liotti, 1983), and still others logically follow from more detailed descriptions of cognitive therapy with other disorders (Beck, 1976; Beck & Emery, 1979; Beck *et al.*, 1979; Ellis, 1962). The preceding sections have outlined specific cognitive methods that have been applied to anorexia nervosa; however, much of the time in therapy is spent applying these and other techniques in the gradual alteration of underlying assumptions (Beck, 1976) that determine much of the patient's dysfunctional behavior. These assumptions are analogues to basic values or organizing principles around which much of the patient's thinking and action revolve. Some of the most important assumptions relate to "self-concept." Before cognitive methods aimed at modifying self-concept deficiencies are described, fundamental principles related to normalization of eating and weight must be dealt with.

NORMALIZATION OF WEIGHT AND EATING

Patients often enter treatment with a sincere desire to recover, yet expressly or implicitly assume that this may be accomplished at an emaciated or suboptimal weight. This assumption has been shared by some therapists, who have recommended that weight and eating should largely be ignored, with the logic that these will become normal once underlying psychological factors have been addressed (Goodsitt, 1977; Solomon & Morrison, 1972; Szyrynski, 1973). However, the *process* of psychotherapy is seriously influenced by weight, in the sense that starvation exerts a profound effect on cognitive and emotional functioning (cf. Garner *et al.*, Chapter 21, this volume). Beliefs and emotions that are salient at a suboptimal weight are often completely different from those that prevail at a normal weight.

A positive and trusting therapeutic relationship is crucial in impelling the anorexic patient to modify her abnormal eating and weight. The therapist must be acutely aware of the patient's contradictory goals of achieving recovery while remaining at a low weight, and must stipulate that weight restoration is a necessary (but insufficient) condition for meaningful change. Although clinical strategies for promoting weight gain have been described elsewhere (Garfinkel & Garner, 1982; Garner *et al.*, 1982; Garner *et al.*, Chapter 21, this volume), several points should be reiterated:

1. A nonnegotiable weight range should be established that is above the patient's menstrual threshold (Frisch & McArthur, 1974) and that takes hereditary, constitutional, and metabolic factors into consideration (see Garner *et al.*, Chapter 21, this volume). This "goal range" of 1–2 kg (2.2–4.4 lb) should be established in advance, and pleas for renegotiation should be met by firmness and the reasoning that this is inconsistent with the goal of recovery.

2. Erroneous beliefs about "control" should be addressed. It is not the therapist's goal to control the patient or to cause her to lose control. A low weight is interpreted by the patient as a sign of "control." However, it may be argued that real control involves being able to exercise a wide range of choices; thus the patient lacks control in the sense that weight *gain* may not be chosen freely. The implications of defining self-control or self-worth in terms of weight have been addressed earlier.

3. It must be understood that outpatient therapy may only proceed if the patient's weight does not fall below a certain level (Bruch, 1982; Garner *et al.*, 1982; Selvini-Palazzoli, 1978) and if the patient is not in imminent danger due to other complications (e.g., hypokalemia, cardiac irregularities, anemia). There are no absolute rules regarding the minimum weight level, since it depends on the patient's overall health; in general, the patient's physical status should be monitored by a physician, and hospitalization must be seriously considered if weight loss approaches 25% below premorbid weight or if the patient becomes "stuck" at a low weight (Garner *et al.*, 1982).

4. The patient's weight should be monitored regularly. We generally recommend to patients who are highly preoccupied with their weight that they do not weigh themselves, but that they be weighed on a weekly basis by the primary therapist, a nurse, or a physician. Presuming a trusting relationship, there are several advantages of having the primary therapist assess weight. First, it emphasizes the interdependence between psychological and physical issues. It is important for the therapist to avoid duplicating the "Cartesian split" between mind and body so frequently observed in the patient's attitudes about herself. Secondly, in the same way that it is inappropriate to ignore the suicidal patient's acts of self-harm, it is inadvisable to disregard the anorexic patient's weight loss. Even if weight fluctuations are not at dangerously low levels, they may constitute a rather primitive means of communicating concerns to the therapist. These must be dealt with openly and frankly in the psychotherapy. Every attempt should be made to convey that weighing the patient is not a punitive action, but rather a reflection of concern about an area that influences the patient's thinking. Finally, regular monitoring of weight provides the opportunity for some patients to be relieved of the burden of weighing themselves repeatedly every day. Often, patients use the "feedback" from the scale in a very destructive fashion. Even when they are committed to the ultimate goal of recovery, they panic at the slightest increase in numbers on the scale. They may prefer to agree upon a rate of weight gain that does not exceed 1.5 kg (3.3 lb) per week, and to be blind to weekly weighings while the therapist records these on a chart to be periodically shared with the patient. This will allow the patient to focus on a consistent caloric intake that is not adjusted in response to diurnal fluctuations in weight.

5. A precise meal plan may be outlined by the therapist or with the assistance of a dietitian who is familiar with the disturbed eating patterns in anorexia nervosa. This should consist of "nonanorexic" foods, which are those that were consumed prior to the onset of the disorder. The patient's tendency to divide foods into dichotomous (i.e., "good" and "bad") categories should be explored, and she should be encouraged to challenge this self-defeating system. This may be accomplished by incorporating small, predetermined amounts of avoided foods into the daily diet. Bulimic patients should consume small amounts of the food typically reserved for bingeing episodes. These foods should be redefined as "medication," which will help inoculate them against bingeing by reducing psychological cravings and by establishing new response tendencies to food that previously only denoted a "blown" diet (Fairburn, 1982; Garner *et al.*, 1982; Garner *et al.*, Chapter 21, this volume; Russell, 1979).

6. Weight gain and modifications in eating patterns should be approached as experiments through which the patient can test particular beliefs and assumptions that have developed with the disorder. The general notion of irreversibility permeates much of the thinking of the anorexic (Garner & Bemis, 1982). Despite years of rigid control over intake, there is the belief that "I am just a doughnut away from a permanently higher weight and more liberal eating habits." It may be helpful to remind the patient that if her attempts to cope with "health" fail, she may choose to lose weight again. The changes are experiments that will help her acquire data to assess her ability to cope with change.

7. As much as possible, changes in eating and weight should be "mechanical." Many patients (just like frustrated dieters) have the best intentions to change their behavior when they are in the therapist's office, but their convictions dwindle when confronted by familiar signals in the environment or rigid cognitive rules for conduct that reappear in the therapist's absence. They have to be taught that, at least for the present in the areas of food and weight, they cannot permit their behavior to be determined by "urges" and transient shifts in thinking. Whereas much of the therapy is devoted to developing trust in individual perception, the patient must come to understand that her perceptions related to food, weight, and her body shape are truly aberrant and untrustworthy. External or cognitive control of intake is necessary until regulation of eating can be more naturally determined by internal signals. Early in treatment, every attempt should be made to help the patient eliminate *choice* in eating, since she will feel obligated to "choose" a dietetic protocol. Precise, mechanical adherence to a prescribed meal plan verified by detailed records may allow the patient to feel less guilty about eating. The mechanical approach to eating may make consuming larger quantities of food more acceptable, since it conforms to a definite plan. Undereating and overeating should be equally discouraged, since they represent loss of control. Again, this strategy presupposes a trusting therapeutic relationship and may be considered premature if the therapist repeatedly hears that the patient has devoured 4500 calories per day and has lost another pound.

Distorted beliefs about food, eating, and weight repeatedly emerge during the course of therapy; they may provide an opportunity for specific cognitive–behavioral interventions. Common beliefs are presented here, with examples of methods for challenging them. As explained previously, certain obviously fallacious ideas may be discredited by their mere articulation. Other, more intractable assumptions require repeated cognitive and behavioral interventions before they are vanquished. The following are concerns commonly expressed by patients and examples of the type of responses that may be offered by the therapist.

PATIENT: Once I reach my goal weight, or once I get into the habit of eating "nondietetic" food, I will not be able to stop and I will catapult into obesity.

THERAPIST: Are the only two options emaciation or obesity? If you have maintained "control" at this weight, where is the evidence that you will not be able to exert similar "control" at a normal weight? Recovered patients do not typically indulge in only high-calorie foods, and very few become obese. Could it be that you are feeling this way because you are *currently* starved—that once you get to a normal weight, you won't be sitting on a powder keg of hunger?[3]

Let's say that you do *want* more cookies or cake after you have a small portion; does this mean that you *must* have more? Is there a way that we can arrange the environment so that you are protected from going overboard? What if you consume the specified amount of feared food here or with a trusted friend so that if you should lose control you could be stopped?

---

3. There may be some logic to the patient's assumption that once she begins eating, she will be more hungry. She may have achieved a mildly ketotic state by limiting her intake, and her true "anorexia" will be reversed by more food. Most patients who gradually gain weight through consistent and planned overconsumption experience a marked reduction in hunger once their weight reaches normal levels. Nevertheless, the patient should be assured that should she "lose control" and fail to stabilize at a normal weight, she would be hospitalized and provided with external controls. Loss of control in this form would be taken as seriously as emaciation. This reassurance often enables the patient to begin to experiment with exercises designed to challenge her beliefs about eating and weight.

PATIENT: I cannot gain weight because it will all go to my stomach or thighs.

THERAPIST: Overeating may temporarily make your stomach bloated, but the weight will redistribute itself. When you lost weight, did it all come off one place? If your stomach were a bit bigger than you would like, what would it mean? What would you be inferring about your overall attractiveness, self-discipline, or self-worth? Where is the evidence for your stomach's being a valid index of these qualities?

PATIENT: I couldn't stand it if my weight got above 100 pounds.

THERAPIST: Many patients have a "magic weight," which is based either on the special meaning that the number holds or on the biological significance of this weight. Knowledge of your concerns that antedated the disorder and your anticipations of new demands that await a mature shape tell us more about why 100 pounds is so significant.

PATIENT: If I gain weight I will have to give up clothes sizes that have taken me months of anguish to achieve.

THERAPIST: Rather than thinking of those clothes sizes as being a reflection of competence, you may want to consider them as a sign of a serious illness. They are a public acknowledgment of a failure to cope with a mature shape. Are there other achievements that might make you feel good?

PATIENT: I must know exactly what my weight is, or I won't be able to get through the day.

THERAPIST: What are you assuming will happen if your weight moves up or down? Many patients display a dire need for certainty and the perception that any deviation from predictability is equivalent to chaos. This leads to the imposition of rigid rules to minimize the likelihood of change. If you move a small distance on the continuum of shape, does this really indicate that you are destined for the other pole? Holding your weight exactly at 105 pounds does not allow for normal fluctuations. It is analogous to maintaining a continuous heart rate of 72 beats per minute or attempting to steer a car in a straight direction by locking the wheel in a rigid position. A stable weight means continual fluctuations within an appropriate range.

In summary, while dealing with eating and weight in therapy may seem like a mundane and "nonpsychological" task, it is essential for several reasons:

1. It emphasizes the interdependence of mental and physical issues.

2. Even the most resistant patient can discuss these areas, and it thereby provides an opportunity to evaluate and begin to alter distorted thinking.

3. Since these topics occupy much of the starved patient's thinking, they provide "common ground" around which therapeutic trust may evolve; however, prudence must be exercised to ensure that these do not become a means of avoiding other psychological issues (we are reminded of one naive therapist who emerged from an initial assessment with 14 recipes for bran muffins).

4. Therapy may only proceed if eating and weight are relatively stable.

5. Once progress has been made in these areas, other psychological issues, such as low self-esteem, inadequate personal trust, anxiety, depression, and poor socialization, begin to emerge; these may be dealt with using cognitive–behavioral strategies.

COGNITIVE BASIS OF SELF-CONCEPT DEFICITS

One of the most consistent clinical observations in anorexia nervosa, even prior to the development of the syndrome, is an abysmal level of self-esteem (e.g., Bruch, 1973; 1978; Casper, 1982; Crisp, 1980b; Selvini-Palazzoli, 1978; Sours, 1980). It has also been repeatedly observed that the patient with anorexia nervosa displays a remarkable lack of trust in the reliability and/or validity of her thoughts, feelings, perceptions, and behavior (Andersen, 1979; Bruch, 1962, 1973, 1978; Frazier, 1965; Garner et al., 1982; Goodsitt, 1977; Lucas et al., 1976; Selvini-Palazzoli, 1978; Sours, 1980; Story, 1976).

The deficits in self-esteem, as well as the apparent inability to identify and respond accurately to inner experiences (i.e., lack of self-awareness or personal trust), may be conceptualized under the broader construct of "self-concept." The "self-esteem" components of self-concept primarily relate to the attitudes, feelings, and perceptions that constitute a person's appraisal or evaluation of his or her value, whereas "self-awareness" refers to the individual's perception and understanding of the internal processes that guide experience (Hall & Lindsey, 1970). We have chosen to formulate our observations in terms of self-concept, because cognitive psychology has begun to develop empirical strategies for investigating the parameters of this construct. Particularly in the study of depression, cognitive methods have begun to strengthen the data-theory bridge by using standardized procedures to draw inferences about the operation of cognitive processes or structures related to the self (e.g., Greiger, 1975; Rizley, 1978).

Modification of what may be defined as cognitive aspects of "self-concept" is a complex task, which must be distinguished from changing simple beliefs and attitudes. Guidano and Liotti (1983) have differentiated shifting more superficial cognitive structures related to food and weight from "deep cognitive restructuring implying a modification of the personal identity" (p. 299). Although, for the anorexic, food and weight issues may become inextricably intertwined with self-concept, the idea that cognitive methods can be employed to alter fundamental aspects of one's self-concept or personal identity is valuable. This parallels Beck's (1976) concept of "underlying assumptions" as basic personal philosophies around which more specific automatic thoughts and irrational beliefs are organized. These assumptions may not be verbalized directly, but can be inferred from patterns of thinking that re-emerge over time.

DEFICITS IN SELF-ESTEEM

The typical patient with anorexia nervosa is highly self-critical and experiences herself as inadequate in most areas of personal or social functioning. This extreme form of self-disparagement has been empirically confirmed by several recent investigations (Casper et al., 1981; Garner & Garfinkel, 1981). Although decreased self-esteem is one consequence of experimental semistarvation (Garner et al., Chapter 21, this volume; Keys et al., 1950), the anorexic's negative self-evaluation appears to precede weight loss and is not ameliorated by simple renourishment. Her poor self-esteem usually occurs despite excellent objective performance and an apparently normal or even ideal childhood.

Although the anorexic subscribes to underlying assumptions about self-worth that are common in other emotional disorders, she also displays some that appear to be distinctive. The most notable is the assumption that weight, shape, or thinness is the "sole or predominant referent for inferring personal value or self-worth" (Garner & Bemis, 1982). Recent investigations have found that individuals tend to organize their social experiences and information about themselves into specific categories referred to as "self-schemata" (Markus, 1977; Markus, Crane, Bernstein, & Siladi, 1982; Rogers, Kuiper, & Kirker, 1977). The anorexic's personal domain is dominated by *weight-related self-schemata*. Within our weight-preoccupied culture, it is easy to imagine how the female adolescent suffering from feelings of inadequacy might select weight as a frame of reference for self-evaluation. In addition to the positive social connotations associated with thinness (cf. Garner, Garfinkel, & Olmsted, 1983), weight itself has properties that may make it an appealing yardstick for self-rating: It is unambiguous, observable, and quantifiable.

Using a standardized methodology from cognitive psychology, several investigators have empirically confirmed that anorexic patients construe themselves in terms of body shape (Ben-Tovim, Hunter, & Crisp, 1977; Button, 1983; Crisp & Fransella, 1972; Fransella & Crisp, 1979). With the repertory grid technique, Button (1983) found marked individual differences among anorexic patients' assessments of the meaningfulness or "self" in terms of the "thin–fat construct." Moreover, strength and uniformity of construing self from weight were negatively related to outcome.

The anorexic's dependence on weight as an index for self-assessment is a reflection of a more general tendency to evaluate herself strictly in terms of external frames of reference. Favorable self-evaluation becomes rigidly bound to positive appraisals from others and extraordinary achievements. This is probably not qualitatively different from the formula employed by many emotionally healthy individuals; however, it is the extreme and absolute nature of this tendency that distinguishes the anorexic patient. Whereas most people are able to shift between external feedback and internal standards, the anorexic is almost exclusively bound to extrinsic factors. Behavior is described as being pulled from outside rather than driven by internal motives. There are probably adaptive applications of perfectionism (e.g., proofreading manuscripts); however, the anorexic's lack of selectivity and the nature of the objects of her perfectionistic pursuits are problematic.

Mahoney (1974) has described a "cycle of inflationary self-evaluations" in anorexia nervosa, in which "replication of past excellence becomes routinely expected and future endeavors must always set new highs" (p. 155). This escalating standard for self-reinforcement is self-limiting. At some point, increments in performance become smaller and more difficult to accomplish. This is epitomized by the anorexic's use of weight as a parameter for self-evaluation. She assumes, "If only my weight were a little lower, then I would feel better." Although she tells herself that the new goal will be sustaining, no weight is permanently satisfying, since it is the *loss* that is reinforcing. As weight declines, further loss becomes more difficult; the process that originally provided frequent rewards becomes the unforgiving purveyor of fear and guilt. Moreover, the anorexic secretly recognizes that accomplishments do not really change what she considers to be a fundamentally flawed character. The negative beliefs about self are extremely resistant to change, because they have been "overdetermined" in the sense that they are the product of a long-standing history of internal reinforcement and are often insidiously supported by parents. For example, one patient was encouraged by her mother to begin dating, but each social foray was followed by a "debriefing" and detailed suggestions for minimizing the possibility of rejection. The patient concluded that the coaching indicated an intrinsic inadequacy that had to be concealed.

Bruch (1961, 1973, 1982) has emphasized the anorexic's paralyzing feelings of ineffectiveness. Although "ineffectiveness" appears to be more closely related to "self-awareness" or "personal trust," which is discussed in a subsequent section, the "self-evaluative" component of self-concept is also implicit in Bruch's ineffectiveness construct. Anorexic patients have been described as ineffective in the sense that they "lack awareness of their own resources and do not rely on their feelings, thoughts and bodily sensations" (Bruch, 1973, p. 255). This leads to their experience of "themselves as acting only *in response* to demands coming from other people in situations, and not as doing things because *they want to*" (1973, p. 254).

It could be hypothesized that these feelings of vulnerability to influence are fundamentally related to self-esteem. Early research on persuasibility found that subjects with low self-esteem were more responsive to influence from the media and individual social interactions (cf. Cohen, 1959). Moreover, results from a number of studies indicate that subjects with low self-esteem also perceived themselves to be more vulnerable to the exercise of power over them in various situations (Cohen, 1959). Thus, it seems plausible to assume that individuals with consistently low self-evaluations may respond more to the demands of others and behave less in response to their own thoughts, feelings, and perceptions. It could also be speculated that by ignoring or not responding to "inner state," one may become less aware of one's feelings, thoughts, and bodily sensations, since these do not function as important determinants of behavior.

Guidano and Liotti (1983) have argued that the most striking quality of the sense of ineffectiveness is that "it is usually expressed as a general expectation of failure," which is not necessarily attributed to personal responsibility or precise external events. This may contrast with the state of the depressed patient, who is predisposed to assume personal responsibility and blame. According to Guidano and Liotti, the anorexic displays an "emptiness in personal identity," as if there is nothing inside to which success or failure could be attributed. There is remarkable similarity between Bruch's and others' descriptions of the ineffectiveness dimension and Lefcourt's (1966) definition of the locus of control (internal–external, or I-E) construct. Lefcourt defines external locus of control as "the perception of positive and/or negative events as being unrelated to one's own behaviors in certain situations and therefore beyond personal control" (1966, p. 207).

Several investigators have administered different versions of Rotter's (1966) original Locus of Control Scale to anorexic patients (Garner, Garfinkel, Stancer, & Moldofsky, 1976; Hood, Moore, & Garner, 1982; Strober, 1982). Although anorexic patients, as a group, are not more external than control samples, externality is associated with various other measures of psychopathology and may be a useful prognostic index (Hood *et al.*, 1982). Nevertheless, the similarity between anorexic and control samples suggests either that existing measures of the I-E construct do not adequately tap the ineffectiveness dimension in anorexia nervosa or that there is no genuine effectiveness deficit in the disorder. We have attempted to operationally define the ineffectiveness construct further by developing an Ineffectiveness subscale to the Eating Disorder Inventory (Garner, Olmsted, & Polivy, 1983a, 1983b). Items on this scale reflect elements of ineffectiveness referred to above, including negative self-evaluation (i.e., "I have a low opinion of myself"), external locus of control (i.e., "I feel generally in control of things in my life" [negatively keyed item]), and poor self-awareness (i.e., "I feel empty inside [emotionally]"). Anorexia nervosa and bulimia patients score significantly higher than normal female college students on the Ineffectiveness subscale of the Eating Disorder Inventory.

STRATEGIES FOR IMPROVING SELF-ESTEEM

Self-esteem deficits identified in the foregoing discussion are reflected in at least three related tendencies displayed by the anorexic patient: (1) An inexorable construing of the self in terms of body shape is pathognomonic for the disorder; (2) self-worth is rigidly tied to external frames of reference; and (3) the self is experienced as ineffective, incompetent, and vulnerable to external control. Guidelines for the conduct of cognitive therapy can be recommended for each of these areas.

Continual assessment and reassessment are required to determine possible functions served by the patient's weight-related self-evaluation. In other words, what are the *meanings* attached to pursuing thinness and avoiding fatness? These may vary considerably among patients; however, some of the more common meanings that serve to maintain the disorder have been described in the earlier section on positive and negative reinforcement contingencies, and others have been elaborated elsewhere (Garner *et al.*, 1982). Patients must gradually understand that their system of meaning makes their disorder *functional*; however, it also requires the maintenance of a disorder that is clearly dysfunctional in the sense that it precludes adaptation in a broader sense. Moreover, the patient must be encouraged to recognize the serious limitations of this unidimensional framework for self-definition. There is some empirical support to suggest that this recognition may be a key ingredient in recovery. Using the repertory grid technique, Button (1983) found that patients who responded favorably at outcome were those whose elaboration of self went beyond the concept of weight; this confirmed an earlier case study by Crisp and Fransella (1972). The therapist may promote the process by gradually helping the patient (1) to identify and modify weight-related self-schemata; (2) to articulate specific beliefs about the meaning of weight; and (3) to challenge the basis for construing oneself in terms of weight or shape, using specific methods described below.

An essential aspect of psychotherapy is the gradual modification of the cognitive appraisal systems and underlying assumptions related to self-esteem. First, the therapist must assist the patient in the examination of her assumptions regarding self-worth. One strategy involves exploring the consequences of making self-acceptance contingent upon external factors. When extrinsically determined, self-worth is ephemeral, in that it may be gained or lost on the basis of daily accomplishments. For example, if self-worth is exclusively tied to acceptance from others, it is easy to see how nonacceptance would produce anxiety and depression. However, acceptance may not be truly satisfying, because there is no insurance against ultimate rejection by others. Moreover, rating one's basic worth in terms of performance is often problematic, since performance is often ambiguous; it is difficult to determine whether an accomplishment is truly deserving of a positive evaluation. Is a B on an exam good enough? Does a particular friend really like you? How many friends are required for proof of acceptability? Basing self-worth on the expectations of others is inherently risky, since standards may change precipitously or may be contradictory if derived from more than one source. Finally, this external orientation leads to perpetual comparisons with others. This is self-defeating, since there is virtually always someone who can display superior performance or traits in a specific domain.

The therapist may guide the patient in her questioning of this formula for self-evaluation. The concept of self-worth may be *operationalized*: "How does one really estimate self-worth? Is it justified to infer such an abstract notion from particular performances? If so, how does one legitimately determine worth based on an inventory of different traits and performances? How can relative weights or units of value be assigned for their past, present and future contributions?" Some writers have argued that self-worth is a complicated and abstract concept that may not be legitimately inferred from simple traits or performances (Ellis & Harper, 1975; Greiger, 1975). It is preferable to direct the patient away from the "balance-sheet" or self-rating approach by concluding that it is arbitrary and unnecessary. The cognitive technique of *decentering* may be used to determine whether the patient evaluates others' worth by the same inflexible criteria that she uses for herself. Here is an example:

PATIENT: I am terrified that I may do worse this year than last year at the university.

THERAPIST: What would it mean if you did do worse?

PATIENT: Well, I guess it would mean that I am not very good as a person.

THERAPIST: You mean your worth as a person is being evaluated—it's reflected by your grades?

PATIENT: Yes—that is why it is so important to do well in everything you attempt. I feel the same way about sports, hobbies, and my friends. In the last year losing weight has become the way for me to feel better about myself.

THERAPIST: The way that you are looking at your worth sort of relates to a philosophical question. How does one really evaluate or measure self-worth? *(Operationalizing the belief.)* You have implied that you base it on your daily performances, but this has some distinct disadvantages. *(The therapist then outlines some of these as listed above.)*

PATIENT: Don't all people judge their worth by what they do?

THERAPIST: We may do this to some degree, but not as literally or harshly as you seem to do, and not on a moment-to-moment basis. In fact, you might ask yourself if you rate others' worth by their performances. For example, do you rate your roommate's worth based on her grades? You haven't seemed particularly concerned about my grades in graduate school. *(Decentering.)*

PATIENT: I just assumed that you did everything well.

THERAPIST: That is hardly the case. If you found that I did things poorly in several areas, would your evaluation of me decline?

PATIENT: Well, no, but you are different.

The patient may be encouraged in the gradual pursuit of activities that are intrinsically enjoyable or fulfilling. The anorexic's basic difficulty in identifying and responding to pleasurable sensations is an obstacle in this task. Nevertheless, therapy is aimed at reinforcing the patient's slow discovery of her own interests and helping her view herself in a more complex and multidimensional fashion. If the "self" can indeed be rated, then it must be done within the context of a wide range of variables (i.e., multiple traits, hobbies, career pursuits, relationships, etc.).

Beyond their faulty system for evaluating self-worth, many anorexic patients are convinced that they are incompetent, ineffectual, and inadequate; they assume that their basic personalities are inherently defective, and all of their efforts at superior behavior are desperate attempts to conceal or rise above this deficit. The degree of self-loathing does not seem to be adequately represented by the notion of poor self-esteem. There seems to be an underlying assumption that intrinsic deficiencies exist in their personality that make them undeserving of approval, respect, and depthful caring. One patient described her self-disgust as so intense that she only felt right when she was punishing herself, since at least it could be said that justice was being served.

Many patients' self-loathing is expressed as a lack of acceptance of their own personality attributes and an idealization of the opposite traits. For example, many patients are quite socially dependent, but they view this trait with the utmost contempt and desperately strive to be independent. They repudiate their derivation of pleasure from nurturance, tactile stimulation, protection, affection, and interpersonal sharing; they expect themselves to be self-reliant in the pursuit of individualistic goals. They place exclusive emphasis on mastery of bodily functioning and the environment. While these autonomous goals are not inherently negative, neither are those reflected in social dependence. A patient's distorted beliefs about the legitimacy or respectability of "social dependence" in general may have led to a lack of acceptance of this trait in herself.

Responding to these concerns and alluding to cognitive mediators, Bruch (1978) recommends that "therapy must help the patient to uncover the error of these convictions, to let her recognize that she has substance and worth of her own, and that she does not need the strained and stressful superstructure of an artificial ultra-perfection" (p. 137). Examination of assumptions and corrective feedback from the therapist may promote the gradual recognition of the acceptability of the anorexic patient's genuine personality traits. Modification of these "deep cognitive structures" (Guidano & Liotti, 1983) requires a trusting therapeutic alliance, in which experiences with the therapist disconfirm the underlying assumptions related to incompetence and lack of value.

The therapist may encourage the development of a sense of effectiveness by carefully observing and reinforcing small signs of independent and competent functioning, which may be distungished from performances that have been strictly the product of other people's expectations. Support should be given for behavior that reflects risk taking, reasonable self-expression, assertiveness, flexibility, the pursuit of purely pleasurable activities, and, occasionally, healthy noncompliance or defiance.

Changing the anorexic's basic view of herself as inadequate is a lengthy process that requires repeated discussion of the same themes over many sessions. The entire process is analogous to learning a new language. In psychotherapy, the patient is exposed to novel concepts and strategies for evaluating self-worth and increasing self-acceptance. These components do not produce meaningful change, just as vocabulary and conjugation of verbs alone are insufficient for language fluency; however, redundancy and practice in the use of new constructs related to "self" may ultimately lead to changes in "deep" cognitive structures.

DEFICITS IN SELF-AWARENESS OR PERSONAL TRUST

Many investigators have described deficits in self-awareness in anorexia nervosa (Bruch, 1962, 1973, 1978; Frazier, 1965; Goodsitt, 1977; Jessner & Abse, 1960; Selvini-Palazzoli, 1978; Wall, 1959; and others). As we have discussed earlier, these deficiencies may, in part, be mediated by low self-esteem; however, they may develop from and be maintained by distorted beliefs or assumptions about stimuli arising in the body. Distorted beliefs related to physiological needs and emotional states pose unique problems, for which specific treatment strategies are indicated. Cognitive distortions may be identified that are specifically related to aspects of internal experience:

1. Identification and expression of affect.
2. Identification and responsiveness to bodily sensations and perception.
3. Identification and responsiveness to beliefs.

The manifestations and cognitive features in each of these areas are described separately and followed by specific recommendations for modifying distortions.

Deficits in the Identification and Expression of Affect

These deficiencies may be manifested in patients' sense of "not knowing how they feel" (Bruch, 1973, p. 338), but are more commonly expressed as a lack of trust in the validity and reliability of affect. There is a conflict between a particular affective state and the belief about the *appropriateness, acceptability,* or *justification* of that emotion.

The confusion about affective experiences is often indicated early in treatment, when patients are asked to talk about their emotional reaction to a particular situation. This may be met by a blank stare or a counterquestion, such as "How should I feel?" When asked about her feelings in a family interview, one patient pointed to her mother and said, "Ask her, she knows me better than I do." Sometimes patients will become frightened, defensive, or openly hostile when asked about their feelings; however, these more expressive reactions often camouflage vagueness, confusion, and a general emotional impoverishment.

Patients frequently report experience as the *absence* of feelings. The complaint of "emptiness" or paucity of inner feelings has been repeatedly observed in the clinical literature (Bruch, 1973, 1978; Garner *et al.*, 1982; Goodsitt, 1977; Selvini-Palazzoli, 1978). Some patients are able to link their preoccupation with shape to this deficit: "I know beauty is only skin deep, but I know that there really isn't anything underneath; at least focusing on my exterior distracts me from the inner void." Apparent superficiality or lack of psychological-mindedness may stem from the inability to describe inner feeling states accurately. The overall lack of confidence in the validity and reliability of emotional experiences results in an overreliance upon others to determine what one *should* feel, as well as the creation of rules to determine when feeling states are acceptable. The inconsistency between the patient's experience of an emotion and her judgments about its appropriateness often leads her to the conclusion that the feeling must not really exist. For example, one patient assumed that anger was only appropriate if its object were malevolent in every regard. In trying to decide whether or not she was angry at her mother, her reasoning followed this syllogism: (1) I could only be angry at my mother if she were a bad person; (2) my mother is not a bad person; and (3) therefore, I must not be angry at my mother. Her "logic" disregarded her experience as sufficient validation of her anger; the result was confusion about the feeling.

Another 20-year-old patient illustrates the difficulty many anorexics have in accurately experiencing and labeling depression. The expression of sadness was completely unacceptable within the patient's family. Her father conveyed the impression that sadness was an unforgivable indication of weakness. Moreover, any other sign of emotion, including warmth and attachment to another person, was viewed as a reflection of inadequacy. Her mother experienced depression related to unfulfilled career aspirations, as well as lifelong rejection from her own mother; however, she preserved the family's "denial" of depression by masking her own unhappiness with superficial optimism. The patient suppressed her own depression by discrediting its legitimacy. Again, her reasoning followed a syllogism: (1) I could only be depressed if I were weak; (2) I am not weak; (3) therefore, I must not be depressed. At the point when she was particularly depressed at the prospect of not being able to cope with university studies, the patient began losing weight and remembers thinking, "Now that I am weak [physically], it is legitimate for me to be depressed." Although her further weight loss did not ameliorate her depression, she reported at least feeling more "honest." Moreover, her attachment in psychotherapy was only acceptable as long as she was at a low weight: Weight gain meant that she would have to be both invulnerable to depression and completely self-sufficient in the sense of not wanting to be involved in a relationship.

The examples we have cited of dependence upon a deductive formula in deciding whether or not an emotion is legitimate reflect a more basic discomfort with emotions. Judgmental attitudes about emotions or idiosyncratic meanings attached to a particular emotion repeatedly emerge during the course of therapy. For example, anger may be intolerable because it means complete loss of control or because it is assumed that the expression of anger will be followed by rejection or retaliation. The beliefs or assumptions attached to an affect make the experience or expression of that emotion simply too threatening. This is exemplified by a 30-year-old patient with a 15-year history of anorexia nervosa and bulimia. Her mother drank excessively and would unpredictably fly into a rage, accusing the patient of vulgar thoughts about sex or assaulting the passive father with an assortment of vile verbal criticisms. The mother's rage would be followed by extreme guilt and obsequious fawning over the father and daughter. At the initiation of treatment, the patient not only denied ever experiencing anger (as well as a number of other feelings and impulses), but was unable even to say the word. Moreover, she insulated herself from anger toward her mother by routinely referring to herself in the second person and her mother in the third person plural. Later in therapy, the patient's beliefs about the inadvisability of experiencing or expressing anger became explicit: (1) Anger will definitely be met by retaliation and alienation; and (2) if I allow myself to experience anger, I may completely lose control and devastate others. Modifying these inappropriate beliefs about the acceptability or justification of emotions is a primary goal of psychotherapy with anorexic patients.

Deficits in Identification of and Responsiveness to
Bodily Sensations and Perceptions

Confusion and mistrust related to bodily sensations have been clinically observed in
anorexia nervosa (Bruch, 1962, 1973, 1978; Frazier, 1965; Selvini-Palazzoli, 1978;
Sours, 1969) and have been empirically documented for some patients (cf. Garfinkel
& Garner, 1982; Garner, Garfinkel, & Moldofsky, 1978). For the purposes of this
chapter, we are interested in the cognitive parameters of these interoceptive deficits;
patients very often report doubts or distorted beliefs about internal state and display
little confidence in the reliability or validity of bodily sensations. It may be that these
cognitions are secondary to fundamental interoceptive disturbances, or that the
anorexic patient's poor overall self-concept results in her questioning the reliability
of all aspects of her experience. The confusion in the area of bodily functioning may
be responsible for the anorexic's compensatory "overcontrol" of natural biological
processes, as well as her reliance upon "rules" and intellectual strategies to determine
what is happening inside her body.

In a manner analogous to that described in the section on affect, patients may
not be able to recognize and respond reliably to bodily sensations because these signals
have acquired a negative or inappropriate meaning. Rather than accepting their simple presence as adequate justification for experiencing them, biological sensations are
evaluated as to whether they are "correct" or "wrong." The most obvious example
of this process relates to the perception of hunger and satiety, which probably become
distorted *after* the disorder has begun to develop. This clinical feature also illustrates
how salient beliefs about particular bodily needs or drives may prohibit patients from
responding appropriately to them and ultimately may interfere with their accurate identification. For the normal individual, food is a positively valenced stimulus and eating
is a positively valenced response, because they are associated with the dissipation of
the unpleasant biological tension brought about by hunger. For the anorexic who has
a morbid fear of fatness, food and eating are *negatively* valenced events because they
lead to weight gain. Therefore, on at least one level, food, eating, and satiety, usually associated with pleasure, become *negative* events, while dieting and hunger acquire
the new positive meaning of "virtue" and "self-control." The need to eat is deprecated
as bad, wrong, or even disgusting. Biological signals indicating its presence are systematically ignored or suppressed. From this converse system of meanings, a myriad of
logically consistent beliefs develop that contradict the bodily messages related to
hunger and satiety. Bruch (1978) has suggested that patients literally "brainwash" themselves into experiencing hunger as "pleasant and desirable" (p. 4). Trust in "natural"
biological processes is replaced with "intrapersonal paranoia" (Selvini-Palazzoli, 1974).
For patients with a long history of anorexia nervosa, the many years during which
the natural causes of eating have been systematically dissociated from satisfaction and
satiety may be responsible for the remarkable confusion experienced during recovery
when they attempt to depend upon "appetite" to regulate eating. One patient who
became voracious rather than satiated after meals described herself as "an infant having
to completely relearn how to eat and what all of the internal signals stand for."

The interaction between beliefs and bodily needs is dramatically reflected in attitudes toward sexual urges. However, it must be underscored that a broad spectrum
of experiences, knowledge, and attitudes is reflected in the psychosexual histories of
anorexic patients (Beumont, Abraham, & Simpson, 1981). Beumont *et al.*'s (1981)

detailed interviews of a group of anorexia nervosa patients revealed a subgroup who described their sexual experiences favorably. However, the majority reported disturbed sexual functioning in some area, and almost 60% believed that their sexual difficulties either precipitated or maintained their disorder. These distorted beliefs about sexuality often may be directly linked to the family. Selvini-Palazzoli (1978) has argued that the families in which anorexia nervosa develops are typically "rooted in the old ways," rejecting modern views of sexuality in favor of puritanical beliefs that urges are bad and should be suppressed or eliminated. These antiquated beliefs are very often uncritically accepted by the anorexic patient, and the experience or anticipation of sexual sensations is a source of grave concern. Because they elicit guilt or panic, such experiences are often denied or suppressed. In the same way that inappropriate responding to hunger cues may confound the natural experience, sexual sensations may not be accurately identified because of the surplus meaning they have acquired. After denying any sexual urges for a year, one 19-year-old college student describer her conflict as follows:

I was terrified by the apparent sexual sophistication of my contemporaries. I feigned indifference to men, believing that by pretending to myself that I did not need anyone, I would not reveal the weakness of wanting affection so badly. To be indifferent, either emotionally or physically, is acceptable to me and reconcilable with my vision of attractiveness being tied to self-sufficiency. I felt trapped by my facade, but also felt helpless to let down my protective barriers and admit the truth. I was, and am, incredibly scared of being rejected for the weakness inherent in my needs and my desires.

In summary, the belief that desires are inherently frightening or are a sign of weakness repeatedly emerge during the course of psychotherapy with most anorexic patients. These attitudes toward specific biological urges and needs are reflected in the patients' general approach to pleasure. It is our clinical impression that the majority of anorexic patients have a history of deriving enjoyment primarily from activities that are "performance-oriented"; they rarely seek pleasure for its own sake. After the disorder develops, the limited sources of pleasure dwindle to weight control and dieting. The quintessential case was a young patient who was given the Lewinsohn Pleasant Events Schedule (Lewinsohn & Graf, 1973) to assess her repertoire of enjoyable activities. After responding negatively to the entire 160 items, she added one item that she could endorse: "Enjoy losing weight." Empirical confirmation of this anhedonic stance in anorexia nervosa has been reported by Garner and Garfinkel (1981), using the Chapman, Chapman, and Raulin (1976) Physical Anhedonia Scale. Anhedonia was related to body size overestimation, and the mean scores for the anorexic patients were greater than those of schizophrenic and college student samples described by Chapman *et al.* (1976).

Deficits in the Identification of and Responsiveness to Beliefs and/or Behaviors

Bruch (1978) has observed that patients with anorexia nervosa "behave as if they had no independent rights, [and seem to believe] that neither their bodies nor their actions are self-directed, or not even their own" (p. 39). The confusion surrounding internal state extends to mistrust of the validity and reliability of attitudes, motives, and behavior. The lack of confidence in thinking processes is reflected in exaggerated self-monitoring and rigidity. Behavior is designed to meet the expectations of others, and is judged by extreme standards of "correctness," "legitimacy," and "justification."

One recovered patient put it simply: "I did all the right things for the wrong reasons—I was like a ship with everyone else at the rudder." She did not trust herself to make decisions because she had no experience in directing her own life. Moreover, she feared that failure would elicit unbearable disapproval. The assumption that her own frame of reference was untrustworthy led to an overreliance on external performance standards, as well as a rigid adherence to altruistic rules and philosophies that were beyond criticism. The wishes of others were often embraced as her own. For example, her parents expected her to pursue undergraduate studies in preparation for law school. The daughter's suggestions of other alternatives were subtly devalued or ignored, and she simply assumed that she would proceed according to her *own wish* to become a trial lawyer. It was only after repeated academic failures, despite her exceptional ability, that she began to recognize that she had absolutely no interest in either the study or the practice of law. This is a fairly typical case where there seems to be a deficiency in the patient's trust of her own thinking, and a resulting dependence on others to set the standards for performance. The doubt about the validity of thinking may not be immediately apparent, since patients will often defend their pursuit of excellence and dismiss as coincidence the isomorphism between their own and their parents' expectations.

This particular aspect of the anorexic patient's self-concept deficiency may be linked specifically to underlying assumptions that she applies to her experience. Common assumptions are "My thinking or behavior may be incorrect, and that would be intolerable or lead to catastrophic consequences" or "In order to evaluate myself favorably, my behavior and thoughts *must* be proper, legitimate, and accurate, and must meet with the approval of others." Other, subsidiary beliefs follow, which are designed to reduce the likelihood of failure (e.g., "I must rely on parents or others to provide direction so that I will not do the wrong thing" or "I must rigidly adhere to rules for conduct"). The anorexic patient's feelings of ineffectiveness and incompetence may be linked to the understanding that her behavior and thinking are not determined by herself, but by the expectations of others. The exaggerated fear of negative evaluation or social rejection is a major determinant of behavior.

In summary, we have postulated that the deficiencies of self-trust may be linked to the anorexic patient's belief system, and particularly to the rules she has adopted for judging what she *should* feel, think, and experience, with the implicit demand that it be *correct*. The anorexic patient's mistrust of internal experiences and inability to function autonomously have been attibuted to specific developmental deficits by a number of prominent theorists (Bruch, 1962; Goodsitt, 1969, 1977; Masterson, 1977; Selvini-Palazzoli, 1978). Although each relies on a somewhat different explanatory system, they share the common feature of assuming that on some level the child's self-expression, initiative, and autonomy have been discouraged rather than reinforced. Family theorists (Caille, Abrahamsen, Girolami, & Sorbye, 1977; Conrad, 1977; Minuchin, Rosman, & Baker, 1978; Selvini-Palazzoli, 1978) argue from a similar point of view, but focus upon interactional patterns within the family. Overprotectiveness and enmeshment both discourage the child's independent functioning. A cognitive approach is not necessarily incompatible with either developmental or interactional theories, and may be viewed as complementary to both. One distinction is that the cognitive model explicitly defines the locus of disturbance as *distorted or inappropriate beliefs* that either "cause" or maintain behavior. It follows that the emphasis in treatment relates to meanings that are currently operative for the patient. The locus of change, regardless of the technique, is assumed to be cognitive. It is not necessary to reconstruct early developmental history to identify many instances in which the anorexic patient's experiences, beliefs, values, and opinions have not been confirmed or authenticated by parents; it is the patient's *current* beliefs about being unable to trust herself that make these family interactions relevant. Furthermore, some patients appear to develop these same opinions about themselves in the absence of an "enmeshed" family system. Their beliefs may have a less traceable origin, but it is obvious that the same set of beliefs may develop from different individual, familial, and cultural sources. Thus, understanding family interactional patterns and developmental events may be helpful in determining the origin of a particular set of assumptions for some patients, but it is the *current belief system* that must be accessed and modified. Various clinical strategies proposed by interpersonal and family therapy may be useful in promoting change in these beliefs.

STRATEGIES FOR IMPROVING SELF-AWARENESS

The general principles for facilitating the development of personal trust are similar to those described for improving self-esteem. The essential features of this process may be broken down into a series of strategies involving the following:

1. Identification of emotions, sensations, and thoughts.
2. Identification of distorted attitudes *about* these experiences.
3. Gradual correction of these erroneous convictions by the cognitive methods outlined earlier.
4. Practice in responding to previously avoided experiences.
5. Reinforcement of the patient's independent expression of previously avoided emotions, sensations, and thoughts.

The anorexic patient's misperceptions, faulty reasoning, and erroneous beliefs about her body must be identified and labeled as such without undermining her confidence that she possesses the ability to think for herself. The therapist must proceed very gradually, correcting distortions and confirming authentic expressions of inner state. Again, Bruch (1978) instructively outlines general parameters of conduct:

[The therapist] must pay attention to the discrepancies in a patient's recall of the past and to the way she perceives or misperceives current events, to which she will respond inappropriately. The therapist must be honest in confirming or correcting what the patient communicates. (p. 136)

The identification of affective or other internal states must be done gradually and often somewhat indirectly. Indications that internal experiences are not being recognized include categorical denial of the presence (ever) of a particular affect or sensation (e.g., "I never feel angry," "I am always on the go; I never get tired," "I never feel pleasurable sensations"). More commonly, the failure to identify internal states is reflected by the absence of affect or sensations under circumstances in which they are seemingly appropriate. For example, one patient commented frequently about her divorced father's unwillingness to visit, but stoically maintained that she had no feelings about his lack of interest. Sometimes the denial is incongruent with other behaviors. A patient emphatically protested that her mother's telephone calls were not upsetting her, yet they were regularly followed by bingeing episodes. Since it is always possible that the patient genuinely may not possess a particular feeling, the therapist must proceed cautiously, without prematurely implying that the patient's experience is distorted. When faced with an apparent discrepancy between affect and content, the therapist can explore the patient's thinking in some detail:

THERAPIST: How did you feel when your mother implied that you couldn't do it yourself?
PATIENT: Nothing—I really did not feel anything.
THERAPIST: What were you thinking?
PATIENT: That she was right; I can't do anything for myself.
THERAPIST: Were you thinking anything else about your mother?
PATIENT: Well—she should let me do things on my own.
THERAPIST: Did this make you feel angry?
PATIENT: No—I can't get angry.

Here, the thought that "she should let me do things on my own" could be expected to be accompanied by some variant of the emotion of anger, and the patient's unwillingness to acknowledge this affect has to do with her belief that anger toward her mother is unacceptable. It is critical to proceed slowly and allow the patient to discover her inner feelings herself. Continued queries begin to elicit "incipient feelings," which should be acknowledged and confirmed. This involves "shaping" through successive approximations of more clearly articulated affect and sensations.

A pervasive problem is the anorexic's tendency to devalue or discredit inner feelings that she feels are illegitimate or "morally wrong." It is necessary to detect negative opinions that the patient has about her feelings, since these may distort her experience. This may be done by untangling the faulty syllogistic reasoning applied to certain emotions. Awareness of the logical error will convince some to begin tentatively testing the expression of the emotion.

Many of the distortions apply to "urges" or "feelings," which are viewed in either negative or extreme terms: "If I enjoy sex, I will become a prostitute," "If I experience pleasure, I will be vulnerable to its being taken away," "If I give in to my hunger, I will not be able to stop," "If I give in to my urge to relax, I will become a degenerate." Using the cognitive methods described earlier, the erroneous convictions underlying these beliefs may be slowly exposed. Pleasure is often disregarded as frivolous in favor of exaggerated self-discipline. One emaciated patient agreed to inhibit all forms of exercise, but when she visited her athletically oriented family, she could not resist thrusting herself into avid competition. Casual "dips in the lake" turned into vigorous time trials; a brisk walk in the morning escalated into a jog. The following dialogue illustrates the therapist's attempts to identify and legitimize the patient's experience of pleasure.

THERAPIST: What makes you change your initial commitment to resist exercise?

PATIENT: I just get caught up with what is going on.

THERAPIST: Do you enjoy the exercise?

PATIENT: I guess I do—I do it.

THERAPIST: But you could do it for other reasons? Is it pleasurable?

PATIENT: I would feel badly if I didn't do as much as my brother or sister. I would feel lazy.

THERAPIST: How do you feel after swimming?

PATIENT: Exhausted. I can't keep up with them.

THERAPIST: So maybe it is *not* highly pleasurable.

PATIENT: I guess not, but it *should* be.

THERAPIST: Are there any aspects of being in the water, other than racing, that you enjoy?

PATIENT: Not really—well, there is one thing, but it sounds silly; it is not really swimming. I like to float and look at the clouds.

THERAPIST: That sounds like pleasure to me.

PATIENT: But it is nothing really.

THERAPIST: Pleasure often comes from something small; it does not have to come from Olympic events.

PATIENT: People *should* get pleasure out of accomplishment; I should like swimming laps.

THERAPIST: It sounds like you have tried to place a value judgment on pleasure. You may end up spending so much time trying to decide if your pleasure is acceptable that you lose it. You like floating—I think that I would agree with the part of you that prefers it over racing.

This passage illustrates the gentle challenging of the patient's tendency to diminish the simple experience of pleasure. It may be followed by encouragement to practice pursuing activities that result in this type of positive sensation. Over the course of many meetings, these new types of "accomplishments" may be reviewed and authenticated. One patient found solace in therapy sessions because the therapist's office was the only place that she truly allowed herself to relax her harsh demands for performance. She would often sit with her eyes closed and simply concentrate on the pleasure derived from "not having to do something productive" for the hour. Legitimizing this activity in the therapist's office gradually was extended to other sensations; over time, her *belief* about the acceptability of leisure changed.

Finally, the therapist may reinforce the patient's independent expression of previously avoided emotions and sensations. Often patients will require tremendous support in their initial diffident expressions of anger or assertions with overprotective parents.

Occasionally, bodily sensations are accurately perceived; however, the patient's interpretation of the meaning of the interoceptive experience is incorrect. For example, with emaciation, the loss of hunger may be interpreted as a lack of need for food; excess energy as a sign of health or new-found inner strength; hyperacuity to light or noise as an indication of improved perception; the absence of menstrual periods and sexual feelings as insignificant; postmeal bloating or nausea as a sign that eating is inadvisable; constipation as an indication for laxatives. Using reattribution techniques, misinterpretations of the meanings of these experiences may be slowly corrected.

CONCLUSION

The present chapter has supplemented previous discussions (Garner & Bemis, 1982; Garner *et al.*, 1982) by including more detailed material on cognitive "setting conditions," such as deficits in self-esteem and self-awareness. These basic assumptions about the self are presumed to have a more remote origin and to operate at less accessible levels of cognitive processing than specific irrational ideas about eating and weight. The role of self-concept deficits in the development of anorexia nervosa is a fertile area for future investigation. However, the question of whether or not cognitive mechanisms can be implicated in the production of anorexic symptoms is both conceptually and methodologically separate from the utility of cognitive–behavioral therapy in treating the disorder. As Hollon and Beck (1979) have noted, "there need be no necessary congruence between the factors that trigger a disorder and the factors that alleviate it" (p. 155). Variables of theoretical significance to the cognitive model, such as weight-related self-schemata, errors in information processing, and the operation of negative and positive self-reinforcement, will continue to be investigated in their own right. In addition, it will be important to study the higher-order beliefs that are hypothesized to precede, to coexist with, and often to persist beyond the disorder itself.

At present, all conceptual and therapeutic models for anorexia nervosa must be considered tentative and provisional. Since the disorder was first recognized as a diagnostic entity, numerous etiological formulations have been proposed; however, there is a remarkable absence of controlled outcome research evaluating the effectiveness of outpatient psychotherapy. The follow-up research on anorexia nervosa has suffered from a myriad of methodological flaws, which have been the subject of recent reviews (Hsu, 1980; Schwartz & Thompson, 1981; Swift, 1982; Vandereycken & Pierloot, 1983). One major obstacle in evaluative research has been that descriptions of the conduct of outpatient psychotherapy typically have not been detailed enough to allow replication.

The techniques we have described have been applied unsystematically in clinical settings, and no rigorous tests have yet been conducted to support or refute our favorable opinion of their efficacy. Nevertheless, we do believe that the results obtained so far are encouraging enough to warrant further examination through a series of more systematic clinical trials and comparative studies. While the tentative nature of our hypotheses about the applicability of cognitive–behavioral methods to anorexia nervosa cannot be overemphasized, we hope that the model presented here and elsewhere is sufficiently specific to be replicated and tested by other investigators.

REFERENCES

Andersen, A. A. (1979). Anorexia nervosa: Diagnosis and treatment. *Weekly Psychiatry Update Series,*
    3, 1–8.
Beck, A. T. (1970). Role of fantasies in psychotherapy and psychopathology. *Journal of Nervous and Mental*
    Disease, 150, 3–17.

Beck, A. T. (1976). *Cognitive therapy and the emotional disorders.* New York: International Universities Press.

Beck, A. T., & Emery, G. (1979). *Cognitive therapy of anxiety and phobic disorders.* Philadelphia: Center for Cognitive Therapy.

Beck, A. T., Rush, A. J., Shaw, B. F., & Emery, G. (1979). *Cognitive therapy of depression.* New York: Guilford Press.

Bedrosian, R. C., & Beck, A. T. (1980). Principles of cognitive therapy. In M. J. Mahoney (Ed.), *Psychotherapy process* (pp. 127–152). New York: Plenum.

Bemis, K. M. (1983). A comparison of functional relationships in anorexia nervosa and phobia. In P. L. Darby, P. E. Garfinkel, D. M. Garner, & D. V. Coscina (Eds.), *Anorexia nervosa: Recent developments* (pp. 403–416). New York: Alan R. Liss.

Ben-Tovim, D. I., Hunter, M., & Crisp, A. H. (1977). Discrimination and evaluation of shape and size in anorexia nervosa: An exploratory study. *Research Communications in Psychology, Psychiatry and Behavior, 2,* 241–257.

Beumont, P. J. V., Abraham, S. E., & Simpson, K. G. (1981). The psychosexual histories of adolescent girls and young women with anorexia nervosa. *Psychological Medicine, 11,* 131–140.

Blue, R. (1979). Use of punishment in the treatment of anorexia nervosa. *Psychological Reports, 44,* 743–746.

Boskind-Lodahl, M. (1976). Cinderella's step-sisters: A feminist perspective on anorexia nervosa and bulimia. *Signs: The Journal of Women in Culture and Society, 2,* 342–356.

Bowlby, J. (1977a). The making and breaking of affectional bonds: 1. Aetiology and psychopathology in the light of attachment theory. *British Journal of Psychiatry, 130,* 201–210.

Bowlby, J. (1977b). The making and breaking of affectional bonds: 2. Some principles of psychotherapy. *British Journal of Psychiatry, 130,* 421–431.

Branch, C. H., & Eurman, L. J. (1980). Social attitudes toward patients with anorexia nervosa. *American Journal of Psychiatry, 137,* 631–632.

Bruch, H. (1961). Family transactions in eating disorders. *Comprehensive Psychiatry, 12,* 238–248.

Bruch, H. (1962). Perceptual and conceptual disturbances in anorexia nervosa. *Psychosomatic Medicine, 24,* 187–194.

Bruch, H. (1973). *Eating disorders: Obesity, anorexia nervosa and the person within.* New York: Basic Books.

Bruch, H. (1975). How to treat anorexia nervosa. *Roche Reports Frontiers Psychiatry, 5,* 1–2.

Bruch, H. (1977a). Depressive factors in adolescent eating disorders. In W. E. Fann, I. Karacan, A. D. Pokorny, & R. L. Williams (Eds.), *Phenomenology and treatment of depression* (pp. 143–152). New York: Spectrum.

Bruch, H. (1977b). Psychological antecedents of anorexia nervosa. In R. A. Vigersky (Ed.), *Anorexia nervosa* (pp. 1–10). New York: Raven Press.

Bruch, H. (1978). *The golden cage: The enigma of anorexia nervosa.* Cambridge, MA: Harvard University Press.

Bruch, H. (1979). Anorexia nervosa. *Key, 7–8,* 60.

Bruch, H. (1982). Anorexia nervosa: Therapy and theory. *American Journal of Psychiatry, 139,* 1531–1538.

Button, E. J. (1983). Construing the anorexic. In J. Adam-Webber & J. Marcuso (Eds.), *Applications of personal construct theory* (pp. 305–329). Toronto: Academic Press.

Caille, P., Abrahamsen, P., Girolami, C., & Sorbye, B. (1977). A systems theory approach to a case of anorexia nervosa. *Family Press, 16,* 455–456.

Casper, R. C. (1982). Treatment principles in anorexia nervosa. *Adolescent Psychiatry, 10,* 86–100.

Casper, R. C., & Davis, J. M. (1977). On the course of anorexia nervosa. *American Journal of Psychiatry, 134,* 974–978.

Casper, R. C., Kirschner, B., Sandstead, H. H., Jacob, R. A., & Davis, J. M. (1980). An evaluation of trace metals, vitamins and taste function in anorexia nervosa. *American Journal of Clinical Nutrition, 33,* 1801–1808.

Casper, R. C., Offer, D., & Ostrov, E. (1981). The self-image of adolescents with acute anorexia nervosa. *Journal of Pediatrics, 98,* 656–661.

Chapman, L. J., Chapman, J. P., & Raulin, M. L. (1976). Scales for physical and social anhedonia. *Journal of Abnormal Psychology, 85,* 374–382.

Cohen, A. R. (1959). Some implications of self-esteem for social influence. In C. I. Hovland & I. L. Janis (Eds.), *Personality and persuasibility* (pp. 102–120). New Haven: Yale University Press.

Cohler, B. J. (1977). The significance of the therapist's feelings in the treatment of anorexia nervosa. In S. C. Feinstein & P. L. Giovacchini (Eds.), *Adolescent psychiatry* (Vol. 5, pp. 352–384). New York: Jason Aronson.

Conrad, D. E. (1977). A starving family: An interactional view of anorexia nervosa. *Bulletin of the Menninger Clinic, 41,* 487–495.

Crisp, A. H. (1965). Clinical and therapeutic aspects of anorexia nervosa: A study of 30 cases. *Journal of Psychosomatic Research, 9,* 67–78.

Crisp, A. H. (1970). Premorbid factors in adult disorders of weight, with particular reference to primary anorexia nervosa (weight phobia): A literature review. *Journal of Psychosomatic Research, 14,* 1–22.

Crisp, A. H. (1977). The differential diagnosis of anorexia nervosa. *Proceedings of the Royal Society of Medicine, 70,* 686–690.

Crisp, A. H. (1980a). *Anorexia nervosa: Let me be.* London: Academic Press.

Crisp, A. H. (1980b). Sleep, activity and mood. *British Journal of Psychiatry, 137,* 1–7.

Crisp, A. H., & Fransella, F. (1972). Conceptual changes during recovery from anorexia nervosa. *British Journal of Medical Psychology, 45,* 395–405.

Dally, P. J., & Gomez, J. (1979). *Anorexia nervosa.* London: William Heinemann.

DuBois, F. S. (1949). Compulsion neurosis with cachexia (anorexia nervosa). *American Journal of Psychiatry, 106,* 107–115.

Ellis, A. (1962). *Reason and emotion in psychotherapy.* New York: Lyle Stuart.

Ellis, A., & Harper, R. A. (1975). *A new guide to rational living.* Englewood Cliffs, NJ: Prentice-Hall.

Fairburn, C. G. (1982). *Binge-eating and bulimia nervosa.* London: Smith, Kline & French.

Frank, J. D. (1973). *Persuasion and healing.* Baltimore: Johns Hopkins University Press.

Fransella, F., & Crisp, A. H. (1979). Comparisons of weight concepts in groups of neurotic, normal and anorexic females. *British Journal of Psychiatry, 134,* 79–86.

Frazier, S. H. (1965). Anorexia nervosa. *Diseases of the Nervous System, 26,* 155–159.

Frisch, R. E. (1983). Fatness and reproduction: Delayed menarche and amenorrhea of ballet dancers and college athletes. In P. L. Darby, P. E. Garfinkel, D. M. Garner, & D. V. Coscina (Eds.), *Anorexia nervosa: Recent developments* (pp. 343–364). New York: Alan R. Liss.

Frisch, R. E., & McArthur, J. W. (1974). Menstrual cycles: Fatness as a determinant of minimum weight necessary for their maintenance or onset. *Science, 185,* 949–951.

Galdstone, R. (1974). Mind over matter: Observations on 50 patients with anorexia nervosa. *Journal of the American Academy of Child Psychiatry, 13,* 246–263.

Garfinkel, P. E., & Garner, D. M. (1982). *Anorexia nervosa: A multidimensional perspective.* New York: Brunner/Mazel.

Garner, D. M., & Bemis, K. M. (1982). A cognitive–behavioral approach to anorexia nervosa. *Cognitive Therapy and Research, 6,* 123–150.

Garner, D. M., & Garfinkel, P. E. (1981). Body image in anorexia nervosa: Measurement, theory and clinical implications. *International Journal of Psychiatry in Medicine, 11,* 263–284.

Garner, D. M., Garfinkel, P. E., & Bemis, K. M. (1982). A multidimensional psychotherapy for anorexia nervosa. *International Journal of Eating Disorders, 1,* 3–46.

Garner, D. M., Garfinkel, P. E., & Moldofsky, H. (1978). Perceptual experiences in anorexia nervosa and obesity. *Canadian Psychiatric Association Journal, 23,* 249–263.

Garner, D. M., Garfinkel, P. E., & Olmsted, M. P. (1983). An overview of the socio-cultural factors in the development of anorexia nervosa. In P. L. Darby, P. E. Garfinkel, D. M. Garner, & D. V. Coscina (Eds.), *Anorexia nervosa: Recent developments* (pp. 65–82). New York: Alan R. Liss.

Garner, D. M., Garfinkel, P. E., Schwartz, D., & Thompson, M. (1980). Cultural expectations of thinness in women. *Psychological Reports, 47,* 483–491.

Garner, D. M., Garfinkel, P. E., Stancer, H. C., & Moldofsky, H. (1976). Body image disturbances in anorexia nervosa and obesity. *Psychosomatic Medicine, 38,* 227–236.

Garner, D. M., Olmsted, M. P., & Polivy, J. (1983a). Development and validation of a multidimensional eating disorder inventory for anorexia nervosa and bulimia. *International Journal of Eating Disorders, 2,* 15–34.

Garner, D. M., Olmsted, M. P., & Polivy, J. (1983b). The Eating Disorder Inventory: A measure of the cognitive/behavioral dimensions of anorexia nervosa and bulimia. In P. L. Darby, P. E. Garfinkel, D. M. Garner, & D. V. Coscina (Eds.), *Anorexia nervosa: Recent developments* (pp. 173–184). New York: Alan R. Liss.

Goldfried, M. R. (1971). Systematic desensitization as training in self-control. *Journal of Consulting and Clinical Psychology, 37,* 228–234.

Goldfried, M. R. (1980). Toward the delineation of therapeutic change principles. *American Psychologist, 35,* 991–999.

Goodsitt, A. (1969). Anorexia nervosa. *British Journal of Medical Psychology, 42,* 109–118.

Goodsitt, A. (1977). Narcissistic disturbances in anorexia nervosa. In S. C. Feinstein & P. L. Giovacchini (Eds.), *Adolescent psychiatry* (Vol. 5, pp. 304–312). New York: Jason Aronson.

Greiger, R. (1975). Self-concept, self-esteem and rational–emotive therapy: A brief perspective. *Rational Living, 10,* 13–17.

Groen, J. J., & Feldman-Toledano, Z. (1966). Educative treatment of patients and parents in anorexia nervosa. *British Journal of Psychiatry, 112,* 671–681.

Guidano, V. F., & Liotti, G. (1983). *Cognitive processes and emotional disorders: A structural approach to psychotherapy.* New York: Guilford Press.

Hall, C. S., & Lindsey, G. (1970). *Theories of personality.* New York: Wiley.

Hollon, S. D., & Beck, A. T. (1979). Cognitive therapy for depression. In P. C. Kendell & S. D. Hollon (Eds.), *Cognitive-behavior interventions: Theory, research and procedures* (pp. 153–204). New York: Academic Press.

Hood, J., Moore, T. E., & Garner, D. M. (1982). Locus of control as a measure of ineffectiveness in anorexia nervosa. *Journal of Consulting and Clinical Psychology, 50,* 3–13.

Horney, K. (1950). *Neurosis and human growth: The struggle towards self-realization.* New York: Norton.

Hsu, L. K. G. (1980). Outcome of anorexia nervosa: A review of the literature (1954 to 1978). *Archives of General Psychiatry, 37,* 1041–1046.

Jessner, L., & Abse, D. W. (1960). Regressive forces in anorexia nervosa. *British Journal of Medical Psychology, 33,* 301–312.

Kalucy, R. S. (1978). An approach to the therapy of anorexia nervosa. *Journal of Adolescence, 10,* 197–228.

Keys, A., Brozek, J., Henschel, A., Mickelsen, O., & Taylor, H. L. (1950). *The biology of human starvation* (2 vols.). Minneapolis: University of Minnesota Press.

King, A. (1963). Primary and secondary anorexia nervosa syndromes. *British Journal of Psychiatry, 109,* 470–479.

Lacey, J. H. (1983). The patient's attitude to food. In M. H. Lessof (Ed.), *Clinical reactions to food* (pp. 35–58). New York: Wiley.

Lefcourt, H. M. (1966). Internal versus external control of reinforcement. *Psychological Bulletin, 65,* 206–220.

Leitenberg, H., Gross, J., Peterson, J., & Rosen, J. C. (in press). Analysis of an anxiety model and the process of change during exposure plus response prevention treatment of bulimia nervosa. *Behavior Therapy.*

Lewinsohn, P. M., & Graf, H. (1973). Pleasant activities and depression. *Journal of Consulting and Clinical Psychology, 41,* 261–268.

Lucas, A. R., Duncan, J. W., & Piens, V. (1976). The treatment of anorexia nervosa. *American Journal of Psychiatry, 133,* 1034–1038.

Mahoney, M. J. (1974). *Cognitive and behavior modification.* Cambridge, MA: Ballinger.

Markus, H. (1977). Self-schemata and processing information about the self. *Journal of Personality and Social Psychology, 35,* 63–78.

Markus, H., Crane, M., Bernstein, S., & Siladi, M. (1982). Self-schemata and gender. *Journal of Personality and Social Psychology, 42,* 38–50.

Marmor, J. (1976). Common operational factors in diverse approaches to behavior change. In A. Burton (Ed.), *What makes behavior change possible* (pp. 3–12). New York: Brunner/Mazel.

Masterson, J. F. (1977). Primary anorexia nervosa in the borderline adolescent: An object-relations view. In P. Hartocollis (Ed.), *Borderline personality disorders* (pp. 475–494). New York: International Universities Press.

Meichenbaum, D. (1974). *Therapist manual for cognitive behavior modification.* Waterloo, Ontario: University of Waterloo Press.

Meyer, B. C., & Weinroth, L. A. (1957). Observations on psychological aspects of anorexia nervosa. *Psychosomatic Medicine, 19,* 389–398.

Minuchin, S., Rosman, B. L., & Baker, J. (1978). *Psychosomatic families: Anorexia nervosa in context.* Cambridge, MA: Harvard University Press.

Mogul, S. L. (1980). Asceticism in adolescence and anorexia nervosa. *Psychoanalytic Study of the Child, 35,* 155–175.

Palmer, R. L. (1979). The dietary chaos syndrome: A new useful new term? *British Journal of Medical Psychology, 52,* 187–190.

Palmer, R. L. (1980). *Anorexia nervosa: A guide for sufferers and their families.* Suffolk: Penguin.

Quaeritur. (1971). Treatment of anorexia nervosa. *Lancet, i,* 908.

Rahman, L., Richardson, H. B., & Ripley, H. S. (1939). Anorexia nervosa with psychiatric observations. *Psychosomatic Medicine, 1,* 335–365.

Rizley, R. (1978). Depression and distortion in the attribution of causality. *Journal of Abnormal Psychology, 87,* 32–48.

Rogers, T. B., Kuiper, N. A., & Kirker, W. S. (1977). Self-reference and the encoding of personal information. *Journal of Personality and Social Psychology, 35,* 667–688.

Rotter, J. B. (1966). Generalized expectancies for internal versus external control of reinforcement. *Psychological Monographs, 80*(1, Whole No. 609).

Russell, G. F. M. (1973). The management of anorexia nervosa. In Royal College of Physicians, Edinburgh (Ed.), *Proceedings of the symposium on anorexia nervosa and obesity* (pp. 43–52). Edinburgh: T. A. Constable.

Russell, G. F. M. (1979). Bulimia nervosa: An ominous variant of anorexia nervosa. *Psychological Medicine, 9,* 429–448.

Schwartz, D., & Thompson, M. (1981). Do anorexics get well?: Current research and future needs. *American Journal of Psychiatry, 138,* 319–323.

Selvini-Palazzoli, M. (1974). *Self-starvation.* London: Chaucer.

Selvini-Palazzoli, M. (1978). *Self-starvation: From individual to family therapy in the treatment of anorexia nervosa.* New York: Jason Aronson.

Slade, P. D. (1982). Towards a functional analysis of anorexia nervosa and bulimia nervosa. *British Journal of Clinical Psychology, 21,* 167–179.

Solomon, A. P., & Morrison, D. A. R. (1972). Anorexia nervosa: Dual transference therapy. *American Journal of Psychotherapy, 26,* 480–489.

Sours, J. A. (1969). Anorexia nervosa: Nosology, diagnosis, developmental patterns and power–control dynamics. In G. Caplan & S. Lebovici (Eds.), *Adolescence: Psychological perspectives* (pp. 185–212). New York: Basic Books.

Sours, J. A. (1980). *Starving to death in a sea of objects: The anorexia nervosa syndrome.* New York: Jason Aronson.

Stonehill, E., & Crisp, A. H. (1977). Psychoneurotic characteristics of patients with anorexia nervosa before and after treatment and at follow-up 4 to 7 years later. *Journal of Psychosomatic Research, 21,* 189–193.

Story, I. (1976). Caricature and impersonating the other: Observations from the psychotherapy of anorexia nervosa. *Psychiatry, 39,* 176–188.

Strober, M. (1980). Personality and symptomatological features in young, non-chronic anorexia nervosa patients. *Journal of Psychosomatic Research, 24,* 353–359.

Strober, M. (1982). Locus of control, psychopathology and weight gain in juvenile anorexia nervosa. *Journal of Abnormal Child Psychology, 10,* 97–106.

Strober, M. (1983). An empirically derived typology for anorexia nervosa. In P. L. Darby, P. E. Garfinkel, D. M. Garner, & D. V. Coscina (Eds.), *Anorexia nervosa: Recent developments* (pp. 185–198). New York: Alan R. Liss.

Swift, W. J. (1982). The long-term outcome of early onset anorexia nervosa. A critical review. *Journal of the American Academy of Child Psychiatry, 21,* 38–46.

Szyrynski, V. (1973). Anorexia nervosa and psychotherapy. *American Journal of Psychotherapy, 27,* 492–505.

Theander, S. (1970). Anorexia nervosa. *Acta Psychiatrica Scandinavica* (Suppl.), 1–194.

Ushakov, G. K. (1971). Anorexia nervosa. In J. G. Howells (Ed.), *Modern perspectives in adolescent psychiatry* (pp. 274–289). Edinburgh: Oliver & Boyd.

Vandereycken, W., & Pierloot, R. (1983). Drop-out during inpatient treatment of anorexia nervosa: A clinical study of 133 patients. In W. R. Minsel & W. Herff (Eds.), *Research on psychotherapeutic approaches* (Vol. 2, pp. 236–241). Frankfurt-Am-Main: Peter Lang.

Vertes, R. (1971). The should: A critical analysis. *Rational Living, 6,* 22–25.

Vigersky, R. A., Loriaux, D. L., Andersen, A. E., Mecklenburg, R. S., & Vaitukaitis, J. L. (1976). Delayed pituitary hormone response to LRF and TRF in patients with anorexia nervosa and with secondary amenorrhea associated with simple weight loss. *Journal of Clinical Endocrinology and Metabolism, 43,* 893–900.

Wall, J. H. (1959). Diagnosis, treatment and results in anorexia nervosa. *American Journal of Psychiatry, 115,* 997–1001.

CHAPTER SEVEN

Behavioral Management for Anorexia Nervosa

KATHERINE A. HALMI

A major criterion for the diagnosis of anorexia nervosa is "intense fear of becoming obese. This fear does not diminish as weight loss progresses." Because of this recognized clinical feature of the fear of becoming obese, anorexia nervosa has been conceptualized as a phobia. Crisp (1965a) thinks that this fear of gaining weight represents a fear of developing an adult female sexual body and thus actually represents a fear of the expected adult female sexual behavior.[1] The strength of his reasoning lies in the fact that the majority of anorexia nervosa patients develop their illness at the beginning, middle, or late stages of puberty (Halmi, Casper, Eckert, Goldberg, & Davis, 1979), and that an age-inappropriate lack of interest in sex and asexuality is a common clinical feature of anorexia nervosa (Halmi, 1974).

Anorexia nervosa has also been conceptualized as an eating phobia:

[Patients] behave rather as though they suffer from an eating phobia — eating generates anxiety, and their failure to eat represents avoidance. In other words, their cessation of eating after ingesting a very small portion of a meal (or removing it from the body by self-induced vomiting) is reinforced by anxiety reduction. From such an analysis, two treatment procedures suggest themselves: deconditioning the anxiety associated with eating and/or shaping eating behavior (and hence, weight gain) by making access to powerful reinforcers contingent on eating. (Brady & Rieger, 1972, p. 1)

Systematic desensitization (Wolpe, 1958), a behavior therapy often used for treatment of phobias, tries to inhibit the anxiety evoked by a gradual series of imagined scenes with concurrent deep muscle relaxation. Leitenberg, Agras, and Thompson (1968) succinctly state,

The assumption [with systematic desensitization] is that the desired behavioral changes in the real situation will automatically occur as anxiety dissipates in therapy sessions. The conditioning strategy, on the other hand, attempts gradually to change overt behavior, the assumption being that each behavioral step forward will reduce anxiety. In essence, the systematic desensitization strategy takes care of anxiety and lets overt behavior take care of itself, while the operant strategy takes care of behavior and lets anxiety take care of itself. (p. 212)

---

1. Throughout this chapter, anorexic patients are referred to as female.

Katherine A. Halmi. Department of Psychiatry and Eating Disorder Program, Cornell University Medical College; and The New York Hospital — Westchester Division, White Plains, New York.

Before presenting pragmatic approaches to the behavioral management of anorexia nervosa, it makes sense to review the strengths and pitfalls of previously reported
studies that have used behavioral techniques.

STUDIES USING BEHAVIORAL TECHNIQUES

There are few reports of systematic desensitization for the treatment of anorexia nervosa. Lang (1965) applied desensitization to several hierarchies of anxiety-producing
social situations associated with inability to eat in a 23-year-old patient. Assertive training was also given. Although Lang reported that the patient gained weight, he did
not report the patient's actual weight after treatment. Hallsten (1965) paired Jacob-
sonian relaxation with graded scenes of eating at home in the treatment of a 12-year-
old. However, Hallsten also restricted visits by relatives and made them contingent
upon weight gain in the treatment of this patient. There is only one case report of
desensitization used without other treatment modalities (Schnurer & Rubin, 1973).
Jacobson's relaxation technique was used to desensitize the patient to her anxiety
associated with progressive weight gain and concomitant changes in appearance. The
patient gained weight steadily throughout the treatment; however, the authors did caution that systematic desensitization alone would most likely only be effective for a
subgroup of anorexic patients.

The first explicit use of the operant conditioning paradigm in the treatment of
anorexia nervosa was reported by Bachrach, Erwin, and Mohr (1965). Initially, social
reinforcements (attention, conversation, and praise) were made contingent upon eating
behavior. Later, weight gain was enhanced by reinforcement deprivation and by making visits and activities contingent on satisfactory eating behavior. The patient's weight
stabilized at 27 kg (63 lb), and it was discovered that she had been secretly vomiting.
At this point, reinforcements were made contingent on weight gain rather than on
the ingestion of food.

Few reports on behavioral treatment of anorexia nervosa include experimental
control procedures. One such report was that of Leitenberg et al. (1968). In one patient during a "non-reinforcement phase," an extinction technique in which complaints
and comments about eating difficulties were ignored, there was no improvement in
weight gain. During the "operant" phase, ward privileges were attached to weight gain;
during this time, the patient gained steadily. In a second case, the patient counted
mouthfuls of food and charted her weight daily, with no facilitation of weight gain.
However, when she was put on a positive reinforcement regimen, she gained weight
steadily. Perhaps the most interesting part of this study was that when contingent
praise and privileges were no longer provided to the second patient for increased eating
and weight, the expected extinction effects were not observed; that is, the patient continued to eat and gain weight. The authors give two explanations. The first is that
the originally distant incentive of leaving the hospital was never withdrawn, so that
the patient knew that if she gained sufficient weight, she would be allowed to leave
the hospital. Another, equally pertinent explanation is that the patient was receiving
constant feedback from her own observations that the desired behavior was being more
closely approximated or gradually increasing in frequency. The patient thus perceived
that she was being successful. After a while, external confirmation and praise from
the therapist may have become unnecessary, and self-observed signs of progressive

improvement may have maintained the course of behavioral change. This is an important consideration to remember in all "cross-over" studies on anorexia nervosa patients.

In a series of five single-case experiments, using the technique of systematic analysis, Agras, Barlow, Chapin, Abel, and Leitenberg (1974) were able to demonstrate the strong effect on weight gain of regular feedback information regarding weight and calorie intake. Without the feedback information, positive reinforcement appeared to be relatively ineffective. In the same study, the effect of negative reinforcement (associating leaving the hospital with weight gain) was removed by contracting a patient for a 12-week stay for "research purposes," whether or not the patient gained weight. Thus, positive reinforcement was shown to contribute independently to weight gain. Pertschuk, Edwards, and Pomerleau (1978) used a multiple-baseline experimental design to show the efficacy of an operant conditioning therapy in anorexia nervosa. Each subject received the experimental behavioral treatment at a different time during hospitalization for a period of 13 days. The outcome, weight gain, was evaluated using the Rn statistic for this multiple-baseline approach. For the group, median weight gain before behavioral treatment was .09 kg (0.2 lb) per day; the weight gain per day over the 13 days of behavior therapy was .32 kg (0.7 lb).

Eight other studies reporting series of patients treated with reinforcement programs are listed in Table 7-1.

Wulliemier, Rossel, and Sinclair (1975) compared the efficacy of an operant conditioning form of behavior therapy with a program of strict isolation, appetite-stimulating drugs, and psychotherapy in 16 anorexic patients. The latter program was not free of behavioral contingencies, since it contained the strong negative reinforcer of strict isolation. In this study, the rate of weight gain was three times as great for those patients receiving an operant conditioning program.

There is only one controlled treatment study with random assignment of patients to behavior therapy or its absence (Eckert, Goldberg, Halmi, Casper, & Davis, 1979). This study was actually designed to compare the effectiveness of behavior therapy and milieu therapy, and of cyproheptadine and placebo. Thus, the patients were randomly assigned to four treatment cells: (1) behavior therapy and cyproheptadine, (2) behavior therapy and placebo, (3) no behavior therapy and cryproheptadine, and (4) no behavior therapy and placebo. The treatment program was an operant conditioning paradigm in which the patients were followed for 35 days. This study was con-

Table 7-1. Behavior Reinforcement Studies in Anorexia Nervosa

INVESTIGATOR	SAMPLE SIZE	TREATMENT
Blinder, Freeman, & Stunkard (1970)	6	Reinforcers contingent on weight gain
Brady & Rieger (1972)	16	Reinforcements contingent on weight gain
Bhanji & Thompson (1974)	11	Bed rest; reinforcers contingent on weight gain
Halmi, Powers, & Cunningham (1975)	8	Reinforcements contingent on weight gain
Kehrer (1975)	8	Token system for food eaten
Pertschuk (1977)	29	Reinforcements contingent on weight gain
Garfinkel, Moldofsky, & Garner (1977)	17	Reinforcements contingent on weight gain
Agras & Werne (1977)	19	Reinforcements contingent on weight gain

ducted in three collaborating hospitals. Across hospitals, there was no overall significant difference in weight gain between the group receiving behavior therapy and the
group receiving milieu therapy. Those receiving behavior therapy gained weight at
a rate of 4.2 kg (9 lb) per month, as compared with a rate of 3.6 kg (8 lb) per month
for milieu therapy. Several explanations were given by the authors for the lack of
efficacy of behavior therapy in this study. Constant reinforcers were used in all patients instead of individualized reinforcers, which may have been more effective. Also,
a schedule of delayed reinforcers given only every fifth day might not have been as
effective as a schedule of more immediate daily reinforcements. It is also conceivable
that various ward milieu programs and isolation, which constituted the form of treatment for those patients who did not receive behavior therapy, may have produced
a maximal possible weight gain, so that behavior therapy could not be expected to
do any better. Also, it should be remembered that the patients were assessed for only
a 35-day period. If these patients had been followed until they reached their target
weight or terminated the treatment program, there may have been a difference in the
rate of weight gain in those patients receiving behavior therapy, compared with those
who had milieu therapy.

PRESENCE OF BEHAVIORAL ELEMENTS IN "NONBEHAVORIAL" STUDIES

The studies reviewed and discussed above have been identified by their authors as
studies of behavioral treatment for anorexia nervosa. Actually, behavioral techniques
have been used in the management of anorexia nervosa in most treatment programs
over the past 100 years. In the 1970s it was fashionable to raise controversies about
the relative merit of using behavioral techniques in the treatment of anorexia nervosa. In these controversies, "behavioral" and "nonbehavioral" approaches to the management of anorexia nervosa were labeled with an ignorance of the fact that the so-
called "nonbehavioral" approaches implicitly or explicitly used behavioral techniques.
Actually, behavior therapy was used in the treatment of anorexia nervosa as early as
1873, when Gull (1874) treated anorexic[2] patients by separating them from their families
and not allowing them access to their families until they had gained weight. This is
an example of negative reinforcement, in which paradigm a patient works (eats) to
remove an unpleasant event (isolation) from the environment.

    In fact, almost all treatment programs for anorexia nervosa have used this type
of behavioral conditioning paradigm without recognizing it for what it is. For example, the nursing care program of Russell (1973) and the psychotherapy program of
Crisp (1965) both required that their patients be put to bed and not allowed out of
bed until they had obtained close to their target weight. The intensive nursing supervision that forms the majority of the so-called "nonbehavioral" hospital treatment
programs actually uses behavioral techniques. For example, Lucas, Duncan, and Piens
(1976) reported that patients ate alone under the supervision of a nurse who used firmness and patience as a direct social pressure. When progress was made, a patient moved
to the regular dining room, where she served herself under gradually diminishing staff
surveillance. It is important to look behind the labels and assess what is actually being done in a treatment program. Maxmen, Silberfarb, and Ferrell (1974) describe

---

2. I do not use the term "anorexic," but rather "anorectic." However, in the interest of achieving uniformity in the current volume, I have adopted the convention in my chapter.

a practical initial management of anorexic patients in the general hospital. In this program, if the patient fails to gain .113 kg (.25 lb) per day, she receives a high-calorie liquid feeding.

One of the early reports on the use of chlorpromazine in the treatment of anorexia nervosa (Dally & Sargent, 1960) was contaminated by the use of a strong negative reinforcement program. There is often a marked discrepancy between what therapists say and think they are doing and what is actually being done in a treatment program. All hospital treatment programs have an implicit form of negative reinforcement: In order to leave the hospital, the patients must eat. Behavioral techniques are also an integral part of most family therapy programs for anorexia nervosa (Liebman, Minuchin, & Baker, 1974).

It is possible to draw some clinical impressions from the various treatment studies reported in the literature; however, it is not meaningful to do a comparison of these studies because of serious methodological problems. One of the problems is that there are large numbers of variables affecting the outcome of anorexia nervosa, irrespective of the type of treatment. Some of these predictors of outcome are age at onset of illness, presence of vomiting, number of previous treatment failures, and degree of laxative abuse (Halmi, Brodland, & Loney, 1973). Thus, a significant difference in the samples being treated would, in and of itself, affect outcome.

Few patients are treated solely with behavior therapy, and no other forms of personal or family counseling and few behavioral programs that occur within the context of a hospital setting continue as a controlled behavior therapy program once a patient is discharged from the hospital. A number of treatment modalities are administered to anorexic patients in outpatient programs, and these undoubtedly will influence the long-term outcomes of the patients. In summary, it is probably not possible to assess the effectiveness of the long-term outcome of a behavior therapy program. To make matters more difficult, the criteria for satisfactory outcome can vary considerably among investigators; different standards of judgment can also be applied to the same criteria, further complicating a comparison of studies in the literature. Patients enter a treatment program at different admission weights (best described as percentages below ideal weights), and they are treated for different periods of time. Ideal weights are calculated differently by different investigators. When all these necessary variables are controlled for, the sample size is often too small to expect any significant difference in the controlled treatment studies of anorexic patients.

BEHAVIORAL MANAGEMENT OF ANOREXIA NERVOSA

The behavioral management of anorexia nervosa can now be discussed in pragmatic clinical terms in the context of the knowledge obtained from previous studies. Behavioral management is most obviously needed and is easily done in the context of a hospital treatment program. At this point it is worthwhile to point out that there has been no randomized control treatment study evaluating or comparing outpatient treatment with a hospital treatment program for anorexia nervosa. The initial decision of whether the patient should be treated as an outpatient or enter a hospital has to be made. It is very likely that outpatient therapy will be effective for the anorexic patient who has been ill for less than 4 months, is not bingeing and vomiting, and has parents who are willing to cooperate in family therapy. At the other extreme, the patient who has previous treatment failures, has been ill for longer than a year, and is engaging in purging behavior should enter a hospital treatment program. There are four general treatment goals for an anorexic patient:

1. To have the patient return to a normal medical condition; this means that the patient must gain weight to a normal level and then maintain it, and also must stop purging behavior.
2. To have the patient resume normal eating patterns.
3. To assess and treat relevant psychological issues.
4. To counsel the anorexic's family appropriately, with emphasis on the family's effect on maintaining the anorexic state of the patient, and to assist the family in developing methods to promote the normal functioning of the patient.

Behavioral management is especially useful for the first two goals, but to some degree it can also be used to accomplish the third and fourth goals.

Hospital Treatment Program

In a hospital treatment program, the immediate aim of treatment should be to restore the patient's nutritional state to normal. Emaciation itself can cause irritability, depression, preoccupation with food, and sleep disturbance (Keys, Brozek, Henschel, Mickelsen, & Taylor, 1950). It is difficult to accomplish a behavioral change with psychotherapy in an emaciated patient who is suffering the psychological effects of starvation. The importance of obtaining a normal medical state should not be underestimated in anorexic patients. In a recent follow-up study, Morgan and Russell (1975) showed that the closer the anorexic patient was to a normal weight, the better were her scores on psychiatric, sexual, and socioeconomic adjustment scales.

For the patients who are hospitalized, daily weight should be measured every morning after the patient has voided and before the first feeding. The effectiveness of daily feedback information of weight has been demonstrated by Agras *et al.* (1974). In an operant conditioning program, weight gain should be reinforced, rather than eating behavior, until the patient is able to maintain a normal weight. The reason for this is that the patient can eat a normal-sized meal, earn her reward, and then induce vomiting; hence, she may never change her weight status. Making positive reinforcements contingent only on weight gain is helpful in reducing staff–patient arguments and stressful interactions over how and what the patient is eating, since weight is an objective measure. An individual behavioral assessment should be made on all patients in order to determine and implement individualized reinforcers. A combination of daily reinforcements with more delayed reinforcements will provide the most effective behavior therapy program. The anorexic behaviors needing correction are defined through observation and discussion with the patient.

In addition to inducing weight gain effectively, behavior therapy can be used to stop vomiting. A response prevention technique is used to stop vomiting. The most commonly used response prevention is to have the patient sit in a day room under the staff's supervision for 1 or 2 hours after every meal. This constant supervision inhibits most patients from vomiting. Another technique is to have the patient use only a chair commode in her room, and not give her access to flush toilets. The patient is instructed that if she vomits she will have to vomit into the commode in her room, and she will have to clean it out herself. This effectively stops vomiting in most patients.

At the beginning of the program, a goal or target weight should be set for the patient. This should be a medical decision and should be a weight high enough to assure the regaining of menses. This weight figure could be obtained from the Frisch and McArthur (1974) weight scales. For some patients the overwhelming negative reinforcement of hospitalization and separation from their families, with the expectation that they cannot leave the hospital until they reach their target weight, is sufficient for the induction of a progressive weight gain. Other patients will need to have an operant conditioning form of behavior therapy. In this type of program, a patient is expected to gain a specific amount of weight each day and then is reinforced by positive reinforcements contingent on the weight gain. The positive reinforcements are usually access to an increasing number of activities and social events. There are some patients, however, who are socially withdrawn and prefer to isolate themselves in their rooms; for these patients, it is better to make access to their rooms contingent on weight gain.

It is important to remember that a behavioral program has to be suited not only to the individual patient, but also to the environment in which the patient is being treated. Thus a behavioral program for a pediatric ward would obviously be different from a behavioral program in a specialized unit for eating disorders in a psychiatric hospital. The specifics described for a program in one setting may not be appropriate at all for another environment. The behavioral management in the medical restoration phase can occur concomitantly with individual psychotherapy and with family counseling. An important factor in the successful behavioral management of anorexic patients is the cooperation of the entire staff. Staff cohesiveness is necessary, especially with the more severely ill patients. A meeting of all staff members involved in the treatment of the eating-disordered patients should occur at a minimum of once a week and preferably two to three times a week. In some settings, there is an advantage to separating the behavioral management of the patient from the psychotherapy. This frees the psychotherapist to deal solely with the psychological issues and to refer the issues of medical and behavioral management to the designated staff (usually the doctors and nurses).

When the patients reach their goal weight, many will have anxiety over being able to maintain that weight. At this time, the behavioral program should change its form: For example, the patients may have increased activities and privileges every day that their weight is within a normal range, but on days when weight falls below that range, they could be restricted to the hospital ward. When the patient reaches her goal weight, it is best to emphasize that she stay within a 2-kg (5-lb) weight range, since this will reflect more accurately the weight maintenance of normal people and will de-emphasize preoccupation with a single weight. During the weight maintenance phase, increasing external control of the diet should be given to the patient. If external controls have been applied (food has been given on trays), then the patient must gradually be introduced to choosing her own foods. After this, she can practice eating in situations alone, with family members at home, and in restaurants before she is actually discharged from the hospital. Sometimes a 2- to 3-week maintenance period is necessary in order to provide a gradual transition to outpatient status. When it is clear that the patient is maintaining her weight, it is often wise to encourage passes home for increasingly longer intervals. The problems involved with transition to the home environment can be identified and addressed before the patient is discharged. It is the clinical opinion of many investigators that patients are at less risk for relapse if they are discharged from a hospital program after they are able to maintain their weight and eat normally. However, there are no controlled studies to prove this.

Aftercare Program

In the aftercare program, it is wise to continue a combined program of behavioral management, personal psychotherapy, and family counseling. Weight maintenance in the aftercare program is best managed with a behavioral contract. For example, for a high-school student who has been physically active, it is often effective to have her weighed by the school nurse every Monday and, on the Mondays that she is below her normal weight, to forbid her to participate in any school sports or in gym classes for that week. (Obviously, for those patients who are not interested in physical activity, another type of contract will have to be arranged.) Behavioral contracts for weight maintenance must also be individualized.

A response prevention technique has already been described for managing the bingeing and purging behaviors of anorexic patients in the hospital. Other behavioral techniques can be used for bingeing and purging in the hospital and then extended to the aftercare program. For example, bulimic anorexic patients can devise a list of alternative behaviors to binge eating. They can practice these behaviors on passes from the hospital, so that when they are discharged they have experience in testing and putting into effect their alternative behaviors. During the hospital phase of treatment, all anorexic patients are placed on a supervised exercising program. This is a program that they can effectively continue on an outpatient basis. The binge-eating anorexic patients often regard exercising as anxiety-relieving and will find it an effective substitute for binge eating. It is important that the anorexic patients learn to exercise in moderation.

Outpatient behavioral programs for anorexia nervosa are always more difficult to enforce and require more ingenuity on the part of the therapist. The same principles of behavioral management for the inpatient treatment program are used in the outpatient treatment programs. It is especially important that the behavioral management be individualized in outpatient therapy. If a behavioral program cannot be enforced, it is useless. Thus one must devise a program that has a reasonable chance of working with the patient and her family. In an outpatient program, it is necessary to have the same treatment goals for the anorexic patient that have been described in the inpatient program. The patient must be restored to a normal medical condition, and in the outpatient program a specific period of time should be allocated for this goal. A reasonable rate of weight gain for an outpatient is 0.5 kg (1 lb) a week. If the patient has not been restored to a normal medical condition by 6 to 8 months, hospitalization should be seriously considered. Response prevention techniques can be used in outpatient treatment to reduce the patient's bingeing and vomiting or purging behavior. Behavioral management techniques may be used in either individual or group outpatient programs.

USE OF MEDICATION

Behavior therapy is frequently combined with medication in the treatment of anorexia nervosa. Almost all open drug trials are contaminated with the concomitant use
of some type of behavioral contingency program. One of the first drugs used in the
treatment of anorexia nervosa was the dopamine blocker chlorpromazine (Crisp, 1965b;
Dally & Sargent, 1960). In both studies the patients were placed on bed rest until they
had gained close to their target weight.

Because anorexia nervosa patients have many depressive symptoms, such as sleep
disturbance, irritability, difficulty concentrating, and (in some) an admission to feeling depressed and frequent crying spells, a variety of antidepressant medications have
been used in the treatment of anorexia nervosa patients. In a randomized double-blind
controlled study of clomipramine (50 mg just before sleep) in 16 anorexic patients,
there was no main effect of the drug on weight gain. It is of interest to note that all
patients reached their target weight in this study, and there was no difference in the
rate of weight gain between the clomipramine group and the placebo group (Lacey
& Crisp, 1980). This study was performed on hospitalized anorexics who were put on
bed rest and informed that they would stay in bed until they obtained their target
weight. It is very likely that the drug could not have any additive effect over this very
strong negative contingency.

There is only one controlled study assessing the efficacy of combining behavior
therapy with medication. This was a multicenter study of 105 anorexic patients who
were randomly assigned to cyproheptadine or placebo and behavior therapy or no
behavior therapy. (Eckert et al., 1979). Thus, as described earlier, there were four
treatment groups in this study: (1) cyproheptadine and behavior therapy, (2) cyproheptadine and no behavior therapy, (3) placebo and behavior therapy, and (4) placebo
and no behavior therapy. Although a subgroup was identified that responded preferentially to cyproheptadine with increased weight gain, and another subgroup was identified that responded preferentially to behavior therapy with increased weight gain, there
was no subgroup of patients that responded to the combination of behavior therapy
and cyproheptadine with increased weight gain. Nor did the patients assigned to the
combination of the two therapies have a greater weight gain, compared to the other
three treatment groups. The fact that there was no main effect for any type of therapy
in this study, but only the identification of certain subgroups that responded preferentially to the cyproheptadine or to the behavior therapy, is most likely due to the enormous heterogeneity of patients that participated in this study. Even though they all
had the diagnosis of anorexia nervosa, there was considerable variation in the population with respect to the severity of the disorder. Perhaps there is a group of anorexic
patients that responds preferentially to the combination of behavior therapy and a
medication. This group probably remains unidentified because the correct variables
have not been analyzed. An area for future research would be to continue to try to
identify more homogenous subgroups that will respond preferentially to a treatment.

In the severely ill anorexic patient, it often makes good clinical sense to combine
medication with behavior therapy. In the emaciation phase of anorexia nervosa, drugs
will affect such anorexic symptoms as decreased gastric emptying time, hyperactivity,
mood changes, obsessionality, sleep disturbance, and some anorexic attitudes. The
"fear of getting fat" may respond best to the exposure to the fear of weight gain by
a behavioral program that requires patients to gain weight. It has been shown that

exposure to weight gain is actually associated with the reduction of the fear of gaining weight and is also associated with general psychological improvement (Morgan & Russell, 1975). After patients regain a normal weight, they must be reassessed for the need to continue medication along with behavioral techniques.

In order to describe more specifically the usefulness of integrating behavior therapy with outpatient, inpatient programs and medication, a typical case of anorexia nervosa is presented here.

Case History

Heidi is a 17-year-old girl who lives with her parents and is a senior in high school. She was first referred for a diagnostic consultation 6 months after she began dieting in order to be more attractive. Heidi is 170 cm (5 ft 7 in) tall and weighed 61 kg (135 lb) before dieting. The lowest acceptable weight range for a woman at this height would be between 54.5 and 57 kg (120 and 128 lb). Heidi gradually lost weight to a low of 40.5 kg (90 lb), which she weighed 2 weeks prior to the consultation. She had never induced vomiting or abused laxatives, but she did exercise a great deal. She started menstruating at the age of 14, and her last period occurred just at the time she started dieting. She emphatically stated that she would like to weigh about 50 kg (110 lb) and not one pound over that. At the time Heidi's dieting behavior began, she also began to have difficulties in school. She started to skip classes and go out with friends. After a few months, however, she began to have arguments and altercations with her friends. Then she began to stay at home; for several months prior to the consultation, she had isolated herself from her peer group and stayed in the house most of the day. She became very interested in cooking and started collecting recipes and cooking for her family. She admitted to feeling depressed and to having occasional crying spells. About 2 months before Heidi began to diet seriously, she broke up with her boyfriend, who had told her she was too fat and should lose weight.

PAST HISTORY

Heidi was the product of a full-term pregnancy with a birth weight of 3.5 kg (8 lb 8 oz). She had no obvious problems until about eighth grade. She was described as being very shy and very slow at getting involved with things. In eighth grade her school marks went down considerably, from average to below average, and remained low since that time. IQ testing showed her to be within an average range.

FAMILY HISTORY

The patient's mother, who is of normal weight and good health, works as a cleaning lady in a women's locker room at a golf club. Her father works with a construction company. He had a heart attack 2 years ago, smokes a lot, and is mildly overweight. A brother who is 1 year older than the patient repeated first grade; he has a learning disability and has been in special classes all through school. Heidi had an older brother who died in a car accident when she was 16. She was very close to this brother and was depressed for a long time after his death.

TREATMENT

Heidi was mildly depressed and preoccupied with the fear of being fat. She stated that she had an obsession with counting calories and was not able to stop her dieting behavior. Heidi was referred to an experienced therapist in her area for outpatient therapy. In outpatient therapy,

Heidi continued to deny any difficulties in the family. Heidi was completely uninterested in treatment. An attempt was made to set up a variety of behavioral contracts, but Heidi refused to cooperate with any of them. After 10 sessions she refused to see the therapist, stating that she would gain her weight back alone. She then began a pattern of eating nothing during the day and then, late at night, eating 10 to 15 pieces of Kentucky Fried Chicken with an extensive amount of salt over about a 2-hour period. Eventually she stayed up through the night, going to sleep at 5:30 A.M. and then sleeping until about 1 or 2 P.M. For a short period, Heidi tried to stop this pattern and attended school all day to make up credits; however, her eating difficulties prevailed, and she eventually stopped going to school entirely.

One year after the initial consultation, Heidi reluctantly came into the hospital for treatment. After the hospitalization, it became obvious that Heidi's mother had a severe problem with alcohol abuse and that there was a strong history of alcoholism and depression in her mother's family. During the first few days after hospitalization, Heidi was very upset and wanted to leave the hospital; however, when her parents supported the continued hospitalization, she became less agitated and more cooperative. During the first few days of hospitalization, she was given a "free diet," and her eating behavior was observed. She was assigned a target weight of 55 kg (122 lb), with the expectation that she would keep her weight within a range between 54.5 and 56.5 kg (120 and 125 lb). Her weight on admission was 40.5 kg (90 lb). She was placed on a liquid formula, Sustacal, with enough calories to maintain her weight plus 50% for activity. She was given this in six equal feedings throughout the day. For the first 15 days of the treatment program, her only form of nutrition was the Sustacal. The amount of calories was increased every 5 days until she reached her target weight.

Heidi needed a great deal of encouragement to interact with her peers. One week after hospital admission, she started attending the hospital school. Because of her desire to isolate herself, a program was put into effect that allowed Heidi access to her room for several hours each day if she gained weight on that day. She gradually became more involved with her peers and her school program, and by the time she reached her target weight was able to eat fairly normally. Initially she was given all of her food on trays; after she demonstrated she could maintain her target weight, the trays were removed, and she was able to choose her own diet.

During individual sessions, it became obvious that the patient had to stay at home to take care of her alcoholic mother. The mother's alcoholism was discussed in the family therapy sessions, and the mother entered a treatment program. Heidi eventually requested to be removed from her single room into a four-bed girls' dorm room on the unit. After a series of visits to her family, Heidi was discharged from the hospital program and transferred to an outpatient therapy program. She is having continued individual psychotherapy, and the family is continuing in family therapy. Heidi also signed a behavioral contract, which she helped design with her outpatient therapist. In this contract she agreed to go to her family doctor's office to be weighed once a week. She agreed to eat three meals a day and not to eat at night. Every week that she had been able to maintain her weight within a normal weight range, she would reward herself by buying some new painting or drawing materials. The family agreed that Heidi could not be responsible for her mother's care. Alternative care programs were set up for the mother.

Behavioral management is an integral part of all effective treatment programs for anorexia nervosa. It is important to look behind the "labels" of treatment programs and carefully analyze what exactly is being done. Often the therapist will designate certain facets of the treatment program as the important factors in establishing a change in the patient, when in fact the actual features contributing to a change in behavior are totally unrecognized by the therapist. This phenomenon is certainly the case with regard to the behavioral management of anorexia nervosa. The challenge to the clinician is to find the right combination of behavioral techniques, personal psychotherapy, and family counseling for the individual patient. There are a great variety of techniques included under the umbrella of behavioral management, in addition to the variety of techniques in personal psychotherapy and family therapy. The research task of identifying subgroups of patients that will respond preferentially to specific therapy combinations is formidable.

REFERENCES

Agras, S., Barlow, D.H., Chapin, H. N., Abel, G., & Leitenberg, H. (1974). Behavior modification of anorexia nervosa. *Archives of General Psychiatry, 30*, 279–286.

Agras, S., & Werne, J. (1977). Behavior modification in anorexia nervosa. In R. A. Vigersky (Ed.), *Anorexia nervosa* (pp. 291–304). New York: Raven Press.

Bachrach, A. J., Erwin, W. J., & Mohr, P. J. (1965). The control of eating behavior in an anorexic by operant conditioning techniques. In L. Ullmann & L. Krasner (Eds.), *Case studies in behavior modification* (pp. 153–163). New York: Holt, Rinehart & Winston.

Bhanji, S., & Thompson, J. (1974). Operant conditioning in the treatment of anorexia nervosa: A review and retrospective study of 11 cases. *British Journal of Psychiatry, 124*, 166–173.

Blinder, B. J., Freeman, D. M., & Stunkard, A. J. (1970). Behavior therapy of anorexia nervosa: Effectiveness of activity as a reinforcer of weight gain. *American Journal of Psychiatry, 126*, 1093–1098.

Brady, J. B. P., & Rieger, W. (1972). Behavior treatment of anorexia nervosa. In *Proceedings of the International Symposium on Behavior Modification* (pp. 1–19). New York: Appleton-Century-Crofts.

Crisp, A. H. (1965a). Some aspects of evolution, presentation and follow-up of anorexia nervosa. *Proceedings of the Royal Society of Medicine, 58*, 814–820.

Crisp, A. H. (1965b). A treatment regimen for anorexia nervosa. *British Journal of Psychiatry, 112*, 505–510.

Dally, P. J., & Sargent, W. (1960). A new treatment of anorexia nervosa. *British Medical Journal, i*, 1770–1778.

Eckert, E. D., Goldberg, S. C., Halmi, K. A., Casper, R. C., & Davis, J. M. (1979). Behavior therapy and anorexia nervosa. *British Journal of Psychiatry, 134*, 55–59.

Frisch, R. E., & McArthur, J. W. (1974). Menstrual cycles: Fatness as a determinant of minimum weight for height necessary for their maintenance or onset. *Science, 185*, 949–951.

Garfinkel, P. E., Moldofsky, H., & Garner, D. M. (1977). The outcome of anorexia nervosa: Significance of clinical features, body image and behavior modification. In R. A. Vigersky (Ed.), *Anorexia nervosa* (pp. 315–330). New York: Raven Press.

Gull, W. W. (1874). Anorexia nervosa (apepsia hysterica, anorexia hysterica). *Transactions of the Clinical Society of London, 7*, 22–28.

Halmi, K. A. (1974). Anorexia nervosa: Demographic and clinical features in 94 cases. *Psychosomatic Medicine, 36*, 18–26.

Halmi, K. A., Brodland, G., & Loney, J. (1973). Prognosis in anorexia nervosa. *Annals of Internal Medicine, 78*, 907–909.

Halmi, K. A., Casper, R. C., Eckert, E. D., Goldberg, S. C., & Davis, J. M. (1979). Unique features associated with age of onset of anorexia nervosa. *Psychiatry Research, 1*, 209–215.

Halmi, K. A., Powers, P., & Cunningham, S. (1975). Treatment of anorexia nervosa with behavior modification. *Archives of General Psychiatry, 32*, 92–96.

Hallsten, E. A. (1965). Adolescent anorexia nervosa treated by desensitization. *Behaviour Research and Therapy, 3*, 87–91.

Kehrer, H. E. (1975). Behandlung der Anorexia Nervosa mit Verhaltenstherapie. *Medizich Klinik, 70*, 427–432.

Keys, A., Brozek, J., Henschel, A., Mickelsen, O., & Taylor, H. L. (1950). *The biology of human starvation* (2 vols.). Minneapolis: University of Minnesota Press.

Lacey, J. H., & Crisp, A. H. (1980). Hunger, food intake and weight: The impact of clomipramine on a re-feeding anorexia nervosa population. *Postgraduate Medical Journal, 56*, 79–85.

Lang, P. J. (1965). Behavior therapy with a case of anorexia nervosa. In L. P. Ullmann & L. Krasner (Eds.), *Case studies in behavior modification* (pp. 217–221). New York: Holt, Rinehart & Winston.

Leitenberg, H., Agras, W. S., & Thompson, L. E. (1968). A sequential analysis of the effect of selective positive reinforcement in modifying anorexia nervosa. *Behaviour Research and Therapy, 6*, 211–218.

Liebman, R., Minuchin, S., & Baker, L. (1974). An integrated treatment program for anorexia nervosa. *American Journal of Psychiatry, 131*, 432–436.

Lucas, A. R., Duncan, J. W., & Piens, V. (1976). The treatment of anorexia nervosa. *American Journal of Psychiatry, 133,* 1034–1038.

Maxmen, J. S., Silberfarb, P. M., & Ferrell, R. B. (1974). Anorexia nervosa: Practical initial management in a general hospital. *Journal of the American Medical Association, 229,* 801–805.

Morgan, H. G., & Russell, G. F. M. (1975). Value of family background and clinical features as predictors of long-term outcome in anorexia nervosa: Four year follow-up study of 41 patients. *Psychological Medicine, 5,* 355–371.

Pertschuk, M. J. (1977). Behavior therapy: Extended follow-up. In R. A. Vigersky (Ed.), *Anorexia nervosa* (pp. 305–314). New York: Raven Press.

Pertschuk, M. J., Edwards, N., & Pomerleau, O. F. (1978). A multiple baseline approach to behavioural intervention in anorexia nervosa. *Behaviour Research and Therapy, 9,* 368–376.

Russell, G. F. M. (1973). The management of anorexia nervosa. In Royal College of Physicians, Edinburgh (Ed.), *Proceedings of the symposium on anorexia nervosa and obesity* (pp. 44–52). Edinburgh: T. A. Constable.

Schnurer, A. T., & Rubin, R. A. (1973). Systematic desensitization of anorexia nervosa seen as a weight phobia. *Journal of Behavior Therapy and Experimental Psychiatry, 4,* 149–153.

Wolpe, J. (1958). *Psychotherapy by reciprocal inhibition.* Stanford, CA: Stanford University Press.

Wulliemier, F., Rossel, F., & Sinclair, K. (1975). La therapie comportementale de l'anorexie nerveuse. *Journal of Psychosomatic Research, 19,* 267–272.

CHAPTER EIGHT

Cognitive–Behavioral Treatment for Bulimia

CHRISTOPHER G. FAIRBURN

INTRODUCTION

The recent emergence of bulimia as a relatively distinct clinical entity raises many intriguing issues. From the practical standpoint, there are two major unanswered questions. The first concerns the prevalence of the disorder and the extent to which it constitutes a source of psychiatric morbidity. Several epidemiological studies have been conducted, but without exception these have had significant methodological limitations (Fairburn, 1983a). For example, all the studies have been cross-sectional in design. Thus it has not been possible to distinguish transitory behavioral and attitudinal abnormalities from more enduring problems. Furthermore, most studies have failed to examine the clinical significance of their findings, yet it cannot be assumed that all those whose eating habits or attitudes are abnormal in the statistical sense necessarily view them as "a problem," or indeed wish to receive help.

The second question of practical importance concerns the treatment of bulimia. Several different psychological and pharmacological approaches have been advocated, but there have been no satisfactory treatment studies, and it is not known whether any intervention influences the long-term outcome. The consensus is that this disorder is difficult to treat (Fairburn, 1982; Russell, 1979; Stunkard, 1980). The present chapter is concerned with a cognitive–behavioral treatment approach.

RATIONALE OF THE COGNITIVE-BEHAVIORAL APPROACH

One of the most striking features of both bulimia and anorexia nervosa is the intensity and prominence of these patients' dysfunctional beliefs and values concerning their shape and weight. This psychopathology is peculiar to these disorders and their variants, and has been variously characterized as a "morbid fear of fatness" (Russell, 1979), a "pursuit of thinness" (Bruch, 1973), or a "weight phobia" (Crisp, 1967). Given the presence of this specific psychopathology, most other aspects of these conditions become intelligible. In bulimia, the extreme dieting, the vomiting and laxative abuse, the preoccupation with food and eating, the sensitivity to changes in shape and weight, and the frequent weighing or total avoidance of weighing are all comprehensible, once it has been appreciated that these patients believe that their shape and weight are of

Christopher G. Fairburn. Department of Psychiatry, University of Oxford, Warneford Hospital, Oxford, England.

fundamental importance and that both must be kept under strict control. Even the apparently paradoxical binge eating can be understood in cognitive terms, since it seems that it may represent a secondary response to extreme dietary restraint (Polivy, Herman, Olmsted, & Jazwinski, 1984). Thus, rather than being simply symptomatic of bulimia, these beliefs and values appear to be of primary importance in the maintenance of the condition. It is therefore likely that change in this specific psychopathology is a prerequisite for full recovery (Fairburn, 1983a). For this reason, a cognitive–behavioral treatment for bulimia has been developed that is designed to produce such cognitive change (Fairburn, 1981, 1983a); for similar reasons, there has been interest in the cognitive–behavioral treatment of anorexia nervosa (Garner & Bemis, 1982; Chapter 6, this volume).

THE EFFECTIVENESS OF THE COGNITIVE–BEHAVIORAL APPROACH

Most patients with bulimia benefit from this form of cognitive-behavior therapy. Preliminary findings on 11 patients were reported in 1981, and the principal data are shown in Table 8-1 (Fairburn, 1981). These patients' mean length of history of binge eating and self-induced vomiting was 3.9 years ($SD = 3.0$ years), and at presentation they vomited on average three times daily. By the end of treatment nine patients had reduced their frequency of binge eating and vomiting to less than once a month, and this reduction was maintained in the seven cases for whom follow-up data were available (mean length of follow-up = 9.6 months). The changes in eating habits were accompanied by a decrease in levels of anxiety and depression and a lessening in the intensity of the dysfunctional attitudes concerning shape and weight. There were no significant changes in body weight. Subsequent experience with over 50 patients has confirmed that the majority of patients do indeed benefit from this cognitive-behavioral approach, with most remaining well and requiring no further treatment.

THE RELEVANT PATIENT GROUP

The form of treatment described in this chapter is designed to suit patients of the type seen by psychiatrists and clinical psychologists in Britain.[1] The clinical features of such patients have been described both in general terms (Fairburn, 1983b; Russell, 1979) and using standardized assessment procedures (Fairburn & Cooper, 1984a). Table 8-2 summarizes the principal clinical characteristics of a representative patient sample, together with comparable data from two large community studies of bulimia nervosa and from a study of healthy young adult women. It can be seen from the table that the subjects in the large community studies, most of whom wished to receive treatment, closely resemble the patient population.

---

1. In Britain, the syndrome equivalent to "bulimia" as defined in the *Diagnostic and Statistical Manual of Mental Disorders*, third edition (DSM-III; American Psychiatric Association, 1980), is termed "bulimia nervosa" (Russell, 1979). The latter may be regarded as a subtype of DSM-III bulimia in which binge eating is accompanied by self-induced vomiting or laxative abuse and abnormal attitudes to body shape and weight. In practice, virtually all patients who meet the diagnostic criteria for bulimia nervosa also fulfill the criteria for DSM-III bulimia.

Table 8-1. Principal Clinical Data on 11 Patients with Bulimia Nervosa Who Received Cognitive-Behavior Therapy

| PATIENT | TREATMENT DURATION (MONTHS) | FREQUENCY OF BINGE EATING AND VOMITING | | | LENGTH OF FOLLOW-UP (MONTHS) | WEIGHT (% MPMW[a]) | | |
		ONSET BEHAVIORAL TREATMENT (PER WEEK)	TERMINATION BEHAVIORAL TREATMENT (PER MONTH)	REDUCTION MAINTAINED AT FOLLOW-UP		ONSET BEHAVIORAL TREATMENT	TERMINATION BEHAVIORAL TREATMENT	FOLLOW-UP
1	6	28	0	Yes	12	113	110	113
2	3[b]	7	0	Yes	12	111	100	104
3	12	>140	>150	No	12	100	104	104
4	7	21	2	Yes	12	89	90	95
5	5	10	0	Yes	7	94	99	92
6	7	7	0	Yes	12	107	101	100
7	5	7	0	Yes	8	90	93	90
8	8	12	0	Yes	12	88	94	95
9	8	14	0	?	–	93	93	?
10	6	7	0	Yes	4	90	97	91
11	6	5	0	?	–	101	104	?
Mean	7[c]					97.8	98.7	98.2

Note. From "A Cognitive Behavioral Approach to the Management of Bulimia" by C. G. Fairburn, 1981, *Psychological Medicine, 11*, 707–711. Reprinted by permission.

[a]Matched population mean weight.

[b]Patient moved home after 3 months in treatment.

[c]Excluding Patient 2.

Table 8-2. Eating Habits, Weight History, and Psychiatric State of Bulimia Nervosa Cases and a Comparison Group of Young Adult Women

	BULIMIA NERVOSA CASES			COMPARISON GROUP OF YOUNG ADULT WOMEN[d] (n = 369)
	PATIENTS[a] (n = 35)	COMMUNITY SAMPLE 1[b] (n = 499)	COMMUNITY SAMPLE 2[c] (n = 579)	
Age in years (mean and SD)	23.5 (±4.4)	23.8 (±5.5)	28.1 (±7.4)	24.1 (±5.5)
Frequency of binge eating:				
At least daily (%)	48.6	27.2	32.9	.5
>weekly, <daily (%)	51.4	32.6	38.3	6.8
Age at onset of binge eating in years (mean and SD)	19.7 (±4.2)	18.4 (±4.5)	20.2 (±6.4)	–
Frequency of self-induced vomiting:				
At least daily (%)	74.3	56.1	47.0	.5
>weekly, <daily (%)	25.7	17.5	23.3	.5
Age at onset of vomiting in years (mean and SD)	20.0 (±3.7)	19.3 (±4.6)	22.1 (±6.7)	–
Laxative use (%)	31.4	18.8	42.3	4.9
Exercise as weight control (%)	28.6	61.3	30.0	7.3
Present weight (mean and SD)[e]	97.3 (±10.3)	97.6 (±11.2)	104.2 (±19.8)	98.0 (±10.3)
Highest weight since menarche (mean and SD)[e]	115.8 (±15.3)	116.2 (±15.4)	127.8 (±25.9)	108.3 (±14.0)
Lowest weight since menarche (mean and SD)[e]	84.3 (±12.4)	86.7 (±10.1)	88.8 (±14.6)	90.3 (±9.8)
Desired weight (mean and SD)[e]	89.4 (±6.5)	88.0 (±7.0)	88.2 (±7.9)	91.5 (±6.3)
EAT score (mean and SD)[f]	48.7 (±16.1)	49.8 (±16.3)	50.7 (+16.6)	11.4 (±11.2)
GHQ score (mean and SD)[g]	14.6 (±8.1)	10.1 (±7.9)	12.0 (±7.9)	4.4 (±6.0)

[a]Fairburn & Cooper (1984a).

[b]Fairburn & Cooper (1982).

[c]Fairburn & Cooper (in press).

[d]Cooper & Fairburn (1983).

[e]Percentage of matched population mean weight.

[f]Eating Attitudes Test (Garner & Garfinkel, 1979).

[g]General Health Questionnaire (Goldberg & Hillier, 1979).

Such patients have grossly abnormal attitudes to their shape and weight, together with markedly disturbed eating habits. Often their eating problem has been present for many years, with few, if any, periods of remission. On the Eating Attitudes Test, a global index of disturbed eating habits and abnormal attitudes to food, eating, shape, and weight (Garner & Garfinkel, 1979), their mean score is similar to that of patients with anorexia nervosa. Despite this, their body weight usually lies within the normal range, although a history of weight disturbance is common. With regard to nonspecific psychopathology, they exhibit a wide range of psychiatric symptomatology (see Table 8-3), with over 75% being rated as significantly psychiatrically disturbed on the Present State Examination (Wing, Cooper, & Sartorius, 1974). The most prominent features are affective in character, with these patients having a level of depressive symptoma-

Table 8-3. Frequency of Present State Examination Symptoms among Patients with Bulimia Nervosa

SYMPTOM	%	SYMPTOM	%
Pathological guilt	94.3	Premenstrual exacerbation	40.0
Worrying	94.3	Free-floating autonomic anxiety	37.1
Poor concentration	80.0	Guilty ideas of reference	34.3
Obsessional ideas and rumination	80.0	Delayed sleep	34.3
Nervous tension	80.0	Early waking	34.3
Tiredness	77.1	Panic attacks	31.4
Self-depreciation	74.3	Loss of libido	31.4
Irritabilility	74.3	Specific phobias	28.6
Situational autonomic anxiety	71.4	Expansive mood	28.6
Subjective anergia and retardation	71.4	Tension pains	28.6
Lack of self-confidence with people	65.7	Subjective ideomotor pressure	25.7
Depressed mood	62.9	Suicidal plans or acts	17.1
Social withdrawal	62.9	Derealization	11.4
Hopelessness	60.0	Grandiose ideas and actions	8.6
Inefficient thinking	60.0	Anxious foreboding with autonomic accompaniments	5.7
Restlessness and fidgeting	54.3	Depersonalization	5.7
Muscular tension	48.6	Morning depression	5.7
Neglect due to brooding	48.6	Obsessional checking and repeating	5.7
Autonomic anxiety on meeting people	45.7	Hypochondriasis	0
Recent loss of interest	42.9	Obsessional cleanliness and rituals	0
Avoidance of autonomic anxiety	42.9		
Simple ideas of reference	40.0		

Note. From "The Clinical Features of Bulimia Nervosa" by C. G. Fairburn and P. J. Cooper, 1984, *British Journal of Psychiatry, 144,* 238–246. Reprinted by permission.

Note. "Loss of weight" was not rated, in view of these patients' grossly disturbed eating habits.

tology similar to that of patients with major depressive disorder. Approximately 25% have had anorexia nervosa in the past; in terms of their clinical features, patients in this subgroup do not appear to differ from those with no such history (Fairburn & Cooper, 1984a).

THE ASSESSMENT OF PATIENTS FOR COGNITIVE-BEHAVIOR THERAPY

The assessment of patients with bulimia is discussed in detail by Johnson (Chapter 3, this volume). However, certain specific points need to be made about the assessment of patients for cognitive-behavior therapy.

Patients must be suitable for treatment on an outpatient basis. There are two contraindications to such treatment. The first is if the patient is thought to be at significant risk of suicide. Although this is relatively uncommon (Fairburn & Cooper, 1984a), suicide risk must be routinely assessed. The second contraindication is if the patient's physical health requires inpatient investigation or treatment. Again, this occurs infrequently. The most common abnormalities of note are metabolic alkalosis, hypochloremia, and hypokalemia, either alone or in combination (Mitchell, Pyle, Eckert, Hatsukami, & Lentz, 1983). Severe hypokalemia is an indication for hospitalization. As with suicide risk, electrolyte disturbance must be excluded as a matter of routine.

In addition, the possibility that there may be a coexisting affective disorder must be considered. Table 8-4 shows the frequency of depressive symptoms among a typical patient sample. It can be seen that depressive thoughts, difficulty in concentrating, and depressed mood are particularly common. The clinical evaluation of such symptoms is complicated by the direct effects of the eating disorder on mood, appetite, weight, sleep, energy, interests, and concentration. Careful history taking usually indicates that the eating disorder began prior to the onset of significant depressive symptoms, and that the patient's mood closely corresponds to the degree of control over eating. This suggests that the mood disturbance is a secondary phenomenon; this proposition is supported by the finding that in practice the depressive features usually respond to measures that enhance control over eating. However, a minority of patients appear to have a coexisting affective disorder; in addition to treatment for their eating problem, they require antidepressant medication. It is important to detect such patients at an early stage, since they do not respond to cognitive–behavioral measures on their own. In general, their depressive symptoms are severe and invariable, and they persist irrespective of changes in the state of the eating problem. For example, self-depreciatory thoughts tend to be particularly prominent, even at times when the patient's eating is under control.

If it appears that a coexisting depressive disorder is present, treatment with antidepressant medication should be instituted. Unfortunately, the choice of drug is not straightforward (Fairburn, 1982). Tricyclic antidepressants have a propensity to induce weight gain and, in some cases, "carbohydrate craving" (Paykel, Mueller, & de la Vergne, 1973), both of which are poorly tolerated by this patient group. On the other hand, monoamine oxidase inhibitors should not be prescribed unless both the patient and the physician are confident that the dietary restrictions will be obeyed.

Table 8-4. Depressive Symptoms in Bulimia Nervosa: Frequency of Ratings of 4 or More on the Items of the Montgomery and Asberg Depression Rating Scale (Montgomery & Asberg, 1979)

ITEM	%
Apparent sadness	5.8
Reported sadness	51.4
Inner tension	25.7
Reduced sleep	35.3
Reduced appetite	—
Concentration difficulties	60.1
Lassitude	51.5
Inability to feel	28.6
Pessimistic thoughts	71.4
Suicidal thoughts	17.2

Note. "Reduced appetite" was not rated, in view of these patients' grossly disturbed eating habits.

Note. The data are from "The Clinical Features of Bulimia Nervosa" by C. G. Fairburn and P. J. Cooper, 1984, *British Journal of Psychiatry, 144,* 238–246. Used by permission.

Once the depressive disorder has substantially resolved, cognitive-behavior therapy can be instituted while the patient continues on medication. Contrary to the experience of others (e.g., Pope, Hudson, & Jonas, 1983), both Russell (1979) and I have found that antidepressant drugs are not an effective treatment for bulimia *per se*: The depressive symptoms lessen in intensity, but the eating disorder persists largely unchanged. The findings of a recent controlled study support this clinical impression (Sabine, Yonace, Farrington, Barratt, & Wakeling, 1983).

One further point needs to be made about assessment. This concerns the patients' desire to change. In Britain, patients presenting with the type of clinical picture described above are almost invariably distressed by their symptoms and are eager to receive help. They react positively to the prospect of starting treatment, and they particularly welcome the initial emphasis on enhancing self-control. In practice, treatment proves acceptable to the great majority, and few drop out. However, patients whose desire to change appears questionable should not be offered a full course of treatment (see "Treatment Procedure," below), but instead an initial series of four sessions. Thereafter, progress can be reviewed and further arrangements can be made.

SOME PRELIMINARY POINTS ABOUT TREATMENT

Treatment is conducted on an outpatient basis and lasts about 5 months. It is semi-structured, problem-oriented, and primarily concerned with patients' present and future rather than their past. It is an active process, with the responsibility for change residing with the patient; the therapist provides information, advice, support, and encouragement.

Three stages in treatment may be distinguished. Each contains several different elements designed to deal with relatively specific areas of difficulty. In the first stage, the main emphasis is on establishing some degree of control over eating, and the techniques used are largely behavioral. In the second, treatment is more cognitively oriented, with particular stress being placed on the identification and modification of dysfunctional thoughts, beliefs, and values. In the final stage, the focus is on the maintenance of change.

It is essential that the patient and therapist establish an effective working relationship, in which they are collaborators with a common goal — namely, overcoming the eating problem. Mutual trust and respect are important. A sound relationship is a prerequisite for successful treatment, since many of the behavioral assignments not only are difficult to accomplish, but also run counter to the patient's system of beliefs and values. The sex of the therapist does not seem to be of relevance to therapeutic success.

The therapist requires some knowledge and understanding of the physiological processes that complicate bulimia and its treatment. These patients have disturbed hunger and satiety; they sometimes experience dramatic rebound water retention on ceasing to vomit or use laxatives; and they are at risk for potentially serious physical complications. During treatment, patients need to learn about such disturbances; in addition, they need to be provided with information about body weight regulation, dieting, and body image misperception, since many harbor gross misconceptions about food and eating and about their shape and weight. Clearly, in order to educate patients, the therapist must be well grounded in such matters.

TREATMENT PROCEDURE

The following program of treatment suits most patients with bulimia. For clarity's sake, a definite treatment "package" is described. In clinical practice, however, treatment should be adapted to suit the needs of the individual patient. Therefore, certain possible modifications are outlined. It is assumed throughout that the patient is female, since the great majority of people with bulimia nervosa are women (Fairburn & Cooper, 1984a).

Stage 1

Stage 1 lasts 4 weeks, and appointments are twice a week. The principal aim is to disrupt the habitual binge eating, self-induced vomiting, and laxative abuse that characterize the more severe cases of bulimia. More specific aims are shown in Table 8-5. Patients who are bingeing on an intermittent basis usually need a less intensive initial intervention. While it is generally worthwhile to arrange the first two or three interviews at 3- or 4-day intervals, thereafter appointments may be weekly. However, the content of treatment should be the same. On the other hand, if the patient's eating habits are extremely disturbed — for example, when vomiting is occurring 10 or more times daily — it is appropriate initially to see the patient three or more times a week.

INTERVIEW 1

Orientation of the Patient. The patient should be provided with the following information.

1. Treatment structure. Treatments last 18 weeks, during which there will be 19 appointments. Stage 1 consists of eight interviews over four weeks; Stage 2 comprises eight interviews at weekly intervals; and Stage 3 consists of three appointments at 2-week intervals. Each interview lasts up to 1 hour.

2. Treatment content. The initial aim is to help the patient regain control over eating. Specific advice is given on how this can be achieved. Once she is bingeing on an intermittent basis, attention is directed to factors maintaining the eating problem. The patient is helped to cope more effectively with the circumstances that tend to result in binge eating; and attempts are made to identify, question, and (where appropriate)

Table 8-5. The Aims of Stage 1

---

1. To establish a sound therapeutic relationship.
2. To disrupt habitual binge eating, self-induced vomiting, and laxative abuse.
3. To introduce a pattern of regular eating.
4. To inform the patient of the physical consequences of binge eating, self-induced vomiting, and laxative abuse.
5. To provide information about the "effectiveness" of vomiting and laxative abuse as means of weight control.
6. To establish regular weekly weighing.
7. To examine the "function" of binge eating and self-induced vomiting.
8. To enlist the cooperation of friends and relatives.

---

to modify habits, beliefs, and values that are perpetuating the disorder. The final stage is concerned with the maintenance of change. The treatment program is designed to ensure that the eating problem does not recur in the future.

3. *Likely outcome.* Using this treatment approach, the majority of patients successfully overcome their eating problem, and the improvement is usually maintained. However, a patient should not expect to be "cured" in the conventional sense. Disturbed eating may remain her response in periods of extreme stress, but between such times it should not be a problem. She may remain marginally more sensitive than the average person about food and eating and about her shape and weight.

4. *Treatment style and need for commitment.* Treatment requires an intensive commitment; it should be given priority in the patient's life. Half-hearted attempts at treatment often fail. Regular homework assignments are set, and she should do her utmost to complete these tasks. The more effort that is put into treatment, the greater the rewards are. The therapist will offer information, advice, and encouragement, but it is up to the patient to make the most of treatment.

History Taking. The therapist needs information about the eating problem and its development. Formal history taking is necessary if the therapist was not involved in the initial assessment. In general, the following topics should be covered: the eating problem and any other current difficulties; previous experience of treatment; the patient's attitude to the eating problem and how it should be managed; her weight and menstrual history; her mental and physical state; her current social circumstances; her eating habits; and her attitudes to food, eating, shape, and weight. In addition, whenever possible, supplementary information should be obtained from an informant. However, at this stage some patients may be unwilling for others to be involved; indeed, it is quite common for no one to know that the patient has an eating problem or that she is seeking help. Under such circumstances, there is no need to insist upon interviewing an informant.

Establishing a Sound Therapeutic Relationship. Considerable effort should be devoted to the establishment of an effective working relationship. However, while genuine interest and concern in the patient and her problems is important, the therapist should be capable of being firm and authoritative, particularly when discussing homework assignments.

Monitoring. Toward the end of Interview 1, the patient should be taught how to monitor her eating. She should be given written instructions on monitoring (see Figure 8-1), together with a typical monitoring sheet (see Figure 8-2). The rationale for monitoring should be explained: Namely, it helps both the therapist and patient analyze the patient's eating habits and the circumstances under which problems arise. It is not uncommon for patients to be reluctant to monitor themselves, especially if they are ashamed of their eating habits. As a matter of routine, the therapist should anticipate this reaction by assuring each patient that there is no need to be ashamed of her behavior, and that recording what actually happens is the first stage in confronting the eating problem and overcoming it.

Weekly Weighing. The patient should be asked to weigh herself once a week on a morning of her choice. In practice, a weekday morning works out best. There is often some resistance to this suggestion. The great majority of patients are overconcerned with their weight, and this concern is evident in their weighing habits. There is a tendency for them either to check their weight daily or oftener, or to avoid weighing

The purpose of monitoring yourself is to provide a detailed picture of your eating habits. It is central to the treatment process. At first, writing down everything you eat may seem inconvenient and irritating, but soon it becomes second nature and of obvious value.

A sample monitoring sheet is shown in Figure 2. A separate sheet (or sheets) should be used each day, with the date and day of the week noted at the top.

Column 2 is for recording *all* the food and liquid you consume during the day. Each item should be written down as soon as possible after its consumption. Recalling what you ate or drank some hours earlier is not sufficient. Obviously, if you are to record your food intake in this way, you will have to carry your monitoring sheets with you. Calories should not be recorded. Instead, you should provide a simple description of what you ate or drank. Meals should be identified using a bracket. A meal may be defined as "a discrete episode of eating that was controlled, organized, and eaten in a normal fashion." Mere snacks should not be bracketed.

Column 1 is for noting the time at which the food or liquid was consumed.

Column 3 should detail where the food or liquid was consumed. If this was in your home, the room should be specified.

Column 4. Asterisks should be placed in this column adjacent to eating that you felt was excessive. It is essential to record all the food you eat during "binges."

Column 5 is for recording when you vomit, take laxatives, or take diuretics (water tablets).

Column 6 should be used as a diary to record events that influenced your eating: For example, if you feel that an argument precipitated a "binge," you should note that down. You may wish to record other important events, even if they had no effect on your eating. You may also like to note down any strong feelings—for example, feelings of depression, anxiety, or loneliness, or feeling "fat."

Column 6 should also be used to record your weight each time you weigh yourself.

Every treatment interview will include a review of your latest monitoring sheets. You must therefore remember to bring them with you.

Figure 8-1. Instructions for self-monitoring.

altogether while nevertheless remaining highly aware of their shape. Both groups find it difficult to adjust to weekly weighing. Patients who have been avoiding weighing should be forewarned that they may well experience a short-lived increase in their concern with their weight.

Weighing at weekly intervals is an essential element of treatment. Since these patients' eating habits change markedly during treatment, and since certain of the behavioral instructions are designed to highlight their fear of becoming fat, it is important that they monitor their weight. However, they also need to counter any tendency to be overconcerned with their weight. Weighing once a week serves both functions. It is also an excellent example of how a simple behavioral instruction can highlight underlying psychopathological features: Indeed, during the more cognitively oriented phase of treatment, patients' reactions to weighing are examined.

INTERVIEW 2

Review of the Monitoring Sheets. Interview 2 and all subsequent interviews should open with a detailed review of the patient's monitoring sheets. Each sheet should be discussed in depth, with the patient guiding the therapist through the day's events. The aim is to get a full understanding of the patient's current eating habits. Episodes of "excessive eating" (signified by asterisks in the fourth column of Figure 8-2) should be discussed in particular detail. It is important to make sure that monitoring is not retrospective; instead, the patient should write down what she eats just before its con-

DAY ...Monday...   DATE 20th September

TIME	FOOD AND LIQUID CONSUMED	PLACE	B	V/L	CONTEXT
7.35	1 grapefruit 1 cup black coffee	Kitchen			Feel really fat.
11.10	1 apple	Work			
3.15	2 Twix 1 bread roll a fruit cake	High St " Market	* * *		Everyone looked at me in the market. I'm out of control.
3.30	2 chocolate eggs 2 bread rolls ½ pint of milk	" Kitchen "	* * *	V	I hate myself. I can't stop crying.
5.10	1 bowl cereal 1 bowl cereal 1 pita bread with cottage cheese. 1 glass water	" " " "	* * * *		
6.00	a baked potato 1 can Tab	Van outside "		V	
9.00	1 cup Slimline soup 1 ice cube	Kitchen "			Weighed myself 9st 8lb -too heavy Feel fat and ugly.
9.20	1 cup coffee	"			
10.00	1 coffee (black)	Sitting room			
11.20	1 coffee (black) 6 shortbread biscuits 4 pieces of chocolate 2 pieces of toast 2 glasses of water	Kitchen " " " "	* * *	V V	Why do I do this? I want to be thin. I can't help it. Weighed 9st 7lb - fat Took 24 Nylax.
				L	

Figure 8-2. A monitoring sheet showing three episodes of binge eating and self-induced vomiting.

sumption or immediately afterward. Accurate monitoring should be praised, especially in those cases where the patient finds the process humiliating or embarrassing.

Other Elements. In Interview 2, it is usually sufficient to concentrate exclusively upon reviewing the patient's monitoring sheets and suggesting means of improving her recording. In addition, the therapist may wish to continue history taking. However, if time allows and monitorng is satisfactory, certain advice may be given regarding eating and its control (see Interviews 3, 4, and 5).

INTERVIEWS 3, 4, AND 5

During Interviews 3, 4, and 5, the therapist should introduce the principal behavioral strategies for regaining control over eating. At the end of each session, the patient should be set a limited number of clearly specified tasks. At the subsequent interview, the therapist and patient should review her attempts to fulfill these assignments, and further tasks should be set. Since patients with bulimia tend to be excessively self-critical, all successes, however modest, should be praised. Sometimes it is worthwhile to ask the patient to make a daily rating of her degree of success at fulfilling each homework assignment—for example, by giving herself "marks out of 10." This counters any tendency to view less than perfect performance as complete failure.

Provision of Information. The patient should be provided with information on the following topics:

1. Body weight. The patient should be told what her weight represents as a percentage of the average weight for her age and height (i.e., standard weight). She should be advised against choosing an exact desired weight, since this would fail to take account of natural day-by-day weight fluctuations. Instead, she should accept a weight range of approximately 3 kg (7 lb) in magnitude. This weight range should not extend below 85% of her standard weight, since at such a weight she will be liable to experience the physiological and psychological sequelae of starvation, which may tend to worsen the eating problem (cf. Garfinkel & Garner, 1982). The patient should also be advised against choosing a weight range that necessitates anything more than moderate dietary restriction, since restraint of this type is likely to encourage overeating. In practice, it is best that she postpone deciding upon a specific weight range until she has regained control over eating, since only then will she be able to gauge the amount she can eat in order to keep her weight relatively stable.

At this stage in treatment, it is also worth discussing the arbitrary nature of most desired weights. These tend to be located just under a threshold figure: Thus, in the United States people often wish to weigh below 100, 110, 120, or 130 lb, whereas in Britain people usually choose to weight below 7, 8, or 9 stone (equivalent to 98, 112, or 126 lb, respectively).

2. The physical consequences of binge eating, self-induced vomiting, and laxative abuse. All patients should be informed of the physical complications of bulimia (Fairburn, 1983b). These are listed in Table 8-6. They should be reassured that most of these physical sequelae resolve once their eating habits have normalized, although in the case of menstruation there may be a significant delay before the onset of regular monthly periods.

3. The "effectiveness" of vomiting and laxative abuse as means of weight control. The main point to emphasize is that "binges" usually involve the consumption of a large number of calories (it can be salutary for patients to calculate the calorie content of a typical binge) and that self-induced vomiting does not retrieve everything that has been eaten. It should also be pointed out that among patients with bulimia, self-induced vomiting is habit-forming, since it encourages overeating: First, since patients think that by vomiting they will avoid absorbing what they have eaten, they tend to relax their dietary controls and overeat; and second, they soon discover that it is easier to vomit if their stomachs are full. As a result, a vicious circle is established, with patients becoming increasingly dependent on vomiting to compensate for

Table 8-6. The Physical Complications of Bulimia

BINGE EATING	SELF-INDUCED VOMITING	LAXATIVE ABUSE
Acute dilatation of the stomach	Metabolic disturbance (hypokalemia is especially important):	
Menstrual disturbance		
Painless salivary gland enlargement (especially the parotids)	Cardiac arrhythmias	
	Tetany and peripheral paresthesia	
	Weakness and lethargy	
	Dehydration	
	Epiletic seizures	
	Renal damage	
	Erosion of dental enamel (periomolysis)	Steatorrhea
	Chronic hoarseness of the voice	Finger clubbing
	Gastrointestinal reflux	(Rebound water retention on stopping)

their increased food intake. Where appropriate, patients should be informed that laxatives have a marginal effect on calorie absorption (Bo-Lynn, Santa-Ana, Morawski, & Fordtran, 1983), and that diuretics only influence fluid balance.

Advice Regarding Eating.

1. The prescription of a pattern of regular eating. The patient should be asked to restrict her eating to three or four planned meals each day, plus one or two planned snacks. Thus there should rarely be more than a 3-hour interval between eating times, and she should always know when she is next due to eat. This eating pattern should take precedence over other activities; irrespective of her circumstances or appetite, the patient should not skip any of the meals or snacks. Conversely, however, between these times she should do her utmost to refrain from eating.

This pattern of regular eating has the effect of displacing the alternating overeating and dietary restriction that characterize these patients' eating habits. Obviously the pattern must be tailored to suit the patient's daily commitments, and usually it needs to be modified to accommodate weekends. Patients whose routine is varied should devise an eating plan to suit each day. If the day is unpredictable, the patient should plan ahead as far as possible and decide upon a time when she can make further plans for the remainder of the day. Patients whose eating habits are grossly disturbed should introduce this eating pattern in gradual stages. First, they should concentrate on the part of the day when their eating is least disturbed, which is usually the mornings; then they should gradually extend the eating plan until it encompasses the entire day.

Some patients are reluctant to eat meals or snacks, since they think this will result in weight gain. They can be reassured that the converse usually occurs, since the introduction of this pattern of eating will decrease their frequency of binge eating and thereby significantly reduce their overall caloric intake. Despite such reassurances, however, it is common for patients to select meals and snacks that are low in calories. There need be no objection to this tendency: *At this stage in treatment, the emphasis should be primarily on establishing a pattern of regular eating.* However, if the patient does seek advice on what foods to eat, she should be encouraged to adopt a varied diet with the minimum number of prescribed foods. Patients should be actively discouraged from counting calories, and especially from any tendency to keep a running total. During treatment, they will discover that they can eat much more than they previously thought without gaining weight; in the past, they had failed to take account of the calories they absorbed when bingeing.

Occasionally patients seek advice about the quantity they should eat, and in particular whether they should eat until they feel full. They should be told that their sensations of appetite, hunger, and fullness are all likely to be disturbed, and that for the meantime these should not be used to determine when they should start or stop eating. Instead, the patient should adhere to the prescribed eating pattern and should consume no more than "average"-sized portions of food. (The size of an average portion can be determined from the eating habits of friends or relatives, from recipes, or from the instructions on food packages.)

A common problem is that patients are liable to feel full after eating relatively small amounts, and that this results in an urge to vomit. Feelings of fullness are especially likely to develop after eating foods perceived as fattening. This reaction is likely to be largely cognitive in nature—the result of paying undue attention to abdominal sensations that would normally pass unnoticed. Patients who are troubled by feelings of fullness after eating often benefit from wearing loose clothes at mealtimes and from engaging in distracting activities immediately afterward. They should be assured that these feelings usually subside within an hour.

2. Stimulus control and allied measures. The well-established stimulus control techniques used in the treatment of obesity (cf. Ferguson, 1975; Mahoney & Mahoney, 1976) should be used to help patients adhere to the prescribed eating pattern. Such measures include not engaging in other activities while eating normally or while bingeing, restricting eating to one room in the house, limiting the amount of food available while eating, practicing leaving food on the plate, and discarding leftover food. In addition, the patient should limit the amount of "dangerous" food in the house (i.e., food liable to be consumed when bingeing), she should make such food relatively inaccessible, and she should have substitute supplies of "safe" food. She should carefully plan her shopping and use a shopping list. She should avoid shopping when she is hungry or when she feels liable to overeat, and she should buy foods that need preparation rather than those that can be eaten immediately. When she senses that her control is poor, she should carry as little money as possible.

3. Alternative behavior. Patients should be asked to construct a list of pleasurable activities. Such activities may be used to occupy the time between meals and snacks, thereby reducing the likelihood of binge eating; in addition, they can help patients cope wth times of difficulty – for example, times of feeling full or "fat." It is especially important to encourage patients to keep "one step ahead of the problem": They should predict when difficulties are likely to arise and then engage in activities incompatible with binge eating. Such activities may include telephoning friends or visiting them, taking some form of exercise, or having a bath or shower.

4. Techniques for controlling the act of eating. Measures for controlling the act of eating are not often required. However, patients with an abnormal style of eating may find them helpful. They include slowing the rate of eating by putting down utensils between mouthfuls, and completing each mouthful before starting another. Patients should also be encouraged to savor their food and to pause at regular intervals during meals. Such pauses may be used to decide whether or not to continue eating. It is also worthwhile to discourage patients from drinking large quantities of liquid with their meals, since this tends to exaggerate feelings of fullness.

A substantial minority of these patients habitually ruminate. Such rumination is not often spontaneously described. It occurs immediately after eating, and it involves the effortless regurgitation of small quantities of food, which are then chewed. Subsequently, the food is either reswallowed or spat out. No specific techniques seem to be required to help patients stop ruminating, since the habit almost invariably ceases once the patient has regained control over eating (Fairburn & Cooper, 1984b).

Advice Regarding Vomiting. Vomiting *per se* does not need to be tackled, since in the great majority of cases it ceases once the patient has stopped overeating. Nevertheless, patients should be instructed to choose meals and snacks that they are prepared not to vomit. As mentioned earlier, if the patient feels tempted to vomit after a particular meal or snack, she should engage in a distracting activity for the following hour or so.

Advice Regarding Laxatives and Diuretics. The patient should be asked to cease taking these drugs, and she should discard her supplies. Surprisingly, simply telling patients to abandon this habit is often successful. Those patients who find this instruction impossible to follow should be given a fixed withdrawal schedule during which the drugs are gradually phased out. A small number experience a temporary period of weight gain, which can probably be attributed to rebound water retention.

INTERVIEWS 6, 7, AND 8

Interviews 6, 7, and 8 are the last three in Stage 1 of treatment. They are primarily concerned with the consolidation of progress. The bulk of each session should be taken up with a detailed examination of both the patient's eating habits and her degree of success at fulfilling the homework assignments. Each assignment should be reviewed, difficulties should be discussed, and new strategies should be explored. Sometimes "failures" may be ascribed to the therapist's having set vague, unattainable tasks or ones that are too ambitious. The emphasis should be on adherence to the pattern of regular eating. The content of the patient's diet and her attitude to food, eating, shape, and weight need not be tackled until Stage 2 of treatment, although the therapist should regularly check that the patient is continuing to weigh herself once a week. As always, all successes should be praised. In addition, patients should be helped to make a realistic day-by-day appraisal of their progress. They should be capable of congratulating themselves when things have gone well, and they should do their best to analyze and learn from apparent "failures." The therapist should counter any tendency for the patient to think in diurnal units, since, following any perceived failure, some patients abandon their efforts for the remainder of that day. Rather than working from one day to the next, patients should work from hour to hour.

Examination of the "Function" of Binge Eating and Vomiting. Once binge eating is occurring on a more intermittent basis, the emphasis of treatment should move toward an examination of the factors maintaining the eating problem. For example, binge eating often conveys certain benefits, including distraction from unpleasant thoughts, short-term relief from dysphoric moods, the occupying of spare time, the induction of sleep, and the provision of a release from the monotony and rigors of extreme dieting. In addition, some patients eat as a means of punishing themselves, or in order to spite others who are trying to help them. Vomiting also has its rewards. Not only does it relieve the abdominal distension that follows binge eating, but it also reduces the amount of food absorbed. A minority of patients find vomiting a potent means of releasing tension, and such patients may induce vomiting whenever they feel anxious.

The idea that binge eating serves a function is novel to most patients. Usually they find this notion reassuring, since it starts to make sense of the eating problem. Each time the patient overeats, she should be encouraged to examine why she did so. This analysis should be conducted as soon as possible afterward, and her conclusions should be written down in the sixth column of the monitoring sheet, together with her views on how overeating might have been avoided.

Interviews with the Patient's Family or Friends. It is advisable to arrange occasional joint interviews with the people with whom the patient lives and shares her meals. These interviews serve two functions. First, they encourage the patient to bring the problem into the open, thereby relieving her guilt over continuing secrecy and deceit. Second, by discussing the rationale of treatment, and in particular the importance of self-control, friends and relatives can be helped to provide an environment that will facilitate the patient's own efforts to overcome the problem. For a variety of reasons, some patients may be reluctant to involve others, but by this point in treatment it should be possible for the therapist to persuade them to divulge the problem and thereby to enlist further help. The only risk is that the friends or relatives will become overinvolved and will usurp the patient's control over her eating. For this reason, the therapist must stress that the patient should remain free to decide what and when to eat.

PROGRESS DURING STAGE 1

In the great majority of cases, Stage 1 results in a marked reduction in the frequency of binge eating and an improvement in mood. In those cases where significant mood disturbance persists, the possibility that there is a coexisting depressive disorder must be reconsidered.

Patients whose eating habits have not shown some improvement by this stage rarely benefit from Stage 2 of treatment. The therapist should therefore review other treatment options. For example, it may be appropriate to offer the patient a period of inpatient care, during which she will be subject to external controls (see Andersen, Morse, & Santmyer, Chapter 14, this volume; Strober & Yager, Chapter 16, this volume). Alternatively, Stage 1 may be extended for a week or so. For example, this is justified when the patient has made significant gains but is still bingeing at least once a day. However, it must be stressed that protracted intensive contact is inadvisable. If by the end of 8 weeks the patient's eating habits have not improved, this form of treatment should be discontinued.

Stage 2

Stage 2 of treatment lasts 8 weeks, and appointments are made at weekly intervals. In comparison with Stage 1, treatment is more cognitively oriented. The principal aims are shown in Table 8-7.

Table 8-7. The Aims of Stage 2

1. To establish and maintain a pattern of regular eating.
2. To reduce dietary restraint.
3. To identify the circumstances that tend to result in binge eating, and to help the patient
   a. to cope more effectively with such circumstances;
   b. to reduce the frequency of their occurrence.
4. To identify and challenge thoughts, beliefs, and values that are perpetuating the eating problem.
5. To help the patient deal with body image misperception and body image disparagement.
6. To raise the issue of termination.

INTERVIEW 9

Some patients react adversely to the decrease in appointment frequency. In such cases, Interview 9 should be concerned with the consolidation of progress, and homework assignments should be similar to those used earlier. However, those patients who continue to make satisfactory progress should move directly on to the first major aim of Stage 2, the reduction of dietary restraint (see below).

INTERVIEWS 10 TO 14

The Maintenance of a Pattern of Regular Eating. The patient should continue to apply the techniques learned in Stage 1. She should use the stimulus control measures and alternative activities to restrict her eating to regular meals and snacks.

The Reduction of Dietary Restraint. Dietary restraint is thought to encourage binge eating, either through secondary cognitive processes (Polivy *et al.*, 1984) or as a result of secondary neurochemical abnormalities (Wurtman, 1983). At present the balance of evidence supports the former mechanism, at least among those who are not significantly underweight.

The therapist should explain the link between dietary restraint (or "rigid dieting") and binge eating. By having strict rules governing what and when she may and may not eat, the patient is inviting failure. She is also encouraging binge eating, since the breaking of these rules is likely to result in the abandonment of self-control. Furthermore, in order to compensate for episodes of overeating, most patients diet even more conscientiously, thereby establishing a vicious circle. To make matters even worse, they blame themselves, rather than concluding that the fault lies in their dietary regimen.

Two forms of dietary restraint may be distinguished. First, many patients attempt to avoid eating for long periods each day, especially if they have recently overeaten. This tendency is countered in the first stage of treatment by the introduction of regular meals and snacks. The second form of restraint consists of attempts to adhere to a highly selective diet from which all "fattening" foods are excluded. Frequently it is these foods that are eaten when the patient loses control. In order to tackle the second form of restraint, such foods must first be identified. The patient should therefore be asked to identify any foods that she likes, but that she nevertheless avoids eating. This may be set as a homework task. She should then be instructed to eat moderate amounts of such food at times when she feels in control. Gradually, over a period of several weeks, the patient should introduce all these foods into her diet. The intention is that she should relax control over the content of her diet, while continuing to adhere to a pattern of regular eating. This practice rarely results in weight gain.

Many patients are reluctant to accept this advice. From years of dieting and reading publications on slimming, they have come to believe that certain foods are inherently fattening. Nevertheless, by insisting upon the introduction of such foods, and by discussing the patient's reaction to the prospect of eating them, it should be possible for the therapist to correct certain misconceptions about food and eating, while at the same time lessening dietary restraint. Patients who find it particularly difficult to eat such foods may remind themselves that by doing so they will be protecting themselves against binge eating.

Patients should not only eat as varied a diet as possible, but they should also relax certain other controls over eating. For example, some patients dislike eating foods whose calorie content is uncertain. They may insist upon preparing all their own food so that they know its precise composition. These patients should be encouraged to eat foods whose calorie content is difficult to determine. In addition, all patients should practice eating in as wide a range of situations as possible — for example, at restaurants, dinner parties, and picnics. Very occasionally, patients are discovered to have a specific phobia that is precipitated by these situations or other food-related environments, (e.g., supermarkets or bakeries). In such cases, graduated *in vivo* self-exposure should be incorporated into the treatment program.

Training in Problem Solving. By Stage 2, most patients are bingeing on an intermittent basis, and usually such binges are occurring in response to adverse events, dysphoric moods, or certain dysfunctional thoughts. The patient should be taught the principles of problem solving in order to help her cope with these events and moods without recourse to binge eating. Ideally, a recent event in the patient's life should be used as an example. The following model of problem solving is used:

Step 1. The problem should be identified and specified as precisely as possible. It may emerge that there are two or more coexisting problems, in which case each should be considered separately. For example, if a patient's plans for the evening are disrupted, she may need to review how she is going to spend the evening and what she will do about eating.

Step 2. Alternative ways of coping with the problem should be identified. The patient should attempt to think of as many potential means of coping as possible, and not simply one or two extreme solutions. The more solutions that are generated, the more likely it is that a suitable one will emerge.

Step 3. The implications of each solution should be considered. Each potential solution should be examined in terms of its practicability and probable effectiveness.

Step 4. One solution should be chosen. Often this process is intuitive.

Step 5. The steps required to carry out the solution should be defined. The patient should rehearse each step in her mind.

Step 6. The solution should be executed.

Step 7. The entire problem-solving process should be evaluated. The same day or soon afterward, the patient should review in detail her attempt at problem solving and decide how the process could have been improved. Patients who tend to devalue their achievements should quantify their degree of success by giving themselves a "mark out of 10."

Having taught the patient the principles of problem solving (and a didactic manner is perfectly appropriate), the therapist should ask the patient to practice problem solving as often as possible. Whenever any difficulty occurs or is foreseen, the patient should write "problem" in the sixth column of her monitoring sheet, and should then write out each of the stages of problem solving on the back. She should be told that problem solving can be applied to any day-to-day difficulty, including mood disturbance. If she uses this approach effectively, it will result in an improvement in her ability to cope with situations that would previously have led to episodes of binge eating. In addition, by encouraging her to look out for potential problems, it should lessen the frequency with which difficulties occur. It should also serve to counter any tendency toward "all-or-none" (dichotomous) thinking by making her generate a range of different solutions to each difficulty she encounters. Lastly, it should help her discover means of changing her mood. Many patients find that they can elevate their mood by listening to certain pieces of music, taking exercise, having a bath or shower, or changing into attractive clothes.

Having taught the patient the principles of problem solving, the therapist should ensure that in subsequent sessions each attempt at problem solving is examined and ways of improving her technique are discussed. In addition, the therapist should consider whether the patient is using problem solving sufficiently often. At first patients tend to underuse the technique, or to use it rather too late in the evolution of any problem. For this reason, they should be encouraged to think ahead and look out for potential difficulties so that they can practice their problem-solving skills. Most patients come to enjoy problem solving and regard it as a challenge. Figure 8-3 shows a monitoring sheet typical of this phase in Stage 2.

The Identification and Modification of Thoughts, Beliefs, and Values That Are Perpetuating the Eating Problem. The therapist should outline the rationale for identifying and examining the patient's beliefs and values concerning her shape and weight. By this point in treatment, virtually all patients accept that these attitudes are of relevance to their eating problem. However, many will be reluctant to discuss their "feelings" regarding their shape and weight, usually because such feelings consist of shame and self-condemnation. Indeed, many patients have never discussed these matters before. Considerable sensitivity on the part of the therapist is therefore required.

The specific psychopathology of bulimia is relatively uniform (Fairburn & Cooper, 1984a). The most prominent feature is a profound fear of becoming fat, which is often accompanied by an extreme sensitivity to weight change. A minority of patients also have an intense desire to be thin. Often these specific features are associated with perfectionistic tendencies and a reliance on external criteria to gauge self-worth. Although such characteristics may be strikingly obvious to the therapist, they may not be recognized by the patient. It is the therapist's role to help the patient identify and, where appropriate, modify these features. The techniques used are similar to those employed by Beck and colleagues in the treatment of depression (Beck, Rush, Shaw, & Emery, 1979). Four elements may be distinguished:

1. The identification of dysfunctional thoughts.
2. The examination of these thoughts.
3. The identification of underlying dysfunctional beliefs and values.
4. The examination of these beliefs and values.

1. The identification of dysfunctional thoughts. On a day-to-day basis, much of the disturbed behavior of these patients (for example, the extreme dieting and fre-

DAY Wednesday DATE 10th November

TIME	FOOD AND LIQUID CONSUMED	PLACE	B	V/L	CONTEXT
7.55	1 grapefruit 1 piece toast 1 black coffee	Kitchen			Due to weigh myself today. Not expecting a change. If there is, I better be careful. 9st 9lb – up two pounds. (Maybe it's because I'm due a period?). Must stick to my plan.
11.00	1 apple	Work			
12.40	1 bread roll with pate. 1 pear 1 black coffee and two pieces of chocolate	Work			– threw the rest of the chocolate away... pleased
4.10	1 cup of tea 2 digestive biscuits	Work			
					Problem – invited out to restaurant with Peter (see over)
6.15	1 glass grapefruit juice 1 piece of toast	Kitchen "			– decided to eat this as we won't be eating until about nine.
8.20	2 glasses mulled wine	Peter's			(Will wear loose dress – it doesn't look too bad).
8.35	1 more glass of mulled wine	"			
9.15 | 11.30	Onion soup Trout (grilled!!) some vegetables 2 glasses white wine 1 Baked apple with custard – NEW	NEW Restaurant			Took some risks, but they were calculated. A successful evening. Glad I went. Need more loose clothes.

Figure 8-3. A monitoring sheet typical of Stage 2.

quent weighing) is governed by certain accessible "dysfunctional" thoughts. These thoughts appear to be expressions of certain abnormal beliefs and values concerning shape and weight. They occur involuntarily, and on the surface they seem plausible. Certain of these thoughts will already have been encountered during treatment, since several of the behavioral interventions are designed to highlight and challenge the patient's beliefs and values. Thus, in encouraging the patient to perform such tasks, the therapist will already have had to confront her reluctance to do so. Indeed, in many cases the ensuing discussions, together with the effects of following the behavioral program, will have resulted in significant cognitive change. However, even in these cases, it is usual for residual dysfunctional thoughts to be continuing to influence the patients' behavior.

In order to identify such thoughts, the therapist should instruct the patient to write down her thoughts (1) when she is reluctant to adhere to an agreed behavioral instruction (e.g., when she experiences a strong urge to overeat, when she wishes to avoid eating a planned meal or snack, or when she wants to weigh herself more or less often than arranged); (2) before she is due to weigh herself and immediately afterwards; and (3) when she "feels fat." At such times, the patient should specify on the back of that day's monitoring sheet her exact train of thought. If the thought took the form of a mental image, she should describe its nature. Whenever possible, she should identify her thoughts then and there. However, if this is impracticable, she should reconstruct the scene later on in the day and note down what passed through her mind at the time.

At first some patients find it difficult to identify such thoughts. It is therefore worthwhile to rehearse the procedure by asking the patient to recall what thoughts usually pass through her mind at such times. In addition, the therapist can elicit thoughts by asking her to imagine what she would think if she were given a "banned" food to eat, if she were asked to weigh herself, or if someone commented on her appearance.

The following thoughts are frequently identified: "I have no self-control," "I might as well give up," "I will get fat," "I look fat," "I am fat," "I feel fat," "I must lose weight," "I must diet."

2. The examination of dysfunctional thoughts. Having identified such thoughts, the patient should be taught to question their validity. There are four steps in this process:

a. The thought should be reduced to its essence. For example, the thought "I feel fat" may have several different meanings, including "I am overweight," "I look overweight to myself," "I look overweight to others"; or it may refer to unpleasant affective states that make the patient feel unattractive.

b. Arguments and evidence to support the thought should be marshaled. For example, if the patient has gained weight, this fact could be said to support the thought "I am getting fat," especially if weight gain in the past has resulted in obesity.

c. Arguments and evidence that cast doubt on the thought should be identified. Using the example above, if the patient has only gained a few pounds in weight, this cannot be equated with imminent obesity. The notion of "getting fat" should be examined and operationalized. The patient should consider such issues as "At what stage does one become fat?", "Can 'fatness' be reduced to a specific shape or weight (for example, clothes size)?", and "If so, am I actually approaching this shape or weight?"

In generating counterarguments, the patient should consider what other people would think, given the particular situation concerned. Would others conclude they were getting fat if they had gained a few pounds in weight? The patient should ask herself whether she is applying one set of standards to herself while applying another, less rigorous set to others. She should check that she is not confusing subjective impression (for example, feeling fat) with objective reality (for example, being statistically overweight). She should look out for errors of attribution: For example, could the weight gain be due to premenstrual fluid retention rather than to overeating? In addition, she should check that her reasoning is not faulty. Often there are errors in the patient's processing and interpretation of events; for example, there may be dichotomous thinking, selective abstraction, or overgeneralization (cf. Beck *et al.*, 1979; Garner & Bemis, 1982).

d. The patient should reach a reasoned conclusion, which must then be used to govern her behavior. This conclusion should provide a response to the specific dysfunctional thought. Some patients may choose to recite this response each time the thought occurs. Here is a brief example: If a patient concluded that, although gaining weight had made her think "I am getting fat," the balance of evidence failed to support this conclusion, it would be inappropriate for her either to chastise herself or to go on a diet. Table 8-8 provides a more complete example of the identification and examination of a dysfunctional thought.

Occasionally it is possible to devise ways of obtaining supplementary information relevant to the particular thought in question. For example, many patients are convinced that they are fat, or that parts of their bodies are fat. Often they have never discussed this thought before. In such cases it may be appropriate to suggest that the patient ask a trusted female friend for her uncensored view on the patient's physique. It is also quite common for patients to insist that on some days they are "fat" and that on other days they are thin, or rather, "less fat." This proposition can be quite easily tested by suggesting that, for a period of a week or two, the patient decide each morning whether or not she is fat, and then see whether this impression matches up with her actual weight. Almost invariably, the two are found to be poorly correlated.

Before proposing such "experiments," however, the therapist should ensure that they will yield findings that will benefit the patient. Obviously, after any experiment, the therapist and patient should examine its implications.

3. The identification of dysfunctional beliefs and values. Dysfunctional beliefs and values concerning shape and weight govern much of these patients' behavior; however, the patients are not necessarily aware of their presence or influence. They are so much a part of a patient's conceptual scheme that she is unable to stand back and analyze them. They are implicit, unarticulated underlying rules. For this reason, these beliefs and values cannot be identified using the technique for eliciting dysfunctional thoughts; instead, they have to be inferred from the patient's behavior (e.g., her avoidance of "fattening foods") and from the nature of her dysfunctional thoughts (e.g., "I feel fat"). Occasionally certain of these beliefs and values are directly expressed during treatment.

Using a Socratic style of dialogue, the therapist and patient should together attempt to identify such attitudes. Typical examples include the following:

Table 8-8   The Identification and Examination of a Dysfunctional Thought: A Clinical Example

---

I have to go to a party tonight. I decided to wear a dress that I have not worn for years. I put it on and found it was uncomfortably tight, whereas it used to fit me well.

Step 1. Thought: "I am fat. That's real, objective evidence."

Step 2. Arguments in favor: "Since the dress can't have changed, I must have gained weight."

Step 3. Arguments against: "Yes, I have gained weight, but that does not make me 'fat.' I know that statistically speaking I am below average weight; moreover, my friends do not think I'm fat. Also, I've ignored the fact that I was markedly underweight when I bought the dress."

Step 4. Conclusion: "It is not that I am too big: rather, it is my dress that is too small! I should give it away. I have many other clothes I like. I must remember that I am below average weight and could not conceivably be thought of as fat."

- I must be thin, because to be thin is to be successful, attractive, and happy.
- I must avoid being fat, because to be fat is to be a failure, unattractive, and unhappy.
- Self-indulgence is bad since it is a sign of weakness.
- Self-control is good because it is a sign of strength and discipline.
- Anything less than total success is utter failure.

It will be evident that such beliefs and values are extreme forms of widely held attitudes: it is their strength, personal significance, and inflexibility that make them dysfunctional.

   4. Examination of dysfunctional beliefs and values. The technique for questioning these morbid beliefs and values is similar to that used when examining patients' thoughts. However, more of the work has to be done in treatment sessions. The therapist's role is to act as a facilitator, helping the patient explore the significance and validity of her underlying attitudes. Seven steps in this process may be identified. The first four are the same as those used when examining dysfunctional thoughts.

   a. The belief or value should be specified precisely.

   b. Arguments and evidence to support the belief or value should be marshalled.

   c. Arguments and evidence against the belief or value should be identified. Again, the patient should be encouraged to check that her attitudes do not entail any errors of reasoning; to consider whether the same beliefs or values would be held by others whom she respects; and to ensure that she is not applying one set of standards to herself and another to others.

   d. The advantages of holding the particular belief or value should be considered. Many of these attitudes have definite benefits for the patient, and it is partly for this reason that they are often so difficult to erode. It is therefore important for the therapist to help the patient examine what she gains by adhering to these beliefs and values. For example, by judging her self-worth in terms of her shape or weight, the patient is provided with a simple measure of her strengths and weaknesses. By showing that she can influence her shape and weight, and overcome her need to eat, the patient is demonstrating that she is capable of exerting control over her life. By concluding that she is "fat," she is providing herself with a convenient excuse for a host of interpersonal problems.

   e. The disadvantages of holding the belief or value should now be reviewed when its advantages are considered, it should be clear that most of the benefits are short-term. In contrast, the long-term consequences are usually disadvantageous. The therapist should try to help the patient articulate these disadvantages. For example, most patients will admit that they are unlikely ever to be satisfied with their shape or weight. Thus, if they are to retain a belief and value system in which shape and weight are given high priority, they are likely to remain perpetually dissatisfied with themselves. In addition, by being preoccupied with shape and weight, patients may fail to recognize and tackle more fundamental problems — for example, lack of assertiveness, low self-esteem, problems in coping with anxiety or depression, or difficulties with relationships.

   f. The origin of these beliefs and values may be explored. To do this, the patient should reflect on the evolution of her eating problem. She should consider its earliest roots, the influence of her family and peers, and the role of social pressures to be slim. She should distinguish between factors that are likely to have contributed to the development of the problem, and factors that have served to maintain it. Diaries, old photographs, and talking to long-standing friends can all facilitate this exploratory process, which may be set as a homework task.

A minority of patients become particularly interested in the influence of sociocultural factors. They may be recommended books such as *Fat Is a Feminist Issue* (Orbach, 1978) and *Womansize* (Chernin, 1983). However, they should be advised against following the advice contained in these books without first discussing the matter with the therapist.

g. Conclusions should be drawn. In general, the therapist should encourage the patient to adopt less extreme and more flexible beliefs and values. For example, with regard to the issue of self-control, the patient may decide that some degree of self-control is desirable, but that it is positively counterproductive to demand of oneself total self-control in all spheres at all times. In certain instances, the patient may wish to obtain supplementary information — for example, by discussing with others her beliefs and values. In helping the patient draw her conclusions, the therapist should place particular emphasis on how short-term gains are likely to obscure long-term disadvantages.

Having reached a reasoned conclusion, the patient should repeatedly remind herself of this conclusion and use it to govern her behavior. Occasionally this may mean behaving in a manner that seems totally alien. For example, if the patient discovers she has gained some weight, she may choose to wear clothes that highlight her figure, rather than clothes that disguise it. Such behavior would be compatible with the conclusion that "I should not evaluate myself in terms of my shape or weight."

5. *"Cognitive restructuring" in practice.* While morbid beliefs and values concerning shape and weight are of central importance in the maintenance of bulimia, formal "cognitive restructuring" is not always required. This is because the entire treatment program is cognitively oriented. For example, significant cognitive change often occurs during Stage 1 and the early part of Stage 2. Certain behavioral interventions, such as weekly weighing and the introduction of avoided foods, are particularly potent in promoting cognitive change, largely because they highlight and challenge the patient's beliefs and values. Thus, if patients are encouraged to obey such behavioral instructions, many of their dysfunctional attitudes become progressively eroded. As a matter of routine, however, patients' beliefs and values should be explored, but the therapist may discover that sufficient cognitive change has occurred for formal cognitive restructuring to be unnecessary. More often it is evident that, although there has been some cognitive change, certain core attitudinal abnormalities remain intact.

Although cognitive resturcturing is presented here as a strictly ordered process that progresses with measured tread through several well-defined stages, in practice the course tends to be highly variable and erratic. For this reason it is essential that the therapist remain clear about the objectives of cognitive restructuring and the means of achieving them; otherwise there is a risk that treatment will degenerate into a series of vague discussions. Each session must contribute toward helping the patient identify and examine her thoughts, beliefs, or values. It is especially important to set patients well-defined, manageable homework tasks: All to often, patients are given imprecise instructions that are impossible to follow.

Some patients are resistant to cognitive restructuring. Usually this resistance stems from a fear of the unknown, a feeling that therapy is becoming unacceptably intrusive, and a realization that certain fundamental and private aspects of themselves are going to be brought out into the open. This reluctance to embark on cognitive restructuring is understandable. Nevertheless, patients must be reminded of the rationale for exploring their thoughts, beliefs, and values, and they must be persuaded to embark upon the enterprise. Usually their reticence diminishes after one or two sessions, especially if the potential benefits of such self-exploration are becoming evident.

A minority of patients seem completely unable to engage in cognitively oriented tasks. While they appear to understand the rationale and are willing to do the necessary homework, they seem incapable of identifying their thoughts, beliefs, or values. This inability to examine cognitive processes effectively precludes cognitive restructuring. With such patients this part of treatment is best abandoned; instead, the therapist should concentrate on those behavioral interventions that seem most likely to promote cognitive change.

Body Image Misperception and Body Image Disparagement. Occasionally a patient with bulimia exhibits unequivocal body image misperception, in which she misperceives the size of part or all of her body. Clinical experience with patients with anorexia nervosa suggests that this abnormality fails to respond to direct modification, and it appears that the same is true of patients with bulimia. Accordingly, using the therapeutic strategies of Garner and Garfinkel (1981), the therapist should attempt to help the patient recognize the phenomenon and function in spite of it. The patient should be provided with all the evidence indicating that she misperceives her shape, and she should be encouraged to attribute this misperception to her eating disorder. She should be told that it is as if she were color-blind with respect to her figure. Whenever she sees herself as fat, she should remind herself that she misperceives her shape, and that she should judge her size according to the opinions of trusted others and the information provided by weekly weighing.

"Body image disparagement" refers to feelings of extreme revulsion toward one's body. It is not often found in anorexia nervosa, but it is present in a minority of patients with bulimia (Fairburn & Cooper, in press). It may coexist with body image misperception. Usually patients with body image disparagement do their utmost to avoid seeing their bodies. For example, they will dress and undress in the dark; they will avoid mirrors; they will wear shapeless clothes; and, in the more extreme cases, they will bathe or shower while wearing a chemise. Treatment involves exposure. Rather than avoiding seeing herself, the patient should look out for opportunities to see and reveal her body — for example, by looking in mirrors, by going to swimming baths or saunas, or by attending aerobics classes.

INTERVIEWS 15 AND 16

Interviews 15 and 16 should continue along the lines outlined for Interviews 9 through 14. However, in addition, the therapist must remind the patient that the end of treatment is imminent and that these sessions constitute the last of the weekly interviews. Patients should be encouraged to discuss their feelings about the prospect of ending treatment. Some are pleased and regard it as a challenge, whereas others are alarmed and view their gains as precarious. The therapist should explain that ending treatment is an important and necessary stage in overcoming the problem.

PROGRESS DURING STAGE 2

In most cases, Stage 2 results in a consolidation of the gains made during the first phase of treatment. Binge eating becomes infrequent or ceases altogether, while dysfunctional attitudes toward body shape and weight lessen in intensity. Occasionally progress is sufficiently rapid to justify abbreviating the course of treatment. However, the therapist should beware of judging progress simply in behavioral terms. It is quite possible for the patient to improve behaviorally while retaining the specific psychopathology that maintains the disorder. In such cases, progress is likely to be spurious and short-lived. On the other hand, if some cognitive and behavioral problems remain despite the completion of Stage 2, this is not necessarily an indication for extending treatment. If definite changes do seem to be occurring, then it is reasonable to prolong this stage in treatment, but rarely by more than an additional four sessions. Experience suggests that little is gained from protracted courses of treatment, whereas patients often continue to improve following discharge.

Stage 3

Stage 3, the final stage in treatment, consists of three interviews at 2-week intervals. The aims of this stage are to ensure that progress is maintained and to prepare for future difficulties.

INTERVIEWS 17 TO 19

The Maintenance of Progress. The patient should be encouraged to practice the techniques learned during Stage 2. She should relax control over the content of her diet while adhering to the pattern of regular eating. She should continue problem solving and cognitive restructuring. The therapist should adopt more of a "back-seat" role, and the patient should take more of the initiative.

The patient should be asked to consider how she will manage once treatment has finished. Obviously, she will not want to continue monitoring herself indefinitely; however, she should be advised to persist in it for the meantime. She should only cease monitoring if she is certain she has complete control over eating, since the desire to stop may stem from a reluctance to acknowledge that there has been a deterioration in the eating problem. The patient should be informed that normal sensations of hunger and fullness will return, if they have not done so already; once these are established, they may be used to help her decide when to eat, so long as a pattern of regular eating is maintained. The patient should be strongly advised against dieting, since this will tend to encourage binge eating.

Preparation for Difficulties in the Future. The therapist should remind the patient that she may experience further difficulties in the future, especially at times of extreme stress. In order to prepare for such times, the patient should construct a plan for use when she senses that her eating is becoming a problem. This may be set as a homework task. Subsequently, the plan should be discussed with the therapist, who should then prepare a formal typewritten version for the patient to keep. A typical maintenance plan is shown in the Appendix.

The patient must be told to expect occasional setbacks. She should be reminded that she has dealt successfully with such difficulties during treatment, and that she therefore has the capacity to do so in the future. She should not be disheartened by an occasional slip-up. However, at such a time she should always consider why the slip-up occurred and how she might prevent similar difficulties from arising again.

FURTHER APPLICATIONS OF THE COGNITIVE–BEHAVIORAL APPROACH

Anorexia Nervosa

Patients with bulimia have many features in common with those with anorexia nervosa, and about 33% of bulimics have had anorexia nervosa in the past (Fairburn & Cooper, 1984a; Pyle, Mitchell, & Eckert, 1981). In particular, the specific psychopathology of the two conditions is similar. Since the cognitive–behavioral approach to the treatment of bulimia appears capable of modifying these abnormal attitudes, it seems reasonable to expect that similar techniques might benefit patients with anorexia nervosa (Fairburn, 1983a). This seems especially true of patients with the bulimic subtype of anorexia nervosa (i.e., those who binge), since they are also likely to benefit from the behavioral strategies used to establish a pattern of regular eating.

For this approach to be used to treat patients with anorexia nervosa, it needs to be modified and lengthened in order to accommodate two major problems. The first is poor motivation. Since the behavior of most patients with anorexia nervosa is consonant with their beliefs and values, many see no need for treatment. Garner and Bemis (1982) have described various ways of increasing the motivation of these patients. They emphasize the importance of establishing a sound therapeutic relationship, accepting the patient's beliefs and values as genuine for her, and adopting an experimental approach in which the therapist and patient together explore the use of various different treatment strategies. In addition, at the outset of treatment, it is worthwhile to review from the patient's standpoint the relative advantages and disadvantages of change. It is particularly important to identify issues that the patient regards as problems. Such issues often include starvation-related symptoms — for example, impaired concentration, sensitivity to cold, preoccupation with food and eating, and sleep disturbance. Once patients understand the origin of these symptoms, they are sometimes more willing to engage in treatment. The issue of motivation is less problematic with the subgroup of patients who binge, since the associated sense of loss of control is invariably a source of great distress. These patients positively welcome the self-control strategies used in the early stages of treatment (Cooper & Fairburn, 1984).

The second problem in applying this treatment to anorexia nervosa is the need for weight gain. Unless the weight loss is extreme or the patient's health is endangered by physical complications, programmed weight gain can be incorporated into the outpatient treatment regimen. Before emphasizing the need for weight gain, it is best to devote several sessions to the establishment of a collaborative working relationship. Thereafter, weight gain must become a nonnegotiable part of treatment. However, patients must understand why they need to gain weight. They need to be informed of the physical and psychological sequelae of starvation, and they need to understand how these sequelae perpetuate their eating problem (cf. Garfinkel & Garner, 1982). It is best to decide on a target weight range in excess of 85% of the average weight for their age and height. Patients should be reassured that care will be taken to ensure that they do not exceed this range and that there is no danger of their losing control over eating. Precisely how they choose to increase their weight is relatively unimportant, so long as the weight gain is gradual (about 1 kg or 2 lb per week) and occurs without contravening other elements of the behavioral program. In effect, this means that they must eat high-calorie foods as part of their meals or snacks. Alternatively, some patients find it easier to drink energy-rich preparations, regarding them as "medicine." This approach is perfectly acceptable during the period of weight restoration, but once the target range has been reached, patients must maintain their weight without using artificial dietary supplements. If weight gain does not occur, the therapist and patient must consider whether hospitalization is indicated. On the other hand, if the patient succeeds in gaining weight and reaches the target range, treatment can follow the guidelines described earlier.

Preliminary experience with this approach has produced mixed findings (Cooper & Fairburn, 1984). Patients with the bulimic form of anorexia nervosa seem to do well, but the restricting patients (i.e., those who do not binge) appear not to benefit. These findings are interesting, since bulimic patients have been reported to respond less well to conventional treatment regimens (Garfinkel, Moldofsky, & Garner, 1977). For this reason, it would seem worthwhile to pursue the application of cognitive–behavioral techniques to the treatment of patients with the bulimic form of anorexia nervosa. However, until effective methods of increasing the motivation of restricting patients have been developed, cognitive-behavior therapy with this subgroup is likely to be relatively ineffective (Cooper & Fairburn, 1984). Cognitive–behavioral methods that form the basis of a longer-term approach to anorexia nervosa have been described by Garner and Bemis (1982; Chapter 6, this volume).

Other Related Disorders

Some patients present with a number of features of bulimia or anorexia nervosa without fulfilling the diagnostic criteria for either syndrome. These patients benefit from elements of this cognitive–behavioral approach. For example, there is a group of patients who diet excessively, induce vomiting when they feel they have overeaten, yet neither binge nor have a weight that is outside the normal range. These patients appear to respond to a treatment that combines the restraint-reducing techniques with cognitive restructuring and training in problem solving.

Obesity

In some respects, this cognitive–behavioral treatment for bulimia may be viewed as a modification of the standard behavioral program for obesity. The main differences are that treatment is more intensive in the initial stages, it is lengthier, and there is a greater emphasis on cognitive factors and the maintenance of change. It is possible that the effectiveness of existing behavioral programs for obesity might be increased by incorporating some of these modifications. It would certainly seem appropriate to use elements of this approach in the treatment of obese people who binge, a population that has been reported to respond poorly to conventional programs (Wilson,

1976). In addition, the techniques employed in the latter half of Stage 2 might benefit the minority of obese people with body image disparagement.

FUTURE DEVELOPMENTS OF THE COGNITIVE–BEHAVIORAL APPROACH

Group Therapy

Since bulimia probably constitutes a significant source of psychiatric morbidity (Fairburn, 1983a), there is a need to investigate whether this cognitive–behavioral treatment can be adapted for use with groups of patients. It might be predicted that there would be positive advantages in treating these patients in groups, since this might help ameliorate their extreme guilt, shame, and secrecy. However, serious doubts must be raised concerning the feasibility of conducting formal cognitive restructuring within the setting of a group. Cognitive restructuring is a subtle and complex process, which not only is by its nature tailored to the individual, but also relies heavily on a Socratic dialogue between the therapist and the patient. Clearly an exchange of this type would not be possible within a group.

This reservation does not apply to most other elements of the treatment program. The behavioral techniques of Stage 1, the measures to reduce dietary restraint, and the training in problem solving could all be conducted in groups. Since these measures alone sometimes result in significant cognitive change, group therapy might therefore benefit a significant proportion of patients, especially those whose attitudes are not significantly disturbed. Patients with grossly abnormal attitudes are likely to require treatment on an individual basis, although this could be combined with group therapy.

Drugs as an Adjunct to Cognitive-Behavior Therapy

The use of antidepressant drugs has been discussed earlier (see p. 165). They are occasionally indicated — not as a treatment of bulimia as such, but rather as a treatment of a coexisting depressive disorder.

Appetite suppressants, however, may prove to be a useful adjunct to the cognitive–behavioral treatment of bulimia; they are unlikely to be an effective treatment on their own. Under laboratory conditions, both methylamphetamine (Ong, Checkley, & Russell, 1983) and fenfluramine (Robinson, Checkley, & Russell, 1983) have been shown to decrease the food intake of these patients, and it has been claimed that this reduction is accompanied by decreased frequency of binge eating. While the last point is open to question, the effect on food intake is nevertheless of potential clinical importance, since it might result in patients' being less likely to break their dietary rules and thereby less likely to binge. If this proves to be the case, such drugs might be useful in the early stages of treatment, when the principal emphasis is on regaining control over eating.

Several points are worth making about this application of appetite suppressants. First, these drugs have a range of different actions and do not simply affect "appetite." They have different effects on food choice (Blundell, Latham, Moniz, McArthur, & Rogers, 1979), eating style (Blundell et al., 1979), stress-induced eating (Antelman, Catggiula, Black, & Edwards, 1978), and possibly satiety (Blundell, Latham, & Leshem,

1976). Thus they could influence the eating of patients with bulimia in various different ways. Clearly, very sensitive research designs would be required to determine the exact nature of their action. The second point concerns their potential for abuse. While this is not a problem with fenfluramine, there is a danger that stimulating appetite suppressants might be abused. Not only are these patients in the age range liable to misuse appetite suppressants (Carabillo, 1978), but it has been suggested that patients with bulimia are particularly prone to abuse drugs (Lacey, 1982; Pyle *et al.*, 1981). In view of this possibility, fenfluramine might seem to be the appetite suppressant of choice. However, this use of fenfluramine might be complicated by its propensity to depress mood, especially when the drug is withdrawn (Oswald, Lewis, Dunleavy, Brezinova, & Briggs, 1971; Steel & Briggs, 1972), since patients with bulimia are vulnerable to depression.

The final point is somewhat speculative. It has recently been proposed that appetite suppressants act primarily by lowering body weight set point and only secondarily by suppressing appetite (Stunkard, 1981, 1982). Since a constitutional predisposition to obesity may prevent patients with bulimia from developing anorexia nervosa, appetite suppressants might therefore have the effect of inducing anorexia nervosa in patients with bulimia. This course of events would be most unusual: If patients change from one of these disorders to the other, it is almost invariably in the opposite direction. The only way to prevent this complication would be to ensure that appetite suppressants are not used in isolation, but instead are combined with measures capable of changing these patients' dysfunctional attitudes concerning their shape and weight.

CONCLUDING REMARKS

While a considerable body of clinical experience supports the use of this cognitive–behavioral approach in the treatment of bulimia, it must be noted that it has not yet been formally evaluated. It is quite conceivable that its effects are nonspecific, and that similar results would be obtained by any credible treatment that provides active support and structure.

Before any treatment for bulimia can be wholeheartedly advocated, its use must be supported by data from controlled outcome studies. Using reputable standardized measures, such studies should assess each facet of the condition, including patients' eating habits, mood, and (most important) their attitudes toward their shape and weight. Unfortunately, as yet there is no satisfactory measure of these attitudes (Fairburn, 1983a). With regard to the choice of control groups, there seems little need to use waiting-list controls, since bulimia tends to run a chronic, unremitting course. Moreover, Lacey (1983) found that the frequency of binge eating and vomiting of 15 patients with bulimia did not change while they were on a 10-week waiting list. On the other hand, attention or placebo controls have definite limitations, particularly as regards the investigation of psychological forms of treatment, since they often have limited credibility. It therefore seems that, when evaluating a psychological treatment for bulimia, the most appropriate control is an alternative form of psychotherapy that differs in terms of one or more postulated essential elements. Alternatively, should evidence suggest that pharmacological treatment benefits these patients, then a control group could receive drug treatment. Finally, the nature of the follow-up period must be considered. Not only should this be of reasonable length (6 months would seem to be the absolute minimum), but account should be taken of intervening events, including, of course, further treatment. No study of the treatment of bulimia has even approached these requirements.

APPENDIX: A PATIENT'S MAINTENANCE PLAN[1]

Eating problems may recur at times of stress. You should regard your eating problem as an Achilles heel: It is the way you may react at times of difficulty.

You discovered during treatment that certain strategies helped you regain control over eating. The strategies you found most helpful are listed below. These should be re-established under two sets of circumstances: (1) if you sense you are at risk of relapse; or (2) if your eating problem has deteriorated. At such times there will often be some unsolved difficulty underlying your relapse or fear of relapse. You must therefore examine what is happening in your life and look for any events or difficulties that might be of relevance. Once these have been identified, you should then consider all possible solutions to these problems and construct an appropriate plan of action. In addition, you should use one or more of the following strategies to regain control over eating:

1. Set some time aside so that you can reflect on your current difficulties. You need to devise a plan of action. Reckon on formally re-evaluating your progress every day or so. Some strategies may have worked; some may not.

2. Recommence monitoring everything you eat, when you eat it.

3. Restrict your eating to three or four planned meals each day, plus one or two planned snacks. Try to have these meals and snacks at predetermined times.

4. Plan your days ahead. Avoid both long periods of unstructured time and overbooking. If you are feeling at risk of losing control, plan your meals in detail so that you know exactly what and when you will be eating. In general, you should try to keep "one step ahead" of the problem.

5. Restrict your food stocks. If you feel you are at risk of buying too much food, carry as little money as possible.

6. Identify the times at which you are most likely to overeat (from recent experience and the evidence provided by your monitoring sheets), and plan alternative activities that are incompatible with eating, such as meeting friends, exercising, or taking a bath.

7. Whenever possible, avoid areas where stocks of food are kept. Try to keep out of the kitchen between meals.

8. If you are thinking too much about your weight, make sure you are weighing no more than once a week. If necessary, stop weighing altogether. If you want to reduce weight, do so by cutting down the quantity you eat at each meal rather than by skipping meals. Remember, you should accept a weight range, and gradual changes in weight are best.

9. If you are thinking too much about you shape, this may be because you are anxious or depressed. You tend to feel fat when theings are not going well. You should try problem solving in order to see whether you can identify any current problems and do something positive to solve or at least minimize them.

10. If possible, confide in someone. Explain your present predicament. A trouble shared is a trouble halved. Remember, you would not mind any friend of yours sharing his or her problems with you.

---

1. From "Bulimia: Its Epidemiology and Management" by C. G. Fairburn, 1983, in A. J. Stunkard and E. Stellar (Eds.), *Eating and Its Disorders* (pp. 235–258), New York: Raven Press. Reprinted by permission.

11. Set yourself limited, realistic goals. Work from hour to hour. One "failure" does not justify a succession of failures. Note your successes, however modest, on your monitoring sheets.

Before seeking professional help, try to use the strategies listed above. Remember, you have used them with benefit in the past.

ACKNOWLEDGMENTS

I am extremely grateful to Dr. Peter Cooper and Dr. Zafra Barkusky for their helpful advice during the writing of this chapter. I am also greatly indebted to Marianne O'Connor for her help with the preparation of the manuscript. Included in this chapter is an abbreviated version of a treatment manual that is being used in a study of the management of bulimia nervosa. This research project is being supported by a grant from the Medical Research Council of the United Kingdom. I am a Wellcome Trust Senior Lecturer.

REFERENCES

American Psychiatric Association. (1980). *Diagnostic and statistical manual of mental disorders* (3rd ed.). Washington, DC: Author.

Antelman, S. M., Caggiula, A. R., Black, C. A., & Edwards, D. J. (1978). Stress reverses the anorexia induced by amphetamine and methylphenidate but not fenfluramine. *Brain Research, 143*, 580–585.

Beck, A. T., Rush, A. J., Shaw, B. F., & Emery, G. (1979). *Cognitive therapy of depression.* New York: Guilford Press.

Blundell, J. E., Latham, C. J., & Leshem, M. B. (1976). Differences between the anorexic actions of amphetamine and fenfluramine: Possible effects on hunger and satiety. *Journal of Pharmacy and Pharmacology, 28*, 471–477.

Blundell, J. E., Latham, C. J., Moniz, E., McArthur, R. A., & Rogers, P. J. (1979). Structural analysis of the actions of amphetamine and fenfluramine on food intake and feeding behavior in animals and in man. *Current Medical Research and Opinion, 6*(Suppl. 1), 34–54.

Bo-Lynn, G., Santa-Ana, C. A., Morawski, S. G., & Fordtran, J. S. (1983). Purging and calorie absorption in bulimic patients and normal women. *Annals of Internal Medicine, 99*, 14–17.

Bruch, H. (1973). *Eating disorders: Obesity, anorexia nervosa, and the person within.* New York: Basic Books.

Carabillo, E. A. (1978). USA Drug Abuse Warning Network. In S. Garattini & R. Samanin (Eds.), *Central mechanisms of anorectic drugs* (pp. 461–471). New York: Raven Press.

Chernin, K. (1983). *Womansize: The tyranny of slenderness.* London: The Women's Press.

Cooper, P. J., & Fairburn, C. G. (1983). Binge-eating and self-induced vomiting in the community: A preliminary study. *British Journal of Psychiatry, 142*, 139–144.

Cooper, P. J., & Fairburn, C. G. (1984). *Cognitive behavior therapy for anorexia nervosa: Some preliminary findings.* Manuscript submitted for publication.

Crisp, A. H. (1967). The possible significance of some behavioral correlates of weight and carbohydrate intake. *Journal of Psychosomatic Research, 11*, 117–131.

Fairburn, C. G. (1981). A cognitive behavioral approach to the management of bulimia. *Psychological Medicine, 11*, 707–711.

Fairburn, C. G. (1982). Binge-eating and its management. *British Journal of Psychiatry, 141*, 631–633.

Fairburn, C. G. (1983a). Bulimia: Its epidemiology and management. In A. J. Stunkard & E. Stellar (Eds.), *Eating and its disorders* (pp. 235–258). New York: Raven Press.

Fairburn, C. G. (1983b). Bulimia nervosa. *British Journal of Hospital Medicine, 29*, 537–542.

Fairburn, C. G., & Cooper, P. J. (1982). Self-induced vomiting and bulimia nervosa: An undetected problem. *British Medical Journal, 284*, 1153–1155.

Fairburn, C. G., & Cooper, P. J. (1984a). The clinical features of bulimia nervosa. *British Journal of Psychiatry, 144*, 238–246.

Fairburn, C. G., & Cooper, P. J. (1984b). Rumination in bulimia nervosa. *British Medical Journal, 288*, 826–827.

Fairburn, C. G., & Cooper, P. J. (in press). Binge-eating, self-induced vomiting and laxative abuse: A community study. *Psychological Medicine.*

Ferguson, J. F. (1975). *Learning to eat: Behavior modification for weight control*. Palo Alto, CA: Bull.

Garfinkel, P. E., & Garner, D. M. (1982). *Anorexia nervosa: A multidimensional perspective*. New York: Brunner/Mazel.

Garfinkel, P. E., Moldofsky, H., & Garner, D. M. (1977). The outcome of anorexia nervosa: Significance of clinical features, body image, and behavior modification. In R. A. Vigersky (Ed.), *Anorexia nervosa* (pp. 315–329). New York: Raven Press.

Garner, D. M., & Bemis, K. M. (1982). A cognitive–behavioral approach to anorexia nervosa. *Cognitive Therapy and Research, 6*, 123–150.

Garner, D. M., & Garfinkel, P. E. (1979). The Eating Attitudes Test: An index of the symptoms of anorexia nervosa. *Psychological Medicine, 9*, 273–279.

Garner, D. M., & Garfinkel, P. E. (1981). Body image in anorexia nervosa: Measurement, theory and clinical implications. *International Journal of Psychiatry in Medicine, 11*, 263–284.

Goldberg, D. P., & Hillier, V. F. (1979). A scaled version of the General Health Questionnaire. *Psychological Medicine, 9*, 139–145.

Lacey, J. H. (1982). The bulimia syndrome at normal body weight: Reflections on pathogenesis and clinical features. *International Journal of Eating Disorders, 2*, 59–66.

Lacey, J. H. (1983). Bulimia nervosa, binge-eating, and psychogenic vomiting: A controlled treatment study and long-term outcome. *British Medical Journal, 286*, 1609–1613.

Mahoney, M. H., & Mahoney, K. (1976). *Permanent weight control*. New York: Norton.

Mitchell, J. E., Pyle, R. L., Eckert, E. D., Hatsukami, D., & Lentz, R. (1983). Electrolyte and other physiological abnormalities in patients with bulimia. *Psychological Medicine, 13*, 273–278.

Montgomery, S. A., & Asberg, M. (1979). A new depression scale designed to be sensitive to change. *British Journal of Psychiatry, 134*, 382–389.

Ong, Y. L., Checkley, S. A., & Russell, G. F. M. (1983). Suppression of bulimic symptoms with methylamphetamine. *British Journal of Psychiatry, 143*, 288–293.

Orbach, S. (1978). *Fat is a feminist issue*. London: Paddington Press.

Oswald, I., Lewis, S. A., Dunleavy, D. L. F., Brezinova, V., & Briggs, M. (1971). Drugs of dependence though not of abuse: Fenfluramine and imipramine. *British Medical Journal, iii*, 70–73.

Paykel, E. S., Mueller, P. S., & de la Vergne, P. M. (1973). Amitriptyline, weight gain and carbohydrate craving: A side effect. *British Journal of Psychiatry, 123*, 501–507.

Polivy, J., Herman, C. P., Olmsted, M. P., & Jazwinski, C. (1984). Restraint and binge eating. In R. C. Hawkins, W. J. Fremouw, & P. Clement (Eds.), *The binge/purge syndrome: Diagnosis, treatment, and research* (pp. 104–122). New York: Springer.

Pope, H. G., Hudson, J. I., & Jonas, M. D. (1983). Antidepressant treatment of bulimia: Preliminary experience and practical recommendations. *Journal of Clinical Psychopharmacology, 3*, 274–281.

Pyle, R. L., Mitchell, J. E., & Eckert, E. D. (1981). Bulimia: A report of 34 cases. *Journal of Clinical Psychiatry, 42*, 60–64.

Robinson, P. H., Checkley, S. A., & Russell, G. F. M. *Suppression of symptoms of bulimia nervosa with fenfluramine*. Paper presented at the annual meeting of the British Feeding Group, Oxford, 1983.

Russell, G. F. M. (1979). Bulimia nervosa: An ominous variant of anorexia nervosa. *Psychological Medicine, 9*, 429–448.

Sabine, E. J., Yonace, A., Farrington, A., Barratt, K. H., & Wakeling, A. (1983). Bulimia nervosa: A placebo controlled double-blind therapeutic trial of mianserin. *British Journal of Clinical Pharmacology, 15*, 195S–202S.

Steel, J. M., & Briggs, M. (1972). Withdrawal depression in obese patients after fenfluramine treatment. *British Medical Journal, iii*, 26–27.

Stunkard, A. J. (1980). Psychoanalysis and psychotherapy. In A. J. Stunkard (Ed.), *Obesity* (pp. 355–368). Philadelphia: W. B. Saunders.

Stunkard, A. J. (1981). Anorectic agents: A theory of action and lack of tolerance in a clinical trial. In S. Garattini & R. Samanin (Eds.), *Anorectic agents: Mechanisms of action and tolerance* (pp. 191–209). New York: Raven Press.

Stunkard, A. J. (1982). Anorectic agents lower a body weight set point. *Life Sciences, 30*, 2043–2055.

Wilson, G. T. (1976). Obesity, binge eating, and behavior therapy: Some clinical observations. *Behavior Therapy, 7*, 700–701.

Wing, J. K., Cooper, J. E., & Sartorius, N. (1974). *The measurement and classification of psychiatric symptoms*. Cambridge, England: Cambridge University Press.

Wurtman, R. J. (1983). Behavioural effects of nutrients. *Lancet, i*, 1145–1147.

CHAPTER NINE

Exposure Plus Response Prevention Treatment of Bulimia

JAMES C. ROSEN / HAROLD LEITENBERG

In this chapter, we discuss a subvariety of bulimia, sometimes called "bulimia nervosa" (Russell, 1979) or "bulimarexia" (Boskind-Lodahl, 1978). This disorder refers to *normal-weight* individuals who habitually vomit or use purgatives (laxatives) after binge eating or after eating even minimal amounts of foods they consider fattening and frightening. Patients with this eating disorder are distinguishable from those anorexia nervosa patients who, in addition to self-starvation, occasionally engage in episodes of binge eating and vomiting (Casper, Eckert, Halmi, Goldberg, & Davis, 1980; Hsu, Crisp, & Harding, 1979). They are also distinguishable from individuals who binge but who do not vomit, such as normal-weight women who alternate between deprivation diets and bouts of overeating (Polivy, Herman, Olmsted, & Jazwinski, 1984). Although binge eating with and binge eating without vomiting are both classified under "bulimia" in the *Diagnostic and Statistical Manual of Mental Disorders*, third edition (DSM-III; American Psychiatric Association, 1980), there is good reason to consider these separately: They may have somewhat different etiologies; the course of the disorder may be different; the degree of associated pathology (both physical and psychological) is different; and the type of treatment that is likely to be effective may be different. It is also generally assumed that binge eating coupled with vomiting is a more severe and recalcitrant disorder than binge eating alone.

Although the exact incidence in the general population is still unknown, recent estimates suggest that 5-10% or more of college women in the United States may be gorging and vomiting on a regular basis (Clement & Hawkins, 1980; Crowther, Chernyk, Hahn, Hedeen, & Zaynor, 1983; Halmi, Falk, & Schwartz, 1981; Schwartz, Thompson, & Johnson, 1982). If accurate, this is a phenomenally large and frightening number.

Bulimia nervosa is a complex disorder, and undoubtedly many different factors contribute to its development and maintenance in a given individual. Given that this disorder is overwhelmingly more prevalent in females than in males,[1] however, an overriding issue is the greater cultural pressure on women to be slim. Individuals with bulimia nervosa invariably report that vomiting after eating began as an attempt to lose

---

1. Because of this prevalence, the feminine pronoun is used to refer to bulimia nervosa patients throughout this chapter.

James C. Rosen and Harold Leitenberg. Department of Psychology, University of Vermont, Burlington, Vermont.

weight or to prevent weight gain. There is thus no question but that bulimia nervosa patients are engaged in a desperate and self-defeating attempt to achieve some idealized version of the perfect slender body. However, as Boskind-Lodahl (1978) argues, women with bulimia nervosa, unlike those with anorexia nervosa, are usually not rejecting their "femininity" or adult sexuality. Instead, they have an exaggerated need to please and obtain approval from others in these areas. This is not the whole story, of course, and the sensitive therapist must also be on the lookout for many other issues, including early histories of parental rejection, low self-esteem in spheres other than appearance, clinical depression, inordinate feelings of guilt about being a selfish and bad person, and a host of other interpersonal concerns. Despite these far-reaching and typically complex clinical issues, however, there also has to be some direct focus on the behavioral features of bulimia nervosa — namely, binge eating and vomiting.

BEHAVIORAL MODELS OF BULIMIA NERVOSA

At the present time, three behavioral models of bulimia are emerging: the eating-habit control model, the interpersonal stress model, and the anxiety reduction model. There are specific approaches to treatment that come from each model, although they are clearly not mutually exclusive. In the first two formulations of bulimia nervosa, binge eating is the primary target problem for treatment, and vomiting is considered only a secondary role in the disorder. In fact, these two models could be applied to individuals with bulimia who *do not* vomit after eating.

According to the eating-habit control model, described by W. G. Johnson and Brief (1983), bulimia nervosa patients have a deficit in knowledge or skill about how to maintain a normal weight through appropriate regulation of food intake and activity. The typical progression of the disorder involves the patient's attempts to lose weight with an unrealistic or drastic diet. When this fails, the patient rebounds and binges (Wardle & Beinart, 1981). The pattern of binge eating after dieting is analogous to the counterregulatory eating of chronic dieters who are temporarily forced to break their restraint in the laboratory (Herman & Polivy, 1980). The patient compensates for binge-eating episodes with subsequent drastic diets. Unable to get out of this cycle and into a moderate form of dieting by eating "normal" amounts of food, the patient may use vomiting. This is much like drastic dieting in that it offsets binge eating and is reinforced by its role in weight regulation. According to the eating-habit control model, the patient in treatment should be helped to resist urges to binge and to establish eating and exercise habits that are realistic in the long term by using behavioral weight control methods similar to those employed for obesity (W. G. Johnson & Brief, 1983). Alternatively, the patient could be encouraged to resist binge eating *and* dieting, lest even moderate forms of restraint precipitate binges in the future (Orbach, 1978; Wardle & Beinart, 1981).

According to the interpersonal stress model, binge eating is triggered by stressful antecedent events. Negative feelings of deprivation, depression, anxiety, anger, and relationship problems involving loss and rejection stimulate the urge to binge; binge eating momentarily reduces these stresses (Abraham & Beumont, 1982; Clement & Hawkins, 1980; Katzman & Wolchik, 1983; Loro, 1980). From this perspective, binge eating fills a void in the patient's interpersonal skills and coping strategies, and eventually develops into an all-purpose mechanism to regulate negative emotions. Binge eating would not occur if the patient were to exercise adaptive coping strategies. When vomiting is present, it can be viewed as a secondary behavior that is used to relieve guilt and other negative emotions after eating. However, vomiting is not considered essential for initiating or sustaining the disorder; it merely offsets the effects of the driving force of the disorder, binge eating. According to this model, the patient in treatment should be helped to resist binge eating in times of stress and to practice other stress-reducing behaviors instead (Fairburn, 1981).

In contrast to the formulations described above, the anxiety reduction model (Leitenberg, Gross, Peterson, & Rosen, 1984; Rosen & Leitenberg, 1982) proposes that vomiting drives binge eating, rather than vice versa, and that to gain control over the disorder, the problem must first be attacked from the vomiting side rather than from the binge-eating side. The remainder of this chapter describes this model, as well as the use of an exposure plus response prevention treatment for bulimia nervosa.

ANXIETY REDUCTION MODEL OF BULIMIA NERVOSA

Some people with bulimia nervosa always binge eat before vomiting. Others may induce vomiting not only after binge eating, but also after moderate food intake. Still others will vomit only after eating certain specific types of food, regardless of the amount. As in anorexia nervosa, there is a morbid fear of weight gain. Eating elicits this anxiety; binge eating elicits it dramatically. Vomiting momentarily reduces it. It could be argued that vomiting in bulimia nervosa serves an anxiety-reducing function similar to compulsive handwashing and checking rituals in obsessive–compulsive neuroses. The bulimia nervosa patient believes that she rids herself of the effects of the "contaminating substance" by the vomiting ritual.

Two studies indicate that the vomiting component of the binge–purge cycle is anxiety-reducing. C. Johnson and Larson (1982) had bulimia nervosa patients rate mood and eating–purging behavior every 2 hours throughout the day for one week. They found that vomiting relieved negative feelings of anger, inadequacy, and lack of control. We (Leitenberg et al., 1984) had bulimia nervosa patients eat a series of meals that they ordinarily would vomit, such as a five-course dinner, a dinner plate of spaghetti, and candy bars. In therapy sessions, the patients were asked to push themselves to eat an amount of food that would elicit a strong urge to vomit, knowing in advance that they would not be able to vomit. In these instances, when the chain was broken and vomiting was blocked, eating was associated with a dramatic increase in anxiety.

A question often asked is this: If bulimia nervosa patients are so anxious about eating and weight gain, why then do they binge? The answer is that they rarely, if ever, do binge unless they are planning to vomit afterward. If circumstances are such that they will not be able to vomit, they will not binge. For example, we (Rosen, Leitenberg, Fondacaro, Gross, & Willmuth, in press) had bulimia nervosa subjects eat the same series of meals as that described above (large dinner, spaghetti, and candy) without vomiting afterward. In this instance, however, they were to eat only what they could comfortably keep down, rather than to push themselves to the point where they would feel they had to vomit. The results were that the subjects did not binge. In fact, they ate a very small amount of food, much less than a group of matched normal controls did. This contrasts with their typical complaint of eating "too much" or binge eating with these foods when they *do* plan to vomit.

In contrast to bulimia nervosa patients, classic obsessive–compulsive handwashers try to avoid initial contact with contaminating substances, even though they know they can wash afterward. Why the difference? One possible explanation is that hand-washing never completely resolves the dread of contamination, whereas bulimia nervosa patients somehow seem to be more secure in the magical protection of vomiting. The faith that bulimia nervosa patients have in vomiting is evident by the misconceptions that they commonly hold. For example, they believe they completely rid themselves of their intake by vomiting, even when vomiting is delayed for an hour or more after a binge begins. Also, they often believe that even if they ate normally, they still would gain a large amount of weight if they did not vomit. Another difference in avoidance behavior between the obsessive–compulsive and the bulimic is that there is no way for the bulimia nervosa patient to avoid the contaminant, food, unless she starves herself and becomes anorexic. Further, in the classic obsessive–compulsive there are no positive consequences of coming into contact with "dirt" or "germs." In fact, there may be secondary gains associated with such avoidance (e.g., control over one's spouse, rationalization for why one cannot deal effectively with the competitive pressures outside the home). In contrast, binge eating in bulimia nervosa does satisfy various psychological, gustatory, and physical needs. The fact that the bulimia nervosa patient will only binge if she can vomit afterward does not negate the pleasurable aspects of binge eating or the contributions of other factors to binge eating (e.g., self-nurturance, boredom and loneliness, feelings of deprivation, depression, anxiety, guilt, etc.). These factors are probably as applicable, if not more so, to people suffering from bulimia nervosa as they are to people in the general population who occasionally binge but who do *not* vomit. However, in women suffering from bulimia nervosa, such distressing feelings are likely to be temporarily relieved only when binge eating is coupled with vomiting afterward. These pleasurable aspects of binge eating can only be realized if they are freed of anxiety by the anticipation of vomiting.

Once it has been established as an escape response, vomiting becomes the driving force that sustains binge eating, not vice versa. In fact, in the typical progression of bulimia nervosa, once self-induced vomiting is learned, binge eating usually becomes more severe and frequent (Abraham & Beumont, 1982). Vomiting is so effective in relieving guilt and the fear of weight gain that it becomes increasingly unnecessary for the bulimia nervosa patient to resist her urges to binge. In other words, anticipation of vomiting frees the bulimia nervosa patient from normal inhibitions against overeating. Based on their sequential analysis of binge eating, vomiting, and stress reduction, C. Johnson and Larson (1982) similarly suggested that vomiting rather than binge eating may be the "primary mechanism for tension regulation" in bulimia nervosa, and that vomiting comes to maintain binge eating, rather than the reverse.

In summary, according to this analysis, binge eating and self-induced vomiting in bulimia nervosa seem linked in a vicious circle by anxiety. Vomiting is an escape response that is reinforced by the subsequent reduction in anxiety about weight and is analogous to anxiety-reducing compulsive behaviors in obsessive–compulsive disorders. Binge eating usually only occurs in anticipation of vomiting, and binge eating becomes more severe as vomiting increases in frequency. In other words, binge eating in bulimia nervosa is more a consequence of vomiting than vomiting is a consequence of binge eating.

EMPIRICAL SUPPORT FOR EXPOSURE PLUS RESPONSE PREVENTION TREATMENT OF BULIMIA NERVOSA

According to the anxiety reduction model, and in line with recent developments in behavioral treatment of obsessive–compulsive disorders (Foa & Steketee, 1979), an exposure plus response prevention model of treatment for bulimia nervosa should prove effective. The two basic ingredients of this treatment paradigm are (1) exposure to the feared stimulus in the presence of a therapist (i.e., eating particular foods or amounts of foods), and (2) prevention of the habitual escape response (i.e., vomiting). In our first study (Rosen & Leitenberg, 1982), we examined the effectiveness of this exposure plus response prevention treatment protocol, using a multiple-baseline design in which therapy sessions were provided in sequence for different food groups (typically a full-course dinner, pasta, sweets). The results of this single-case experimental analysis were unusually clear: As each of three food groups was treated in turn, the amount the subject could eat without vomiting increased, and the anxiety and urge to vomit decreased for only that particular food group. By the end of treatment, vomiting outside of therapy was eliminated. Without specific instructions to do so, the subject also stopped binge eating. This final result supports the notion that in bulimia nervosa patients, habitual binge eating may be more a consequence of vomiting than vice versa. In a second study (Leitenberg et al., 1984), we found further support for the anxiety reduction model and exposure plus response prevention treatment: namely, that in the absence of the opportunity to vomit, food intake and associated thoughts and feelings about weight gain provoke anxiety. Also, in accord with behavioral treatments of other anxiety-based disorders, repeated exposure to feared stimuli (eating without vomiting) eventually leads to both decreased anxiety while eating and an increased ability to eat more normal amounts of food. The specific findings were as follows:

1. Within treatment sessions while subjects were eating, self-reported anxiety and the urge to vomit increased; after subjects stopped eating, self-reported anxiety and the urge to vomit eventually declined even though subjects were not permitted to vomit.

2. Across treatment sessions, the mean anxiety provoked by eating tended to decrease, as did the mean urge to vomit.

3. Across treatment sessions, the mean amount of calories consumed in therapy sessions tended to increase.

4. As treatment progressed, self-statements about eating problems (self-statements were analyzed from tape recordings of responses to probes to "think aloud and say whatever comes to mind") tended to become more positive and/or less negative.

5. Reductions in anxiety and negative self-statements across successive sessions were not prerequisites for increased eating behavior, or vice versa.

6. In four out of five subjects, binge eating and vomiting at home were substantially reduced or entirely eliminated, even though the focus of treatment sessions was primarily on vomiting rather than binge eating.

7. Finally, there were other positive effects of the treatment, including improvements on the Eating Attitudes Test (Garner & Garfinkel, 1979), the Beck Depression Inventory (Beck, Ward, Mendelson, Mock, & Erbaugh, 1961), the Lawson Social Self-Esteem Inventory (Lawson, Marshall, & McGrath, 1979) and the Rosenberg Self-Esteem Scale (Rosenberg, 1979), even though the focus of treatment sessions was primarily on the binge–purge cycle rather than on these more global variables.

BEHAVIORAL ASSESSMENT AND PRETREATMENT EVALUATION OF BULIMIA NERVOSA

There are two essential eating behaviors that need to be determined in bulimia nervosa: (1) the foods avoided when vomiting is *not* possible; (2) the type and amount of food consumption that usually results in vomiting. In addition to these eating behaviors, bulimia nervosa patients also report an extreme fear of obesity and hold many misconceptions about what is "too much" food, their susceptibility to weight gain, their bodily appearance, the nutritional and metabolic effects of foods, and the importance of vomiting in controlling their weight. A behavioral assessment should include an analysis of all three of these characteristics of bulimia nervosa: food avoidance, vomiting after eating, and irrational beliefs. These same three behaviors are the targets for an exposure plus response prevention treatment for bulimia nervosa. In the assessment of eating behavior, one may use the usual methods of interview, questionnaires, and recording of at-home eating behavior to obtain relevant information. In addition, it can be quite illuminating to "test" the patient's eating behavior and beliefs in a controlled way, both at home and in the laboratory.

Food Diary and Interview

In a daily food diary, the patient should record all food and liquid intake: the time of day, type of food, how it was prepared, and the amount eaten. Patients also rate anxiety for each eating episode on a 0–100 scale, where 0 is defined as "no discomfort or anxiety" and 100 is defined as "extreme discomfort or anxiety." Further, they rate their urge to vomit after every eating episode on a 0–100 scale, where 0 is defined as "no urge to vomit" and 100 is defined as "an overwhelming urge to vomit." Patients should also record whether or not they consider an eating episode a binge and whether or not they vomit. These records should be collected for at least 2 weeks prior to treatment, as well as throughout treatment, to determine the patient's current pattern of eating, food avoidance, and vomiting.

EATING AND VOMITING AT HOME

The overall frequency of vomiting is one of the significant characteristics of bulimia nervosa, as it most likely relates to the severity of the disorder and to associated problems. Frequency of vomiting varies tremendously among patients. Some vomit as much as several times a day, every day of the week. Others only vomit several times a week (Pyle, Mitchell, & Eckert, 1981). We have evaluated a number of patients who vomit more than 10 times per day. The patient who vomits several times per day is likely to be more preoccupied with eating and may have less concentration, time, or inclination to handle the demands of work, school, or social life, thereby worsening her psychological functioning. In our sample of bulimia nervosa patients, a high frequency of vomiting is associated with lower self-esteem on the Lawson Social Self-Esteem Inventory and the Rosenberg Self-Esteem Scale. It is unknown at this time whether the frequency of vomiting is a prognostic indicator independent of the duration of the disorder.

In addition to the frequency of vomiting, it is important to determine which foods the patient will vomit after eating. Typically, these foods include large meals, sweets, salty snacks, and other high-carbohydrate foods, such as pasta or bread (Abraham & Beumont, 1982; Basow & Schneck, 1983; Pyle *et al.*, 1981). In order to extinguish fears of eating and weight gain, the foods to be used as stimuli in the exposure procedure must include those that elicit the greatest anxiety. These can be identified by observing which foods are usually if not always eaten before the patient vomits, and which foods therefore are avoided unless vomiting is planned. Furthermore, the patient should help to arrange the foods in a hierarchical order for their anxiety-provoking properties.

If the coupling of eating and vomiting is weak (e.g., if there are no foods that regularly provoke vomiting, and the frequency of vomiting is very low), it can be concluded that neither the anxiety nor the escape response is well developed. In this instance, there are minimal fears to extinguish, and an alternative to an exposure plus response prevention therapy should be used.

There are at least two other patterns that may contradict the usefulness of the exposure plus response prevention paradigm. The first is the case of a patient who is literally unable to eat anything without vomiting afterward. Such a patient has too many opportunities to engage in the escape response (vomiting) outside the therapy session in relation to her opportunities to practice eating without vomiting in the therapy sessions. It may be necessary in this instance to intensify the prevention of vomiting beyond what is possible with the outpatient approach described here, by using instead a more controlled environment, such as an inpatient setting. Further, this patient, who may be trying to avoid digesting any food, may have features that are more akin to anorexia nervosa. Accordingly, treatment approaches that are employed with anorexia nervosa patients with bulimia episodes could be used.

The second pattern for which exposure plus response prevention therapy may not be appropriate is the case of a patient who is very inconsistent: For example, sometimes she vomits a particular food or amount of food, and other times the same food or amount of food is retained. The therapist should try to determine what conditions are associated with the episodes of eating that are followed by vomiting. For example, a particular patient sometimes vomits after eating potato chips but sometimes does not. She keeps potato chips down if she has not eaten much during the previous meals of the day. If she has been "good" and has restrained her eating earlier, she may not feel so anxious about weight gain from potato chips. The likelihood of this patient's vomiting is influenced in part by that day's caloric preload. Another example is a patient who vomits after eating a food when she anticipates having to eat a large meal later in the day. If she is not planning to eat again, she may not vomit. The exposure plus response prevention therapy might be viable in cases of inconsistent vomiting so long as a consistent set of "rules" for the decision to vomit can be ascertained, as in these examples. Furthermore, to provoke anxiety during eating in the therapy session, it must also be possible to program these conditions (e.g., a specific caloric intake before or after the session) into the treatment format.

BELIEFS AND FEELINGS

The reasons for the decision to vomit during the day and the feelings associated with the urge to vomit should be explored. Distorted beliefs about their bodies, food, and eating behavior are cognitive mediators that serve to sustain vomiting in bulimia nervosa patients. A patient's decision to vomit is usually governed by her own set of "rules" about what are safe or acceptable foods to "keep down." The cognitive process involved and the control that it exercises over vomiting is similar to the cognitive process described in restrained eaters who overeat in the laboratory when they think they have "blown" their diet (Herman & Polivy, 1980). Knowledge of the patient's rules for unacceptable food will help the therapist to construct an eating situation that will expose the patient to the salient cues for anxiety, such as in the example above involving potato chips. These beliefs can also be earmarked for the patient to challenge later as she accumulates evidence that it is safe *not* to vomit.

In her eating diary, the patient records whether she considers an eating episode to be a binge. In actuality, "binge" does not always refer to.eating an enormous amount of food, at least not in the objective sense of the term. What bulimia nervosa patients usually mean by "binge" is that they have eaten "too much" in relation to their ideal of what their consumption should be. We allow this use of the term "binge" as a means for the patient to label anxiety-provoking eating. Furthermore, it provides the therapist with an opportunity to discuss the patient's rules for acceptable versus unacceptable eating. In addition to beliefs, other emotional and bodily sensations (e.g., feeling fat, protruding, or bloated) that are cues for vomiting should be identified, as these are the experiences of the patient that are to be provoked during the therapy session.

ASSOCIATED INTERPERSONAL EVENTS

The eating diary sometimes reveals "good" days and "bad" days. It can be helpful in reviewing these diaries with the patient to discover whether certain specific events, such as particular interactions or thoughts about spouse, children, parents, and coworkers, tend to trigger the desire to eat and vomit.

Test Meals

In addition to the interview and self-recording, a standardized laboratory behavioral measure of eating behavior can also be used in the assessment of bulimia nervosa. This can add valuable information in assessing the severity of the disorder prior to treatment, and thus in gauging improvement following treatment. With respect to the goal of assessing anxiety about eating and avoidance of food, we have used a series of "test meals," in which the patient has the opportunity to eat frightening foods with the intention of not vomiting afterward. A measurement of consumption and anxiety in the test meal situation would be similar to a behavioral avoidance test (Lang &

Lazovik, 1963), such as has been used in the assessment of a variety of phobias (Taylor & Agras, 1981). However, to provoke anxiety and avoidance behavior in the individual with bulimia nervosa, the escape response (vomiting) must be prevented. This assessment is similar to the use of behavioral avoidance tests in obsessive–compulsive disorders, in which approach to the feared stimulus or to discriminative stimuli for rituals is measured while the individual is being prevented from engaging in the ritual (Rachman, Hodgson, & Marks, 1970). It would be predicted that a woman with bulimia nervosa would be unable to eat *normal* amounts of frightening foods if she knew that she would be unable to vomit. The more food has acquired anxiety-provoking properties, the less the individual should be able to eat if vomiting is prevented.

TEST MEAL PROCEDURE

The foods for the patient to eat and other conditions (e.g., caloric preload) for the test meals should be tailored to the individual patient. The patient should arrange to eat three test meals on three separate days. One meal is a large dinner obtained from a restaurant and served by the evaluator in the laboratory or clinic. For instance, it can consist of a meat entree, cooked vegetables, salad with dressing, a potato or rice, and two rolls with butter. The patient eats this meal alone in an office while the evaluator is in another room. The other two test meals are unsupervised and eaten at the patient's home when she is alone. One meal is typically a spaghetti dinner or some other "fattening" food that is high in carbohydrate. The other test meal is a sweet snack, such as candy bars, ice cream, or doughnuts. The patient is instructed to eat what she normally would prior to the time of the meal and not to vomit for at least 1½ hours beforehand. She should consume the at-home test meals alone and without engaging in any other activity at the same time, such as watching television or reading. The patient is to agree not to vomit for at least 2½ hours after the test meal. She is instructed that this will allow enough time for her to digest the food. With this in mind, the patient should eat as much of the meal as she comfortably can, as much as she thinks she can keep down without vomiting afterward.

Although the instructions for this behavioral test with bulimia nervosa are straightforward, many patients make the meals much less threatening than they are designed to be, or eat more food than they can comfortably handle and vomit afterward. Some patients try to avoid the anxiety that they anticipate will occur in the test by choosing "safer" foods or versions of the meal. For example, the patient might select a broiled fish entree rather than a beef dish, which would trigger a greater urge to vomit, or she may fail to add the dressing to the salad. To prevent this from happening, the evaluator should carefully specify the foods in advance or even provide the food for the patient. Another possible occurrence is that the patient may not even face the food; she simply does not carry out the test, because she expects to be unable to eat anything under this condition. Even if the patient says that she is certain she will not be able to eat any of this food without vomiting, she is to go through the motions of sitting down with the meal; at least it will be possible to get some idea of the anxiety that the patient experiences when faced with the *opportunity* to eat without vomiting. In fact, about 50% of the patients in our sample ate nothing during at least one out of three test meals.

In contrast to completely avoiding the meal or to altering the meal in some way such that it is less threatening, some patients *over*challenge themselves and eat more than they really want to, and as a result are unable to refrain from vomiting afterward. In addition to *deliberately* overeating, some patients *inadvertently* overeat during test meals. The patient may have no idea in advance what a "comfortable" amount of food is, because it has been so long since she has eaten these foods without vomiting. As a result of these factors, some patients vomit after the test meals or eat their meals with other people, so that the social situation constrains them from vomiting even if the urge to do so is strong. This is why we emphasize to the patient that she not feel compelled to push herself to the point where the urge to vomit is very strong, or that she not push herself beyond the "safety zone." In fact, it is this boundary between a safe and unsafe amount of food that we want to determine. As a final comment on test meals that are not carried out properly, one hidden advantage of this occurrence is that it will give the therapist a clue for how the patient might resist the exposure plus response prevention procedure during the treatment phase.

SIGNIFICANCE OF TEST MEALS

The results of our study of test meals indicate that our bulimia nervosa patients ate very little in these situations. Specifically, they ate approximately 27%, 15%, and 12% of the large meal, spaghetti, and candy, respectively. This is much less than the consumption of matched normal controls, who ate approximately 70% in each test meal (Rosen *et al.*, in press). Previous studies have also shown that recovered bulimia nervosa patients increase their consumption in the test meals after therapy ends (Leitenberg *et al.*, 1984; Rosen & Leitenberg, 1982).

The information revealed by the test meal results is similar to information revealed by the eating diary. Test meals provide a measure of the severity of food avoidance. Usually they are consistent with what can be surmised from the eating diary. If a patient habitually vomits specific foods eaten at home, she can be expected to eat only a small amount of these foods without vomiting during test meal situations. Another useful function of the test meals is to test different foods for their anxiety-provoking capabilities in order to select the most appropriate foods for stimuli in therapy sessions. Finally, the test meal in the laboratory presents a good opportunity to assess the patient's beliefs, emotions, and physical sensations that are associated with eating frightening foods. We collect 2 minutes of thought sampling periodically during and after eating by having the patient say aloud into a tape recorder whatever she is thinking. This is a more precise sample of cognitions than the patient can provide from a description of an eating episode that took place at home. It is also possible to code these thoughts for positive and negative food-related content, for the purpose of comparing the patient's pretreatment and posttreatment status on these variables (Leitenberg *et al.*, 1984).

Other Purging Behavior

Another assessment issue involves whether or not vomiting is the only method of purging that the patient is using. In particular, is the patient primarily using laxatives rather than vomiting? A special characteristic of laxative use is that the purge is not completed for several hours after eating. In contrast, the more common method of purging, vomiting, can be performed immediately after eating. Do patients who use laxatives experience anxiety while they wait for the laxatives to take effect? Alternatively, do these patients feel so secure about the effects of laxatives on weight regulation that the delay of the purge is of no consequence to them? If the patient is prevented from using a laxative after eating in an exposure plus response prevention therapy session, how long will it be before anxiety is provoked? It may be that the duration of the exposure plus response prevention session will have to be greatly increased in order for the patient to experience anxiety. The effects on anxiety of using or being prevented from using laxatives have not been studied. To date, there is no report of exposure plus response prevention treatment in a case where laxative use is the sole purging behavior.

Other Psychological and Physical Pretreatment Evaluations

It can be helpful to evaluate other psychological factors that are pertinent to this population by including several broad-band measures in the pretreatment evaluation, such as the Beck Depression Inventory, the Eating Attitudes Test, the Eating Disorder Inventory (Garner, Olmsted, & Polivy, 1983), the Lawson Social Self-Esteem Inventory, and the Rosenberg Self-Esteem Scale. Also, if there are any questions about current physical status, such as the possibility of the patient's being hypokalemic, a medical evaluation is indicated.

TREATMENT

Treatment Format and Rationale for the Patient

In the beginning phase of treatment, the sessions are scheduled frequently (e.g., three sessions per week). Massed therapy sessions give the patient practice in eating frightening foods without vomiting several times within a short period. This speeds the patient's learning about the effects of this change on her weight and eating behavior. Furthermore, in exposure plus response prevention treatment of obsessive–compulsive disorders, massed sessions have been shown to be more effective than less frequent sessions (Foa & Steketee, 1979). The frequency of sessions should eventually be reduced in relation to the patient's improvement. In our previous studies, the treatment schedule was standardized for research purposes. The patients participated in three sessions per week for 6 weeks before weekly sessions were scheduled. If we had been able to individualize this schedule, some people would undoubtedly have benefitted from a more gradual shift from multiple sessions a week to weekly sessions, to biweekly sessions, and so on. The therapy may be provided on either an individual or a group basis. In the treatment studies previously summarized, the procedure was carried out on an individual basis. However, we have subsequently treated most of our research patients in a group format. At first glance there do not appear to be any significant disadvantages with this approach, and patients seem to benefit from the mutual feedback and support. However, we have not yet made a direct comparison of the group versus the individual format to determine whether one is more or less effective than the other.

The treatment rationale given to the patient during the initial sessions covers the following main points: She is told that binge eating is being maintained by vomiting; that if she learns to gain control over vomiting, binge eating will not be as likely to occur; that therapy sessions are designed to allow her to get in touch with the anxiety she experiences when eating; and that she will learn to overcome her anxiety without vomiting. This conceptualization often goes against most patients' theories of their disorder. Typically, patients argue that they would not vomit if only they did not binge; that once they start eating, they cannot stop; and that therapy should help them to control their eating, not their vomiting. Our response has been to tell the patient that our experience has been otherwise — that if they are not able to first learn to control their vomiting, they seldom can learn to control their eating. We reiterate that if they did not plan to vomit, they would probably eat too little, not too much, but that we understand that this is hard for them to believe. Although it might take some time before the patient believes the treatment rationale, the education process should begin in the first session.

In sum, each treatment session has two basic parts: (1) exposure to the feared stimulus (i.e., eating particular foods or particular amounts of food), and (2) prevention of the habitual escape (i.e., vomiting). During each treatment session, the patient is encouraged to eat an amount of food that causes a strong urge to vomit, beyond the point where vomiting would ordinarily occur. The patient knows in advance that she will not be allowed to vomit and that the therapist will stay with her until the urge to vomit is under control. The patient is told that treatment will be most beneficial if vomiting does not occur within 2½ hours after the end of any treatment session, so as to allow enough time for the food to be digested; and that it is best to stay with the therapist until she feels she can safely leave without vomiting afterward. At the beginning of therapy, a 2-hour session is usually needed for the patient to eat and gain control over the anxiety. Later sessions can be much shorter.

Eating in the Therapy Session

The types of foods to be used in the therapy sessions are those that have been found to be most anxiety-provoking during the pretreatment evaluation. It is best to give the patient as much variety in food as possible, as long as the patient's choice will enable her to face some fear of eating. For example, under the category of snack food, a patient might need to alternate practicing with ice cream, brownies, granola, and tortilla chips if she usually vomits after eating each one. The amount of food to be brought in by the patient or presented to the patient in the therapy session should always be a "normal" amount, or only slightly above the range most people could eat comfortably. It is not necessary for the patient to binge in the session in order to become anxious. In the absence of vomiting, even small quantities of food are typically defined by patients as "too much" and provoke intense anxiety. It should be recalled that baseline consumption in test meals is very low (Rosen *et al.*, in press). Initially, the patient only needs to eat slightly more than she did in the test meals. As therapy progresses, the patient should be encouraged to eat even more. However, it is also best to avoid extremely large amounts of food, so that the patient does not use these as standards for later consumption. Three pieces of pizza, a submarine sandwich, or three cups of macaroni and cheese will provide the patient with a sufficient range in amount with which to practice without being excessive. The order in which different foods are used depends on how much anxiety they provoke. The more frightening eating situations should be introduced after the patient has adapted to less frightening ones. One final guideline in regard to eating is that it may be better for the therapist not to eat with the patient during the session. To do otherwise could distract the patient from being aware of her feelings about eating and could influence the amount she eats.

Therapeutic Intervention

While the patient is eating and after she has finished, the therapist directs the patient's attention to whatever anxiety-provoking thoughts and sensations are being induced. The specific concerns that are provoked during the exposure procedure vary from session to session. The topics for discussion and intervention, however, typically fall into several recurring categories, which include misconceptions about the following:

1. *Susceptibility to weight gain.* Many patients fear that if they eat normally and do not vomit, they will gain an enormous amount of weight; that they will gain weight if they eat even 100 calories more than they think they should at any particular point; and that transient, slight increases in weight are always due to eating "too much," as opposed to other factors, such as decreased exercise or fluid retention during the menstrual cycle.

2. *Bodily appearance.* Patients may feel that certain body parts are too large or that they bulge immediately after eating; that slight weight fluctuations are noticeable; or that by losing weight it will be possible to alter other physical characteristics, such as a large frame.

3. *Nutrition and metabolic processes.* Many patients believe that certain foods (e.g., pasta) have no "nutritional value" and may even be harmful, or may lead to immediate and large weight gains; or that certain foods make them fat whereas other foods do not, even if the calories are the same.

4. *Effectiveness of vomiting.* Patients may think that vomiting after even long delays will prevent food eaten beforehand from being digested. In therapy sessions, after 30 minutes have gone by, we continually remind the patients that the food "has gone its way" and that vomiting now is too late.

The process of modifying these irrational beliefs and overcoming the anxiety that is provoked by eating is structured by the therapist. Information, feedback from other people, and various types of challenges to the patients' misconceptions are used. As therapy progresses and the patients have had repeated practice in eating without vomiting, the therapist tries to help the patients make several discoveries and reconceptualizations of their problems:

1. *Anxiety.* The anxiety patients experience after eating forbidden foods is not as overwhelming as they first thought it would be, and is capable of diminishing to tolerable levels even if they do not vomit. The changes in self-reported anxiety after eating in the therapy session and the time it takes to overcome the urge to vomit can be useful indicators of progress for a patient.

2. *Binge eating.* In the absence of planned vomiting, patients do not have an uncontrollable craving to consume huge amounts of food; instead, they have an obsessive craving to be slim, to eat as little as possible, not to gain weight. It is most important

to have the patients analyze the effects of not vomiting on their eating behavior in order for them to see that in their own experiences binge eating is more a consequence of vomiting than vice versa. Response prevention, which is carried out independently at home, away from the security and structure of the therapy session, is especially helpful in demonstrating to the patients that they do not binge if they do not plan to vomit, and that their problem is not that they eat "too much," but that they do not allow themselves to eat enough without vomiting.

3. Physical sensations. Physical sensations of immediate weight gain or being bloated, and feelings of gross changes in bodily appearance (particularly stomach, thighs, and buttocks) following consumption of normal or even less than normal amounts of food, are distorted; furthermore, these feelings are capable of being relieved without recourse to vomiting. In order to develop realistic perceptions of their weight and body size, patients should be encouraged to accept feedback about their appearance from one another, to reinterpret some unpleasant physical sensations as normal feelings of fullness after a meal, and to realize that such sensations will dissipate after digestion even if they do not vomit.

4. Pressure to be thin. The obsessive desire to achieve a "perfect" slim body usually stems from a complex mix of disturbed family relationships, low self-esteem and associated fears of rejection and abandonment, a variety of guilt feelings, and cultural values and stereotyped beliefs about appropriate feminine appearance and behavior. Interventions that can help the patient control the drive for thinness include the following:

a. Support and encouragement to fight against the social pressure for thinness and the conception that if a woman is not exceedingly thin, that automatically means she is fat.

b. Critical evaluation of the patient's current and ideal weights with respect to norms and her own weight history.

c. Feedback that some physical characteristics that the patient disparages may in fact exist, but that they are unalterable by weight loss (e.g., "Yes, you are big-boned," "Yes, your hips are proportionately larger than your chest," "Yes, your stomach has a round contour").

d. Encouragement to stop avoiding other situations besides eating that provoke anxiety about appearance, such as wearing shorts, looking in the mirror, or allowing a sexual mate to look at or touch certain body areas, and to face these situations without vomiting beforehand.

e. Promotion of a longer-range view of factors affecting weight gain (i.e., one's appearance will not change overnight, and one's appearance does not change as a function of minor fluctuations of weight).

f. Assurance that one's personality and worth as a person do not hinge on whether she loses or gains a few pounds.

5. Dieting. Patients' desire to maintain a strict diet and their criteria for "bad" foods, "having eaten too much," or "having blown it" are distorted and serve to trigger the impulse to eat even more and to vomit afterward. Several experiences can help the patient to control drastic, deprivation forms of dieting. The patient should be encourged to accept that some of her "bad" foods really are her preferred foods, and that to eliminate them permanently from her diet is unrealistic, unnecessary, and even harmful from the standpoint of preventing binge eating and vomiting in the future. These foods should not be avoided, but should be deliberately programmed into her diet so she can learn to eat these foods without "having to" vomit afterward. Erroneous ideas about the caloric value of certain foods should be corrected (e.g., "A doughnut does not contain 800 calories"). The patient's belief that in the absence of vomiting she will always "have to diet" (e.g., never eat more than 1200 calories) in order to maintain a normal weight should be challenged by giving her nutritional information and by having her sustain a "normal" caloric intake long enough to study the effect on her weight. Furthermore, the patient should be encouraged to exercise rather than to restrain or vomit. In our previous studies, some patients who have overcome bulimia nervosa have indeed gained several pounds, but have stayed within the normal range for weight. Others have not shown any change in weight.

Exposure Plus Response Prevention at Home

The patient should be given recommendations about increasing intake and decreasing vomiting at home, in order to promote transfer of the gains made during the treatment sessions to the patient's at-home eating behavior between treatment sessions. The timing and the nature of the recommendations for changing eating patterns at home should be individualized. Generally, the recommendations should be introduced when the patient has demonstrated improvement during the treatment sessions by reporting less anxiety and a lower urge to vomit after eating, and by consuming a greater amount of food. The instructions should begin with avoidance behavior. The patient should practice eating a certain food or eating at a time of the day that has been avoided up to that time in treatment. For example, a patient who only eats in the late evening and who avoids breakfast and lunch may be asked to begin eating some small amounts of breakfast on a regular basis without vomiting. After some reduction in avoidance of eating has occurred, a set of assignments to reduce the frequency of vomiting across the weeks should be provided: for example, "This week, try not to vomit on one day of the week." It is often more effective to have the patient skip 1 day of vomiting instead of skipping several vomiting episodes in separate days of the week. This will give the patient a more accurate idea of what her daily dietary intake might be if she stopped vomiting. At the beginning of treatment, most patients evaluate their day as being all "good" or all "bad" with respect to eating and vomiting. This all-or-none thinking might make it easier for the patient not to vomit for the entire day than to vomit only one time less on a given day. We also often eventually encourage midmorning and midafternoon snacks with "safe" foods (usually fruit); as mentioned earlier, for those individuals not already involved in any exercise, we encourage exercise as well.

CONCLUSIONS

We have tried to summarize briefly the essence of our anxiety reduction model of bulimia nervosa, which places heavy stress on the maintaining role of vomiting in this disorder. Based on this analysis, we have developed a treatment program that involves practice in eating without vomiting, while the therapist concurrently explores with the patient anxiety-provoking feelings and thoughts under this exposure plus response prevention condition. Our initial series of studies with this approach has been promising. However, we have not yet completed a large-scale controlled evaluation; thus we are not in a position to say that this is the most effective treatment paradigm available. Much more empirical development and evaluation are needed before any treatment paradigm can be said to be demonstrably the treatment of choice for this very serious and complex disorder. It might also be worth reiterating that we have been exclusively concerned in our research with normal-weight individuals who binge and vomit. Also, our population has been restricted to adult women aged 18 to 45, usually living autonomously and far away from their parents; this has made family therapy approaches impractical, even though family issues are still often salient concerns.

REFERENCES

Abraham, S. F., & Beumont, P. J. V. (1982). How patients describe bulimia or binge-eating. *Psychological Medicine, 12,* 625–635.

American Psychiatric Association. (1980). *Diagnostic and statistical manual of mental disorders* (3rd ed.). Washington, DC: Author.

Basow, S. A., & Schneck, R. (1983). *Eating disorders among college women.* Paper presented at the meeting of the Eastern Psychological Association.

Beck, A. T., Ward, C. H., Mendelson, M., Mock, J., & Erbaugh, J. (1961). An inventory for measuring depression. *Archives of General Psychiatry, 4,* 53–63.

Boskind-Lodahl, M. (1978). The definition and treatment of bulimarexia in college women: A pilot study. *Journal of the American College Health Association, 27,* 84–97.

Casper, R. C., Eckert, E. D., Halmi, K. A., Goldberg, S. C., & Davis, J. M. (1980). Bulimia: Its incidence and clinical importance in patients with anorexia nervosa. *Archives of General Psychiatry, 37,* 1030–1035.

Clement, P. F., & Hawkins, R. C. (1980). *Pathways to bulimia: Personality correlates, prevalence, and a conceptual model.* Paper presented at the meeting of the Association for the Advancement of Behavior Therapy.

Crowther, J. H., Chernyk, B., Hahn, M., Hedeen, C., & Zaynor, L. (1983). *The prevalence of binge-eating and bulimia in a normal college population.* Paper presented at the meeting of the Midwestern Psychological Association.

Fairburn, C. G. (1981). A cognitive behavioral approach to the treatment of bulimia. *Psychological Medicine, 11,* 707–711.

Foa, E. B., & Steketee, G. A. (1979). Obsessive–compulsives: Conceptual issues and treatment interventions. In M. Hersen, R. M. Eisler, & P. M. Miller (Eds.), *Progress in behavior modification* (Vol. 8, pp. 1–53). New York: Academic Press.

Garner, D. M., & Garfinkel, P. E. (1979). The Eating Attitudes Test: An index of the symptoms of anorexia nervosa. *Psychological Medicine, 9,* 273–279.

Garner, D. M., Olmsted, M. P., & Polivy, J. (1983). Development and validation of a multidimensional eating disorder inventory for anorexia nervosa and bulimia. *International Journal of Eating Disorders, 2,* 15–34.

Halmi, K. A., Falk, J. R., & Schwartz, E. (1981). Binge-eating and vomiting: A survey of a college population. *Psychological Medicine, 11,* 697–706.

Herman, C. P., & Polivy, J. (1980). Restrained eating. In A. S. Stunkard (Ed.), *Obesity* (pp. 208–225). Philadelphia: W. B. Saunders.

Hsu, L. K. G., Crisp, A. H., & Harding, B. (1979). Outcome of anorexia nervosa. *Lancet, i,* 61–65.

Johnson, C., & Larson, R. (1982). Bulimia: An analysis of moods and behavior. *Psychosomatic Medicine, 44,* 341–351.

Johnson, W. G., & Brief, D. (1983). Bulimia. *Behavioral Medicine Update, 4,* 16–21.

Katzman, M. A., & Wolchik, S. A. (1983). *Behavioral and emotional antecedents and consequences of binge eating in bulimic and binge eating college women.* Paper presented at the meeting of the Eastern Psychological Association.

Lang, P. J., & Lazovik, A. D. (1963). Experimental desensitization of a phobia. *Journal of Abnormal and Social Psychology, 69,* 519–525.

Leitenberg, H., Gross, J., Peterson, J., & Rosen, J. C. (1984). Analysis of an anxiety model and the process of change during exposure plus response prevention treatment of bulimia nervosa. *Behavior Therapy, 15,* 3–20.

Lawson, J. S., Marshall, W. L., & McGrath, P. (1979). The Social Self-Esteem Inventory. *Educational and Psychological Measurement, 39,* 803–811.

Loro, A. D. (1980). *Binge eating in overweight populations: A clinical behavioral description.* Paper presented at the meeting of the Association for Advancement of Behavior Therapy.

Orbach, S. (1978). *Fat is a feminist issue.* New York: Paddington Press.

Pyle, R. L., Mitchell, J. E., & Eckert, E. D. (1981). Bulimia: A report of 34 cases. *Journal of Clinical Psychiatry, 42,* 60–64.

Polivy, J., Herman, C. P., Olmsted, M. P., & Jazwinski. C. (1984). Restraint and binge eating. In R. C. Hawkins, W. J. Fremouw, & P. F. Clement (Eds.), *The binge/purge syndrome: Diagnosis, treatment, and research* (pp. 104–122). New York: Springer.

Rachman, S., Hodgson, R., & Marks, I. (1970). Treatment of chronic obsessive–compulsive neurosis. *Behaviour Research and Therapy, 8,* 385–392.

Rosen, J. C., & Leitenberg, H. (1982). Bulimia nervosa: Treatment with exposure and response prevention. *Behavior Therapy, 13,* 117–124.

Rosen, J. C., Leitenberg, H., Fondacaro, K. M., Gross, J., & Willmuth, M. (in press). Standardized test meals in assessment of eating behavior in bulimia nervosa: Consumption of feared foods when vomiting is prevented. *International Journal of Eating Disorders.*

Rosenberg, M. (1979). *Conceiving the self.* New York: Basic Books.

Russell, G. F. M.(1979). Bulimia nervosa: An ominous variant of anorexia nervosa. *Psychological Medicine, 9,* 429–448.

Schwartz, D., Thompson, M., & Johnson, C. (1982). Anorexia nervosa and bulimia: The sociocultural context. *International Journal of Eating Disorders, 1,* 20–36.

Taylor, B., & Agras, S. (1981). Assessment of phobia. In D. H. Barlow (Ed.), *Behavioral assessment of adult disorders.* New York: Guilford Press.

Wardle, J., & Beinart, H. (1981). Binge eating: A theoretical review. *British Journal of Clinical Psychology, 20,* 97–109.

PART FOUR

Group Treatment

CHAPTER TEN

Group Psychotherapy for Anorexia Nervosa

ALYSON HALL

Group therapy is frequently mentioned in descriptions of treatment programs for anorexia nervosa, particularly as a component of inpatient treatment (Bruch, 1973; Crisp, 1980; Garfinkel & Garner, 1982). There remains, however, a paucity of detail in the literature about treatment techniques in, indications for, and limitations of group therapy. Many major inpatient treatment centers incorporate small groups and milieu therapy in their treatment programs, but often the expectation is that these offer the opportunity for the anorexic to interact with other people and that these experiences can then be explored in individual therapy (Bruch, 1973). Self-help groups have sprung up in North America and Britain over the last 10 years, but their effectiveness has not so far been evaluated.

Although it is not unusual for selected individual anorexic patients, after body weight has been restored, to be placed in groups with nonanorexic members, outpatient treatment groups for anorexics are rarely advocated and even less often described. This contrasts with recent reports of the successful use of outpatient groups for patients with bulimia nervosa at normal body weight. Lacey (1983) has described the use of groups in a 10-week outpatient treatment program, which included the maintenance of dietary diaries, as well as individual and group therapy sessions. The treatment was structured and initially involved a behavioral approach, moving to a more psychodynamic approach as eating patterns became less chaotic. The Women's Therapy Centre in London has a long experience of a similar reduction in bulimic symptoms with short-term therapy groups, often in conjunction with individual therapy. Both centers report that patients with a previous history of anorexia nervosa have a poorer outcome in their groups, compared with normal-weight bulimic patients.

THE DIFFICULTIES OF GROUP THERAPY WITH ANOREXICS

What are the characteristics of patients with anorexia nervosa that make them so difficult to treat in groups? Despite restoration of body weight, the anorexic often remains withdrawn, anxious, rigid, egocentric, and preoccupied with body weight and food, and has extreme difficulty in identifying and expressing her feelings.[1] These char-

---

1. Throughout this chapter, anorexic patients are referred to as female.

Alyson Hall. Consultant in Child and Adolescent Psychiatry, The London Hospital, London, England.

acteristics make individual therapy difficult, but facing a group of such individuals is a daunting task for any therapist, no matter how experienced he or she may be either in the treatment of anorexics or as a group therapist.

Patients who might seem superficially socially competent are so limited in their ability to form and benefit from meaningful social relationships that they often cannot begin to use a group. They recognize these interpersonal difficulties and are often enthusiastic about the suggestion of group therapy. However, their poor self-esteem and hypersensitivity to the feelings of others, particularly to criticism that may be more imagined than real, results in a mobilization of anxiety in the group setting. Unable to express these feelings and usually unconscious of them, the anorexic responds by losing weight or running away, both of which make her unavailable for psychotherapeutic change. Her capacity for intellectualization makes her more inaccessible to the therapist: "The others in the group are different from me," or "The group doesn't seem to be helping anyone, so there's no point in going." Sometimes her reasons for not attending may be accurate: "The group made me feel more depressed," or "I always feel much worse after the group, and my eating gets worse." The implication is always that feelings must be avoided rather than experienced and increasingly coped with. The therapist may collude with the patient because of his or her own lack of confidence in a treatment that does not promote rapid results in terms of weight gain, unlike inpatient treatment or family therapy.

Certain assumptions about anorexics in groups have been held up as reasons for not using group therapy. This may have more to do with poor selection of patients and inappropriate therapeutic techniques than with group therapy *per se*. The patients are likely to be silent, or preoccupied so much with food that this may be the sole topic of discussion; in fact, they may launch headlong into a competition to be the thinnest group member. Such disastrous results can be avoided with proper patient selection, appropriate therapeutic approach, and a therapist who is confident, experienced, and well supported. Nevertheless, the difficulties even for the most experienced therapist cannot be minimized. This form of therapy may be one of the most demanding and anxiety-provoking and least rewarding of the psychotherapies in general, and of those treatments currently in use for anorexia nervosa in particular. When it is successful, however, I believe it can offer the patient the opportunity for lasting change in social relationships, increased self-awareness, and ability to cope with emotions in a way that acts protectively against relapse, as individual therapy alone may fail to do.

Few psychoanalysts and even fewer group analysts have successfully worked with anorexics, and it is difficult to construe the characteristics described above in terms of traditional psychoanalytic concepts. Bruch (1973) and Selvini-Palazzoli (1974) have contributed substantially to our understanding of how early disturbances in mother–infant relationships contribute to the development of the personality structure associated with anorexia nervosa, and how the defective ego must be recognized and strengthened in psychotherapy in a way similar to the approaches used with borderline, narcissistic, or schizophrenic patients. Bruch herself says,

I find it difficult to compare my concepts to one or other schools of psychoanalytic thought, except to say that most of the differences appear to be more theoretical constructs than based on factual events. Controversies between libidinal or interpersonal theories have no realistic basis, since biological development requires close and continuous interaction with another person. It is a mere abstraction which neglects the facts of human development to speak of "drives" without relation to the interpersonal environment, or of "interpersonal relations" without a biological body attached to them. (1973, p. 64)

She describes how absent, contradictory, or inaccurate confirmation and reinforcement of the infant's relatively differentiated needs and impulses results in the infant's growing up unable to differentiate between disturbances in biological, emotional, and interpersonal experiences. The infant will become an individual deficient in a sense of separateness, with diffuse ego boundaries, and will feel helpless under the influence of external forces. Both Bruch and Selvini-Palazzoli identify the mother as a typically overprotective, rigid, and insensitive person who cannot respond to her developing daughter as an individual. The daughter in turn fails to express her needs and individuality, simply anticipating and responding to her mother's own expectations and needs. In my view, constitutional personality characteristics may contribute to problems in a mother's relationship with a particular infant, and this is supported by the findings of a twin study (Holland, Hall, Murray, Russell, & Crisp, in press).

The task for the adolescent of separating and individuating while coping with the emergence of uncontrollable needs and impulses becomes insurmountable for the potential anorexic, especially when it is further complicated by the parents' own resistance to and nonacceptance of these changes in their daughter.

Selvini-Palazzoli explains this further in object relations theory. In early infancy, the anorexic has incorporated and repressed the bad aspects of her mother object, leaving a good externalized mother object with whom she identifies during latency. The ego develops with its libidinal aspects split off and attached to the incorporated bad object with its bodily needs. The remaining central ego, associated with superego components, becomes identified in latency with an asexual, acarnal, and essentially powerful image. In adolescence, when bodily needs begin to emerge and are more difficult to ignore, the body "bad object" threatens to overwhelm the fragile ego. For the anorexic, the body becomes the infantile bad object as it was experienced at a stage of overwhelming helplessness when she was incapable of satisfying her own vital needs. The anorexic starves her body to keep it under control and to prevent it from swelling and overwhelming her precarious sense of self. At the same time, she maintains a positive view of the world and preserves her incomplete relationship with a "good mother" object.

In its early stages, the daughter's anorexia nervosa provokes concern and nurturing in her family; this nurturing is often primed by overwhelming guilt, which reinforces enmeshed family relationships and prevents the challenge to the deficient ego structure threatened by adolescent development. Her mother may now be given the opportunity to compensate in the short term for the difficulties she had in her early relationship with her daughter, particularly if these were related to comprehensible circumstances — a bereavement, for example — and if she can cope with her guilt, freeing the two of them to develop further. If her own ego strengths are inadequate and were responsible for the disturbed relationship in the first place, this development is not possible, and her daughter will remain identified with an idealized woman who cannot express her feelings or respond in intimate relationships and is invested in preserving her good image in the eyes of the world. Her personality structure is characterized by an underlying sense of ineffectiveness, similar to that of her daughter, but it is defended against by a fragile sense of identity maintained by her view of herself as a successful, caring mother. In order for the anorexic daughter to recover, she needs to recognize and externalize those bad aspects of her mother that she has incorporated and associated with her body. This may prove an intensely threatening experience for her mother. Without these changes, the anorexic cannot develop the autonomy and sense of personality identity necessary for separation from her family and full adult life.

An understanding of these dynamics helps to explain the difficulties of group therapy with anorexics. In individual work, a warm, flexible therapist has the opportunity to allow the anorexic to begin to identify and express her conflicts and negative feelings in a safe private relationship, so that she no longer needs to act them out by losing weight. The open, relaxed female therapist, in accepting and responding to the anorexic, is likely to be experienced differently from the mother, facilitating the development of a trusting but ambivalent relationship with a more complete object with whom identification can take place. The therapy can take place at the patient's own pace with avoidance of transference interpretations, criticism, and confrontation, which would challenge her fragile ego and reinforce her poor self-esteem. In a group, this approach is much more difficult, not least because the therapist is shared with others and is constrained by the group setting. It is not so easy for the therapist to be warm, relaxed, open, and responsive to each group member, and he or she will be experienced as even less so by the intensified transference situation. The therapist may be experienced as a good but unavailable parent or as a negative, controlling, uncaring, critical, or threatening parent. These feelings, largely inaccessible to the patient and concealed from the therapist, serve to reinforce the anorexic's sense of personal ineffectiveness and to mobilize denial, intellectual defenses, or flight into low body weight or nonattendance. While the therapist is the central focus for the individual member, other group members may be experienced as much more competent competitors for the therapist's attention and also may threaten to challenge or confront her. The structure of the group and the needs of each group member make flexibility difficult. The group has its own pace, unpredictability, and intensity, minimizing the sense of effectiveness for each member and increasing the feeling of being controlled and influenced by others. There is the added complication that a group member's sense of identity as an anorexic may become pronounced by identification with other anorexic members.

GENERAL TREATMENT TECHNIQUES

Having examined the difficulties in some detail, let us now explore the possibility of avoiding some of the pitfalls and facilitating the opportunity we can give patients for major shifts in self-expression and personal relationships through the use of group therapy with appropriate techniques. Just as a traditional psychoanalytical approach fails with anorexics in individual psychotherapy, so does a formal group analytical approach. In general, the group needs to be experienced as safe, nonconfrontative, and warm, allowing room for individual attention and support from the leader for each member, in order to facilitate self-expression with encouragement of gradual interpersonal interaction. One could argue, of course, that any psychotherapy group should be like this, but in order for change to take place in the type of patients usually selected for outpatient group therapy, a mobilization of anxiety, intensification of the transference, and frank interchange among group members seems to be essential. Only the highly defended patient may experience the group as safe and comfortable and will thus avoid change. The anorexic would be too anxious to use such a group, and various adaptations of the group structure and therapeutic approach are required in order to titrate the level of anxiety, contain the patient, avoid retreat into anorexia nervosa, and maximize change.

Selection of Patients

Unless patients are carefully selected, taking into consideration the type of group therapy available, the majority of anorexics will terminate treatment prematurely or deteriorate dramatically in their eating behavior. In either case, the patients will not benefit from treatment, and both they and the therapist will part seriously discouraged. Factors related to the individual's course of anorexia nervosa and underlying personality strengths, which may have been modified by previous treatments, all have to be taken into account in the assessment of an individual's suitability for a group.

There are two absolute contraindications for any kind of group therapy. First, the patient must not be at a stage of extreme inanition requiring medical management, and the symptoms of starvation should have begun to be ameliorated by resumption of eating before group therapy in an inpatient setting is begun (Hedblom, Hubbard, & Andersen, 1981; Sclare, 1977). Secondly, the patient must accept that she is ill, must want help, and must have moved beyond the stage of denial, emotional blandness, and extreme rigidity associated with the early stages of anorexia nervosa and/or low body weight. Inpatient groups that are continuing alongside management of eating behavior and other psychotherapeutic treatments can accommodate more emotionally restricted, socially restricted, and withdrawn patients, since psychological change will in most cases accompany restoration of body weight. Selection of outpatients, even when group therapy continues alongside individual therapy, must be considerably more rigorous.

The majority of the characteristics associated with high dropout rates in groups in the studies reviewed by Yalom (1975) are cardinal features of anorexia nervosa: high denial, high somatization, lower motivation, lower psychological-mindedness, and social ineffectiveness. The only exceptions in his list are lower social class and intelligence.

Grotjahn (1972) found that 40% of his dropouts fell into three categories: (1) patients with diagnoses of manifest or threatening psychotic breakdowns; (2) patients who used the group for crisis resolution and dropped out when the emergency had passed; and (3) highly schizoid, sensitive, isolated individuals who needed more careful, intensive preparation for group therapy. The third category closely resembles many anorexic patients. However, in severe anorexia nervosa, threatened or sudden deterioration is likely to precipitate premature termination, just as psychotic illness or threatened breakdown is likely to do. Similarly, anorexics who have rapidly achieved symptom resolution are often unwilling to pursue anxiety-provoking psychotherapy and mobilize their denial mechanisms in their impatience to put anorexia nervosa behind them. Patients in this group are vulnerable to relapse or can only survive without anorexia nervosa by leading very restricted lives. Yalom (1966) established nine major factors that were associated with early dropout from groups:

1. External factors
2. Group deviancy
3. Problems of intimacy
4. Fear of emotional contagion
5. Inability to share the doctor
6. Complications of concurrent individual therapy
7. Early provocateurs
8. Inadequate orientation to therapy
9. Complications arising from subgrouping

The first five of these are relevant to the selection of anorexic patients, while the last four are more related to therapeutic technique.

Since anorexics are experienced rationalizers, external factors are often given as reasons for not attending. Often these reasons are associated with core problems, such as their inability to reveal their difficulties to others, conscientiousness, rigidity, and lack of assertiveness, as well with their ambivalence about treatment. They thus have a terror of asking their bosses if they can leave work early, or of refusing to attend because of a conflicting activity, be it work or social. Pending examinations wreak havoc on a group of young anorexics. Time spent in anticipating these difficulties and developing strategies is well worth while, both before an anorexic joins the group and during the course of therapy. If these difficulties are successfully coped with and the anorexic is engaged in the group, she will often travel great distances in order to attend and will feel able to return after such interruptions as examinations or changes of employment. External emotional stresses do not seem to have the same disruptive effect on anorexic groups as Yalom has described for groups in general. They seem to find it easier to justify attending and taking up time in the group when there is a concrete, conscious emotional issue comprehensible to others, such as a bereavement or illness in the family.

Although a group of anorexics obviously has the same presenting problem and many features in common, certain characteristics that distinguish one individual from other group members may be associated with failure to engage in the group. These are not always deviant factors associated with failure in nonanorexic groups; they include marked denial, lack of previous treatment, extreme social withdrawal and isolation, or complicating disturbances (e.g., personality disorder, substance abuse, or obesity). Features mentioned by Yalom (1975) — lack of psychological sophistication, of interpersonal sensitivity, and of personal psychological insight, all of which are usually associated with denial — are frequently found in anorexia nervosa, but an individual who markedly differs from other members in these dimensions is likely to drop out or lose weight and would be unable to make use of the group in any case. Marked deviance of a single group member in other features, such as age, chronicity, marital status, type of eating disturbance (bulimia or restriction), or educational level should be avoided, and these factors should be taken into consideration in the composition of the group.

It goes without saying that the anorexic has problems with intimacy; these are usually demonstrated by withdrawal because of her inability to identify and express her feelings and to communicate generally, and because of a constant, pervasive dread of self-disclosure related to her poor self-esteem. Occasionally, she will help and support others and sometimes the therapist, often driven by guilt, but she will eventually drop out or lose weight, frustrated by her failure to get her increasingly conscious emotional needs met. These core difficulties with intimacy, difficulty in sharing the therapist, and fears of emotional contagion — all associated with an inability to recognize and cope with negative emotions, coupled with extreme sensitivity to the feelings of others — probably present the greatest challenges for the therapist: first, in holding the patient in the group, and, second, in helping her to change. They have important implications for therapeutic technique, which are explored later in the chapter.

Having looked at exclusion criteria, let us identify features in anorexic patients that might be associated with potential successful use of a group. Yalom, Houts, Newell, and Rand (1967) found that two factors predictive of success in outpatient group therapy were the patients' attraction to the group and their general popularity in the group. While these are certainly variables that would also predict success for anorexics, they are difficult to predict at assessment unless the anorexic has already had experience of a group while in a hospital. Motivation is crucial, but it is extremely difficult to judge its predictive value in anorexia nervosa. Most anorexics, who find the relative isolation and increasing emotional sensitization they experience in the hospital unbearable, are enticed by the possible distraction of a group. Outpatients who have had experience of a wide range of treatments, including inpatient groups, become increasingly aware of their own interpersonal difficulties and their inability to reveal their illness and depressive feelings to others; these patients usually positively welcome the suggestion of group therapy where they can "meet others with the same problem." What they do not anticipate is their extreme inhibition about opening up in the group, even with other anorexics, or the strong negative emotions (particularly anxiety and depression) that are aroused. In addition, their compliant natures, lack of assertiveness, and eagerness to please make it unlikely that they will express reservations easily, particularly to a professional whom they have come to trust, respect, and depend on. Unfortunately, the referral to a group may be provoked by hospital discharge, an individual therapist's leaving, or a general feeling that treatment can progress no further. Both the therapist and the patient see the group as the last straw, with the therapist enthusiastically suggesting it and the patient eagerly clutching at it for fear of abandonment. These are not good reasons for group therapy, unless the patient is highly suitable and genuinely motivated.

Group popularity is almost certainly associated with positive feelings toward a patient by professionals previously involved in her care. A patient who has consistently aroused frustration, pessimism, boredom, or high anxiety in individual work or on an inpatient unit will certainly arouse similar feelings in both the therapist and other group members. As with nonanorexic groups (Yalom, 1975), initial negative countertransference may be diluted or worked through more easily than in individual therapy, but it must be taken into consideration in patient selection, since anorexic groups have so many other unrewarding aspects for the therapist. More specific factors that Yalom et al. (1967) found to be precursors of popularity — high previous self-disclosure, high activity in the group, and the ability to be introspective — may help in selection if information from previous therapists, especially from those conducting inpatient groups, is available.

Since so many of the characteristics associated with poor group therapy outcome in general are typical of anorexia nervosa patients, it is not surprising that few group therapists have chosen to work with anorexics in mixed groups or have started outpatient groups specifically for anorexics. I could find no mention of the disorder in

Yalom's seminal work (1975); moreover, in discussing outpatient group therapy for anorexics with colleagues, I found that both experienced group analysts and specialists in anorexia nervosa tended to be skeptical of its value, either from their experience of the difficulties encountered with such patients in groups or from assumptions resulting from their experiences in individual therapy. However, since few large centers in the world have long-standing experience with anorexic groups, pessimism in these early days should not deter us too much from attempting to select the most appropriate anorexic patients for group therapy. We can conclude broadly now which anorexics are most likely to benefit from a group:

1. Those who are not severely ill, but are gaining weight or are relatively stable.
2. Those who are highly motivated.
3. Those who have benefited psychologically from other treatments.
4. Those who are not totally isolated or withdrawn.
5. Those in whom denial or intellectualization is not predominant and who show some capacity for psychological-mindedness, ability to reveal feelings, and sensitivity to others.
6. Those in whom another treatment approach is not indicated (e.g., admission or family therapy) or where a combination of the other treatment with group therapy is practical.
7. Those who are liked by the therapist and have the potential to be liked by other group members.

Size and Group Composition

It is my own experience and that of colleagues who have run outpatient groups, including self-help groups, that anorexics function best in a small group. The optimal number is four to six, in contrast to seven or eight, the number that maximizes member interaction and likelihood of change in most outpatient therapy groups. Anorexics seem to function better in larger groups in an inpatient setting where there is interaction on a daily basis, greater support, and usually a dilution effect by nonanorexic group members.

The problem remains as to how one can select a group of four to six outpatients who will attend regularly and at least maintain their weight from a group of patients who are highly likely to do neither. Even with a large and appropriate group of patients from which to choose, dropouts are to be expected. It is therefore wise to select approximately 10 for a closed outpatient group. Obviously, new members can be introduced into an open group whenever members drop out, but early dropouts should be anticipated by selecting at least eight. Members do tend to appear intermittently or to return after long periods of absence, and this factor needs to be taken into account. Consistent, regular attendance by anorexics for individual or family therapy, which has been my experience, is no predictor of group attendance rates for individual patients, and the overall attendance rate of group members is likely to be much poorer than their previous attendance record for appointments.

There are several important issues when considering the composition of a group (at this juncture I ignore inpatient groups and mixed outpatient groups, which are discussed later). All patients should probably have a history of anorexia nervosa even if they are presently at normal body weight. A bulimic patient who has not had anorexia nervosa generally has a different personality structure. She will be more able to express her feelings and to interact with other members, and is more likely to be engaged in a fairly satisfactory social and sexual life. She may dominate the group because of her ability to express herself, and she is likely to be frustrated by the limitations of the other members, which will be exacerbated by the anxiety she provokes through her anger or confrontations. Generally, the proportion of bulimics and restricters should be approximately equal; this is similar to the proportions experienced in anorexic populations attending major treatment centers. Since restricters may develop bulimia and are terrified of this complication, while bulimics want to become restricters and sometimes achieve this, it is advisable to have both represented in a group for educative reasons.

A group of restricters would be an enormous challenge for any therapist, as they are even less able to identify and express their feelings (particularly depression and anxiety) than bulimics, and, unless they have responded to previous treatment, will show more withdrawal, denial, and intellectualization. A group consisting entirely of bulimics would not present the same problems for the therapist and has been described by Leichner and Harper (1983a). Their group was older than average, and many members were married or in stable relationships. Attendance was better than had been the therapists' experience with a younger mixed group of anorexics and bulimics, and required less energy on the part of the therapist because of greater group cohesiveness. In their experience, bulimic patients who have not had anorexia nervosa fit into such a group more easily than into a group containing several restricters. Leichner and Harper also describe how their older bulimic patients dealt with different issues in their group: They were more concerned about marital and child-rearing matters, careers, and related problems with assertiveness and perfectionism in these roles. Leichner and Harper conclude that separate groups should be formed for these patients who are likely to ignore, exclude, or unintentionally intimidate younger anorexics who are involved with early adolescent issues (e.g., relationships with parents, leaving home) and have not yet established any role in a career or a relationship to protect them from their feelings of ineffectiveness. In general, we can conclude that group members should have several issues in common, aside from the eating disorder. A group containing young teenagers probably should exclude patients in their late 20s or older, and vice versa.

Another important mix is connected with the stage of the illness. Although patients at very low weight, extremely chronic patients unlikely to change, or patients who have only recently become ill will be excluded by selection factors, it is wise to include at least one patient who has achieved and maintained normal body weight, as well as patients who are gaining weight or are strongly motivated to do so. The emphasis of the group can then shift away from issues of weight and eating toward psychological problems associated with or underlying the disorder. Including partially recovered patients who are able to express themselves more easily is facilitating, but, more importantly, it underlines the difficulties that anorexics face after body weight is restored. Such a patient may also benefit enormously from the group; she can continue to identify with other members' eating and psychological difficulties, protecting her from relapse, while her self-esteem is enhanced by her ability to use the group effectively and help the others. Frequently, such an individual becomes a leader in self-help groups.

Organizational Aspects

As for any psychotherapy group, the physical setting should offer privacy and freedom from distraction, with the patients seated in a circle of comfortable chairs. If the group involves physical or other activities, such as social skills, training, or art therapy, space and materials should be provided. If the sessions are to be tape-recorded or viewed through a one-way screen, the group's permission must be obtained in advance. Anorexics seem to ignore the screen more than most other groups of patients; this may be related to their denial, compliance, and lack of assertiveness. The availability of a viewing screen is extremely important if the group is conducted by a single therapist. Such a group can be a lonely, demanding experience, and the opportunity for supervision or discussion of the group with colleagues is invaluable.

The group should be designated as open or closed at its inception. If an outpatient group is planned to run for over 1 year or indefinitely, it is inadvisable for it to be a closed group, because of high dropout rates and the lack of opportunity to bring in appropriate patients at a later stage. Inpatient groups are usually open, unless a closed short-term group is organized for a specific purpose. If the number of suitable patients is small, it is certainly better to organize an open group than to include inappropriate patients. In addition to the chance of losing patients who fail to engage in the group, many patients in their late teens or 20s are likely to move for college or employment, especially if they are doing well.

The length of each session depends on the stamina of the therapist. All those with experience of anorexic groups with whom I have spoken describe how slow the groups are to start, how they seem to be functioning maximally after 1 hour, and how difficult then they are to stop. Probably 1¼ hours should be a minimum length, with a maximum of 2 hours. Since these patients seem highly sensitive to interruptions, an outpatient group should meet weekly with as few breaks as possible. Infrequent longer breaks are preferable to frequent short ones, both for the patients and for the therapist. Inpatient groups can and should meet more frequently.

In contrast to the successful use of short-term group therapy in bulimia nervosa, short-term therapy seems of little value in anorexia nervosa except in an inpatient setting, for highly selected older patients with bulimia, or possibly for physically recovered patients who are highly motivated to improve their self-expression and social interactions. One or both therapists should be able to commit himself or herself to running a group for a year at least, with a suitable therapist available to take over if an open group continues after that.

While most group therapists prefer their patients not to be in concurrent individual therapy because of the complications it produces in treatment, group therapy in anorexia nervosa must be seen in the context of a variety of other forms of treatment in a specialized program. Most other forms of treatment can and should continue while a patient attends a group; intermittent family sessions are particularly facilitating, especially if the therapists are the same for both. Individual sessions are very valuable for anorexics, as they may be able to deal with feelings provoked by the group in preparation for revealing them later, rather than responding by fearfully running away from them and the group. An intellectual, or ideally an emotional, understanding of these feelings can help the patient to accept and recognize them more easily in the future; such an understanding often cannot be achieved in the group alone because of her inability to reveal her feelings. It is not always practical for the same group therapist to see all the patients individually, although it is preferable. Leichner and Harper (1983a) had some anorexics in their groups who were in individual treatment with one of the group therapists, while the rest had other therapists. This mix did not cause major complications, and the patients were encouraged to keep the boundaries of their two forms of weekly therapy separate. In order to do this, the therapists need to be quite clear about the goals of the different treatments. Anorexics, in my experience, seem to have fewer difficulties in making use of different therapies, once they are committed to treatment, than have other patients. So enormous are their needs and their difficulties in meeting them that they benefit from different approaches, and they do not seem to play off therapists against each other destructively, provided they are not still engaged in manipulations about food. This is seen most clearly in the inpatient setting, where a multiplicity of treatment approaches are found to enhance one another and to prove maximally beneficial (Crisp, 1980; Garfinkel & Garner, 1982; Hedblom *et al.*, 1981).

The Therapist

Finding even one suitable therapist willing to run an outpatient group for anorexics may prove even more difficult than selecting a group of patients. At least one therapist in a cotherapy situation should have experience in individual psychotherapy with anorexics, as well as group experience. A less experienced cotherapist must feel comfortable with allowing the more experienced partner to set the tone of the group, especially in the early stages. Support and supervision from an appropriately experienced professional who is not committed to a group analytical model should be available. A highly skilled therapist working alone needs support, at the very least, and observers using the one-way screen serve to alleviate some of the loneliness and hunger that seem to be provoked in the therapist. This hunger is literal: Some therapists have actually found themselves bringing food to eat before the session or taking it into the session. Observers, too, report a tendency to eat while watching. This is a powerful countertransference phenomenon that I have not heard described for other groups; it must be related to the physically and emotionally draining experience of such work, as well as to the patients' intense needs. Therapists must obviously be mature and free of conflict about their own eating behavior, weight, and shape. Indeed, patients occasionally ask about the therapist's own eating behavior and attitudes. Maralyn Lawrence (personal communication), from The Women's Therapy Centre of London, talks specifically of "normal women's eating problems." Frankness is essential and helps the anorexic to see her disorder on a continuum.

Stamina for this kind of work is required. Anorexics find terminations difficult to work through until they themselves are ready for them; if there is a possibility that a therapist will leave within the first year, two therapists are preferable to avoid a major setback. Cotherapy needs to be free from its potential hazards because of the sensitivity of these patients to tension between therapists. Both need to be comfortable with the style required and comfortable with each other; they can then offer each other considerable mutual support and encouragement and can maintain the required energy levels. If there is anxiety rather than enthusiasm about a possible partnership, one therapist may offer the other much more support from behind the one-way screen than could be gained from being in the room together.

So far, specific reference has only been made to the experience of female therapists and female patients. Inpatient groups containing patients of both sexes may work well with therapists of either sex, but therapists with experience of outpatient anorexic groups have told me that the presence of male therapists consistently inhibits discussion of sexual issues, which are discussed only with difficulty with female therapists. Lacey (1983) found that two female therapists were associated with greater treatment success and patient satisfaction than was a male–female combination for bulimic patients at normal weight.

For all types of groups, the therapist must be comfortable with an approach that differs markedly from the traditional interpretative model with a relatively silent reflective stance. Instead, the therapist needs to encourage (very actively) discussion of situations and interactions both inside and outside the therapy setting, in an attempt to help the group members to reconstruct events and associated feelings. In order to give the anorexic the consistent experience that she is being listened to (Bruch, 1982), great attention must be paid to minutiae of verbal expression in the group; this requires both intense concentration and verbal activity on the part of the therapist. The therapist's style must facilitate both individual expression and interpersonal interaction, at the same time that it encourages a sense of autonomy and effectiveness. Warmth and flexibility are essential, so that the therapist is experienced as sensitive, encouraging, and responsive rather than as controlling, demanding, and critical.

THE GROUP PROCESS

Preparation

The effectiveness of preparation for group therapy has been demonstrated by Yalom *et al.* (1967), who found that after a 30-minute preparatory session, patients had more faith in therapy and engaged in significantly more group and interpersonal interaction than nonprepared patients did. Anorexics are more likely than most patients to experience crippling anxiety related to the uncertainty they face in the group, coupled with their own feelings of inadequacy; careful preparation for the important but precarious early sessions is crucial to prevent discouragement and early termination.

Group therapy must be presented as the challenge it really is. Without denigrating the progress made in treatment so far, the patient's continuing difficulties in establishing and maintaining close and gratifying relationships should be explored. The possibility of honest interpersonal exchange that a group offers can help the individual to begin to express both positive and negative feelings and to receive feedback and encouragement from others. The anorexic clearly sees the value of meeting others with the same disorder in reducing isolation and facing up to the difficulties of changing eating patterns and gaining weight. Patients should be warned, however, that observing the difficulties in personal relationships and expression of feelings that their peers experience may make them even more painfully aware of the same feelings in themselves. They may be afraid of these feelings and may be tempted to avoid them by not attending, but if they can allow themselves instead to begin to recognize and express them in the group, the feelings will become less threatening and painful. In contrast to the relationships experienced in their own families, they can now begin to enjoy the opportunity of having their feelings recognized and accepted by others and of beginning to experience the resulting trust, closeness, and emotional support.

It is essential that the difficulties be emphasized, together with the length of time required for change to take place. While the goal is the expression of feelings as they are experienced toward group members and the therapist, it is anticipated that this expression will take time to achieve. The first step will be for the anorexic to begin to recognize her feelings in other situations or in previous group sessions and to attempt to reveal them gradually. The patient should be forewarned of feelings of discouragement and bewilderment in the early stages and should be advised to try to hang on, attending regularly, even if she is unable to express these feelings. Although she may be anxious and emotionally withdrawn in the group, the therapist will make every effort to help her to begin to express herself. Previous knowledge of the patient and her family assists the therapist, and permission should be requested to refer to material in a general way whenever it may help her. The issue of confidentiality among group members should be emphasized, and there must be discussion of the use of the one-way screen and tape recording.

Overall, the group should not be "sold" to the patient. Its difficulties and potential long-term benefits should be frankly discussed in the context of progress made so far. It should not be experienced as an abandonment or relegation, but as the next but difficult step that the patient needs to negotiate in her progress towards autonomy and sense of personal effectiveness. She should not be pressed to make an immediate decision about joining a group, but should be given another appointment and a deadline by which she must decide. If the starting point is some time hence, or if the group is open, the issue can be gradually worked with in individual therapy until the patient feels ready. Individual difficulties, especially with regard to the day and time of the group, should be fully explored in advance. The meeting place needs to be clarified with written directions and signposting, as failure to locate the first meeting, anxiety about making inquiries, or lateness are strong disincentives for attendance.

The First Meeting of an Outpatient Group

The first group meeting presents a major challenge to the therapist and to the members. A large number of patients are likely to be present and can only be helped to feel comfortable and included in the group by structure, support, and activity on the part of the therapist. Introductions should begin the session and should be repeated for latecomers, who will feel especially anxious and easily isolated. Introductions tend to become more personal and detailed with each round, as members move from names and occupations to brief histories of their illness and treatment and sometimes to descriptions of their families.

Soon members will discover common experiences: admissions to hospitals, therapists or patients they have known, or bulimic symptomatology. Groupings will occur, with those sharing experiences beginning to relate to one another. The therapist must pay attention to and clarify these divisions, drawing in group members who have remained silent, so that no individual is excluded from a grouping on one dimension or another. From here, the members can begin to explore their common and differing experiences of treatment, course of illness, and eating behavior, and then slowly begin to move toward wider issues less obviously connected to their illness, such as their experiences at work or in their families. They are very unlikely to express feelings spontaneously and will tend to talk concretely about issues. Those who appear more confident and verbal will begin to talk to similar group members, and the therapist must attempt to draw in silent members, often using previous knowledge of them to enable them to make a positive contribution. They seem to welcome the invitation, which relieves them of anxiety about whether their potential contribution is sufficiently relevant or important to be expressed. Again, the therapist must encourage responses from group members to individual contributions, so that everyone can experience being listened and responded to.

The goals of the first session should be to assist each member to begin to get to know every other member and to discover mutual experiences both related to anorexia nervosa and apart from it. Minimizing anxiety and actively encouraging all members to participate (by going around the room if necessary) are essential to this process. Sufficient time must be allowed toward the end of the group for each member to discuss her experience of the group session, how it accorded with her expectations and her fears. Emphasis must be laid on both the positive and negative aspects, and opportunity must be given for any member who feels different or has doubts about the value of the group to express these feelings rather than go away with them. Encouragement to attend and warm inclusion by other group members is invaluable in reducing the number of dropouts that inevitably occur after the first session.

The therapist should mention that he or she will contact any members who have not attended the first session to encourage them to come next time, and should anticipate that ambivalence about attending may occur among those present. Even though they may have felt relieved during the session, their fears and feelings of inadequacy may become sufficiently powerful for them to dread returning. The purpose of the group and its difficulties should be reiterated as expressed during the preparatory sessions; the therapist should also provide the group with some general feedback, essentially encouraging but accurate, about how the members have met or exceeded her expectations of the first session.

Early Stages: Structure

Just as the first session needs to be highly structured, with time allotted to all the important issues mentioned above, the early sessions continue to require structure and considerable activity on the part of the therapist. The nature of the structure and the rationale for it should be frankly explained; the therapist should stress that whenever it becomes a hindrance to, rather than a facilitator of, the group process, it should be changed or abandoned. The group members should be encouraged to participate in the development of the structure, which should be tailored to the needs of the group at each stage.

Yalom's (1975) description of a group in its first few sessions applies to a group of anorexics, particularly in the first half of each session, over a very long period of time. There is a search for similarities, symptom description, and discussion of the meaning of therapy. Seeking and giving advice may be the main interaction, but this is often directed initially through the therapist. The group remains enormously dependent on its leader, and the members continue to look overtly to the therapist for structure, answers, approval, and acceptance even after many months of therapy. Since anorexics are highly sensitive to any response on the part of the therapist that they can interpret as rejection or criticism, it is important for the therapist to acknowledge the importance of every issue raised before deflecting it to other members. The interaction can be most useful if the initiator and those who respond feel listened to and taken seriously, and this can be assisted if the therapist reiterates the original issue and discusses the responses in relation to each member in a nonjudgmental manner. While group interaction is restricted, anorexics do not seem to deal with their inhibitions by stereotyped "cocktail party" discussion of trivial issues. They usually cannot conceal their anxieties and tend to deal with them by withdrawal, discussion of weight and eating, or verbose intellectualizations. Fairly early on, the therapist should frankly comment on these defenses, but in a generalized way: "Everyone seems to be talking a lot about food this week, but I wonder what other things have been going on in your lives?" If the therapist makes an interpretation that directly relates the defense to underlying anxiety, this will be a repetition of the anorexic's experience with her own mother, who always "knew what she felt."

In the early stages, the structure should be geared to encourage participation of all members. Going around the room to include all members who have not yet made an observation on an issue before moving on to another issue that may have been raised facilitates general participation, and underlines the importance of the minutiae of each member's personal experience. At first, especially early in each session, the group may feel to the therapist like individual therapy for each member, but slowly the members begin to listen more carefully to one another and to respond spontaneously. By the end of the session, the group will feel "like group therapy should feel," with the therapist able to take a back seat. However reluctant the therapist may be to interrupt this process, he or she must take over the steering wheel near the end and bring the group to a close, again by checking out with each member how she feels and how she has experienced the group session. It is essential that the therapist should be able to be flexible about the finishing time, as it is devastating for a patient to begin to express any feelings, particularly negative ones, only to be curtailed by an abrupt ending. Unfinished business should be clearly acknowledged at the end and brought up by the therapist at the start of the next session. Early in each meeting, it is useful to ask the patients how they feel, how the week went, and whether they wish to bring up any issue from last week. Gradually they will, with varying difficulty, begin to be able to bring up major issues early in the session. If the therapist can help each member to take responsibility for identifying needs early in the session, a flexible agenda can be prepared by the group members, allowing those needing more time and attention to receive it after some space has been given to all the members. Positive encouragement to express needs, and a planned sensitive response that does not ignore the needs of others, are very rewarding experiences. As an anorexic's own needs begin to feel overwhelming, she is terrified of "hogging" the group and provoking the hostility of others. Intense guilt becomes linked to the uncontrolled outpouring of emotion, which is thus in danger of becoming totally unacceptable just as it begins to become possible.

In the early stages of therapy, introductions may need to be repeated so that members who have attended sporadically feel included. Late arrivals need acknowledgment before the group resumes its business. Such a level of structure, encouragement, and sensitivity should be clearly distinguished from the rigid overprotectiveness that the patient has experienced in her relationships with others. A frank, gentle pressure to help her to explore and express her feelings is different from the anxious, nonverbal reaction to them so frequently demonstrated by family members and sometimes by therapists. It is important to encourage every effort and to accept the level of expression that the individual is capable of at the time, and the therapist must avoid the temptation of expressing feelings for her and of interpreting them. The patient may be helped if a variety of possible responses to a situation are suggested by the therapist or preferably other group members, so that she can see the range of possible and acceptable reactions and perhaps select one that most closely approximates her own. "If I were in that situation, I would be annoyed, but maybe it doesn't bother you, or you have some other feelings?" is vastly preferable to "You must have been angry." Even if it is obvious to the therapist that the patient was angry, she may not be aware of it, or may only be aware of anxiety or an associated change in eating behavior.

Exploring the possible practical responses to different situations begins to encourage the anorexic to develop a range of alternative strategies. She is so afraid of the disapproval of others that she has lost sight of the possibility that her actual behavior may be less acceptable to others than new solutions. Honest expression of attitudes by group members and the therapist alike help her to realize that individuals feel differently. She can learn that she cannot please everyone, but that it is important and acceptable that she can begin to please herself.

While these principles are closely related to those of transactional analysis and Gestalt therapy, the technique of role play or other techniques to facilitate emotional expression do not seem to offer much for anorexics, unfortunately. They tend to refuse to attempt them, in one of their few expressions of independence and autonomy; this refusal must reflect the intense anxiety that these techniques provoke, which is related to self-consciousness, fear of failure, and loss of control. Leichner and Harper (1983a) started their first group using largely a transactional-analytical approach, but have abandoned this in favor of the approach already described, which encourages an attitude of acceptance of feelings and their gradual recognition and expression. Specific techniques may prove more valuable in the inpatient setting, or for older bulimic patients who are more in touch with their feelings, but who have difficulties in expressing them appropriately or in asserting themselves.

Contact with Members and Therapists outside the Group

Contact with group members outside the group for support and mutual encouragement should be actively encouraged. A list of addresses and phone numbers can be produced after the first meeting and distributed, with periodic updating. Anorexics, even in self-help groups, do not often seek one another out for social contact, but may travel together after sessions or arrive early, and this allows extended contact in the waiting room. As trust and concern for one another's well-being develop, they begin to telephone one another to encourage absent members to return to the group or to support members who have been especially distressed during meetings. It takes regular attendance, close relationships, and a long time before they begin to phone other members when they themselves are experiencing difficulties. They turn to the group therapist or their individual therapists much more easily for this, although after the group has ended they may use mutual contact more freely. They are much more able to express themselves in writing, and may write to the therapist and/or group regularly if they are unable to attend for a period of time. Contact outside the group, both with the therapist and other members, may help an individual to deal with ambivalence about attending, to retain cohesiveness during absences, and to begin to express needs that she is unable to bring up in the group. Provided that the therapist resists the temptation to conduct therapy outside the group by describing any contact made by members outside the group during the next session, the members will use these contacts to facilitate the introduction of issues in the group that they have felt anxious about by obtaining permission and encouragement in advance. Members are encouraged to discuss their contacts outside the group with other members or separate individual therapists, but with the option to preserve privacy. It is so difficult for them to discuss negative feelings that any means by which they can begin to do so should be accepted, as should their right to private relationships outside the group; these may be strikingly different from their experiences with their families. It is a great advantage if the group therapist has been or can continue to be the therapist seeing all the group members in individual or family therapy. If this is not possible, external therapists should encourage the anorexic to raise issues in the group that have been explored individually, and should assist her with the difficulties she experiences in the group. It is very important that the group therapist remain openly in contact with other therapists involved with members; anorexics seem to welcome this, perhaps because it facilitates communication, which has been so stifled in their own families.

Management of Dropouts and Introduction of New Members

A high dropout rate is to be expected in an anorexic group, and often the group may find its own level of comfort in small numbers. However, this number may be too low to maintain a functioning group over time, or too low for the therapist's own morale, which needs to be supported. The highest dropout rate will occur during the first few sessions, but dropouts will continue as patients move, change jobs, recover, or inappropriately attempt to prove independence as they sense their growing dependence on the group. Members find it difficult to return after a break, and written reminders are useful. The therapist will require time and energy to maintain and restore contact with absent members, particularly in a closed group. In an open group, with motivated patients waiting for a place, the therapist can more comfortably afford to take the risk of asking the recalcitrant or reluctant patient to make a decision one way or the other about group attendance.

A balance needs to be found among badgering the absentee, allowing more contact outside the group than within it (which may exacerbate the problem), and offering the opportunity for discussion of difficulties to facilitate the patient's return to and use of the group. Interpreting ambivalence directly is experienced as criticism, and it is much more constructive to explore practical problems with attending the group, which is the level of difficulty that the patient consciously experiences: "It really becomes a choice between taking the risk of asking your boss for permission to leave early and attending the group. If you would like to come to the group, other members may have some suggestions to help you deal with your boss, but first let us try to understand how you expect your boss to react." Pressure to attend may feel like forced feeding, and members should be encouraged to return to the group when it becomes more practical or when they would like to. It is surprising that an occasional anorexic may progress well with infrequent group attendances, and it may be encouraging for other members to see the changes so clearly.

As the group progresses, the patients may begin to contact other members when they do not attend. Who will take this responsibility needs to be clarified in the sessions, particularly as patients may be reluctant to admit they do not know some members well enough to contact them personally.

The proposed introduction of a new member should be discussed fully in the group well in advance, and the group should be offered a genuine opportunity to decide whether they would like to expand the group. Numbers that are comfortable for the members may be less comfortable for the therapist, who must be open about this. The group as a whole can then take responsibility for committing themselves to more regular attendance and drawing in irregular attenders whom they are often concerned about, or for accepting a new member. As with any group, the timing is important, and the most favorable time is when numbers are dwindling or when the work of the group is somewhat stagnated. There is an advantage in introducing two members at the same time. The introduction of new members and the return of absent members are often natural times for the group to take stock of their progress, and this can be very productive.

Issues in the Group

"To weigh or not to weigh" is an important issue, which must be decided and discussed before the group starts. Much depends on whether the patients' weight and eating behavior can be dealt with outside the group, in which case the group can expressly focus on other issues, and discussion of weight is specifically excluded. This has been the successful approach used by Leichner and Harper (1983a), who were able to provide weekly individual and group therapy, which seemed acceptable to their patient population. My own experience with relatively chronic patients who have already received a lot of individual therapy is that they are ready to commit themselves to group therapy alone, and I have incorporated a weighing session each month before a group meets. Time is set aside that week to review weight, eating patterns, and menstrual function, and to relate their progress in those areas to the patients' general functioning. I have found that the patients begin to challenge one another more effectively than any therapist can, and I have heard them giving advice to one another that they have found difficult accepting as applicable to themselves in individual work. This seems to be the area in which they are able to confront one another most easily and productively, at the same time as they are being honest about their own behavior, which they see reflected in others. Anorexics begin to see the effect of conflicts and emotions on eating behavior in the group setting and to feel comfortable about seeking out underlying issues in themselves. Those who are at a normal weight enhance this progress by beginning to admit the more subtle responses that persist in themselves, even when to other members they appear recovered. Although initially a mixed group may divide itself into subgroups of bulimics and restricters, over time the distinctions become blurred as members recognize the potential for both behaviors in themselves and acquire a better perspective on both: The restricters become less enviable, and bulimia becomes less feared. Members recognize the denial and withdrawal associated with reduction of food intake, despite its "safety," and begin to see bulimia as less frightening, more normal, and potentially controllable.

Aside from issues directly related to anorexia nervosa, common themes emerge in relation to associated psychological difficulties and issues that are much more generally age-appropriate.

Issues characteristic of anorexics include problems with assertiveness, fear of displeasing others, recognizing and handling anger, social isolation, emptiness, and hopelessness. These are increasingly dealt with, but only in the later stages of the group do members begin to recognize and discuss negative feelings experienced in the group, and then often only the week after such an experience. Discussion of family issues provides considerable group cohesiveness as members discover experiences in common: intrusive parents, sibling rivalry, overprotectiveness, and covert family conflict.

Transference interpretations, when such difficulties are reflected in the group, dampen this process. In time, however, the therapist can begin to express his or her own feelings (negative as well as positive) in the room, moving from general reactions to gentle specific responses to an individual. Invariably the person concerned will overreact, feeling criticized; however, this can be discussed with other members, producing a less threatening, more supportive, but accurate analysis of the interaction. Negative reactions toward the therapist are expressed more easily than those toward other members, unless they feel an individual is retreating into anorexia nervosa or denial, in which case the issues tend to be expressed in a concerned manner in that member's absence. Thus, the stage of conflict, dominance, and rebellion described by Yalom (1975) is scarcely reached in a group of anorexics, who tend to blame themselves for lack of progress rather than to become overtly disenchanted with the leader.

Nevertheless, the leader may go through a phase of disenchantment, which may reflect projected feelings and the general hopelessness of the group. This is an important phase in the group, and the therapist requires support so that it can be worked through. Despite the progress that the group makes in expressing fundamental problems with despair, intimacy, and a greater group cohesiveness, the pattern described in the early stages prevails to a greater or lesser extent, especially when restricting anorexics are present. Each group meeting tends to begin with multiple individual interactions directed toward or initiated by the therapist, which become interwoven with intermember interactions until the group is proceeding with considerably less input from the therapist. However, less structure is required in the sessions as time goes on, although considerably more is needed than is usual for outpatient groups.

Certain issues differentiate younger restricting anorexics and older bulimic patients. The first group will be more involved with education, career choice, relationships with parents, leaving home, and the problems associated with developing and maintaining relationships with friends, particularly of the same sex. Older patients who are married or in stable relationships may be more concerned with asserting themselves, recognizing and expressing their needs in their relationships, and issues of self-esteem in their roles of career woman, wife, and mother. Most patients find it exceedingly difficult to reveal their eating disorders and feelings of inadequacy to the outside world, where they are often seen as highly competent, successful individuals. The group becomes a testing ground for revealing both sides of themselves; this generalizes fairly rapidly, enhancing social relationships in which they no longer live a lie. Although relationships with men may be discussed in older bulimic groups, attitudes towards sexuality are often avoided. Groups with male therapists seem to avoid these issues completely. My own group, all members of which had discussed sexual issues with me individually, did not seem to have so much difficulty, and a few were beginning to form sexual relationships before the first session.

Termination

Termination of treatment in anorexia nervosa is rarely planned for adequately, and the appropriate time is not easily agreed upon by both patient and therapist. As Selvini-Palazzoli (1974) writes,

Once the initial problems have been solved and the patient's ego has been sufficiently strengthened, psychoanalysis proper can be begun. However, this happens far too rarely. . . . Most of these patients prefer to terminate treatment as soon as their symptom has been cured, certain that they can do the rest by themselves. Often it is better to agree with them and, rather than arouse their hostility and undermine their self-confidence, to express one's faith in their character. (p. 129)

This flight into precarious autonomy, with its avoidance of continued dependence and an increasingly challenging therapeutic approach, is both an expression of health and an avoidance reaction, similar to that seen in sudden termination of therapy by adolescents. Some anorexics will do well, but many will remain somewhat limited in their range of psychological expression and will be vulnerable to relapse. In individual work, ideally the patient should make the final decision to leave and negotiate an appropriate ending phase. Like many adolescents, patients may choose a series of less frequent appointments — a weaning process — or they may end abruptly but often re-initiate friendly contact subsequently. This genuine opportunity for choice in an important intimate relationship seems highly therapeutic and contrasts starkly with the rigid expectations of their enmeshed family relationships.

In individual therapy, such a termination may be impractical because of the availability of the therapist, and it is usually impossible in a group. A group may have a fixed length, which ideally should be determined in advance. Alternatively, the therapist may wish to end the group because of a move, because of dwindling numbers, or, unfortunately, because he or she feels dissatisfied or exhausted by the therapeutic role. The therapist needs to set the termination date at least 3 months ahead of time, preferably taking into consideration the group members' feelings about it. It is difficult to restart a group in its termination phase after a break, and so it is best to have the last meeting coincide with a natural break, such as the summer vacation.

An open group run or supervised indefinitely by a single therapist, even with a series of cotherapists, has distinct advantages. Each patient has the opportunity to deal with her own termination, which she can tailor to her needs; indeed, she may choose to return to the group if appropriate at a later stage, or to remain in contact with group members or the therapist. Termination is not such a powerful issue if individual therapy continues, but it should be dealt with carefully in the group. My own experience is that it can be a very productive phase, just as it is in individual therapy: Issues of dependency, separation, fears of future relapse, sadness, anger, and future unmet needs may be tackled, and progress made may be evaluated realistically. It is considerably enhanced if the therapist discloses his or her own feelings about the ending, particularly ambivalence. Follow-up appointments may be planned, or alternatively, the patients may be invited to contact the therapist by telephone or letter if they wish to. It must be clarified whom they should approach if they require further help in the future.

FORMS OF GROUP THERAPY

Inpatient Groups

Inpatient groups are often mentioned in the literature as valuable adjuncts to treatments aimed at restoring body weight, as well as to individual and family therapy. Small and large groups may form the major therapeutic approach for the treatment of all types of patients on adolescent units or wards with a "therapeutic community" approach. In the past, anorexics have joined groups once their target weight has been restored (Crisp, 1966). However, I support the view proposed by Hedblom *et al.* (1981) and Sclare (1977) that group therapy should begin after the stage of extreme starvation is over, when the patient has started to eat normally and made a commitment to remaining in the hospital. Her ability to use the group will increase as she gains weight; she will move from a position of silence through intellectualization and exclusive helpfulness toward others, and ideally will enter a stage where she can begin to express her feelings and relate more fully to others. Even total silence can be valuable, and, as Bruch (1973) and Crisp (1980) suggest, the group sensitizes the anorexic and enhances individual and family therapy. Apart from groups for mixed patients of both sexes, more focal groups have been described, such as an assertiveness group by Grossniklaus (1980), and a related closed "trust" group by Crisp (1980). Both types help patients to begin to recognize and express feelings in a safe, controlled environment. Other groups, usually run by occupational therapists, use art, drama, relaxation, and dance; these groups have proved valuable for some anorexics. A "femininity" group, organized by nurses at Crisp's unit in London, helped a selected group of female anorexics and other patients to begin to discuss sexual issues more comfortably. Polivy (1981) has also described groups specifically for anorexics, in which patients discuss their feelings connected with the disorder and how it has affected them. The setting provides support and acceptance, as well as models of coping, peer feedback, and education. Hedblom *et al.* (1981) describe a weekly luncheon group that patients may continue to attend after discharge. The main problem in a hospital setting may be to find therapists with sufficient experience, and a balance has to be found between consistent expertise and the training needs of staff and students. Conflict often occurs when a doctor confident in his or her therapeutic approach for nonanorexic patients begins to run a group containing anorexics with an experienced nonmedical cotherapist. Skilled supervision may prevent some of these difficulties. Despite the problems encountered in group therapy with anorexics, the patients often seem to be able to use groups more effectively in the hospital, because of the high level of support and continuous interaction with other patients and staff. Change usually occurs most rapidly during admission. The crunch comes when they face the outside world alone after discharge, finding it very different from the therapeutic world of the hospital and different from the world they experienced as anorexics. It may be hoped that group and milieu therapy will have provided some preparation.

Outpatient Groups

Apart from groups for bulimics, only Leichner and Harper (1983a) have described outpatient groups for anorexics. Both their experience in Winnipeg and that of Maralyn Lawrence of The Women's Therapy Centre in London are very similar to my own, and discussion with them has substantiated my description of the group process. They differ in that Leichner and Harper ran open groups for an indefinite period, while Lawrence ran short-term groups. We all now concur that an open long-term group approach probably offers more to anorexics, particularly restricters. While Leichner and Harper began with techniques of transactional analysis, Lawrence came from a group analytic background, and my own experience was eclectic with a bias toward family work, we all developed a similar style in anorexic groups—gentle, warm, and active, with an emphasis on an educative role and structure. We experienced an unusual group process: The group unconscious was not apparent, and its mood was often hard to define in the early meetings. It was hard to identify the transference, and while feelings were present, they were not allowed to enter the room. Role play and silences proved counterproductive. In general, the approach we evolved helped lower anxiety, so that other feelings could be recognized, the right to them could be accepted, and then the feelings could be gradually expressed. Leichner and Harper (1983a) described how the patients felt they were sharing in the group and experienced the group as supportive and trusting, contrary to the experience of the therapist; this serves to highlight the different expectations of patients and therapist. The patients' body weight on average changed little, with some patients gaining, some losing, and some remaining the same. After 1 year, the main changes were that the patients were less anxious, more understanding of others, and slightly more assertive and confronting.

Anorexics in Mixed Outpatient Groups

Once a normal eating pattern has been restored and maintained after hospital discharge, both bulimic and restricting anorexics may benefit from outpatient group therapy with nonanorexic patients. Suitable patients are those who have shown a capacity for enduring psychological change in psychotherapy, and those who have been able to use inpatient groups in more than an intellectual or altruistic way. A few conditions seem to apply: The group therapist has to accept the need for individual or family therapy and monitoring of weight outside the group, and should be warned that the patient may be relatively silent in the group, despite her abilities to express herself in the one-to-one situation. Weight may fluctuate, and change may only take place slowly and imperceptibly. The individual therapist is much more likely to see any progress, and the therapists should maintain regular contact. Long-term groups may prove valuable, particularly if the patient is highly motivated to continue to look at herself, to cope with painful feelings, and to improve relationships with others.

Parents' and Spouses' Groups

Groups for parents of anorexics undergoing outpatient or inpatient treatment have been developed by Rose and Garfinkel (1980) and by Piazza, Piazza, and Rollins (1980); a group for spouses of bulimic patients with a past history of anorexia nervosa has been described by Leichner and Harper (1983b). All are particularly useful when family or marital therapy is not possible, and in some cases they facilitate the introduction of these approaches at a later stage. They begin with an educative function: Participants are anxious to learn about the syndrome and to meet others with similar experiences. Piazza *et al.* (1980) limited their goals to support and help for parents to work constructively with hospital staff. The two other groups described moved on to a stage of catharsis, when parents and spouses express their despair and frustration with coping with their eating-disordered family members; this in itself offers therapeutic possibilities, as the expression of feelings may generalize to family and marital relationships. Rose and Garfinkel (1980) have described the effect of having a recovered anorexic as a cotherapist who provided a symbol of hope, but also a testing ground for parents to attempt new ways of relating to and understanding the patient. An open group provided the possibility for parents to experience different stages of treatment and recovery, each with their own characteristic pressures. In contrast to the parents, the spouses coped to a greater extent with insight into their own relationship with their wives, all of whom had developed their eating disorders after marriage and were attending their own group. Leichner and Harper (1983b) comment that the relationships and possibilities for such treatment are likely to be more restricted when anorexia nervosa is already present at the time of marriage, because of the nature of men who choose to marry anorexics (see also Crisp, 1980).

Self-Help Groups

Many anorexics who are determined not to seek professional help, who have had unsatisfactory experiences (such as being discharged following weight gain without adequate support), or who are already engaged in treatment have received considerable support from self-help groups, such as Anorexic Aid in Britain, and Anorexia Nervosa Aid in the United States. Some have benefited both physically and emotionally as a result, while others have become more motivated to seek professional help (Slade, 1983). Such groups have an important place in providing long-term support following treatment if insufficient psychotherapeutic resources are available. Anorexic Aid also runs groups for families of anorexics, and attempts to dispel feelings of isolation by offering friendship to sufferers and their families. Local groups are coordinated by a volunteer "contact" who serves as a liaison with the national committee and with local health services, social services, and community groups. The arrangements locally are variable, but most offer weekly meetings with two leaders – a professional counselor and a "recovering anorexic." Such a group has been described by Vaughan (1979), and the guidelines for group leaders highlight an approach similar to the one described in this chapter:

   a) It is difficult for anyone, and especially for anorexics, to be open and expose their emotions to others in a group. It is necessary to encourage trust within the group. The group leaders can facilitate this by being honest and open themselves, and by being prepared to expose and explore their own weaknesses.

   b) Give attention to one person at a time, trying to enable them to be aware of their own feelings. Allowing people to talk things out will release tension and help them to see a pattern in their reactions to everyday situations. Try to keep conversation centred on the person's own feelings rather than the situation and people around them.

   c) Practise listening attentively and allow each person true expression of feelings rather than judging or consoling them. Realise that feelings such as depression aroused in yourself by another in the group were not produced by contact with that person, they were simply exposed from where they were buried in your subconscious.

d) Try to effect changes for people by encouraging them to aim for goals which they set and which they need to work towards but can achieve. Progress should be assessed at each session and the goals reset.

e) Encourage people to write. It does release tension and clarify feelings in a way that thinking cannot. Also it is useful to read things (again) after progress has been made.

f) Practising self-relaxation does enable people to cope with episodes of great tension. It can free the mind when it is running round in circles powered by excess nervous energy. (Schiller, 1978)

Usually a group starts with an informal get-together over coffee for anorexics and their families, who then attend separate meetings. The groups function best when they are small, and usually the leaders structure the early part of each meeting following introductions. Both restricters and bulimics usually attend in equal proportions, with the latter finding it easier to express feelings. Discussion of weight and eating is usually avoided.

Counselors have found that those who do not do well in such groups include early adolescents, those who are chronically ill or hostile, those with disordered personalities, and married women for whom the group serves as a support in their isolated lives with typically doting husbands. Many who do well get in touch with the groups before hospital admission, then maintain contact during and after treatment. The groups often serve as a place to express anger and disappointment about their treatment. Many anorexics may attend once or twice and then drop out, while others come and go; still others attend for up to 2 years, sometimes taking on a leadership role. The leader is often seen as "one of us," and her gentle confrontations seem to be more easily accepted than those of professionals. A group often becomes dependent on a leader, who may have difficulty extricating herself once she has reached the point at which she wants to put her illness behind her. At this point, the group is vulnerable to folding, so that attempts are made to select a leader in advance; sometimes the group is maintained by a nonanorexic leader until a new leader emerges.

CLINICAL MATERIAL FROM AN OUTPATIENT GROUP

A closed group for relatively chronic anorexics was started when the limitations of their long-term individual and family therapy became obvious, in terms of both their social development and the frequency of sessions possible. A total of 14 patients were invited to join a group, which ran for 13 months. Two patients declined to join; one wished to continue in individual therapy, and one wanted to try to go without treatment. Two patients dropped out after the first meeting. The first, who was largely recovered, moved abroad, and the other discontinued because she felt out of place in the group, as she was now considerably overweight. Of the remaining 10 patients, four attended the group regularly and six intermittently. All of the patients had suffered from anorexia nervosa for at least 2 years, and five for more than 5 years. All had received treatment in the department for 1 to 2 years, and three had been admitted to a hospital for a few months. Other than very infrequent family therapy, none received any other treatment after the start of the group. I had seen them all for assessment and family therapy, and had seen most of them individually; this proved invaluable in my role as sole therapist. For the first 7 months, skilled observers watched through the one-way screen. The last 6 months, when observers were only occasionally present, proved lonely and demanding. The group members did not comment on the screen in any meeting.

The sessions were very much as I have described earlier in the chapter, but I highlight here some of the issues mentioned. The first group had an atmosphere like the first day at boarding school, and the members initially discussed their eating patterns and experience during admissions to St. George's Hospital or elsewhere. Surprisingly, they moved on to relating their attitudes about weight to relationships with men; some felt that they become more desirable as they gained weight, which was an incentive for them, while others admitted their fears of such relationships. They all said that they did not like being at low weight but were terrified of not being able to stop gaining weight. Apart from discussing their difficulties in eating in the presence of their families, they mentioned them very little. Toward the end, they began to talk about their menstrual periods, remembering their first one and the difficulties that most of their mothers had had helping them with it. The group was difficult to stop, and one member came back afterward—a pattern that persisted for her.

The early part of the second session was dominated by two bulimics, who discussed the difficulties of their relationships with married men, while the latter part alternated between themes of loneliness and social difficulties and the relationship of both to eating. The end was very tense, with one patient reluctantly admitting that she had wanted to be alone after the group and did not wish to travel with another member, while another patient expressed her hopelessness about recovery. Her distress made it difficult to allow time for other members to describe their feelings and deal with unfinished business.

The group settled down to a cohesive core of six members, who began, over the next few months, to become more able to express feelings and to support and gently confront one another, especially in the second half of each session. All but one were gaining or maintaining their weight, and their eating patterns improved. Three resumed menstruation; two of these became involved in stable relationships and (with difficulty) discussed starting the contraceptive pill. One patient, who had previously made excellent use of a hospital admission and psychotherapy, began to develop a role as "assistant leader." This was interrupted when she felt unable to refuse a long paid holiday abroad, which she knew would set her back. She was able to deal with her distress and indecision in the group, but, as she feared, she lost weight while away and was very depressed during the final 2 months of the group. Her absence, the diminishing numbers, and a lack of support for the therapist contributed to a rather pessimistic middle period for the group.

One member who started the group immediately after hospital discharge rapidly lost weight and dropped out, assuring the others that she could manage better alone. She had, however, managed to establish herself in a career of her own choice and to move away from her family. There was an uncomfortable relationship between a successful teacher, who was the most overtly anxious member, and a relatively confident 16-year-old schoolgirl, who in contrast returned to target weight and made excellent use of the group. This was resolved when the two were alone during the early part of one session. Both progressed well and were particularly sad when the group ended, although they have since continued to progress. One member, who came to the group with her weight slowly increasing above her target weight, managed to cope with her anxiety about her weight without dieting. She aroused the most covert hostility in the group, but as she became more sensitive to others, less obsessed with food, and more insightful, she was well liked, and her weight decreased to a few pounds above her target weight.

Four members attended sporadically; of these, two made dramatic progress between sessions in terms of weight gain and increasing openness. Toward the end, both cried each time they attended. Two attended sporadically, because they could not put their treatment before their academic aspirations, but both had been ill for more than 7 years and had refused hospital admission. After the group ended, both deteriorated and were willing to accept treatment.

The end of the group was very productive. Interestingly, it was preceded by five bereavements — a father, two grandmothers, an aunt, and a grandfather. All were significant figures, and the members were able to mourn them together in the group. This seemed to prepare the way for the end of the group, when a great deal of sadness and anger was expressed about the loss of contact with me as their therapist, as well as their fears about relapse. They reviewed their progress and made realistic assessments of how they would cope in the future, making arrangements to keep in touch with one another. All had been able to reveal their feelings increasingly with one another, and this had generalized to their relationships outside the group. They had largely developed greater independence from and insight into their family relationships, and all were coping appropriately with their education or careers. Six of the 10 were maintaining their weight gain and were close to target weight.

In general, those patients who did well in the group were those who had been able to make significant changes in terms of either weight gain or psychological development in previous individual and family therapy. Those who developed a healthy, trusting transference relationship and began to express their feelings freely in the one-to-one situation did particularly well.

REFERENCES

Bruch, H. (1973). *Eating disorders: Obesity, anorexia nervosa and the person within.* New York: Basic Books.

Bruch, H. (1982). Anorexia nervosa: Therapy and theory. *American Journal of Psychiatry, 139,* 1531–1538.

Crisp, A. H. (1966). A treatment regime for anorexia nervosa. *British Journal of Psychiatry, 112,* 505–512.

Crisp, A. H. (1980). *Anorexia nervosa: Let me be.* New York: Grune & Stratton.

Garfinkel, P. E., & Garner, D. M. (1982). *Anorexia nervosa: A multidimensional perspective.* New York: Brunner/Mazel.

Grossniklaus, D. M. (1980). Nursing interventions in anorexia nervosa. *Perspectives in Psychiatric Care, 18,* 11–16.

Grotjahn, M. (1972). Learning from dropout patients: A clinical view of patients who discontinued group psychotherapy. *International Journal of Group Psychotherapy, 22,* 306–319.

Hedblom, J. E., Hubbard, F. A., & Andersen, A. E. (1981). Anorexia nervosa: A multidisciplinary treatment program for patient and family. *Social Work in Health Care, 7*(1), 67–86.

Holland, A. J., Hall, A., Murray, R., Russell, G. F. M., & Crisp, A. H. (in press). Anorexia nervosa: A study of 34 twin pairs and one set of triplets. *British Journal of Psychiatry.*

Lacey, J. H. (1983). Bulimia nervosa, binge eating and psychogenic vomiting: A controlled treatment study and long term outcome. *British Medical Journal, 286,* 1609–1613.

Leichner, P., & Harper, D. (1983a). *Group therapy for patients with anorexia nervosa and/or bulimia.* Manuscript submitted for publication.

Leichner, P., & Harper, D. (1983b). *Group therapy for spouses of women with anorexia nervosa and/or bulimia.* Manuscript submitted for publication.

Piazza, E., Piazza, N., & Rollins, N. (1980). Anorexia nervosa: Controversial aspects of therapy. *Comprehensive Psychiatry, 21,* 177–189.

Polivy, J. (1981). Group therapy for anorexia nervosa. *Journal of Psychiatric Research and Treatment Evaluation*, *3*, 279–283.

Rose, J., & Garfinkel, P. E. (1980). A parents' group in the management of anorexia nervosa. *Canadian Journal of Psychiatry*, *25*, 228–233.

Schiller, M. S. (1978). *Running a self-help group*. High Wycombe, Bucks, United Kingdom: Anorexic Aid National Headquarters.

Sclare, A. B. (1977). Group therapy for specific psychosomatic problems. In E. D. Wittkower & H. Warnes (Eds.), *Psychosomatic medicine in clinical applications* (pp. 107–115). Hagerstown, MD: Harper & Row.

Selvini-Palazzoli, M. (1974). *Self-starvation: From the intrapsychic to the transpersonal approach to anorexia nervosa*. London: Chaucer.

Slade, P. D. (1983). The role of counselling and self-help groups in the management of anorexia nervosa. In E. Karas (Ed.), *Current issues in clinical psychology* (Vol. 1, pp. 73–82). New York: Plenum.

Vaughan, E. (1979). Counselling anorexia. *Marriage Guidance Journal*, *18*, 230–236.

Yalom, I. D. (1966). A study of group therapy dropouts. *Archives of General Psychiatry*, *14*, 393–414.

Yalom, I. D. (1975). *The theory and practice of group psychotherapy*. New York: Basic Books.

Yalom, I. D., Houts, P. S., Newell, G., & Rand, K. H. (1967). Preparation of patients for group therapy. *Archives of General Psychiatry*, *17*, 416–427.

CHAPTER ELEVEN

Intensive Outpatient Group Treatment for Bulimia

JAMES E. MITCHELL / DOROTHY HATSUKAMI /
GRETCHEN GOFF / RICHARD L. PYLE /
ELKE D. ECKERT / LAURENE E. DAVIS

There has been a long-standing interest in eating disorders at the University of Minnesota Department of Psychiatry. This interest has traditionally centered on treatment of and research with patients who have anorexia nervosa, some of whom have bulimia as a symptom (Casper, Eckert, Halmi, Goldberg, & Davis, 1980). However, in 1979 there was a perceptible shift in the types of patients coming for evaluation to the outpatient clinic. The staff noted that an increasing number of patients were of relatively normal weight but had problems with binge eating and self-induced vomiting (Mitchell & Pyle, 1982). This trend toward an increasing number of patients with bulimia in the population seeking help in our clinic has continued. The majority of the patients we now see for evaluation of eating difficulties have bulimia.

In this chapter, we summarize our experiences in treating these patients and the evolution of our current programs for nonanorexic patients with bulimia. We focus on what we call our intensive bulimia treatment program. This particular program is an outpatient group approach; it currently represents our major treatment effort with these patients. An overview of our earlier experiences with these patients may serve as a useful introduction to our current approach.

EARLY CLINICAL WORK

The first few patients we treated for bulimia either were hospitalized on one of our inpatient psychiatric wards or were treated with outpatient individual insight-oriented psychotherapy. We experienced variable success with these approaches.

With individual psychotherapy, the focus frequently drifted to the dysphoria and interpersonal problems commonly seen in these patients. Both patients and therapists all too often seemed to find it most comfortable to avoid dealing directly with the eating problem. Hence, eating behavior often was unchanged following individual psychotherapy.

Our initial experiences with hospitalization were instructive when we compared treatment approaches on two different adult psychiatric wards. We experienced little

James E. Mitchell, Dorothy Hatsukami, Gretchen Goff, Richard L. Pyle, Elke D. Eckert, and Laurene E. Davis. Department of Psychiatry, University Hospitals, Minneapolis, Minnesota.

success when we hospitalized patients in our general psychiatric ward, which used a traditional milieu approach. The staff members commonly found themselves involved in struggles with patients over issues of control of eating behavior. Although staff sought to establish an environment that would preclude binge eating by controlling access to food, it was very difficult to maintain such a milieu on a mixed adult inpatient service. Patients met with little success in stopping their abnormal eating behavior. Even if they were successful, abstinence from binge eating and other abnormal eating-related behavior often did not generalize to the natural environment after patients were discharged. Patients would frequently relapse.

We had better success in stopping abnormal eating behavior when patients were hospitalized on another adult psychiatric ward, one that used a behavior therapy–token economy milieu. On this ward, there were previously established programs for the treatment of anorexia nervosa and chemical dependency. In this setting it was possible to control access to food, and with structured diets and close patient monitoring, almost all patients controlled their eating behavior while in the hospital. Once the eating behavior was under control, attempts were made to shift responsibility for this control to the patients by a gradual expansion of privileges contingent on eating behavior. With this approach, some patients were able to re-enter their natural environment and maintain normal eating behavior. However, relapses were frequent. This seemed in part due to a lack of appropriate follow-up programs. We also found ourselves increasingly concerned about removing the responsibility for controlling eating behaviors from the patients by hospitalizing them. It seemed paradoxical that we were hospitalizing and hence controlling patients who needed to learn to control themselves. Because of these concerns, and because of an increasing number of patients who were presenting to our clinic with bulimia, we decided to shift to an outpatient group treatment approach.

Although group work remains the major therapeutic technique in our program, we have subsequently become interested in both hospitalization and individual psychotherapy as treatment options, and readily acknowledge the worth of both of these alternatives as they have been developed at other centers (Fairburn, 1981; Lacey, 1983; Russell, 1979). However, most of our experience remains in the area of group work, and our work in this area provides the material for the rest of this chapter.

To return to our historical overview, a number of staff members had become interested in bulimia and offered to assist in our group treatment program. In an effort to gain experience and to evaluate various group techniques, we next conducted seven different groups over a 1½-year period. Each group was comprised of one or two group leaders and between 6 and 12 patients with bulimia. Nine different therapists, including psychiatrists, a psychologist, nurses, and social workers, were involved in the various groups. There was considerable variety in the types of treatment strategies employed, ranging from a nondirective psychodynamic approach to an operant behavioral approach. Five of the groups were time-limited (usually 12 weeks), and two were open-ended.

The experiences in these groups were discussed in an ongoing weekly conference, which involved all the participating therapists. Out of these conference discussions emerged the following conclusions concerning the group treatment of bulimia. These were later to be integrated into the intensive bulimia treatment program.

1. The problem of the eating behavior should be addressed directly in the therapy. In many of the groups, patients seemed quite comfortable not discussing their eating behavior, even if it remained a major problem. It was our impression that there was little or no substantive change in eating behavior in groups that did not address the abnormal eating behavior directly. We also concluded that the eating behavior should be dealt with early in the course of treatment. As a corollary, it was noted by several therapists that patients seemed less able to work effectively on other problems when the eating disorder remained active.

2. A second conclusion concerned the problem of the timing of attempting abstinence from bulimic behavior. The original design in two of the groups had been to encourage a stepwise reduction in bingeing–vomiting each week for 4 weeks, using goal setting. Two other groups adopted the expectation of complete abstinence from the beginning of the first week of treatment. Several groups set no clear requirements regarding binge-eating behavior. Based on our limited experience in these groups, it appeared to us that an approach requiring abstinence from the initiation of group treatment seemed most effective.

3. Although self-esteem and mood seemed to improve considerably when patients became abstinent from bulimia, additional work on self-concept was frequently indicated for many patients. Techniques found helpful included modification of maladaptive cognitions, the teaching of assertiveness skills, and the use of relaxation training.

4. Many patients reported that they found it helpful to be involved in support groups such as Overeaters Anonymous, in addition to the group treatment program itself. This was eventually encouraged by the staff.

5. Group members frequently reported that it had been helpful for them to interact outside the formal group setting. This was also eventually facilitated by some of the groups, and in the later groups an exchange of phone numbers among members was organized early in group treatment. Patients were encouraged to contact each other, particularly when needing support to avoid binge eating.

6. Most patients frequently would be able to abstain from binge eating and vomiting for several days following a group meeting, but some would be unable to sustain this effort and would relapse toward the end of the week before the next group meeting. For many patients, abstinence was sporadic at best. Because of this finding, it was concluded that a more intensive program was needed.

Because of the tentative nature of these conclusions based on early experiences, and our increasing interest in and reliance on behavioral constructs and techniques as a method to understand and treat bulimia, the intensive bulimia treatment program was initiated.

The intensive program remains only one facet of our Eating Disorders Clinic. Before turning to a more in-depth discussion of the intensive program, two additional areas are covered. The first is a discussion of the relative role of the intensive program in the clinic, and, in particular, how and why patients are placed in this particular treatment program. The second is a brief discussion of some of the theoretical principles that underlie the program in its present format.

EATING DISORDERS CLINIC

Patients referred to the University of Minnesota for eating problems are usually evaluated in the outpatient Eating Disorders Clinic. Prior to coming for evaluation, patients are mailed information about the clinic and are also sent self-report forms, which instruct them to self-monitor their eating behavior prior to evaluation. The evaluation itself includes a psychiatric interview with one of the staff psychiatrists or the staff psychologist, and the completion of several patient-rated instruments, including a detailed data base concerning medical and psychiatric history and a detailed eating history form. Patients also receive screening laboratory work and physical examinations, and are offered dental evaluations.

At the completion of the evaluation process, patients who meet the criteria for bulimia are referred to one of several treatment options. These options, and the usual reasons for which patients are referred to them, include the following:

1. Hospitalization. Fewer than 5% of our nonanorexic patients with bulimia are hospitalized at the time of evaluation. Indications for hospitalization include medical instability (particularly severe fluid/electrolyte disturbances), psychiatric instability (severe depression and/or high suicide risk), or failure to demonstrate any significant improvement in an outpatient treatment program. The inpatient treatment program for bulimia is not discussed in any depth in this chapter.

2. Weekly group psychotherapy. Patients who have less severe eating problems, such as those who are bingeing and vomiting only a few times a week, are often referred to a once-a-week group. Also, patients who would be more appropriate for the intensive program but who are unwilling or unable to make the necessary time commitment may be referred to a weekly group.

A variety of types of weekly groups are offered through the clinic. These are specialized to handle certain types of patients. For example, at any given time, one group is composed of "abstinent" members who have been free of binge eating or vomiting for at least 2 months. The focus of such a group is on prevention of relapse. Patients may graduate to this group from other weekly groups composed of "nonabstinent" members who have recently been evaluated in the clinic. There is also a weekly group for laxative abusers, which focuses on the particular problems associated with laxative withdrawal.

3. Individual psychotherapy. This is only infrequently utilized as an initial primary treatment approach. Where obvious and severe psychopathology not directly related to eating behavior appears to be the dominant problem, this approach may be used. However, most patients who are referred for individual psychotherapy within the Eating Disorders Clinic are actually referred following some other primary treatment for the eating problem. It is generally the philosophy of the clinic that other psychological problems can be better addressed after the eating behavior has been brought under control.

4. Medications. Because of both clinical and research interest in the use of antidepressants in patients with bulimia, the Eating Disorders Clinic maintains an active medication clinic. Patients seen in this clinic may be receiving either tricyclic/tetracyclic antidepressants or monoamine oxidase (MAO) inhibitors. There appears to be a relationship between primary affective disorder and bulimia (Hudson, Laffer, & Pope, 1982), and current research supports the utility of antidepressant drugs in the treatment of bulimia (Pope, Hudson, Jonas, & Yurgelun-Todd, 1983; Walsh, Stewart, Wright, Harrison, Roose, & Glassman, 1982). However, it is currently difficult or impossible to predict which patients with bulimia will respond to these drugs. Presently, only patients with histories suggestive of primary affective disorder or with severe depressive symptomatology are treated with these drugs in our clinic.

Patients can be seen for medication in addition to other parts of the treatment program. For example, a patient may be seen for antidepressant drug therapy while participating in the intensive treatment program. Antidepressants are currently used in only a minority of our patients with bulimia.

   5. Intensive bulimia treatment program. Patients with bulimia who are seen on an outpatient basis for evaluation and who are not thought to require hospitalization, but are thought to have severe problems with their eating behavior, are usually referred to this program. Patients in the intensive program are usually bingeing and vomiting at least once a day and have been actively bulimic for several years. Most of these patients have been seen in other treatment programs outside our facility, and many have been through some sort of counseling experience before coming to our clinic for their eating problems.

   6. Meal-planning clinic. This group is led by the clinic dietician. Patients are taught an exchange system of dietary management. Patients usually come to this clinic for a few weeks while they master the meal-planning material, and are usually seen in this clinic in addition to some other group placement.

INTENSIVE BULIMIA TREATMENT PROGRAM

Theoretical Principles

The initial design and the subsequent modifications of the program as it has been in operation have reflected certain theoretical biases as to treatment approach, and these biases have reflected the backgrounds of the staff members involved. A variety of backgrounds are represented in our eating disorder team, including psychiatry, psychology, social work, chemical dependency counseling, and psychiatric nursing. Although all of these disciplines have influenced the program to some extent, two major influences can be discerned. The first of these is the chemical dependency treatment model widely used in our area, which is based on the Alcoholics Anonymous (AA) model (V. E. Johnson, 1973). The insistence upon abstinence upon entry into the program, the focus on the behavior itself, the assumption that other problems will become easier to contend with following correction of the eating problem, the use of an intensive approach, and the use of group pressure and confrontation to reinforce abstinence all underscore the similarities between the intensive treatment program and many chemical dependency treatment programs. The use of this model is strengthened by the finding of similarities between bulimic behaviors and other substance abuse problems, such as alcohol abuse, as has previously been reviewed (Hatsukami, Owen, Pyle, & Mitchell, 1982).

   The other major theoretical influence in our program has been behavioral psychology, both cognitive and operant. In our experience, bulimic behavior can conveniently be viewed using a behavioral model, and many of the techniques designed for obesity treatment can be adopted to the problem of bulimia (Ferguson, 1976; Jeffrey & Katz, 1977; Smith, 1981; Stuart & Davis, 1972). Specific behavioral paradigms that have been incorporated into the intensive treatment program, many of which have been advocated by other researchers in this area, include the following:

   1. Educational techniques are used to inform patients about bulimia and its consequences (Fairburn, 1981; Long & Cordle, 1982). This process begins at the time of evaluation, when certain basic information is provided, and continues throughout the program. Lectures and handouts are frequently employed as educational techniques.

2. Self-monitoring techniques are used (Boskind-Lodahl & White, 1978; Dixon & Kiecolt-Glaser, 1981; Fairburn, 1981; Long & Cordle, 1982; Mizes & Lohr, 1983; Welch, 1979). These are used to increase awareness of bulimic behavior in particular and eating patterns in general. The patients are mailed forms prior to evaluation, on which they record both normal and abnormal eating behavior. The form used for this purpose, the Eating Behaviors III form, represents a modification of an instrument we have used previously in research (Mitchell, Pyle, & Eckert, 1981). The patients monitor their eating behavior for a period of approximately 2 weeks prior to evaluation, continue to monitor it between the time of evaluation and the time of entry into the intensive program, and keep monitoring it during their tenure in the intensive program.

3. There is a strong emphasis on the need to analyze behavioral antecedents to bulimic behavior (Fairburn, 1981; Mizes & Lohr, 1983). The concept of this analysis is originally introduced by lecture and remains a focus of the group work throughout the program. Types of antecedents that are discussed include situational factors, social factors, emotional factors, cognitive factors, and physiological factors.

4. A directive approach is used to change eating behaviors. The use of structured meal-planning techniques, the prescription to eat three meals a day, and the directive to avoid foods that are associated with binge-eating episodes are all employed (Fairburn, 1981; Lacey, 1983; Long & Cordle, 1982; Mizes & Lohr, 1983).

5. Patients are taught various mechanisms to manipulate antecedents of behavior in order to avoid binge-eating episodes. These include the avoidance of stimulus cues, the delay of binge-eating response to a cue, and the use of competing alternative behaviors to binge eating as a way of responding to certain cues (Fairburn, 1981; Grinc, 1982; Smith, 1981). This material is originally introduced in the lecture series and remains a focus of the group discussions throughout the program.

6. Patients are introduced to the need for other adaptive skills. Lecture topics include discussions of stress management and assertiveness training. There is also a discussion of the need for behavioral problem-solving techniques (Rimm & Masters, 1979).

7. Patients are taught to manipulate the consequences of their behavior in order to reinforce adaptive eating habits (Mizes & Lohr, 1983). For example, they are taught to reward themselves cognitively and materially for abstinent behavior.

8. Part of the program is devoted to the need to reshape cognitions (Beck, 1976; Dixon & Kiecolt-Glaser, 1981; Ellis, 1962; Grinc, 1982; Welch, 1979). These cognitions may directly relate to eating behavior, such as erroneous notions about food, weight, and body image. These cognitions may also involve self-concept and the ability or inability to exert control over one's behavior.

General Stucture of the Program

The program lasts for 2 months. Approximately 10 bulimic patients constitute a treatment group. All sessions are held in the evening so that patients will be occupied in the clinic during the evening hours, when many are most likely to binge (C. Johnson, Stuckey, Lewis, & Schwartz, 1982). The schedule is outlined in Table 11-1. For the initial week the patients are seen every evening, Monday through Friday, for a period of 3 hours, from 5:00 P.M. to 8:00 P.M. As the program progresses, the frequency and duration of the sessions gradually decreases to the point where, during the second month of treatment, the patients are meeting twice a week for 1½ hours each visit. Patients are also seen individually for a session at the end of the first month and at the end of treatment to evaluate their progress in the program and to determine recommendations for follow-up.

During the first 3 weeks of the program, there are three segments to each of the evening sessions. Patients first spend 45 minutes in a group hearing a lecture and participating in a group discussion of a topic related to bulimia. (These topics are discussed in more detail later in this chapter.) In the second segment of each evening's activities, the group eats dinner with one of the staff members in a dining room in the hospital, which is contiguous with the hospital cafeteria. The last segment is a 1½-hour group therapy session, which focuses on a discussion of the lecture material and a review of the homework from the previous session.

A total of nine different staff members participate in the program; they perform various functions, such as lecturing or leading groups. Included are three psychiatrists, one psychologist, one social worker, two nurses, one dietitian, and one chemical dependency counselor. The staff members meet weekly as a group to discuss the program and the progress of each intensive group.

Specific Components of the Program

FOCUS ON EATING BEHAVIOR

The program expects abstinence from binge eating and vomiting from the time of the first session. Patients are informed prior to beginning the program of this expectation. Patients also sign a contract that they will be financially responsible for the entire program even if they should leave prematurely, unless their departure is for medical reasons.

The program focuses primarily on eating behavior and stresses three main points:

1. Patients need to maintain a stable weight if they plan to stabilize their eating patterns. Any desired weight change should be postponed until the eating pattern has stabilized. It should be recalled that patients who are significantly low in weight are not treated in this program.

2. Patients need to eat three balanced meals a day.

3. The meals need to be planned in advance, using specified meal-planning techniques. Patients initially should not eat in response to hunger and should not cease eating in response to satiety, but instead should eat what they have planned to eat in their meal plans.

Beginning with the first night, the patients are instructed in meal-planning techniques, the use of a dietary exchange system, and the necessity of eating three meals a day. This is reinforced at each group session. Meal planning for the next day is integrated into each evening's group; patients read their meal plans aloud at the end of the group and hear suggestions from other group members about their plans.

The necessity to have adequate caloric intake during recovery is also stressed. Patients are required to eat a minimum of 1200 calories a day and are strongly dis-

Table 11-1. Schedule for the Intensive Bulimia Treatment Program

First Week: Monday–Friday (5 sessions)	
Monday–Thursday	Lecture and discussion
	Dinner and informal discussion
	Group therapy and assignments
Friday	Dinner
	Open support group
	Group therapy and assignments
Second Week: Monday, Tuesday, Thursday, Friday (4 sessions)	
Monday, Tuesday, Thursday	Lecture and discussion
	Dinner and informal discussion
	Group therapy and assignments
Friday	Dinner
	Open support groups
	Group therapy and assignments
Third Week: Monday, Wednesday, Friday (3 sessions)	
Monday, Wednesday	Lecture and discussion
	Dinner and informal discussion
	Group therapy and assignments
Friday	Open support group
Fourth Week: Monday, Wednesday, Friday (3 sessions)	
Monday	Group therapy
Wednesday	Group therapy
Friday	Open support group
Fifth–Eighth Week: Tuesdays and Fridays (2 sessions per week)	
Tuesdays	Group therapy
Fridays	Open support group

couraged from any attempt at weight loss while they are in the program. A caloric level is calculated by the patients to encourage weight maintenance. They are also informed that any significant fluctuation in their weight will be discussed by the treatment team and that significant weight loss during the program may be grounds for termination from the group. They are weighed at 2-week intervals during the program. Patients are also instructed at the beginning of the program to avoid high-carbohydrate foods and any other foods that may trigger binge eating.

As part of the evening's activities, the group eats with a therapist, usually the person who has been responsible for the lecture and discussion. For this meal, foods are selected in a cafeteria setting, and the group eats in a separate dining room. During the dinners, the discussion from the preceding hour may be continued. There is also discussion concerning what individual patients have selected to eat, and suggestions may be offered if some patients are having difficulty selecting proper foods.

The focus on eating behavior continues throughout the program. As the group progresses, therapists strongly encourage group discussion about healthy eating habits, and attempt to expose irrational ideas about eating and food.

Initially, patients are usually very concerned about their weight and insist that they will gain weight if they eat regular balanced meals. In our experience, many patients think that they cannot eat breakfast, cannot tolerate regular meals, or have some other problem with their eating that they feel is unique to them and that they feel we have not anticipated. The usual approach in the program is to insist that patients follow our model. In our experience, the vast majority are able to do so successfully.

A sequence of 11 lectures is given as part of the program; these are coordinated with homework assignments. The contents of each of these lectures are briefly reviewed here.

Introduction. The first lecture serves as a general introduction to the topic of bulimia and to the treatment program. The medical literature on the bulimia syndrome is briefly reviewed, and a basic outline of the treatment program is offered. The various patterns of abnormal eating behaviors are discussed. Patients are given introductory material on meal planning. The requirement for abstinence from bulimic behaviors is stressed. Rules for participation in the group, such as the necessity for regular prompt attendance, are distributed in written form.

Cues and Chains. Behavioral antecedents and chains of behavior associated with binge eating are reviewed. The discussion centers around the need for an awareness of the cues of various types (environmental, emotional, etc.) that are associated with binge eating, vomiting, and/or laxative abuse. The necessity for manipulating antecedents and finding substitute behaviors is underscored. The homework assignment includes the completion of a list of "cues and chains" leading to binge eating behavior (on a prepared sheet), and the making of a list of alternative behaviors to break the chain leading to binge eating (Ferguson, 1976). Furthermore, both the positive and the negative consequences of binge eating, vomiting, and laxative abuse are examined, and methods to reinforce adaptive eating behavior are taught.

Nutrition. The program nutritionist reviews and further discusses nutrition, meal planning, and a simple food exchange system. Patients practice making meal plans and continue this practice as a homework assignment. Misconceptions about nutrition are addressed.

Depression and Associated Behavior. General information on depressive symptomatology in bulimia is provided (Hudson *et al.*, 1982; Pyle, Mitchell, & Eckert, 1981; Russell, 1979). The relationship between bulimia and affective disorders is discussed, and the use of cognitive techniques in the management of depression is introduced (Beck, 1976). The relationships among bulimia, drug abuse, stealing, and lying are also reviewed (Mitchell & Pyle, 1982).

Making a Plan of Action. This lecture falls on the evening before the first weekend of the program. Each patient makes a detailed plan for the weekend; this includes meal plans, as well as plans for relaxation, exercise, and time to contact other group members. The group is encouraged to meet outside the clinic over the weekend.

Stress Management. This lecture offers various definitions of stress and describes the implications of stress for bulimia. A stress inventory is administered and discussed. Stress management techniques, including the use of relaxation techniques and regular exercise, are discussed. The homework assignment is to develop a plan of stress management and regular exercise.

Assertiveness Training. Definitions of terms associated with assertiveness are reviewed. Specific situations where problems with assertiveness may arise are discussed, including apologies, compliments, criticisms, and saying "no." Problems with assertiveness in bulimic patients are described. Homework involves completing an assertiveness worksheet, and a book on assertiveness is assigned (Alberti & Emmans, 1978).

Family Systems Theory. The lecture and discussion center on family systems theory and the way in which such theory relates to eating disorders. Group members are encouraged to discuss their roles in their families and to identify family rules that may be influencing their eating behavior.

Self-Help Groups. Information is provided about self-help groups in the community. Patients are encouraged to become active in community groups and to develop a plan for follow-up care after leaving the program. Patients are encouraged to begin these groups prior to leaving the intensive program.

Rational–Emotive Techniques. A general introduction to rational–emotive techniques is presented, and information is provided for further study in this area (Ellis, 1962). Cognitions about eating and body weight are examined as possible examples of irrational thinking. Homework involves worksheets designed to encourage patients to examine their own irrational beliefs about food, weight, and self-concept.

Relapse Prevention. The course of bulimia, the patterns of recovery, and the dangers of relapse are reviewed. Patients are assigned to make written plans of what they will do to avoid relapse, as well as plans to implement if they do experience relapse.

GROUP THERAPY AND GROUP SUPPORT

The last 1½ hours of each evening's activities are devoted to group therapy. The group retains a focus on eating behavior. The group is usually opened by the therapist asking all patients who have been abstinent since the previous group meeting to raise their hands. Generally, members are then asked in turn to discuss how they are progressing in the group. The therapist verbally reinforces abstinence in each individual and strongly encourages patients to discuss what factors are helping them to maintain their abstinence. Patients who have "slips" of binge eating and vomiting, or who are having difficulty eating regular meals, are allowed to present this information briefly but are not reinforced with a large amount of the group's time. They are asked to describe what they will do differently in the future to prevent recurrences, and they may receive suggestions from other group members. Lengthy discussions of breaches of abstinence are discouraged; the therapist attempts to direct group discussion to the patients who are doing best. The lecture topic is frequently discussed further, and homework from the previous evening is reviewed.

The last 20 minutes of each group session are devoted to making meal plans for the next day. As mentioned previously, these are read aloud in the group, and group members make comments or give criticisms to one another's plans.

In addition to the group experience, patients are strongly encouraged to contact one another outside the group and to see one another socially. Eating and grocery shopping together at other times are particularly encouraged. We require that members contact at least two other group members during each 24-hour period. They are particularly encouraged to contact other group members if they are afraid they will have a binge eating episode. During the course of the program, the group usually becomes quite cohesive and socially active as a unit.

INVOLVEMENT OF FAMILY AND FRIENDS

During the first 4-week period, two sessions are held for family members or interested friends. These are held during the evening hours and are conducted by clinic staff. Patients are strongly encouraged to invite the people most closely involved with them.

During the first session, family members and friends are provided information about bulimia and the treatment program, and are also allowed to ask questions. Patients are not present during this initial meeting. During the second meeting, patients and their families and/or friends meet together in a large group. They are encouraged to discuss family relationship or other relationship problems that have been associated with the bulimia or that may have arisen during the course of treatment. Individuals are encouraged to discuss ways that they have devised to deal with these problems.

Through these meetings, families and friends are able to meet others who are in similar circumstances and to express common concerns and misconceptions. These meetings may make it more difficult for patients to return to bulimic behaviors, since concerned people in their lives are more likely to recognize early signs of relapse and to encourage them to return to treatment.

RELAPSE PREVENTION

As mentioned earlier, by the end of the program, increasing emphasis is being given to the issue of relapse. It has been our impression that there is a high relapse rate during the 2- to 6-month period following treatment for this problem. Because of this, we strongly recommend that patients continue in some form of supportive care, and that they continue for several months to make meal plans and avoid foods that might trigger an eating binge. In particular, we stress that if they do relapse, there are things they can do to re-establish abstinence, including the reinstitution of meal plans and the contacting of other recovering bulimics. We stress that isolated "slips" after treatment indicate the need for further care and should not be interpreted to mean that the patients have lost the struggle and are destined to return to their previous pattern.

THE PROBLEM OF CHEMICAL DEPENDENCY

There appears to be a significant risk of chemical dependency problems in patients with bulimia (Mitchell & Pyle, 1982). Patients who have active problems with alcohol or other drugs are not accepted into the intensive treatment program unless they have been abstinent from drug abuse for several months. We strongly encourage continued participation in AA groups for those individuals with a history of drug abuse while they are in our program.

As a general rule, the patients are instructed that they should not drink alcohol or use other drugs during the intensive program. In our early experiences with these patients, we found that some seemed to turn to drugs as an alternative when binge eating was proscribed by the program. Also, the disinhibition of alcohol seemed to predispose some patients to binge eating.

PREMATURE TERMINATION

Patients are informed at the outset that their progress will be reviewed weekly by the treatment staff, and that if they demonstrate uncontrolled binge eating beyond a few isolated "slips," they may be asked to leave the program. They are also informed that if they fail to cooperate with the program in other ways, such as missing sessions or failing to complete homework assignments, they may be asked to leave. Approximately 6% of the patients who first enter the program are asked to leave before finishing. This usually happens in cases where patients do not achieve abstinence and fail to cooperate with the other parts of the program, such as meal planning. A large number of patients are warned as to possible termination and are told what we specifically expect in terms of behavior change if they are to remain in the program. Patients who are terminated prior to completing the program are usually offered hospitalization as an alternative treatment method.

VOLUNTEER PROGRAM

Patients who have been abstinent from bulimic behaviors for a minimum of 3 months can become volunteers for the program. Volunteers are utilized in many of the outpatient groups as well as the intensive program. By incorporating recovering bulimics as volunteers, we are able to provide other patients with good role models for recovery. One or two volunteers are permitted to attend the groups in the intensive program. Volunteers also participate in the family groups and act as speakers at a general outpatient support group held on Friday nights. They sometimes serve as role models for recovery in these groups. If a question comes up as to the value of making meal plans or eating three meals a day, a volunteer's endorsement of these behaviors is generally well accepted by the group. Volunteers have frequently stated that participation helps them to maintain their abstinence from bulimic behaviors.

In addition to the volunteers' involvement in group activities, another role is to serve as "food sponsors." Outpatients will occasionally be assigned to a food sponsor, whom they can call in the evening after making their meal plan in order to have the plan reviewed. The volunteer can offer suggestions and encouragement to the patient.

Outcome

Studies are currently in progress to examine the effectiveness of the intensive bulimia treatment program. Only preliminary data are available, and these are from short-term follow-up. A survey of 104 patients who recently completed the intensive treatment program in its present form revealed that 47% reported being abstinent throughout the program, 25% reported between one and three "slips" of vomiting during the program, and 11% reported four or more slips. Overall, these patients represent 83% of those who started the program, and are regarded as successful completers. Of the remainder, 11% dropped out before the end of the second month of treatment. Most of these can be assumed to have been actively bulimic at termination; however, a few left early for reasons unrelated to their eating. An additional 6% were asked to leave for reasons of noncompliance with the program.

An examination of the weights of patients going through the program also proves interesting. In a sample of 35 patients who were abstinent during the first 2 weeks of the program, 66% lost weight during this period (mean weight loss of 1.6 kg or 3.5 lb, range of .2 to 6.7 kg or 0.4 to 14.7 lb) and 31% gained weight (mean weight gain of 1.2 kg or 2.6 lb, range of .6 to 2.0 kg or 1.3 to 4.4 lb). The remaining 3% experienced no change in weight. A large gain in weight does not appear to be a major problem during the early phases of the treatment.

While the short-term outcome results are encouraging, long-term outcome data are not yet available. We are now routinely following up patients at 1 year after evaluation in order to study the effectiveness of these treatment methods.

In terms of outcome, it should be reiterated that during the program it is stressed to the patients that 2 months of abstinence are only a beginning. Patients are strongly encouraged to continue to attend the support groups that are offered in our clinic, as well as in the community at large. It is of note that a number of self-help groups in the local area have been formed by former patients in our program.

Although the focus of the program is on issues related to eating behavior, the by-products frequently include a marked decrease in depressive symptoms and a marked increase in self-esteem. Studies are under way to quantify such changes and to assess how lasting they are.

In conclusion, the intensive bulimia treatment program as it is currently constructed represents a synthesis of previous experiences with different types of group techniques, a growing knowledge of patients who have bulimia, and behavioral principles. The task before us now is to document the effectiveness of this treatment approach and to compare it with alternative treatment methods.

REFERENCES

Alberti, R., & Emmans, M. (1978). *Your perfect right*. San Luis Obispo, CA: Impact.
Beck, A. T. (1976). *Cognitive therapy and the emotional disorders*. New York: International Universities Press.
Boskind-Lodahl, M., & White, W. C. (1978). The definition and treatment of bulimarexia in college women: A pilot study. *Journal of the American College Health Association, 27*, 84–97.
Casper, R. C., Eckert, E. D., Halmi, K. A., Goldberg, S. C., & Davis, J. M. (1980). Bulimia: Its incidence and clinical importance in patients with anorexia nervosa. *Archives of General Psychiatry, 37*, 1030–1040.
Dixon, K., & Kiecolt-Glaser, J. (1981, May). *Group therapy for bulimia*. Paper presented at the meeting of the American Psychiatric Association, New Orleans.
Ellis, A. (1962). *Reason and emotion in psychotherapy*. New York: Lyle Stuart.
Fairburn, C. G. (1981). A cognitive behavioral approach to the treatment of bulimia. *Psychological Medicine, 11*, 707–711.
Ferguson, O. M. (1976). *Habits not diets*. Palo Alto, CA: Bull.
Grinc, G. A. (1982). A cognitive–behavioral model for the treatment of chronic vomiting. *Journal of Behavioral Medicine, 5*, 135–141.
Hatsukami, D., Owen, P., Pyle, R. L., & Mitchell, J. E. (1982). Similarities and differences on the MMPI between women with bulimia and with alcohol or drug abuse problems. *Addictive Behaviors, 7*, 435–439.
Hudson, J. I., Laffer, P. S., & Pope, H. G. (1982). Bulimia related to affective disorder by family history and response to the dexamethasone suppression test. *American Journal of Psychiatry, 139*, 685–687.
Jeffrey, D. B., & Katz, R. C. (1977). *Take it off and keep it off*. Englewood Cliffs, NJ: Prentice-Hall.
Johnson, C., Stuckey, M., Lewis, L. D., & Schwartz, D. (1982). Bulimia: A descriptive survey of 316 cases. *International Journal of Eating Disorders, 2*, 3–16.
Johnson, V. E. (1973). *I'll quit tomorrow*. New York: Harper & Row.
Lacey, J. H. (1983). Bulimia nervosa, binge eating, and psychogenic vomiting: A controlled treatment study and long term outcome. *British Medical Journal, 286*, 1609–1613.
Long, G. C., & Cordle, C. J. (1982). Psychological treatment of binge-eating and self-induced vomiting. *Journal of Medical Psychology, 55*, 139–145.
Mitchell, J. E., & Pyle, R. L. (1982). The bulimic syndrome in normal weight individuals: A review. *International Journal of Eating Disorders, 2*, 61–73.
Mitchell, J. E., Pyle, R. L., & Eckert, E. D. (1981). Frequency and duration of binge-eating episodes in patients with bulimia. *American Journal of Psychiatry, 138*, 835–836.
Mizes, J. S., & Lohr, S. M. (1983). The treatment of bulimia (binge-eating and self-induced vomiting). *International Journal of Eating Disorders, 2*, 59–65.

Pope, H. G., Hudson, J. I., Jonas, J. M., & Yurgelun-Todd, D. (1983). Bulimia treated with imipramine: A placebo-controlled double-blind study. *American Journal of Psychiatry, 140*, 554–558.

Pyle, R. L., Mitchell, J. E., & Eckert, E. D. (1981). Bulimia: A report of 34 cases. *Journal of Clinical Psychiatry, 42*, 60–64.

Rimm, D. C., & Masters, J. C. (1979). *Behavior therapy*. New York: Academic Press.

Russell, G. F. M. (1979). Bulimia nervosa: An ominous variant of anorexia nervosa. *Psychological Medicine, 9*, 429–448.

Smith, G. R. (1981). Modification of binge-eating in obesity. *Journal of Behavior Therapy and Experimental Psychiatry, 12*, 333–336.

Stuart, R. B., & Davis, B. (1972). *Slim chance in a fat world*. Champaign, IL: Research Press.

Walsh, B. T., Stewart, J. W., Wright, L., Harrison, W., Roose, S. P., & Glassman, A. H. (1982). Treatment of bulimia with monoamine oxidase inhibitors. *American Journal of Psychiatry, 139*, 1629–1630.

Welch, G. J. (1979). The treatment of compulsive vomiting and obsessive thoughts through graduated response delay, response prevention and cognitive correction. *Journal of Behavior Therapy and Experimental Psychiatry, 10*, 77–82.

PART FIVE

Family Therapy

CHAPTER TWELVE

Family Therapy for Anorexia Nervosa

JOHN SARGENT / RONALD LIEBMAN / MICHAEL SILVER

INTRODUCTION

Anorexia nervosa is a powerful interpersonal phenomenon. An individual single-mindedly refuses to care for his or her body[1] in an obvious way by becoming danger-ously thin, denies any problems, and resists the entreaties of others to stop. When challenged, the individual can become defiant, secretive, and highly emotional. The anorexic's behavior is beyond others' control and also is highly compelling and engag-ing to people involved with the patient. The family is an individual's primary social context, and anorexia nervosa in a family member becomes a focal point for family concern. Family behavior can reinforce the symptoms of anorexia nervosa, or the family can interact in a way that diminishes these symptoms while encouraging more adaptive behavior in the patient and other family members. This chapter describes anorexia nervosa as a problem of family organization and functioning; it outlines methods for intervening in family behavior and helping the family to resolve the disorder and ensure ongoing development of all family members.

A Model of the Family

The therapist confronting a debilitating, intractable, and potentially chronic or fatal condition, such as anorexia nervosa, needs a theory of behavior and treatment to guide his or her efforts toward inducing change. Family therapy is based on a con-ceptualization of the family as a biosocial system. The basic principles of general systems theory are a framework for understanding family functioning. The family is an organism itself, greater than the sum of its individual members. It has tasks and goals, and its functioning can be evaluated in relation to those goals. The family operates on the basis of predictible patterns of interaction of family members, in which each behavior is an interpersonal communication. These patterns form a chain of cir-cular causality, in which every action is a reaction to other actions, and change in one family member affects other members. The patterns of family interaction in the pres-

---

1. Since anorexia nervosa is far more common in females than in males, the feminine pronoun is used hereafter to refer to anorexic patients.

John Sargent and Ronald Liebman. Philadelphia Child Guidance Clinic, Children's Hospital of Philadel-phia; and Departments of Child Psychiatry and Pediatrics, University of Pennsylvania School of Medi-cine, Philadelphia, Pennsylvania.

Michael Silver. Philadelphia Child Guidance Clinic, Children's Hospital of Philadelphia; and Department of Psychiatry, University of Pennsylvania School of Medicine, Philadelphia, Pennsylvania.

ent are of major importance in determining the outcome of current family tasks. These patterns are related to one another in a mutually reinforcing fashion. The family acts to maintain stability and promote change and growth. These goals exist both for the family as an organization and for individual members. The family provides a sense of belonging and support, at the same time that it encourages increased differentiation and adaptation to the larger culture.

Minuchin (1974) has developed a structural model of family organization to clarify how the family accomplishes the goals of maintaining integrity as a unit, promoting individual development and allowing for the negotiation of affection, intimacy, and mutual respect. Major concepts in Minuchin's model are hierarchy, subsystems, and boundaries. Hierarchy within the family provides leadership, direction, and is a reflection of the different skills, abilities, and responsibilities of family members based on age and developmental stage. In Minuchin's view, the family is organized into smaller subsystems based on function and role. Membership to these subsystems may vary among different families, according to differences in family composition, but their functions remain analogous. The terms "spouses," "parents," and "siblings" refer in what follows to whoever assumes those roles within the family.

The spouse subsystem allows for the negotiation of physical and psychological intimacy and provides for support of individual adult experiences within and without the family. The parental subsystem has primary responsibility for child rearing. Parents provide nurturance to the child, and maintain expectations for the child's behavior. These expectations are based upon the child's developmental stage and the demands of both family life and the larger society. Parents also assist the child in developing a sense of competence and self-esteem, which is based on the child's accomplishments in the family and in the outside world. This sense of competence and self-esteem provides the foundation for autonomy and ultimate separation from the family. The sibling subsystem is an area in which children learn and experience competition and cooperation among peers. Each individual in the family also can be viewed as a subsystem, balancing adherence to the family context with the autonomy to participate successfully in the external world. Boundaries around the family and within the family between its subsystems are the patterns of family interaction, which allow for the independent and effective functioning of each of the units. Negotiation, resolution of disagreement, and a commitment to the achievement of goals are necessary for effective functioning of the family and its subsystems.

The family therapist treating anorexia nervosa should also be aware of the role of the family in promoting autonomy in its members. As the child grows toward and into adolescence, the peer group gains greater salience. The patterns of family interaction must be increasingly flexible to allow for these new influences, limiting some influences and encouraging others. The child's physical development and increasing sexuality must be integrated into family life. The ultimate development of autonomy and self-reliance for an adolescent or young adult is a three-person process. The parents must enforce independent action, change from a position of direct control to supervision, and learn to respond increasingly to the child's cues for involvement and independence. The parents need to move away from the child when the child does not need them, and yet must be available to provide support or limits when necessary. Family interaction also must allow for adequate mutual support for the parents and must encourage their satisfaction in the extrafamilial world. Lack of collaborative effort by the parents inhibits this process. At the same time, the parents may be facing other stresses, including failing health of their parents and increasing awareness of their own physical vulnerability. The child participates in this process by seeking more independence and developing his or her own belief system. The child's efforts can be increasingly refined and revised through parental input. The child has the opportunity to test his or her strength through disagreement within the family and through meeting the demands of parental supervision. If the child has difficulties in relating to the peer group, if the child's position in the family is too compelling, or if the child is uncomfortable with assertiveness, disagreement, and mood changes, the child's contribution to the process of separation is lacking. The parents then have increased responsibility to encourage the child to develop autonomy.

For young adults, the role of the family is less obvious, but no less important. Interaction among parents and child must lead to increased self-reliance and to the development of intimacy with others. There need to be increasing expectations of assertiveness, adjustment, and personal problem solving for the young adult as the parents adjust to life without him or her. Problems in adulthood continue to require effective direction from parents. Parental assessment of development and the need for intervention and assistance must be based on behavior and not age. The parents may have their own difficulties personally, with each other, or with other children, and they need to resolve these without reinvolving their young adult offspring in a way that interferes with his or her development. At the same time, the young adult may need to have his or her perspective on problems in the family recognized and appreciated.

The Family with an Anorexic Member

Authors (Bruch, 1973, 1978; Crisp, 1980; Selvini-Palazzoli, 1978; Sours, 1980) who have described anorexia nervosa and its treatment have uniformly described difficulties within the family. Bruch (1973, 1978) describes the family as functioning as if members could read one another's minds. Yager (1981) describes the family as focused on high achievement, communicating along narrow lines and failing to recognize the anorexic child's individuality. Sours (1980) has emphasized the need of the family to maintain harmony and to disavow distress or upset. These comments have been derived primarily from clinical observation and retrospective analysis. Minuchin and colleagues (Minuchin, Baker, Rosman, Liebman, Milman, & Todd, 1975; Minuchin, Rosman, & Baker, 1978) investigated the interaction of families with anorexic members at the time the symptoms were present by having each family participate in a standardized series of tasks and a diagnostic stress interview. Five predominant characteristics of family interaction were identified as excessively present and detrimental to overall family functioning: enmeshment, overprotectiveness, rigidity, lack of conflict resolution, and involvement of the sick child in unresolved parental conflict. It is important to note that these characteristics are not static pictures of family relationships; rather, they create a matrix of ongoing behavior in the present for all family members.

"Enmeshment" refers to a tight web of family relationships in which family members are highly sensitive to one another. They often infer moods and needs of others and submerge individual interests for the good of the whole. Overt criticism is rare. Enmeshment characterizes appropriate relationships between parents and young infants, but is inappropriate in the relationships between spouses or parents and adolescents or young adults. "Overprotectiveness" describes a relationship in which autonomy is sacrificed and highly nurturant interactions predominate. A stronge sense of vulnerability is felt among family members. The anorexic patient is often as highly protective of her parents and siblings as they are of her. Within these families, the interactions of enmeshment, protectiveness, and conflict avoidance are rigidly preferred. Even at times of stress or necessary developmental change, one observes that a family utilizes, repeatedly and ineffectively, a narrow range of behavior. In dealing with the anorexic child, the family members respond as they would to a much younger child. Families with anorexic members have marked difficulty allowing for and encouraging the resolution of disagreement or conflict. One member of a disagreeing pair may abandon the conflict, or other family members may enter, preventing mutually satisfying agreement. As these disagreements remain, a chronic state of tension and stress develops. These characteristics are mutually reinforcing, creating a family organization that is fragile and unable to respond effectively to the symptoms of anorexia nervosa. The final common feature of these families is involvement of the symptomatic child in unresolved parental conflict. The patient, by joining the side of one parent in a stable coalition against the other parent, by providing a focus for common concern and action through her symptoms, or by being caught between her parents in a loyalty conflict, plays a role in maintaining family integrity. Meanwhile, the family characteristics listed previously provide the context within which the anorexic symptoms develop and are maintained.

These family characteristics describe a context in which the primary psychological features of anorexia nervosa as described by Bruch (1975, 1978) fit and are adaptive. If the family is highly overinvolved with the anorexic, she need not perceive her own sensations. Others may recognize them first or deny their presence. The child must also be vigilant to perceive and respond to the signs of distress from others. In a context where everyone is vulnerable and protection is necessary, interpersonal trust does not develop. Where conflict and distress are denied or are not resolved, the child does not develop a sense of competence, and problem-solving skills are underutilized. The demands of family interaction reinforce developmental lags, which make adaptation to the extrafamilial world more difficult. This magnifies the importance of the family, which further acts to maintain the symptoms. As the symptoms worsen, they tend to draw further involvement and overprotectiveness from family members. The obvious vulnerability of the anorexic inhibits challenges to the patient to act in a more mature fashion.

The parents have difficulty collaborating, due to unresolved marital conflicts and mutual distrust. They can counteract each other; this reinforces their opposing positions. Hierarchy and leadership, which could lead to resolution of conflict and improved self-definitions in the family, are lacking. Effective boundaries between family subsystems are absent, while the boundary that separates the family from the outside world is too restrictive. Ultimately, the family system is failing to meet its goals.

This review describes the family phenomena that maintain and reinforce the syndrome of anorexia nervosa. It does not attempt to explain its etiology, nor does it exclude the influence of individual physiological or psychological features in bringing on or reinforcing the symptoms. It highlights the fact that all family members are involved in the disorder, and it does suggest specific aspects of family interaction that will need to be altered by the therapist in order to assist the family in resolving the symptoms.

TREATMENT

Overview

The family therapy for anorexia nervosa is directed at changing the behavior of all family members, not just the patient. It is based on the techniques of structural family therapy as developed and elaborated by Salvador Minuchin and colleagues (Minuchin, 1974; Minuchin & Fishman, 1981; Minuchin *et al.*, 1978). The goal is to alter the family organization through limiting some patterns of family interaction while encouraging others. The focus of the therapy is family behavior in the present. Through therapy, the family can take responsibility for the resolution of the symptoms, as well as promote the patient's further development. By involving the family in treatment, the therapist has access to a significant context that reinforces the anorexic symptoms. The family can be transformed to participate in and reinforce the patient's recovery. The family's efforts at effectively promoting the health and development of all its members, especially the patient, can extend into the family's behavior outside therapy sessions with appropriate therapeutic assistance.

The Therapist

Family therapy for anorexia nervosa is difficult work. The therapist needs to be able both to participate in and to direct the action of therapy. He or she needs to be in control of the treatment, with a clear sense of the goals of therapy, and to establish a plan to achieve them. The family therapist must be spontaneous within a framework of concepts about how families work well and techniques to help families achieve competence. He or she must be able to attend more to what occurs between people — the process of interaction — than to what happens within any one person, or to what people *say* happens between them, while recognizing the effect of changes in family interaction upon individual family members. This attentiveness to the feedback of the family is a primary attribute guiding the therapist's efforts, plans, and goals. The strengths and weaknesses of all family members will need to be recognized, and alternative truths and realities will need to be considered and proposed.

Therapy for anorexia nervosa is an optimistic and hopeful proposition — that everyone in the family can be more competent and lead more satisfying lives, together and separately. The therapist conveys this belief through respect for family members, for their vulnerabilities, for their capabilities, and for their view of the perils of change. The therapist utilizes warmth and sensitivity to establish close relationships with each family member, inducing change through support, tenderness, humor, and playfulness. He or she can model flexibility by accommodating to family requests, acknowledging his or her mistakes, and perhaps modifying the course of treatment when it is too threatening to the family. The therapist will need to bring to treatment the full range of his or her behavioral and emotional repertoire, including patience with himself or herself and the family when progress is slow, and the self-respect to challenge himself or herself and the family when change is not occurring. At times, consultation and supervision will be necessary, and at times a particular family may do better with another therapist. Therapists who maintain their focus on the best *possible* outcome for each family and patient will be satisfied with their efforts, including both successful interventions and mistakes. Therapists can also be helped immensely by having supportive colleagues with whom to discuss difficult cases.

A therapist must be comfortable with creating and escalating conflict to the point of resolution, even when disagreement is feared by family members. The therapist must be capable of indirection and subtlety, as well as of concretely maintaining a simple focus until a task is accomplished. This may extend even to the point of being firm and unfair to one or another family member at certain times. As long as they appreciate the therapist's professionalism, dedication to a positive outcome, and underlying respect for them even when he or she criticizes their behavior, the family members will accept and welcome directness. Since families contain members of both sexes, any therapist will need to establish strong and respectful relationships with both men and women in treatment. We believe that the sex of the therapist is not an important determinant in working with families with an anorexic member. What is important is that the therapist possess the ability to be both gentle and firm with both men and women. The therapist should also be able to relate to different family members in different ways, but with equal concern and respect.

Arranging Family Participation

Effective family therapy for anorexia nervosa is a collaborative effort by therapist, physician, and family. Successful treatment requires that involved family members be recruited to participate in a responsible and meaningful fashion. Usually the family is willing to participate as a complete unit. However, since families with anorexic members have the tendency to be overprotective and rigid and to have serious unresolved conflict, there are occasions when a therapist becomes aware of these features as he or she requests participation of the entire family. The therapist can use this opportunity to begin to challenge those family characteristics as he or she requests that everyone involved be prepared to participate.

We request that everyone living with the anorexic patient come to treatment. This includes parents, other parental figures, grandparents, and siblings. We find that it is usually easier to reduce participation after treatment has begun than to struggle with the family to arrange that Father or Grandmother come to sessions. No family member living with the patient is unaffected by willful starvation. The therapist must recall that only the perspective of the person requesting treatment is being presented over the phone. If the anorexic patient's physical condition is serious, this can increase the authority of the therapist to request participation. In order to carry this out, the therapist will need to present confidently his or her willingness to help, interest in their problem, and potential for being effective if his or her recommendations are followed. This then begins the process by which the family changes from a unit committed to preserving their way of doing things to a unit committed to resolving the anorexia nervosa with the therapist's assistance.

The therapist can identify the request for family participation as part of an evaluation process — an assessment of what goes on at home — to enable him or her to understand the disorder completely. The therapist can also suggest to family members that their concern for the patient is an important element in best helping the patient. If a family member protests that someone's health or job renders him or her unable to participate, this can reflect a disagreement that must be dealt with as treatment begins.

The therapist should rely on personal judgment about when to push for resolution of this matter. The therapist must arrange for effective leadership in the family in order to treat the anorexia nervosa, and he or she must resist the family's wish that he or she treat the anorexic individually. If the parents are separated or divorced, we attempt to gain agreement that both natural parents will participate in treatment at the therapist's request prior to beginning treatment. In some situations, postseparation or postdivorce animosity between natural parents may be significant, and resolution of the patient's relationship with both parents may be part of the ongoing therapeutic process. If the therapist feels that it may be too threatening to require participation of both natural parents prior to beginning treatment, this request can be deferred. In situations of serious difficulty in one parent, such as alcoholism, psychosis, history of physical or sexual abuse, and the like, that parent may be included in treatment after the therapist has held individual sessions with him or her. In these sessions, the therapist can let that parent know that only responsible participation in treatment to help the patient is acceptable.

The patient who is married or living in a steady relationship with a boyfriend or girlfriend comes to treatment with the spouse or lover, and the patient's parents may be involved in treatment later. If the anorexic lives alone outside the parents' home, initial participation depends on who calls to initiate treatment. If a parent calls, we request that both parents come with the patient for initial sessions. If the patient asks for treatment independently and resists bringing the parents, we agree to meet with the patient alone, remembering that we may need to insist on the parents' participation if improvement does not occur.

If participation appears to the therapist to be a difficult issue, he or she can agree to a consultation concerning who is to come to sessions. This can only be done when the patient's physical condition is medically stable. The therapist can meet with both parents, one parent, or the patient (if the patient has called personally requesting treatment). In this meeting the therapist's focus on positive results can be presented, and family members present can be reminded that the therapist can be most helpful to them when involved family members are present in therapy sessions. Again, the therapist's focus is on helping the family to resolve the anorexia nervosa. The family must take responsibility for ensuring collaborative effort among its members.

Medical Evaluation and Treatment

The physician is an integral member of the treatment team. Medical evaluation, treatment, and surveillance of the patient's physical condition must be integrated into the therapist's approach to the family, and the physician's efforts must be coordinated with those of the therapist. The physician must understand that the medical evaluation, diagnosis, and recommendations must be made with the family and not just the patient in mind. The goals of the medical evaluation of the anorexic patient are as follows: (1) identification of underlying disease processes (if any) present at the time of referral, and ascertainment that no physiological process explains the weight loss; (2) clarification of the patient's physiological condition and the nature of any metabolic difficulties resulting from the patient's symptoms that require immediate remediation; (3) effective preparation of the patient and family for the inception of psychotherapy.

The medical evaluation is generally performed on an outpatient basis. The presence of all parental figures is required; this underscores their need to be involved in the treatment, emphasizes the seriousness of the symptoms, and allows for initial observation of family interactions. The parents' presence also insures that all relevant physical concerns can be raised at the time of initial evaluation. The evaluation proceeds as usual, with opportunity to gain history concerning development of the symptoms, methods utilized to achieve weight reduction in general, and current dietary practices of the patient. Also, the physician can readily obtain information concerning the patient's psychosocial adaptation, family medical history, recent changes in the home environment, and previous family efforts to reverse the symptoms. A complete physical examination with necessary laboratory studies is performed. After becoming certain of the diagnosis, the physician determines a healthy weight for the age and height of the patient and suggests appropriate daily caloric intake and rate of weight gain. In our program, the physician meets with the family and the therapist to begin therapy. During this meeting, the physician reviews the physical findings and informs the family of the seriousness of the situation. He states that there is no physical cause for the symptoms and that the family will now need to work with the therapist to help the patient return to normal physical health. The presence of both the physician and the therapist at this meeting allows the therapist to encourage family members to ask questions of the physician, while the physician lets the family members know that they will be able to reverse symptoms by working with the therapist. Answers to questions of why the symptoms have occurred and how they can be reversed should be deferred to the therapist and psychotherapy. The physician will then be available to the patient, family, and therapist during treatment if medical questions or difficulties arise.

The physician and the therapist serve as consultants to each other concerning the physical and psychological aspects of treatment, and their collaboration serves as a role model for the parents. If the physician cannot be present at the initial therapy session, the therapist should be aware of what the physician has told the family and should be prepared to direct the family back to the physician if unanswered medical questions arise. It is important for the physician and the therapist to communicate regularly during treatment and for each to be prepared to help the family work in a collaborative fashion with the other. During treatment, the physician and the therapist will need to help the family address questions to the appropriate person as the family learns to resolve disagreements directly. The physician and the therapist will need to support each other's efforts with the family when the family is uncomfortable with the direction of treatment, as well as to work together to resolve any disagreements between them concerning treatment. Ultimately, they can build a supportive relationship to help each other with difficulties during treatment.

Hospitalization and the Family

Family therapy for anorexia nervosa generally involves outpatient therapy aimed at improving family effectiveness at home and the patient's effectiveness at school or work and in social relationships. Outpatient treatment also concretely emphasizes family involvement in and responsibility for improvement in the symptoms. If hospitalization is necessary, inpatient treatment must be carried out in a way that is consistent with the overall family therapy approach to anorexia nervosa. The hospital is an arena where the family can gain sufficient control of the symptoms and begin to reverse them with hospital staff support. The authority and responsibility for the efficacy of hospitalization rest with both the family and the staff. Disagreements among members of the treatment team (including family members) concerning any aspect of inpatient treatment should be addressed and resolved directly. Any hospitalization for any reason should further the goal of improving family functioning as the symptoms are dealt with.

The specific indications for hospitalization and goals of inpatient treatment should be agreed upon with the family. Potential reasons for hospitalization include (1) to clarify the patient's medical diagnosis or physical condition; (2) to treat acute physical complications brought on by the weight loss, such as dehydration, electrolyte imbalance, or other metabolic difficulties; (3) to help the parents and other involved adults recognize the seriousness of dangerously low weight and to initiate weight gain for the patient; (4) to respond to complicating psychiatric symptoms, such as psychosis or suicidal ideation or behavior; and (5) to create a crisis when treatment is not progressing on an outpatient basis by changing the context of treatment and raising its intensity. Hospitalization will need to occur in an environment where medical and psychiatric surveillance and treatment is possible and where family involvement is expected. We utilize the medical services of the Adolescent Medical Surgical Inpatient Unit of the Children's Hospital of Philadelphia for diagnostic evaluation and reversal of acute metabolic abnormalities, and the Child and Family Inpatient Service of the Philadelphia Child Guidance Clinic for more prolonged hospitalizations, directed toward weight gain coupled with interventions in family functioning and efforts to help the patient gain increased autonomy and effectiveness. The two institutions share staff members and are located under the same roof. Transfer between the two units is easily accomplished when clinically necessary. Psychiatric hospitalization is necessary in approximately 10–15% of cases treated at our facility; it generally lasts from 3 to 4 weeks.

The treatment plan in the hospital should allow for evaluation of family interaction and should center on treatment goals for the family, even though only the anorexic patient is hospitalized. These can be to encourage parental leadership, collaboration and mutual support, to help the patient become more autonomous, and to challenge the family's sense of helplessness or denial through the acquisition of new problem-solving skills and communication patterns. The hospitalization offers the family an opportunity to become effective. It should not solely allow the hospital staff to treat the patient. If that occurs, the parents may feel that their protectiveness is justified, that their helplessness is ratified, and that their reliance on the hospital to resolve problems with their child is reinforced at the same time as the patient's status as symptom bearer is reified. In order to avoid these pitfalls, careful planning is necessary. Clear communication and resolution of disagreements among staff and family are essential. Regular team management meetings are necessary to ensure consistency in applying the treatment plan and to minimize staff splitting.

Hospitalization begins with a meeting with the entire family, where concrete behavioral goals for the patient and the family are outlined and agreed upon. The patient is encouraged to participate in this process, to the degree to which her goals are responsible and realistic. The goals must include both weight gain (when necessary) and psychosocial improvements for the patient. The therapist can assist the family in developing these goals by focusing attention on the patient's behavior in admission sessions and by encouraging the parents to decide together what changes they require before they are willing to have the patient back home. As the parents set goals in collaboration with the therapist and physician, enmeshment, parent–child coalitions, and poor conflict resolution within the family are challenged, and the beginnings of change occur. The family members are not blamed for past mistakes; rather, their concern for their child is stressed, and they are told that they need to change to help the patient. The focus is on observable behavioral change, not on increased understanding, and the change is monitored through observation of family interaction. Family therapy meetings are held regularly two to five times per week; they are the forum for reviewing, altering, and intensifying the treatment plan. The parents are instructed to discuss plans and persist in this discussion until they are both committed to the plan and to their evaluation of progress. Only when the parents agree are they then directed to the patient to present their ideas and expectations.

The patient is encouraged to negotiate and disagree verbally and to offer alternative suggestions while ultimately accepting her parents' decisions. The patient earns the right to influence parental decisions by demonstrating her ability to take care of her body and by demonstrating social competence with other patients in the unit. Our inpatient milieu includes other patients with eating disorders, as well as patients with other behavioral and emotional difficulties. The daily routine includes individual therapy, group therapy, art and recreational therapy, and nutritional instruction and assistance. Daily activities are task-oriented and usually involve collaboration with peers; assertiveness and direct resolution of disagreements are encouraged. Psychotropic medications are used only if necessary for acute organic psychosis. Within the unit, the patient gains increased independence through a series of steps based on her behavior. Each patient sets individual goals on a daily basis and reviews her own performance with staff and peers. We have found being with other patients with differing social backgrounds and difficulties to be very helpful for anorexic patients. The patient can learn that she has special talents and attributes beyond her ability to lose weight — attributes that can be valued and respected by others.

During family therapy sessions, the therapist must be adept at encouraging conflict and preventing premature capitulation of one family member in a discussion. This can be done by directing the person who has "won" the argument to make sure that true agreement and commitment have been reached. The therapist will need to monitor participation in discussion, limiting it to two disagreeing partners. Limit setting and conflict resolution are supported during hospitalization and establish the foundation for later successful outpatient treatment.

Family lunch sessions (see below) are further forums for family change and intervention. Weight gain programs, diet selection, and exercise are items discussed with the family in therapy sessions. Parents are informed that it is possible to require daily weight gain of their child, with bed rest necessary if a minimum weight is not gained (usually .227 kg or .5 lb per day). However, the parents may develop any plan to insure steady weight gain *as long as it works*. Discharge weight is negotiated with the parents and patient and usually is approximately halfway between admission and target weight. However, we attempt to help the parents to develop behavioral and psychosocial criteria for discharge, in addition to gaining a specified amount of weight. The parents can also supervise their child's participation in peer group activities in the unit, reinforcing her efforts at learning assertiveness, social competence, and appropriate responses to disappointment. The parents are challenged if they are unrealistically harsh or lenient with their daughter. As the patient gains weight and demonstrates increased interest in peer activities and maturity within the hospital milieu, she is supported by the staff to help her parents recognize these accomplishments. The therapist can then help the patient to negotiate increased autonomy and independence effectively, while also supporting the parents for their successful supervision.

The parents can use the time of hospitalization to develop increased mutual support, and the therapist can encourage this through therapy sessions just with the parents. Parental and sibling participation with the patient in unit activities and on passes home prior to discharge are further vehicles to induce and monitor family change. The therapist and treatment team can support the development of improved relationships between the patient and individual family members by requesting specific visits or passes for the patient with only the mother, the father, or a specified sibling. The team can then supervise the patient and that family member in planned therapeutic tasks. Hospitalization will be successful only if therapist, treatment team, and family (including the patient) work together to achieve its goals. Since our hospital program is short-term and geared toward inception of family change, and since our view is that resolution of anorexia nervosa depends on change maintained in daily life by all family members, we strongly recommend outpatient family therapy after discharge from the hospital.

Outpatient Treatment

BEGINNING THERAPY

At the time of initial outpatient family therapy sessions, the therapist is aware of the patient's physical condition and is prepared to recommend hospitalization if concerned about dangerously low weight or metabolic consequences of starvation. If the patient is medically stable, we have three major goals for the initial sessions: (1) to establish a therapeutic relationship with all family members; (2) to formulate an evaluation of the family and the patient; and (3) to establish a contract for treatment with the family, centering primarily on the problems of the anorexic patient. In this phase of treatment, the therapist establishes his or her position in charge of the treatment. Families confronted with willful starvation are usually tense and distraught. Family members have attempted to get the patient to eat without success and may feel helpless. The parents may be confused and startled by the patient's problem. Family members often have theories about the cause of the anorexia, and often parents feel guilty or threatened by the occurrence of this problem in their family. The patient is often upset by the disturbance in the family, as well as bent on continuing to lose weight, and the siblings often also are scared and feel helpless. The family system is out of control, yet family members frequently maintain a facade of normality, stating that everything would be fine if only the patient would eat. Through professional conduct and respect for the concern of family members for the patient, the therapist can establish initial control. Further, by conveying a sense of familiarity with anorexia nervosa and an expectation that the situation can be resolved with effort by everyone, the therapist can begin to create a therapeutic system — family *and* therapist.

In beginning treatment, the therapist should spend some time getting to know the family members as individuals — their occupation or academic level, their interests and their competencies — and should express an interest in what they enjoy. Family members should be put at ease and encouraged to make themselves comfortable, and each person should be contacted by the therapist. In doing this, the therapist can note who interrupts, who speaks for whom, and whether the patient and siblings are able to enter a nonthreatening discussion with the therapist. The therapist can also note what kind of independent action is encouraged and accepted by the family.

At this point, the therapist inquires about the problem. The therapist should begin with the parents and obtain from each parent his or her view of their child's difficulty, what each has tried to do to resolve the problem, how the patient and other family members have responded to his or her efforts, and how the child's illness has affected that parent. Often one parent will have been much more involved with the problem. It is extremely important also to obtain the impressions of the other parent in some detail. The therapist will then begin to convey that both parents will be involved in the process of recovery. The therapist should not be deflected from this by one parent's saying "My wife [husband] knows more about this," but should continue in a respectful way, saying, "I need to know your view." It is important here for the therapist gently to discourage interruptions. The therapist should pay particular attention to differences of opinion, approach, and tone between the parents. These differences will reflect any split between the parents that the therapist will need to resolve.

The patient and siblings are then asked similar questions about the problem and its effect on each of them. When questioning the patient, the therapist should help her to speak as directly as possible in the presence of the family about dieting, methods of weight loss, weight goals, and feelings about her parents' concerns. We recommend that the therapist not allow challenges of these statements. The therapist can also ask the patient about weight goals that have been recommended by the physician and the patient's view of these recommendations. The therapist can state agreement with the physician's goals, but should not enter an argument with the patient about this. The patient should also be asked about emotional problems and suicidal ideation. If possible, the patient should be encouraged to explain the weight loss. If the patient expresses self-critical ideas or a feeling of personal incompetence or ineffectiveness, the therapist can empathize with this and convey to the patient his or her acceptance of her view of herself, while not accepting her reliance on weight reduction as the sole method of self-improvement. In families with anorexia nervosa, the parents often try to reassure the patient, to "make her happy;" the therapist begins to challenge this by allowing the possibility that the patient may be unhappy or dissatisfied with herself and her life. By not offering immediate solutions, the therapist also begins to suggest that the patient may be the best authority about herself and may need to be encouraged by the parents to resolve her own difficulties in a constructive fashion.

The initial evaluation of the family should include an assessment of each of the family's subsystems — spouse, parents, siblings, and individuals — and the stability of boundaries between them. The developmental level of the children, including the patient, should be assessed. The therapist should gather impressions about how the parents work together concerning the patient and other children, as well as how they support each other as spouses. The therapist should ascertain who seems to direct the family's behavior and how much control the patient exerts through her symptoms. Also, the therapist should attend to the degree of involvement (positive or negative attention) the patient has with each parent and whether the patient participates in an alliance with one parent to the exclusion of the other parent. It is our impression that the developmental level of all the children, the degree of mutual respect and cooperation between the parents (exclusive of issues concerning anorexia nervosa), and the emotional and physical stability of each parent are prognostic guides for the therapist. The therapist should also note the family's willingness to follow his or her directions (e.g., respecting his or her choice of whom to speak with, etc.). Other aspects of the evaluation include how family members assess and respond to each other and the degree to which verbal and nonverbal communications of family interaction convey congruent or discrepant messages.

The treatment contract should be concrete, specific, and problem-centered. It should be focused on the difficulties of the anorexic patient, with other problems such as marital discord, even if obvious, deferred until later in treatment. The therapist should highlight concern for the patient's emotional and social difficulties in addition to the weight loss, and treatment goals should reflect psychosocial issues as well as weight gain. These goals can be defined in developmental terms: "Sally needs to learn how to take responsible care of her body; she needs to learn how to deal with bad moods; she should be able to make her wishes heard," and the like. Treatment then can be a learning process for the patient and family. This is less threatening for the family than a process that is labeled as an exploration of deep-seated psychopathology or serious "family conflicts"; it maintains the focus on normalization and reintegration of the patient into the world of peers. The treatment contract should involve all family members, with the parents' and siblings' roles in helping the patient outlined clearly. Progress will be monitored and changes in the plan made in future therapy sessions. We ask that family members call the therapist if problems develop between sessions, instead of changing the program independently or failing to adhere to it. Additional family meetings can be arranged to resolve these difficulties, and the family distress engendered can be utilized to further desired family change.

The treatment contract should specify provisions for consistent weight gain by the patient. The therapist suggests to the family that the patient can and should gain .454 to .908 kg (1 to 2 lb) per week. The parents are encouraged to negotiate together the amount of weight the patient should gain and how they will respond if she fails to accomplish this. They are advised to establish a behavioral consequence that they will enforce if she fails to achieve appropriate weight gain. This consequence can be restriction from physical activity or sports participation, "grounding" for the weekend, or even (if necessary) the requirement that the patient remain home from school or work at bed rest. We suggest that the therapist help the family to start with a less restrictive consequence and increase the restriction if the patient challenges the program through not gaining weight. It is important for the therapist to avoid engaging in repetitive discussions with one parent, but to involve both parents together in a process of negotiation and agreement upon a plan. The therapist should help the patient understand that it is her responsibility to gain weight and that she will gain freedom of activity and increased autonomy from her parents as she pursues weight gain successfully. The therapist can identify and support the patient's knowledge of nutritional information (usually excellent) and can encourage her to choose how, what, and when to eat. The parents can then be instructed to allow the patient to eat food of her choosing, with her performance to be measured through weighing prior to the next therapy session. We suggest that the therapist weigh the patient, unless the physician is easily accessible and can communicate the patient's weight directly to the therapist. The patient's weight is one measure of the family's response to treatment and is used by the therapist to help the family as a unit to review problem-solving skills.

It is important, in setting the treatment contract, for the therapist not to allow the family to be overly pessimistic or to become embroiled in arguments with the patient about the program. The therapist can advise the parents to notify him or her if they are concerned that the patient is not following through or is losing weight during the week. A crisis-oriented session can then be scheduled with the family. The therapist's goal here is to use the process of setting the treatment contract to decrease family enmeshment and to begin to create a boundary between the parents and the patient. The parents' job is to establish, agree upon, supervise, and enforce the program; the patient's task is to meet the expectations of the contract through her own efforts. If successful, all are supported for their competence: the parents for helping their daughter to grow, and the patient for demonstrating her responsibility for herself and her right to independence.

Family lunch sessions (Liebman, Minuchin, & Baker, 1974a, 1974b; Liebman, Minuchin, Baker, & Rosman, 1975; Liebman, Sargent, & Silver, 1983; Rosman, Minuchin, & Liebman, 1975) have been described as a specific method of identifying family interactions concerning eating and of helping the patient to eat in the presence of her family, thus beginning the process of disengaging the patient from her parents. We recommend that a lunch session be held with the family when there is family concern about the patient's ability to eat without undue distress or when the patient is losing weight following agreement upon a treatment contract. The goal of the lunch session is for the patient to eat autonomously under collaborative parental direction, but without unnecessary parental intrusiveness. The therapist helps the parents identify what the patient should eat and then engages the parents in discussion, while the patient can eat without parental interruption or nagging. Only if the patient refuses to eat within a specified period of time are the parents instructed to work together to help her follow their directives. In this process, the therapist's goal is to increase mutual support and collaboration between the parents. The therapist may note that one parent becomes angry and threatening, while the other comforts and pleads with the patient. If this occurs, the therapist needs to help the parents coordinate their efforts. Again, the goal is for the patient to experience her parents' and the therapist's direction that she eat. This process requires both the therapist's experience and careful planning. Family lunch sessions may be required subsequently at times of crisis in the initial phase of treatment, when there is concern about the patient's weight or about her willingness to follow her parents' direction to gain a healthy amount of weight. Steady weight gain by the patient will allow the therapist to prevent the patient's eating symptoms from focusing and directing family activity and maintaining enmeshment and overprotectiveness.

MIDDLE PHASE OF TREATMENT

Once the patient is gaining weight steadily (even if slowly), the therapist should help the family to shift the focus of sessions to the psychosocial developmental difficulties of the patient and unresolved family conflicts. The therapist can help the family utilize the previously successful approach to weight gain if the patient loses weight or progress ceases. The therapist can help the family identify stresses that might have led to the patient's weight loss. Once these stresses are identified, the parents and patient can be challenged to find alternative methods of coping with stress, other than weight loss for the patient and predictable reinvolvement of the parents in enmeshed relationships with the patient. As the patient approaches her goal weight, she can decrease the rate of weight gain and can also gain more complete control over her weight with the therapist's support.

At this point, the therapist should be particularly attentive to content that can be used in the therapy process to further the therapeutic goals of fostering mutual support and conflict resolution between the parents and increased autonomy and self-respect for the patient. The therapist helps the patient to speak for herself, to disagree with her parents, and to express in her own words the difficulties she is experiencing. Often as the patient begins to gain weight, she begins to experience again her feelings of ineffectiveness, her feeling of being excluded from the world of peers, and other concerns that she finds troubling and believes to be out of her control. She may become depressed, even to the point of considering suicide. Both the patient and the family should be prepared by the therapist for this possibility. If both the family and the patient believe that awareness of troubling emotions is a sign of progress, they will bring these concerns to therapy sessions. There, the therapist can help the patient to develop methods of responding to unhappiness, while the parents encourage her in this form of mature problem solving. If the therapist has not prepared parents and patient, the patient's moods can become a new focus for parental enmeshment, and the patient can be frightened by her emotional responses and seek further involvement with her parents through continued symptoms.

The therapist further helps the family recognize that disagreements between parents and children are part of family life; that separation is a painful process that must be undertaken by parents and children; and that increased autonomy for the patient requires that she demonstrate responsibility and earn parental trust. These issues become the background of interactions that the therapist encourages among family members in therapy sessions. As the therapist listens to these interactions, he or she can help the parents individually to be supportive of the patient and to reinforce her competence. Whether the content of the discussion is courses at school, work problems, rejection by peers, or dating or love relationships, the parents are instructed to find out from the patient what assistance she needs from them and to expect that the patient resolve her difficulties independently. At the same time, the therapist can help the parents accept their increasing distance from the patient; the futility of trying to prevent her pain; and their need to encourage her in her life and her choices, even though they may not always agree with her.

The therapist should also begin to explore with each parent his or her personal concerns. As the patient's symptoms improve, often the parents become increasingly aware of individual and marital concerns. Difficulties at work, problems with their own parents, issues of redirecting their energies away from parenting toward increased involvement in their own lives, and intimations of marital discord can be addressed in sessions and added to the agenda of therapy. Resolution of these issues becomes part of the therapeutic contract. Lack of resolution of these problems may lead to recurrence of the anorexic patient's symptoms or to the development of symptoms in another family member. Problems among the siblings, difficulties between mother or father and patient, and individual problems brought up by the patient (including dissatisfaction with her increasingly mature body) can be highlighted. The therapist should feel a solid, separate, and different relationship with individual family members and should experience boundaries between the various subsystems of the family. The therapist can then shift to marital therapy for the parents and individual therapy sessions for the patient. Sessions can also be scheduled for the siblings as a group. As these sessions are being planned and arranged, the therapist can support family subsystems by encouraging the parents to support each other when upset rather than looking to the children (especially the patient) for validation and approval, and by instructing the siblings to support their sister rather than attempting to parent her (by telling her to eat, not to get so upset, etc.). Changing the focus of therapy to marital and individual therapy constitutes the final phase of treatment.

FINAL PHASE OF TREATMENT

The family systems therapist carries out individual therapy for the anorexic patient and marital therapy for the parents with his or her knowledge of the entire family system in mind. Experience with the family as a whole helps the therapist to work with the parental couple and the patient in a way that furthers the family's overall goals as well as helping the spouses and the patient. We recommend that the same therapist perform the individual, marital, and family therapy, because of the need for these efforts to be integrated. If a different individual therapist is sought for the patient by the family, that therapist must collaborate with the original family therapist. The therapist should meet regularly with the entire family on a monthly basis while pursuing couples and individual therapy to ensure that changes for the patient and the parents are meshing successfully in the family unit. The therapist should also request family meetings when issues raised in individual or marital therapy require resolution with other family members. The therapist should defer discussions concerning family members who are not present until family sessions for direct negotiation of these problems. The therapist can then further support the patient and parents in separate meetings to enable them to be assertive and direct in the family sessions.

Individual therapy with the patient has the focus of maintaining the patient's disengagement from parental conflicts and encouraging her development of self-care, self-esteem, and interpersonal trust. The therapist can encourage the patient to make her own arrangements for transportation to sessions and to schedule appointments for herself. The therapist should maintain a stance of support for the patient, and should slowly help her to identify features of her experience that she can change and to develop strategies to change them. As family problems are discussed with the patient, the therapist can use three approaches: (1) Assist the patient, to develop methods to change how family members treat her, with discussions in therapy sessions used to evaluate their success; (2) help the patient plan ways of minimizing her role in repetitive, nonproductive interactions with family members; (3) help the patient recognize that particular aspects of family life may not change, and then help her identify what she can do to improve her own life outside the home. The therapist usually combines these strategies in the treatment of any patient. The therapist can also wonder with the patient whether family conflicts and concerns about her parents may be a distraction from difficulties in her relationships with peers that need to be dealt with.

The process of individual therapy should be directed toward assisting the patient in making choices, resolving ambivalences, and learning to recognize her emotional experience. She should be encouraged to interact with the therapist in an assertive way. The therapist can admit errors and lose arguments while modeling negotiation and compromise with the patient; however, he or she should avoid power struggles with the patient. The therapist can also attend to ways in which he or she reacts to the patient as one or the other parent does and can modify his or her own responses accordingly. The therapist should maintain a problem-solving focus, encouraging the patient to specify the difficult aspects of situations with peers, at school or work, in dating or love relationships, and so forth. The therapist will need to challenge the "all-or-none" logic associated with the patient's perfectionism, and to provide strong support for her competence and success while assisting the patient in accepting mistakes and disappointments. The therapist supports emotional, cognitive, and behavioral flexibility in the patient. The therapist can also help the patient develop physical and psychological self-monitoring skills, while helping her to accept fluctuations in mood and weight as part of life. The patient can then be encouraged to attend more to external sources of enjoyment and satisfaction for their own sake as she learns to supervise herself and become truly autonomous.

Marital therapy for the parents is centered on the need of the spouses to attend to themselves, their future, and their relationship. The therapist develops and maintain a focus on negotiation, compromise, and the possibility of mutual support and respect within the marriage. Often past resentments and perceived injustices must be identified. The husband and wife then negotiate forgiveness for these past resentments, with the therapist's support. The therapist monitors spouse interactions to encourage true agreement and commitment; he or she does not allow one parent to capitulate, and disagreement and resentment thus to become submerged again. The therapist should strongly discourage the spouses from involving the patient or siblings in their disagreements at home. Spouses can also be instructed to plan time together and to agree upon issues of child rearing. Each spouse needs to develop and engage in satisfying ways of spending time and achieving successes as the patient becomes more involved outside the family and is less available to the parents for support and interaction. The husband can learn to distract his wife from engaging in nonproductive interactions with the patient, and vice versa.

Occasionally one or both spouses will become aware of incompatibilities in the marriage and will discuss separation. If this occurs early in treatment, prior to weight gain or the inception of developing autonomy for the patient, we strongly recommend that the therapist discourage separation, reminding the parents of their shared responsibility for the patient's recovery. Discussion of this issue is deferred until the patient is successfully disengaged from the parents. At that time, if the spouses continue to wish to separate, the therapist can assist them with this in a way that helps them maintain collaborative efforts in child rearing and minimizes deleterious effects on the patient and her siblings. The therapist can also help the children with their responses to this in therapy sessions.

Termination of treatment can occur at different times for different family subsystems. We generally hold follow-up sessions monthly with the patient and with the family for 2 to 4 months, when the patient, the spouses, and the entire family are functioning effectively; we may maintain phone contact with patient and family for some time after that. We try to help family members to experience their own resources in dealing with stresses and transitions. We move to decrease our therapeutic involvement as these stresses are negotiated by family members with little disruption in other family members or subsystems. Often the therapist's assistance is sought by the patient or a parent when future stresses or developmental challenges occur. The patient who developed and has recovered from anorexia nervosa as an adolescent may request the therapist's assistance with difficulties occurring in young adulthood. One parent may seek individual therapy for himself or herself concerning issues that arise in middle age. The therapist can best appreciate these requests as indicative of the family's respect for his or her skills, and should welcome these opportunities to assist the family further in managing their development through the family life cycles.

Special Problems in Family Treatment

During the course of family therapy for anorexia nervosa, problems and difficulties may arise for the therapist. Also, special circumstances occur in individual cases, and these require that the therapist make some modifications in the approach presented above. We find that it is important for the therapist to be clear in his or her thinking about the family in these situations and to spend time planning therapeutic efforts carefully. Some of the more common of these problems are discussed in this section.

LACK OF PROGRESS IN THERAPY

How should the therapist deal with therapy that is not progressing? The family comes regularly to sessions, does not change, and appears unconcerned about this.
This situation occurs as the therapist has decreased the tension level in the family while the guardedness of family members has limited their personal involvement with therapy. The therapist may find himself or herself engaged in power struggles with family members and becoming increasingly frustrated and angry with the family. The therapist needs to establish some distance between himself or herself and the family, and to start again with fresh ideas. Supervision or consultation with a trusted colleague is especially valuable here. A series of questions can be considered during this review of the previous therapy:

1. What is the therapist's understanding of the family and the role of the symptoms within the family? Are there issues that the therapist does not understand fully?
2. Do the family members appreciate their responsibility for the success of therapy, or are they subtly expecting that the therapist will resolve the anorexia nervosa without real change occurring in the family?
3. Are important family members who do not live at home exerting pressure on the nuclear family that counteracts the efforts of the therapist? Can these individuals be involved actively in therapy?
4. Are there particular aspects of this family that make it a difficult one for the therapist to work with? Can the therapist accept these phenomena, or are they so compelling to the therapist that they continually engage him or her in power struggles? Is transfer to another therapist necessary?
5. Is hospitalization necessary to alter this stagnation?
6. Is the therapist aware of the fear of change that the family experiences? Can the therapist gradually diffuse this apprehension and help change occur more slowly with less anxiety?
7. Do individual family members have a relationship with the therapist based on respect and concern for the problem? Can the therapist, when becoming defensive and angry with a family member, move closer to that person and understand that person more completely?

8. Is there an unresolved disagreement within the family about the seriousness of the symptoms or the potential efficacy of therapy that has not been resolved and that must be stated and dealt with explicitly?

9. Should the therapist vary the composition of attendance at meetings in order to get fresh ideas?

10. Is the therapist too active, or too insistent upon change? Is the therapist's aggressiveness inducing a resistant, protective attitude on the part of the family?

As these questions are considered by the therapist, he or she will be able to develop new approaches to the problem that can be effective. In difficult cases, this review may be necessary regularly.

THE SINGLE-PARENT FAMILY

What approaches can be developed to work with the single-parent family with an anorexic child or young adult?

The parent should make clear his or her desire that the patient gain weight and improve psychologically. Two other strategies are also very helpful. First, the therapist should determine whom the parent relates to and relies on in his or her own life (extended family, friends, community members, etc.). These individuals can support the parent, may attend therapy sessions, and can help in the process of disengaging the parent from the patient. If the parent reports that he or she is isolated and without support, the therapist should stress that support is an essential part of the patient's treatment and should help the parent build supportive relationships with adults. The patient can also develop a supportive network of friends who can attend therapy sessions if necessary.

Second, the therapist himself or herself can act as a boundary between parent and patient by developing strong relationships with both individuals and by requesting that he or she be involved in serious disputes until they can resolve disagreements successfully. Therapy with isolated, highly involved parent–patient dyads can be a long and difficult process. The therapist can also develop strategies with the parent and patient to encourage the child to act independently, such as participating in social groups, attending camp, or preparing for college. The patient can then plan with the therapist and parent how she can be successful in these experiences.

PREMATURE TERMINATION OF TREATMENT

How should the therapist respond when the patient gains weight readily and the family and patient decide to terminate treatment prior to resolving emotional and family problems?

The patient's rapid weight gain can again focus family attention away from unresolved conflicts, relieving anxiety and decreasing the family's motivation for change. If the therapist believes that further treatment is needed, he or she should state this clearly. The physician and other involved resources can be informed and enlisted to help encourage the family to continue treatment. If this is not successful, we recommend that the therapist review with the parents and the patient their assessment of the patient's physical *and* psychological status, as well as of the overall quality of family life. The therapist then can review with the parents normal developmental milestones for adolescents and young adults. The therapist lets all family members know that they are responsible for monitoring and supporting the patient's development, and that the therapist is available to the family and the patient to help when they request his or her assistance.

NONCOMPLIANCE OF ONE PARENT

What should the therapist do when one parent cannot or will not become involved with therapy because of physical or emotional difficulty?

After the therapist has investigated the situation and agrees that the parent cannot be involved in treatment, the therapist should carry out treatment with family members who can come and should inform the absent parent of progress regularly by phone. These phone contacts can reinforce that parent's lack of involvement and restate the therapist's concern for that parent's well-being. The therapist should also help participating family members to discuss and resolve lingering ambivalence and resentment toward the parent who is not participating. What is most important here is that all family members are following the treatment contract, not who is attending specific therapy sessions.

The following case example demonstrates how a therapist maintained the family-oriented perspective advocated here while responding to the problems encountered in a difficult case. Through flexible adherence to the goals of treatment and the assistance of colleagues, the therapist was able, over time, to help the family toward a successful resolution of the anorexia nervosa, subsequent emotional and behavioral problems of the patient, and long-standing family difficulties.

CASE EXAMPLE

Karen was 15 years old when she began to diet while a sophomore in high school. She lived with her parents and younger brother in a middle-class suburb outside the city. The father was 48, the mother was 38, and the brother was 10 at this time. This was her father's second marriage. He had two adult daughters from his first marriage, who are professionals in another city. His first marriage had ended in divorce 20 years prior to this. The father was a managing partner of a retail business and was away from home 1 week monthly for his business. The mother was a homemaker, and the younger brother had been a family concern for several years because of mild mental retardation and the need for special education.

Karen had been an excellent student and a successful athlete throughout her childhood. She was about 4.54 kg (10 lb) overweight prior to beginning her diet, and her diet persisted as she lost 15.91 kg (35 lb) to a weight of 43.18 kg (95 lb) (her height is 160 cm, or 5 ft 3 in) over 4 months. At this point, she was eating mostly salads and consuming 500 calories daily. She was taking five to ten laxative tablets daily, but did not induce vomiting. She had given up social and sports activities and had become highly emotional and disruptive at home. Her dieting had become a major concern for the family, leading to frequent explosive arguments. The father would become impulsively angry, make excessive threats, and then not carry them out. The mother would become upset and overwhelmed, and would either argue with her husband or withdraw to her room. Both maternal and paternal grandparents were involved, although they did not live with the family. The grandparents would call regularly and argue with the mother about how to help Karen eat. Karen would become distraught and firmer in her resolve to continue dieting. The patient was finally evaluated by her pediatrician and referred to a therapist with a diagnosis of anorexia nervosa.

In the first session, the therapist noted a high level of tension within the family, and in initial questioning became aware of the impulsiveness of both parents and the patient. Family members were quick to argue with one another, and the focus on the patient was intense. The younger brother seemed overwhelmed, confused, and highly upset. Each parent and the patient were more interested in disagreeing among themselves than in relating to the therapist. Interruptions were frequent and emotionally charged as the therapist attempted to establish control and develop a plan to begin the patient's weight gain. The family gradually developed a plan, and a lunch session was scheduled. At this point, the patient announced that her mother regularly engaged in binge eating and induced vomiting, and that the mother needed help more than she did. The therapist briefly asked the mother about this and learned that the mother had been bulimic for 10 years since the death of her younger sister. She reported that she was in psychotherapy for this problem and agreed that the therapist could contact her therapist. Her husband and the therapist supported the mother and re-established focus on the adolescent patient's anorexia nervosa. The patient ate spontaneously in the lunch session, but lost weight between sessions. The parents agreed to limit the patient's use of the stereo and television because of the lack of weight gain, and they limited laxative use by the patient. During the next five weeks, the patient's weight dropped to 39.5 kg (87 lb), despite weekly family therapy sessions. The parents did not carry out restrictions in response to the weight loss, and family arguments persisted. The therapist confronted the family concerning their failure to follow through with their plan and suggested that a new plan be developed. The parents then, in collaboration with the therapist and the referring pediatrician, recommended hospitalization for the patient.

Karen was admitted to the medical inpatient unit, where her metabolic status was evaluated and stabilized. In the medical unit, Karen began to eat more regularly, but she remained easily upset and angry. She was then transferred to the psychiatric unit with her parents' agreement, where she continued to gain weight, where family therapy continued twice weekly, and where she participated in peer group activities. Karen did not like the hospital, and her parents remained both impulsive and evasive in therapy sessions. Karen's weight rapidly went up to 47.72 kg (105 lb) within 2 weeks, and her parents requested her discharge, although Karen remained emotionally immature. The family then went on a summer vacation and did not immediately pursue outpatient treatment, despite the staff's recommendation. The therapist was aware that the situation was not resolved and maintained phone contact with the parents.

Two months later, the mother called the therapist to say that Karen continued to have severe moodiness and was overeating, and that family disruption persisted, although Karen's weight was now 53.64 kg (118 lb). The family agreed to return to therapy. Karen now appeared depressed and reported that she felt unable to control her appetite. The therapist inquired how the patient could seek support from her parents when she felt out of control. The father's evasiveness and the mother's sense of incompetence became apparent again, and the parents were encouraged to help each other change. However, attendance at therapy sessions was sporadic. Finally, although recognizing Karen's continued symptoms, the parents requested that therapy be discontinued due to financial stresses brought on by the dissolution of the father's business partnership. The therapist reiterated that the parents were responsible for Karen and that he did not agree with discontinuing treatment.

Subsequent to this, Karen ran away from home and then, upon return, took a small overdose of medication in a suicide attempt. At this time, the family again requested that Karen be admitted to the psychiatry inpatient unit. This was 1 year after her first admission. The hospital staff helped the therapist evaluate the course of treatment. The therapist recognized that the parents' inconsistency in following treatment plans and their inability to work together for Karen needed to be challenged and altered. The therapist held several sessions with the parents and Karen, highlighting the seriousness of Karen's situation and the danger inherent in her disordered and self-destructive behavior. The parents were assisted in helping Karen take more responsibility for her emotional state and her behavior. The parents began to focus increasingly on the quality of Karen's behavior and required that she demonstrate self-control and develop methods of dealing with sadness and helplessness. Karen responded to the increased parental concern and availability. Karen participated more actively in unit activities, and her parents were more personally involved in her treatment. The mother and father each spent time with Karen individually in the hospital, and therapy sessions were held with just the mother and Karen and the father and Karen, as well as with the entire family. Karen's mother also brought her own mother to a session to resolve chronic disagreements about how to deal with Karen; the grandmother was instructed to follow the mother's lead in caring for Karen. Karen was discouraged from complaining to her grandmother when she became upset or worried about her mother. Karen was also encouraged to invite classmates from school to visit her in the hospital and meet her therapist with her, which she agreed to readily. The hospitalization lasted 3½ weeks, and Karen was discharged with significant improvement in her mood as she prepared to return to school and complete final exams. The level of impulsiveness and enmeshment in the family had diminished significantly, and family communication patterns had improved.

Following discharge, the family continued regular outpatient therapy. Sessions were held with the family, Karen individually, and the parents alone over the next two months. Karen planned a 1-month camp experience which she completed successfully. Her overeating stopped, and her weight stabilized at 54.5 kg (120 lb). She did not become involved in arguments between her parents. The mother continued her own therapy; she resumed college, and her bulimia diminished. The father's new retail business became increasingly successful. Eighteen months after referral, Karen was a senior in high school, was planning to attend college away from home, worked at a part-time job, and engaged in regular social acitivities including dating. She met with the therapist once monthly and described herself as a "regular teenager."

CONCLUSION

The syndrome of anorexia nervosa is associated with characteristic dysfunctional patterns of family interaction. The family therapist conceptualizes anorexia nervosa in relation to the organization and functioning of the entire family (including the patient); organizes a therapeutic system, including patient, family, therapist, physician, and hospital staff; and plans the therapeutic interventions to induce change in the family. The therapist carries this out with concern and respect for the family, compassion, patience, persistence, and flexibility. Outcome studies (Minuchin *et al.*, 1978; Rosman, Minuchin, Baker, & Liebman, 1977; Rosman, Minuchin, Liebman, & Baker, 1977) have demonstrated the efficacy of family therapy for anorexia nervosa. The family can, with the therapist's assistance, act to resolve the symptoms and foster the continued development of all its members.

REFERENCES

Bruch, H. (1973). *Eating disorders*. New York: Basic Books.
Bruch, H. (1978). *The golden cage*. Cambridge, MA: Harvard University Press.
Crisp, A. H. (1980). *Anorexia nervosa: Let me be*. New York: Grune & Stratton.
Liebman, R., Minuchin, S., & Baker, L. (1974a). An integrated treatment program. *American Journal of Psychiatry, 131*, 432–436.
Liebman, R., Minuchin, S., & Baker, L. (1974b). The role of the family in the treatment of anorexia. *Journal of the American Academy of Child Psychiatry, 13*, 264–274.
Liebman, R., Minuchin, S., Baker, L., & Rosman, B. L. (1975). The treatment of anorexia. In J. H. Masserman (Ed.), *Current psychiatric therapies* (pp. 51–57). New York: Grune & Stratton.
Liebman, R., Sargent, J., & Silver, M. (1983). A family systems orientation to the treatment of anorexia nervosa. *Journal of the American Academy of Child Psychiatry, 22*, 128–133.

Minuchin, S. (1970). The use of an ecological framework in the treatment of a child. In J. Anthony & C. Koupernik (Eds.), *The child in his family* (pp. 41–57). New York: Wiley.

Minuchin, S. (1974). *Families and family therapy*. Cambridge, MA: Harvard University Press.

Minuchin, S., Baker, L., Rosman, B. L., Liebman, R., Milman, L., & Todd, T. (1975). A conceptual model of psychosomatic illness in children. *Archives of General Psychiatry, 32*, 1031–1038.

Minuchin, S. & Fishman, H. C. (1981). *Family therapy techniques*. Cambridge, MA: Harvard University Press.

Minuchin, S., Rosman, B. L., & Baker, L. (1978). *Psychosomatic families: Anorexia nervosa in context*. Cambridge, MA: Harvard University Press.

Rosman, B. L., Minuchin, S., Baker, L., & Liebman, R. (1977). A family approach to anorexia nervosa: Study, treatment, outcome. In R. A. Vigersky (Ed.), *Anorexia nervosa* (pp. 341–348). New York: Raven Press.

Rosman, B. L., Minuchin, S., & Liebman, R. (1975). Family lunch session: An introduction to family therapy in anorexia nervosa. *American Journal of Orthopsychiatry, 45*, 846–853.

Rosman, B. L., Minuchin, S., Liebman, R., & Baker, L. (1976). Input and outcome of family therapy in anorexia nervosa. In J. Claghorn (Ed.), *Successful psychotherapy* (pp. 128–139). New York: Brunner/Mazel.

Selvini-Palazzoli, M. (1978). *Self starvation*. New York: Jason Aronson.

Sours, J. A. (1980). *Starving to death in a sea of objects*. New York: Jason Aronson.

Yager, J. (1981). Psychological aspects of anorexia nervosa. In A. D. Schwab (Moderator), *Anorexia nervosa*. *Annals of Internal Medicine, 94*, 371–381.

CHAPTER THIRTEEN

Family Therapy for Bulimia

RICHARD C. SCHWARTZ / MARY JO BARRETT /
GEORGE SABA

At first glance, the phenomenon of bulimia in normal-weight individuals seems perplexing and enigmatic. Why would anyone eat so much and then immediately try so desperately to get rid of what was just eaten? The behavior does not seem to make any sense.

Many glances later, however, this symptom begins to make a great deal of sense, and does so from many different vantage points. To us, bulimia is more than a set of eating disorders. It is a rigid and extreme pattern of thinking, feeling, and relating to others—a self-image and a life orientation that develops in certain family and sociocultural contexts, and is maintained by and maintains the functioning of the bulimic's current context at many different levels. Fully understanding bulimia requires a grasp of the interconnections among many different systems, including the interplay of physiological, intrapersonal, familial, extrafamilial, and sociocultural factors. That is, bulimia can be seen as being embedded in rigid sequences in each of these levels of systems, which both mirror and affect the other levels. For example, the extreme peaks and valleys of blood glucose levels that are intrinsic to the bulimia experience can be seen as isomorphic to and contributing to the bulimic's emotional lability, which is also reflected in polarized interaction patterns in her family, and so on.[1]

If viewed from each of these levels of systems, bulimia seems understandable. This is part of bulimia's fascination. There is something for everyone, from the researchers who like symptoms they can count to the philosophers who like to analyze society. Consequently, there are increasing numbers of "blind" men and women, ourselves included, who are feeling different sections of the bulimic "elephant" and giving very different descriptions of what it feels like.

Depending on the level of one's focus, bulimia can, with some validity, be viewed in any one of the following ways and more.

---

1. Since the vast majority of bulimics we have treated are female, we use feminine pronouns to describe bulimics in general, with the recognition that some percentage are male.

Richard C. Schwartz. Family Systems Program, Institute for Juvenile Research; and Department of Psychiatry, University of Illinois College of Medicine, Chicago, Illinois.

Mary Jo Barrett. Midwest Family Resources, Chicago, Illinois.

George Saba. Behavior Sciences Program, Division of Family and Community Medicine, University of California School of Medicine, San Francisco, California.

1. As an addiction maintained by (and maintaining) extreme oscillations of glucose levels, or by the relief of tension that a binge–purge episode can temporarily afford.

2. As a way to avoid facing depressing feelings, intimacy, or stressful life decisions by becoming obsessed with weight or with the bulimic patterns; as a way to comfort or nurture oneself when upset.

3. As an excuse for not performing well or for being irritable or moody in a family where any of these behaviors are not acceptable.

4. As the "passive" rebellion of a person who cannot rebel more directly against overprotective, intrusive parents, in a family where eating has special significance.

5. As a way to protect the patient's parents or marriage by providing a focus that distracts them from their conflicts or their depression; to provide an upper threshold for overt conflict (e.g., "Stop fighting, we are upsetting her").

6. As an attempt to get nurturant attention or to demonstrate the severity of one's problems in a family that denies any problem and/or in which siblings are extremely competitive.

7. As the response of a family that has become extremely isolated and intradependent, due to the mobility and competitiveness of American culture or due to being detached from its kin network.

8. As a desperate attempt to control one's weight in a society where low weight is closely tied with personal worth; as an example of the extremes to which women are willing to resort in order to please men in a male-dominated society; as a symptom of the contradictory pressures facing contemporary women to be competitive and "nice" at the same time.

We have been groping and probing the bulimic "elephant" for the past 4 years in an attempt to discover what it is and to what it responds. During this period we have treated or supervised the treatment of over 100 normal-weight bulimic individuals and their families; we have studied 30 of these units intensively. Over the course of this exploration, we have encountered evidence pointing to each of the hypotheses or "partial realities" regarding bulimia that we have outlined above. We believe that most cases of bulimia fit into one or another combination of these hypotheses, and we have been struck with the degree to which these themes are present across the wide variety of families and individuals we have observed. And yet we strongly believe that, aside from a few general characteristics, any single profile for "the bulimic" or "the bulimic family" is oversimplified and does not do justice to the diversity of family and personality presentations. It follows, then, that treatment approaches can contain some standard themes across cases, but must also be flexible enough to accommodate variation. In this chapter, we hope to acquaint the reader with both the commonality and the variety of our experience with bulimia, and to outline the model of treatment that these families have taught us.

BULIMIC INDIVIDUALS AND THEIR FAMILIES

The characteristics of individuals suffering from anorexia nervosa have been studied and described for many decades. Various authors have speculated about the involvement of family members (usually the mother) in the problem, but it was not until the characteristic interaction patterns of the families of anorexics were actually provoked

and observed through family therapy that a relatively clear picture of the family context of anorexia nervosa began to emerge. Since Minuchin, Rosman, and Baker (1978)
reported their observations of anorexic families and their impressive outcome results,
it has become commonplace to find some form of family therapy as at least a part
of many treatment programs for anorexia nervosa.

One would expect that in light of the apparent advances made in the understanding and treatment of anorexia nervosa after the context of the problem was examined
more fully, the families of bulimics would have been carefully scrutinized by now. To
the best of our knowledge, this is not the case. Aside from case studies (Madanes,
1981; Saba, Barrett, & Schwartz, 1983; Schwartz, 1982), we have found no descriptions of bulimic families that rely on more than the reports of patients. This absence
of consideration of family context in the literature on bulimia may be partially explained by the high average age of most samples of bulimics, relative to anorexic
samples. That is, because they are older, many bulimics are no longer living with their
families of origin; therapists are thus less likely to include them in treatment. In addition, many bulimics try to be secretive about their symptoms, and may claim that their
families do not know about the bulimia and hence should not be involved (Lacey &
Phil, 1982). This attitude is epitomized by a recent unsupported statement about
treating bulimia by Donald Keppner (quoted in Cunningham, 1984).

"Most of the time family therapy is totally out of the question . . . the family would totally,
utterly refuse to come into treatment. . . . Changing the system you're in isn't a real good
philosophy. I think we should learn to cope with the people in our environment and not hope
they will change." (p. 17)

Needless to say, we disagree. We have also found that while it is often true that a bulimic believes her family does not know about the bulimia, it is rare to find that family
members actually do not know, and even more rare that they are unwilling to participate. In addition, we have treated many bulimics who live away from home, and
have found that despite their geographical separation, they are still quite involved with
their families. Thus, we believe that it is just as important to understand bulimia in
the family context as it is to do so for anorexia nervosa.

Minuchin et al. (1978) described five interaction patterns that they believe characterize anorexic families, as well as other psychosomatic families. These include enmeshment, overprotectiveness, rigidity, lack of conflict resolution, and involvement
of the patient in parental conflict. These five characteristics have been quite apparent
in nearly all of the bulimic families we have studied, and to this list we would add
three more: isolation, consciousness of appearances, and a special meaning attached
to food and eating. In this section of this chapter, we describe the different types of
bulimic families and individuals, indicate how these characteristics appear in each type
of bulimic family, and provide a model that attempts to explain how many of these
families got to be the way they are/were.

We have noticed that while all the families have been, for example, enmeshed,
hyperconscious of appearances, or overprotective, the issues around which these characteristics have been played out largely depend on the degree to which a family holds
a strong ethnic identity or is "Americanized" (i.e., striving to achieve the dominant
values of our culture) or is in between (i.e., holding some ethnic and some American
values). Among our intensively studied sample of 30 families, about one-third (33%)

were clearly "ethnic" families; about 40% showed a blend of ethnic and American values ("mixed" families); and about 27% were clearly "all-American" families. Below we describe the way in which the characteristics of bulimic families were differently manifested in each of these three types of families.

"All-American" Families

The "all-American" families tended to place extreme importance on appearing stylishly attractive and inordinately successful at all times and at any cost. These values were reflected in a constant pressure to dress fashionably, to get good grades, to make or marry into a lot of money, and to look healthy and attractive (which means to look thin). In some families that subscribed to these values, all members were subjected to this pressure, and the parents held each other up as models of these standards for their children. In others of these families, one or both parents had failed to achieve one or more of these ideals and expected the children to succeed where they had not.

In these "all-American" families, a very pleasant and polite style of social interaction belied an extreme level of competitiveness with the neighbors and within the families themselves. Family members were perpetually on guard to avoid looking bad or sad. Thus, in spite of the appearance of social involvement in some of these families, all of these families were isolated in the sense of not having supportive or affectionate extrafamilial involvement.

This combination of isolation, competitiveness, ambition, and appearance consciousness produced intrafamily relationships that were enmeshed, in the sense that they were characterized by extreme degrees of intrusiveness regarding issues of children's achievement, neatness of dress and of the house, and, of course, weight and attractiveness. Children were commonly compared to one another or to a parent or another relative, and sibling and parent–child rivalry abounded. Conversations between family members rarely strayed from comparative discussions of someone's appearance or level of success. Thus, while at one level these relationships were closely enmeshed, they were at the same time painfully distant, in the sense that family members would show one another or see in one another only the masks of happiness and success.

Since financial achievement was so highly valued in these "all-American" families, fathers' approval was desperately desired but rarely given in an unqualified way. Often a patient's father had been or was currently especially close to the patient, and they were highly reactant to each other's moods. The father was quite interested in how his daughter (and women in general) looked and how much she achieved. He might vacillate between doting on his "little girl" and pouting or raging at her. The patient often expressed worry about his well-being, for which she felt she had a lot of responsibility.

Since the mother usually did not have a rewarding outside-the-home career, her competence was reflected in the attractiveness of the children and house; consequently, eating and neatness became arenas for picky and intrusive struggles with the patient. Thus, the mother would appear to be enmeshed in the classic sense, while the father often presented a misleading air of detachment. Often, the patient reported identifying with and yet being disdainful of the negative aspects of her mother's personality.

The patients in the "all-American" families were expected to go to the best colleges, be members of the best sororities, and attract men of the highest quality. To achieve these ends, these women were imbued with high levels of competitiveness, particularly toward other women, while at the same time they were socialized to be "nice"—to be nonassertive and deferential, especially toward men. These contradictory extremes were reflected in the constant conflictual internal dialogue that most patients reported and in their behavioral vacillations between aggressive outbursts and passivity. In these families the leaving home of these "all-American" daughters was expected, although the parents remained highly child-focused while she was away, calling and visiting often.

"Ethnic" Families

The "ethnic" families we observed were equally isolated, enmeshed, and appearance-conscious, but these characteristics were focused on a different set of issues than in the "all-American" families. These families were far less obsessed with the ideals of the mainstream American culture; instead, they were preoccupied with maintaining the values of the ethnic culture or extended family network from which they emerged. Thus, within these families, there was a high degree of appearance consciousness, but it was manifested in pressure to maintain traditional roles. The lives of offspring in these families were circumscribed into the proper roles of their ethnic cultures, and powerful sanctions were invoked for straying from these roles. Family members were imbued with the conviction that everything they did was, in some way, a reflection on "the family"—that they constantly represented this all-important entity.

In contrast to the "all-American" families, the "ethnic" families showed far less aversion to fatness; indeed, it was common to find several obese family members. A mother's competence was often defined by how well her family ate, and a father's by how well he "brought home the bacon." Food, and what family members did with it, became one of the most important arenas for defining relationships—for expressing love and anger.

These families also showed less interest in achievement or success in the mainstream American sense than they did in conforming to acceptable cultural or family roles—that is, in marrying an acceptable mate whose career was secure, or in embarking on the kind of career that the family had been involved with for years. Thus, personal ambitions were always to be sacrificed for security and acceptability. College, if it was valued at all, was only important as a step toward an acceptable career or marriage, and, while in college, a patient usually lived at home and commuted to school.

Where the isolation of the "all-American" families was maintained by competitiveness, the "ethnic" families inculcated a strong distrust of, and occasional disdain for, the extrafamilial. They kept rigid boundaries around their families that were difficult for us, as therapists, to penetrate; these boundaries made for special crises in such families at transition points, when children wanted to leave home or even to marry. Many of the "ethnic" families had left the larger network and, consequently, were alone, without the support of relatives or acceptable friends.

"Mixed" Families

The third group, which we are calling "mixed" families, was torn by the pull of contradictory ethnic and American values, with some family members trying to protect the old, others pushing to explore the new, and still others caught in the middle. In many of these families each parent advocated a different set of values, so that the patient's behavior became a reflection of her allegiance to one parent or the other. For example, her father's approval might be contingent upon her personal achievement, while her mother disapproved of activities that took her away from the family and out of the nurturant role.

As one might expect, the profile of a patient varied according to the type of family to which she belonged. For example, bulimics from "all-American" or "mixed" families often showed a wider range of behaviors than those from "ethnic" families. Patients from "all-American" or "mixed" families were more likely to vacillate between the extremes of dependent, passive, young behavior on one hand and a precocious sophistication and pseudoconfidence or rebelliousness on the other. The "ethnic" patients more often presented only their young, dependent side.

In spite of these differences among groups, many characteristics were shared by the bulimics; these are described more fully, although perhaps in different terms, in other chapters of this book and so are only mentioned here. These included (1) a feeling of being unable to control the direction of their lives or of all-important relationships; (2) an inability to know what they really wanted or who they really were, a sense of constant mental turmoil and confusion at having to wear a mask of happiness for others; (3) relatedly, an obsession with the way they looked, a strong fear of getting fat, and a state of chronic depression over the bulimic pattern; (4) an overriding feeling of obligation toward or protectiveness for certain other family members; and (5) an orientation toward polar extremes of thinking, affect, and behavior (e.g., elation at getting some approval, devastation when it was withdrawn).

While these characteristics were evident in all cases, they were particularly severe for a number of the most difficult cases; for these patients, bulimia was only one of several symptoms, which might include alcohol or drug abuse, shoplifting, phobias, or excessive promiscuity. Not surprisingly, the families of this group correspondingly displayed more extreme versions of the characteristics of families outlined in this section.

THEORY

Why are the families of bulimics so enmeshed, overprotective, appearance-conscious, triangulating (e.g., involving children in the parents' marriage), rigid, and so forth? Why are the patients so nonassertive, dependent, afraid to grow up? Is it because of deep-seated intrapsychic pathology that permeates the character of key family members? Family therapists would like to think not, but we have few useful alternative explanations. In this section, we briefly outline a hypothesis that attempts to account for the evolution of these characteristics — one that not only fits the evidence in many of these cases, but also implies directions for treatment.

If a family's lineage is traced far enough, one will usually find that at one point or another in its history, the family was embedded within a stable kin network. The families within many such networks will have many characteristics that are functional and adaptive for existence in that context but are not so adaptive outside the networks. For example, there is little need for, nor is it easy to have, a close, intimate relationship between the parents of a family surrounded by close relatives. The father has his "amigo network," the mother spends time with her mother and sisters, and everybody is involved in everybody else's conflicts. The children will not leave the network after they become adults, so there is little need for parents to support each other in preparation for an empty nest. Network loyalty is paramount; as a result of historical invasions by or conflicts with other groups, the extrafamilial is feared. Children are raised to be obedient and loyal rather than personally ambitious. Finally, food is a central focus of interaction and ritual within the network.

The family structure and values described above, which are fully adaptive for a stable network, may create problems if the family leaves the network and becomes a part of bountiful, mobile middle America, unless its structure can change rapidly. The family is likely to maintain its distrust of strangers, and consequently to become extremely isolated. The parents, not knowing how to get close to each other or not being oriented to do so, are likely to become overinvolved with their children and to discourage them from leaving. The children will get large doses of the loyalty ethic and yet will feel the pull of values for personal success and independence permeating their environment outside the family. After some time, the parents may give contradictory push–pull messages as one or both of them become imbued with ambition, yet do not adapt their family structure to permit its fulfillment.

This isolation, lack of marital closeness, and child-centeredness will lead family members to "feed off" one another. They will be so interdependent that the family will become hypersensitive to any threat to the marriage or demeanor of the parents, or to the possible departure of key members. In short, they believe that the cohesion of the family is quite delicate, and they organize to avoid change. After several generations adrift in the American mainstream, values of competitiveness and vogue appearance may prevail in the family, but the basic structure may still be retained from the network. Thus, the three types of families described earlier, the "ethnic," "mixed," and "all-American," are not seen as discrete categories of families; instead, they are ranges of variation on a continuum of family values and structural evolution.

The following interchange illustrates the predicament of an "ethnic" family that has not adapted. It took place when one of the authors consulted on a case of a withdrawn 22-year-old bulimic and her first-generation Italian parents.

CONSULTANT: (*to mother*) Sally [the patient] says she is very worried about you and about your husband. She thinks you wouldn't make it if she grew up.

SALLY: (*weakly*) That's right.

MOTHER: That's crazy. Why should she worry about our relationship? Nobody's happy all the time.

CONSULTANT: I don't think she worries about you two splitting up; I don't think there's much chance of that. I think she thinks you will be sad. You have been a mother a long time. You have four kids? How old is the youngest?

MOTHER: Eighteen.

CONSULTANT: Sally seems to worry that soon they will be gone, and then what will you do?

MOTHER: That's crazy. I don't want her worrying about me—she has her own problems. I never worried about my mother. She had 10 kids and they never worried about her.

CONSULTANT: Was your mother's mother around then? And her sisters and friends?

MOTHER: Yes.

CONSULTANT: Then no wonder you didn't have to worry about her. Is your mother around?

MOTHER: No.

CONSULTANT: Any sisters or brothers around?

MOTHER: No, they are all still in Italy.

CONSULTANT: Do you have many friends?

MOTHER: I see what you're getting at, but I don't want her worrying about me. She has her own life to think of.

This model of evolution of enmeshed families and their associated problems is not intended to apply to all families with eating disorders. Instead, it is presented as an overarching framework that implies that if the therapist is able to help the family or individual change or better accommodate to their context, then the problems will abate. In some cases, this may mean getting the parents to support each other; in others, it may mean helping them open their boundaries to establish a new network. In yet others, it may be possible to help the patient establish a network for herself apart from the family without having to involve other family members directly. In general, however, this model implies a view of the bulimic symptom as an adaptive solution for a family whose structure has not fully adapted to its context.

Moving down from the macro level of our conceptualization of this problem to our basic theoretical orientation toward treatment of bulimics, we are philosophically influenced by the structural school of family therapy (Minuchin, 1974; Minuchin & Fishman, 1981; Minuchin et al., 1978). Structural family therapy has been unfairly stereotyped by many practitioners in the field of eating disorders who have seen or heard about a few dramatic videotapes ("Structuralists? Oh yeah, they're the people who force anorexics to eat hot dogs!"). What such stereotypes miss in that assessment is a way of viewing people that is extremely optimistic and allows the therapist to scan for and elicit the strengths rather than the deficits in people. The idea is that an individual's context, of which the family is a very significant part, will limit and shape a person's experience in such a way that certain "partial selves" (i.e., aspects of their personality and orientation to life) will be overdeveloped and other "partial selves" underdeveloped. This belief implies that change can result from a restructuring of that context, so that underdeveloped partial selves are activated and supported.

As applied to bulimia, this model suggests that in spite of appearing to be hopelessly nonassertive, self-deprecating, or enmeshed with her family, the patient has the ability to behave and think in very different, more competent ways. This is possible if the therapist can activate partial selves of competence and strength and can help her family to accept them, possibly by activating other partial selves within family members. Thus, large doses of education, insight, behavior modification, or medication need not be doled out by the therapist, because it is assumed that the individual and family already have within them the ability to be competent, and will do so if released from habitual interaction patterns and orientations that have fostered the fear of change.

This model of change translates into a directive style of therapy where, in family sessions, family members are both encouraged and challenged to interact in new ways to see themselves and one another differently. Relationships that have been blocked or interfered with in the past are re-engaged and strengthened. The reinforcing aspect of this process is that family members get to know and affirm one another beyond the masks (partial selves) they habitually show one another. This is an extremely important part of working with bulimic families, because the family members tend to have very rigid images of themselves and one another.

Where a bulimic's family is inaccessible, as is the case with many older bulimics, the therapy process is similar, in that the task of the therapist is to use his or her relationship with the patient to activate new partial selves in the patient and to get her to hold on to those new behaviors and orientations in the face of predictable out-of-session reactions from her context. She becomes the architect of new relationships with significant others, including peers, work associates, and spouse or boyfriends, as well as family members.

In addition to the structural orientations described above, we have also been conceptually and technically influenced by strategic family therapies and their concern with and respect for (1) the ambivalence that families and individuals have regarding change; (2) the consequences of change; and (3) the importance of the sequences of interactions and thinking that surround the symptom (Fisch, Weakland, & Segal, 1982; Haley, 1976; Madanes, 1981; Selvini-Palazzoli, Boscolo, Cecchin, & Prata, 1978). As we worked with bulimic families, these considerations became increasingly salient as we recognized the degree of fear that many patients had about giving up their symptoms and that many of the families had about their daughters growing up. In addition, we became increasingly aware that in certain cases the symptoms would persist well beyond the point where we believed that the families had been successfully restructured. In those cases, we had to turn toward symptom-specific strategies to reach complete remission.

The techniques of strategic family therapists reflect both their concern about using or not provoking the family's or individual's resistance to change and their search for interactional solutions to specific problems. Regarding the first concern, families or individuals are sometimes restrained by the therapist from changing too fast. They may be asked to devote a great deal of thought to the possible negative consequences of symptom remission or various structural modifications. As the therapist promotes this protective restraining position, the family members and/or the patient often open up enough to explore the validity of their fears and inclinations to protect one another, and the stronger, more hopeful side of their ambivalence about change will enter the foreground.

Regarding symptom-specific directives, strategic family therapists have developed a wide variety of interventions designed to alter the specific patterns of thinking or interaction that they believe to be maintaining a problem. The interventions we have found particularly useful in treating bulimia, and the timing of these interventions relative to various stages of treatment, are discussed in the next section of this chapter.

Combining the complementary aspects of structural and strategic family therapy conceptual frameworks and techniques has not been a smooth process and is not recommended to the inexperienced family therapist. The style of therapy that has evolved from this process is one in which the therapist's position will alternate between advocating changes and warning against the same changes, in rhythm with the oscillation of the ambivalence of the family or patient. The degree of restraining necessary has varied considerably from case to case, but having that position as an alternative provides the therapist with a great deal of flexibility, so that he or she can avoid being inducted into power struggles centering on change.

The successful implementation of this rhythmic restraining–encouraging stance requires some reorienting of the therapist's attitude toward change. If the therapist views the symptom as a family's and/or an individual's response to a particular predicament, rather than as a problem to be eradicated as quickly as possible, it will be easier for the therapist to focus on and nurture changes in the "big picture" (i.e., patterns of interaction and orientation), rather than becoming attached to the waxing and waning of the symptom itself. The therapist will be able to restrain with sincerity rather than with ulterior motives because he or she, along with the family, is aware of and respectful of the dangers in overly abrupt change. To adopt such an attitude, it is important for the therapist to understand the symptom at many levels simultaneously — that is, to view it in its full context, which may include many or all of the "partial realities" enumerated at the onset of this chapter.

The level of understanding advocated above is not essential to the successful treatment of some cases of bulimia. This is because, from case to case, there is a wide range in the level or degree of systems involvement in the problem. Thus, some cases can be lastingly improved with approaches that are not particularly context-sensitive. We are convinced, however, that in many cases we have encountered, the symptoms would not have improved or would have improved only temporarily if the patients were treated without awareness of their context.

The treatment model we have developed for bulimia is difficult to summarize because we have tried to incorporate enough flexibility to accommodate the wide variation in the patients' ages, living situations, degree and length of involvement in family-of-origin conflicts, and type of family. In the rest of this chapter, we outline many of the themes, techniques, and stages of treatment that are common to many cases in which a patient is living with her family; we also give some sense of how these might vary where her circumstances are different.

TREATMENT

Goals

As described in the first section of this chapter, we hold a relatively complex conceptual formulation of bulimia, involving several levels of systems. Consequently, our goals of treatment are correspondingly difficult to state simply.

As family therapists, we are oriented toward the goal of helping the whole family evolve to the point where the symptom is no longer necessary — where the patient and family have "grown out" of the interaction patterns that fostered it, and have explored new alternatives. In many cases, this goal is appropriate and realistic. In many other cases, however, this goal has to be revised because the circumstances of the case do not permit its realization or because that broad a goal is unnecessary.

For example, where the patient's family is geographically unavailable, the goal becomes to help the patient deal with and view her family in new ways, so that she feels more differentiated, more grown up, and more in control of family and other relationships. This process will have an impact on the rest of the family, but, for example, if they reassemble to focus on another child, there is little that the therapist can do from a distance. Thus, in some cases the goal is not so much the restructuring of the whole family of origin as it is to help the patient change in the face of or in spite of the lack of change in her family or significant others.

In addition, our focus is not exclusively interpersonal. We track and attempt to change rigid patterns of thinking as well as rigid patterns of interaction that maintain the symptom. In this way, our defintion of family therapy is broadened beyond its stereotype. The number of people in the therapy room is far less relevant than the therapist's objectives to change rigid patterns and introduce alternatives at any level of system.

Thus, in some of our 30 cases, family members were never present in sessions, and the work was done with the patient alone or at times with her friends. Where the patient was married and/or had children, the couple or family of procreation became the main unit of in-session treatment, with the focus shifting to the family of origin at various stages of treatment. In cases such as these, the initial goal is to improve the functioning of the couple or family of procreation, and later to include members of the family of origin in sessions if they are available; or if not, to send the couple on out-of-session tasks with the patient's family, designed to prevent the erosion of the improvements.

In sum, the overarching goal becomes to activate nonapparent "partial selves" within the patient, so that the patient takes more direct control in significant relationships and in the direction of her life; becomes less protective of and elicits less protectiveness from her family; allows herself to become genuinely close to people both inside and outside of her family; and, finally, lets go of the dependent, sick, incompetent identity that the bulimia both symbolizes and maintains. To achieve and maintain these changes, the patient's family of origin and/or procreation, as well as her general interpersonal context, either must also change or must at least be attended to.

To achieve these changes fully, the patient needs to feel in control of the bulimic pattern. Complementarily, she will not feel in control of this symptom until she achieves some of these changes. For us, total abstinence from bingeing is not necessarily the goal here. Of much greater importance is a change in the patient's relationship with and attitude toward food and her weight, which parallels the changes she makes in other relationships and thinking patterns. An obsessive fear and avoidance of sugar can be as disabling as being a slave to it. Thus, we have incorporated into our model of treatment symptom-specific techniques aimed at getting control of rather than totally eliminating the bingeing. With many patients, the point of feeling in control does not arrive until they are bingeing once a month or less and not purging at all. In general, they come to view bingeing and the part of them that encourages it very differently—not as a dreaded enemy, but either as a signal that something needs to be taken care of, or as an old friend with whom they like to keep in touch.

In the remainder of this chapter, we describe the treatment model as it applies to patients who are living with or still very dependent on their parents. We have chosen to use this space to describe the work with this group in some depth, rather than to give more brief descriptions of our approach to patients who live alone or with their spouses and/or children as well as this living-at-home group, because we have found the "at-home" group to be the most difficult and because many themes for this group apply directly to the other groups. In the section of the chapter titled "Special Issues," these other groups are briefly addressed.

Stages

We have found that the timing of interventions over the course of treatment is extremely important to successful outcome. For example, if a symptom-specific intervention is made at the outset of therapy it may have no effect, whereas the same intervention may be very effective if it follows other changes in the family or individual. For this reason, we have divided the treatment model into three stages, each of which contains different goals and techniques:

1. Creating a context for change.
2. Challenging patterns and expanding alternatives.
3. Consolidating change.

These stages are offered as a flexible framework of guidelines and considerations, rather than as the specific steps that must be taken in this order in every case. The length of each stage will vary considerably, and, depending on the dynamics of the family or individual, a whole stage or several interventions within a stage may not be needed.

Treatment Model

Before we describe the stages of treatment, some general statements about our approach may help orient the reader. This model is designed for outpatient treatment, although in a few cases, we have hospitalized patients very briefly. As nonphysicians treating a life-threatening problem, we have gone to great lengths to cultivate close working relationships with internists, pediatricians, and family practitioners who are familiar with bulimia and who can support our treatment. We involve one of these physicians from the outset of treatment, and he or she consults with us regularly throughout the course of therapy. We strongly believe that such a supportive collaboration should be in place before any treatment of bulimia is attempted.

In cases where the patient lives with her parents, or is single and lives apart but the family is available, we often alternate between individual sessions with the patient and sessions with the family and patient. We have found that at least some individual contact with the patient is important, for a variety of reasons that we clarify below.

In general, we have found the treatment of bulimics to take a long time, compared to our work with many other problems, although there is a considerable range in length among cases. In our study of 30 cases, the average number of sessions for those who completed treatment was 33, spread over 9 months. The varied lengths of treatment reflect the complex and difficult nature of many of these cases and our emphasis on working in stages. That is, we usually will wait until the patient has achieved a certain degree of differentiation from her family before directly targeting the bulimia. We do this because, until that is the case, the symptoms can or will be reactivated by family patterns, and the intervention will become just another attempted solution that has failed. Thus, in summary, the treatment process includes (1) motivating the family and patient for differentiation; (2) guiding the differentiation; (3) targeting the symptom; and (4) inoculating the system against relapse.

Stage 1: Creating a Context for Change

GOALS

The goals and tasks of the therapist during this first stage of treatment may be summarized as follows:

1. To introduce himself or herself as an expert the family can trust.
2. To establish a restrain—advocate rhythm regarding change that anticipates and respects the family and patient's ambivalence.
3. To get close enough to key family members, including the patient, that he or she can use the strength of his or her relationship with them as leverage for change.
4. To assess the rigidity of family and individual patterns of interaction and thinking that maintain the symptom.
5. To introduce a framework of themes and redefinitions in both family and individual sessions that challenge or block existing patterns.

THEMES

As mentioned earlier, experience with bulimic families and individuals has taught us to be acutely sensitive to their ambivalence regarding any of the changes the therapist might advocate. This is true even for those families that initially appear to be eager to cooperate and in a hurry to change.

It is easy to overestimate how well engaged or joined family members are, and their initial warmth or sociability can quickly dissolve if they are pushed too forcefully or rapidly by the therapist. On the other hand, the therapist can become paralyzed by the family's fearful cues and can thus fail to affect the symptom-maintaining system. To avoid these pitfalls, during this early stage we attempt to straddle the fence in regard to change. By asking pointed questions and commenting on family interaction, the therapist begins to develop two sets of themes: (1) that the symptom is related to family processes, such as overprotectiveness, escalating power struggles, or the inability of family members to really know each other; and (2) that changing the symptom or any of these processes related to it may have some negative consequences, which must be seriously considered before change is attempted. An example of this fence-straddling therapist position lies in the dialogue presented earlier in the chapter from the session with the Italian family. In that example, the therapist established the theme that the patient was extremely protective of her mother, while implying that this protectiveness might be warranted and important.

In other words, it is the task of the therapist in this stage to establish a framework of themes that are challenging to the family's structure and world view, and yet do not activate them to expel the therapist. Many structural family therapists are oriented toward disengaging enmeshed relationships; for example, a common goal for a patient who is in a highly intrusive relationship with her father is to decrease the time they spend together and their emotional involvement. We do not disagree with this ultimate goal, but we have found that once the family becomes aware that the therapist's intention is to make them less close, they close ranks against him or her. An alternative approach to these relationships during this stage is for the therapist to imply that he or she wants to make them closer, but that if they are to come closer they will have to change the way they interact. This theme is illustrated by the following dialogue, which is also taken from the session with the Italian family.

CONSULTANT: (*to father and patient*) I don't think you two really know each other at all. You are together a lot, but you are strangers. You (*to father*) only know the part of your daughter that she's been showing you now—the part that acts 13. And you (*to patient*) only know the part of your father that lectures.

FATHER: I don't think we know each other, but she won't talk to me any more.

CONSULTANT: I think you both would love to get closer to each other, and that is one of our goals, but to do that, you (*to father*) have to let her show other parts of her—let her be 22 with you. And you (*to patient*) have to stop protecting him. Now, tell him what he does that keeps you from getting to really know him.

Here, the emphasis the family placed on closeness was respected, and yet the father and daughter were challenged to evolve their relationship.

RESTRAINING

In individual sessions with the patient during this first stage, the therapist may also take a restraining position regarding the bulimia as a symptom: "Are you sure you are ready to give up this behavior that has been such a large part of your life? I want you to think hard about what might happen if you suddenly let go of this part of you. Perhaps we should work on helping you adjust to it if it is too dangerous to quit."

We were initially surprised at the relief many patients expressed at this restraining posture. "I was so terrified that you'd give me a pill or press a button and it would be gone forever." Now we recognize that most bulimics have grown intimate with the symptoms and the identity they signify, and have very mixed feelings about what the loss of the bulimia would imply—growing up, getting close to people, upsetting the family, and so on.

Through this restraint, the themes for individual sessions will emerge. These often include the patient's facing the direction of her career or life; her patterns of interaction with both male and female friends; and her fears of being incompetent—unable to support herself or control her appetite.

In recommending concurrent individual sessions with the patient, along with family sessions, we recognize that we place the therapist in a precarious position—having to walk a tightrope between not appearing to or actually allying with the patient against her family, and vice versa. For example, if the daughter begins to express anger toward the parents, they are likely to attribute this to the individual discussions with the therapist and to become suspicious and defensive. In an effort to avoid this situation, we usually refrain from discussing the patient's difficulties with her family during individual sessions in this first stage of treatment, and instead focus on the themes mentioned in the paragraph above. Themes related to her family are developed during family sessions.

SYMPTOM SEPARATION

Nearly every bulimic family we have encountered is involved in a rigid, repetitive sequence of interaction with the patient in regard to eating. Even when the purging aspect of bulimia is ostensibly a secret, family members may be hypervigilant about how much or what kind of food she is consuming or how much she weighs. Where the purging is overt, family members will resort to threats, pleading, or guilt inducement to try to control this behavior. Very often, we believe that this excessive focus on the patient's eating is a method for the family and patient to avoid more threatening issues. Food is a safe battleground that permits family members to express feelings indirectly and to stay enmeshed with and protective of each other.

As one might imagine, making this arena of enmeshment unavailable to the family can be a potent but difficult intervention. At some point during this first stage, we commonly attempt such a move by (1) tracking the family's attempts to solve this problem, (2) emphasizing and empathizing with their frustration and ineffectiveness, and (3) giving them "a vacation" from these efforts. That is, at least temporarily, the therapist and the medical consultant are to be the only ones trying to help the patient with her bulimia, and are to do so during the individual sessions. The family can still help her to grow up in other ways, and family sessions are to be devoted to those issues.

The family, including the patient, will often have trouble accepting or sticking to this arrangement. For example, the patient may sporadically raid the food supplies of the rest of the family, which will reactivate their involvement; or the mother may back off for a brief period, only to explode with concern and frustration, saying she cannot just sit by and watch her daughter hurt herself.

The degree to which the family is able to disengage from the symptom is often a prognostic indication of the rigidity and enmeshment of the family. If they cannot disengage, then this failure can become more evidence for the therapist's theme of overprotectiveness. If they can, then a central form of communication will have been disrupted, and other issues among family members are likely to emerge and become more accessible to the therapist.

In the individual sessions during this symptom-separation phase, the therapist maintains the restraining position described earlier regarding the bulimia. His or her basic stance is this: "You will not and should not try to give up the symptom until you are clear about what the ramifications of doing that are and are sure you can commit to give it up in spite of those ramifications." Another therapist position at this point is this: "You will be in control of your symptoms when you are in more control of your life and relationships, and not until then." It is important for the therapist to be sincere in these statements—not to be attached to the fluctuations of the bulimic pattern during this stage, and instead to watch for changes in interaction and belief patterns. It is not uncommon for the symptoms to disappear temporarily for as long as a month at times during the symptom-separation stage. If the therapist becomes excited along with the patient and family over this change, then he or she will become equally discouraged at the inevitable relapse. If the therapist is genuinely unfazed by the course of the symptoms during this stage, he or she can help the patient and family get off the bulimic roller coaster so that they can focus on other issues.

This attitude of detachment does not imply that the therapist treats the symptom as if it were not serious or ignores it. On the contrary, it is important for the therapist to help the patient fully face what she is doing and avoiding. Many patients, while chronically upset that they are at the mercy of this problem, at the same time try to forget about or disown the part of them that engages in the symptomatic behavior. If this protective dissociation can be blocked, and if the patient looks carefully at what she is doing, acknowledges that it is she who is doing it, and shares this awareness with the therapist, her motivation to let go of the symptom will increase. Similarly, if she allows herself to experience some of the feelings that the symptom has helped her avoid, she will be more motivated to try to change the aspects of her context that are related to those feelings.

DIRECTIVES

With these goals in mind, the therapist may, during this stage, make several prescriptions. First, the patient may be asked to keep a journal detailing the time, place, and intensity of her binges and purges, and also exploring the emotional or interactional context preceding each episode. This journal will also provide the therapist with data regarding the course of the symptoms. There is, however, a danger inherent in the use of such a journal: Because of its focus on the bulimic symptoms, the therapist will have to struggle to maintain an attitude of detachment and to help the patient accept what she is doing without feeling devastated or elated about it. Indeed, it is our belief that it is not so much the binge–purge behavior itself, but the extreme self-denigration that follows the symptom, that perpetuates the cycle at the individual level. So the therapist's detachment from the symptom must be conveyed in the way he or she reacts to and uses the patient's journal.

A second intervention we have often used at this point in treatment is to prescribe that the patient try to become depressed, for a specific period of time each day or week, about the issues that she should be feeling depressed about (e.g., lack of real closeness to anyone, dissatisfaction with the direction of her life, issues with her family, mourning of losses). In addition, her family is instructed to help the patient do this by giving her privacy for the necessary period of time and by not trying to keep her from being sad. The family and patient are told that if they and she can allow her to get upset about these things, she will do something about them, and if they and she cannot allow this, then she will not grow up.

This intervention will affect the family system on several levels. First, it redefines depression for the patient and family as something that can be useful rather than dangerous. If this redefinition is accepted, the family's rigid interaction sequences, organized by their attempts to avoid depression in the patient or other family members, will be broken. At least for a moment, the masks of cheeriness can be dropped and the blanket of protectiveness can be lifted, so the patient can show her distress to her family and to herself.

Second, this prescription for depression gives the patient some privacy — a rare and undervalued commodity in enmeshed families. A boundary is created between patient and family for the prescribed period of time; the family must get used to respecting it, and the patient must get used to enforcing it.

Third, we have found that the rationale given the family for this exercise is valid. That is, if the patient can become depressed about the issues in her life that are not related to food or weight or guilt, she will gain motivation to do something about them. Dormant or underused "partial selves" will be activated.

As with the symptom-separation intervention, the family's and patient's ability to follow this depression directive is often an indication of the rigidity of their avoidance sequences, and hence of the difficulty of treatment.[2] If compliance breaks down at any level, the therapist can use this to fuel his or her other themes, and can reintroduce this intervention at a later stage of treatment when its success is more likely.

A third intervention during this stage is to heighten the patient's awareness of the conflict in her head—the incessant internal argument with which, it seems, all bulimics are cursed—and to redefine the meaning of that conflict. If encouraged to do so, a bulimic can usually identify at least two separate "voices"[3] in these internal dialogues, which represent two fairly distinct parts of her. Usually one of these parts is hypercritical and demands perfection, while another is rebellious, is impulsive, and advocates extremes of indulgence. Not surprisingly, these parts and their interaction are often isomorphic to patterns within the family.

The bulimic is asked to become aware of the interaction of these parts and to identify the events that activate or interrupt their conflict. Usually the patient has a great deal of disgust for one or more of these parts (often the indulgent part) and a mixture of resentment and respect for others. The therapist can help her accept these parts more easily and decrease the intensity of their conflict by redefining them as follows: Each part has a different and valuable message that she needs to hear, but a message has become extreme or exaggerated because of the conflicts among the parts, or because she has not listened to the message. She is instructed to begin listening to each part separately (i.e., to block interference from other parts), in order to try to grasp its nonextreme message. This intervention has relatives in many schools of psychotherapy, but is most clearly derived from the reframing work of Bandler and Grinder (1982). The prescription for depression described above complements this intervention nicely, because the depression time can be framed as being spent listening to disowned parts.

Sometimes events in the patient's context activate the parts conflict to such an extent that she cannot get enough perspective to identify, much less listen to, each part. Where this is the case, the therapist works to untangle the context or to distance her from it first, and then returns to this intervention.

Stage 2: Challenging Patterns and Expanding Alternatives

Depending on the family, the shift to the second stage may begin after only a few sessions or may not begin for some months. As previously mentioned, the boundaries between stages in our model are arbitrary and diffuse rather than discrete and binding. Aspects of stages often overlap, and the therapist should feel free to move back and forth between stages.

2. It may also be a reflection of the therapist's skill in delivering these directives, but, of course, it is always less threatening to focus on the family's resistance.

3. This term is not used in the sense of disembodied voices of psychotics, although in a few of our 30 cases the voices had been disowned to that point.

CHALLENGE

As the themes of the previous stage begin to take hold, and the therapist senses more trust and interest in change from the family, he or she begins to intensify the challenge to their interactions and beliefs, building on the new framework of themes. At this point, the therapist temporarily moves away from the alternating restrain-advocate rhythm regarding change and takes a firm position on one side of the fence or the other, depending on the rigidity of the family. In most cases we have moved toward the side of more directly advocating changes and doing less restraining. We have encountered enough families in which the direct approach has been unsuccessful, however, that now in cases where the fear of change is extreme and intractable, we move to a position of "hard" restraining (i.e., implying that perhaps the family should not change, while positively connoting everyone's motives). In the rationale given to the family for this restraining, the network of interprotectiveness within the family and the feared consequences of the changes are laid out. This is a potent intervention that we reserve for very difficult families, and we restrain therapists from attempting it until they are thoroughly familiar with the principles behind its use and have adopted the contextual view of this problem outlined earlier in this chapter (for more information on this approach, see Selvini-Palazzoli et al., 1978). Without this awareness, therapists tend to use these so-called "paradoxical" techniques to punish families for not complying with their directives; in these situations, the techniques are not only ineffective, but potentially destructive.

In the many cases where the therapist senses enough leverage in his or her relationship with family members to advocate interactional changes directly, the therapist uses this leverage to help family members. He or she uses the themes established in Stage 1, to help the family break dysfunctional patterns of interaction and to redirect their energies more effectively. If the symptom-separation intervention has been successfully introduced in Stage 1, non-symptom-focused conflicts among various family subsystems may become more accessible to the therapist, since the symptom-focused sequences of avoidance of these conflicts have been broken. The therapist translates these conflicts into issues centering on family members' ability to permit one another and themselves to grow up, to stop protecting one another, or to permit closeness with people outside and inside the family. Once these conflicts have been identified in this way, the therapist, often beginning with the patient–mother or patient–father dyad, holds the members of the dyad in conflict well beyond their previous threshold for dealing with each other. That is, the therapist prevents distractions or intrusions by other family members, the changing of the subject, or the premature withdrawal of one member of the dyad. In addition, he or she challenges both members to interact in new ways and to help each other change by changing themselves. The following dialogue from the session with the Italian family is illustrative of this process:

CONSULTANT: (*to father*) These two women [the mother and daughter] are convinced that you are so delicate that you would be terribly sad if they ever disagreed with you. That seems crazy to me, because I know you are a strong man. Am I right? Or do they need to protect you?

FATHER: I don't know why they would think that. I want to know what they think.

CONSULTANT: (*to patient*) Can you talk to your father like a 22-year-old — without protecting him? He wants to get to know you.

PATIENT: It's my fault, really — I just can't communicate with people. I get all tied up when I try to talk to people.

CONSULTANT: That's nonsense. You communicate very well when you want to. You just don't want to right now, because you're afraid to make your father sad, but he said he can take it.

PATIENT: O.K. Well (*pause*), all you ever want to talk about is politics! I get tired of that, and I don't like the way you stare at me or sneak up on me sometimes!

As was true in this case, we have found that when the patient or other family members are challenged to deal directly with an issue, they move from one extreme to another — in this case, from passively blaming oneself to overaggressively attacking the other. This is consistent with the general orientation toward extremes in these families, and it becomes the therapist's task to help the dyad become comfortable with a middle-ground style of interaction that permits conflicts to be resolved and relationships to evolve.

In some cases, these moves to improve the boundaries around the patient–parent dyad and the tolerance of conflict within it are enough to improve the functioning of the dyad dramatically. In other cases, family alliance or competition prevent the evolution of one or both of these relationships. For example, the patient may be competing (often winning the competition) with her mother for access to and approval from her father. Where this is the case, the chronic, picky skirmishing between mother and patient probably will not abate even with the best boundary-making moves until the therapist has helped the patient to withdraw from the competition. Pursuing this example, the therapist may try to create more distance between the father and patient in many ways, including getting him to take a firm stand with her regarding her inappropriately young behaviors (excluding eating); increasing the patient's involvement with friends; getting her to deal with him age-appropriately, without protecting him; and tarnishing the halo he wears in the patient's eyes by highlighting his weaknesses and her mother's predicament. This tarnishing process need not be an overt pointing out of the father's failings, because we have found that commonly during this stage the patient begins to see both her parents in a more balanced, less good-versus-bad light. Thus the therapist need only strategically agree with her new observations.

DIFFERENTIATION

Another way to reduce the patient's dependence on her family is to permit dependence to increase with the therapist. In general, bulimics are quick to form dependent relationships, and the therapist should view the patient's growing dependence on him or her as an inevitable and potentially useful part of this stage. At the same time, however, the therapist takes care not to neglect his or her relationships with other family members. Inherent in the process of getting closer to the patient is the danger of losing one's systemic perspective and, instead, beginning to see various family members as villains and the patient as their victim. The therapist must find a way to combat this tendency, such as consulting with a colleague, or else he or she will (often intentionally) lose the family members and continue to work with the patient individually.

It is important at this point to differentiate between allowing the patient to depend on the therapist for emotional support and allowing her to behave dependently. In other words, the patient will often attempt to get the therapist to fight her battles or make decisions for her. While initially some of this may be necessary to wean the patient from her family, it is crucial that the therapist not remain in this position; instead, he or she should gradually activate and support her competent partial selves.

As the patient is encouraged to and actually does begin to stop protecting either of the parents or the parents' marriage,[4] the marriage will often begin to "heat up." We have found that the hostility or distance in the parents' marriage in bulimic families is usually less covert than in the "united-front" anorexic families, but it is still elusive. The parents might enter loud arguments, but they are quickly defocused or detoured onto the patient. During Stage 2, this marital conflict is more accessible to the therapist. Now the therapist must decide between pursuing marital issues or keeping the focus of conflict between the parents in the safer parental domain. This decision should be based on an assessment of the parents' readiness to face these issues. Whichever direction the therapist chooses, if he or she can hold the parents in marital or parental conflict to the point of resolution in the presence of the patient, the patient will feel less obliged to be their therapist and can trust that role to the therapist. If the parents have previously (perhaps in Stage 1) worked together successfully to help their daughter be more responsible, then the likelihood of their being able to resolve marital issues is greater.

LAUNCHING

Once the parents have begun to deal with each other directly, and the patient feels less protective of them and has begun to develop a network of friends, has a job, or is in school, the stage is set for her potential launching from the family. Up to this point, the therapist may have had to maintain an ambivalent or even restraining posture regarding the patient's actually moving out of the house, in order to avoid activating the family's fears. She can "grow up" without "growing away." At this point, however, the therapist has a choice: If he or she believes the family needs further preparation or motivation for launching, a strong message of restraint may be appropriate again ("Be careful; if she feels too independent, she may want to move out prematurely"). If, on the other hand, the family and patient seem ready for the transition, the therapist throws his or her weight behind the patient's moving out and tries to comfort everyone as they go through it.

We have found that it is far more difficult for a bulimic to give up her symptoms while she is living in her parents' home and dependent on them. If she is living on her own, or is even living with her family but has a solid date of departure, symptom control is easier. Thus, successful launching becomes an important step in symptom control. Many bulimic families suffer through a series of aborted or temporary launchings, which compound the image of the patient as incompetent and dependent. Therefore, it is crucial that, once launched, she stays launched.

No matter how well prepared the family has become for this step, the therapist should expect and gird for a tumultuous period in the months following the launching. After a short period of euphoria at her new freedom, the patient may become

---

4. A powerful intervention in this direction is to point out to the patient how her well-intentioned protecting of her parents is actually making their marriage worse.

very depressed at the prospect of facing the world by herself, and her symptoms may intensify dramatically. The family may heighten their concern and encourage her to return home. The therapist needs to be especially active and available during this period to help the family weather this storm and reorganize after it. He or she directs the patient to lean on the extrafamilial support network she has developed in preparation for this move, rather than on her family. He or she also helps the parents support the partial selves of each other that want their daughter to grow up.

We have often observed that there seems to be a critical period of stress as the whole system panics over this major change. If pressure to abort the change can be resisted through this period, the system will readjust relatively quickly. Gradually the parents may report and appear to the patient to be getting along better. Moreover, being forced to rely on herself, the patient will find she has resources she never believed possible. At this point the therapist may increase the individual work with the patient in order to support and nurture her new-found strength; he or she may also either work with the parents separately on their marital issues if they are so inclined, or, if not, cut back on the frequency of family sessions.

SYMPTOM-SPECIFIC INTERVENTIONS

Gradually, during the process of differentiation outlined above, the experience of bulimia will begin to change for the patient. The therapist will notice less ambivalence in her reports about wanting to be rid of it. She may hint that "it's just not the same any more," like the lament of a former lover. She may express less disgust with herself for being so weak or impulsive, and more irritation that the symptoms are hanging on while she is changing. These are signs that the timing may be right to address the symptom more directly, although it is not uncommon for the symptoms to have remitted by this point without the direct assistance of symptom-specific interventions.

We have used a number of different symptom-specific interventions at this point, and we outline some of the most successful ones here. Again, the ultimate goal of these interventions is not necessarily elimination of all bingeing. Instead, the goal is to break the sequence of behaviors or thoughts involved in the syndrome, and thereby to give the patient more control over the symptom. This can be achieved by either changing the meaning of the bulimic behaviors and thoughts, or changing the interpersonal and/or intrapersonal interaction sequences that precede or follow the symptoms.

There are many ways to change the meaning of a binge–purge episode. The first step in many of these is to heighten the patient's awareness of the sequences of thoughts, feelings, or interactions with others that typically surround it. This process can begin through the interventions described in Stage 1, such as the use of a journal, the depression prescription, and the tracking of the conflict among internal parts; the therapist may want to prescribe one or all of these again. Once such an expanded awareness of the context of the symptoms is achieved, several different interventions are possible. For one, the therapist may redefine the bulimic episode as a helpful signal to the patient that a part of her is not being taken care of. She is to listen carefully to discover what that part might really want for her, and to write down several alternative ways to acting on that intention that do not involve food. Similarly, she can listen to other parts of her and find other alternatives. Some common examples of these alternatives include finding time to relax and allow herself some enjoyment, asserting herself where she has not, clarifying a chronically ill-defined relationship, getting close to someone, or working toward a goal that is her own and not her family's. Initially she is asked just to write these alternatives down, and she is restrained from acting on them until she is certain she is ready to give up the bulimic identity and all that goes with it. Gradually permission and encouragement is given to try out some of these new behaviors, but not, at this point, to deprive herself of the binge–purge sequence. Later, as she tries alternatives, she may be asked to schedule binges so that they are more convenient for her, but still not to give them up. This will enhance her feeling of control.

At this point, depending on the therapist's sense of the patient's readiness, he or she may ask her to stop bingeing for a period of time and to increase her alternative behaviors. Or the therapist may prescribe rituals to go with the symptoms that exaggerate the bulimia to absurdity or make it more of an ordeal. These include having her make all the preparations for a binge–purge sequence (buying the food, clearing some time) and then simply throw the food away without eating it. Significant others may be asked to join in the experience of an episode, to be with her through one, so as either to heighten the ordeal aspect of the experience or to take away its aura of mystery.[5]

Once the family and patient have evolved to the point at which the side of their ambivalence that wants to let go of the symptoms is particularly strong, and at which the patient clearly wants the help of others to break the sequence of events culminating in the symptoms, the patient may contract for the active and noncoercive help of significant others. It is best for the patient to take the lead in deciding who will help and in what way. The type of help may range from discussing and supporting the alternative behaviors the patient has chosen to being available when she feels out of control. It is important that this help be defined as only a small phase of her overall effort to let go of the bulimic identity. The ability to accept help and not to feel or be made to feel incompetent is a part of this process.

This contracting intervention is a delicate one and should not be suggested without a good deal of forethought and vigilance. It is important that this helping does not replicate or reactivate previous power struggles centered on food; thus the therapist needs to be certain that the system has changed enough for these sequences to be different.

On a few occasions we have used a 1- to 2-week hospitalization on a medical-nutrition unit in a similar helping-contract way. Again, care must be taken to be sure that the timing and meaning of this step is correct — that is, that the patient, family, and therapist view it as a way to "get over the last hump," rather than as indicative of the patient's inability to control the problem herself.

To summarize this second stage of treatment, it is the period during which the family is helped to evolve relationships, reduce levels of protectiveness, and, if appropriate, launch the patient successfully. In addition, the symptom is redefined; if it does not fall under the patient's control during this process, it becomes the target of symptom-specific interventions after the family has differentiated sufficiently for this to be successful.

---

5. See Madanes (1981) for further examples, as well as guidelines for the use of these rituals.

Stage 3: Consolidating Change

We believe that, in many cases, it is not enough to achieve the desired changes in family and individual functioning temporarily. For these changes to last, they must be nurtured and tested, and the family and patient must come to believe in and know how they can maintain them. This postchange, consolidation stage will vary considerably in length, according to the degree of lag in the social development of the patient and the family's adaptation to her differentiation.

GOALS

The goals of this stage are (1) to help the patient find and maintain some nontherapy, extrafamilial, close relationships; (2) to heighten the family's and patient's awareness of and vigilance for the interaction patterns that form the context of the bulimic symptoms, and to heighten their motivation to continue avoiding those patterns; (3) to solidify the new image the patient is developing of herself and the family's new image of her; and (4) to transfer agency for change from the therapist to the patient and family, while remaining available to them at future points of crisis.

EXTRAFAMILIAL NETWORK

The content of both individual and family sessions is likely to shift outward from the family issues during this stage. Left without the distraction of her symptoms or the protecting of her parents, the patient should be helped to face and deal with the more age-appropriate issues of intimacy with both male and female peers, the direction of her career, and the stability to behave responsibly, assertively, and competently in the world.

Without some input, many patients may quickly enter relationships with men that mirror their parents' relationship and that will erode the incipient changes. Out of terror at her aloneness now that she is out of the family, the patient may rapidly look for the shelter of another dependent relationship and may never realize that she can care for herself. It is important, therefore, that the therapist help her develop a network of nonromantic intimates first. The importance of such a network is usually alien to bulimics, who have spent much of their lives competing with or feeling inferior to other women, and have only appearance-oriented, superficial relationships with men. The therapist emboldens the patient to take risks with potential friends and provides support and perspective when some risks result in rejection or pain. Friends are sometimes brought into sessions, and boyfriends usually are. The themes of such sessions are often similar to those of the previous family sessions, but their repetition is often important during this stage of building new relationships.

CEMENTING CHANGES

In general, the therapist helps the patient struggle with the vestiges of her orientation toward isolation, dependence, protectiveness, and self-deprecation. Those parts of her will be activated frequently during this stage, and the therapist should predict this, help her plan for these times, and help her practice strategies for pulling herself out of them.

An effective intervention in this direction is for the therapist to prescribe a relapse, in the sense of directing the patient and her family to recreate the patterns of interaction and thinking that form the bulimic context. Compliance with this directive is often not required for it to be effective. Rather than trying to forget or deny the existence of those patterns, the family is pushed by this suggestion to discuss that context, how they would know when it was being recreated, and how they would each change to pull them all out of it. The therapist may predict points at which the family will have to struggle particularly hard to avoid a contextual relapse.

During this stage the therapist may spend sessions with the parents, helping them face and resolve issues they could avoid through activating old patterns. Often the goal of creating an intimate, non-child-centered relationship out of the parents' marriage is an unrealistic and unnecessary one. It may be sufficient for them to achieve a means for resolving conflict without triangulating others and, perhaps, for each of them to find more rewards outside the family. Progress on these goals is usually more rapid after the patient has been launched.

THERAPIST WITHDRAWAL

As the changes become more thoroughly consolidated, the therapist should notice and encourage a difference in the form of the session. Increasingly the family members and/or the patient may use the session to report and receive feedback on the problems they have identified and the solutions they have come up with and tried out, instead of receiving direction from the therapist. During this shift, the therapist increasingly congratulates them for taking charge of their lives and downplays his or her role in their change. The therapist increases the interval between sessions and deliberately decreases the giving of advice. Eventually the interval between sessions becomes a month or longer, or therapy is terminated. In our model, however, this termination is not permanent. Patients and/or families are encouraged to return for a few sessions at future transition points, and many do. In nearly all of those cases, a few sessions are all that is needed, and overdependence on the therapist does not become a problem. Relatedly, it is not uncommon for a patient, after a long period of feeling fully in control of the symptoms following termination, to phone in a panic after a string of episodes. Again, we have found that one or two sessions are all that is needed to help her recognize the meaning of the symptoms and make an effective plan. After experiencing one such minor relapse and pulling out of it, the patient's confidence in her new self-image and abilities is greatly solidified. Thus, as structural family therapists profess, our role at this point in treatment is similar to that of the family practice physician's role for medical problems: We are available to the family or individual throughout the life cycle.

OUTCOME

While developing the treatment model described above, we studied the process and outcome of therapy very carefully with 30 consecutive referrals. The details of this study are reported elsewhere (Schwartz, Barrett, & Saba, in press), but we present a summary of the results most relevant to this chapter here.

Since our goals for treatment are complex, our outcome criteria are multidimensional, involving ratings on four categories: (1) control over the symptoms, (2) change in family relationships, (3) change in life goals or career, and (4) change in the patient's behavior in extrafamilial relationships. For purposes of brevity, we report only on the first criterion here: control over the symptoms. "Control" was defined as a combination of the patient's self-reported feelings regarding being in control and the number of binge–purge episodes per week. We found that the frequency of binge–purge episodes was correlated to attitudes about control in roughly the following way:

1. Nearly always in control, and one or fewer episodes per month.
2. Usually in control, and two episodes per month to one per week.
3. Control somewhat a problem, and two to four episodes per week.
4. Control a big problem, and more than five episodes per week.

In our sample, the mean frequency of episodes was 19.3 per week, with a range of 5–63 per week, and every patient felt very much out of control. Thus, every patient began at the fourth level. The mean chronicity of the sample was 6.8 years, with a range of 1–23 years.

Of these 30 cases, 29 are now closed.[6] At the point of closing, 19 (66%) were at the first level, 3 (10%) at the second level, 3 (10%) at the third level, and 4 (14%) at the fourth level.

In addition, all cases have been followed beyond closing at regular intervals. At this writing, the mean length of follow-up is 16 months, with a range of 1–42 months. All of those who closed at the first level maintained those improvements through the follow-up. Two of the three who closed at the second level had relapsed to the third level, however. Those at the third or fourth level at closing remained at those levels. The mean number of sessions through the course of treatment was 27, with a range of 2–90.

In discussing our results, several trends are worthy of mention. First, symptom chronicity was not an obstacle to successful outcome. This may be explained in part by the fact that the more chronic patients tended to be older and less likely to be living with their parents. We had more difficulty with those who began and closed therapy while still living in their parents' home. Second, of the seven cases closed at the third or fourth level, four were dropouts completing fewer than eight sessions, and were early referrals in the study, so they were treated while we were struggling to develop our treatment model. We expect that our results would be better if the study were begun today.

SPECIAL ISSUES

A number of issues, considerations, or types of therapy are important in working with this problem group and have not been covered above. In this section, we discuss some of these briefly and encourage the reader to carry his or her thinking on them further than space permits here.

6. A case is defined as closed at the point after which the patient is seen no more than once a month.

Support Groups

Most bulimics are extremely reluctant to distance themselves from their families without some extrafamilial support network to move toward. A support group can provide this kind of network. Ideally, the group can provide a safe context for experimenting with assertive or intimate behaviors, for exploring and making life decisions, and for feeling less alone or strange (see Boskind-White & White, 1983).

For these purposes, we have sometimes referred patients to groups during the second stage. There are inherent drawbacks in the use of groups, however, and the type or content of the group will make a big difference in the degree to which these drawbacks become a problem. We offer the following advice, based on our experience with many different group formats.

First, groups that (1) focus primarily on controlling the bulimic symptoms, (2) foster the bulimic-as-lifelong-addict identity, or (3) see family members as villains or adversaries are not complementary to our approach. A more productive focus is on issues of growing up and getting close to people.

Second, no matter what the format or content, a group is still an artificial assemblage. It is always better for the patient to develop a nontherapy network, because she can always disqualify the group experience as not normal and thus can avoid changing her self-image. In addition, dependence on the group may develop, and this may actually stifle motivation for nontherapy relationships. In short, certain groups may be useful at certain points in therapy, but they should be used with care.

Marital Treatment

As mentioned earlier, a bulimic's marriage tends to mirror both the bulimic's parents' relationship and her relationship with her father. Since many characteristics are so similar, the themes for the marital therapy are often the same as for the family-of-origin treatment. The couple is encouraged to drop the masks of protectiveness and appearance consciousness, and to stop triangulating food, parents, or children into their conflict.

Often, a patient has never been given full permission to marry. For example, she may still be "married" to her father's approval, so that any real closeness in the couple threatens the larger system as well. As long as the husband joins the rest of the family in treating her like a patient, stability can be maintained. Thus, the husband is challenged to be her husband rather than her father, doctor, or therapist. Similarly, the patient is asked to relate as a wife rather than a daughter or a patient. The therapist may warn them, however, not to let either family-of-origin know they are really "getting married," for fear of destabilizing the system. Once really "married," even temporarily, they can help each other differentiate themselves from their respective families.

Siblings

The sibling subsystem is often overlooked by family therapists, and, to some degree, we have perpetuated this mistake by giving this subsystem so little attention in this chapter. Because of the extreme competitiveness and need for parental approval in the families of bulimics, sibling issues abound and are very powerful. The bulimic's lack of differentiation is often fostered by the fear that if she thinks for herself, she will lose irretrievable ground in the "best child" competition. "Well" siblings often resent the special attention and enormous power to control the family that the bulimia affords, and yet they fear that if the patient improves they too will lose ground. Parents commonly intrude into sibling conflicts, siding with one and attacking another; this also prevents any conflict resolution. For these reasons, sessions with the patient and various combinations of her siblings without the parents are, whenever possible, a part of treatment.

The special issues touched on above, as well as many others (including male bulimics, hospitalization, medical considerations, medication, nutritional education, and the treatment of isolated individuals) are explored more extensively elsewhere (Schwartz *et al.*, in press).

EPILOGUE

In conclusion, not surprisingly, our experience with bulimia has been characterized by extremes: fascination and frustration, conceptual crisis and clinical gratification. By focusing on a single intriguing symptom group, we have been pushed to expand our thinking about and definitions of family therapy, outcome, the evolution of problems, the significance of food, and American society. These changes have affected our lives as well as our therapy, and we are grateful to these families and individuals for their patience and instruction.

ACKNOWLEDGMENTS

We gratefully acknowledge the assistance of the following people: Vivian Meehan and Anorexia Nervosa and Associated Disorder (ANAD) for many referrals; Lynn Selby, PhD, for her work in the project; the staff and associates of the Family Systems Program for their support and guidance; and Nikki Holloway for typing.

REFERENCES

Bandler, R., & Grinder, J. (1982). *Reframing*. Moab, UT: Real People Press.
Boskind-White, M., & White, W. C. (1983). *Bulimarexia: The binge/purge cycle*. New York: Norton.
Cunningham, S. (1984, January). Bulimia's cycle shames patient, tests therapists. *APA Monitor*, pp. 16–17.
Fisch, R., Weakland, J., & Segal, L. (1982). *The tactics of change*. San Francisco: Jossey-Bass.
Haley, J. (1976). *Problem-solving therapy*. San Francisco: Jossey-Bass.
Lacey, J. H., and Phil, M. (1982). The bulimic syndrome at normal body weight: Reflections on pathogenesis and clinical features. *International Journal of Eating Disorders, 2*, 59–66.
Madanes, C. (1981). *Strategic family therapy*. San Francisco: Jossey-Bass.
Minuchin, S. (1974). *Families and family therapy*. Cambridge, MA: Harvard University Press.
Minuchin, S., & Fishman, H. C. (1981). *Family therapy techniques*. Cambridge, MA: Harvard University Press.
Minuchin, S., Rosman, B., & Baker, L. (1978). *Psychosomatic families: Anorexia nervosa in context*. Cambridge, MA: Harvard University Press.
Saba, G., Barrett, M. J., & Schwartz, R. (1983). All or nothing: the bulimia epidemic. *Family Therapy Networker, 7*, 43–44.

Schwartz, R. (1982). Bulimia and family therapy: A case study. *International Journal of Eating Disorders, 2*, 75–82.

Schwartz, R., Barrett, M. J., & Saba, G. (in press). *The treatment of bulimic individuals and their families*. New York: Guilford.

Selvini-Palazzoli, M., Boscolo, L., Cecchin, G., & Prata, G. (1978). *Paradox and counterparadox*. New York: Jason Aronson.

PART SIX

Inpatient Treatment

CHAPTER FOURTEEN

Inpatient Treatment for Anorexia Nervosa

ARNOLD E. ANDERSEN / CATHY L. MORSE /
KAREN S. SANTMYER

INTRODUCTION

Anorexia nervosa frequently requires inpatient treatment. As long ago as the time of Sir William Gull (1874), it was suggested that patients suffering from anorexia nervosa may improve more when separated from family and friends and treated with nutritional rehabilitation and psychological counseling. The goal of this chapter is to describe an effective, safe, and practical program for the inpatient treatment of anorexia nervosa, with a rationale for its employment.

In this chapter, anorexia nervosa is defined according to the criteria of the *Diagnostic and Statistical Manual of Mental Disorders*, third edition (DSM-III). Where appropriate, discussion focuses on one of the two anorexic subgroups, either the food restricters or the binge-and-purge (bulimic) group. These two subgroups of anorexic patients are part of a spectrum of eating disorders (Andersen, 1983) and share fundamental features, but at times are best described separately for the purpose of treatment. Diagnostically, we have emphasized the finding of the central psychopathological feature of anorexia nervosa, the fear of fatness, in order to make a confident diagnosis. Even though a patient may not meet the technical criterion of a loss of 25% of body weight, where the fear of fatness is present with substantial weight loss, resistance to weight gain, and perceptual distortion, the diagnosis is rarely anything but anorexia nervosa and should be made confidently.

It is essential to remember that inpatient treatment is only one phase of the long-term treatment for anorexia nervosa. The preadmission assessment, perhaps a trial of outpatient treatment beforehand, and close follow-up for several years afterward are all important phases of treatment bracketing the inpatient experience. Another introductory point to be stressed is the great probability of improving patients through inpatient treatment, but the limited possibility of achieving a complete "cure." A fundamental understanding of the illness is lacking, although many contributing factors to the disorder are appreciated. The challenge of inpatient treatment is to restore normal weight safely, effectively, and promptly, and to make substantial progress toward the psychological well-being of the patient and the family in preparation for extended outpatient follow-up.

Arnold E. Andersen, Cathy L. Morse, and Karen S. Santmyer. Henry Phipps Psychiatric Service, The Johns Hopkins Medical Institutions, Baltimore, Maryland.

The past decade has seen many changes in our understanding and treatment of the eating disorders. There has been an appreciation of the differences between the restricting and the bulimic categories; diagnosis has become confident and reliable; treatments have emphasized a combination of nutritional rehabilitation and psychological work; and the close relationship between the eating disorders and the affective disorders has been recognized. This increased knowledge has provided the basis for the beginnings of real understanding of the disorder.

THE DECISION TO ADMIT FOR INPATIENT TREATMENT

Difficulties of Admission

The decision to admit may be a difficult one. Referral for inpatient treatment may be seen as a failure of outpatient therapy or as a failure of the patient to work hard enough, and therefore may become a source of guilt. It may also be taken as an indication of special seriousness of illness. The decision to admit often produces fears and fantasies about what the treatment program is like on the part of the patient. The usual fear is that weight gain is out of the individual's control. Admission is usually best presented as a practical necessity for which the patient can make preparations.

Indications for Admission

WEIGHT LOSS

Weight loss is the most common cause for admission. The systemic effects of weight loss are related to both the severity and the rapidity of the weight loss. The most damaging situation results from total starvation. Levels of weight loss seemingly unsupportive of life can be attained in a slow, chronic fashion with surprisingly few ill effects.

Patients meeting the weight criterion for anorexia nervosa — that is, loss of more than 25% of their body weight — usually require inpatient admission, unless they started losing weight while moderately obese. Several weeks of weight loss of 1.8–2.3 kg (4–5 lb) per week or more usually indicate a need for admission. The most common resulting symptoms are difficulty in concentration, coldness, lowering of vital signs, and weakness.

Example A. Susan is a 14-year-old young woman who is 168 cm (5 ft 7 in) tall and wanted to decrease her weight from 58 to 50 kg (128 to 110 lb). She kept losing weight by almost complete starvation until she was at about 45.5 kg (100 lb). Despite promises to begin eating normally, she continued her rapid weight loss and by the time of admission felt uncomfortably cold, despite wearing wool flannels outside on a hot summer day. This clearly is a potentially prefatal situation. Her core temperature was below 35°C (95°F).

Example B. Mrs. Smith is a 40-year-old married white female, referred from the southeastern United States for treatment of 20 years of anorexia nervosa. She gradually had lost almost 50% of her body weight, from slightly over 45.5 kg (100 lb) to about 25 kg (55 lb). She sustained this weight loss fairly well, but had multiple metabolic abnormalities, including abnormal liver function tests and chronic anemia, as a result of the weight loss.

LOW SERUM POTASSIUM AND OTHER SERIOUS MEDICAL PROBLEMS

Low serum potassium and other serious medical problems secondary to bingeing and purging are other causes for admission. The repeated purging of the body, whether by vomiting, laxatives, or diuretics, causes a hypokalemic alkalosis, with possible cardiac arrhythmias as a result. Most of the other symptoms of purging, such as esophageal and gastric distress and swelling of the parotid gland, are uncomfortable rather than dangerous. The low potassium level, however, is one of the reasons for death in acute anorexia nervosa, the others being starvation and suicide.

Example C. Josephine is a 17-year-old high school student who made a transition from the restricting to the bulimic phase of anorexia nervosa shortly after its onset several years ago. Boxes of laxatives were found by family members, despite her denial of using them. After dinner she purged in the shower. During a series of recent stressful events, she began taking more laxatives and vomiting more frequently. She requested hospitalization herself because of weakness. She was admitted for the third time at a weight of 33.2 kg (73 lb), down from a maximum of 50 kg (110 lb), with a potassium level of 2.6 meq/L. Her serum potassium was restored to normal levels after admission, and she gained several pounds rapidly by rehydrating the water that she had lost.

SEVERE PSYCHOLOGICAL DISTRESS

Severe psychological distress on the part of the patient and/or the family may also be a reason for admission.

Depression with suicidal thoughts or intents is a painful psychological symptom that anorexic patients may experience and that may require hospitalization. While depression can often be treated in an outpatient clinic, the combination of depression and low weight together is usually best treated in a hospital.

Persistent, intrusive thoughts about food and weight can occupy much of the patient's mental life and can be overwhelming and relentless. A variety of behavioral problems can also lead to admission, especially relentless, driven exercising and limit testing that the family cannot handle.

Example D. Zelda is the 14-year-old daughter of an ophthalmologist. She had had several prior admissions to well-known Midwestern treatment programs without significant improvement in her low weight. She managed in the outpatient setting to frustrate multiple therapists and her parents. When urged to eat, she threw food and milkshakes on the walls and kicked individuals who tried to help her eat. Her behaviors required hospital treatment more than her weight did. During a difficult but successful hospitalization, her weight improved from 29.5 to 43.2 kg (65 to 95 lb), with a considerable decrease in her limit-testing and aggressive behaviors. The approach taken was to reward constructive behavior and to ignore or limit behavioral abnormalities.

LACK OF RESPONSE TO OUTPATIENT TREATMENT

Sometimes a patient does not respond to a well-organized outpatient treatment program that has been tried for months or years. In this situation, the patient may be more helped by a structured, organized inpatient approach. Asking outpatients to eat the very food they fear, and thereby gain the weight they already feel they have too much of, is a bit like asking patients phobic of elevators simply to walk into many elevators. Surprisingly, many anorexic outpatients do make progress, but not all. If a patient is admitted because of lack of response to outpatient treatment, the staff should take a nonblaming approach toward the referring therapist and the patient. The practical fact is that sometimes inpatient treatment proceeds more successfully.

LACK OF OUTPATIENT FACILITIES

The better the outpatient facilities and the more experience the treating staff has, the more seriously ill the patient can be and still do well in outpatient treatment. In some areas, however, there are no experienced personnel and no organized facilities, and so inpatient treatment, either locally or at a more distant referral center, may be the only way to get adequate improvement.

THE PROCESS OF ADMISSION

We encourage patients to have as large a role as possible in deciding to seek admission. Although there are times, especially with young adolescents, that treatment must be started without the complete cooperation of the patients, it helps to have the patients participate in the decision about admission, with encouragement for the patients to identify something that they would like to get out of treatment personally. Hilde Bruch has emphasized the patient's need for a personal sense of effectiveness in helping to choose admission. The area in which a patient wishes to be helped may not be weight gain, but something like better social skills or improved self-esteem.

A preadmission tour helps to decrease the fears and fantasies of patients. They benefit from a tour of the facilities and a chance to have the program explained in detail. A preadmission orientation also decreases the chances of a sudden request to leave the hospital against medical advice shortly after admission. We ask patients considering admission to talk privately with current inpatients in order to answer any questions, since we feel they will trust these answers more than those from staff. We ask prospective patients to sign a brief statement (see Figure 14-1) of willingness to participate in all phases of the treatment program. Very few people decline to be admitted after having had a tour. They often feel more motivated and less fearful.

If a patient refuses treatment and is not critically ill, then a period of additional waiting is helpful in order to let the patient make a firm commitment. If a patient is very ill, however, and refuses treatment, then a court order may have to be sought, or the patient can be committed to a state facility. Many patients will come into the hospital if they know that the only alternative is a court order.

The setting of mutual goals and expectations can be planned by discussion with patients and staff. The goals obvious to the staff may not be the ones the patients wish to work on, as noted above. The staff expectations are that patients will eat all foods as prescribed, will not use laxatives or diuretics or induce vomiting, and will not use drugs or alcohol. They will stay in the hospital as long as is needed, which in our program is about 3 months. The patients will participate in all aspects of the program, and their families will participate in weekly family sessions. Any research

Date _____

To: Treatment Team, Eating and Weight Disorders Program

I have visited the ward and had a chance to become acquainted with the program. I recognize this program may or may not help me. I wish to be admitted for treatment. I am willing to eat all foods as prescribed by staff (except for three specific foods that I can name), and to accept the goal weight range set by the staff. I will stay as long as necesssary (the average stay is about 3 months). I have my doctor's permission to travel if my physical health is poor.

My family agrees to attend family therapy weekly. If admitted to another ward, I will not be transferred to Meyer 4 at a later time. I will not use laxatives, diuretics (water pills), or any other medications unless they have been prescribed by your staff. I will be responsible for all expenses associated with my treatment.

Patient name _____

Family member _____

Telephone number _____ Home _____ Work

Address _____

Therapist _____

Family doctor, internist, or pediatrician _____

Figure 14-1. Statement of willingness to participate in inpatient treatment.

procedures that require a separate informed consent will be described in detail and an opportunity given for participation.

It is essential to avoid premature promises about the length of time required for treatment, the number of calories to be prescribed, or the weight goals to be attained. Patients latch on to premature promises, even though casually stated, and deal with them as if they were facts.

EVALUATION OF THE PATIENT AFTER ADMISSION

An admission protocol is listed in Figure 14-2. The basic features of the evaluation are a complete history and mental status examination, a physical examination, appropriate laboratory studies to determine the physical state of the patient, and a period of close observation.

Psychiatric History

The psychiatric history should elicit a complete picture of the present illness, including the circumstances surrounding the onset of dieting, the precipitants to weight loss, the course of illness, the onset of bingeing and purging, the loss of menses for female patients, and psychological symptoms of starvation. Other aspects of the history are elicited from outside informants as well as from the patient, including the predisposing features of the patient's personality, the family dynamics, past treatment efforts, and family history of eating disorders or depressive illness.

Studies to be repeated routinely at discharge are indicated by D. Studies to be done at discharge only if results are abnormal on admission or for other specific indications are indicated by D*.

1. Routine Psychiatric Evaluation: History, mental state examination. (See semistructured interview.)
2. Physical Examination: Note emaciation, vital signs (especially bradycardia), lanugo hair, acrocyanosis, height, weight, edema, parotid gland tenderness, hair loss, nail softening, jaundice, scars on dorsum of hand, abdominal tenderness.
3. Laboratory Studies:

(Check) *Admission*	(Check) *Discharge*
____ Heme-7 with differential	____ D*
____ Urinalysis with micro	____ D*
____ SMA-6	____ D*
____ SMA-12	____ D*
____ Growth hormone	____ D*
____ LH	____ D*
____ FSH	____ D*
____ Thyroid: T_4, T_3 RU, and Plasma T_3	____ D*
____ 8 A.M. Plasma cortisol	____ D*
____ Chest X-ray	____ D*
____ EKG	____ D*
____ Bone age (if growth retardation present)	____ D*
____ Testosterone (males)	____ D*
____ Chromosomal studies (if indicated)	Not repeated
____ Dexamethasone suppression test (if indicated)	____ D*
____ Serum estradiol	____ D*

4. Psychological Tests:

(Check) *Admission*	(Check) *Discharge*
____ MMPI	____ D
____ General Health Questionnaire (Goldberg)	____ D
____ Eating Disorders Questionnaire (Andersen)	____ D
____ Mini-Mental Examination	____ D*
____ IQ (WAIS): After nutritional rehabilitation	Not repeated
____ Perceptual Distortion Test	____ D
____ Montgomery–Asberg Depression Scale	____ D
____ Zung Depression Scale	____ D
____ Nutritional Quiz	____ D
____ EDI (Garner, Olmsted, & Polivy)	____ D

5. Additional Documentation and Research Studies:

(Check) *Admission*	(Check) *Discharge*
____ Patient photographs	____ D
____ †Eating disorders dental evaluation	____ D*
____ †Satiety studies	____ D*
____ †Gastric emptying	____ D*
____ Additional research studies	____ D

6. Social Work:

____ Family evaluation: Semistructured interview
____ Psychological functioning of family members
____ Social functioning of family members

7. Other: _____

Figure 14-2. Anorexia nervosa: Evaluation (admission and discharge). †Informed consent required (research studies).

Mental Status Examination

The mental status examination includes a complete cross-sectional evaluation of the patient. Specific notes should be made of the presence of alteration in the state of consciousness due to starvation, alteration in mood state, obsessional and compulsive features, the fear of fatness, pursuit of thinness, and the presence of perceptual distortion. In our experience, we have never found a patient with anorexia nervosa to have truly "psychotic" features. Many patients have peculiar ideas about what food does in their stomachs and certainly have distortions in body image, but they are not deluded. When asked to draw (Draw-A-Person Test) a picture of themselves as their doctors see them, patients all draw themselves as being very thin. They *feel* fat but *know* they are thin.

Physical Examination

The physical examination should especially note changes in vital signs, such as bradycardia, hypotension, hypothermia, and bradypnea. Although the pulse may dip into the 30s in some patients, we have not found any cardiological intervention, such as pacing, necessary where no prior cardiac disease exists. The stigmata of purging include swollen parotid glands; scars on the knuckle from inducing vomiting with the hand, as Russell (1979) has pointed out; complaints of burning in the esophagus; and nonspecific gastrointestinal symptoms on palpation.

Psychological Tests

A combination of intellectual testing by the Wechsler Adult Intelligence Scale (WAIS), personality testing with the Minnesota Multiphasic Personality Inventory (MMPI), and general screening inventories such as the General Health Questionnaire and the Eating Disorder Inventory (EDI) of Garner, Olmsted, and Polivy (1983) provide a relatively thorough battery of testing. In practice, we have not found the projective tests very useful. Their interpretation in anorexia nervosa remains uncertain and varies among testers; often the application to therapy is not made unless the therapist is trained in using projective tests. Specific tests to rate depression are indicated, especially where a research orientation prevails or protocols are being tested.

STAGES OF TREATMENT

Hedblom, Hubbard, and Andersen (1981) have described a systematic, staged approach to inpatient treatment of anorexia nervosa. Although these stages are described separately, they overlap in practice. A consensus among treatment programs over the last decade has been reached that nutritional rehabilitation is essential before effective psychotherapy can proceed. Our approach to treatment is team-oriented, with a multidisciplinary staff, using a multifactorial concept of the origin of anorexia nervosa. The staff includes psychiatrists, psychologists, nurses, social workers, nutritionists, occupational therapists, and educators.

The four stages of treatment are (1) nutritional rehabilitation; (2) psychotherapy (individual, group, and family); (3) maintenance; and (4) follow-up.

Nutritional Rehabilitation

SETTING THE GOAL WEIGHT RANGE

There are several approaches to setting the goal for desired weight gain. In general, we try to strive for a thin–normal weight, which is slightly under mean-matched population weight. The two standards we generally use are (1) the Metropolitan Life Tables (Metropolitan Insurance Companies 1983) and (2) the nomograms devised by Frisch and McArthur (1974) for the necessary weight for return of periods in females (see Table 14-1 and Figure 14-3). A reasonable compromise is 95% of the weight on the Metropolitan Life chart for a given height (with appropriate age correction). Many times we use the weight indicated by Frisch and McArthur for at least a 50% chance of return of menstrual periods. It should be noted that the weight for return of periods is higher than the weight required to begin cycles during normal development. For younger patients, weights may be chosen from pediatric development charts.

Picking a number from a chart is not the whole answer, however; some attention should be given to the weight at which the patient functioned well if he or she had a time of stable weight without increase in height prior to the illness. A fact not accepted by most people is that weight is normally distributed around a central point with an upper and a lower shoulder. The average anorexic patient begins at about 5% above the matched-population weight at the onset of dieting. Although we have compromised in our treatment by setting a "thin–normal" weight as a goal, there is a rationale for setting the goal weight at slightly above the mean-matched population weight, since many of these patients may in fact be biologically normal only when slightly above average in weight. Few patients would accept this reasoning in practice, although they may agree in theory.

Where practical considerations dictate a short treatment period, moderate weight gain (85–90% of normal) may have to be accepted as the goal, with close follow-up required in the outpatient department. Certainly anything less than 85% of a mean-matched population weight is too low. A goal weight *range* rather than a single point should be set, so that patients can fluctuate comfortably within this 1.4- to 2.3-kg (3- to 5-lb) range. Other factors include bone structure, but in practice very few patients are extremely petite or very large-boned, so usually the weights for average build can be used. Anorexic patients often ask that charts for petite figures be consulted.

The weight goal is not set as soon as the patient comes into the hospital, but only after treatment has been under way for several weeks. It is made as a staff decision among the team members. Occasionally nursing staff will comment that a patient nearing the goal looks plump or chubby, and the weight goal may be modified by a few pounds. Since it is our practice not to tell patients of the goal weight range until they are in the middle of it, these changes can be made by staff without incurring the wrath or fears of patients that come from perceived breaking of promises about a given weight. Our "track record" of discharging people in the thin–normal range is good enough that we feel comfortable asking patients to accept our weight range for them and to be notified about it only when they are in the middle of it. They find that the

Table 14-1 1983 Metropolitan Height and Weight Tables

	MEN				WOMEN		
HEIGHT	SMALL FRAME	MEDIUM FRAME	LARGE FRAME	HEIGHT	SMALL FRAME	MEDIUM FRAME	LARGE FRAME
5'2"	128–134	131–141	138–150	4'10"	102–111	109–121	118–131
5'3"	130–136	133–143	140–153	4'11"	103–113	111–123	120–134
5'4"	132–138	135–145	142–156	5'0"	104–115	113–126	122–137
5'5"	134–140	137–148	144–160	5'1"	106–118	115–129	125–140
5'6"	136–142	139–151	146–164	5'2"	108–121	118–132	128–143
5'7"	138–145	142–154	149–168	5'3"	111–124	121–135	131–147
5'8"	140–148	145–157	152–172	5'4"	114–127	124–138	134–151
5'9"	142–151	148–160	155–176	5'5"	117–130	127–141	137–155
5'10"	144–154	151–163	158–180	5'6"	120–133	130–144	140–159
5'11"	146–157	154–166	161–184	5'7"	123–136	133–147	143–163
6'0"	149–160	157–170	164–188	5'8"	126–139	136–150	146–167
6'1"	152–164	160–174	168–192	5'9"	129–142	139–153	149–170
6'2"	155–168	164–178	172–197	5'10"	132–145	142–156	152–173
6'3"	158–172	167–182	176–202	5'11"	135–148	145–159	155–176
6'4"	162–176	171–187	181–207	6'0"	138–151	148–162	158–179

Note. From *1983 Metropolitan Height and Weight Tables* by the Metropolitan Life Insurance Company, 1983, New York: Author. Reprinted by permission of the Metropolitan Life Insurance Company.

Note. Weights at ages 25–59 based on lowest mortality. Weight in pounds according to frame (in indoor clothing weighing 5 lb for men and 3 lb for women; shoes with 1-in heels).

Note. To make approximation of your frame size, extend your arm and bend the forearm upward at a 90-degree angle. Keep fingers straight and turn the inside of your wrist toward your body. If you have a caliper, use it to measure the space between the two prominent bones on either side of your elbow. Without a caliper, place thumb and index finger of your other hand on these two bones. Measure the space between your fingers against a ruler or tape measure. Compare it with these tables, which list elbow measurements for medium-framed men and women. Measurements lower than those listed indicate you have a small frame. Higher measurements indicate a large frame.

Men		Women	
Height in 1" heels	Elbow breadth	Height in 1" heels	Elbow breadth
5'2"–5'3"	2 1/2"–2 7/8"	4'10"–4'11"	2 1/4"–2 1/2"
5'4"–5'7"	2 5/8"–2 7/8"	5'0"–5'3"	2 1/4"–2 1/2"
5'8"–5'11"	2 3/4"–3"	5'4"–5'7"	2 3/8"–2 5/8"
6'0"–6'3"	2 3/4"–3 1/8"	5'8"–5'11"	2 3/8"–2 5/8"
6'4"	2 7/8"–3 1/4"	6'0"	2 1/2"–2 3/4"

weight set by staff has always been slightly below average for height and age, and this information is passed on to new patients.

HOW FAST SHOULD WEIGHT BE GAINED?

Keys, Brozek, Henschel, Mickelsen, & Taylor (1950), in their historic monograph on experimental starvation, noted that nutritional rehabilitation can take place at a pace of about 5000 calories a day with a gain of 1.4–2.3 kg (3–5 lb) a week without

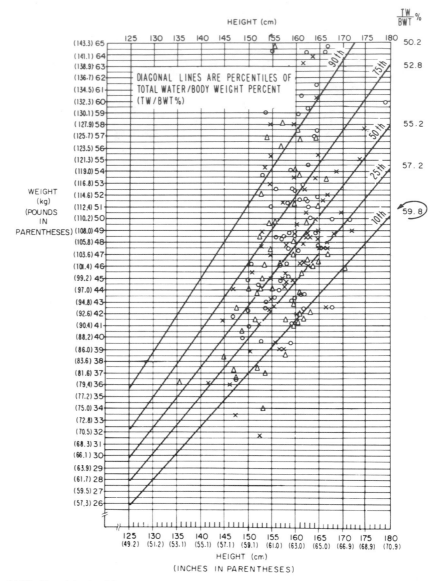

Figure 14-3A. The minimal weight necessary for a particular height for onset of menstrual cycles is indicated on the weight scale by the 10th-percentile diagonal line of total water/body weight percent, 59.8%, as it crosses the vertical height lines. Height growth of girls must be completed or approaching completion. For example, a 15-year-old girl whose completed height is 160 cm (63 in) should weigh at least 41.4 kg (91 lb) before menstrual cycles can be expected to start. Symbols are the height and weight at menarche of each of the 181 girls of the Berkeley Guidance Study (O); Child Research Council Study (X); and Harvard School of Public Health Study (△). Figure 14-3B. The minimal weight necessary for a particular height for the restoration of menstrual cycles is indicated on the weight scale by the 10th-percentile diagonal line of total water/body weight percent, 56.1%, as it crosses the vertical height line. For example, a 20-year-old woman whose height is 160 cm (63 in) should weigh at least 46.3 kg (102 lb) before menstrual cycles would be expected to resume. ⊙ 1-9, weights while amenorrheic of patients of one of us (J.W.M.); ⊗ 1-9, their weights at resumption of regular cycles. When two weights are given for a patient, the lower weight is at first resumed cycle. ⦸, the weights before occurrence of amenorrhea of subjects cited by Lundberg et al., and ⊙, their weights while amenorrheic. (From ''Menstrual Cycles: Fatness as a Determinant of Minimum Weight for Height Necessary for Their Maintenance or Onset'' by R. E. Frisch and J. W. McArthur, 1974, Science, 185, 949–951. Copyright 1974 by the American Association for the Advancement of Science. Reprinted by permission of the authors and publisher.)

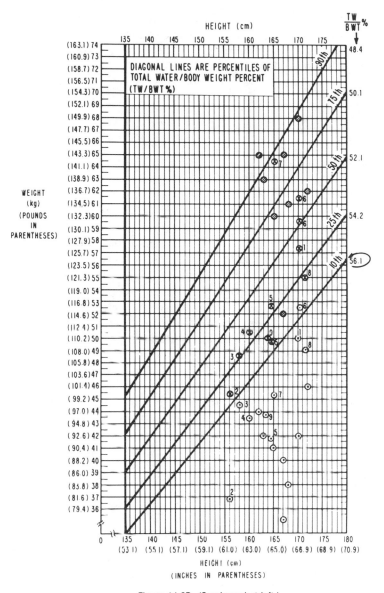

Figure 14-3B. (See legend at left.)

adverse medical consequences. Our first 100 patients gained weight at an average of 1 kg (2.17 lb) per week. In the last year or so, the weight gain has been increased to about 1.4 kg (3 lb) per week, a brisker pace, but considerably less than could be achieved following the example of Keys *et al.* (1950).

WHERE SHOULD TREATMENT TAKE PLACE?

Treatment is usually best accomplished on a psychiatric ward with a team approach. Several reports of successful treatment on pediatric or medical wards (Maxmen, Silberfarb, & Ferrell, 1974) suggest that treatment may proceed in a nonpsychiatric setting. Our experience has been that it is difficult to secure the support of medical nurses, many of whom do not understand the need for supervision during and after eating. An example of successful treatment on the pediatric wards is the program at Children's Hospital in Washington, D.C.

HOW TO ACHIEVE WEIGHT GAIN

Concepts. The essential concept of this phase of our program is the following: Food is prescribed as medication. It is eaten in normal form, with only occasional use of milkshake-type products. Within 24 hours of admission, all of our patients have begun to eat normal meals. The kind of information contained in Figure 14-4 is discussed with the patients, and we hope that it helps them to understand this approach. Nurses and nursing assistants stay with patients for 24 hours a day for as long as necessary, until the eating pattern has been established and a round-the-clock assessment of the patients' psychological and physical state has been obtained. Nurses sit with the patients and encourage them to eat. Force is not used. No threats of tube feeding are used. The emphasis is on empathizing with the patients' fear of fatness, giving much support, and utilizing the milieu for group support. A promise is made that patients will not be allowed to get overweight; we understand that they are fearful of losing control of their eating. They will not be allowed to eat more than is prescribed for them. No discussion of weight or calories is permitted; rather, the emphasis is on the patients' feelings. Fears of fatness are interpreted as symptoms of illness, and our record of not having discharged patients above weight is pointed out. This combination of an empathic nursing-supervised approach to refeeding, using normal food in a milieu setting, results in patients' beginning to eat three meals a day with only moderate anxiety. About half of our patients receive a small amount of antianxiety agent (lorazepam, 0.5 mg 1 hour before meals) for a week or two.

Figure 14-4. Summary of talk given to patients upon entry to the Eating Disorders Program on Meyer 4, the Henry Phipps Psychiatric Service, Johns Hopkins Hospital.

You have an illness that has changed your perception about your body's size and your body's need for food. We are going to ask you to trust us to prescribe your food like medication. This may be difficult for you because of your fear that you may lose control, eat too much, and become overweight. Our goal, however, is never to make anyone overweight, and we won't let you gain too much. But we will ask you to accept our judgment about your nutritional needs and to eat everything that we prescribe for you. You may be anxious during part of the program, but we will have nurses with you much of the time to give you support and encouragement.

We do not know where this illness comes from. It seems to come from many factors, including some features of your personality, such as perfectionism; some family stresses; perhaps some biochemical changes in your body; and going on a diet. Whatever the cause, we don't consider anybody to blame. We think people are often blamed for this problem, but we don't feel your parents are to blame or you are to blame.

Please be honest with us and trust us. We know that there is a great temptation to dispose of your food secretly or to vomit to avoid the effects of eating. We want to concentrate not on your gaining weight, but on your losing your starvation. We think that your hands and feet will be less cold; you will have more energy and less restlessness. Your thinking will be clearer. Our goal is to make you a happier and healthier person. You may experience some discomfort as you go through the nutritional rehabilitation, but we will try to make you as comfortable as possible. We want you to regain control of your life and to continue your growth and development.

Alternatives to Refeeding. A number of other alternatives to refeeding have been described and should be considered.

A behavioral program with rewards for specific amounts of weight gain is one possible alternative to refeeding, especially where staff is limited (Agras, Barlow, Chapin, Abel, & Leitenberg, 1974; Halmi, Powers, & Cunningham, 1975). Bruch (1974) has warned about the danger of patients' eating their way out of the hospital, however. Most large treatment programs receive the failures from other treatment programs. Those coming to us from behaviorally oriented programs have told us the many tricks they learn to increase their weight artificially and thus to get out of the hospital sooner.

Hyperalimentation has been advocated for the extremely thin patient. In our practice, this has not been found to be necessary even with extremely starved patients; it has been associated with a high rate of morbidity and occasional mortality. We have not used hyperalimentation or a nasogastric tube for any of our more than 170 patients.

A number of methods are completely unacceptable, including forcing patients to eat, using a passive interpretive psychotherapy alone without any attention to the eating pattern, or use of appetite-stimulating medications alone without psychological support. Medicines designed to increase appetite are fundamentally misdirected, since anorexia nervosa does not involve a true loss of appetite. When patients are asked whether they would be freer to eat if food had no calories, they usually say yes. Patients with cancer and other illnesses involving true medical anorexia do not care about how many calories food contains. "Anorexia nervosa" is a phrase that probably will remain with us in the English language, but the alternatives of "weight phobia" or *Pubertätsmagersucht* ("pubertal passion for thinness") should be considered.

Food Prescribed. The initial food prescribed is usually between 1200 and 1500 calories per day, according to the patient's admission weight. The diet is low in fat and lactose. We have been able to decrease the nonspecific gastrointestinal symptoms during the refeeding phase by beginning with low-fat, low-lactose foods. The enzymes for digesting fat and milk products take time to increase after starvation, and the body should not be overwhelmed with these products until the inducible enzymes have been regenerated. No diet foods of any kind are allowed; no skim milk, diet sodas, or dietary dressings are used. See the Appendix for more details.

The nutritionist plays an essential role in relating to both patients and staff. The nutritionist takes a complete history from the patients upon admission, and after that does not discuss directly with the patients any aspect of treatment until their weight is in the maintenance range. Every day, however, the nutritionist is present at staff rounds to help make decisions about changes in dietary programs. If the nutritionist and the patients are allowed to interact directly during nutritional rehabilitation, the patients make endless requests for changes in menu. We allow patients to name three specific foods to delete from their menu, but other than these three choices, they are not allowed to determine the foods prescribed. During the maintenance phase, the nutritionist becomes active again in direct conferences with patients regarding the choosing of balanced meals.

Calories are increased by 500 to 750 calories a week until a maximum of between 3500 and 5000 calories per day is achieved. The exact number will depend on the rate of weight gain, the size of the patient, and the presence of discomfort.

If too many low-calorie foods are allowed in the diet, then the physical quantity occupied by 5000 calories a day is enormous. Once nutritional rehabilitation has been underway for several weeks, most calories are in fairly dense form, including a moderate number of fats and sweets; we do not resort to "junk foods," however.

A detailed program for nutritional rehabilitation is listed in the Appendix, with specific suggestions for food items.

Exercise Program. A graduated exercise program is introduced within a week or two after admission. This must be adjusted to the physical status of the patient. It is a big source of encouragement for patients to begin stretching and walking soon after admission. It also makes sense that weight gain will be better distributed if there is moderate, appropriate exercise. Compulsive, driven exercise is discouraged, and strenuous exercises such as aerobics are not introduced until a patient is in the maintenance range.

General Comments. The person supervising a patient at a given meal makes the final decisions. Endless discussion about the contents of the tray are not allowed. If there is something obviously wrong it is changed, but beyond that, the supervising staff member makes decisions. Signs of staff splitting are watched for carefully, and comments about what other staff members have "allowed" are not attended to. The key is consistent, empathic, insightful supervision, with encouragement of development of normal eating patterns. Two additional points need to be emphasized.

First, an increase in weight does not automatically produce a normal eating pattern. Specific teaching about balanced patterns of nutrition, role modeling, and working out the patient's fears of fatness in psychotherapy are all important in achieving normal eating patterns as well as normal weight.

Second, weight gain is a means to an end and not an end in itself. The reasons for weight gain are to eliminate symptoms of starvation; to help patients, once in a normal weight range, to understand their illness; and to help the patients to live life in a more healthy, direct way. Many confusing symptoms are produced by starvation, and psychotherapy is ineffective in the starved patient. But weight gain by itself is only the beginning of the process of healing, and not an end in itself.

Specific Problems and Suggestions. A patient may refuse to eat. A confident, supportive approach by the nursing staff almost always overcomes this refusal. Group encouragement from other patients is helpful. We have not had any of about 170 patients refuse to eat in the past 7 years. See the Appendix.

At times the staff members worry about whether their weight influences the patients. We try to avoid hiring grossly overweight or severely emaciated nurses, but in general, we ask patients to deal with their own problems and not with those of the staff.

If patients induce vomiting so quickly that it cannot be prevented, we ask them to help the staff clean up. The approximate volume vomited is replaced by an equal volume of a nutritious milkshake. Most of the time, the patients express relief that they are not allowed to vomit. Nurses accompany them to the bathroom and stand outside the stall while the patients void or defecate. They stand to the side of the shower while a shower is taking place.

Occasionally a patient is very behaviorally disordered and attempts to strike out at a staff member. This is discouraged by time in the Quiet Room and again with a supportive, empathic, but firm approach. Several times we have devised a behavioral program of rewarding positive behavior and not attending to negative behavior where abusive behavior by patients has persisted. These programs have generally been effective.

Frequent staff meetings are necessary to deal with the staff's feelings about the patients' attitudes and behaviors. The more knowledgeable the staff members are about this illness, the more confident they are, and the more regularly weight gain proceeds in patients they supervise.

Most medical consequences of nutritional rehabilitation are transient, and are mild to moderate. The commonly occurring peripheral edema is treated by elevation of feet, by limiting salt in the diet, and at times by holding calories constant for a week without increases. No diuretics are needed. One patient out of 170 developed gastric dilatation, a potentially fatal problem.

Role of Medications in Treatment. The use of medicines to stimulate appetite, as noted above, is fundamentally misdirected. Antidepressants have been advocated and may well have a role (Needleman & Waber, 1976; Pope, Hudson, Jonas, & Yurgelun-Todd, 1983). Our practice has been not to prescribe antidepressants until patients' weights are normal, their eating patterns are normal, and they have had experience with intensive psychotherapy. If they meet the criteria for major depressive illness after these three approaches have been tried, then antidepressants are prescribed. About 15% of bulimic patients and about 7% of anorexic patients have received antidepressants in our series of more than 170. The reports in the literature are not sufficiently convincing yet to suggest that antidepressants have a role during the starvation phase of all patients.

Figure 14-5 suggests that obsessional and depressive symptoms decrease in direct proportion to weight gain in some patients. Although this illustrative case may not apply to all patients, there are many whose depressive and/or obsessional symptoms improve substantially with weight gain alone.

As mentioned earlier, about half of our patients are prescribed a small amount of antianxiety medicine for 1 to 2 weeks during the early phase of treatment. The usual dose is 0.5 mg of lorazepam (Ativan). This is only done after discussion with the patients. It is done to decrease the anxiety that centers on eating and to help patients feel less distressed when eating. They are told that it does not increase appetite and it does not take away their will; it only allows them to make choices with less anxiety. With three or four patients, we have used small amounts of chlorpromazine. In one very behaviorally disordered 14-year-old, 10 mg of chlorpromazine three times a day proved helpful during the phase of very abusive behavior. But, in general, few medications are used for an extended period of time.

Retrospective Comments. Using the nursing-supervised management of nutritional rehabilitation as described above, we have had a consistent weight gain of 9 to 12 kg (20 to 26 lb) on the average per patient. There have been no deaths. There have been no incidences of congestive heart failure. As noted, one patient had gastric dilatation, which was treated appropriately. Transient pedal edema and nonspecific gastrointestinal symptoms of the "irritable bowel" kind have occurred fairly often, but have responded quickly to conservative treatment. Patients are told about these symptoms in advance and anticipate them when they occur.

Older patients begin to show improvement in their chronic abnormalities of liver and bone marrow functioning after weight has increased to about 90% of their goal range. At times, anemia in the chronically starved anorexic patient persists even longer after normal weight is achieved. Here again, a conservative approach to treatment has been used, with minimization of invasive tests unless absolutely necessary. Male patients show a dramatic increase in testosterone (Andersen, Wirth, & Strahlman, 1982), often increasing 10-fold in their testosterone levels. This increase is accompanied

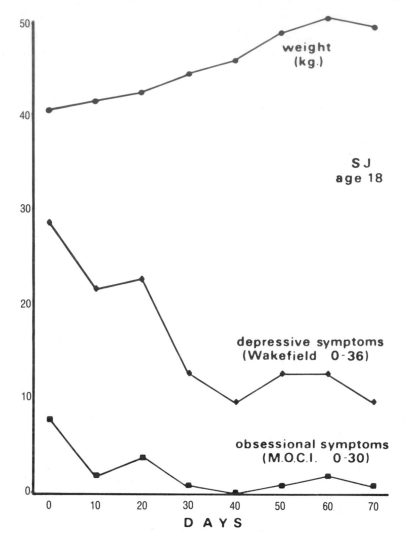

Figure 14-5. Relationship between weight gain and depressive and obsessional symptoms in an anorexic patient. (From "A Study of Correlates of Weight Gain during the Treatment of Anorexia Nervosa by S. Channon, 1982, unpublished master's thesis, University of London. Reprinted by permission of the author.)

by a return of sexual fantasies, erections, and a sense of sexual drive. A small percentage of female patients achieve return of menstrual cycles while in treatment; most of the time this does not occur until after discharge, if it occurs at all (Andersen, Hedblom, & Hubbard, 1983).

We have inquired of patients during their follow-up interviews after treatment about their feelings toward the treatment program. Most feel that the close initial supervision was difficult because of the lack of privacy during the first week or two of treatment. They feel, however, that it is an essential part of the program and that they would have found a way to avoid weight gain if other methods had been used. Most agree that leaving the hospital and getting back to everyday life are even more difficult.

Psychological Treatment of Anorexia Nervosa during Inpatient Status

OVERVIEW

The earliest papers by Morton, Gull, and Lasegue all acknowledged that patients with anorexia nervosa were troubled people and needed some approach to psychological treatment as well as nutritional rehabilitation. For a while in the early and middle part of this century, the pendulum swung in the direction of giving only psychological treatment without attention to nutritional rehabilitation. Some programs have since gone entirely toward refeeding without dealing with psychological issues. Adequate treatment clearly involves both nutritional and psychological work, and the last decade has been helpful in the development of programs that integrate these two necessary components of treatment.

Another basic principle to be followed is the recognition of the multiple psychological factors in anorexia nervosa and the avoidance of a single dynamic interpretation as the explanation of illness. The early analytic work on anorexia nervosa focused on the concept of "fear of oral impregnation" as an underlying motif. Recent empirical studies have noted the frequency of predisposing personality factors in these patients (Halmi, Goldberg, Casper, Eckert, & Davis, 1979) and a multiplicity of family dynamics at about the time of illness onset, as well as familial genetic contributions (Gershon, Hamovit, Schreiber, Dibble, Kaye, Nurnberger, Andersen, & Ebert, 1982).

SOURCES OF PSYCHOLOGICAL SYMPTOMS OF PATIENTS

The following are some of the sources of psychological symptoms of anorexia nervosa patients. An appreciation of these multiple sources allows for more specific treatment.

Starvation. Keys *et al.* (1950), in their historic monograph, documented the psychological symptoms associated with starvation in their experimental subjects. Many nonspecific symptoms, such as difficulty in concentration and loss of emotional expressivity, occurred almost invariably. Interestingly, male volunteers who did not have signs of an eating disorder or a professional interest in nutrition began to focus on food. Thinking about food was pervasive; trading menus and talking about food among the subjects were common events. Their behavior showed typical "anorexic" symptoms: cutting food in small pieces, hoarding food, procrastinating at mealtimes. It is clear that many of the symptoms of anorexia nervosa come from starvation rather than from the psychopathology of the illness. This is important for staff members to know, so that they do not spend too much time talking about food, but deal instead with the core illness.

Personality. Many (but not all) patients prior to illness have perfectionistic, self-critical, and obsessional traits. In general they are above average in intelligence, although usually not extremely gifted. Often there is repugnance at sexual development, as noted by King (1963). They have been praised as model children by families for their compliant behavior and their attainment of good grades in school. Associated with the perfectionistic personality are an all-or-none kind of reasoning and the setting of unattainable goals. There is an interaction between starvation and the pre-illness personality. Many personality features are amplified or caricatured in the setting of starvation. Hence, a firm diagnosis of personality disorders should not be made while the patient is starved, or in general while the patient is a young teenager and still developing. The preillness personality and the changes in personality secondary to starvation both contribute to the psychological symptoms noted during inpatient treatment.

Anorexia Nervosa Per Se. The anorexic illness itself, of course, contributes to psychological symptomatology. The cardinal features are the fear of fatness and the closely allied pursuit of thinness. Russell (1979) has emphasized the fear of fatness as a central feature, while Bruch (1974, 1978) has noted the pursuit of thinness. Perceptual distortion is frequently but not invariably present. This is a symptom that is so obviously present that it can be elicited without difficulty, and yet has so many uncertainties in its measurement and meaning that it is hard to quantitate or understand. It is certainly not unique to anorexia nervosa. Pregnant patients, the formerly obese, and a number of normal individuals have perceptual distortion. There is disagreement about the best technique for quantifying this symptom. Some patients do not have it at all and recognize that they are dreadfully thin, but they remain terrified at the thought of gaining weight. The terror has been described as being "of delusional proportions." This concept of delusional symptoms in anorexia nervosa is a matter of continuing controversy. In our experience, we have never found an anorexic patient who truly was deluded about his or her body size. Patients may have a tremendous sense of "dysmorphophobia," with *feelings* of being overweight. But when asked if they are truly medically overweight, they respond that they are in fact quite thin.

Consequences of Chronic Illness. There are psychological consequences from chronic illness whether the illness is physical or psychological in origin. The "sick role" legitimizes dependency needs and at times serves to accomplish fundamental goals, such as keeping parents together who otherwise might divorce or separate. There are social consequences from chronic illness, especially lack of development of age-appropriate social skills, that may be difficult to remediate.

Patients with anorexia nervosa generally are bright to normal in intelligence; they are often very verbal, but with an associated emotional immaturity. There is clearly an overlap between the psychological features of the restricting and bulimic subcategories, but there are some differences. Table 14-2 lists the typical features of the prototype restricter in contrast to the prototype patient with bulimic features.

In assessing the psychological symptoms of patients with anorexia nervosa, it is important to recognize the multiple origins of these symptoms and the implications for treatment. A passive interpretive psychotherapy, for example, will not help the starvation-induced symptoms. The depressive affect or lack of emotional response that goes with starvation may not respond to antidepressants, but it may respond to nutritional rehabilitation without medication. Caricatured personality features may improve with reversal of starvation.

ASSESSMENT

Tools of Assessment. The primary tool for psychological assessment is an extended history from patient and family and a complete mental status examination. The more informed the examiner is about the natural history of these disorders and their modes of presentation, the more complete the history and examination will be. Several psychological tests are useful, especially the following:

1. The WAIS should be used to assess intelligence. Since many patients have ex-

Table 14-2 Comparison of Anorexia Nervosa and Bulimia

ANOREXIA NERVOSA (FOOD-RESTRICTING)	BULIMIC PATIENTS (BINGEING AND PURGING)
No vomiting or diuretic/laxative abuse	Vomiting or diuretic/laxative abuse
More severe weight loss	Less weight loss
Slightly younger	Slightly older
More introverted	More extroverted
Hunger denied	Hunger experienced
Eating behavior may be considered normal and source of esteem	Eating behavior considered foreign and source of distress
Sexually inactive	More sexually active
Obsessional features predominant	More hysterical or borderline features as well as obsessional features
Death from starvation (or suicide, in chronically ill)	Death from hypokalemia or suicide
Amenorrhea	Menses irregular or absent
More favorable prognosis	Less favorable prognosis
Fewer behavioral abnormalities	Stealing, drug and alcohol abuse, self-mutilation, and other behavioral abnormalities

pectations of performance beyond their ability, it is useful to have an assessment of intellect. This should be done after most of the weight has been regained.

2. The MMPI, while a flawed instrument in many respects, has so much empirical research behind it that it often can serve as a dependable tool for identifying symptoms, personality traits, and prognostic implications (Strober, 1981).

3. The General Health Questionnaire, the SCL-90, the Middlesex Inventory, and other general screening devices can identify levels of general psychological distress.

4. The Eysenck Personality Inventory is one example of the measurement of traits rather than states.

5. The recently published EDI by Garner *et al.* (1983), and the Eating Attitudes Test that preceded it, represent the first valid and reliable tests specifically for eating disorders. The EDI gives a differentiation into bulimic and anorexic categories, and also gives measurements of such categories as ineffectiveness and fears of maturation, which are central theoretical constructs of the illness.

Diagnostic Considerations. The first question is whether the patient satisfies DSM-III criteria for anorexia nervosa. In theory, this provides a consistent criterion for interinstitutional comparisons, and for most purposes it works very well. Some patients, however, do not quite fit the criteria; for example, some may have lost only 20% of body weight instead of the required 25%. When in doubt, the finding of the central psychopathological feature of fear of fatness, associated with substantial weight loss and an abnormality in reproductive endocrine function, should be sufficient for a diagnosis. Technically, patients who do not meet DSM-III criteria but have the essential features of anorexia nervosa would meet the diagnosis of "atypical eating disorder." Occasionally patients will meet the DSM-III criteria, but because they started losing weight when moderately obese, they clearly are not very thin at the time they meet the technical criteria. It is uncertain whether the diagnosis of anorexia nervosa should be used in a person who is not very thin; here, the features of the case should guide the diagnosis and treatment, rather than the DSM-III criteria. In the fourth edition of the *Diagnostic and Statistical Manual of Mental Disorders*, many of these features will probably be clarified, but for most purposes DSM-III serves as a reliable guide to diagnosis. Russell (1979) has used the term "bulimia nervosa" for former anorexics who binge and purge, and has noted the implications of this group for therapy. Diagnostically, patients with bulimia nervosa overlap the categories of classical restricting anorexia nervosa and bulimia, and may be called anorexics or bulimics by various investigators.

Associated diagnoses should be made cautiously. There is a tendency to make early diagnoses of personality disorder, since features of personality disorder are often strikingly present. Clinicians should remember, however, that personality disorder diagnoses should be cautiously made in young adolescents and that much of the symptomatology present may change as weight improves. For these reasons, a firm diagnosis of personality disorder probably should only be made in those of late adolescent years or older and in weight-recovered patients.

The next most common associated diagnoses are those of depressive illness and schizophrenia. When charts for 20 or more years ago were reviewed, we found that the diagnosis of chronic and undifferentiated schizophrenia was often made in association with anorexia nervosa. This diagnosis was made partly for theoretical reasons, reflecting the biases of the earlier decades, and partly because of looser diagnostic criteria. Lately there has been a tendency to overdiagnose major depressive illness in the setting of untreated anorexia nervosa. Here, again, the diagnosis is best made after weight has been restored if it is to have meaning. We have not found any individual in several hundred inpatients and outpatients having anorexia nervosa who has also met the criteria for schizophrenia. A few have continued to meet the criteria for major depressive illness after weight gain.

Dynamic Formulation. A dynamic formulation is essential to a complete assessment. The dynamic formulation is an attempt to postulate a central conceptualization of the purpose that the eating disorder serves in view of the patient's personal history, defenses, and maturational stresses. Bruch (1978) and Crisp (1980) both give helpful conceptualizations of anorexia nervosa that are broad enough to accommodate most patients in an individualized manner. For example, Crisp's concept of anorexia nervosa is that it occurs when the individual's defenses and coping skills are overwhelmed at times of maturational crises. The breadth of the concept allows one to use this idea in understanding the illness in older patients. A middle-aged male who is faced with the loss of children going off to college, the dissolution of a marriage, and increased demands at work is facing in many ways crises similar to those faced by adolescents. In this setting of multiple changes, we have found numerous older people who have developed anorexia nervosa as a means of increasing their sense of effectiveness and control. Dynamic psychiatry has never solved the problem of symptom choice, however, and many people with the typical preconditions of anorexia nervosa do not go on to develop anorexia nervosa.

INDIVIDUAL PSYCHOTHERAPY

The individual psychotherapy of the patient with anorexia nervosa begins in a similar manner for most anorexic patients, but then becomes individualized for different patients. In the beginning, all patients need support, realistic encouragement, and reassurance. They need to know that the members of the treating staff understand their symptoms and appreciate their fears. A sense of empathy for their struggle against perceptual distortion and fear of fatness is essential. The therapist needs to appreciate the mourning that patients go through as they give up the fantasy that thinness will solve their problems; this appreciation will help create a bond between therapist and patient.

Effective individual psychotherapy will avoid either a purely supportive approach or a passive interpretive approach. There are a number of relatively recently described detailed approaches to psychotherapy, especially cognitive therapy, that can be learned in a reasonable time. The choice of a method of psychotherapy will depend very much on the qualities the patient brings to treatment. The patient's age, capacity for insight, and psychological maturity are all factors that should influence the move toward a more dynamic psychotherapy.

For many patients, applied cognitive methods as described by Garner and Bemis (1982), which build on the work of Beck and others, are very useful. This therapy begins with the concept that patients utilize faulty interpretations of environmental stimuli, which lead first to painful emotions and then to abnormal behavior. Role playing is often helpful, especially as the patient prepares to leave the hospital and to face family, friends, school, and work. A framework for a long-term psychodynamic approach can be built within the hospital. Unless a patient remains in the hospital for 6 months or longer, the central work of inpatient individual psychotherapy does not focus on the interpretations of the transference neurosis. This more classical approach may be applicable to long-term outpatient treatment for mature individuals.

Goals for treatment should be identified early so that progress toward them can be identified. A central goal of inpatient individual psychotherapy is to help patients deal directly with life's challenges, rather than indirectly through the "pseudosolution" of anorexia nervosa. Most patients can meaningfully understand the idea that anorexia nervosa is a pseudosolution to very real and important problems. But it is a solution that ultimately does not work and that has a high price tag. The problems patients try to solve with anorexia nervosa are real and not imaginary; the goals patients seek from the illness are very sincere goals; but the temporary solution is inherently flawed and unstable. Because of their perfectionistic qualities, these patients may have a hard time letting go of the fantasized solution to life's stresses via thinness; accepting a more open-ended, ambiguous search for maturity and a sense of personal effectiveness means having to develop more mature patterns of coping.

Treatment will usually involve helping patients develop a less intellectualized approach to life and an increased awareness of and comfort with inner emotions. Whether anorexic patients have an immaturity of feelings, whether they are frightened of identifying them, or whether they are simply inexperienced, the fact is that they generally are not able to identify their emotions accurately. They may look and sound angry, frightened, or depressed, and yet may maintain that they are perfectly normal in mood. Giving patients a safe environment in which to identify and deal with feelings is an essential goal of treatment. Anorexic patients have been identified as having the problem of "alexithymia."

Individual therapy can accomplish only a limited amount in each patient in regard to symptom reduction. Sometimes symptoms essentially disappear, but many times, patients are left with some fear of fatness, some perceptual distortion, and the tendency to turn toward starvation in the setting of stress. While these symptoms can be diminished only to a certain point, there is no limit except intrinsic capability as to how much personal growth patients can experience. While anorexic symptoms may be present to some degree, they can and should occupy a smaller and smaller fraction of the patient's psychological life. This means placing emphasis on individuation and separation, to use concepts of Eriksonian stages, as well as on symptom reduction. If residual symptoms are the numerator, the fraction can be made smaller by increasing the denominator, the patient's total psychological development.

The following are some specific suggestions regarding individual psychotherapy. Therapy in the beginning should be planned to take place every day, but with short (15- to 30-minute) sessions. As the starvation is diminished and patients are better able to concentrate, then longer sessions three times a week become practical. A focus on food and calories should be avoided, although allowing the patient a few minutes at the beginning of the session to ventilate feelings and fears may be helpful. Some therapists are concerned that if they both serve as psychotherapists and manage the patients' nutritional rehabilitation, then patients will be unable to relate psychotherapeutically to them. In practice, we have not found this to be true. Some wards may want to have a separate medical manager for the patients, but this is not necessary. One practical way to avoid the split between therapist and manager roles is to have all decisions about nutritional rehabilitation and program management be made by the treating team as a whole.

Some of the problems encountered in treatment are the following: patients who will not talk because of anger or fright; patients who talk excessively about food or calories; the use of intellectualization; and attempts to split staff members by quoting one against the other. There is nothing specific to anorexia nervosa regarding these issues; they should be approached with the techniques found useful in all psychiatric patients. It is important to point out to a patient that the therapist is not the patient's parent; while the patient may treat the therapist as a parent, the hope is that the patient will be able to develop a new therapeutic relationship with the therapist that will not duplicate the maladaptive ones of the past. The goal is to help patients understand themselves and feel better and more effective as individuals. Inevitably issues of transference occur, and the interpretation of this transference on an occasional basis may be useful, but only if the patient is able to deal with this level of insight.

GROUP THERAPY

Group therapy is an effective and valuable adjunct to individual and family therapy. As with individual therapy, extreme approaches should be avoided. In our experience, the most effective leadership is provided by a combination of male and female therapists who are active facilitators but not dominant. There is some concern that patients will learn new techniques of weight loss through group interaction, and this is true to a limited extent. The positive side of group interaction, however, is much greater than the negative side, and the risk should be addressed directly. A group can provide support and honest feedback. Patients say that they feel accepted for the first time and do not feel strange when they are in a group of other eating-disordered patients. Often, some patients in the group can put words to feelings in a way that others may not be able to do yet. We have found that two 90-minute sessions a week, focusing on helping patients identify and deal directly with feelings and emotions have been very productive of growth. Patients also benefit from work on assertiveness and anger management.

FAMILY THERAPY

Much has been written about family dynamics in anorexia nervosa and approaches to family therapy. The most important guideline is to deal empirically with families rather than theoretically. There is no single family model that predisposes individuals to anorexia nervosa. Hedblom *et al.* (1981) noted that a large number of families with anorexic members fit the model of emotionally reactive, overly close families. But a substantial number of families are rather distant emotionally, and a fair number show no psychopathology at all. Some assumptions to work on in family therapy are the following: Parents generally have a mixture of feelings, including guilt, anger, and the sense of being overwhelmed by the illness; generally, families have done their best to help the patients but have not succeeded; they usually want to help, but are tired of the effort and need relief and guidance.

Our family therapy begins by reviewing the nature of the illness and giving support for the family's efforts. Issues concerning the whole family that need improvement are identified. These usually include communication skills within the family as a whole, as well as between the parents and the patient. Effective parenting is often a concern. At times the father is distant and unavailable, and the mother is left to deal with parenting alone but has become overwhelmed in the process. In separate sessions, issues between the parents as a couple can be identified and discussed. Here again, goals should be set early for treatment so that progress can be identified. Most parents are very worried about having the patient return home; they are concerned about doing the "right thing." We place the responsibility for eating on the patient rather than the parents, but encourage parents to create a normal atmosphere without focusing on the patient's symptoms.

FAMILY SUPPORT GROUP

Goodwin and Mickalide (in press) and Rose and Garfinkel (1980) have described an effective family support group, which allows parents to meet with one another to give and receive support and to make progress on shared problems.

SUMMARY OF PSYCHOLOGICAL TREATMENT

Figure 14-6 summarizes in diagrammatic form the interrelationship of the various kinds of psychological treatment for inpatients with anorexia nervosa.

Maintenance Phase of Inpatient Treatment

The term "maintenance phase" refers to the last phase of treatment, during which the controls are returned to the patient. The goal is to have the patients assume more and more control over choices regarding food, weight, and exercise, and to internalize the structure of the ward so that inner controls can be taken with them after they leave. While nutritional rehabilitation seems difficult to achieve, it proceeds surprisingly well; the maintenance phase in many ways is more difficult because of the transfer of responsibility back to the patient. There is a realistic danger in creating prolonged dependence by taking over controls for a patient during the initial phase, but we feel there is no practical alternative with the very starved person. The alternative is to have

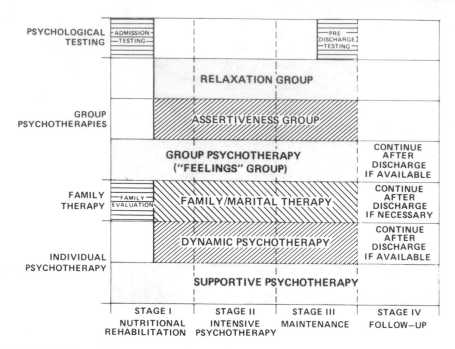

Figure 14-6. Inpatient psychotherapy program for anorexia nervosa and bulimia. The figure schematically describes the variety of psychotherapeutic treatments that a patient receives during each of the four stages of treatment.

patients, while severely ill, make choices about which they are already conflicted and that they are incapable of altering.

The challenge of taking away controls for eating is that they eventually have to be given back. In practice, we have found that this can be done in a systematic manner with a high degree of success. First, when the time for returning controls comes, patients are more prepared to accept responsibility than when they are starved. Having been helped through the starvation phase and engaged in an intensive psychotherapy experience, they are clearly more able to accept responsibility for choices concerning food and weight, and, most importantly, life in general. They are often surprised at how comfortably they can manage weight maintenance and food selection and how much food they need to eat to maintain weight. As noted in the Appendix, patients are first asked during maintenance to choose *kinds* of foods and then to choose *quantities* of foods. Finally they can choose both, vary their weight, and practice an individual exercise program.

Choosing appropriate-sized "healthy" clothing is a difficult task for patients initially. There is often a psychological investment in a certain size of clothing as representing a real achievement. Nurses go with patients to choose "healthy" clothes and encourage them to give away or throw away old clothing. Clothes that are too tight invariably get interpreted as a proof of fatness, and these clothes should be discarded. Gains in psychotherapy will be minimized when patients wear tight clothes that make them feel constantly overweight.

We encourage patients to go to restaurants and fast-food chains to practice eating normally and in a social context. At first they are accompanied by nurses, then by family members, and then by friends; finally, they go on their own. Clearly there are aspects of desensitization involved in this phase. Meal preparation with an occupational therapist is accomplished by starting at the market, bringing food back to the ward kitchen, and preparing and eating a meal with the occupational therapist. The emphasis is on balance and moderation in food choices rather than on calories.

The nutritionist re-enters the scene here and works directly with the patient. All through this final phase of treatment, support is given for healthy behavior; perceptual distortion and fear of fatness are identified as symptoms when they persist. Patients gradually learn to choose a healthy pattern of eating, even though they *feel* they are slightly overweight. They learn to trust the scale and the comments of peers about appearance, instead of their fears. They develop a healthy skepticism about their perceptions. A major goal of the maintenance phase is to set up an effective follow-up program. This is more difficult when patients come from a distance and when there is either no therapist available or a therapist who is not acquainted with current methods of treatment.

Follow-Up

This last phase of treatment will often take several years. Most patients are discharged in an improved but not a "cured" state. We maintain a 24-hour availability for patients, who can call collect and know they will talk to a member of the staff who knows them, at any time after discharge. The first several days are a shock to most patients, no matter how well prepared they are for the transition. The perfectionistic tendency of patients, which may result in the temptation to abandon effective weight control because they have made a single mistake, often appears in the first week. We encourage patients before leaving to structure their time as well as their food patterns and to practice the techniques learned in assertiveness training and relaxation training. They keep records of foods eaten and of feelings and experiences associated with eating, so that therapy can begin with their actual experiences and then move to more dynamic issues.

Bulimic patients with anorexia nervosa are especially vulnerable when leaving the hospital. They leave a supportive environment where their dependency needs are gratified. Practice trips to restaurants, no matter how well planned, tend to have a classroom quality, and there is often a rude reintroduction to reality when leaving the hospital. A combination of plans is helpful: setting up a therapy session for immediately after discharge; a structured approach to time and eating; giving support and encouragement for progress; and providing empathy for the continuing struggle to deal directly with their inner psychological state and the outer world.

SUMMARY

Inpatient treatment of anorexia nervosa is necessary for a large number of patients. Early recognition and effective treatment of anorexia nervosa have resulted in a tremendous decrease in early mortality. It is rare now to have a patient die from acute anorexia nervosa unless there is undetected hypokalemia. Mortality is often as low as 1%. A number of methods are plausible for the treatment of anorexia nervosa. Our method derives from Gull (1874) and Russell (1979), among others, and has as a goal the restoration of biological and emotional health and the capacity for individual growth, with minimization of adverse side effects from treatment. The first rule of medicine is always "Above all, do no harm."

Our practical assumption is that anorexia nervosa is the outgrowth of a number of different factors, including vulnerabilities in personality; a societal emphasis on thinness as a means of feeling effective and successful; a family that is often emotionally overreactive or distant; a possible family history of affective disorder; and a crisis in life that overwhelms the patient's defenses and ability to cope. Sociocultural influences shape the form of these historic, age-old issues in maturation.

A nursing-supervised program in nutritional rehabilitation; an intensive experience in individual, group, and family psychotherapy; and a gradual reintroduction of the patient back into the everyday world result in great improvement for most patients, with few side effects. This staged approach to treatment can be divided into interrelated role functions practiced by different staff members, which can be applied in any inpatient psychiatric setting and in some medical settings. Most medications used in this treatment are adjuncts to nutritional rehabilitation and psychotherapy, but there is some possibility that antidepressants may play a larger role in the future, if early data are confirmed. Patients can usually be greatly improved in inpatient treatment, but they seldom are cured. Most patients remain vulnerable and should be treated for several years after discharge.

While anorexia nervosa may present as a severe, life-threatening disorder, it often responds well to treatment. On the positive side, many patients who have suffered from this illness may eventually become more effective people than if they had never had the illness. Many of these individuals are talented people with considerable potential for growth, who can be helped by guiding them to respond in a direct rather than indirect way to life's challenges. The lack of complete response in many patients, however, reminds us that much remains to be discovered about the fundamental causes of anorexia nervosa and truly effective treatment. In the meantime, the 10-fold reduction in acute mortality that has occurred over the past decade, and the improvement in empirical treatment methods in many centers, suggest that there is considerable hope for the future for the truly effective treatment of anorexia nervosa.

APPENDIX

A Summary of the Eating Disorders Program of Meyer 4 Unit of the Henry Phipps Psychiatric Service (HPPS), Johns Hopkins Hospital: Nursing Care Plan

FOR STAFF USE ONLY
NOT TO BE GIVEN TO PATIENTS

Prepared by Karen Santmyer, Head Nurse, and Cathy Morse, Senior Clinical Nurse.

The purpose of this booklet is to provide guidelines for the staff members who work with patients suffering from anorexia nervosa or bulimia. These patients may be divided into four general categories:

1. Anorexia nervosa — Patient accomplishes and maintains a low weight by food restriction primarily. May use laxatives and/or diuretics, vomiting or excessive exercise as further means to maintain low weight. Has morbid fear of fatness.

2. Anorexia nervosa complicated by bulimia — Patient accomplishes and maintains low weight by combination of behaviors described under anorexia nervosa. Also experiences binges (i.e., powerful and intractable urges to overeat). Has morbid fear of fatness.

3. Bulimia I — Patient has history of anorexia nervosa but is not currently seriously underweight. Repeated episodes of bingeing and purging. Has morbid fear of fatness. (Termed by some experts "Bulimia Nervosa.")

4. Bulimia II — Patient has no history of anorexia nervosa. May be normal or overweight. Repeated episodes of bingeing and purging. Has morbid fear of fatness.

Because these eating disorders involve different behaviors, each category is treated separately in many ways. Our goal is to structure a program with guidelines that will benefit each patient and that will assist the staff in maintaining a consistent approach, while still allowing flexibility for treating each patient individually.

Upon admission of any eating-disordered patient — regardless of the category — the nursing staff will utilize a very structured approach designed to maintain consistency of treatment during the stressful first hours and days and to identify unhealthy behaviors in the patient. The approach will be maintained until an individual treatment plan is devised by the treatment team (i.e., therapist, primary nurse, social worker, occupational therapist, and dietitian).

Therefore, upon admission, all controls for food and weight maintenance are taken from the patient, and the following measures go into effect:

1. Patient is placed on constant observation for 24 hours a day.

2. Patient may leave unit with staff only (does not include family members).

3. Patient is weighed with back to scale and may not see weight or know goal weight range (GWR).

4. Patient is not permitted to discuss weight or calories. Excessive discussion of food is interrupted by staff.

5. Patient's food is selected for him or her by the dietitian; patient may indicate to dietitian three specific foods he or she does not like. Patients may not follow a vegetarian diet while in the Meyer 4 program.

6. Patient must eat all food presented to him or her by staff (i.e., meals and snacks). Patient must eat meals within a 1-hour time limit. Patients who run over this limit will be expected to finish the meal away from the rest of the community, with a staff member present to give support. The Quiet Room may be used for this purpose.

7. Patient is seen by the occupational therapist and may begin attending occupational therapy (OT) groups as agreed upon by the occupational therapist in conjunction with the physician writing the orders.

Family involvement is extremely important in the treatment of patients with eating disorders. For this reason, families are asked prior to admission if they are willing to participate in family meetings with the social worker and other members of the treatment team. If they are unwilling to participate in such meetings, the patient is usually not admitted. If after admission the family refuses to participate in such meetings, discharge of the patient is considered.

Please see page 340 for the policy on constant observation presently in effect in the HPPS. You may hear the staff refer to this as 1 : 1, but it is different from the policy of 1 : 1 Observation for Suicide in the HPPS Policy Manual.

Constant observation is one area of the program that requires flexibility, so that decisions are consistent with each patient's unhealthy behaviors. Twenty-four-hour constant observation should be reduced as soon as possible, unless something mitigates against it. A minimum of 3 days of 24-hour constant observation is the general guideline. Three days are usually sufficient to provide staff with adequate information about unhealthy behaviors to make a decision regarding the need for constant observation at night. Patients who only starve themselves usually do not need to continue 24-hour constant observation past 3 days. Patients who have used vomiting or excessive exercise as a means to control weight may need to remain on 24-hour constant observation for a much longer period of time.

Patients on constant observation must be accompanied by a staff member when using a bathroom. The door to the bathroom is left partly open so the staff person may observe the patient. The staff person flushes the toilet. Frequency and description of the stools should be documented in nursing progress notes or on a patient data flow sheet. Patients on constant observation must request use of the bathroom *before* 7:45 A.M., 11:45 A.M., and 4:45 P.M., so the staff is free to check the meal trays when they arrive on the floor.

The guidelines for reducing constant observation to mealtimes, 1 hour after meals, and visits to the bathroom are similarly dependent on each individual patient's level of anxiety and behavior. This reduction should occur as soon as possible after a regular pattern of weight gain is apparent. If a patient is off constant observation except at meals and snacks, 1 hour after meals and snacks, and visits to the bathroom, but his or her weight gain stops or slows dramatically, it is usually an indication that the staff needs to assume more control, and the patient is put back on constant observation for either 24 hours a day or from 8 A.M. to 8 P.M.

Most patients are not taken off constant observation completely until they reach the middle of the GWR. The overweight bulimic patient may be an exception and may be maintained on constant observation for a longer time while impulse control is a problem.

The GWR should be set after a few weeks of hospitalization. The patient is given verbal assurance that we will not make him or her fat. He or she is not allowed direct input regarding the range itself (i.e., a patient cannot say that he or she will only agree to weighing 95 pounds); no bargaining is done with the patient. Utilizing the premorbid history and various weight charts, a range is set that is related to regaining the menses in female patients. We presently aim for getting patients to a weight higher than the weight at which they first menstruated, as a minimum. Individual decisions are made on the basis of the patient's ability to tolerate the weight emotionally, as well as her desire to regain menses. It may not be realistic to insist that an older woman with children reach a weight that allows her to regain menses. We realize, too, that this marker may not be used in every patient; some will not regain menses regardless of weight gain, or it may take many months at a normal weight for menses to be regained.

Prepubescent females will have GWRs set consistent with pediatric weight charts. Likewise, weight charts for men will be utilized to set the GWRs for males.

Patients are not permitted to see their weight or know their GWRs until they reach the *middle* of the GWRs.

Passes for patients on constant observation are decided upon on a very individualized basis. Initially, passes are given between mealtimes only. When a pass involves a mealtime, the key to the decision is whether the friend or relative with the patient can reproduce what happens in the hospital (e.g., constant observation at meals and snacks and on visits to the bathroom). Ideally, passes that involve eating with significant others will not occur until after a patient has eaten in a public place at least once with his or her primary nurse. The dietitian will provide box lunches for meals eaten while on pass when the staff requests this as part of the treatment plan.

Specific questions regarding mealtime protocol and patient behavior frequently arise. Please see page 341 for mealtime protocol. Other specific guidelines include the following:

1. Eating-disordered patients frequently mix foods in a way most people would find abnormal. Mixing of foods should be discouraged in general, but it is always at staff discretion, which may at times lead to some inconsistency. Sensible, normal eating behaviors should be encouraged by staff, with the following yardstick applied: "Would you mix these foods together in a public restaurant?" Fruit on cereal, fruit in cottage cheese and yogurt, and ice cream on pie are examples of acceptable mixing of foods. Even these may be carried to the extreme (e.g., cutting apples into very small pieces and putting them into yogurt). Again, the staff member with the patient at the time will decide what is appropriate mixing. Peanut butter on fruit is not considered appropriate mixing and is discouraged.

2. Dicing food into small pieces is another behavior frequently noted by staff in patients who wish to delay their meal. Foods are to be cut and eaten in bite-sized portions. Again, this is interpreted individually by staff members, and there may be a slight discrepancy among staff members. Patients need to learn that slight differences may occur, but that they must follow the instructions of the particular staff person with them at the time; they cannot draw other staff members into a discussion about "what is bite-sized?" If patients continue to have difficulty with dicing of food after staff reminders to the contrary, this should be reported to the therapist and primary nurse as soon as possible so that they can confront the behavior in therapy sessions.

3. Patients are required to drink the fruit syrup that accompanies a serving of canned fruit.

4. Patients are *not* required to drink the liquid left after vegetables are eaten. An exception would be the patient who deliberately melts butter pats on vegetables in order to avoid eating them.

5. Patients may request one cup of ice and one cup of water in addition to the fluids on their trays at each meal.

6. Diet drinks (anything with an artificial sweetener) and skim milk are prohibited unless the eating-disordered patient (usually an overweight bulimic) is on a weight reduction diet. Sometimes when a patient reaches maintenance (GWR), his or her prescribed calories are decreased; this does not constitute a reduction diet.

7. Patients are allowed one 8-ounce serving of an approved beverage in between meals, but not within 30 minutes of a meal (e.g., one cup of coffee or tea before breakfast, an 8-ounce beverage between breakfast and lunch, another between supper and bedtime). These guidelines may be modified in response to unhealthy patient behavior and/or difficulty with refeeding edema.

8. Patients are required to eat chicken skin unless it is one of their three food dislikes. Large amounts of fat do not need to be eaten, nor does gristle on meat. New servings of meat may be ordered at the discretion of the staff if a portion contains excessive fat and/or gristle.

9. Patients are expected to eat their meals within 1 hour after beginning the meal. If they do not, they are taken to a quiet area to complete the meal. Occasionally, patients do not adjust to this requirement and continue to take over an hour to eat each meal. Consequences are not initially discussed with the patient, nor are they used as a threat; staff members offer support and encouragement. Continued difficulty will be discussed; the treatment team will then develop a plan to assist the patient to comply with the 1-hour limit. Ultimately, discharge will be considered as an option offered to the patient. The option of feeding via a nasogastric tube will *not* be considered.

"Maintenance" is defined as the period of time prior to discharge which begins when the patient reaches the middle of his or her GWR. If the patient is ready to assume some control, he or she may begin selecting *types* of foods when the bottom of the GWR is reached. This should not occur until teaching has been done by the dietitian and the patient's primary nurse. A minimum of 1 week should elapse between the time a patient begins selecting *types* and *amounts* of foods. The exception to this rule again may be the overweight or normal-weight bulimic, who needs extensive education regarding selection of types and amounts of foods and who may begin selecting before reaching the GWR (in the case of the overweight bulimic).

Patients may see their menus when they begin selecting types of foods. Trays of patients in maintenance are checked by staff to make sure all items ordered are on the tray. Staff may give the patient verbal feedback at this time regarding selections, but should not make changes. When it is noted that the patient is selecting in an unhealthy manner, the specifics of the situation should be reported to the therapist and the primary nurse. Patients in maintenance have had the opportunity to select their menu in advance. They are to eat what they selected and not make substitutions. They should turn their menus in to the staff, with the foods they ate clearly marked. Patients may not delete items at their meals unless a specific treatment plan for deleting has been developed by the therapist and the primary nurse. If it becomes apparent that a patient is having difficulty deciding what to select and/or in eating what he or she has selected, the therapist and the primary nurse should be told as soon as possible.

The patients in the Eating Disorders Program are encouraged to engage in a normal, healthy exercise program. Some guidelines have been developed, because patients frequently use exercise to induce weight loss and have difficulty developing a normal program for themselves.

1. An exercise program is not begun until it is discussed at staff report. Time periods for exercising are prescribed by the resident or psychologist with staff input.

2. The occupational therapist is to specify the exercises to be done. These are listed in the patient's chart under "Consults."

3. The patient is given a list of exercises and a book describing the exercises and specifying the number of times each exercise is to be repeated.

4. No patient is permitted to exercise without his or her book and list at his or her side (even those not being supervised for exercises).

5. Exercises are, in general, supervised until the patient reaches the middle of his or her GWR. These patients must follow the prescribed plan; the staff reserves the right to question activity.

6. Supervised exercise times are provided twice a day at staff discretion. Patients must wait 2 hours after meals before exercising.

7. Exercising is permitted in the activity room only; no patients are allowed to exercise in their bedrooms. Exercise times should not be scheduled during visiting hours. No other patients or visitors should be present during exercise periods.

8. Patients who miss a scheduled exercise period may not extend their next exercise time.

9. Physical activity class (OT) does not count as exercise time.

10. Patients may participate in games in the gym in the evening or on weekends with staff supervision. The therapist and the primary nurse should be consulted if a staff person thinks that a patient is exercising excessively.

11. Patients on constant observation may take as many as two walks on campus with staff each day according to staff availability. The length of the walk is at staff discretion.

12. Patients on or off campus alone have no restrictions on number of walks a day unless otherwise specified by their therapist and primary nurse.

This booklet has been designed to answer some questions you may have about the Eating Disorders Program. If you have other questions that have not been addressed here, or if you need clarification on any item, please feel free to consult us.

CONSTANT OBSERVATION

Purpose

To provide close staff supervision to patients for their safety. This observation will not be utilized in the situation of a patient with suicidal thoughts.

Method

1. This nursing intervention will be instituted by physician or nursing order. The order will be written specifically to state the purpose of this intervention: for example, (a) constant observation for 24 hours a day for eating-disordered patient; (b) constant observation for reality testing; (c) constant observation for elopement precautions.

2. One staff member may be assigned the responsibility of more than one patient on constant observation. Patient/staff ratio may range from 2 : 1 to 5 : 1.

3. Night shift staff members will station themselves in the alcove areas of Corridor A to observe patients on constant observation.

MEALTIME PROTOCOL

1. Mealtimes will be announced when trays arrive on unit.

2. Patients on constant observation should be prepared to begin meals at 8 A.M., 12 noon, and 5 P.M.; they are allotted 60 minutes to complete the meal. Patients not on constant observation should plan mealtimes that end by 9:30, 1:30, and 6:30, *or* by the time OT activities begin.

3. The trays of eating-disordered patients are checked by a staff member to determine correctness of items and to allow for necessary corrections.

4. Eating-disordered patients on constant observation are not permitted near trays until staff indicates it is time to begin eating; the seating arrangement for patients will be decided by staff.

5. Only those patients who have begun selecting foods may see their menus.

6. Eating-disordered patients on constant observation may not alter food on trays. The only exception is if they receive one of their three documented dislikes.

7. Staff will toast bread if requested by patients on constant observation (even if they are in maintenance) before the meal begins. Condiments are placed on the table by staff and removed after patients have made their selections. Eating-disordered patients are limited to the following: (a) one salt and one pepper only, (b) three packages of condiments only (e.g., ketchup, lemon juice); (c) two packages of sugar.

8. Patients may have one cup of ice and one cup of water in addition to fluids on trays if desired.

9. Stirring, dicing, or combining of foods will be stopped. Patients will comply with the decision of the staff person with them at that particular meal if one of these behaviors is interrupted.

10. Chicken skin must be eaten unless it is a documented dislike.

11. When lettuce is used as a *garnish* under other foods, it does not have to be eaten. Lemon slices need not be eaten, but orange slices must. Olives are no longer used as a garnish.

12. Bananas, oranges, and grapefruit may be peeled; other fruit skins must be eaten.

13. Only patients on weight reduction diets may use dietetic foods, artificial sweeteners, or diet drinks.

14. Patients on maintenance may not substitute foods; they are to eat the foods they selected from the menu. They are to turn in their menu after the meal, with the items they ate clearly marked. Patients may delete items only if this is part of a written treatment plan.

15. During meals, discussion of food or weight will be interrupted by staff; patients who experience difficulty in this regard may talk to staff after the meal.

16. The trays of eating-disordered patients on constant observation are checked by staff after the meal.

17. Patients who take more than 60 minutes to complete their meal will be removed to a quiet area to finish it.

18. Food may not be brought into the hospital by or for eating-disordered patients.

19. The kitchen door is locked unless a staff person is in the kitchen. *Any* patient on constant observation must be observed by staff while using the kitchen.

ADDENDUM TO SUMMARY OF EATING DISORDERS PROGRAM

Over several months' time, it has become apparent that eating-disordered patients who are in the maintenance stage of their program and are selecting types and amounts of food are proficient at selecting fewer than the number of prescribed calories by persistently selecting foods low in calories. We have partially resolved the problem by insisting that these patients select foods from *the regular hospital menu only* at the beginning of the maintenance stage. The "Special Items" list and the deletion of items are used as described in the following teaching plan, which is utilized by the primary nurse and the dietitian with each eating-disordered patient.

We are now conceptualizing the maintenance stage of our program as a two-phase process. The emphasis in Phase 1 will be on determining how many calories a patient needs to maintain his or her weight in the GWR. We will stress honesty (i.e., the importance of the patient telling us if he or she is taking in fewer or more than the maintenance calories). If the patient consistently deletes or adds calories without our awareness, the possibility exists that the person may be maintaining his or her weight on a significantly different amount of calories than we have ordered. Consequently, we may then discharge the person on a lower or higher number of calories than is really needed to maintain weight. In order to monitor this situation further, we will collect the menus of all eating-disordered patients in maintenance, with all necessary corrections made on them. During the first 10 days of maintenance, the patient will remain on constant observation at meals to determine what exactly they have eaten. The dietitian will randomly select menus for 3 days out of the 10 to determine the exact calories the patient is eating.

During Phase 2 of maintenance, the patient should be encouraged to make changes in his or her diet (under the supervision of the outpatient therapist if this occurs after discharge) so that he or she will experience fluctuations in weight. This will allow the person to see the consequences of changing the prescribed pattern. This can help the person to learn that he or she can allow weight to go up and down a few pounds without losing control of his or her behavior and eating too much or too little.

Staff Responsibilities during Maintenance

1. Dietitian:
   - Phase 1: Educate patient; monitor caloric intake.
   - Phase 2: Provide discharge meal pattern.
2. Primary nurse:
   - Phase 1: Educate patient (see teaching plan); confront patient for unhealthy eating behaviors; monitor selections and encourage patient to order high-calorie foods that are feared (i.e., desserts).
   - Phase 2: Make decision with primary therapist, dietitian, and occupational therapist to begin Phase 2 while person is an inpatient, based on progress. Provide appropriate teaching for Phase 2. Give emotional support. Provide telephone support and follow-up teaching as needed after discharge.
3. Therapist
   - Phase 1: Order constant observation at meals for first 10 days of maintenance; reinforce teaching done by dietitian and primary nurse. Encourage meal planning, shopping, and preparation with the occupational therapist.
   - Phase 2: Decide with primary nurse, dietitian, and occupational therapist if Phase 2 is to begin while person is an inpatient. Contact follow-up therapist and give summary of hospitalization, with description of our treatment approach if this therapist is unfamiliar with our program. Describe Phase 2 of maintenance and stress importance of close monitoring of patient during this time. Suggest that outpatient therapist assist patient to experience fluctuations of a few pounds in weight by making assignments (e.g., patient is to adjust calories so that he or she gains or loses 2 pounds).
4. Occupational therapist
   - Phase 1: Teach menu planning; plan trips to grocery stores to purchase food; teach meal preparation; eat prepared meal with patient.
   - Phase 2: Teach meal planning for after discharge.

REFERENCES

Agras, W. S., Barlow, D. H., Chapin, H. N., Abel, G., & Leitenberg, H. (1974). Behavior modification of anorexia nervosa. *Archives of General Psychiatry, 30*, 279–286.

Andersen, A. E. (1983). Anorexia nervosa and bulimia: A spectrum of eating disorders. *Journal of Adolescent Health Care, 4*, 15–21.

Andersen, A. E., Hedblom, J. E., & Hubbard, F. A. (1983). A multidisciplinary team-treatment program for patients with anorexia nervosa and their families: Preliminary report of long-term outcome. *International Journal of Eating Disorders, 2*, 181–192.

Andersen, A. E., Wirth, J. B., & Strahlman, E. R. (1982). Reversible weight-related increase in plasma testosterone during treatment of male and female patients with anorexia nervosa. *International Journal of Eating Disorders, 1*, 74–83.

Bruch, H. (1974). Perils of behavior modification in treatment of anorexia nervosa. *Journal of the American Medical Association, 230*, 1419–1422.

Bruch, H. (1978). *The golden cage.* Cambridge, MA: Harvard University Press.

Crisp, A. H. (1980). *Anorexia nervosa: Let me be.* New York: Grune & Stratton.

Frisch, R. E., & McArthur, J. W. (1974). Menstrual cycles: Fatness as a determinant of minimum weight for height necessary for their maintenance or onset. *Science, 185*, 949–951.

Garner, D. M., & Bemis, K. M. (1982). A cognitive–behavioral approach to anorexia nervosa. *Cognitive Therapy and Research, 6*, 123–150.

Garner, D. M., Olmsted, M. P., & Polivy, J. (1983). Development and validation of a multidimensional eating disorder inventory for anorexia nervosa and bulimia. *International Journal of Eating Disorders, 2*, 15–34.

Gershon, E. S., Hamovit, J. R., Schreiber, J. L., Dibble, E. D., Kaye, W., Nurnberger, J. I., Andersen, A. F., & Ebert, M. (1982, March). *Anorexia nervosa and major affective disorders associated in families: A preliminary report.* Paper presented at the meeting of the American Psychopathological Association, New York.

Goodwin, R., & Mickalide, A. (in press). Increased perception of mutual support from other parents in a support group for eating disorders parents, *Children's Health Care.*

Gull, W. W. (1874). Anorexia nervosa. *Transactions of the Clinical Society* (London), *7*, 22–28.

Halmi, K. A., Goldberg, S. C., Casper, R. C., Eckert, E. D., & Davis, J. M. (1979). Pretreatment predictors of outcome in anorexia nervosa. *British Journal of Psychiatry, 134*, 71–78.

Halmi, K. A., Powers, P., & Cunningham, S. (1975). Treatment of anorexia nervosa with behavior modification. *Archives of General Psychiatry, 32*, 93–97.

Hedblom, J. E., Hubbard, F. A., & Andersen, A. E. (1981). Anorexia nervosa: A multidisciplinary treatment program for patient and family. *Social Work in Health Care, 7*, 67–85.

Keys, A., Brozek, J., Henschel, A., Mickelsen, O., & Taylor, H. L. (1950). *The biology of human starvation* (Vol. 2). Minneapolis: University of Minnesota Press.

King, A. (1963). Primary and secondary anorexia nervosa syndromes. *British Journal of Psychiatry, 109*, 470–479.

Maxmen, J. S., Silberfarb, P. M., & Ferrell, R. B. (1974). Anorexia nervosa: Practical initial management in a general hospital. *Journal of the American Medical Association, 229*, 801–805.

Metropolitan Life Insurance Company. (1983). *1983 Metropolitan height and weight tables.* New York: Author.

Needleman, H. K., & Waber, D. (1976). Amitriptyline therapy in patients with anorexia nervosa. *Lancet, ii*, 580.

Pope, H. G., Hudson, J. I., Jonas, J. M., & Yurgelun-Todd, D. (1983). Bulimia treated with imipramine: A placebo-controlled, double blind study. *American Journal of Psychiatry, 140*, 554–558.

Rose, J., & Garfinkel, P. E. (1980). A parents' group in the management of anorexia nervosa. *Canadian Journal of Psychiatry, 25*, 228–232.

Russell, G. F. M. (1979). Bulimia nervosa: An ominous variant of anorexia nervosa. *Psychological Medicine, 9*, 429–448.

Strober, M. (1981). The relation of personality characteristics to body image disturbances in juvenile anorexia nervosa: A multivariate analysis. *Psychosomatic Medicine, 43*, 323–330.

CHAPTER FIFTEEN

Special Problems of Inpatient Management

PAUL E. GARFINKEL / DAVID M. GARNER /
SIDNEY KENNEDY

Anorexia nervosa and bulimia continue to pose many therapeutic challenges. This is partly because these are serious illnesses with significant mortality and frequent chronicity, and partly because a range of issues must be considered in understanding and managing patients with these eating disorders. Furthermore, until recently, their etiologies were poorly understood, and this led to diverse approaches to treatment. Recently, there has been an increasing consensus on certain aspects of treating these eating disorders. For example, most clinicians would acknowledge the need for the patient to gain weight in order to benefit properly from psychotherapy; most would also agree that therapy must be tailored to the individual's needs, and that this necessitates family involvement. In spite of these areas of accord, controversies and special problems in treatment persist. We have chosen to focus on four areas that may present obstacles to effective inpatient management: (1) psychological characteristics of people with anorexia nervosa; (2) features of the family; (3) staff-related problems; and (4) limits in our current level of understanding of anorexia nervosa and bulimia.

Examples of difficulties due to the characteristic psychological disturbances of people with eating disorders are as follows:

1. Lack of cooperation and reluctance to allow staff control over behavior.
2. A basic mistrust of oneself and others.
3. The presence of depression.
4. Competition among anorexic patients in a hospital ward.
5. Attitudes of nonanorexic toward anorexic patients on a ward.
6. Medical complications.

Family-related difficulties include the following:

1. The cycle of hostility–dependency and helplessness that may evolve.
2. Separation fears.

Staff-related difficulties include the following:

Paul E. Garfinkel, David M. Garner, and Sidney Kennedy. Department of Psychiatry, Toronto General Hospital; and the University of Toronto, Toronto, Ontario, Canada.

1. Re-enactment of family conflicts.
2. Countertransferrence issues; splitting and rescue fantasies.

Other areas where present knowledge is limited are as follows:

1. The optimum management of time during an inpatient admission.
2. The ideal target weight for an individual.
3. The role of medication.
4. The best approach to the chronic relapsing patient.

While many other concerns and problems develop in treating anorexics, these are the most common ones encountered in the hospital setting.

These problems on an inpatient ward are discussed within the context of our own particular approach to inpatient management; however, this chapter does not review in detail our model of inpatient treatment, as this has been done elsewhere (Garfinkel & Garner, 1982). Inpatient management must be considered within the overall context of a broad-based psychotherapy that includes outpatient treatment.

Our approach to inpatient treatment is based on our understanding of the pathogenesis and evolution of the illness as multidetermined (Garfinkel & Garner, 1982), and it shares many points in common with contributions from other clinician/investigators in this area (Andersen, Morse, & Santmyer, Chapter 14, this volume; Bruch, 1973; Crisp, 1980; G. F. M. Russell, 1977; Selvini-Palazzoli, 1974; Strober & Yager, Chapter 16, this volume).

It is our belief that anorexia nervosa and bulimia can be viewed as illnesses with multiple predispositions; these result in a particular individual's being at risk. Predispositions may be arbitrarily and somewhat artificially thought to occur in the individual, the family, and the culture. The various risk factors have been discussed in detail elsewhere (Garfinkel & Garner, 1982). They ultimately lead to dieting, which is intended to enhance the individual's sense of self-control and self-worth. As weight declines further, starvation and a variety of other factors supervene to perpetuate the illness. Factors that sustain the illness may be very different from the ones that serve as predisposing or initiating factors. Common sustaining factors include the presence of the starvation syndrome, relying on vomiting as a means of controlling weight, the familial relationships that change during the illness, the person's social and vocational skills, and others (see Garfinkel & Garner, 1982).

The overall aim of treatment must be to restore the patient's health and to prevent recurrences of the illness. It must be emphasized that this requires a multifaceted treatment, which varies according to a particular patient's individual needs. Therefore the treatment team must display considerable flexibility in dealing with individual patients. Within this context, several issues must be regularly addressed. These include the following:

1. The need for weight restoration, so that individuals may be freed from the cognitive, affective, and behavioral consequences of starvation and can begin to face their phobia of body size.

2. The need for ongoing psychotherapy to prevent recurrences and to allow for the emerging sense of personal identity.

While patients with weight loss must regain weight, not all patients with anorexia nervosa require hospital admission. Many patients can gain weight outside the hospital, with regular weighing, support, guidance, and the initiation of psychotherapy. In an earlier study, we found that 62% of our patients required admission to a hospital (Garfinkel, Moldofsky, & Garner, 1977); however, today fewer than half of our patients are admitted. This is probably related to several factors:

1. The earlier diagnosis and referral process, resulting in a larger proportion of less severely ill patients seeking consultation.
2. An increasing familiarity with the problem, resulting in greater comfort in managing more severely ill patients outside the hospital.
3. The reduced availability of inpatient beds.

Criteria for admission have been described elsewhere (Garfinkel & Garner, 1982).

Hospital treatment aims to establish a controlled rate of weight gain in a setting of emotional support. This involves a graduated level of activity, often beginning with bed rest and dietary re-education. There is emphasis on weight gain, but this is applied within the context of comprehensive treatment for particular individuals and their unique situations. This individualized treatment involves a relationship type of individual therapy, occupational therapy, and, at times, group therapies and family therapy. This type of inpatient management has been described in detail elsewhere (Garfinkel & Garner, 1982).

CHARACTERISTIC PSYCHOLOGICAL DISTURBANCES OF THE INDIVIDUAL

Patients with anorexia nervosa are a heterogeneous group, as are any group of patients with a psychiatric syndrome. Although psychological themes vary across patients, there are common issues. These include fears of maturity because of the increased personal responsibility that maturity requires. However, these maturational fears are rooted in earlier problems. Generally, these involve a failure to develop a sense of mastery or control over oneself and one's world; dieting then becomes an isolated area of personal control. Closely related is a relative lack of awareness of bodily processes, including inner feelings and changes in one's body shape (Bruch, 1973). Because of these problems, the body is not a source of comfort, nor is it viewed as natural; rather, it is perceived as something foreign and something that must be artificially controlled (Selvini-Palazzoli, 1974).

Two other psychological phenomena are common. These relate to the regulation of self-worth and a characteristic thinking pattern. People with anorexia nervosa are very dependent on external phenomena for the maintenance of their self-esteem. Performance and achievement are tied to pleasing others rather than pleasing oneself. This makes anorexics particularly vulnerable to the influences of culture, family, and peer group. Cognitively, they display a variety of abnormalities (Garner & Bemis, 1982). Of particular importance is a dichotomous or "all-or-nothing" thinking style. A patient may feel, "If I gain 1 pound, it might as well be 100 pounds." Similarly, eating is all-or-nothing; but this style extends beyond food and weight and involves other behavior (studying, exercise, relationships with the opposite sex), attitudes to the self (patients view themselves as all good or all bad), and attitudes to others (others may be idealized or vilified). Because of these particular psychological disturbances, admitting anorexic patients to the hospital may increase the likelihood of specific management problems.

Refusal to Cooperate

Some patients may resist or refuse totally to accept inpatient treatment; moreover, once in the hospital, they may not cooperate with the parameters of the inpatient regimen. There are several reasons for this initial lack of cooperation. Denial may play a major role, especially for many patients who have the restricting form of anorexia nervosa. In spite of their severe emaciation, these individuals report feeling well and deny that their bodies are in some way changed. This denial of illness may not have been confronted on the preadmission interviews; or preadmission interviews may have been impossible to conduct, because of extreme starvation or medical complications. It is our impression that confronting the denial prior to admission, and actively attempting to elicit the patient's cooperation in working toward the inpatient treatment goals, are beneficial in reducing resistance.

Another factor contributing to the lack of cooperation is the ego-syntonic nature of the individual's symptoms. Many of the features of anorexia nervosa are not disturbing to patients; not only do they not wish for change in these features, but they may actually derive rewards from them. For example, dietary restraint and observing the scales recording decreasing weights regularly provide pleasure from the resulting sense of control and accomplishment. If the physician focuses entirely on these symptoms (e.g., the weight), it is unlikely that a patient will agree to cooperate. Prior to admission and again at the time of admission, the treatment team and the patient must carefully enumerate goals upon which all can agree. Detailed descriptions of the components of treatment (meals, rate of weight gain, privileges, etc.) will facilitate the development of more realistic expectations on the part of the patient.

Some patients continue to refuse to be admitted to the hospital. Generally, they are encouraged to gain weight over several weeks; if the individual fails to gain weight, it will provide further evidence to such individuals that they are no longer in control of their weight. If they again refuse hospital treatment, it may be arranged to continue to see them for supportive care outside the hospital, but such patients and their families should clearly understand that meaningful psychotherapy cannot occur until the symptoms of starvation have been alleviated. This general support should not be misconstrued as a psychotherapy aimed at prevention of relapse. On infrequent occasions, severely emaciated patients have to be admitted involuntarily because of the risk of death. Involuntary hospital admission has the disadvantage of at least initially impairing the development of trust in the treatment team. Nevertheless, it may confront a patient therapeutically and be life-saving.

Mistrust of Oneself and Others

Most patients with anorexia nervosa have little trust in physicians, who are thought to be interested in controlling them rather than in alleviating their suffering. Often they also mistrust themselves, particularly with regard to their ability to control bodily functions naturally. Earlier, they have often felt helpless in dealing with other individuals, and their stubborn sense of defiance may conceal the feelings of helplessness these patients later describe when they have improved. The fact that most people with anorexia nervosa are mistrustful of others, and the fact that the low body weight is ego-syntonic, mean that great care must be taken to create a gradual sense of trust. The development of a working alliance must begin with the initial interview through the demonstration of a patient, yet firm, noncritical approach. Informing the patient about the illness, normal physiology, and the effects of starvation help. It is useful for the therapist to communicate in clear language and to avoid jargon or simplistic interpretations of symptoms. A kind, firm, but nonauthoritarian approach is helpful; a stern, formal approach may increase the patient's resistance. On the other hand, excessive and inappropriate warmth can be viewed by the patient as seductiveness or manipulation. Consistency and a sensitivity to the varied needs of the individual are essential. It is important for the patient to recognize that treatment does not only revolve around weight. The therapist must be prepared to reassure the patient that the commitment to treatment is for as long as is required and is not tied to the patient's low body weight.

We recently treated a patient who illustrates the problems of reluctance toward admission and a basic mistrust. When first seen, she weighted 24kg (53 lb) and totally denied the presence of illness. She required involuntary admission and nasogastric feeding. When she reached 37 kg (80 lb), she was made an informal patient. Despite her assurance that she had developed a working alliance with the treatment team and planned to reach her target weight above 45kg (100 lb), she signed out of the hospital against medical advice the following day.

The Presence of Anorexia Nervosa with Severe Depression

The treatment of the severely ill patient with coexisting anorexia nervosa and major depression with melancholia poses a special problem. Attempts to involve the individual in any behavioral program where motivation and reward are essential components are unlikely to succeed. The patient with psychomotor retardation may not want time out of bed, and the suicidal patient may gain weight but cannot be given privileges to leave the unit unaccompanied or to work toward further independence. In such cases, treatment using antidepressant drugs may be required before further progress can be achieved in the specific treatment of the anorexia nervosa.

Competition among Patients with Anorexia Nervosa

There are many advantages to treating patients in a setting in which the staff members have experience and expertise in managing anorexia nervosa and bulimia. The fact that the staff is dealing with a common problem generally results in a sense of cohesiveness in working toward a common goal. Even within an ideal treatment environment, some problems may arise. An important obstacle to treatment is competition among patients. They may compete for staff time, or they may begin to act out in a variety of other ways. For example, patients may compete directly for their primary therapist's time; worse, they may contend for the "specialness" of being the most seriously ill anorexic through increased caloric restriction, bulimia, or self-mutilation. These may interfere with the unit's overall atmosphere and with individual patients' therapy. They must be openly addressed both in the individual and group psychotherapies.

Attitudes of Other Patients toward Anorexics

There is no one hospital setting that is ideally or uniquely suited to treating patients with anorexia nervosa (G. F. M. Russell, 1981). Previously we worked in a small investigative ward, where 8 or 9 of the 11 beds were devoted to patients with anorexia nervosa. Currently we work in a large teaching general hospital, where 4 of 42 psychiatric beds have been segregated for eating disorders within a clinical investigative unit for mood and nutrition. Work in both settings and elsewhere has confirmed the notion that a variety of hospital settings can be developed to treat anorexic patients. What is important is that there be a particular model of the illness and that this be conveyed in terms of an atmosphere on the ward. An atmosphere of consistency, understanding, and firm limits is needed. The staff should be familiar with the management of anorexia nervosa and should have a clear and consistent philosophy and understanding of the disorder and its treatment (Bruch, 1973). This enables the treatment team dealing with the patient to act in uniform fashion and minimizes staff "splitting," patients' manipulations, and concomitant crises.

The main problem in the larger unit with a heterogeneous group of psychiatric patients lies in the fact that anorexic patients require more staff time and may be viewed by other patients as "special." A sense of neglect and anger may arise in other patients, and this may become focused on the group of anorexic patients. Sensitive handling of ward community meetings is required to resolve these concerns. One marked advantage to the mixed population lies in the fact that anorexic patients, for the first time, may have the opportunity to develop relationships with adults who share none of their misconceptions about eating or weight. In several instances, mutually beneficial relationships have developed in the hospital between anorexic and nonanorexic patients and have continued following discharge.

Medical Problems

Since these patients are seriously ill from a physical point of view, or may rapidly become ill, they pose special concerns to the staff, especially in a psychiatric unit. Staff members must gradually learn to feel comfortable in dealing with young adults who may be very ill and yet may not appreciate the severity of the disturbance. For example, M. C. Brotman, Forbath, Garfinkel, and Humphrey (1981) described a woman with bulimia and a drive for thinness who regularly misused ipecac for purposes of weight control. Ipecac contains emetine, which is a poison to skeletal muscle in general. This woman presented with a marked peripheral and cardiomyopathy and denial of the fact that she was not capable of walking up two flights of stairs. After an initial weight restoration, withdrawal from ipecac, and psychotherapy, this patient presented to the inpatient unit in a very similar fashion — again, with myopathy and denial — 1 year later.

Cardiac arrest secondary to hypokalemia is the most common cause of death in anorexia nervosa and bulimia. When the body is already in a generalized deficiency state due to starvation, rapid and harsh assaults from purgatives, diuretics, and the effects of bingeing and vomiting can be life-threatening. Bradycardia and hypotension occur in the majority of patients (Silverman & Krongrad, 1983). In a recent case report, A. W. Brotman and Stern (1983) emphasized the severity of the bradycardia in one patient, who had a pulse of 28 beats per minute when first seen for a medical evaluation in the emergency department; this increased to a rate of 60 beats within 48 hours of hyperalimentation.

Regular monitoring of serum potassium is usually advocated, but it is unclear how closely serum levels relate to total body potassium (D. M. Russell, Prendergast, Darby, Garfinkel, Whitwell, & Jeejeebhoy, 1983). While potassium supplements may be required for some patients, there is a danger with noncompliant patients, who may forget to take supplements for several days and then "overdose" on the day that the electrolytes are monitored. In the hospital, a supervised diet usually provides an adequate replacement of potassium as long as there is staff observation of the patients to ensure that they are not vomiting.

Gastrointestinal symptoms are common and may limit the rate of weight restoration. Gastric dilatation and occasionally perforation (Browning, 1977) may follow rapid refeeding of starving people. For this reason, most anorexics are initially placed on a 1500-calorie diet, and this is gradually increased as the patient can tolerate it. As weight begins to increase, many patients report on an altered sense of satiety, with bloating, nausea, and distention after even small amounts of food; this has been related to delayed gastric emptying (Dubois, Gross, Ebert, & Castelli, 1979; Holt, Ford, Grant, & Heading, 1981). As gastric emptying is controlled, both by cholinergic activity through the vagus nerve and by dopamine activity, dopaminergic-blocking drugs could well have a role in treating these symptoms. Metoclopramide inhibits gastric relaxation produced by dopamine, but has a high propensity to produce both neurological side effects and depression (Baeyens, Van de Velde, De Schepper, Wollaert, & Reyntjens, 1979).

Domperidone is a new compound that enhances gastric peristalsis and has antiemetic properties. It is believed not to cross the blood–brain barrier at therapeutic levels. We recently reported the successful use of domperidone in a patient with anorexia nervosa who also complained of severe bloating after eating (D. M. Russell, Freedman, Feighlin, Jeejeebhoy, Swinson, & Garfinkel, 1983). This was confirmed objectively by showing a marked delay in solid-phase gastric emptying. Both subjective and objective measures showed a marked improvement within 2 weeks of treatment with the drug. We are currently carrying out a double-blind cross-over study (domperidone vs. placebo) to clarify the value of the medication.

Because many of the patients' gastronintestinal complaints may be corroborated by altered physiology, some staff members become quite hesitant about being firm in having the patients complete their meals as prescribed. It is important for all staff members to recognize that these altered gastrointestinal functions will permanently improve after the starvation has been treated.

Recently we have seen several patients for whom bulimia was initially undiagnosed in insulin-dependent diabetes. These patients had been attending a diabetic clinic where attempts to achieve stabilization were exceptionally difficult. A central aspect of treatment proved to be establishing a normal eating pattern while the patients learned to avoid bingeing and vomiting, and a stable insulin dosage was then obtained. The relationship between eating disorders and diabetes is not yet clearly understood, but it is interesting to note that the refeeding edema commonly seen may be due to a direct effect of insulin on renal tubules, as well as glucagon action on aldosterone.

Edema is common in anorexia nervosa, especially when severely emaciated patients are rapidly refed (Morgan & Russell, 1975). The mechanism is not well understood: While the edema is often attributed to low plasma proteins, these are generally normal in anorexia nervosa (Garfinkel & Garner, 1982). At times the edema can be a result of particular behaviors of a patient. For example, patients have been known to ingest large quantities of salt in order to provoke excessive weight gain; others drink huge quantities of fluids in order to reduce their sense of hunger; a few patients stand all the time, in the belief that this will expend more calories than sitting, and thus there may be a postural component to their edema. Increased aldosterone levels may also be important. The development of edema may be important here for two reasons: (1) It may be frightening to patients, in regard to the rate of gain and distribution of their increased body size; and (2) it plays havoc with contingency systems that utilize weight gain as a basis for daily rewards. The edema can be minimized by (1) initially keeping the patient on bed rest, since there is usually a diuresis associated; (2) gradually increasing the patient's diet; and (3) teaching the patient postural exercises and providing support and explanation when edema does occur. Diuretics should be avoided here.

There are abnormalities in other systems (see Garfinkel & Garner, 1982, for a review). Gynecologists frequently see anorexic patients before other medical specialists do when the patients present with primary or secondary amenorrhea. There is no specific treatment for the induction of ovulation during hospital treatment. Reaching a target weight and maintaining this for several months are usually adequate. Similarly, hematological indices are frequently low: Normochromic, normocytic anemia, leukopenia, and thrombocytopenia may occur. Generally, these indices reverse with weight gain.

The possibility of developing many physical disorders increases the complexity of the management of these patients, emphasizes the need for a close liaison between psychiatrists and other medical specialists, and demonstrates that those directly involved in the treatment must be prepared to deal with physical as well as emotional problems.

FAMILY-RELATED ISSUES

Breaking the Negative Cycle and Resistance to Change

Patients may initially comply with treatment and yet be taken out of the hospital against medical advice because of parental anxieties. The families of anorexics are quite heterogeneous (Rakoff, 1983); there is no one type of family relationship or family structure unique to anorexia nervosa. Rather, there may be a number of risk factors related to the family. We have identified disturbed interactional patterns as common in families with anorexic children, although it is not clear whether this is a cause or a consequence of the disorder (Garfinkel, Garner, Rose, Darby, Brandes, O'Hanlon, & Walsh, 1983). These disturbances specifically relate to communication, affective expression, expectations, and performance of roles. At times, parental psychological difficulties may be enhanced as patients begin to improve in the hospital (Crisp, Harding, & McGuiness, 1974). Because of this, it is not uncommon to have parents subtly undermine treatment by encouraging patients to act out or even to press for premature discharge.

Because of this, contact with a patient's family must begin at the time of the initial assessment and must be maintained through the period of hospitalization. The parents must receive an explanation for the illness that does not include criticism or blame, and they must be informed of their child's progress while complying with specific rules — for example, to keep the family removed from day-to-day management while the patient is in the hospital. The family is not allowed to bring food in to the hospital or to phone during meal times. However, family members are generally encouraged to visit and to participate in family therapy. The timing of this must be individualized, but usually can occur once the patient has started to gain weight and develop some control over eating. If it does not occur relatively early in the hospital stay, the risk of the parents' encouraging premature departure from the hospital may be increased.

For the family therapist, a delicate balancing of conceptual frameworks is required. The family therapist works to understand how anorexic pathology has evolved and what pathological function it may serve within the family, and argues against having "a sick patient and a well family." At the same time, however, the therapist must acknowledge that the anorexic patient is indeed ill enough to be in the hospital, receiving the kind of close supervision and monitoring required by those who are severely ill. In addition to weight gain, enlisting family support during hospitalization may be one of the most important factors for therapeutic success.

Separation Fears

At times, a further factor in the patient's lack of willingness to be admitted or the desire to leave the hospital immediately after admission is the fear of separation from the parents. Many patients will agree to hospital admission if the physician focuses on symptoms that the patients themselves find distressing, if the family is cooperative, and if the goals and plans for the hospital stay are outlined completely.

Preadmission interviews in which the patient (and, at times, the family) meets various staff members and receives an explanation of their role in treatment are often very useful. The interview can be an effective mechanism for describing the details and rationale of the hospital treatment and for eliciting an initial commitment from the patient to be an active collaborator in treatment. An information booklet is provided that outlines the general principles. For some, without this initial introduction and assessment of suitability for hospital treatment, valuable time may be wasted negotiating with staff over every detail of hospital management, or the hospital stay may be terminated prematurely because of enormous expectations from the treatment program.

STAFF-RELATED DIFFICULTIES

The initial process following admission requires that staff members take control over individuals who have failed to demonstrate personal control, as exemplified by their eating and at times their becoming slaves to vomiting and laxative abuse. Patients who suffer from functional disorders of such severity but who fail to acknowledge the seriousness of their disorder may produce a sense of therapeutic helplessness in the treatment team. When patients re-enact deceitful behavior, such as hiding food, vomiting, or exercising when on bed rest, it is easy to understand how such behavior may be viewed as malicious; the staff must guard against repeating the family's desire to punish such a patient. In contrast, staff members who have difficulty being consistently firm may avoid confrontations about deceptive behavior entirely. Such staff members, often out of a desire to be liked by the patients, may wish to deal only with the psychological issues. This facilitates the patients' manipulations, and again treatment may break down. Both extremes in staff attitudes will cause problems and will result in escalation of the patients' deception and subsequent further weight loss.

Such actions must be interpreted not as signs of malice, but of the patients' extreme fears of weight gain. Other responses common in these situations are feelings of inordinate power over patients or a desire to infantilize them, facilitated by the patients' small size and at times regressive behavior.

Staff members must continually convey an understanding that the illness makes the patients do things that are out of character when they are fearful of gaining weight, but that they will not be allowed to behave in these self-defeating ways (G. F. M. Russell, 1973). Throughout treatment, the staff must be understanding and supportive, but firm. A punitive and angry approach will merely increase the patients' resistance and destroy any therapeutic alliance. A patient who has been deceptive about hiding foods, vomiting, or excessive exercising must be confronted in a nonjudgmental manner. Staff members must act sympathetically, with a great deal of support and understanding, yet always with recognition of the reality of the situation. They must not change the treatment plan merely because they are sympathetic. The treatment may be jeopardized if one member of the staff feels it is wise to bend the rules a little and win the patients' favor by being less firm. Because of the difficulty anorexics have in seeing "in-betweens," they tend to view staff members as being all good or all bad. Some may be consistently idealized; others may be severely criticized. Staff members often recognize these as reflections of the patients' disordered thinking, but may become caught in their desire to win the patients' favor. The patients' attempts to split their perceptions and project them onto the staff must be recognized by all staff members. It is important that they not respond to these defenses (Sadavoy, Silver, & Book, 1979).

A further problem may develop when patients have been in therapy and continue this therapy with individuals outside the inpatient team. Again, the patients' tendency to view situations as all good or all bad may result in idealization of the outside therapists and negation of the efforts of the inpatient team. For some patients, it may be necessary to suspend outpatient treatment during the inpatient phase. However, others may continue this, provided that the outpatient therapists maintain very close contact with the inpatient team and are in complete agreement with the treatment philosophy. Outpatient therapies proceeding independently of the inpatient plans will generally result in the inpatient therapy's being sabotaged.

These problems with the staff can be minimized if there is a clear understanding of the treatment philosophy and the rationale upon which it is based. Regular staff seminars are important in this regard, as is a sense of open communication within the treatment team (Book, Sadavoy, & Silver, 1978).

PROBLEMS DUE TO THE CURRENT LEVEL OF KNOWLEDGE

How Patients Deal with Free Time in the Hospital

Bed rest is often beneficial for a period of time following admission. This allows the physician to assume greater control over patients' disturbed eating and to reassure the patients that their lack of personal control will be contained by the staff. Bed rest is useful both for restricting patients who must gain weight and for bulimics whose pattern of overeating and purging requires control from others. Activity is very limited during bed rest, and this may pose problems for people who have been extremely active. Moreover, the inactivity is disturbing to many anorexic patients, who have frequently defined themselves entirely in terms of achievement. Their self-worth is tied to concrete things, such as lowered readings on the scales, higher grades, and the number of sit-ups they can do per day. Being prohibited from engaging in these activities may create a sense of despair.

Enforced inactivity may lead to anxiety in some patients, both because of their terror at increased weight and because they may feel empty as a result of no longer being "productive." It is important to have such patients begin to confront the panic that inactivity produces and not to give in and flee from it, as they have so often done prior to hospital admission. Considerable emotional support from the nursing staff is required during this period. At the same time, some activities are useful, both during bed rest and as patients are gradually being introduced to the ward. It is important, however, not to structure every moment; rather, patients should gradually learn to accept and enjoy relaxing times when they do not have to be "productive."

Occupational therapies should be introduced for each individual—not merely to pass the time, but to encourage the development of particular skills. Crafts may be utilized for self-expression and as a realm of satisfaction outside of body shape and appearance. Patients often enjoy sewing clothes. These should not be made in their emaciated sizes, but rather in their anticipated healthy sizes. This helps in a small way toward acceptance of the inevitable changes in body shape, and also indicates that there are rational limits to the weight gain. For some patients, cooking lessons with ' a dietitian may be appropriate, but only after the starvation symptoms are no longer present. Other patients benefit from interpretative dance classes or yoga, but only after the target weight has been achieved. Physiotherapy may also help to provide pleasurable sensations from a body that is dichotomously viewed as "fat" and "all bad" following weight gain; such therapy helps to promote positive bodily perceptions and acceptance of a new shape. Furthermore, a few patients can begin a program of graded exercises after weight restoration. If this can be begun prior to discharge, it may demonstrate to the patients that they can appropriately control their exercise, rather than become slaves to it. Many patients, however, are not able to tolerate this and may have to defer any exercise program until they have recovered. Throughout, the patient must be viewed as an individual whose unique skills will be enhanced, not as someone to be slotted into all programs that are available.

The Role of Medication

The dispensing of medication remains a controversial issue. Perhaps the only agreement is that no single drug has a generalized application in the treatment of anorexia nervosa. Chlorpromazine, once claimed as the mainstay of treatment because of its antipsychotic properties in attacking near-delusions, as well as its antiemetic and appetite-stimulating properties, has only a very limited role. Many patients are determined to resist oral "mind-altering substances," and these views, together with such side effects as hypotension and sedation, restrict the value of neuroleptics. They are also not helpful in improving the patients' beliefs about their bodies.

A recent controlled trial of pimozide found a modest role for it in improving the rate of weight gain induced by a behavioral program and in improving some attitudes of patients (Vandereycken & Pierloot, 1983), but these results must be interpreted cautiously until further studies have been reported. Where marked anxiety before meals continues to interfere with progress and does not improve with continued emotional support, there may be some merit in prescribing either a small dose (25–50 mg) of chlorpromazine or a short-acting benzodiazepine such as oxazepam (15–30 mg). We have been reluctant to use benzodiazepines in the bulimic subgroup because of their great potential to develop addictions.

Other drugs have aroused and continue to arouse interest. Cyproheptadine, lithium, bromocriptine, naloxone, and cannabis have all been studied; none of these has been found to be a clearly indicated drug. The role of anticonvulsants in treating bulimia is quite unclear. Following initial favorable reports (Green & Rau, 1974) on diphenylhydantoin, larger controlled series (Green & Rau, 1977; Wermuth, Davis, Hollister, & Stunkard, 1977) have found a smaller group responsive to anticonvulsants; this responsiveness is not clearly related to electroencephalogram (EEG) abnormalities. This work must be pursued, as should a preliminary report that carbamazepine may be useful for bulimics with a strong affective component (Kaplan, Garfinkel, Darby, & Garner, 1983).

Of all drug treatments, the role of antidepressants remains the most hotly debated. The existence of depressive symptoms in patients with anorexia nervosa has been recognized for many years (Kay, 1953). More recently, by using a semistructural interview (the Schedule for Affective Disorders and Schizophrenia), Piran, Kennedy, Owens, and Garfinkel (1983) found that 85% of anorexics and bulimics at some time in their pasts met rigorous criteria for an affective disorder. This type of information has led some authors to view anorexia nervosa as a variant of affective disorder (Cantwell, Sturzenberger, Burroughs, Salkin, & Green, 1977); more recently, similar claims have been advanced about bulimia (Hudson, Pope, Jonas, & Yurgelun-Todd, 1983). This work has been supported by evidence that affective disorders and alcoholism are more common in these families than one would expect to occur by chance alone. For example, Piran et al. (1983) found a prevalence of affective disorders of 50% in parents of anorexics (which is as high as that of the parents of bipolar probands), and of alcoholism of 27%. The evaluation of depressive symptoms is complicated by direct effects of starvation on subjective mood state, energy level, interests, and concentration. Where symptoms of major depression persist after refeeding, and especially when this coexists with a positive family history of affective disorder, antidepressant drug treatment is considered in our unit. Often these patients have had a previous history of depressive episodes not related to weight and starvation, and have a strong family history of affective disorders. It may be possible in the future to rely on abnormal cortisol responses to dexamethasone to help predict which patients could benefit from antidepressant medication (Musisi & Garfinkel, 1983).

Antidepressants may not improve the rate of weight gain, and for amitriptyline the reported increased carbohydrate craving (Paykel, Mueller, & De la Vergne, 1973) may make patients more at risk for developing bulimia. The tricyclic antidepressants are not without other problems in this group; for example, hypotension is a common side effect and may contribute to falling in a group that is otherwise at risk for hypotension. Glassman and Carino (1984) has presented some evidence to suggest that nortriptyline may produce less hypotension than other tricyclics. Because of the strong fears of loss of personal control that anorexics and bulimics experience, they are very likely to stop taking any of the sedating tricyclics; those with the least antihistaminic and anticholinergic properties should be selected in this group. Preliminary results with the monoamine oxidase (MAO) inhibitor isocarboxazid in bulimics demonstrated significant improvements in depression and anxiety ratings, as well as improved eating behavior (Kennedy, Piran, Owens, Garfinkel, & Musisi, 1983). This relationship between tricyclic or MAO-inhibitor response, in terms of both mood and eating behavior, requires clarification over the next few years.

Target Weight and Weight Gain

It is generally agreed that any psychotherapy that ignores weight loss and fails to confront patients' phobia about being in a "normal" weight range is doomed to failure. Similarly, any treatment that focuses purely on weight gain without emphasizing other aspects of treatment is likely to have only limited success. To establish a patient's target weight, two options are available: Either the average weight for individuals of this age and height can be obtained from tables (Health and Welfare Canada, 1959), or an attempt may be made to clarify the patients' own "normal weight range." In view of the wide variation in statistical norms, it is probably preferable to use the second method. In this regard, the final target weight should be a range in which (1) the patient can maintain the weight without undue emphasis on dieting, (2) there is a return of normal hormonal functioning, and (3) the cognitive and affective sequelae of starvation are improved.

A detailed eating and weight history is required to clarify the point at which weight loss began. Was dieting an issue at that time? What was the desired weight, and what means were used to obtain this (purging, dieting, using anorexic drugs)? What was the subsequent course of weight change, and did menses cease at any time? It is often possible to see a clear weight level that the patient must reach to expect a return to normal health. This illustrates the importance of a wide range of treatment approaches. Here, not only is the educational component in informing patients of the uniqueness of their own set weight important; an overall attack on the social pursuit of thinness through fashion magazines and the like may also be indicated (Garner, Rockert, Olmsted, Johnson, & Coscina, Chapter 21, this volume). If physiological "markers" could be identified that would help specify when the target weight range has been attained for any individual, it would represent a major aid in helping patients accept the gain of weight to a specified end point.

A weight gain of 1 to 2 kg (2 to 4 lb) weekly is considered adequate; where patients attempt to gain weight more rapidly, this is usually an attempt to eat their way out of the hospital and represents poor motivation for further psychological treatment. Remaining in the hospital for several weeks after the target weight has been reached is often resisted by patients who have already had a lengthy hospital stay. It is important to clarify this expectation from the beginning of treatment and to encourage the patient to become involved in previously feared activities while still a hospital patient, in order to develop means of maintaining weight during this time.

The Chronically Ill Patient

For some patients (perhaps up to 30% of those attending specialized eating disorders clinics), anorexia nervosa has been a persistent disorder for many years. For such patients, admission to a hospital is often only requested at times of life-threatening weight loss or complications. To avoid clashes between staff members and such patients, it is important to clarify what can realistically be expected of a hospital stay. Preadmission interviews, in all cases, serve a useful role; in particular, they may enable realistic goals that are acceptable to both patients and staff to be clarified. It may be possible to set a target weight that a patient can accept, and yet one that does not represent collusion with the patient's denial process. Such patients are likely to feel intense shame and guilt about having to come into the hospital time after time to deal with their weight gain. If a sense of dignity and self-importance can be conveyed to them, this may help these individuals to develop trust and eventually to deal with perpetuating issues that have previously been avoided.

Some patients with strong obsessional characteristics may be able to settle at a relatively low though not immediately dangerous weight and to function reasonably well outside the hospital. Periodically they may lose weight and require admission. For these individuals, it is the change in weight rather than the weight they reach that poses the problem, and it may be realistic to recognize hospitalization for this purpose only. Both patient organizations and other professional community organizations have an important role and are likely to have a growing role in the future in supporting some individuals who in some way have to learn to "live with anorexia nervosa." This group of patients with chronic illness has not been adequately studied to date. Further efforts must enable such patients to learn to live with the illness with dignity and to let it have as little impact on their day-to-day lives as possible.

REFERENCES

Baeyens, R., Van de Velde, E., De Schepper, A., Wollaert, F., & Reyntjens, A. (1979). Effects of intravenous and oral domperidone on the motor functions of the stomach and small intestine. *Postgraduate Medical Journal, 55*, 19–23.

Book, H. E., Sadavoy, J., & Silver, D. (1978). Staff countertransference to borderline patients on an inpatient unit. *American Journal of Psychotherapy, 35*, 521–532.

Brotman, A. W., & Stern, T. A. (1983). Case report of cardiovascular abnormalities in anorexia nervosa. *American Journal of Psychiatry, 140*, 1227–1228.

Brotman, M. C., Forbath, N., Garfinkel, P. E., & Humphrey, J. (1981). Ipecac syrup poisoning in anorexia nervosa. *Canadian Medical Association Journal, 125*, 453–454.

Browning, C. H. (1977). Anorexia nervosa: Complications of somatic therapy. *Comprehensive Psychiatry, 18*, 399–403.

Bruch, H. (1973). *Eating disorders*. New York: Basic Books.

Cantwell, D. P., Sturzenberger, S., Burroughs, J., Salkin, B., & Green, J. K. (1977). Anorexia nervosa: An affective disorder? *Archives of General Psychiatry, 34*, 1087–1093.

Crisp, A. H. (1980). *Anorexia nervosa: Let me be*. New York: Grune & Stratton.

Crisp, A. H., Harding, B., & McGuiness, B. (1974). Anorexia nervosa. Psychoneurotic characteristics of parents: Relationship to prognosis. A quantitative study. *Journal of Psychosomatic Research, 18*, 167–173.

Dubois, A., Gross, H. A., Ebert, M., & Castell, D. O. (1979). Altered gastric emptying and secretion in primary anorexia nervosa. *Gastroenterology, 77*, 319–323.

Garfinkel, P. E., & Garner, D. M. (1982). *Anorexia nervosa: A multidimensional perspective.* New York: Brunner/Mazel.

Garfinkel, P. E., Garner, D. M., Rose, J., Darby, P. L., Brandes, J., O'Hanlon, J., & Walsh, N. (1983). A comparison of characteristics in the families of patients with anorexia nervosa and normal controls. *Psychological Medicine, 13*, 821–828.

Garfinkel, P. E., Moldofsky, H., & Garner, D. M. (1977). The outcome of anorexia nervosa: Significance of clinical features, body image and behavior modification. In R. A. Vigersky (Ed.), *Anorexia nervosa* (pp. 315–329). New York: Raven Press.

Garner, D. M., & Bemis, K. (1982). A cognitive–behavioral approach to anorexia nervosa. *Cognitive Therapy and Research, 6*, 123–150.

Green, R. S., & Rau, J. H. (1974). Treatment of compulsive eating disturbances with anticonvulsant medication. *American Journal of Psychiatry, 131*, 428–432.

Green, R. S., & Rau, J. H. (1977). The use of diphenylhydantoin in compulsive eating disorders: Further studies. In R. A. Vigersky (Ed.), *Anorexia nervosa* (pp. 377–382). New York: Raven Press.

Glassman, A. H., & Carino, J. S. (1984). Use of antidepressants in the geriatric population. In H. C. Stancer, P. E. Garfinkel, & V. M. Rakoff (Eds.), *Guidelines of the use of psychotropic drugs* (pp. 19–30). New York: SP Medical and Scientific Publications.

Health and Welfare Canada. (1959). Canadian average weights for height, age and sex (pamphlet). Ottawa: Nutrition Division of the Department of Health and Welfare.

Hudson, J. I., Pope, H. G., Jonas, J. M., & Yurgelun-Todd, D. (1983). Family history study of anorexia nervosa and bulimia. *British Journal of Psychiatry, 142*; 428–429.

Holt, S., Ford, M. J., Grant, S., & Heading, R. C. (1981). Abnormal gastric emptying in primary anorexia nervosa. *British Journal of Psychiatry, 139*, 550–552.

Kaplan, A. S., Garfinkel, P. E., Darby, P. L., & Garner, D. M. (1983). Carbamazepine in the treatment of bulimia. *American Journal of Psychiatry, 140*, 1225–1226.

Kay, D. W. K. (1953). Anorexia nervosa: Studies in prognosis. *Proceedings of the Royal Society of Medicine, 46*, 669–674.

Kennedy, S., Piran, N., Owens, M., Garfinkel, P. E., & Musisi, S. (1983, September). *Anorexia nervosa and bulimia: Response to MAOI therapy.* Paper presented at the 33rd Annual Meeting of the Canadian Psychiatric Association, Ottawa.

Morgan, H. G., & Russell, G. F. M. (1975). Value of family background and clinical features as predictors of long-term outcome in anorexia nervosa: A four year follow-up study of 41 patients. *Psychological Medicine, 5*, 355–371.

Musisi, S., & Garfinkel, P. E. (1983, September). *Dexamethasone suppression test measurements in bulimia.* Paper presented at the 33rd Annual Meeting of the Canadian Psychiatric Association, Ottawa.

Paykel, E. S., Mueller, P. S., and De la Vergne, P. M. (1973). Amitriptyline, weight gain and carbohydrate craving: A side effect. *British Journal of Psychiatry, 123*, 501–507.

Piran, N., Kennedy, S., Owens, M., & Garfinkel, P. E. (1983, September). *The presence of affective disorder in patients with anorexia nervosa and bulimia.* Paper presented at the 33rd Annual Meeting of the Canadian Psychiatric Association, Ottawa.

Rakoff, V. M. (1983). Multiple determinants of family dynamics in anorexia nervosa. In P. L. Darby, P. E. Garfinkel, D. M. Garner, & D. V. Coscina (Eds.), *Anorexia nervosa: Recent developments in research* (pp. 29–40). New York: Alan R. Liss.

Russell, D. M., Freedman, M. L., Feighlin, D. H. I., Jeejeebhoy, K. N., Swinson, R. P., & Garfinkel, P. E. (1983). Delayed gastric emptying in anorexia nervosa: Improvement with domperidone. *American Journal of Psychiatry, 140*, 1235–1236.

Russell, D. M., Prendergast, P. J., Darby, P. L., Garfinkel, P. E., Whitwell, J., & Jeejeebhoy, K. N. (1983). A comparison between muscle function and body composition in anorexia nervosa: The effect of refeeding. *American Journal of Clinical Nutrition, 38*, 229–237.

Russell, G. F. M. (1977). General management of anorexia nervosa and difficulties in assessing the efficacy of treatment. In R. A. Vigersky (Ed.), *Anorexia nervosa* (pp. 277–289). New York: Raven Press.

Russell, G. F. M. (1981). The current treatment of anorexia nervosa. *British Journal of Psychiatry, 138*, 164–166.

Russell, G. F. M. (1973). The management of anorexia nervosa. In Royal College of Physicians, Edinburgh (Ed.), *Proceedings of the symposium on anorexia nervosa and obesity* (pp. 43–52). Edinburgh: T. A. Constable.

Sadavoy, J., Silver, D., & Book, H. E. (1979). Negative responses of the borderline to in-patient treatment. *American Journal of Psychotherapy, 35*, 404–417.

Selvini-Palazzoli, M. (1974). *Self-starvation*. London: Chaucer.

Silverman, J. A., & Krongrad, E. (1983). Anorexia nervosa: A cause of pericardial effusion? *Pediatric Cardiology, 4*, 125–127.

Vandereycken, W., & Pierloot, R. (1983). Combining drugs and behavior therapy in anorexia nervosa: A double-blind placebo/pimozide study. In P. L. Darby, P. E. Garfinkel, D. M. Garner, & D. V. Coscina (Eds.), *Anorexia nervosa: Recent developments in research* (pp. 365–375). New York: Alan R. Liss.

Wermuth, B. M., Davis, K. L., Hollister, L., & Stunkard, A. J. (1977). Phenytoin treatment of the binge-eating syndrome. *American Journal of Psychiatry, 134*, 1249–1253.

PART SEVEN

Multicomponent Treatment Programs

CHAPTER SIXTEEN

A Developmental Perspective on the Treatment of Anorexia Nervosa in Adolescents

MICHAEL STROBER / JOEL YAGER

The past decade has witnessed a burgeoning interest in understanding the essential nature of anorexia nervosa and the principles relevant to its treatment. These efforts have been guided by new speculations and theories, and varying points of view on the validity of different methods of intervention. Still, the human misery and confusion that surround this disorder persist. Indeed, to many, it appears that theoretical sophistication and increased acquaintance with the clinical and biological nature of anorexia nervosa have outstripped understanding of the interventions necessary to effect meaningful therapeutic change. Faced with increasing disablement and the compelling need for help, the prospective patient and her family[1] can find themselves sorting through quite disparate schools of thought and treatment methods, each over-zealously defended by its proponents as uniquely effective, despite the dearth of objective evidence to support these claims.

Considering its complex and multifactorial nature, it is hardly surprising that anorexia nervosa invites vastly different approaches to treatment. True, it is often the case that different therapeutic adaptations are necessary to address the many problems needing remediation in the patient and her family. However, while a variety of approaches have rational appeal and deserve serious consideration, we are reminded that the somatic, intrapsychic, familial, and cognitive aspects of anorexia nervosa are not equivalently independent or self-determining phenomena; rather, they interact along complex and multiple pathways (Garfinkel & Garner, 1982). For this reason, we reiterate cautions voiced by other authorities (Bruch, 1973; Crisp, 1980; Garfinkel & Garner, 1982) that adherence to theoretical rigidities, or the selective use of one treatment paradigm or another, runs the danger of rearguard and limited intervention, which bears but a tenuous relationship to long-term outcome.

---

1. Throughout this chapter, anorexic patients are referred to as female.

Michael Strober. Teenage Eating Disorders Program, Neuropsychiatric Institute, School of Medicine, University of California at Los Angeles, Los Angeles, California.

Joel Yager. Adult Outpatient Eating Disorders Program, Neuropsychiatric Institute, School of Medicine, University of California at Los Angeles, Los Angeles, California.

A DEVELOPMENTAL PERSPECTIVE ON TREATMENT THEORY AND TECHNIQUE

Our particular philosophy of treatment begins with a statement of the obvious: that anorexia nervosa and the circumstances surrounding its onset and perpetuation are inextricably tied to matters of development. In the most obvious sense, anorexia nervosa is a distinctly adolescent phenomenon—instigated, or at least set in motion, by pubertal changes, shutting down psychobiological maturation; in adaptational and existential terms, it can be viewed as an attempt, however extreme and inexplicable, to resolve the crisis of adolescent identity (Crisp, 1980). Thus, apart from the shocking and seemingly bizarre nature of their presentation, the core psychopathological elements of weight phobia and deficits in autonomy and self-regard do bear a notable parallel to normative adolescent preoccupations with physical appearance, emancipation, and mastery.

Mindful of these parallels, it is germane to approach matters of treatment through an integration of clinical observation with established developmental theory. The advantages of such a perspective are both heuristic and therapeutic. Contrasting the psychopathology of anorexic teenagers with developmental tasks normally achieved during the adolescent years brings into sharper focus the adaptive vulnerabilities that predispose the anorexic to illness, and expands our appreciation of the developmental field in which deficits in autonomous functioning and body image evolve and are played out. In this way a developmental perspective organizes clinical data more parsimoniously, and it lays the foundation for a model of treatment that has wide applicability and whose goals reflect the pursuit of deeper and meaningful change.

In restating the problem in developmental terms, we first take brief note of the major hallmarks of adolescence that prepare the individual for integration into the adult world (Blos, 1962, 1965; Malmquist, 1978; Petersen & Taylor, 1980). These are as follows:

1. The initiation of physical and sexual maturation. In addition to changes in bodily appearance and biological capacity, the advent of puberty is signaled by changes in the intensity and quality of drive activity, increased stimulus seeking, and sexualization of peer attachments.

2. Cognitive shifts from concrete operations to progressive utilization of reflective thought and propositional logic. This shift to formal operations is reflected behaviorally in the adolescent's ability to appraise and resolve dissonance, and to consider the potential for growth and change—in effect, to gain greater autonomy from the here and now.

3. Increasing physical and psychological autonomy. This is witnessed by the deidealization of and disengagement from parental values, a growing sense of one's uniqueness, and the search for physical and emotional gratification in settings outside the home.

4. The emergence of a stable and cohesive self-structure. This overarching achievement involves a synthesis of multiple developmental processes, including the internalization of self-esteem, integration of self and object representations, and the commitment to a system of personal beliefs and values.

In examining the relationship of adolescence to anorexia nervosa in a developmental framework, it becomes important, for reasons that are both theoretical and clinical, to take note of the variables that normally influence and mediate psychological adaptation to puberty. Theoretically, this informs our knowledge of vulnerability factors, as well as possible sources of heterogeneity among patients. Clinically, it suggests guidelines that give focus to and guide clinical interventions.

As summarized by Petersen and Taylor (1980), these influences are multiple and interactive. In the realm of personality, they include attitudes toward growth and maturity established throughout childhood; self-esteem anxieties; characteristic patterns of psychological defense, tension reduction, and regulation of drive and affect states; reliance on self versus environment for approval; the quality of internalized parent identifications; and focal conflicts in the area of gender acceptance and physical appearance.

Family and peer influences affecting the adolescent's acceptance or repudiation of pubertal developments have also been described. Most fateful are peer rejection and the parents' intolerance of the adolescent's unfolding unrest and emotional displays. As various students of adolescent development theorize (Blos, 1965; Kestenberg, 1968; Schonfeld, 1971), a family's imposition of strict and prohibitive controls on the adolescent's challenges and quests for separateness can arouse conflict and anxiety in regard to various aspects of pubertal development, including body change. Also germane in this regard are speculations of psychoanalytic writers (Jacobson, 1964) that, in certain cases, an adolescent's dissatisfaction with body change may signify a far deeper and primitive struggle to free himself or herself from an early and sustained fusion with parental objects by repudiating physical resemblance to that parent.

Clearly, the developmental achievements in adolescence do not proceed in smooth or continuous fashion. In actual fact, development from latency to early adulthood is characterized by certain shifts and reversals in regulative behaviors. These discontinuities become evident during the adolescent period and have been shown empirically to be predictive of adult psychological health; this suggests that they play a crucial role in mastery of drive expression (Peskin, 1972). We would suggest, therefore, that long-term prospective observations on adolescent development deserve far more attention than they have received in the clinical literature on anorexia nervosa, insofar as they shed light on the nature and directionality of developmental functions that must be therapeutically encouraged. Hence, we quote at length from Peskin and Livson (1972) concerning results from the Berkeley Guidance Study on adolescent predictors of adult psychological health:

Most dramatically, all adolescent behaviors which predict health do so in a direction opposite from their preadolescent effects. For girls, four preadolescence to adolescence sequences that maximize adult psychological health are: (1) from rare to frequent whining, (2) from high to low self-confidence, (3) from independence to dependence, and (4) from impulse control to explosive temper. . . . Children who carry into adolescence no outer evidence of unrest appear to have built up excessive defenses against the quantitative increase in drive activity. . . . These "inconsistencies," or developmental transformations, take on the appearance of detours or disruptions, where autonomy and mastery in preadolescence is apparently given up for adolescent passivity and emotionality. . . . In Deutsch's ego terms, the girl's development of ego strength in preadolescence allows her to experience the affectivity of adolescence without ordinarily being overwhelmed by its emergence. In short, the ego's capacity for impulse control makes it safe to bring such expression to the surface. . . . It is just such tolerance for affect and control that females low on psychologic health cannot sustain in adolescence. The lowest scores . . . belong to girls who moved toward more control, i.e., who became less whiny, more self-confident, more independent, and less explosive as they moved into the adolescent period. Theirs was a more iron-clad defense against affective states, as if a permissive attitude toward them would have led to uncontrolled regressions. The peremptory quality of this resistance to pubertal affect implies that these girls had failed to experience the sense of preadolescent confidence and competence upon which the safety to explore feelings of passivity is based. (pp. 347–349)

To summarize, we would propose that these developmental notions bring fresh awareness to the adaptational deficiencies that render the adolescent vulnerable to anorexic pathology. Put succinctly, it is these very hallmarks of pubertal adaptation and adult psychological health — the formation of a stable self-structure, tolerance of ambiguity and emotional intensity, and increasing plasticity of cognitive–psychological functioning — that are absent, or at least incompletely formed or consolidated, in the anorexic teenager (Strober, 1981). Against the backdrop of inhibited self-expression and the unstinting pursuit of external recognition, adolescence imposes heavy challenges and adds new burdens to vulnerability already sensed. In the face of these pressures, maturation is viewed as painfully disruptive and intrusive — a further catalyst to fears of exploitation and control by outside elements (Casper, 1982; Goodsitt, 1977; Selvini-Palazzoli, 1978). Thus, however ruthless and brutalizing it may seem to others, self-starvation is positively valued: It serves as an affirmation of discipline and self-determination, dampens threatening signals of physical change, and greatly simplifies matters of existence (Crisp, 1980).

As a point of departure, this framework also suggests something of the therapeutic mechanisms of change relevant to the anorexic patient — specifically, increasing openness to drive and affective experience; greater tolerance of the uncertainties of change and growth; encouragement of introspection, abstractness of thought, and realistic appraisal of limitations, competencies, and potentials; increased understanding of experiential and dynamic factors inhibiting separation–individuation; and acceptance of a therapeutic relationship that combines dependency with security as a necessary prerequisite for independence. In short, therapy must work toward the establishment of developmental trends that normally link adolescent achievements to a healthy adult adjustment.

FROM THEORY TO TREATMENT: PARAMETERS OF INTERVENTION

The parameters and goals of treatment may now be considered in greater depth.

Multicomponent Treatment Structure

It is an inescapable fact that no single modality of treatment is apt to be sufficiently comprehensive to address the problems inherent to anorexia nervosa. Hence, our philosophy is that treatment is best served by exposure to diverse treatment methods — individual, medical–nutritional, family, and group. We do not advocate such exposure because we feel more is better, because we question the comparative worth of any one approach, because we strive to avoid partisan dichotomies, or because we advocate the principle of specificity — that patients naturally favor certain treatments over others. Rather, we believe that these multiple contexts for expression and behavior change are interdependent, and that their use reflects an appreciation of the need for change at intrapsychic, family, and peer group levels. In this respect, the treatment program is comprehensive and multidimensional; the foci, process, and structure inherent in these efforts are believed to enhance, stimulate, or recapture lines of development that have been arrested or delayed.

Also, from a more strictly dynamic point of view, such a treatment structure has the advantage of reducing a tendency—not uncommon among adolescents generally, but often problematic for anorexic patients—to channel involvement and dependency demands unilaterally onto one person. Ultimately, the success of these many different efforts hinges on the presence of a core professional staff whose members adhere to a reasonably consistent and uniform treatment philosophy. In the absence of such integration, therapeutic efforts in one area may run the danger of being nullified by treatment aims in another.

For ease of exposition, general goals and technical aspects of each modality are described separately.

Restoration of Body Weight

On this point there is general agreement, although we recognize that there is no single ideal formula for its accomplishment. However, within our framework, the functions and implications of weight restoration deserve closer scrutiny. First, starvation debilitates the patient, physiologically and mentally. From a purely functional standpoint, the recovery of body weight is necessary to reduce starvation-induced perseveration and concreteness of thought, obsessionality, and depression. In short, without some capacity for reflective comprehension and experiencing at more abstract levels, a psychotherapeutic process cannot exist. Second, the more normal hormone status and physical appearance brought on by weight gain revives maturational anxieties associated with feeling states and relational issues not previously accessible in the psychobiologically regressed state. In essence, the patient is now pressed to make use of more developmentally mature adjustive methods to cope with reawakened maturational conflicts. Clearly, this is a delicate time. As feelings of passivity and ineffectiveness return, the patient is likely to view weight gain as a destructive attack, and may increase her resistance to examining her vulnerabilities more directly. Yet, at the same time, the "crisis" serves to heighten the patient's emotional involvement with the therapist, to bring into focus her fear of dependence on others for support, and to highlight the ways in which she has psychologically distanced herself from others. These points are illustrated by the following excerpt from the third week of treatment of a 16-year-old anorexic who had been ill nearly 18 months.

PATIENT (*in tears, appearing frantic*): I can't stand the way I look; how can you sit there and tell me I'm not fat? You're supposed to help me, not torture me.

THERAPIST: This is going to be a difficult period; it's going to test your ability to accept my word that you will not become fat.

PATIENT: Why should I trust your word?

THERAPIST: I don't anticipate that you can trust very much of anything—my words, your body, your parents, or yourself. (*Long pause.*) It's frightening to think that you need to rely on my support and reassurance, isn't it?

PATIENT: Yes. (*Continues to sob.*)

THERAPIST: Are you afraid that I'll deceive you, or trick you — that I won't be honest?

PATIENT: I don't know; I really don't know you.

THERAPIST: That's true, but you haven't permitted yourself to know anyone, and you've already told me that you won't let anyone get close to you.

PATIENT: I like it that way.

THERAPIST: I imagine that your weight gain makes it more difficult for you to set yourself apart from others.

PATIENT: I don't want to be like other people or look like them; why can't I be left to do what I want?

THERAPIST: You can't escape being human, even though to look like other girls, to feel the same things as they feel, is so frightening.

Finally, weight restoration is necessary to reduce what is an intolerable anxiety for parents and siblings — an anxiety that overburdens their capacities, and only encourages further blurring of boundaries and avoidance of change. As noted elsewhere (Yager, 1981), while anorexia nervosa may reveal defensive operations of the family in bold relief, the continuing fear and tension it creates can deplete its resources and strengths and can encourage further enmeshment. Plagued by what they sense is an intractable and potentially fatal situation, members remain frozen in an undifferentiated state, unable to examine the disharmonies that perpetuate it.

Individual Psychotherapy

In working with anorexic teenagers, we are compelled to agree with other writers (Bruch, 1979; Kalucy, 1978; Selvini-Palazzoli, 1978) that classical psychoanalytic techniques are to be avoided. However, our basic formula is dynamic; it involves the recognition, analysis, and resolution of persistent distress created by patterns of thought, coping, attribution, and relatedness that are limiting and maladaptive. The goals are to foster autonomy, tolerance of affective expression, uncertainty, psychobiological maturity, and a durable sense of mastery.

Naturally, this will involve many nuances of process and technique. In a dynamic and structural sense (and in keeping with our developmental frame of reference), the therapeutic relationship provides critical holding functions (Winnicott, 1965): The therapist, without threatening intrusion and loss of identity, remains empathically tuned to the patient's needs and fears, intuits her inner "voice," absorbs her experiences of frustration and internal disruption, and tolerates her rage and ambivalence. This is especially crucial during early phases of treatment, when suspicion and control struggles abound, and dependency is resisted.

THERAPIST (*speaking to a 15-year-old anorexic female who has come to acknowledge her terror of loss of control, and of being "faceless"*): I know this may be difficult for you to believe, but I can try to understand something of your fears.

PATIENT: I don't talk about my feelings; I never did.

THERAPIST: Do you think I'll respond like others?

PATIENT: What do you mean?

THERAPIST: I think you may be afraid that I won't pay close attention to what you feel inside, or that I'll tell you not to feel the way you do — that it's foolish to feel frightened, to feel fat, to doubt yourself, considering how well you do in school, how you're appreciated by teachers, how pretty you are.

PATIENT (*looking somewhat tense and agitated*): Well, I was always told to be polite and respect other people, just like a stupid, faceless doll (*affecting a vacant, doll-like pose*).

THERAPIST: Do I give you the impression that it would be disrespectful for you to share your feelings, whatever they may be?

PATIENT: Not really; I don't know.

THERAPIST: I can't, and won't, tell you that this is easy for you to do. I imagine that you've felt that because things often seemed easy in the past, you never really believed you could take control when things got stressful, as they typically are in adolescence. But I can promise you that you are free to speak your mind, and that I won't turn away.

As noted earlier, although adolescence naturally evokes powerful strivings toward separation–individuation, dependency needs are still centered on parental figures. For the anorexic, however, the struggle against passivity and for self-determination is reflected in her scorn of dependence on others (Casper, 1982). Likewise, the relationship with the therapist is not infrequently marked by intense ambivalence, embodying all the classic elements of transference. Thus, the dynamics of transference can have cogent significance for the majority of the young anorexics we see, who ultimately declare, though with considerable reluctance, their need for acknowledgment and substantiation. The therapist's recognition of these needs (such acknowledgment does not imply indulgence) and their transferential elements is integral to other efforts aimed at building genuine self-acceptance and autonomous functioning. These points are illustrated in the following excerpt, taken from the 16th week of treatment of a 17-year-old anorexic patient.

PATIENT (*sounding bitter*): I always get hurt when I get close to people.

THERAPIST: Does that apply to everyone — friends, parents, teachers?

PATIENT: Everyone.

THERAPIST: And what exactly is this hurt that you speak of?

PATIENT: Disappointment.

THERAPIST: You're not being very clear. Do you feel the need to be guarded now — with me?

PATIENT: No.

THERAPIST: How is it with you here — our talking together like this for the past several months?

PATIENT: This is different; you're different.

THERAPIST (*feigning a look of confusion*): Do I take that as a compliment or a curse?

PATIENT (*smiling*): You know what I mean.

THERAPIST: Yes, I think I do. I think you're saying it's easier for you to talk and be understood here; it's very different from what takes place at home with your parents. You can feel more genuine.

PATIENT: My parents don't express their feelings. Nobody talks at home.

THERAPIST: How do you think this affected you? My sense of it is that you came to believe that feelings are intolerable; that you had to be controlled and disciplined.

PATIENT: Discipline! I hate that word! I hate trying to control everything.

THERAPIST: And yet you believed that it was a way to gain approval, to fight off the fear of being unacceptable.

PATIENT: I was always angry. I never let it show.

THERAPIST: And if you had let your anger show?

PATIENT: I don't think they could handle it.

THERAPIST: You doubt your ability to tolerate your feelings as much as you doubt your parents' ability to be emotional.

PATIENT: I guess that's true.

THERAPIST: Are you still distant from your feelings?

PATIENT: Not like before, but I still feel unsure about myself.

The session continued with a discussion of how the patient's low self-esteem and denial of affect and personal needs were related to attitudes toward control and dieting. The transferential elements in the excerpt given above are self-evident.

Although the therapist does his or her best to be a reliable and soothing figure, it is plainly necessary to take note of and actively to challenge faulty modes of construing and thinking. Indeed, a vitally important aspect of treatment is the modeling of an apparatus for logical and reality-oriented thinking, perceiving, and hypothesis testing so as to mediate better between inner needs and outer reality (Bruch, 1978, 1979; Garner & Bemis, 1982). Though conceptually distinct, the dynamic and cognitive dimensions of therapy are pursued simultaneously in practice, and are synthetic. For teenagers in particular, the readiness to accept, (without feeling ridicule) therapeutic confrontations designed to bring maladaptive patterns into focus, and to utilize these insights to behave differently, hinges on the therapist's empathic availability and capacity to instill trust.

The brief example that follows illustrates an attempt to reframe the meaning and functional significance of dietary restriction and body image distortion in one patient. The excerpt is from the fourth week of treatment of a 16-year-old patient, who was 157.5 cm (5 ft 2 in) tall and weighed 44.6 kg (98 lb) at the time. Note how the therapist makes parallel use of cognitive and dynamic approaches in guiding the patient from concretistic thought and perception to redefinition at a more abstract level of conceptualizations.

THERAPIST: You express a fear of being too heavy — of needing to watch what you eat or else you'll get fat. Am I understanding you correctly?

PATIENT: Yes, I'm fat. Can't you see? (*Gesturing at her stomach.*)

THERAPIST: What I can see is that we have very different perceptions about the way you look. I suspect it may be difficult for others to see what you do, in the same way that you don't permit others to know what you think or feel. (*The therapist avoids debate and overt disagreement, but instead relates perceptual disturbance to other aspects of the patient's behavior.*)

PATIENT: I know my mother thinks I'm fat; I can tell she sees it.

THERAPIST: So you think she's deceiving you? Why, if she truly thought you were too heavy, does she express concern about your physical condition? Is she always this difficult to read?

PATIENT: No, she doesn't want to hurt my feelings; she's a very sensitive person.

THERAPIST: She senses you're in some distress. What is it that she senses? I think it's unfortunate that her sensitivity makes it difficult to be straightforward and honest.

PATIENT: I don't know; I'm not really sure.

THERAPIST: Do you think it concerns your physical condition, or has she been concerned about your troubles at school, or your withdrawal? If, just for the moment, we set aside your concern about becoming fat, has it been a difficult time for you — say, the last 2 months? (*The therapist redefines the context of the patient's symptoms.*)

PATIENT: In a way, I guess.

THERAPIST: You can't be sure of what you have been feeling?

PATIENT: I know.

THERAPIST: That's a good sign, then. But maybe it's difficult for you to talk about it. You've felt the need to keep things under wraps for quite a while. In a way, considering how depressed and lonely you've been, how much you've worried about your parents — how hard they are working, all the strain of taking care of the kids — it's remarkable that you've held out so long. You have strength when it comes to putting up a front.

PATIENT: I just couldn't do everything; help out at home, finish my school work. I never had time for friends. That's why I stopped eating.

THERAPIST: So it [the dieting] had something to do with being overwhelmed — of not feeling right inside. Once it started, how did the dieting make you feel? (*The symptom is reframed and redefined.*)

PATIENT: I didn't feel anything. I don't know what you mean.

THERAPIST: Did you notice that you felt worse, or maybe better, after you started to diet?

PATIENT: Better.

THERAPIST: How would you describe "better"? Say it in a way that would make it clear to me what you felt.

PATIENT: I felt better about myself, that's all.

THERAPIST: Other girls say that dieting makes them feel a new kind of discipline, a success — something that no one, other than yourself, can control.

PATIENT: Yeah, that's a good description.

THERAPIST: You don't want to give that up, do you — the feeling of success, of being able to resist and fight off pressures from others?

PATIENT: Why should I? What's wrong with feeling those things?

THERAPIST: You're saying something different now about the dieting, about your reasons for it. Can you sense that?

PATIENT: Well, maybe I wasn't fat when I started, but if I keep going I will be. (*Displaying more anger.*)

THERAPIST: So if you convince yourself that you are indeed fat, you have a justification for continuing to do what makes you feel in control; it helps you feel less unsure about yourself. (*At this point, there is a long pause.*) You've got to believe that because you're afraid you have no other way to cope — to be in control, or effective.

The session continued with the patient alternating between protest and begrudging acknowledgment of her fragile self-esteem and compliance with parent wishes. The therapist persisted in gently pointing out how difficult it was for her to "think" about her situation in emotional terms, at the same time noting the pain she was experiencing.

In essence, we think of the individual psychotherapy in developmental terms as an adaptation-evoking context (Langs, 1982), which provides sound holding and containment for patients with extreme mistrust of their physical self and inner needs. The creation of and adherence to this frame of reference conveys, over time, an inherent security that invites previously resisted feelings of passivity and dependency to emerge and become acceptable. Again, noting that the normal developmental sequence in adolescence reveals control and security giving way to affectivity and introspection (Peskin & Livson, 1972), the psychotherapeutic process confronts these rigidly inflexible, constricted, and externally bound teenagers with a sense of their internal state—as something that defies attempts at easy categorization, that is abstract, and that is evolving. Insofar as the therapist demands nothing materially, sets no performance standards, and expresses no disappointment, the emergence of these feelings is less threatening to the patient, since she does not sense, as she has so frequently in the past, that some vital aspect of her self must be sacrificed or denied to obtain recognition or acceptance. Some of these points are noted in the following exchange with a 16-year-old patient who had been anorexic since age 13 and was in her 10th month of treatment.

PATIENT: Giving up my anorexia is like giving up my identity. I feel totally lost without it.

THERAPIST: Your identity is an illness?

PATIENT: In many ways it is—was, maybe.

THERAPIST: You seem uncertain. Do you feel like you're in a state of transition? That's my impression.

PATIENT: Yeah.

THERAPIST: But uncertain.

PATIENT: Yeah.

THERAPIST: Do you feel threatened by it?

PATIENT: By what? The uncertainty?

THERAPIST: The uncertainty that usually goes with learning about yourself.

PATIENT: Sometimes I do, but then I think it's good.

THERAPIST: How so?

PATIENT: Well, I'm not like I was. I hated it—always thinking about others and being rigid.

THERAPIST: I don't really see how you can be certain about your identity. It seems that you're beginning—God forbid—to become like many other teenagers.

PATIENT: What do you mean?

THERAPIST: Considering who you are—your future, values, things like that. There aren't any clear, easy answers to these things.

PATIENT: I can see that.

Family Therapy

Apart from matters of diagnosis and classification, anorexia nervosa cannot be viewed as a fixed or self-contained entity. When the family is viewed as a self-regulating system with characteristic transactions, redundancies in communication, and subsystems composed of members aligned by age, role, and other common qualities, the anorexic patient's symptoms can be thought of as being evoked, supported, and reinforced by certain system transactions; the symptoms can be seen to play a part in the family system's entire psychological economy. Yet, while family system formulations may help to explain how symptoms can be provoked and sustained once they appear, they do not account specifically for the appearance of anorexia nervosa, except for those rare families in which there is modeling of anorexic symptoms by a relative. Nor do they account for intermediate mechanisms whereby these family patterns might bring about the altered self-perception, desire for thinness, early amenorrhea, behavioral hyperactivity, and other clinical features of the syndrome. Thus, unlike other writers (e.g., Minuchin, Rosman, & Baker, 1978), we consider family therapy as one component of a total, multimodal treatment plan. Certainly, many of the developmental formulations described above provide a clear rationale for family therapy. To the extent that such family operations as enmeshment, overprotectiveness, rigidity, avoidance of conflict, weight preoccupation, and the like are thought to be pathogenic or even only sustaining of symptoms, then a determined attempt to alter these operations, either directly or by working through their psychopathological underpinnings, might reasonably promise therapeutic benefit.

Goals for family therapy have been implied in much of the previous discussion. With respect to individuals within the family, the first intention is to maintain each person's self-esteem and to help each person deal with issues of worry, panic, and shame that derive from the impact of the anorexic process on the family. In general, family therapy strives to help each family member (including the patient) become more autonomous and less enmeshed, to strengthen appropriate coalitions, and to enable family members to resolve conflicts at their proper locus, usually generation boundaries. Such therapy will attend to the concerns, anxieties, and depression in each family member — features that may have preceded or may be consequent to the appearance of anorexic symptoms. Over time, the family is assisted in allowing the adolescent to develop autonomy, to individuate, and to function independently. To this end, the therapist insists that members assume responsibility for their own views and desires; overdirective patterns are pointed out and interrupted; triangulations, detouring maneuvers, and coalitions are pointed out and scrutinized for their dynamic meaning and function; individual autonomy and spontaneity of emotional expression are underscored and provoked.

As is so often the case with psychological disorders, the family constellations associated with anorexia nervosa are variable. A review of our families suggests two broad groupings. In one, a centripetal process occurs, which is typically expressed through excessive cohesion. The hallmarks of this pattern are lack of permissiveness, reduced emotional expressivity, and limits placed on outside contacts. Generally speaking, the need for cohesion is extreme, due to the enormous threat posed by separation. By way of contrast, a significant number of the families we see are highly conflicted or broken well before the onset of anorexic symptoms. Relationships are typically characterized by threats of abandonment, clinging dependency, expressions of disappointment, or angry demands; marital discord is openly apparent, and there are predominant themes of dyscontrol.

The therapeutic implications of these system differences are self-evident. Our point is that interventions need to be empirically pragmatic and guided by individual family assessments. Increasing elasticity of functioning, encouraging spontaneity, and

promoting separation may be a fitting set of goals for one family type; a more controlled and rigid expression of affect, and increased proximity between members, will
be sought for another.

Group Therapy

The group setting offers an approximation of the normal developmental experience
of exploring and experimenting with emotional involvement outside the family, as
well as of confronting disillusionments with parents that have interfered with individual
commitments. In actual fact, the functions served by group treatment are multiple,
and are fueled by gains established in the individual and family arenas. These include
the recognition and examination of deficits in self-expression, dependence on external
objects for guidance and affirmation of self, confused and uncertain personal and
social values, and family conflicts that have stood in the way of individuation. The
group setting is particularly helpful to those adolescents who are socially phobic: For
many, this is the first experience of sharing "secrets" and disillusionment with themselves and others.

Equally important, it has been our experience that the anorexic's tendency toward
denial or minimization often yields more readily to peer confrontation in this setting.
To this end, the therapist initially orients group members to the discomforts generated
by starvation and the toll it has taken on school functioning, family, and peer relations. Invariably, these teenagers acknowledge relief in being able to unburden themselves. Further challenging resistance and perceptual distortions, the therapist notes
the paradox of how perceptive and helpful each group member can be in unsolicited
observations about others, while remaining so apparently distorted in her own self-
view. Gradually, this is reframed as but another example of increased sensitivity to
external surroundings at the expense of self-understanding, and it is discussed against
the backdrop of what has otherwise been a rather isolated or sham social existence.
As group interactions become more relaxed and nonthreatening, deeper and more intimate self-revelations are encouraged. This taking of perspectives is painful for the
majority of patients, although the capacity to render more autonomous and genuine
statements concerning identity issues is a necessary ingredient for developmental progress and continuing growth.

THERAPIST: This must seem very odd to all of you. You look at yourself and you
see fat. You look at the person sitting next to you and you are shocked. (*All of the
patients note this discrepancy.*)

PATIENT 1: Yeah, that's so strange. The same thing happens when I look at a
picture of myself—you know, taken when I was thin.

THERAPIST: Are you suggesting that you are no longer thin? Group, help her out.

PATIENT 2: You're not as thin as before, but you're far from overweight!

PATIENT 1: Okay, when I was thinner. I still can't understand that. Why does
it happen?

THERAPIST: I can't say that I have an answer. However, in many ways it's like
other aspects of your behavior—you know, the way you act: being more tuned into
others—what they want or expect of you—and overlooking the meaning or importance
of what you are experiencing. No wonder you're all so confused.

ESTABLISHING THE THERAPEUTIC ALLIANCE

A common assumption that runs through much of the psychiatric literature on adolescence is that barriers to treatment loom large. As we know all too well, the anorexic patient and her family require a great deal of the therapist, whose task is fraught with innumerable difficulties and challenges. Thus, the therapist working with this population requires a number of attributes to move the process along without serious disruption or premature termination.

First, it is essential for any clinician undertaking this work to command an extensive knowledge of the anorexic condition — its developmental antecedents, biological correlates, and the family experiences believed to permit and maintain its symptoms. The therapist cannot hold back impressions or appear evasive; nor can he or she appear disapproving or critical of the patient's or family's perspective. Rather, the therapist must be able and prepared to respond to questions directly, and to instill trust and confidence.

Coupled with this openness, attributes facilitative of work with the anorexic are not different from those germane to therapeutic work with adolescents generally. These include a firm grasp of therapeutic principles, a mode of relatedness that conveys empathy, tolerance of painful emotion and challenges to the therapeutic contract, and extreme patience. The treatment of anorexics is tedious and patchy. The therapist must be able to keep in check any impulse to blame or scold — to see the patient as stubborn, spoiled, or manipulative — or to act precipitously to alleviate the patient's suffering with promises or quick remedies. He or she must also be intuitive, and must know how to monitor and pace interventions — when to probe gently and when to hold back and wait patiently. Above all, the therapist must evidence genuine spontaneity and humor, along with a flair for the dramatic — characteristics deeply felt and shared by adolescents generally, and needing to be evoked in the anorexic. Thus, the therapists who tend toward strict neutrality and distance, who are rigid, who are put off by challenges and provocation, or who require some tangible evidence of the fruits of their labor may be ill-suited for work with this population, and are well advised to avoid it.

There are critical tasks, both initiated and accomplished, in the first contact with the patient. In our center, the first session is focused explicitly on establishment of rapport, a sense of confidence, and therapeutic alliance. It is almost invariably the case that the family arrives for the initial visit apprehensive, or in a state of panic; many fear that this will only continue a prior pattern of fault-finding, ridicule, and blame. Similarly, the patient often assumes she is to blame for every trouble and is loath to reveal the truth about herself or family circumstances. Considering the residual harm each family member has experienced from past treatment failures (90% of our patients have previous treatment contacts), the therapist is cognizant of being scrutinized very closely. At this point, discussion of these experiences and the probable consequences of each is useful. In so doing, we empathize with their confusion and move to soften the harsh judgments under which they labor.

Deferring assessment until later, we begin with a most comprehensive discussion of the syndrome — its history, biological and clinical characteristics, relation to developmental stresses, association with impaired self-esteem and autonomous functioning, and common family correlates. We first retrace the preadolescent experiences common to the girls we work with: apparently stable and functioning well in school; studious; respectful of others; good-natured and unusually sensitive to the needs of others, and concerned about the adequacy of their performance; rarely disruptive, yet often shy or emotionally reserved. The therapist goes on to state that from the girls now in treatment with us, we know that this period was not entirely trouble-free. Rather, it was a time of self-doubt, which the patient concealed from others who she felt would not understand or accept; during this period, she constantly questioned whether the praise and admiration she received was deserved, whether she could continue to live up to other people's expectations of her, and whether she was truly capable of any independent thought or action. We go on to note how this painful self-appraisal still causes her to fear any hint of dependence on others, even though she remains very sensitive to her surroundings and the rules governing "proper" behavior. In this context, we then describe how and why dieting and weight loss have come to be so central a concern in her life: It restores a sense of discipline, control, and specialness; it is something that few people can accomplish with ease, and something that resists control by others; it is a statement that she can do what she wants in her own way. The therapist then proceeds to describe the natural evolution of the disorder, and the types of cognitive and physiological discomforts the patient may well be experiencing, due to her starved state.

In building up this developmental and clinical picture to reveal the symptoms in their true light, the therapist continues by discussing the immense influences that different patterns of family interaction can have on each member; the role played by parents in the child's development of self-esteem and preparation for independent functioning, critical in adolescence; the ways in which the designated patient's condition now affects the family structure; and the ways in which this present stress may function to bring underlying tensions to the surface. Of late, our experience is that when this area is broached, the patient and her family concede (albeit with some reluctance) to the notion that the teenager's symptoms make some sense in terms of the prior events and family circumstances that are now being described, and display a willingness to explore the problem further along these lines. Of course, for some parents such ideas are unpalatable and rejected as irrelevant or nonsensical. Some eventually alter their opinions with time; some remain intractable.

The evaluation proceeds with individual assessments of the teenager and her parents. With the teenager, we use a detailed structured interview to obtain information on the following:

- The chronology of anorexic symptoms
- Precipitating factors associated with dieting
- Degree of preoccupation with food and calories, and involvement in food preparation
- Weight history
- Topography of eating behavior (e.g., periods of abstinence, extent of dietary restriction, periodicity and duration of eating binges, temporal aspects of feeding, meal content and calorie intake, precipitants of eating binges, vomiting behavior
- Evidence of substance abuse, including laxatives and diuretics
- Attitudes toward physical body development, sexuality, femininity, and ideal body weight
- Personal-developmental traits (e.g., shyness, separation anxiety, reactions to novelty and change, emotional restriction, perfectionistic strivings, general temperament, compulsivity, capacity for independent thought and action, reliance on others, locus of control, socialization patterns)

• Evidence of concomitant or previous nonanorexic psychopathology, especially depression, mania, obsessive illness, and depersonalization (assessed using the Schedule for Affective Disorders and Schizophrenia—Spitzer & Endicott, 1975)
• Current capacity for emotional separation from parents and autonomous functioning
• Future aspirations and goals
• Perceptions of strengths, interests, and hobbies
• Current peer relations (number of friends, quality of relatedness, frequency of contacts spontaneously initiated)
• Regulation of drives, affect, and impulses (e.g., evidence of self-mutilative acts, suicidality, degree of irritability or brittleness of affect, sexual acting out)
• Quality of object relationships (e.g., detachment, object constancy, degree of empathy)
• Perception of individual family members and overall family structure
• Concerns, hopes, fears, and motivation in respect to treatment and the prospect of weight gain

The teenager also completes the Eating Disorder Inventory (Garner, Olmsted, & Polivy, 1983), which is used to derive factor scores for the major anorexic symptom clusters.

In meeting with the parents, we assess the following:

• Individual perceptions of their children (e.g., strengths, weaknesses) and aspects of each child's behavior they admire or find troublesome
• Their aspirations for the children
• Their views on adolescence (e.g., emancipation, contacts outside the home, sexuality)
• Impact of their daughter's illness on the family life style, marital relationship, and family relations generally (e.g., activation of separation fears, abandonment, etc.)
• Their own personal-developmental histories (early self-esteem and maturational problems, relationship with parents and siblings, ongoing intergenerational problems)
• Familial psychiatric disorders
• General organizational structure of the family (e.g., power structure, parental coalitions, clarity of boundaries, efficiency of problem solving and negotiation, clarity of expression of individual thoughts and emotions, responsibility for individual actions, degree of emotional closeness among members, expressiveness, general emotional tone, degree and intensity of conflict, and degree of empathic responsiveness; see Lewis, 1978)

Throughout this phase of the evaluation, the therapist remains respectful of the patient's and parents' need and right to be informed, and never hesitates to discuss the relevance of the information being sought to the patient's condition and the family's treatment needs.

Upon completion of the individual evaluation sessions, the therapist summarizes the historical information presented, pinpoints the nature of the patient's and family system's problems, and formulates treatment plans for the teenager individually and the family collectively. In this respect, the rationale, function, and potential benefits of individual, group, and family therapies are detailed along the lines described above. It is most important that the therapist alert family members to the possibly stressful changes in their accustomed equilibrium that may result from treatment initiatives, while providing reassurance of his or her continuing availability. At the same time, the risks of superficial and hasty treatment are noted; the idea is reinforced that symptomatic relief measured in weight gain cannot be the principal criterion for judging resolution of individual or systemic conflicts.

In principle, the therapist has already accomplished a number of operations during this initial encounter. The basic approach—conveyed through word and demeanor—has been inherently and implicitly supportive, recognizing and carefully measuring the patient's exquisite sensitivity to control issues and fears of intrusion. Without directly challenging the patient's point of view or her denial (to do so would only amplify mistrust and resistance), the therapist has decisively reframed the meaning, derivation, and context of her weight phobia and bodily symptoms; furthermore, in noting that the information presented on the disorder and its significance reflects insights coming from other patients and families now benefiting from treatment, the therapist holds out the prospect of active involvement, improved self-understanding, and change, while emphasizing the importance of therapeutic collaboration. Last, the dual process of seeing the teenager individually and the family as a whole brings into focus two complementary treatment objectives: (1) the teenager's gradual disengagement from parents and reliance on outside supports to assist her progression toward greater separation and individuation, and (2) the realignment of family boundaries along more maturationally appropriate and functionally adaptive developmental lines. In doing this, the therapist has, in effect, depicted anorexia nervosa simultaneously as a sign of individual maladjustment and as a sign of systemic disruption.

DETERMINING LOCUS OF TREATMENT: OUTPATIENT MANAGEMENT

Anorexia nervosa represents a broad range of presenting symptomatology and family dysfunction (Strober, 1983). These variabilities inevitably give rise to questions concerning the ideal setting for initiating and fostering change. Over the years, we have found that patients meeting the following general criteria are likely to respond favorably to outpatient treatment:

1. Evidence of insight into anorexic cognitions and behaviors
2. Expressed motivation to change and to tolerate anxieties inherent in weight gain without significant regression or decompensation
3. Evidence of meaningful and sustained peer relationships and ability to be affectually responsive to the therapist
4. Absence of severe depression, suicidal ideation, characterological defects, or metabolic instabilities resulting from vomiting or use of purgatives
5. Weight loss not exceeding 25% of ideal weight
6. Family commitment to treatment and parental support and encouragement of the patient–therapist alliance.

Once outpatient treatment is believed possible, a more specific contract is established. For the majority of patients, this involves being seen twice a week, in one individual and one family session, and participating in group therapy on a biweekly basis.

However, our general practice is to begin by seeing the teenager and other family members, individually and in subsystems (teenager and siblings; parents). In this way the therapist begins slowly to challenge enmeshment, assures the differentiation of family members, and demarcates the naturally occurring boundaries within the family. It is important to bear in mind that when family members are seen alone, each may appear at least somewhat different to the therapist than when seen in the context of the whole family. To be seen alone invites the teenager, her siblings, and her parents to share sentiments, fears, complaints, and secrets they may not yet be comfortable addressing in a whole-family meeting, where they may feel unbearable guilt or intimidation by other individuals or coalitions. Frequently, meetings with individual family members allow the therapist to gauge more accurately the characteristic transactions taking place among family members. Most importantly, these initial individual sessions afford each family member an opportunity to develop a trusting dyadic relationship with the therapist. In sum, when all family members are viewed sympathetically and heard out, and their plight and self-perceptions are acknowledged, an arena of safety is established that enables the family sessions to be more fruitful and communications to occur less defensively and with less venom. Generally speaking, family therapy proper begins between the second and fourth week of treatment.

Managing Diet and Weight

As noted, the decision to begin treatment outside the hospital presupposes some commitment on the patient's part, however tenuous, to the restoration of body weight. Our strategy, one that has been practical and successful, is to have the patient's weight, diet, and overall physical status monitored initially on a weekly basis by a pediatrician–nutritionist team that is highly experienced in the medical and psychological aspects of anorexia nervosa. The team, operating with the absolute support of the therapist, establishes a target weight (approximately 90% of average for age and height); when necessary, it provides menu planning and didactic information and feedback relevant to the patient's often distorted ideas on nutrition and mechanisms of digestion. As Garfinkel and Garner (1982) recommend, we take great care in this initial phase (especially with the premorbidly overweight patient) to elicit the patient's fear of potential obesity that is being set in motion by weight restoration, and we provide continual reassurance that her weight gain and dietary needs will be closely monitored and carefully moderated until self-control is firmly established. The patient is further reassured that under no circumstances will the target weight be increased as therapy progresses, and that if it proves too difficult to stem the weight loss or to restore body weight gradually, it will be essential to lend added support and structure by continuing treatment in the hospital. Under such circumstances, hospitalization is recommended by the therapist without equivocation.

Initially, the prescribed caloric content of the patient's diet is what is sufficient to maintain weight at its current level. By not emphasizing or enforcing immediacy of weight gain, we move quickly to allay the patient's worst fear: that, despite words to the contrary, she will be deceived; that the therapist's main and unspoken goal is breaking her resolve and forcing her capitulation — forcing her into our own framework of rules and opinions about normal body weight and physical appearance. In addition, it serves to reiterate a point made earlier: that change, if meaningful, is inevitably slow and tedious. Thus, in these initial weeks, it is crucial to acknowledge the patient's possible mistrust of therapeutic intentions and fears of deception, and her dread of "giving up" the sense of virtue, potency, effectiveness, purity, and autonomy of control previously achieved through dietary restriction and weight loss.

At some juncture, usually after 3 to 4 weeks, it can usually be determined whether or not the patient has been responding and will continue to respond favorably to therapeutic efforts at establishing secure ground rules and boundaries in the outpatient program. If so, calories are increased in graduated fashion to establish a slow yet steady rate of weight gain. The patient is weighed only once a week, yet is encouraged to check herself at home more frequently if this will help temporize fears of loss of control. Meetings with the pediatrician and nutritionist continue during this period to reinforce the importance of normalized and sensible eating habits and to challenge behaviors that are obviously deviant. For patients with binge eating, nutritional, cognitive, and behavioral strategies (Fairburn, 1981; Garfinkel & Garner, 1982) are implemented as necessary to promote and reinforce improved self-regulation. On the average, and depending on the absolute amount of weight gain necessary, it will require between 2 and 5 months for the patient to achieve her target weight on this program.

The Progress of Therapy

During this middle phase of treatment, the therapist and patient establish a fresh perspective on the dynamic and experiential underpinnings of her distorted sense of personal worth and value, her compliant manner, and her inhibition of self and affective expression. Through the therapist's more active use of cognitive–behavioral maneuvers (Garner & Bemis, 1982) and inductive questioning, coupled with increasingly intensified support of the patient's efforts at introspective exploration, individuated thoughts, impulses, and feeling states are authenticated and explored against the backdrop of previous self-attributions of inadequacy and extreme dependence on external standards of performance and accomplishment.

Of course, movement in this direction is complemented by therapeutic efforts in the group and family areas as well. The group therapy is now providing a measured and safe environment for enactment of developmentally mature attempts at assertion, genuine self-expression and disclosure, and discussion of interpersonal and psychosexual concerns, especially fears of identity confusion in times of closeness and intimacy. By the same token, more active steps are undertaken in family therapy to provoke open and spontaneous displays of affect and personal opinion, and to uncover more deeply rooted and threatening conflicts fueling the family's static expectations and tendencies toward enmeshing, overcontrolling, intrusive, or distancing behaviors and dysfunctional communications. In this respect it becomes clear that as the patient's symptomatic behavior continues to recede, a redefinition of the problem originally presented by the family is likely. Therapeutic interventions, therefore, may have to be seen and approached from different angles. In particular, the therapist must be able to grasp the greater complexity of the therapeutic situation brought about by shifts in family homeostasis and the surfacing of parental psychopathology, and to manage the treatment crises that ensue. In some cases, it will be necessary to meet in separate sessions with parents or siblings to explore in greater depth neurotic failures, personality deficits, or relational disturbances that, if not treated resolutely, may short-circuit or abort the teenager's and family's task of further differentiation. Ultimately, the parent's ability to acknowledge nondefensively and take hold of the management of their personal and relational problems is indispensable to other family members' efforts at growth and change.

An illustration of these points is drawn from the following excerpt from the family therapy of a 16-year-old anorexic; she has two sisters, aged 15 and 19 at the time. The mother was 41 years of age and employed full-time as a schoolteacher. She had suffered chronically low self-esteem since her own adolescence and was highly enmeshed with her daughters. The father was 47 years of age and quite successful in his profession. Despite his genuine caring and concern for everyone's well-being, he was a truly peripheral member of the family. The session occurred in the sixth month of treatment. The patient had been maintaining her target weight for some 2 months and was becoming increasingly capable of owning her own conflicts and self-contradictions, as well as the stresses inherent in the family. Sessions with the parents alone had focused on the mother's long-standing depression, the father's remoteness, and the parents' lack of sexual fulfillment. Note the therapist's attempt to block the mother's attempts at re-enmeshment with the daughter and to bring the father to a position of greater centrality in the family system.

MOTHER: I think I know what S. [the identified patient] is going through: all the doubt and insecurity of growing up and establishing her own identity. (*Turning to the patient, with tears.*) If you just place trust in yourself, with the support of those around you who care, everything will turn out for the better.

THERAPIST: Are you making yourself available to her? Should she turn to you, rely on you for guidance and emotional support?

MOTHER: Well, that's what parents are for.

THERAPIST (*turning to patient*): What do you think?

PATIENT (*to mother*): I can't keep depending on you, Mom, or everyone else. That's what I've been doing, and it gave me anorexia.

THERAPIST (*turning to the father*): Is it true that your wife knows what S. is going through—every detail of her feelings?

FATHER: I would imagine she does; she's quite close to all the kids, you know.

THERAPIST: So close that she knows what is usually very private, very intimate. Or do the kids reveal to you both exactly what they think? Does your wife know exactly what you (*turning to father*) think and what you go through? Are you as open to her as the kids are?

OLDER SISTER: I don't tell her everything. I love my parents and Dad's right, Mom is very sensitive, but I always keep certain things very private.

THERAPIST: Do you think your mom would prefer that there be no secrets between her and the kids—an open door, so to speak?

OLDER SISTER: Sometimes I do.

THERAPIST (*to patient and younger sister*): How about you two?

PATIENT: Yeah. Sometimes it's like whatever I feel, she has to feel.

YOUNGER SISTER: Yeah.

THERAPIST (*to mother*): How does it make it better for you to be so close and involved with your kids?

MOTHER: I don't see what's so wrong. You seem to be condemning me for being a conscientious parent.

THERAPIST (*turning to father*): I think your wife needs your perspective on this. Do you have a sense of what is happening with her now?

FATHER (*looking a bit uncomfortable*): I think so. M. [the mother] gets a certain kind of emotional fulfillment through her children; it's something we've talked about in the past. I keep telling her she has to let them go. (*Older sister interrupts at this point; the therapist quickly instructs the father to quiet her and continue with his comments.*)

THERAPIST (*to father*): I wonder where you fit in? What stops your wife from turning to you? Again, I wonder if your wife is as sensitive to your needs and what you go through. Also, why aren't you as available to her as she is to everyone else in this family?

FATHER: I would say, probably not. I'm a pretty reserved fellow.

THERAPIST (*to the girls*): Is that the way it is with him?

OLDER SISTER: Dad, you need to express what you think more.

THERAPIST: I wonder what prevents this person (*pointing to father*) from being a participating and emotionally vital part of this family.

PATIENT: I know what I don't like — not what I like, but what frustrates me: your lecturing (*laughter*); it really bothers me. I just want you to listen.

FATHER: But I always listen!

THERAPIST: And then after you listen, you lecture. I've seen you do it here. Look, on the one hand you feel your wife is too close, overinvolved with the kids; yet you are on the fringe, uninvolved.

MOTHER: He cares.

THERAPIST: You're a dear, sweet lady. But you're the most visibly depressed person in this room; you're in no position to extend yourself to others. Do you seek out his support?

MOTHER: I . . . he's there when I need him.

THERAPIST: Great! He's just a little better than the police. I sense you're being a bit guarded and very protective of this man.

FATHER: I think you're right; I'm not as involved as I should be with my wife or the kids (*becoming flushed and teary-eyed*).

THERAPIST (*to mother and father*): The kids can't come between you. (*Turning to father.*) They can't be a buffer for your difficulties in expressing your feelings directly and working out your problems with M. [the mother]. And M., you can't live your life through your kids. Also, there are far better ways to deal with your depression and loneliness. True, the children are concerned about you, and they have every right to be. But they are not, and should never be, part of your medicine.

THE INPATIENT PROGRAM

As noted, hospitalization need not be the pre-eminent consideration in treating the anorexic patient. However, recent criticisms of hospital-based methods — spurred on in part by the family therapy *Zeitgeist* — and the consequent reluctance of many therapists to consider hospital admission are seriously at odds with clinical realities. It is not simply competing theoretical philosophies or polemics that are at issue here. Rather, we must ask what criteria identify that subgroup of anorexics for whom an intensive and multifaceted inpatient program is both essential and the treatment of choice.

In our program, hospitalization is recommended when one or more of the following circumstances are present:

1. Grossly impaired initiative and spontaneity and restricted flexibility of thought. Generally speaking, these are teenagers so walled off from others by social isolation that their separateness threatens to harden into a more enduring life style. It is usually the case that they are premorbidly shy or obsessive–compulsive, with an impoverished sense of identity expressed by pervasive feelings of inadequacy, helplessness, and void.

2. Extreme separation anxiety and fears of abandonment.

3. Multiple past treatment failures or refractoriness to treatment in our outpatient program.

4. Severe disturbances in impulse regulation (e.g., self-abusive behavior, unremitting binge–purge cycles, substance abuse.

5. Suicidal ideation or incapacitating depression.

6. Extreme malnutrition — weight loss exceeding 25% of ideal weight.

7. Severely pathological familial relationships. In these cases, the family has — actually or seemingly — reached a malignant stalemate and thus cannot generate or sustain the conditions under which change is possible. On the whole, these families are wracked by open and divisive conflict, or are kept rigidly enmeshed by chronic marital dissatisfaction or parental depression.

Characteristics of the Milieu

For the past 20 years, anorexic teenagers requiring hospitalization have been admitted to the adolescent service of the UCLA Neuropsychiatric Institute. This is a 19-bed coed, unlocked, and voluntary intensive treatment unit, serving a wide spectrum of diagnostic problems common to the adolescent period. Irrespective of diagnosis, patients are admitted to this unit on the basis of ability to respond to verbal restraint and control and to comprehend the significance of interpretive comments about their behavior.

The unit is organized around a dynamically conceived psychotherapeutic milieu whose characteristics are similar to other adolescent units described in the literature (e.g., Kolb & Shapiro, 1982). There is a full complement of treatment modalities provided, including individual, group, family, and couples therapy, in addition to community meetings, a fully accredited school program, and daily recreational activities. Adolescents are responsible for maintaining their living quarters, keeping to their daily schedule, and participating cooperatively with other residents in community–milieu functions.

The unifying theoretical–technical principle of the milieu is strengthening of secondary-process ego functioning. Hence, therapeutic interventions focus on self-reflection and appraisal; understanding of intrapsychic and intrafamilial conflict, externalized in interactions with milieu staff members and therapists; reinforcement of discriminatory thoughts, feelings, and task mastery; and acquisition of developmentally appropriate peer relations. Behavioral strategies, such as contracts, point systems, and token economies, are not routinely employed. For the anorexic in particular, our sense is that these methods only encourage further ritualistic observance of rules and external expectations and seem inimical to the goal of autonomous and self-directed thought. Needless to say, an element crucial to the therapeutic interaction, beyond matters of theory and technique, is the milieu staff. Staff members are selected for their skill, experience, and, above all, dedication to working with adolescents; they commit themselves to a deep understanding of the phenomenology and therapeutic management of the anorexic patient.

We grant that there is no universally agreed-upon prescription for hospital treatment of anorexia nervosa. We do not here argue for the superiority of our approach to other methods, but seek instead to relate aspects of theory and treatments derived from them to clinical and developmental aspects of the patient and her family. Thus, reflecting on the history of our program, we continue to believe that the decision not to sequester anorexics in a specialized medical or psychosomatic unit is valid, insofar as the overridingly important aims and methods of treatment for seriously disturbed anorexic and nonanorexic teenagers are closely similar. In short, we believe that the treatment of anorexic teenagers in a psychotherapeutic milieu that is congenial and stimulating to developmental tasks is most consistent with the theoretical formulations stated above.

As we see it, the benefits afforded by such a treatment setting are several. First, coexistence with nonanorexic peers brings into sharp relief the anxious, closed-off, and superficial quality of the anorexic's relationships and the maneuvers she uses to set herself apart from the adolescent experience. In a more positive vein, as the peer group's support, encouragement, and nonhostile confrontation come to be perceived as genuine, distance and isolation begin to feel too restrictive and become less desired. Second, exposure to other teenagers who are struggling with parent–child tensions, who also express concerns over acceptance, and who may externalize separation–individuation conflicts through defiance, provocation, and challenging of boundaries and limits permits the anorexic to sense that however peculiar and "different" her symptoms may appear on the surface, she indeed shares the developmental concerns and dilemmas faced by other teenagers. Hence, living in close proximity to teenagers with different coping and expressive styles—teenagers who may articulate their subjective experiences more clearly—provides modeling for alternative methods of problem solving and encourages greater spontaneity and genuineness of self-expression and affective expression. Gradually, with time and treatment progress, these experiences, along with the holding and empathic elements of the milieu, evoke and illuminate the anorexic's intense conflict over issues of control, autonomy, and dependence, while serving as a context for an ever-widening expansion of perceptions fostering self-awareness, object relatedness, and an increased ability to deal openly with uncertainty and change.

Managing Diet and Weight

Upon admission, we make it clear to the patient that the automatic, fixed quality of her symptoms is due simultaneously to her starved and malnourished state and to the gratifications obtained from attributions of discipline, control, and self-sacrifice.

Rather than entreating the patient to eat, our strategy is to affirm that her symptoms express much suffering, confusion, and lack of control, and to lessen her discomforts about eating by assuming temporary responsibility for all matters concerning her diet and weight. She is told that while this may cause her some alarm, it will guarantee a slow and predictable return of normal eating and weight, at the same time as she participates in the therapy program. Reflecting on this strategy, one might be tempted to think it preferable to restore self-regulation of eating as soon as possible. On the contrary, however, our experience with these severely disturbed young anorexics suggests that such an approach could be counterproductive. True, the majority of patients protest abdication of control with considerable intensity. But at the same time, in nearly every case, they eventually come to report that being relieved of this reponsibility helps decrease food-related anxieties to more manageable proportions, and in the long run actually facilitates involvement in the therapeutic program. Said one 18-year-old upon her discharge: "I never wanted to admit it, but I'm glad you took care of my eating and weight. I would never have been able to concentrate on my therapy if I had to deal with the guilt of eating on my own."

The elements of our weight management program are now described. Each of the following points is carefully explained to the patient at the time of admission.

1. Upon admission, the patient meets with a dietitian, who helps her plan a nutritionally balanced diet according to the daily caloric requirement prescribed by her physician. Patients are encouraged to consume solid foods and not to rely on liquid supplements. For the initial week or two, the caloric requirement remains stable at 1500 to 1800 calories; thereafter, calories are increased in graduated steps to establish a maximum weekly gain of .908 kg (2 lbs) until target weight is achieved. The target weight (as with outpatients, about 90% of average for age and height) is established at admission and is not altered. The majority of patients require 2 to 4 months to achieve their target weight on this program.

2. The daily caloric requirement is, for most patients, divided evenly into three meals. Half an hour is allotted to complete each meal. If the patient is unable to finish within the time allotted, the total amount of intake is figured and the remaining calories are offered in liquid supplement. She is given 15 minutes to consume the supplement. If she fails to do so, gastric tube feeding is automatically initiated. Clearly, this is distressing for both the patient and the staff, and every effort is made to facilitate the patient's cooperation with the program. At the same time, it is enforced without hesitation to reinforce the seriousness with which we regard her condition.[2]

3. The patient is observed closely during mealtime to prevent deceptive hiding or disposal of food, and remains under direct observation for 1 to 2 hours following the meal to prevent vomiting. Should vomiting occur while the patient is on observation, all of the calories required for the meal are replaced by liquid supplement; the patient is again allotted 15 minutes for replacement.

4. The patient is weighed in her hospital gown twice a week in the morning, prior to breakfast and after voiding. Depending on their degree of emaciation and general health status, patients may be put on moderate bed rest. If health is not grossly impaired or endangered, open access to the milieu and participation in all regular activities are permitted, although exercising is discouraged and is actively prevented

2. In actual practice, tube feeding is rarely necessary. During the past 10 years, it has been required for fewer than 5% of our patients.

if necessary. At no time are privileges or reinforcers of any type made contingent on increments of weight gain or other aspects of eating behavior.

5. Patients remain on mealtime supervision until signs of rigidity, discomfort, and peculiar eating habits diminish. Generally, this is signaled by decreasing preoccupation with calories and body weight and an increasing ability to engage more spontaneously in mealtime conversation with staff and peers. Naturally, the rate at which this occurs is variable. In our experience, a longer period is required for patients with particularly severe characterological deficits and interpersonal maladjustment. However, for the majority of patients hospitalized in our facility, between 3 and 5 months of supervision are required before self-regulation of diet and weight is restored.

6. After coming off the program, the patient must be able to maintain her target weight without significant loss for a minimum of 1 month before discharge home is considered possible. Naturally, this is but one criterion used to judge her readiness to return home with minimal vulnerability to relapse. Once off the program, she receives any informational feedback deemed necessary, including menu planning, caloric intake required to maintain target weight, and increments in caloric intake that would be necessary to compensate for anticipated patterns of exercise outside of the hospital.

The Phases of Treatment

Over the years, it has been our practice to effect a complete separation of the patient from other family members and peers at the time of admission. However drastic or atheoretical this approach may seem, we believe it is fully justified by its strategic and therapeutic possibilities. The separation is time-limited; the desired effects are generally achieved over a 6- to 8-week period.

In a number of ways, separation permits us to dramatize both individual and parental dysfunctioning and their systemic relationships. In the case of the teenager, especially one who is strongly characterized by mimicry and uncritical assimilation of parental models, separation brings into view her extreme dependence on parental influences and the corresponding lack of inner resources and self-reliance. In the dynamic–affectual sense, the separation "crisis" permits the therapist to take up a position of active involvement with the patient very early, giving her support and containment while accepting the intensity of her rage, disapproval, and fear. The therapist's presence, expressions of genuine concern, and efforts to buffer the many anxieties evoked by separation all serve to congeal the therapeutic alliance and allow a necessary dependence to proceed apace.

At the same time, separation quickly provokes a dynamic instability within the family as a whole, bringing to light clues about the system's overall rigidity, and thus opening up potential therapeutic angles (Andolfi, Angelo, Menghi, & Nicolo-Corigliano, 1983). To the extent that the patient has been the center of a peculiarly intense parental awareness, her sudden absence creates an unanticipated disruption of the family's usual homeostatic pattern. In this light, the functional role of the patient and her symptomatic behavior can be more readily discerned; the family's capacities for reorganization and change can be tested; and reasons for immobility and resistance to change can be identified. With most families, the separation brings to light previously denied patterns of overinvolvement and enmeshment, as parents voice doubt about their child's well-being and question the adequacy of care provided by the hospital staff. As these are exposed and discussed by the therapist, parents come to acknowledge, albeit with great reluctance, major rifts between them on approaches to child rearing. In other cases, separation triggers significant depression in one or more family members and in the patient as well, who expresses anguish at the grief and loneliness of the relative who, she believes, suffers most by her absence. This pattern is especially common in families where an absence of belonging and togetherness has been masked by overinvolvement or extreme boundness with the identified patient.

Thus, we do not enforce separation because we see the patient or family as a pernicious influence. Rather, it is a therapeutic choice—an explicitly provocative agent of change (Andolfi *et al.*, 1983) that actively challenges the binding ties annulling growth and individuation, and that helps the family face the need for greater flexibility.

Above everything else, the early phase of treatment must emphasize the establishment of contact and therapeutic alliance. We have found that these young patients are most effectively approached with a full and open discussion of their possible concerns about the staff's motivations and intentions, rather than waiting for them to come forward and voice such anxieties on their own. Rarely will this allay their fears, but it does go some way to establish the therapist and treatment team as consistent, reliable, honest, intuitive, and trustworthy. Most importantly, the therapist and nursing staff should communicate to the patient patience, sensitivity, tact, genuine caring, and the possibility that she can be understood.

During these early weeks, it is best to avoid giving deep interpretations to the patient's symptoms, lest she view the therapist as an omniscient figure to whom she should submit passively and repeat parrot-like what has been said. Rather, it is more useful to center attention on the significance of her urgent search for rules and structure, the impact of separation on her sense of self, the difficulty she seems to have in judging herself and her appearance accurately, and her criticisms of the staff for not giving objective feedback on what she must do to "get better" or sense improvement. The staff, with great patience and sensitivity, conveys an understanding of how mistrust of personal ideas and perceptions causes her great alarm and makes her fear control by others; staff members provide continual reassurance that her weight will be carefully regulated and that they will be available at all times to listen to her thoughts and to provide another point of view if necessary. In this respect, the staff emphasizes an overriding interest in her individual thoughts and feelings, rather than in her ability to follow explicit rules and instructions, while acknowledging that she may not be accustomed to speaking openly about private matters. They point out that such a dialogue, even if it centers on her complaints or objections, is an important step toward establishing a sense of who she is and the validity of her own thinking and emotions.

As an increasing degree of shared understanding of the patient's vulnerability is achieved, therapist and staff take up a more directive and dynamic style in clarifying behavioral patterns that are self-defeating. Still, this "unlayering" of anorexic behavior and cognitions is undertaken in a gentle manner, considering the ease with which symptoms are so easily re-entrenched in these patients. It is a delicate period, insofar as the patient is now coming to view her compliant and restrictive nature with scorn and ridicule. At the same time, since her dependence on the staff has not caused her to be exploited in any way, she is encouraged to assume an increasing autonomy in the therapeutic alliance and to begin examining some of the sources of interpersonal, family, and self-esteem difficulties. As always, it remains necessary for the therapist to tailor the pace and style of interventions flexibly to the patient's individual needs. Also at this time (generally 2 months postadmission), family therapy is instituted, thereby creating a further stimulus for the patient to reformulate her view of herself in the family context and to consider the restrictions imposed upon her individuality. Though it is a period of considerable stress and painful realization, it sets the stage for all family members to seek out healthier alternative behaviors, roles, and interactive patterns.

Throughout this middle phase of treatment, progress is heralded by increasing initiative in milieu activities, greater social engagement, and more assertive and individuated affective expression. Naturally, the rate of change among patients is highly variable. But in the majority of patients, behavior becomes more decidedly "adolescent"—humorous, provocative, and sometimes sexual. The patients may take risks to challenge staff and overstep rules (e.g., use of foul language); these are signs of an incipient sense of identity and mastery and a more internalized self-esteem. Although the patient is not complimented or reinforced for these changes, they are nurtured by the staff's own challenging and teasing responses and the setting of limits on grossly disruptive behavior. Many patients report that this is the first time they have dared to be boisterous or defiant, and that they feel good about not being approached as though they were too fragile to manage confrontation. Typically, they reveal these "exploits" to the parents in great detail. Some parents are truly relieved to see their daughters giving up rigidity for greater spontaneity; others react with considerable alarm, expressing fear that their previously well-mannered and dutiful children have been irreparably harmed and tainted. Such reactions only serve as further grist for therapeutic confrontation of the family's inhibition of growth and change.

For the majority of our patients, the final phase of hospitalization begins between 4 and 7 months after admission. The patient has started to assume complete responsibility for diet and weight maintenance, has weekend passes home on a regular basis, and exercises her privilege to leave the hospital grounds during unscheduled periods. Clinically, body image concerns and weight preoccupation have receded into the background. Although they are still present in many patients, they are not generally at the level of symptomatic distress; dieting is no longer viewed as an acceptable means of regulating self-esteem. Her role in the family has been decentralized, even though the emotional interplay between members is intensified and often painful. Psychotherapeutically, issues of identity, intimacy, sexuality, and the family's acceptance and tolerance of her changes predominate. Thus, while anxious anticipation of the future is a natural accompaniment of this stage, her improved autonomy and self-regard and her ability to approach future uncertainties without recourse to weight control signal a readiness for discharge.

For other patients, generally the most schizoid and chronically depressed, improvement occurs slowly and requires considerably more effort. Hospitalization is sometimes protracted, lasting 9 to 12 months. Even then, some remain limited to some degree by persistent self-doubt, fear of change, and extreme ambivalence about body weight. In such cases, the hospital staff must decide what reasonable treatment goals should be, and when current hospitalization has reached a point of diminishing returns. This does not imply that hospitalization has failed. While relapse and additional hospitalizations are not uncommon in this group, our follow-up suggests that many respond to subsequent interventions in a more productive manner.

ACKNOWLEDGMENTS

The development of the Teenage Eating Disorders Program is the outcome of an interdisciplinary team effort by the faculty, staff, and students of the Division of Child Psychiatry, UCLA Neuropsychiatric Institute. We are especially grateful to the following colleagues: Stacey Adelman, Linda Beliz, Lynda Benjamin, Paul Bolita, Ellen Bowen, Dawn Broughton, Jane Burroughs, Basil Bernstein, Sally Duran, Robert Diamond, Virginia Estrella, Ira Farmer, Roberta Freeman, Jacqueline Green, Yvonne Ferguson, Harry Hoberman, Nancy Horvath, Ginnie Cruz, Bobbie Jackson, Carrie Jacobs, Susan Josephson, Joann Kucharic, Lloyd Lebow, Paul Montgomery, Wendy Morrell, Diana Miller, Judy Preble, Barbara Salkin, Al Santos, Margi Stuber, Tracy Goodglick, and Lee Pezzuti. We also thank Dr. James Simmons, Director of the Division of Child Psychiatry, for his support and encouragement of our efforts.

REFERENCES

Andolfi, M., Angelo, C., Menghi, P., & Nicolo-Corigliano, A. M. (1983). *Behind the family mask: Therapeutic change in rigid family systems.* New York: Brunner/Mazel.

Blos, P. (1962). *On adolescence.* New York: Free Press.

Blos, P. (1965). The initial stage of male adolescence. *Psychoanalytic Study of the Child, 20,* 145-164.

Bruch, H. (1973). *Eating disorders: Anorexia nervosa, obesity, and the person within.* New York: Basic Books.

Bruch, H. (1978). *The golden cage: The enigma of anorexia nervosa.* Cambridge, MA: Harvard University Press.

Bruch, H. (1979). Island in the river: The anorexic adolescent in treatment. In S. C. Feinstein & P. L. Giovacchini (Eds.), *Adolescent psychiatry* (Vol. 7, pp. 26-40). Chicago: University of Chicago Press.

Casper, R. C. (1982). Treatment principles in anorexia nervosa. In S. C. Feinstein, J. G. Looney, A. Z. Schwartzberg, & A. D. Sorosky (Eds.), *Adolescent psychiatry* (Vol. 10, pp. 431-450). Chicago: University of Chicago Press.

Crisp, A. H. (1980). *Anorexia nervosa: Let me be.* New York: Grune & Stratton.

Fairburn, C. G. (1981). A cognitive behavioural approach to the treatment of bulimia. *Psychological Medicine, 11,* 707-711.

Garfinkel, P. E., & Garner, D. M. (1982). *Anorexia nervosa: A multidimensional perspective.* New York: Brunner/Mazel.

Garner, D. M., & Bemis, K. (1982). A cognitive-behavioral approach to anorexia nervosa. *Cognitive Therapy and Research, 6,* 1-27.

Garner, D. M, Olmsted, M. P., & Polivy, J. (1983). Development and validation of a multidimensional eating disorder inventory for anorexia nervosa and bulimia. *International Journal of Eating Disorders, 2,* 15-34.

Goodsitt, A. (1977). Narcissistic disturbances in anorexia nervosa. In S. C. Feinstein & P. L. Giovacchini (Eds.), *Adolescent psychiatry* (Vol. 5, pp. 304-312). New York: Jason Aronson.

Jacobson, E. (1964). *The self and the object world.* New York: International Universities Press.

Kalucy, R. S. (1978). An approach to the therapy of anorexia nervosa. *Journal of Adolescence, 1,* 197-228.

Kestenberg, J. (1968). Phases of adolescence with suggestions for a correlation of psychic and hormonal organizations: III. Puberty growth, differentiation, and consolidation. *Journal of the American Academy of Child Psychiatry, 7,* 108-151.

Kolb, J. E., & Shapiro, E. R. (1982). Management of separation issues with the family of the hospitalized adolescent. In S. C. Feinstein, J. G. Looney, A. Z. Schwartzberg, & A. D. Sorosky (Eds.), *Adolescent psychiatry* (Vol. 10, pp. 343-359). Chicago: University of Chicago Press.

Langs, R. (1982). *Psychotherapy: A basic text.* New York: Jason Aronson.

Lewis, J. M. (1978). The adolescent and the healthy family. In S. C. Feinstein & P. L. Giovacchini (Eds.), *Adolescent psychiatry* (Vol. 6, pp. 156-170). Chicago: University of Chicago Press.

Malmquist, C. P. (1978). *Handbook of adolescence: Psychopathology, antisocial development, and psychotherapy.* New York: Jason Aronson.

Minuchin, S., Rosman, B. L., & Baker, L. (1978). *Psychosomatic families: Anorexia nervosa in context.* Cambridge, MA: Harvard University Press.

Peskin, H. (1972). Multiple prediction of adult psychological health from preadolescent and adolescent behavior. *Journal of Consulting and Clinical Psychology, 38,* 115-160.

Peskin, H., & Livson, N. (1972). Pre- and postpubertal personality and adult psychologic functioning. *Seminars in Psychiatry, 4*, 343–353.

Petersen, A. C., & Taylor, B. (1980). The biological approach to adolescence: Biological change and psychological adaptation. In J. Adelson (Ed.), *Handbook of adolescence* (pp. 117–158). New York: Wiley.

Schonfeld, W. A. (1971). Adolescent development: Biological, psychological and sociological determinants. In S. C. Feinstein, P. L. Giovacchini, & A. A. Miller (Eds.), *Adolescent psychiatry* (Vol. 1, pp. 296–326). New York: Basic Books.

Selvini-Palazzoli, M. (1978). *Self-starvation*. New York: Jason Aronson.

Spitzer, R. L., & Endicott, J. (1975). *Schedule for Affective Disorders and Schizophrenia*. New York: New York State Psychiatric Institute and Columbia University.

Strober, M. (1981). A comparative analysis of personality organization in juvenile anorexia nervosa. *Journal of Youth and Adolescence, 10*, 285–296.

Strober, M. (1983). An empirically derived typology of anorexia nervosa. In P. Darby, P. Garfinkel, D. Garner, & D. Coscina (Eds.), *Anorexia nervosa: Recent developments* (pp. 185–198). New York: Alan R. Liss.

Winnicott, D. W. (1965). *The maturational process and the facilitating environment*. London: Hogarth Press.

Yager, J. (1981). Anorexia nervosa and the family. In M. Lansky (Ed.), *Family therapy and major psychopathology* (pp. 249–280). New York: Grune & Stratton.

CHAPTER SEVENTEEN

Intensive Outpatient and Residential Treatment for Bulimia

SUSAN C. WOOLEY / O. WAYNE WOOLEY

INTRODUCTION

Eating disorders are first and foremost a cultural phenomenon that, like hysteria, results from an impossible conflict between cultural demands and biological drives. And, like hysteria, eating disorders appear to be part of a breakdown in the transition from sexual and social immaturity to adulthood among well-educated young women, who are most sensitized to and responsive to cultural expectations. If the social changes accounting for the rise of hysteria are now complete, those accounting for the rise of eating disorders are at their peak.

Beautiful Women, Good Women

For centuries, girls have been socialized to be dependent and "narcissistic"—that is, they have been culturally conditioned in such a way that self-esteem (self-estimation, self-evaluation) is tied directly to physical appearance. Society has been structured such that power, prestige, privilege, deference, and attention are granted to "beautiful" women (Dworkin, 1974, 1979; Gilbert & Gubar, 1979; Griffin, 1981; Olsen, 1965). There has probably always been, since earliest historical times, a fairly coherent ideology of what constitutes physical beauty in women and what the beautiful woman is "like." This ideology provides a standard or model for lucky and privileged young girls to pattern their own bodies, selves, ideals, and ambitions after.

The ideology of the beautiful woman has almost always excluded any of the so-called "manly" virtues or attributes: strength, action, effectiveness, creativity; open, demonstrative expression of certain emotions, such as anger; love of competition. None of these would add to, and most would detract from, the image of a beautiful woman. As Ambrose Bierce (1911/1958), speaking for the entire culture, has said:

> To men a man is but a mind.
> Who cares what face he carries?
> Or what form he wears?
> But woman's body is the woman.

Susan C. Wooley and O. Wayne Wooley. Eating Disorders Clinic, Psychiatry Department, University of Cincinnati Medical Center, Cincinnati, Ohio.

If a woman cannot be beautiful, she can be "good"—that is, she can put other people's (especially her own children's) needs ahead of her own; she can be self-sacrificing, self-effacing. Of course, a beautiful woman could be "good" if she wanted to, but she does not have to be; she has a choice, insofar as she properly appreciates the gift of her beauty and is willing and able to use the power it bestows. Recent changes in the ideology of women have combined to bring about great increases in the number of women with disordered eating. Thinness has come to be seen as essential *to both beauty and goodness*, so that it is an inescapable criterion of value for women, whether they aspire to social power or moral worth (Selvini-Palazzoli, 1978).

Numerous indices document a changing standard that has required ever greater degrees of thinness as this century has progressed (Garner, Garfinkel, Schwartz, & Thompson, 1980; Mazur, 1983). Data from *Glamour* magazine's 1983 Body Image Survey ("Feeling Fat," 1984) (prepared and interpreted by us in cooperation with the *Glamour* staff) showed that 76% of the respondents considered themselves too fat, including 45% of those classified as underweight according to the Metropolitan Life Insurance Company's (1959) tables of desirable weight, which advocate a degree of slenderness now regarded as unhealthy. Indeed, to many, it appears that the ideal of feminine beauty comes each year to resemble the adolescent male physique more closely; this suggests that the shift in fashion may be a function of a broader social change, in which women are beginning to compete with men for power and prestige. This creates for young women a formidable challenge: to mimic men both physically and behaviorally, and to resolve intense conflicts over identification with their mothers and fathers. They are the first generation of women to be raised by highly weight-conscious mothers who have experienced themselves as failures by the prevalent standards. In the 1983 *Glamour* Body Image Survey, only 13% of the respondents thought that their mothers had liked their own bodies.

The mother's loss of confidence in herself—both physically and in the face of radically redefined roles for women—has powerful repercussions for the daughter. These include the direct learning, through identification, of body hatred; insecurity and rage produced by the inevitable monitoring and criticism of the daughter's size; and guilt produced in the daughter by the mother's (real or projected) envy of her youth, beauty, and greatly expanded opportunities. Undoubtedly, such feelings have always passed between mother and daughter, but never so strongly as now. Dieting may serve simultaneously as identification, differentiation, revenge, and penance. By interesting herself in diet, the daughter "acts like a woman," imitating her mother and affirming her identification with her. By assuming firm control of her own body, she differentiates herself from her mother and emulates the "control" exercised by men, especially her father. If she succeeds in getting thinner than her mother, she enjoys revenge for past criticism. And finally, suffering and self-denial alleviate her guilt over abandoning and surpassing her mother; dieting is a way to be "good" that avoids the loss of self she has observed in her mother.

In a survey of women at Miami University (Ohio), the second strongest predictor of bulimia in female students (after self–body evaluation) was the daughter's belief that her mother was critical of the daughter's body (Debs, Wooley, Harkness-Kling, & Wooley, 1983). In the 1983 *Glamour* survey, a respondent's perception that her mother's attitude toward the respondent's body was "mainly negative" was associated with numerous measures of poor body image, self-consciousness, and severity of dieting techniques.

But the problem is not solved by shifting from identification with a critical, self-disparaging, and often depressed mother to identification with the father. In fact, many bulimic women appear to have been strongly identified with their fathers in childhood, leading to role conflict at puberty. Fear of womanhood may be less a fear of sexuality than of woman's role. But the male role is also unacceptable. Women long for the advantages enjoyed by men, but rarely feel comfortable emulating their behavior. It is too great a leap from the mother's self-effacement and from her desire to please and serve others to the father's ability to use the (largely unreciprocated) emotional support of others to achieve his own goals. If bulimic behavior expresses this dilemma, the condition of bulimia temporarily resolves it, for no movement is possible: The painful choices are avoided altogether.

Starvation

However one interprets the social causes for increased weight obsession and dieting, the phenomenon itself is undeniable. Nearly all young women feel too fat; in an effort to reduce the discrepancy between their perceived actual body size and ideal body size, nearly all of them diet (Nylander, 1971; Thompson & Schwartz, 1982). Eating disorders ensue when a rational attempt to exert conscious cognitive control over food intake falters, and the individual loses control entirely or cannot relinquish control. The outcomes are predictable responses to prolonged food deprivation.

Our contention is that, in the current cultural climate, *dieting (starvation) itself may be a sufficient condition for the development of anorexia nervosa or bulimia.* Relative vulnerability is a function of (1) intensity of perceived social and familial pressure to be thin, and accompanying body image disturbance; (2) genetic and constitutional variability in the body's responses to starvation and weight loss (e.g., the severity of anhedonia produced by food deprivation and the extent and rapidity with which metabolic rate slows, appetite increases, etc.); and (3) the extent to which eating disorders serve to express the conflicts over parental identification experienced by young women (i.e., become a suitable language [Shoenberg, 1975] for such unarticulated feelings as the longing for power, rage over powerlessness, apprehension over loss of the female role and its protective cloak, and guilt over abandonment of female qualities of "goodness").

As publicity about anorexia nervosa increased during the 1970s—and this publicity, by and large, portrayed it in glamorous terms, as the "golden girl" disease—and as dieting took on the dimensions of a cultural mania, more and more girls and women began to starve themselves. The great increase in the number of cases of bulimia is one result of these developments. The message is this: One way to get attention, to be deemed a "golden girl," to get a little power in this world, is to starve—to stage a hunger strike.

However, more women ultimately failed in the art of starvation than succeeded; many learned that it was easier to lose or maintain weight through vomiting or laxative abuse, and thus became bulimic. It could be said that it is their lesser strength and discipline, or their greater flexibility and instinct for self-preservation, that caused them to "fail" in the pursuit of self-starvation and to invoke other methods of weight control. Each interpretation is probably applicable in some cases. Some bulimics have poor impulse control; many are alcoholic, sexually promiscuous, and habitual stealers.

But many are not: Many are conscientious (even compulsive) and productive; some are relatively well adjusted apart from their eating disorder. Rightly or wrongly, however, bulimics regard themselves as failures, characterologically inferior to "starvers."

However, a classical study of the mental and physical effects of semistarvation (Keys, Brozek, Henschel, Mickelsen, & Taylor, 1950) shows that starvation creates conditions that could foster bulimia even in people with strong "superegos" and "firm ethical standards." This study from the University of Minnesota first showed that the self-starving men became profoundly "neurotic." These men were conscientious objectors, of apparently sterling character, and tested out as high in "ego strength"; yet, after they lost 25% of their body weight, their MMPI results showed highly significant increases in hypochondriasis, depression, and hysteria. Secondly, the Minnesota study showed that constant, tormenting, obsessive thoughts of food are an inevitable result of starvation: 19 of the 34 men read cookbooks and collected recipes; 11 of 34 saved money for food after the experiment. Thirdly, starvation predisposes one to binge, to lose control of eating, and having done so, to vomit, to purge oneself of the "sinful" food. Fourthly, once a starvation period is over, the predisposition to binge becomes an uncontrollable reality. In the refeeding ("rehabilitation") part of the Minnesota study, all subjects showed a loss of control of appetite; they gorged themselves and sometimes vomited.

There is still more to be learned from this monumental study. The effects of starvation on work capacity ("energy level") observed in the Minnesota study were profound, with a deterioration in 24 weeks to 28% of control values. Recovery of work capacity was very slow. *Five months* after refeeding began, only one (of the 12-man subsample studied that long) had scores indicating good physical fitness. These findings, when contrasted with the hyperactivity and reported lack of fatigue in emaciated anorexics, suggests how successfully anorexics deny and transcend physical debilitation.

Other starvation effects relevant to the understanding of anorexia and bulimia include edema during the starvation period, and the slowing of metabolic rate and attendant "hyperlipogenesis" (Tepperman & Tepperman, 1964) during the refeeding period. It was observed that, without any improvement in nutritional status, subjects tended to stop losing or even to gain weight as a result of edema. The effects of accumulation of fluid in cells were thought to be especially damaging to heart and brain tissue. Of particular significance to eating disorders were the compensatory metabolic adaptations to starvation. Metabolic rate (oxygen consumption) was lowered by 39% at the end of the starvation period. Also, abnormal levels of fat were deposited during rehabilitation. Eight months after the conclusion of starvation, the men were 10% heavier on the average, with 40% more adipose tissue than during the baseline period. These effects are, of course, experienced as disastrous by "dieters." Many anorexics ("starvers") no doubt become bulimic as a result of wanting to get well. Once an anorexic decides to stop starving and to regain some weight, she is subject to the rapid weight gain and disinhibition of appetite observed in the Minnesota study.

Bulimia resolved itself spontaneously in the subjects of the Minnesota study when they had eaten enough to return to (or to exceed) their original weight. For today's young women, this is not an acceptable solution. Losses of control, while trying to remain below spontaneously regulated weight, represent crises that must be dealt with. The first purge usually occurs after an unintentional lapse at a family celebration or some occasion where prolonged exposure to food cannot be avoided. The young woman remembers or hits upon the idea of vomiting or taking laxatives to "undo" the damage. For a while, this pattern continues: Purging is used only as a method of undoing. In time, however, hunger and greater confidence in the technique of purging allow a subtle change: Binges are planned, with the intent of purging. At this point things begin to change rapidly. Binges quickly escalate in frequency. They become the major form of dealing with hunger, and often the major means of meeting nutritional needs, since considerable food can be absorbed despite purging. Bingeing is used to reduce tension produced by hunger, and soon to reduce tensions generated by other causes. Purging relieves guilt engendered by overeating and comes, in most bulimics, to serve as a general relief stimulus.

Inherent in the bulimic's dilemma is the fact that she cannot eat satisfying amounts of food and remain at an acceptable weight. As long as her food intake (absorption) is sufficiently low to maintain an artificially low weight, she will, like Keys *et al.'s* subjects, be continually subject to voracious appetite and lapses of control. It appears, moreover, that with time the bulimic's appetite increases, even in those instances where normal weight has been restored.

This progression in appetite requires explanation. One possibility is that over time the body adapts to an abnormal diet in ways that perpetuate the problem. Most bulimics eat relatively little between binges. Foods eaten in binges are generally high in sugar content, and it is primarily sugar that can be absorbed before purging. Thus, bulimic women may, in effect, be on nearly pure sucrose diets for periods of months or years. Habituation to such a diet could include the release of large amounts of insulin shortly after initiation of eating. Insulin, of course, increases appetite and promotes fat storage. To stop eating prematurely might well produce a hypoglycemic state, helping to explain the bulimic's experience that to eat one cookie is to unleash uncontrollable hunger. This, paired with the disinhibition of *cognitive* restraint caused by eating a forbidden food, conspires to guarantee a binge.

Second, and perhaps more important, is a conditioning process by which satiety is progressively impaired. In normally feeding animals and humans, the experience of satiety appears to be a conditioned response to the sensory properties of food whose nutritional effects are "known" by the body through repeated pairings of flavor, texture, and other properties with metabolic effects (Booth, 1977; LeMagnen, 1971). Thus, for example, a rat's body "learns" how much of a food marked by a distinctive flavor is required to meet nutritional needs, so that within a meal, feeding is appropriately terminated long before the food's effects are fully experienced. This phenomenon can be demonstrated by altering the information received by the body about the food's nutritional effects — for example, by following intake of a distinctively flavored food by an injection of glucose or insulin. In these instances, the animal learns to eat less or more, respectively, of the food. This effect persists well past discontinuation of the experimental manipulation, until the body has relearned the correct information about the food's intrinsic effects.

In bingeing–purging, the body receives continual misinformation. It learns that a bag of cookies or a dozen doughnuts provide 100 or 200 calories. The figure will vary, depending on the timing of the purge and the foods eaten. Because macronutrients clear the stomach and are absorbed at different rates, there is probably a pattern to the misinformation, with sugar-containing foods most likely to register nutritional effects and fatty ones least likely. This model predicts that in time neural satiety signals will adapt to the actual calories absorbed in binge eating, so that hunger will not be satisfied (despite sensations of distension) until enormous quantities have been consumed. Attempts to eat normal amounts of food should provide very little satiety, especially foods low in sugar or carbohydrates (e.g., proteins and fats).

This model helps to explain both the voracious appetite of the bulimic and the strong preference for sweets. It also explains one of the problems in recovery: namely, that impaired satiety is likely to persist for some time past the point when purging is discontinued, until the body slowly relearns the metabolic consequences of eating every food formerly purged. This process appears to take several months, although it is helpful to reassure patients that within 6 weeks there may be sufficient change to ease hunger to tolerable levels.

It is easy to understand how a bulimic can maintain exaggerated fears of becoming fat when she knows how voracious her appetite is. To the extent that this abnormality is attributed by patient and therapist entirely to the effects of emotion, the patient must despair of change, for it is a chronic state that in fact yields minimally to improved mood or appropriate behavioral change, such as expression of feelings and improved interpersonal skills.

The position taken here is that voluntary caloric restriction (dieting, starvation) causes eating disorders; it causes weight loss, which, in the present climate of intense fear and hatred of fat, acts as a strong reward or reinforcement of further caloric restrictions. If one interprets the social effects of weight loss in "superego" terms (i.e., self-control), then Eisnitz's (1980) remarks are relevant:

The crucial advantage resulting from superego development is that . . . narcissistic support can be accomplished internally even in the face of external frustration or disapproval. . . . Examples of the facilitating effect resulting from this function of the superego can be seen in the tremendous levels of work which can be accomplished when one feels dedicated to working for a special cause, or in the increase in work capacity which follows the resolution of a *moral conflict*. The manic-like elation which some people experience during periods of high creative activity is also a reflection of similar processes. (pp. 379, 380; italics added)

The process of dieting is addictive. Weight loss produces euphoria, but to maintain the euphoria, more weight must be lost. Because metabolic rate decreases as a compensatory response to deprivation, even greater degrees of food restriction must be effected. This process is comparable to the development of "tolerance"; like an addiction, it eventually requires frankly self-destructive behavior in order to maintain psychological equilibrium. "Withdrawal" from dieting produces intolerable symptoms, including rapid weight gain, physical pain and discomfort, and extreme dysphoria.

The present account of the current anorexic–bulimic epidemic, then, goes like this: Most young women go on a diet. It is not a great mystery why they diet: They have been made to feel that normal female bodies are unacceptable and will doom them to the social powerlessness of "woman's role"; they observe that to escape this problem, everyone is dieting. Many become dependent on weight loss for a sense of well-being and competence, and persevere long enough to suffer the effects of starvation. *Their capacity for other gratifications is so impaired by starvation that the pleasures of weight loss (or at least the maintenance of slenderness) assume an importance with which little else in life can compete.* The onset of starvation-produced anhedonia may be regarded as the point of no return.

But one of the symptoms of starvation is the virtually uncontrollable urge to binge. To manage this alarming symptom, many learn to vomit or use laxatives. They learn that in doing so they suffer no apparent injury, and they feel better both physically and psychologically. Whatever shame is experienced is preferable (at least in the short run) to the alternatives. Dieting and management of the effects of starvation thus become the fabric of a young woman's life into which new threads may be gradually woven: the receipt of special attentions; a safe means of expressing aggression; the means to control feelings of "goodness" and "badness" through manipulation of a single behavior; and, above all, the conviction that through her suffering she will eventually achieve something of inestimable value. That the anticipated external rewards never materialize is scarcely noticed, for they have been supplanted by internal ones and the unshakeable belief that triumph is just a few more pounds away. The original reasons for dieting are long forgotten, and the capacity for normal pleasures is wholly lost; the process has become an end in itself.

Body Image

The distortions of body image that lie at the heart of anorexia nervosa and bulimia are notoriously refractory to change by conventional therapeutic techniques. We know relatively little about the determinants of body image, especially as they pertain to sensations of fatness in eating-disordered women, but research from other areas allows the formulation of some tentative hypotheses.

Aside from the cultural belief that thinness is preferable, the most obvious difference between the circumstances confronting young women of this generation and those faced by young women of 50 years ago is that the modern women have experienced life in many "bodies." Before the advent of widespread dieting, the experience of the body was relatively continous for most women, marked only by the gradual change of normal growth, by a period of rapid qualitative as well as quantitative change at puberty, and by pregnancy. Both of the latter, especially puberty, are widely acknowledged to represent times of stress, in which bodily change engenders confusion, and body image distortions are more likely to occur. Puberty has, of course, been the time most often associated with the onset of anorexia nervosa, and both puberty and pregnancy are associated with the onset of obesity (perhaps, but not necessarily, as a result of metabolic changes).

For young women today, the trauma of puberty is typically compounded by a discontinuous experience of the physical self. The majority of young adolescents go on weight loss diets, and, of course, the majority of weight loss diets are followed by regain of the lost weight, often with an "overshoot." Thus by midadolescence young women have cognitive and sensory memories of many forms of the body–self. This constant change may set the stage for the development of persistent susceptibilities to distortion. The individual's dissatisfaction with her body at the beginning of dieting may be relatively casual; but, whether it is great or not, it becomes intensified as a result of dieting and weight fluctuations.

Body image is more than an abstract concept; it is a many-layered, evolving set of memories. It is an integral part of the integrative function of the mind (Brown, 1959; Bychowski, 1943; Castelnuovo-Tedesco, 1973; Frick, 1982; Horowitz, 1966; Kaywin, 1955; Kubie, 1934; Shontz, 1974). Assessments limited to estimation of body width or change (Cappon & Banks, 1968; Crisp & Kalucy, 1974; Garner, Garfinkel, & Moldofsky, 1978; Hsu, 1982; McCrea, Summerfield, & Rosen, 1982; Pearlson, Flournoy, Simonson, & Slanney, 1981) ignore vestibular (Frick, 1982; Schilder, 1930), kinesthetic, proprioceptive (Kolb, 1975; Schilder, 1950), auditory (Bunker, 1934; Horowitz, 1966), and tactile (Biven, 1982) aspects of body image, not to mention affective, evaluative, and cognitive aspects.

"Phantom phenomenon," upon which the body image concept was originally based (Critchley, 1950; Hoffman, 1954), can occur following the loss of any body part or function (Dorpat, 1971; Jarvis, 1967), apparently to the degree that the part or function has been represented in consciousness (Bromage & Melzack, 1974; Melzack & Bromage, 1973; Riding, 1976). Thus, in addition to the frequent reports of phantom limbs, patients have had phantom experiences of the genitals and of orgasm (Heusner, 1965; Money, 1969); of lost facial features (Hoffman, 1955); of intestines (Druss, O'Connor, & Stern, 1972); of the uterus; of the bladder, with accompanying sensations of micturition (Dorpat, 1971); of the colon and anus, with sensations of defecation (Critchley, 1959); and of the stomach, with persistent feelings of hunger referred to the absent stomach and alleviated by eating (Szasz, 1949; Wangenstein & Carlson, 1931).

It is interesting to speculate whether tissue lost in starvation may have a continuing representation, which may account for persistent and irrational feelings of fatness. Some years ago, Stunkard and his associates (Stunkard & Burt, 1967; Stunkard & Mendelson, 1967) reported that body image disturbances persisted even after loss to a normal weight in individuals with juvenile-onset but not maturity-onset obesity. Weiss (1958) equates persisting feelings of fatness after weight loss with phantom limb phenomenon: "Any change in the body image, even a very positive one, is difficult for the personality to assimilate" (p. 25).

Of particular interest is the fact that such phantom experiences vary with physical and emotional condition. Riddoch (1941) reports that a phantom that has faded with time may temporarily reappear if the patient's health becomes impaired from, say, influenza, fatigue, or worry. Ill health or emotional disturbance can reduce "central inhibition," with "resultant reappearance of a phantom that has gone" (p. 199). (See also Halpern, 1965; Jessner & Abse, 1960; Lukianowicz, 1967; Murphy, 1957; Pankow, 1974; Peto, 1972.)

Finally, phantom phenomena can appear in the absence of any stimulus (Dorpat, 1971). The condition common to all phantom phenomena is "the interruption of afferent input from part of the body to the brain"—that is, a reduction of sensory input (as in sensory deprivation or anesthesia) from any body part that has a "mental representation." Noting that phantom phenomena are the norm, appearing in as many as 98% of some study series, Dorpat asks the question: "Could it be that the interruption of sensory input causes the central nervous system to initiate its own sensory discharge, experienced as a hallucination?" (p. 33). It is interesting to speculate whether the loss of sensations produced by starvation may lead to the creation (hallucination) of compensatory ones. The inordinate preoccupation with food might be due to central nervous system-initiated representations of eating or even of specific "favorite foods" (Wooley & Wooley, 1981). The preoccupation with the stomach, and the often inexplicable perception of bloat and distension, may be attempts of the brain to represent the missing functions and sensations normally associated with eating.

In summary, then, an examination of the literature on phantom representation of missing body parts and functions suggests that body image disturbances in patients with eating disorders may be in part attributable to specialized phenomena. These include continuing experience of lost body fat as a "phantom body part"; intensification of such experiences during emotional stress, fatigue, and illness; regression to earlier body images (Jessner & Abse, 1960; Lukianowicz, 1967; Pankow, 1974; Peto, 1972); and exaggerated representations of food and gastrointestinal sensations caused by the sensory deprivation of starvation.

What are required, both in terms of increased understanding and therapeutic access, are techniques that begin to reveal the "layers" of body image carried by women, as well as the early experiences that have influenced these representations. It is generally believed that cultural attitudes, as transmitted through the family, are crucial to stable self-image in the face of bodily changes (Kolb, 1975; Lussier, 1980).

If indeed the current cultural climate has shaken the comfort of mothers with their own bodies, thus creating tension and anxiety in their relationship to the bodies of their daughters, even early self-representations may be anxious, ambiguous, or negative. When cultural pressures further induce the daughters, during the already unstable period of puberty, to attempt further modifications of their bodies, the conditions for body image disturbances are maximized.

Concern over the child's body in the mother–child interaction is likely to vary with the mother's body image and eating behavior. One wonders how the starving mother is apt to deal with the feeding of her child: to withhold food; to feed normally, as if food were not the central issue of her life; or to overfeed in response to her own preoccupation with food and projection of her hunger onto her child. In the absence of any evidence, the most probable assumption is that the process of feeding is marked by inconsistency and is greatly emotionally charged. For example, a mother who sometimes "loses control" by allowing herself the scraps of food left on a child's plate must watch each bite with grim intensity—sometimes hoping that the child will rid her of the temptation, at other times resenting her more with each disappearing morsel. Holding her daughter and feeling her bones or flesh must profoundly affect her, for this is all but part of her body, the closest she comes to feeling herself. Does it invoke acceptance, envy, revulsion, rage, sorrow?

The profound importance of the mother's attitude toward her daughter's body, as perceived by the daughter, is illustrated in the findings of a survey of college women (Debs et al., 1983). The rated degree of negativity of the mother toward the daughter's body was correlated at the .0001 level on all but one of the Eating Disorder Inventory (EDI) scales, which are predictive (among other things) of bulimia and body dissatisfaction (Garner, Olmsted, & Polivy, 1983). While most (92%) of the college women rated their mothers' attitudes toward them, as persons, as "mostly positive" or better, only 43% rated their mothers' evaluation of their *bodies* this highly.

Body image disturbances are probably the commonest problem among women today, and are all but universal in the increasing numbers of women affected by serious eating disorders. Our view is that the gradually intensifying cultural pressures to meet a biologically unrealistic standard level of thinness has created a generation of mothers who find not only their roles and purpose in life outmoded by rapid social change, but also their desirability and acceptability as traditional wives and mothers threatened. The transmission of this discord to their daughters has produced a second generation of weight-obsessed women, subjected to conflict and anxiety over their bodies and food intake from the moment of their birth.

The lack of unswerving and unambivalent acceptance of their physical selves, compounded by unprecedented efforts to alter their bodies, creates a condition of great vulnerability in which bodily insecurities drive young women into starvation, withdrawal, regression, and the reactivation of early negative body images. Unfortunately, weight loss does not "work"; it does not lastingly produce the longed-for sensation of thinness, as lost fat continues to be experienced as a real body part. Eventually the efforts to restrict food intake exceed biological capabilities, and voracious bouts of eating produce sudden, frightening shifts in body size and abdominal sensations. Purging permits temporary relief of these traumatic sensations, while at the same time leading to a progressive destruction of the capacity for normal satiety.

Arriving for treatment, these women struggle to tell us how life in their bodies is experienced — as a series of nightmarish transitions from relative calm to revulsion and loathing; how tenuous and fragile is their capacity for control; how much effort they expend to maintain control for even a few hours; and how purging, for all its horrible effects, is all that stands between them and an anticipated loss of all self-worth. They accept the pain of purging rituals gladly, as the only remaining test of endurance they know they can pass.

To succeed in a world now requiring male toughness, their ability to starve and purge becomes the only remaining vestige of toughness to which they can point. Emotionally, physically, and socially enfeebled, they dread a future of dependence and mediocrity, but doubt their capability for anything else. If they fear growing up and facing the demands of adult life, it is not only because they do not know what to be, but also because they no longer have the energy reserves to "be" anything.

TREATMENT

The Eating Disorders Clinic at the University of Cincinnati Medical Center offers two separate programs of treatment for bulimic women. The first, in existence since 1974, is an outpatient program, without specific time limits, in which treatment is composed of combinations of individual therapy, group therapy, family therapy, and a newly developed body image treatment group. The second program, begun in 1983, is a 3½-week residential outpatient program for groups of six bulimic women whose symptoms are severe enough to warrant concentrated attention but whose level of functioning is high enough to permit them to be treated outside a hospital. This patient selection allows intense, multidimensional, multitherapist attention to be focused on the bulimic symptoms. This program, the Intensive Treatment Program for Bulimia (ITPB), is described in a separate section. However, the same staff and many of the same treatment strategies used in the regular programs are employed.

Therapists

The clinic staff includes five permanent therapists and 13 part-time ones. The majority of therapists are female, but some are male. We do not agree with the view that only women can treat women's problems, but we do feel that men working in this area (as well as women) must undertake considerable self-examination to be sure that their responses are not influenced by sex-role stereotypes — specifically, a greater acceptability of appearance concerns as a fact of life for women; a conscious or unconscious endorsement of the cultural view that women must be slender to be happy; or a lesser emphasis placed on achievement for women than for men.

The reinforcement of cultural prejudices by therapists is devastating. One strategy found helpful is to give all therapists exposure to overweight patients who function at high levels of self-confidence and competency, to make real otherwise empty assertions about the irrelevance of body size to body image and social adjustment, and to avoid any tendency to regard bulimic and anorexic (i.e., thin) patients as the elite.

Format of Therapy

Following is a list of therapy components, to be described in greater detail in later sections. This introduction covers only aspects of format.

INITIAL INTERVIEW

All patients are seen for one or more diagnostic interviews, whether they are self-referred or referred by a therapist, physician, or other source. Initial interviews are conducted by the therapists of the clinic, and an attempt is made to elicit enough information in the initial telephone contact to assign the patient to a therapist with whom she can continue, either in group or in individual therapy.

INDIVIDUAL THERAPY

Individual therapy is generally in the form of weekly, 1-hour sessions, though frequency may be increased to two to three sessions per week for patients in crisis or manifesting more severe disturbances.

THERAPY GROUPS

Therapy groups are co-led by two therapists, contain four to six patients, and have weekly meetings lasting 2 hours each. Patient selection for groups is based on age, maturity, and symptoms. The symptoms patients must have in common to function optimally as a group are weight obsession and intermittent loss of control of eating. Whether "binges" are large or small, or whether they are compensated by purging, fasting, or exercise, is of relatively little importance. Pure "restricters" can be included, but often feel "different." Envy and hostility directed toward them by others in the group will have to be dealt with. Similarly, the weight of patients may vary, but the more extreme the variability, the more time will need to be devoted to management of the feelings about size difference. Thin patients may fear influence by, or feel contemptuous of, heavy ones. Fat patients may find their capacity for empathy tested by the body loathing of thin patients.

Age groupings are based on common developmental concerns, with the following general categories: (1) Ages 15–18. These patients are still living at home, concerned with adolescent issues, and preparing for separation. (2) Ages 19–25. These patients are adjusting to separation and dealing primarily with issues of schooling, career choice, and the development of intimate relationships. (3) Ages 25 and up. These women have generally completed the first round of career choice and choice of part-ners. Issues include review of these choices, marital problems, child rearing, and career advancement. Women between the ages of 21 and 30 may be placed in the second or third categories, according to predominant life concerns rather than chronological age.

FAMILY THERAPY

Family therapy usually consists of weekly 1-hour sessions led by male and female cotherapists. When relatives must travel a great distance, 2-hour sessions are held and may be scheduled on consecutive days. Family therapy has been made a requirement for treatment of any anorexic or bulimic patient who is 18 or younger, or who is liv-ing at home for an indefinite period.

BODY IMAGE THERAPY

Body image therapy techniques are incorporated, to a limited degree, into regular therapy groups. However, their main use is as a separate offering for patients who have had some group or individual therapy, who no longer require close monitoring of or assistance with eating, but who are blocked from further progress by unresolvable distortions of body image. Body image treatment has been offered in closed, medium-term groups (i.e., 4–8 months), and plans are under way to offer 2-day intensive sessions.

COMBINED THERAPIES

Patients may be in any or all of these therapies, simultaneously or consecutively. The usual case is that after the initial consultation, the patient is assigned to group or individual therapy. Groups are generally regarded as the more beneficial; therefore a decision in favor of individual therapy will reflect the patient's reluctance to join a group, unavailability of a place in a suitable group, or some unusual feature of the problem that requires further diagnosis and individual attention. Patients who join groups may elect to continue prior individual sessions if there is an apparent need for concentrated work on a problem outside the scope of the group. As noted above, all patients aged 18 or younger or living at home are required to have family therapy. Marital therapy or family-of-origin sessions are optional (but encouraged) additions to the treatment of independent adults, usually undertaken in the middle of or late in the course of therapy.

Initial Interview

The main purpose of the initial consultation is to get to know the prospective patient — to put her at ease as much as possible, so that she may tell her story in her own way, and relate the events she deems relevant in the order in which she wants to relate them. As she tells her story, specific information is noted (or elicited at appropriate times) concerning peak, lowest, and ideal weights; frequency, nature, and severity of binges and purges; hospitalizations, precipitants, family history, past achievements, present ambitions, and inhibitions; body image attitudes; current eating patterns (e.g., frequency of "normal" meals that are not purged); current dieting and exercise patterns; present and past marital, educational, employment, sexual, and social difficulties.

At the same time that the therapist is getting to know the patient, the patient is getting to know the therapist and making a judgment as to whether the therapy that will follow is likely to be beneficial. Nothing does more to increase the confidence of the patient than to have the interviewer ask questions or make comments that convey an understanding of the *phenomenology* of the eating-disordered patient's experience. It is as though the woman is lost in the woods and receives a signal that she has been sighted; help may not be there yet, but someone knows where she is. The success of the interviewer in imparting this feeling will be a major determinant in how much of her inner experiences the patient chooses to share (then, or ever), and it may be decisive in the choice to pursue therapy. The interviewer should never be timid about inquiring about unusual behaviors or feelings, since the very questions reassure the patient that the therapist knows the terrain, and they give the patient permission to be more self-disclosing without risk of shocking the therapist. It is amazing how frequently patients have been in prior therapy and have not revealed their symptomatology, or have minimized it in response to a baffled, shocked, or judgmental response on the part of the earlier therapist.

As in all therapy, the patient must be met where she is. It is important from the first contact to encourage patients to take the lead in drawing connections. Most patients have a great deal to say, and will provide useful information if asked near the end of the first interview an open-ended question, such as this: "You have lived with this problem for a long time, and you know yourself better than anyone. What do *you* think caused this? Why did you, in particular, develop this problem; and why do you think it has been so hard to give up?"

Duration of Therapy

For most bulimic patients, therapy takes about a year, although a few progress more rapidly, and many choose to continue more than a year to work on other problems. We have moved away from the use of time-limited groups to "open" ones, in which members are replaced as they depart. This allows needed flexibility, and the mix of advanced and beginning patients seems advantageous.

Length of treatment obviously depends on the severity of the problems and the extent to which patients elect to broaden the goals of therapy to encompass other problem areas — a choice that is generally encouraged. Some of the factors that appear to have a bearing on duration of treatment are as follows: Patients with severe character disorders (i.e., borderline or narcissistic) who have been bulimic for several years may not be able to give up their symptoms for a long time, until extensive therapeutic work has been accomplished. Patients coerced into therapy may be resistant and slow to trust the therapist, so that a long time is required to establish a working relationship with them. The greater the patient's sense of coercion and stance of rebellion, the more autonomy must be granted, including the freedom to ignore eating-related issues. Power struggles do no good; the patient's resistance is expressive of an urgent need to direct her own affairs. Later, gently, the patient is encouraged to set her own timetable for addressing her eating problem.

As a general rule, the more secretive and shame-ridden the patient's bingeing–purging is, the more she has to gain by giving it up. If she quits, she will no longer have to expend so much energy keeping the secret, "planning around" the symptom, and risking the shame of exposure. Thus, paradoxically, patients who make rapid gains are often ones with long-standing covert problems and no history of prior therapy (usually because of fears about confidentiality). Conversely, patients whose bulimic habits are long known to significant others, to whom "the worst" has already happened, and who enjoy a high degree of tolerance of their behavior may be slow to improve.

Obviously, adopting a pattern of secrecy versus visibility is indicative of important characteristics of the patient and her social environment. The secretive patient is usually able to exert somewhat more control over her symptoms and tends to be more conscientious and guilt-ridden. Secondary gain, if it exists, is limited to avoidance of anxiety-producing behaviors. The patient who divulges or "exhibits" her symptoms is apt to be more comfortable with them, to be generally more impulsive, to use symptoms expressively as a form of communication, and to be deeply enmeshed in complex secondary gains. The adaptation of others to her symptoms may indicate the importance of the symptoms in maintaining a pathological family structure, or may reflect indifference or despair. It is not unusual for relatives of patients with very long-standing disorders to take the position that they have "given up," and even to state that they expect the patients to die. In cases where the familial and social networks are deeply involved in a bulimic's illness, their involvement in therapy is almost always required.

Obviously, many patients will still have "problems" even after they give up or begin to give up their symptoms; dealing with these will, of course, extend the length of therapy. For one thing, the onset of illness may have led to gaps in normal development. Crucial learning experiences have been lost, and the missing skills (and attendant confidence) must be made up. These areas include dating, sexual activity, the development of a style of dress and "self-presentation," and preparation for and entry into a career.

If the patient became anorexic–bulimic before learning any culturally relevant skills (or if her family life did not instill in her any appreciation of such skills for women), and if she has made a "career" out of her illness, treatment will have to deal — either directly or by way of consultation — with career problems. People who have spent many years oscillating between the heights of grandiose ambition and the depths of humiliatingly low self-confidence may be unable or unwilling to face the reality of work, or to acknowledge the value of self-sufficiency. One patient, a 30-year-old aspiring actress/singer, said that giving up her bulimia was like a grieving process; it represented all she had to show for what she saw as 15 years of futility and failure — that is, by keeping her thin, it kept her hopes alive. (She is presently studying to become an art therapist.)

The main goal of many patients, the one that brings them to therapy in the first place, is to figure out why they have done what they do for so long — in other words, to make sense out of their lives and to gain a sense of identity. But often they are inarticulate about the very thing they and their therapists most want to know about: the "meanings" of their experience. Story (1976) describes this problem in one of his patients:

[She] cared only about radiating an impression of high virtue and industry. As she herself most sadly knew, she was preoccupied with herself and the despairing economics of eating, could think of nothing but exercise and eating schedules, and by that time cared for nobody. Weight, calories, fatness, meals, and efforts to balance them off had all been rendered intrinsically meaningless by her particular obsessional pattern and they had become almost totally abstract and beyond the limits of spoken communication. (p. 181)

It is probably in the nature of this experience to be resistant to verbal articulation. Szasz (quoted by Shoenberg, 1975) speaks of the "language of hysteria," and the same applies to anorexia nervosa: "[It is] the language of illness, employed either because another language has not been learned well enough [i.e., the 'language of anger'] or because this language happens to be especially useful" (Shoenberg, 1975, p. 512). Because of the limitations of language in these matters, nonverbal therapies are often startlingly effective in reviving memories, feelings, perspectives, motivations, and fears; when these are "processed," a fresh sense of understanding and hope is engendered. Extending therapy past the point of symptom remission to allow the patient to fully reconstruct the meaning of this phase of her life helps to create a sense of intellectual identity, future, and purpose, which is ultimately the surest safeguard against relapse.

General Educational Aspects of Treatment

Although it is doubtful that patients are able to make use of excessive and/or ill-timed informational input, recovery requires that they obtain a better understanding of the realities of dieting, weight regulation, and appetite mechanisms. At carefully chosen points in treatment, the following topics are covered:

1. *The recovery process.* The distortion of appetite through purging and the anticipated stages of the return to normal eating are described. The knowledge that all food retained retrains the body to experience satiety provides hope and gives the patient a road map. Physical symptoms accompanying recovery must also be discussed; these are more distinct in patients who abruptly discontinue purging, but are experienced to some degree by nearly all patients. The symptoms include dramatic weight shifts, due to rehydration and to an apparent disturbance of the regulatory mechanisms for fluid retention, which seem to correct themselves with time; gastrointestinal symptoms, such as distension, gas, constipation, and diarrhea, which can be treated symptomatically with simple nonprescription remedies (e.g., simethicone to relieve gas distention, and bulk-forming, nonirritant laxatives); and other transitory symptoms, including sleep interruption (due in part to the newly experienced necessity to void fluids during the night), early morning awakening (from unknown causes), increased body temperature, and heightened lability of mood with the reinstatement of normal hormonal activity and menses.

2. *Weight regulation.* The concept of "set point" must be introduced, and the effects of falling below set point described: The reduced metabolic rate that results slows weight loss and increases appetite. That both effects are reversible with weight gain is important for patients to understand, and sometimes assists in a minor way with their willingness to tolerate some weight gain, since these facts argue against the feared eventuality of relentless appetite and weight gain on low intakes.

3. *Effects of starvation*. Education about the physical and psychological symptoms of starvation is useful in sensitizing patients to recognize and to develop an aversion to them. This information also allows reattribution of some of the experiences that they may have taken as evidence of personality problems or chronically depressed mood with which they would always be confronted. In fact, a myriad of difficulties are often alleviated by a return to adequate nutrition.

4. *Effects of bulimia on health*. Patients should be familiarized with the health risks of bulimia in sufficient detail that they can insure that they receive necessary medical testing at the time of treatment and in future years. They should know enough to request specific tests and to see that records are maintained and transferred to new physicians. Considering our limited knowledge of the long-term effects of bulimia, the bulimic patient should be more closely monitored than others. Potentially useful information may include (in addition to tests included in regular medical examinations) any or all of the following: electrocardiograms (EKGs) and cardiac echograms, bone studies, comprehensive renal studies, and gastrointestinal workups. Although the decisions must rest with the patient and physician, we believe it is important to prepare the patient to be an informed participant.

Treatment of Eating Problems

At the conclusion of the diagnostic session(s), patients are shown how to keep food records. Information about the amount and type of food eaten, time of eating, anxiety level before and after eating, guilt level before and after eating, degree of bloat, and whether or not the food was purged is collected daily by the patient, using food records designed to address those aspects of eating usually experienced as important to the patient. The very questions asked make the patient feel that her problem is understood, and compliance in keeping food records tends to be high. The recording of all food eaten in binges is de-emphasized in favor of an accurate record of food eaten between binges and a notation that a binge occurred. If the patient protests that record keeping, by increasing her preoccupation with food, is too anxiety-producing, it is deferred until the anxieties are explored and resolved. Frequently, as treatment progresses, patients express a desire to wean themselves off the compulsive concern symbolized by psychological or actual "scorekeeping," and this choice is always supported.

The main goal of treatment is a *permanent* resolution of the patient's eating/weight problem. *The effort is made to transform a moral problem into a physiological one.* In anorexia and bulimia, the patient is caught between her fear of getting fat on the one hand, and obsession with food and the urge to eat on the other. She experiences chronic hunger that will not be relieved for very long by *any* amount of food, but only by reconditioning of satiety through abstinence from purging, restoration of normal weight, or both.

Most patients with eating disorders not only binge and vomit, abuse laxatives, and/or binge and starve; they also do not or cannot eat "regular" or conventional meals. They are phobic of all but a few "safe" "diet" foods. Any time they allow themselves to eat and keep down a normal-sized meal, they feel "bloated" and "fat." These feelings are "real" in two senses: First, the digestive tracts of anorexics and bulimics are unaccustomed to processing so much food, and so greater discomfort *is* experienced; second, body image distortions can intensify the feelings. The scale often confirms that they are "fatter," because, without so much water loss through vomiting and starving, it may register a considerable gain of water weight. This, of course, intensifies the fear of large weight gains, which in turn brings about a return to vomiting, starving, and laxatives—the familiar vicious circle.

Many patients' fear of losing control of their eating (i.e., fear of binges) is of course realistic; the further they are below their set point, the easier it is for binges to be set off. Often they have tried to eat "normal" meals, only to discover that once they start eating, they cannot stop. So any suggestion by the therapist to "eat in moderation" falls on deaf ears; besides, parents and friends have already told them this many times.

Nearly all patients have learned two ways of eating: (1) A "controlled" mode, which is usually a low-calorie, low-carbohydrate regimen consisting of "good" foods (i.e., lots of salad—with diet dressing—and other diet foods, such as yogurt, apples, and diet colas). While eating this way, the patient loses weight and feels "in control." (2) An "uncontrolled" mode, in which all the "bad" foods (i.e., sweets, breads, red meat) are eaten in large quantities, but are then vomited or purged with laxatives. During these episodes, the patient is often gaining weight or maintaining a weight that makes her feel "too fat."

The patient usually believes that her "controlled" eating is a healthy way to eat. She sees other women eating this way, and to the casual observer she herself appears to eat this way, too; in other words, this is her public way of eating. "Controlled" eating is "ego-syntonic." The "out-of-control" eating is not; the patient does not feel "herself" when bingeing.

The therapeutic task, once trust exists, is to convince the anorexic–bulimic patient to give up her own means of weight control and to try a different, more normal approach—one that will be compatible with a more conventional social life, for example. If the patient does not already realize it, she must be persuaded to give up her ideas about her "good" way of eating; no foods are forbidden, but encouragement is given to add foods to the "safe" list. The patient must come to understand that she cannot adhere to her "controlled" mode indefinitely. When she eats that way, she loses weight and feels good, but she also insures that she will either "lose control" and binge, or will lose so much weight that someone will step in and take her freedom of choice away from her; she will be hospitalized and force-fed, if only as a last resort.

One approach to getting the patient who is afraid of rapid weight gain to try "unsafe" foods is to explain that when she binges, especially on sweets, she does absorb *some* calories (patients often erroneously believe that by vomiting they rid themselves of all ingested calories); that the longer she has binged, the more calories she is likely to be absorbing with each binge; that the digestive mechanism may adapt in such a way that the early stages of digestion are speeded up and more is absorbed as the habit develops. It can then be pointed out that she can substitute a smaller meal (which she retains) for a binge of the same food (which she vomits) and not gain any fat. However, a gain of water weight may occur, and the patient must be prepared for it.

If a patient is vomiting during all her free time and is unable to make any progress, she is encouraged to set a goal of waiting some amount of time after waking each day before she starts bingeing. Then a time is set after which she will not vomit any more that day. Eventually, binges become restricted to a given time period each day;

during the remaining time, small meals or snacks are planned in such a way that the patient feels in control; these meals/snacks are then gradually built up, while binge time is reduced.

The patient who alternately binges and starves must come to understand that the starvation phase causes the binges, while the shame and humiliation of the binges motivate the starving. Once the patient understands that she must give up her "good" eating as well as the "bad," she decides what pattern of meals and snacks she wants to try to follow (e.g., three meals a day with a snack at night; two meals and two snacks; etc.). Typically, the patient can forego bingeing at first and restricts herself to "good" eating. While she is being "good," she is encouraged to add to one meal or snack a formerly forbidden food — for example, a dessert with dinner; buttered toast or some protein at breakfast; regular (nondiet) dressing on the lunch salad. This is the beginning step in increasing the variety of "safe" foods. The patient is helped to anticipate the effects of eating and retaining food that have been described in the preceding section. She is warned that these distressing effects may trigger a binge, but that they are an unavoidable aspect of recovery, requiring six or more weeks to subside.

Above all, the patient's anxiety about weight gain must be dealt with from the beginning. A flooding–desensitization model is used to assist the patient in undertaking systematic exposure to particular foods so as to extinguish the anxiety. She is reassured that a few anxious trials without the feared consequences (large, rapid, and irreversible weight gain) will allow her to master the food, which now masters her. If necessary, a staff member helps her through the anxiety reaction by having her eat just before or during sessions, or, in some cases, by accompanying her to an ice cream parlor or restaurant and remaining with her till the panic induced by eating subsides. Nurse therapists, familiar with phobia treatment, are helpful in conducting *in vivo* flooding sessions as described above.

The patient must also be made aware that, even if she consciously wants to give up her symptoms (i.e., the symptoms are no longer ego-syntonic), she may find herself choosing to binge and vomit anyway. At this point, it is important to emphasize to her that she is *choosing*; that is, she must "own" the symptoms and begin trying to understand why they are so valuable to her. Sometimes the symptoms are valuable only as a means of weight control; the therapeutic task then shifts to an examination of why thinness is so valuable. Patients who are quite open to questioning the value of thinness for everyone at any cost may have much difficulty modifying their feelings about their *own* thinness. In many cases the symptoms are valuable, even precious, to the patient for idiosyncratic reasons; they are the patient's way of being unique and special, and may have "meanings" that the patient cannot or is ashamed to articulate. The therapeutic task is to help the patient understand and articulate these meanings by identifying how the symptoms function in her world. This identification becomes much easier once the patient is not bingeing and purging every day. Against a background of normal eating, a binge–purge episode can be more easily analyzed.

If, in spite of these efforts, the patient continues to lose control and binges, it may be that she is too far below set point to tolerate the associated level of chronic hunger, and so she must gain weight in order to be able to stop bingeing. Her "premorbid" weight is as good a guide as any as to what her set point might be. It is at this point, when a patient *must* gain weight, that the most resistance will be met. Her choice is essentially to remain "sick" (i.e., anorexic–bulimic; Hall, 1982), or to become "too fat"—the very thing she fears most. In cases like this, we believe, the therapist must in all honesty first make the choice clear and then leave it up to the patient. Part of making this choice clear, however, involves helping the patient understand the causes of her fear of fat.

This choice must, of course, be opposed if starvation or purging becomes life-threatening, at which point hospitalization is required. Patients who are hospitalized are placed on a behavioral program in which access to social interactions and privileges is contingent on weight gain. Tube feeding or hyperalimentation are used only in the rare instances where these measures fail. Despite the disadvantages of rule setting in behavioral programs, they are preferable to forced feeding in that the patient does *choose* (albeit under coercive conditions) to eat rather than having food imposed on her, and this is somewhat more compatible with the goal of encouraging autonomy.

A special problem that occasionally arises is a patient's complaint of "panic attacks," accompanied by hot flashes, rapid heartbeat, and weakness, after eating normal portions of certain foods. It is explained that she may have triggered off an oversecretion of insulin. The body has "learned" that when a particular taste, say sweet, is tasted, large quantities of carbohydrates are customarily ingested, and that therefore large quantities of insulin must be secreted to handle the influx. If the food is then vomited, or if large quantities are not ingested at one particular time, the bloodstream is left flooded with insulin, which can cause a panic attack by bringing blood sugar down. The therapist must take such episodes seriously, as they sometimes progress rapidly into agoraphobia.

Complete remission of symptoms is possible only when the patient's body image is such that dieting is no longer considered desirable, necessary, or even helpful. A patient can reach this point in more than one way: She can change her attitude toward the ideal body image (i.e., decide that it is not ideal for her). She can change her attitude toward her own body (i.e., decide that even if it is not ideal, she loves it anyway). She can de-emphasize appearance in her life and let self-esteem rest on other attributes. She can decide that being thin and adhering to a low-calorie but nutritionally sound diet are "worth it." This is especially true in certain occupations requiring thinness, such as modeling, dance, and competitive athletics.

Group Therapy

Group therapy can operate in either of two somewhat overlapping modes, depending on the number of functions it has to serve. The first mode, in which education and the management of eating are tasks of the group, has a somewhat tighter agenda and more direction by the therapists. If, on the other hand, the issues related to weight and eating are managed in a separate group, are dealt with in concurrent individual therapy, or have been substantially resolved when the group begins, it is possible to use the group primarily as a laboratory for interpersonal experience. Both models have their advantages, with the choice depending primarily on the larger treatment format. They are discussed separately here.

WORKING GROUPS

The first model, which is referred to here as the "working group," is a complete treatment that can be successfully used alone. At the time of entry, each patient begins keeping food records; these are distributed to the group for discussion each week, continuing as long as necessary. In a newly created group, the therapists will have to assume the primary responsibility for posing questions that allow each patient to increase her understanding of the psychological and circumstantial variables that control her eating; the therapists also make suggestions for gradual changes. Since groups are "open" (members are replaced as they terminate), in time advanced patients are able to share this role, including the educational functions. Because sessions are relatively widely spaced (a week apart), patients are discouraged from attempting changes that are likely to be too difficult. The goal is to minimize the experience of failure and to provide a slow, steady transition from disordered to orderly eating, making substantial use of specific, individualized advice and group support.

The task orientation of working groups lends itself to a format in which patients take turns describing the events and issues of their week and formulating goals for the following week. However, discussion need not always center around food and eating. As patients make progress in this area, they tend increasingly to turn their attention to other areas, and they begin to discuss various problems in their lives. Sometimes new lines of discussion are prompted by the attempt to understand an unexpected loss of control with food; sometimes they are selected because, with the reduction in anxiety over eating, energy is freed to look at broader meanings of their behaviors or to examine previously unidentified problems. Sometimes even new patients are best permitted or encouraged to discuss general concerns, leaving the eating behaviors untouched.

Some therapeutic skill is involved in sensing when a patient should be firmly encouraged to deal with her eating problems and when the subject should be ignored. If disordered eating has come to be symbolic of power and autonomy, the therapist must not become an adversary, but must give the patient "permission" to work exclusively on the issues she deems important, while arranging that her weight and physical health are unobtrusively monitored. A useful sign that attention to eating will be counterproductive is the failure of patients to act on eating goals, especially when these have been self-set. The protest is almost invariably subtle; the patient rarely if ever says, "I don't really want to do this." Rather, she thanks the group and the leader for excellent suggestions. She avoids describing her failure; instead, on inquiry, she explains that, for various reasons, she was unable to enact her plans that week.

It is precisely the patients with the most difficulty in asserting their own real preferences and needs who must be helped to articulate them and to tell the group and the leaders, "No, I don't want to do this, or to follow your (or anyone's) suggestions." If this is done, and if the leaders can convey a sense of genuine comfort with such a patient's decision, then she almost inevitably returns to the problem of her own accord, ready to undertake change. The time lapse may be as short as a few weeks or as long as 6 months, depending on the success she is having in becoming more expressive and assertive in the group and in her outside life.

Despite the constraints of this group format, patients reveal and explore surprisingly sensitive issues as time goes by. Some stay on long after they have stopped bingeing to examine such problems as their compulsivity, their needs to feel special, their inability to handle intimacy, their sexual dysfunctions, and their distrustful or hostile responses to people in their lives. By composing groups of patients in similar developmental phases, this process is facilitated.

Groups such as these tend to get better over time. Norms of conduct and values favoring free expression and productivity are established and transmitted from patient to patient. One such group, in existence for over 5 years, has graduated dozens of patients. The leaders are probably truly needed only in the diagnostic phase, to help elucidate to the group the nature and ramifications of a new patient's difficulties. The patients are as good as the therapists (and sometimes better) at pursuing the "cure."

Relationships and interactions among group members are often examined as a means of clarifying habitual emotional and behavioral responses to others. Patients may, for example, offer the information to a particular group member that they have felt discouraged from giving advice or attempting greater closeness; that they are frustrated and annoyed by the alternate declaration and denial of problems; that they repeatedly become fatigued and have difficulty concentrating on what the person is saying; that they are inexplicably angry. Such interchanges are useful in understanding both the speaker and the object of the comments; they help to reveal excessive fears of control or intimacy, conflict and guilt over expression of hostility, masked depression, covert hostility, rivalry, reactivation of unresolved familial conflicts, and so on. Such encounters are encouraged and facilitated by leaders, but it should be noted that the working agenda of these groups does not lend itself as readily as some to the full expression and examination of the feelings generated within the group.

The affective tone of such groups is absorbing, but rarely reaches the excruciating peaks of intensity in the group format to be described next. But groups such as this work, and work hard. They are usually very successful in achieving cures of bulimia, with the average length of tenure being about a year. It is our impression that the group's success depends on keeping the size very small, and on using leaders who have had considerable experience in treating eating disorders and who are able to use special techniques as required (analyzing food records; goal setting, shaping, and fading; flooding and desensitization; role playing and Gestalt techniques; and nonverbal therapies). Careful judgment is required in introducing special methods to amplify emotional expression and to produce behavior change. The techniques must not be disruptive or "take over" the group, but they should be used to keep things moving. To leave any patient in an emotional or behavioral rut for too long drains the group of vitality.

INTERPERSONAL GROUPS

These groups, similar to groups known by many other names (e.g., Yalom, 1975), are but one *component* of complete treatment, in which education and management of eating are handled elsewhere, leaving the group free of any set tasks. We regard these groups as laboratories in which patients may experiment with interpersonal relationships without risking the permanent consequences that could occur in the outside world. Many theoretical models can be used to conceptualize such groups, but we view them as an infinitely more vivid and challenging alternative to behavior therapy directed at altering interpersonal behaviors (e.g., social skills training, assertion training), and to self-examination as carried out in most forms of individual therapy. For many patients, this will be the first experience with total honesty and true intimacy they have ever had.

The goal of the group is explained to patients at the beginning, in these terms:

If you will make an effort to say exactly what you really feel in here about the things that happen, and how you are reacting to the other members, you can learn all you need to know about the interpersonal problems you have had and are still having in your real life. If it happens out there, it will happen in here. Just be yourselves, and don't try to anticipate where it will lead.

From this point on, the task of the therapists is straightforward, albeit difficult to implement: to encourage and amplify, in every way possible, the expression of feelings. William Strunk's famous dictum on writing is applicable to the therapist's task: "Omit needless words! Omit needless words! Omit needless words!" (see Strunk & White, 1979, p. xiii). Chatting, explaining, intellectualizing, equivocating, or qualifying, harmless enough in some contexts, are deadly in this one. They bring the therapeutic process to a standstill. If the therapist has something to say, it should be said clearly and succinctly, since the therapist's ability to be direct becomes the model for the patients.

While it is occasionally useful to point out connections missed by the group, the patients' own tendencies to move away from the immediate to the analogous are so strong that they need no help from the therapists. The relevance of group experience to past events and chronic concerns will emerge readily enough, and the task of therapists is to avoid colluding in premature closure. The risk is not that too much feeling will be generated, but too little—that incomplete expression of feeling will create unresolved tensions that perpetuate fear. As in flooding, one must never back off when anxiety is at its peak, since the immediate reduction of anxiety so accomplished only reinforces avoidance. As risky as it may feel, it is safe to assume that patients who open themselves fully to the group will always be supported; genuineness is moving and endearing to anyone whose responses are not distorted by a painful history of prior interaction. Nor does the response need to be unanimous to be effective.

To achieve the required completeness of expression, it is necessary to interrupt the efforts of patients to rescue one another, for the whitewashing, minimizing, or smoothing over of feelings is often the way in which they have been chronically deterred from emotional expression in the past. They have learned to comply with the implicit message "Keep your pain to yourself," and have been made to believe that such salves are administered for their own good. Thus they are usually unable to protest without the assistance of the therapist.

In one early session, a patient began tearfully to describe her feelings of inferiority to others who had not binged since the last meeting. Another patient, guilty over her success and struggling with a history of being envied for her family's wealth, social standing, and the "privileges" she had received, rushed to the rescue. She reassured the patient that this was only one example; that she herself often failed; in fact, she was sure she would fail again soon, and so on. The "failing" patient smiled with gratitude and stopped crying. Then one of the therapists asked her, "How does it feel to receive all this good advice and support from someone who is doing better than you?" After a brief moment of disbelief at the question, a torrent of emotion was released. "It feels horrible," she screamed. "That is what my whole life has been like. No one can face the fact of my failure—even me. All I get is reassurance and good advice."

This led eventually to important insights about the "failing" patient's role in her family and was the beginning of her ability to stop acting and say what she really thought. Not surprisingly, it also produced great anger at the therapist for attacking someone who was "only trying to help." The analysis of such efforts to help became an important theme in this group, and members eventually learned how to really help one another by encouraging their inner search.

Much later, the same patient began to relive a series of early losses. She wept; she stopped and started; she complained that one minute she was hot, the next cold. "When I close my eyes I am overwhelmed by images," she sobbed. The others silently gathered around her, and the only interruptions were such comments as "Keep going," "Whatever you're feeling, you need to face." When she was through, and only when she was through, did she embrace each one and thank them for their help.

Therapists can facilitate this process by finding alternatives to "talking about" things. For example, talking about a conflict can be replaced by a dialogue between the two conflicting internal voices. Descriptions of a family event can be replaced by a re-enactment of it, in which group members and therapists are cast in roles. Patients are discouraged from *describing* feelings about other members and are encouraged to talk *to* them. If a patient's intellectual defenses are so strong that they can produce only "word storms," movement activities may be substituted. In general, techniques can be invented to suit the situation. The clue that a new tactic is required is a feeling of frustration or boredom engendered in the therapist. But it should be acted on quickly.

Groups of this type afford unique opportunities for intimacy, but are, of course, also susceptible to the development of restrictive norms—different from, but as oppressive as, the ones the patients are trying to escape. Groups are rarely "of one mind," and the therapist must be alert to the needs of the patient who is not in line with the predominant mood.

A particularly difficult feeling to express, requiring therapist facilitation, is that of detachment and indifference to another's pain. One patient was helped to say after a particularly moving event, "I wanted to feel, but I didn't. It's like being at a funeral and knowing you should be sad, should cry, but not caring." This admission allowed several patients to reveal doubts about their ability to love, and ultimately to understand and resolve the barriers to feelings (and to relinquish the idea that they must care about everyone, all the time).

The unique value of a group such as this for patients with eating disorders is that it transfers the burden of expression from the body by allowing the mastery of anxiety associated with direct expression. To learn the *techniques* of assertion and expression does nothing to insure that they will ever be used when they are needed most—in emotionally charged situations, in which there is typically an enormous, unarticulated fear of repercussions. We find it useful to provide skills training, but only after a group experience in which patients have become desensitized to the danger of saying what they mean. Ironically, patients typically love assertion training and say, "Why didn't you teach us this sooner?" This may be one of the few instances of patient feedback we find to be misguided, for in our experience they embrace these techniques precisely because they have acquired the emotional strength to use them for purposes more pressing than sending back an overcooked steak.

As already noted, the conditions under which a group such as this can operate are fundamentally incompatible with the requirements of providing concrete assistance with eating and ongoing life events, which must be provided somewhere. And yet some groups manage to effect a fairly successful merging of the two styles. This is most often accomplished in groups in which patients have had some prior therapy and have achieved some mastery of their eating problems, and in which the therapists are experienced in both modalities. Sometimes groups conduct their "business" in the first 30 minutes, then move on to encounter. Sometimes patients quickly check out one another's needs and make a decision about how to use the meeting. To be able to do that is a sign of considerable sophistication, insofar as it requires patients to identify and make known their needs without cajoling or exploration, and to understand the different requirements and benefits of the two styles of working.

Body Image Therapy

Despite their obvious importance to patients with eating disorders, body image concerns are rarely explored in any depth in group or individual therapy. There are probably several reasons for this. First, neither patients or therapists really know what they are looking for. The only experience readily accessible to the typical patient is body loathing, which seems to require no explanation—it is a natural consequence of having a loathsome body, and she expects the therapist to understand this as she does. Furthermore, bodily perceptions, by their very nature, do not readily lend themselves to articulation. And finally, as we have discovered in the development of body image therapies, there is great resistance to exploration. Feelings about the body are evidently so painful or shame-producing, or communication of them so threatening, that any retreat will be sought. This is expressed variously: in repeated requests for explanations of goals, in the introduction of other "pressing" topics, in intellectualization, and in group boycotts (in the form of giddiness or division into subgroups). Therapists sometimes report that the patients ignore them, and sometimes the group succeeds in dividing cotherapists, so that they are in disagreement among themselves whether to pursue the agenda at hand or give in to requests to discuss other material.

Despite the difficulties in starting up such a group, patients usually settle into working and later see the therapy as having been of great value. This is especially true of less verbal patients (or ones less confident of their verbal abilities), who often surprise the therapists by the richness of expression contained in drawings, the vividness of imagery, and the capacity for bodily expression. For a few patients, it may be the only therapy that truly takes hold.

The aims of body image therapy are both diagnostic and therapeutic. It permits better understanding of a given patient's difficulties. Over time, it helps to clarify recurrent themes, permitting the tentative development of theory about the nature and origins of body image disturbances. Our experience to date is consistent with the view that bodily inadequacy is first experienced early in life and that it is intensified with puberty and/or the onset of dieting. A woman's history of bodily feelings is closely interwoven with memories of her mother's attitude to her own body and the body of her daughter.

Finally, a surprising theme has been the intense conflict over which parent the patient is identified with. Abstract depictions (e.g., collages) representing the family usually reveal much greater perceived similarities between father and daughter than between mother and daughter. Patients discover much anxiety connected with this issue: They are aware of having their father's ambition and of an ambivalent wish to reject their mother's selflessness. Reaching the age of womanhood at puberty, they feel a sense of loss and condemnation to an unwanted role; at the same time, they feel bound to support and protect their mothers, and this makes it difficult to separate, or to express the contempt or pity they may feel for their mothers. These phenomena, as noted earlier, appear to be understandable consequences of the dramatic social changes of the last 20 years, in which women's traditional roles have been rejected. The way these themes emerge in body image therapy is described below.

Following are some of the goals of body image therapy, with examples of techniques that we have used to try to facilitate them.

AWARENESS OF DISTORTION

The first aim of body image therapy is to create greater awareness of the distortion in body image, with the aim of lessening the distortion and clarifying the relationship between negative body image and disordered eating.

In one exercise patients are asked to stand in front of a large piece of paper attached to a wall and, pretending that it is a mirror, draw a line around the imaginary image of themselves. Other patients may be asked to draw an outline on the same paper, depicting how they see the person. Finally, the patient stands against the paper, and the therapist makes an actual tracing. Intervals between the patient's and the therapist's actual tracing are colored in to highlight the discrepancy between the perceived and the real. In one group, the two patients with a history of anorexia were stunned by the distortion and sat staring at the pictures for a long time. The heavier bulimic patients showed a lesser degree of distortion. The exercise can be amplified by questions: "If you saw this person how old would you think she was? What are the advantages and disadvantages of being that age, that size?"

A very different way of providing such feedback is to show patients videotapes of themselves. We often begin with a tape of them seated at a table in a group therapy session; this procedure generates less threat than filming movement or whole-body shots. Although responses are variable, they are often more positive, or less focused on body size, than patients anticipate. Comments have included such remarks as "I look too thin and too nervous," and "I am more expressive than I expected; it is sort of fun to watch." In one session, we asked patients to focus on and make notes about an assigned "buddy" during the first viewing, then to watch themselves in a second. This broadened the context of interest and permitted comparison of the sets of reactions.

Filming of movement can be used for special purposes, as in this example: Patients already comfortable with movement therapy were asked to dance in pairs. They were then instructed to imagine themselves gradually getting fatter. As they did so, they acted out an almost clownlike clumsiness. They were then told to imagine getting thinner, and their movements became more fluid and graceful. Then they were pushed further: "Lose another pound . . . now another." As this progressed, a change occurred: ever so gradually, their movement slowed; the pairs disintegrated. One patient moved to a window and stared out silently. Finally they were at a near halt. In discussing this experience and watching the tapes, they reported that the re-enactment of starvation put them in touch with forgotten sensations and feelings; they felt drained and completely incapable of interaction.

AWARENESS OF MOTHER–DAUGHTER BODY IMAGE RELATIONSHIPS

A second goal of body image therapy is to heighten awareness of the relationships between the mother's body image and the daughter's body cathexis.

An exercise related to this goal is to guide patients in imagining (or remembering) how they felt about their own bodies, how they ate, and how their mothers felt about *their* own bodies at selected developmental points, emphasizing especially times of separation and differentiation.

One patient's mother had always been extremely thin. The mother was very private about her body, always covering it around the daughter. The patient remembered a time in college after she had gained weight, sitting across the table from her mother and feeling hatred toward her. Later, recognizing her mother's shame, she came to feel superior, capitalizing on this difference with an exhibitionistic style of dress.

Another patient whose mother was very thin resented her mother because she felt she competed with her for the attention of her dates. She could remember her father saying, "Eat like your mother; she has it down pat." By vomiting, she stated that she too had it "down pat." She did not know if she wanted to be like her mother or not.

One patient whose mother was overweight recalled that as her mother gained weight, she lost weight. She knew the sight of her body upset her mother and made a point of undressing in front of her. Asked what she thought her body was saying, she replied, "I have a problem." And what was her mother's body saying? "I have a problem too." She commented, "I try to take such good care of my body by dieting and exercising to make up for my mother's mistreatment of hers . . . maybe it will take weight off her body."

Perhaps the greatest affect was connected with the patients' recollections of the onset of menstruation, which was experienced very negatively by all. None of their mothers had told them about it; this possibly reflected ambivalence over the daughters' maturation, hostility, and competition ("You have so much; you can do this without my help"). Above all, they experienced this as a time of losing their fathers, as a directive to leave the fathers' world and join their mothers. One patient remembered her father telling her brothers not to play with her any more.

DECREASING OF BOUNDARY DIFFUSION

The third aim of body image therapy is to decrease boundary diffusion with significant others by providing therapeutic experiences in which women describe and interpret their own internal sensations, as well as the specific, individual ways they utilize their bodies as expressive objects.

Exercises developed to foster this goal have centered primarily around differentiation from the mother.

Patients were asked to envision moving inside their mothers' bodies. They all expressed hatred for the way their mothers moved — their gestures, pace, and expressions, which they regarded as fake, proper, and ladylike. They felt their mothers' bodies said, "I know who I am; I know what I want; but don't get too close, there is a 'wall.'" And yet they were all aware that they imitated her. Asked to sit as their mothers did, they would demonstrate, then make a deliberate shift to another position. Soon they would be back in the position of their mothers, often without awareness. They were disturbed by this.

When "in their mothers' bodies" they felt out of touch with internal cues: "If angry I would smile; if hungry I would diet." They observed that their mothers' experience was not that different from their own experience: "If you look within my mother, she is totally out of control; but she constructs a wall around herself to hide it." At one point, asked to make the part of their body where their mothers reside more powerful, they refused.

To assist them in recognizing similarities and differences, the patients were videotaped while "being their mothers" and "being themselves." They explored, at the therapists' suggestion, the ways in which they would like to be the same or different from their mothers—what they wanted to keep or to change. They were encouraged to be clear about this.

USE OF IMAGERY, ART, AND MOVEMENT

A fourth aim of body image therapy is to utilize imagery, art, and movement as a means of assessing feelings about the body and reworking psychohistorical material relating to body image development. A number of techniques have proven effective in reviving forgotten aspects of body image, sometimes unintentionally. Often, direct efforts to produce such recall fail, but indirect methods achieve the goal.

In one imagery exercise (taken from Stevens, 1971), patients are asked to imagine themselves in a darkened room before a mirror, and then gradually to form an image of themselves in the mirror. Further instructions guide a dialogue between the self and the image, without suggesting any content.

One woman "saw" an image of herself as a toddler, familiar from photographs, and always regarded by her as chubby and repellent. However, during this exercise, she looked carefully at the child and rejected her previous negative view, instead feeling overwhelmed by love for her. She later recounted tearfully, "She—I—was not an ugly child. She was beautiful. I loved her—I just wanted to reach out and cradle her in my arms." In a similar experience of acceptance, a declaration of love was made by a patient who had seen her body only as trailing shining filaments, believed to represent an earlier body image. For both, this reconciliation with an earlier self was a profound emotional experience.

Family portraits, in which patients are instructed to create abstract collages (from geometric shapes of colored paper) depicting their families, are frequently revealing of important themes in the history of the body and the self.

One patient, who displayed some of the classic symptomatology of the anorexic who "does not know who she is," gave little definition to herself in her family portrait. Asked in the second stage of this exercise to select the family member with whom she had the most intense relationship and to elaborate on it, she could not separate her parents, but depicted them as a single entity, and herself as a faint symbol. Shortly thereafter, she announced to them a decision that she felt would serve her own interests but would disappoint them.

A startling handling of the mother was carried out by one patient, who, having completed the representation of her mother, ripped off part of her stomach, giving the outer perimeter to her father and the center to herself. In an elaboration of her relationship to her mother, her mother was shown open at the top, with pieces of herself floating away, and without a heart. She had shown all the males in her family on wheels instead of feet. This same patient had put nothing on her own arms or legs in an earlier collage. One could scarcely more clearly represent the belief that men are mobile and powerful, while women are paralyzed and disintegrating.

An exercise developed specifically to reveal historical landmarks of body image is the sculpting of figures with modeling clay. Patients are instructed to represent their bodies as they were before the eating disorder began, as they were at the time of onset of the disorder, as they are in the present, and as they will be at a future time when they have been "cured."

Most of the figures from the period before development of an eating disorder showed beginning development of the characteristics of womanhood. One was clearly sensuous; one was large, and the patient referred disparagingly to this figure as "the Incredible Hulk." Representations of the time of onset of the eating disorder were notable for splits and dismemberment: One figure was divided vertically down the middle; one was a simple "T." Depictions of the current condition reflected debilitation: One was a small shapeless character; another was a figure without arms, with splayed legs. Images of the "cure" were perhaps most revealing. One was a shapely yellow body. Another was an assertive figure, with her hands on her hips and strong boundary definition. But a third was a cross. The patient explained that she didn't want a body; she wanted to be totally spiritual. The image of death is of course, undeniable and disturbing.

POTENTIAL FOR CONTROL OF BODY IMAGE

A fifth goal of body image therapy is to impart a sense of the malleability of body image and the potential for each woman to control her perceptions and feelings about her own body.

In one exercise, the therapist instructs the patients to picture themselves differently along a variety of dimensions: to become larger, smaller, of a different race, lacking a body part, or larger or smaller in particular places. The therapist also asks the patients to imagine how they looked at ages 5 and 10, how they look now, and how they will look at 80.

Not surprisingly, patients were scared to imagine themselves larger, and were particularly frightened by enlargement of their thighs. In discussing the exercise, they were unanimous and clear in their understanding of how you *should* look in this culture: tubular. They described how being small was associated with being alone, having no demands placed on you. When large, "You have to take care of everyone else." There was great apprehension about the selflessness and nurturance implied (demanded) by largeness. It was not an image of strength or independence, but of enslavement.

Variations for such an exercise could include visualization of the body before and after eating, or after academic and social success or failure. Such exercises might clarify the causal effect of feelings of control and efficacy on body perception.

Actual mirror viewing of the self partially clothed, a widely used exercise, can bring about dramatic changes if the patient can tolerate the experience. We have found that most patients stop early, as soon as they have achieved a state of maximum aversion and anxiety. They come back and report in detail the flaws and signs of deterioration they have uncovered. However, the occasional patient who has spent at least 20 minutes viewing herself finds that the anxious, evaluative responses begin to fade and are replaced with calmer objectivity. Compliance cannot, of course, be forced; the patient must choose to attend and experience her feelings. If she does so, the experience is much like an *in vivo* flooding session.

One surprisingly simple way to achieve new flexibility in body image is to send patients shopping for clothes. We have found local stores cooperative in providing a private setting and assistance from one of their staff without pressure to make any purchases. The requirement of this exercise is that the patients try on some items selected by others, whatever their own opinion may be about how they will look, and leave them on for several minutes. Interest can be enhanced by imagery and discussion in preparation for the trip. Patients often recognize an ambivalent wish to appear more grown up, more sexual and womanly. Some are able to identify specific fears about this — for example, that they will be seen as "too powerful and enviable" and will be rejected. Fear of sex itself has not figured prominently in the anxieties of bulimic women, but rather the meanings (e.g., competition, rejection, self-indulgence) attached by others, or the general demands for assuming responsibility for others implied by a mature appearance.

AWARENESS OF SOCIOCULTURAL ISSUES

A sixth goal of body image therapy is to heighten awareness of the sociocultural issues involved in negative body images of women.

It is our impression that premature introduction of this issue may delay or mitigate the exploration of personal and familial sources of poor body image. Nevertheless, discussion at an appropriate point in therapy — if possible, coincident with group examination of their own and others' goals for them — can be very useful. We have used such devices as showing educational films about portrayal of women in the media, distributing feminist articles, and having patients rewrite advertising copy that capitalizes on stereotypes of women.

CREATION OF MORE POSITIVE BODY IMAGES

The final goal of body image therapy is to create more positive body images by increasing movement repertoire and by developing healing symbols through imagery, movement, and therapeutic art exercises.

To recover from eating disorders, most women have to develop new metaphors for their bodies that do not define "good" and "bad" by size. The fully developed body must be symbolized not in terms of failure, weakness, and enslavement to the needs of others, but in terms of success, strength, and resiliency. Although suitable metaphors will inevitably be highly individualistic, they can be encouraged in the therapy process. Movement, similarly, can be used to rediscover and redefine strength.

In one exercise, patients were asked to demonstrate what their bodies do when angry. One anorexic young woman was at a loss and could do nothing at all. Another patient, who had recently described an angry interchange with her own mother, challenged the first: "Punch my hands." She responded, suddenly, by punching so hard that the therapists suggested instead she push against the other patient's hands. She began to talk to her mother, saying, "Get out of my space; leave me alone, let me be," then began to cry. But still she kept pushing with such force that both therapists were required to support the (much larger) patient who had initiated the exercise.

Asked later what she had done to get such strength, the anorexic patient explained, "I put my foot out, defined my space, and stood my ground." Not only was she able to relate this to her struggle with her mother, but therapists and patients alike noticed an immediate and lasting change in her body carriage.

These techniques, though still experimental, are clearly powerful, and are likely to prove an important component of the treatment of eating-disordered women. By bypassing words, they permit truer expressions of feelings and new methods by which to integrate past and current experience. Not every exercise is experienced as useful by every patient; indeed, the variability is striking. But nearly every patient finds something of great value in at least one facet. In one group, every modality (video, art, imagery, movement) was given the lowest possible rating by at least one patient and the highest possible rating by at least one other. As therapists learn how to tap the potential of these experiences more effectively, reactions may be less variable, but they will probably always be highly personal and perhaps inherently unpredictable.

Family Therapy

Family therapy often proves crucial to the successful treatment of patients living at or near home. This fact seems so indisputable that many therapists have argued that family therapy should always be the primary, if not the *only*, treatment modality. This conclusion may be artifactual. It is sometimes impractical or impossible to assemble the families of adults living away from home for family therapy, nor do patients often want to do this. We do not know how useful such therapy would be if done. What we do know is that among family members accessible for treatment (usually those living with or having close ties to the eating-disordered patient), involvement in treatment is often decisive of success. Whether this reflects a universal truth — that the family, whether literally present or not, is always present at the core of the problem — or whether it reflects important differences in patients who have and have not successfully negotiated separation in an unresolved question.

For adolescents, the issues of separation and autonomy are age-appropriate and inevitable. They are no doubt made worse by the onset of illness, whether that illness reflects a breakdown in the normal separation process due to unresolved family problems or is a relatively independent occurrence. For parents and siblings, fear, protectiveness, anger, and intense involvement will surely be evoked by a serious, seemingly self-inflicted illness in a child. The debilitating effects of illness erode whatever degree of preparedness for separation the child may have achieved, fostering regression and dependency.

Attempts to reconstruct and understand the family's mode of functioning prior to the illness are based on inference. If one projects the family's current behavior into the past, it may certainly appear to constitute a sufficient condition for the development of illness. But it is a projection. In our opinion, it is possible that the development of disordered eating may depend as much on factors only loosely related to the family experience — the method of dieting and the physiological makeup of the child, or cultural attitudes transmitted by the family, for example — as on (commonly defined) pathogenic factors within the family.

We would hardly question the fact, however, that the family's response to the onset of illness creates a complex field of force in which every behavior takes on new and intensified meaning, thus acquiring greater expressive and manipulative potential. Old problems are likely to be revived and new ones created. In the case of the adult patient living at home, this argument is even stronger. Her continued presence at home is proof that separation has not been accomplished; because delayed, it is likely to be more difficult than usual. Moreover, the greater tenure of her illness as a central family event insures that everyone's stake in her behavior will be maximized. With each move, she affirms or denies someone's cherished opinion or hope, and, as such, acquires an extraordinary degree of power. Often it is the power to keep the family together by diverting attention to her symptoms. Again, whether the attainment of power is an underlying motivation of the illness or only a secondary phenomenon, it becomes important, especially as she experiences the progressive loss of power that is based on strength and genuine accomplishment. The family may "use" her illness (e.g., to distract themselves from other problems, or as a vehicle for the expression of feelings they can so avoid "owning") or may abhor it, trying to dispel her and her illness from their lives. Both extremes of response impede recovery, and the appropriate middle ground is undoubtedly hard to achieve.

For all these reasons, to ignore the family context in which the illness occurs is to choose lesser over greater comprehension, less rather than more leverage. At the same time, it is advisable to keep an open mind about what is occurring in the family, and to avoid premature diagnosis of the classic "anorexigenic" constellation, since many adaptations are possible and, in our experience, many are found.

This is especially true in treating families of bulimics. Most of the literature on the treatment of families with eating-disordered patients refers to anorexics, usually young ones. When "bulimia" is included in the patient sample, it may be bulimia that is secondary to anorexia nervosa (i.e., as a later stage). The ex-anorexic bulimic naturally resembles the anorexic in the predominance of obsessive–compulsive traits and needs for control and achievement. Nonanorexic bulimics are seemingly more variable: Sometimes they resemble anorexics; sometimes they have a surprisingly good social and occupational adjustment; sometimes they fall at the other end of the spectrum from anorexics, displaying poor impulse control, low achievement motivation, and hysterical or borderline personality features (the last being especially common among laxative abusers).

One would not expect to find the same characteristics in families of bulimics without a history of anorexia as those found in families of anorexics. In fact, two recent studies support this point. Using the Moos Family Environmental Scale, C. Johnson (personal communication October, 1983) found families of bulimics to resemble control families in having high standards of achievement, but to differ from the controls in being less cohesive and having more conflict. In a recent survey of university students using the same scale (Debs *et al.*, 1983), bulimia was found to be positively correlated with familial conflict, control, and achievement orientation, and negatively correlated with cohesion.

In contrast to the picture of ersatz harmony often presented by anorexic families, we have seen a number of bulimic families in which conflict and disintegration, even explosion, predominate. A number of these families have undergone rancorous divorces; those that are still intact are often characterized by frequent, bitter fights and extramarital affairs. The bulimic daughters have been pulled into uncomfortable alliances with one or both parents, being asked to spy (e.g., tape phone calls, intercept mail), to cover for the activities of parents spending nights with lovers, or to replace the mother as the father's "date" at official occasions. One was told by her father that he had bought a gun, but she did not know why. The daughters have often been found to be the targets of verbal and physical abuse from desperately unhappy parents.

Although enmeshment or "explosion" are not fundamentally incompatible concepts at a theoretical level, they certainly conjure up different images, and therapists do well to anticipate scenarios other than "the perfect American family" with "the best little girl in the world." In our experience, a substantial proportion of bulimic families have long since smashed the white picket fence, even if they have not achieved genuine emotional separation. Conflict in the families described above is very evident; in others it is less so, but becomes revealed in therapy, sometimes leading to separation or divorce.

We have seen daughters permitted by their fathers to treat their mothers like siblings, enjoying equal rights to adult privileges. Daughters frequently express contempt for their mothers, especially their appearance, labeling them as "too fat" or "out of control." The mothers' competition has been expressed by secret study of their daughters' food records, wearing their daughters' clothes, flirting with the daughters' dates, and going out with men who are their daughters' contemporaries. In some families the mothers show exaggerated pride in their perfect housekeeping, perfect grooming, perfect figure, and perfect diet. When the daughters have usurped the fathers' attention, mothers have retaliated by withdrawal of interest in the daughters and their problems, withholding of money, public criticism of their appearance and eating behavior, and the assignment of unreasonable household duties.

Stierlin (1981) describes a helpful model of three levels at which a child can be bound to parents. In the first, there is dependence on the parents for gratification of the most primitive needs and no move toward separation. In the second level, the child is bound through cognitive confusion. She is told how much she is loved, and cannot recognize or reconcile hostile, rejecting, or ambivalent behavior by the parents. In the third level, the child's loyalty to the family is exploited, and guilt is induced at transfer of affection away from the family to peers. Most bulimic families we have seen display elements of the second or third levels. The cognitive confusion may result from the parents' contradictory wishes to love and heal their children and to rid themselves of their problems, or may reflect lifelong competitive and/or exploitive relationships. The guilt that binds daughters usually seems to center around having more than their mothers — sometimes more of their fathers' attention, usually more opportunity for self-fulfillment and achievement. The problem is intensified when a patient feels that her mother is unsupported by her father.

In treatment sessions, focus is taken off the eating disorder and redirected to the entire family's interactions. When this is done, many of the functions that the bulimic's symptoms have come to serve are lost; they no longer bring her attention and power or evoke anger and censure. They no longer protect other family members from self-examination or recognition of conflicts. If problems in the parents' relationship can be resolved, or at least addressed, and limits on the child's influence in this relationship can be firmly established, the child will find it easier to work on her problems and make her own way. Treatment relies on the development of trust in the therapist–client relationships, and on a system of operating in which every member's views and emotions are acknowledged and treated as valid within the context of a therapist-structured process. Healing through encounter is based upon the establishment of an individuating dialogue. Shame- and guilt-laden topics, sources of anger, family secrets, disappointments, and injustices eventually can be faced with the recognition that anxiety does not harm people (Bowen, 1978).

Acknowledgment by the family of problems unrelated to the eating disorder (but concealed, expressed, or intensified by it) is tremendously freeing for the identified patient, who often bears much guilt for creating overt or covert problems. It also releases her from the role of parental mediator. With the rest of the family receiving support from a therapist, the daughter feels more free to leave, and the family often has a renewed capacity to assist her.

Whether or not these goals can be achieved through individual therapy alone, family involvement is of considerable benefit if it accelerates the process. All treatment, but especially treatment of adolescents, is a race against time. Chronicity saps enthusiasm and hope, makes the eating disorder a cornerstone of the patient's identity, and results in ever more developmental lag. There is, in the final analysis, a limit to the amount of psychological "catch-up growth" that is possible.

Intensive Treatment Program for Bulimia (ITPB)

The ITPB was initially developed in response to an apparent need for brief treatment on the part of patients living in areas where professional help, particularly specialized help, was unavailable. The program was designed as a 3½-week treatment package that would interrupt the cycle of bingeing–purging and begin the exploration of psychological issues related to the eating disorder, a process to be continued in follow-up therapy upon return to the home environment.

A maximum of six patients at a time are accepted for treatment. Criteria for acceptance (assessed from a detailed application form and contacts with previous therapists) include the ability to live independently for several weeks; sufficient severity of bulimia to warrant this form of treatment; and absence of strong suicidal tendencies, drug or alcohol addiction, or severe borderline character disorders. During their stay patients reside in apartments with fully equipped kitchens in a residential hotel near the medical center. On weekdays, they are involved in 6–8 hours per day of scheduled activity, and spend much of the remaining time together. On weekends, they are permitted to go home or do as they like, though many use the time to be alone and think, to call old friends, to talk to family members, or to go through old photographs and memorabilia in an attempt to reconstruct their past.

What has been found is that the concentration of therapy has unexpectedly powerful effects: The whole is greater than the sum of its parts. The availability of constant support seems to encourage patients to take greater risks. Because they can give their undivided attention, the therapy process is more absorbing, more compelling. It generates more emotion and encourages more introspection. It is as though the miniature world created within the program becomes the stage on which each patient re-enacts the story of her life, pausing frequently to examine the players, their motives, and the direction that the script (unless rewritten) will take.

At the start of the program, patients are given a complete medical examination, a battery of psychological tests, and whole-body calorimetry to determine current caloric maintenance needs. If, as has often been the case, medical abnormalities are uncovered, additional testing may be continued throughout the program. It is quickly learned that the first 2 days are highly stressful, evoking fears about physical damage and psychological problems, and the schedule needs to include time for discussion of these feelings, for discussion of eating, and for a presentation by the staff of what to expect during the program. On the first day, patients are given blank bound books (diaries) and are encouraged to begin recording feelings and ideas for their own use only. Nearly all patients take up the suggestion, and many continue keeping journals after the program ends. By the third day, the program settles into a regular schedule, which includes the following components:

1. Eating group. This group meets daily from 9 A.M. to 10 A.M. and is devoted to analysis of food records from the previous 24 hours and planning for the next 24 hours. The principles employed and the problems that emerge closely parallel those described earlier in the section on management of eating. An important difference, however is that the modal response to entry into the program has been an abrupt discontinuation of bingeing–purging. Thus, attention is focused less on the weaning process and more on the establishment of adequate eating habits and the examination of relapses.

2. Psychotherapy group. This group follows the model for an interpersonal group described earlier and meets daily from 10:15 A.M. to 12:00 noon. Not surprisingly, it operates at very high levels of intensity. In fact, by the second or third day, it resembles groups that have been in operation for 6 to 12 months. Reasons for this undoubtedly include the greater tension and greater trust produced by near-continuous interaction among members, the frequency of meetings, and greater risk taking by therapists (which the program structure makes possible).

3. Body image and expression therapies group. This group meets four times a week for 2 hours in the afternoon. This group has been developed to deal with body image problems and employs the methodologies already described in the section on body image therapy. However, because of the context in which it takes place, the selection of material and the techniques employed must be responsive to the overall group process and the progress of each individual.

4. Individual therapy. Each patient is assigned a therapist who is part of the core ITPB staff (i.e., a regular leader of one of the groups); a patient and therapist meet two to three times weekly. In the context of ongoing, intense self-examination, these sessions can be particularly productive. Despite the availability of many "projection screens," the individual therapist occupies a special role for the patient; as in all therapies, he or she becomes an object of transferred fears, angers, longings, and anxieties, which can be explored and sometimes substantially resolved within the time constraints of the program.

5. Educational seminars. These are held two or three times a week and cover the following topics (in order): the process of recovery from bulimia; the concept of "set point" and its implications; the effects of starvation on metabolism, physical functioning, personality, and mood (two sessions); feminist views of women and weight (two sessions); and assertion training (two sessions). Patients are given articles to read before each session. and optional additional materials are made available.

6. Family therapy. However difficult the arrangements and often despite considerable resistance, patients are encouraged to undertake one or more family-of-origin therapy sessions, usually during the second and third weekends. These sessions assist the therapists in understanding the patient's problems and usually permit substantial resolution of some of the problems. In a few cases they have revealed family problems so severe that their resolution appears unattainable. If this is the case, it is best that the patient acknowledge the problems *during* the program, while support and assistance are available, rather than maintaining unrealistic fantasies of reconciliation and openness such as they have experienced within the group.

Objections to family meetings are revealing and surprisingly consistent. Patients who have heretofore portrayed their fathers as giving and tolerant now state that their fathers would never tolerate such a proposal. The implication seems to be that it is a threat to the fathers' authority and indisputable judgment on all matters. An even stronger (at least more poignant) concern is that their mothers will be hurt—presumably by the patients' expression of anger or disappointment. However critical they may feel of their mothers, they are protective of them. They may be contemptuous of their weakness or annoyed by their stance of martyrdom, but at the point of confrontation they revert to a view of their mothers as victims requiring their loyalty, and loyalty means suppression of problems and feelings. Whether or not the sessions are ever held, discussion of the possibility quickly brings to the surface unrecognized fears and contradictions, including suppressed or denied problems (e.g., maternal alcoholism and/or depression).

7. *Special events.* Evening events are scheduled twice a week. These have included meetings with recovered patients, discussions of sexuality and "attractiveness" with male peers, a concert and discussion of women's music, and a consultation on "professional dress." Patients choose from a list of suggestions the events which interest them.

The fact that most patients discontinue regular bingeing–purging at the start of the program undoubtedly contributes to the intensity of their involvement. Stripped of their habitual means of dissipating feelings or avoiding them altogether, they are "wide open." They cannot escape experiencing strong affects, and they are given many channels for expression of them. It may be worth noting that the absence of rules and policies that, of necessity, characterize hospital wards discourages displacement of feelings onto trivia or manufactured issues. There is really nothing in the program to rebel against; tension, anger, and pain must be "owned" and examined. With very rare exceptions, staff members are perceived as allies rather than authorities. Patients must regard their actions—for better or worse—as ones they have chosen, not ones "required" by the system. This is not to dispute the value of hospital programs, for clearly not all patients can be treated in a setting such as this; but for those who can, it may be therapeutically preferable as well as more cost-effective.

Themes and issues are carried from one group or session to the next, each offering a new method or approach. Although the patients themselves impose a continuity on the experience, we have found it useful to have staff members meet in the middle of every day to keep abreast of the often dizzying sequences of events. The patients' use of the varying modes of therapy to explore issues and seek resolution of them is illustrated in two vignettes.

The first concerns an 18-year-old patient, J., the youngest we have treated in this program. The oldest of three children, she had been severely bulimic for several years and explained in the application process that one of her concerns was that bulimia had made her a liar and a thief and she wanted to change. J. successfully navigated the first week without bingeing. Somewhat reticent about seeking attention, she gained rapid acceptance within the group through her enormous and obviously sincere capacity for empathy. She rarely watched another patient cry without crying herself, and found it easy to say "I love you." She expressed apprehension about going home the first weekend, worried that her parents would not listen to her or approve of her. Indeed, they did not come home as planned, and she had no opportunity to talk to them. She ate half a jar of peanut butter, but did not vomit; instead, she called her boyfriend.

Her excessive guilt over wrongdoing was illustrated the second week, when anger on the part of her roommate because she had identified them both as members of the "food program" to a hotel bellboy led to a dream in which she first saw her roommate lying dead in the adjacent bed; then she saw her rise from her deathbed and chase her with a knife.

J.'s first binge occurred early in the day before her first family therapy session. This session revealed apparent indifference on the part of her father, who disparaged his daughter and stated, "I do what I want to do. That's it." Indeed, his work had required the family to move every year of the children's lives, and his frequent affairs were not concealed. This stance may have been a surprise to the therapist, but it was not to J.; she left the session drained, but impressed, above all, with the need for her to provide more support for her siblings, who she realized were as distressed as she.

At home alone the following weekend she allowed herself to eat a brownie, no longer a particular challenge for her, and proceeded to binge. Her interpretation of this the following Monday was uncharacteristically centered around the food itself; the "bad" part of her urged her to keep eating, while a "good" part struggled in vain to give her permission to enjoy a few brownies without self-retaliation. Due to a pressured agenda that day, the therapists suggested she write out a dialogue between the parts of herself.

That afternoon in the body image group, she composed a family portrait (collage) in which she expressed a similarity between herself and her father. Both contained an area of "red" which represented aggressive self-interest, and a smaller area of "blue" which was "love." Neither had any "green," which was "understanding" and which was possessed by all the other family members but floated outside her father and herself.

In an elaboration of her relationship to her father, his body loomed large above hers, pouring "red" into her. Her immediate alarm was partially alleviated when someone suggested she turn the drawing upside down, thus creating the image of herself able to move up and away from the red stream. She commented about her father, "I don't think he'll ever get his 'green' together."

The following morning she asked to speak. She began to talk about "red" and "blue." We suggested she do a dialogue. She immediately made her hands into puppets that spoke to each other. The first round involved a struggle between "blue" who urged her to "eat a brownie or two," and "red" who said, "take more; take more; take all you want." Red won, but it did not really sound like a struggle. Asked to make "blue" more assertive, she successfully subdued "red" but experienced no relief. Maybe she wanted to keep some "red." The therapists commented that "red" was like her father, while "blue" was like herself and/or her mother. At first she denied the suggestion, but then began to agree, seeing the parallel: "Blue" loved "red," but "red" always told "blue" how worthless she was. We asked her if "blue" would try expressing her love for "red." "No," she said, "red doesn't understand love." She tried without success to make "red" feel loved, receiving only rebuffs.

"Could you tell 'red' you love him even if he doesn't understand or accept it?" She did this and was overcome with tears. "It's 'red' crying," she finally offered. "He can't accept 'blue's' love because he feels so worthless. He has the world on a string but he has nothing. 'Blue' can't help. 'Red' has to accept himself." She had understood that her father did not love himself and that "red" and "blue" were really fighting themselves, not each other.

She consoled "red" by stroking her hand. Finally the leader asked if "blue" needed support. She nodded and the group came over, embracing her and expressing admiration for her persistence and insight.

J. has not binged since that time; she tries to avoid arguments by meeting the family's demands at home, but asserted her need to get to therapy. She recently left for college, confident she could make a success of it.

For J., body size had never really been a critical issue, and the institution of normal eating was easily accomplished. The cessation of bingeing instead required resolution of chronically unmet needs for approval and caring, as well as of her identification with her rejecting father. As in so many other instances, she found little to identify with in her mother, whom she saw primarily as a hopeless victim, and whom the therapists regarded as depressed, drinking fairly heavily and doing very little at home or elsewhere.

The second vignette concerns a patient for whom weight had always been indeed a major issue.

S., a college student, was among the youngest in a very large family of nearly all girls, all of whom but her were petite. From early childhood she had regarded herself as awkward and lacking the social skills possessed by others. In the group she was quiet and somewhat self-effacing, but scrupulously honest.

On the second day of the program, her body tracing not only made clear the fact that she was the largest member of the group, but was distorted because her loose clothing had not been pressed to her body when the drawing was made by a fellow patient. At the sight of the tracing, she began to cry. The patient who had drawn it was overcome with remorse and tried in every way to argue away her feeling. S. finally said, "Wait, I think I want to face this." She later changed the line to a more realistic proportion.

At the meeting of the food group the following morning (which was videotaped), she was very subdued, explaining that she had found the prior day's experience unsettling and was further upset that morning when she tried to examine her partially clothed body in a mirror (an assignment).

In the psychotherapy group immediately following, other members brought up the experience, still trying to deny the validity of her feelings. Asked by a therapist to describe how she had felt, she said, "Like the Elephant Man." "Be the Elephant Man," she was instructed. She stepped right into the role, explaining through a stream of tears her inexpressible grotesqueness and her desire to take a knife and hack the flesh from her chest. Another patient became so agitated and tearful that it was necessary to interrupt for a few minutes to allow her to express her horror at S.'s self-hatred.

Then S. was asked how she learned that she was grotesque. She couldn't answer, nor did further questions about the history of familial and peer responses to her body elicit anything of much importance. "What *was* grotesque when you were a child?" she was asked. "Dinnertime!" she replied without hesitation. This was followed by a re-enactment of a family dinner, with group members and therapists acting roles assigned and explained to them by her. (As an interesting aside, J. was cast as the father, and 10 minutes into the play let out a piercing scream. "I can't stand it," she cried.)

This enactment revealed normal family conflict, and competition for the floor elevated to an almost absurd degree. Of most relevance to S. was the futility of her childhood efforts to bring issues and problems to resolution. Again and again she was left in the dust, appearing awkward, helpless, and out of step with the other family members, who seemed to thrive on this cacophony. Re-experiencing the event, S. found herself laughing and was pleased by the group's ability to recreate the ambience of her childhood home.

She reported in the body image group that afternoon that she had gone back to her apartment and tried the mirror exercise again, this time feeling much calmer about her body. On viewing the videotape made earlier that day, she observed that she looked detached, but that was okay since she *had* been detached, and that her thighs did not look nearly as large as she had imagined.

S. was able to give up her wish to diet, and was therefore very successful in avoiding binges, eating adequately, and permitting herself "splurges" during the remainder of the program. She took advantage of the shopping trips to buy several items uncharacteristic of her previously casual and "androgynous" look.

These two examples scarcely begin to illustrate the seemingly catalyzing effects of the different modes of therapy. For some patients, discoveries seem to be made in discussion and "worked through" nonverbally. For others, it is the opposite: Problems revealed in art, imagery, and movement are discussed in group and individual therapy. The momentum is remarkable. One evening, for example, when a problem arose involving a group member who had to leave town early the next day, the group held their own 2-hour meeting at 10:00 P.M. One group that went through this program became so cohesive that the members took a trip together a month after the program, and they remain in frequent contact.

Caution has to be exercised that the headiness of this experience does not leave members unprepared for some sense of letdown upon return to the home environment. Brief remissions are not unusual, and ongoing therapy is without question required. Nonetheless, patients appear to achieve in less than a month what might otherwise take a year, and they make excellent use of therapy after the program. Not enough time has elapsed to collect long-term follow-up data, and any suggestion that this program is a panacea is unintentional. Nonetheless, it appears to be a promising addition to other treatment modes currently available.

ACKNOWLEDGMENTS

We wish to acknowledge the following contributions to this chapter: Ann Kearney Cooke developed the goals for body image treatment and many of the exercises described; Kathy Myszak and Michelle Dolnick developed many of the other exercises and prepared the sequence used in the Intensive Treatment Program for Bulimia; Kay Debs and Kip Alishio assisted in the preparation of the section on family therapy.

REFERENCES

Bierce, A. (1958). *The devil's dictionary*. New York: Dover. (Original work published 1911.)

Biven, B. (1982). The role of skin in normal and abnormal development with a note on the poet Sylvia Plath. *International Review of Psychoanalysis, 9*, 205–229.

Booth, D. A. (1977). Satiety and appetite are conditioned reactions. *Psychosomatic Medicine, 39*, 76–81.

Bowen, M. (1978). *Family therapy in clinical practice*. New York: Jason Aronson.

Bromage, P. R., & Melzack, R. (1974). Phantom limbs and the body schema. *Canadian Anaesthetists' Society Journal, 21*, 267–274.

Brown, D. G. (1959). The relevance of body image to neurosis. *British Journal of Medical Psychology, 32*, 249–260.

Bunker, H. A., Jr. (1934). The voice as (female) phallus. *Psychoanalytic Quarterly, 3*, 391–429.

Bychowski, G. (1943). Disorders in the body-image in the clinical pictures of psychoses. *Journal of Nervous and Mental Disease, 97*, 310–335.

Cappon, D., & Banks, R. (1968). Distorted body perception in obesity. *Journal of Nervous and Mental Disease, 146*, 465–467.

Castelnuovo-Tedesco, P. (1973). Organ transplant, body image, psychosis. *Psychoanalytic Quarterly, 42*, 349–363.

Crisp, A. H., & Kalucy, R. S. (1974). Aspects of the perceptual disorder in anorexia nervosa. *British Journal of Medical Psychology, 47*, 349–361.

Critchley, M. (1950). The body image in neurology. *Lancet, i*, 335–340.

Debs, K., Wooley, O. W., Harkness-Kling, K., & Wooley, S. C. (1983). Unpublished study in preparation.

Dorpat, T. L. (1971). Phantom sensations of internal organs. *Comprehensive Psychiatry, 12*, 27–35.

Druss, R. G., O'Connor, J. F., & Stern, L. O. (1972). Changes in body image following ileostomy. *Psychoanalytic Quarterly, 41*, 195–206.

Dworkin, A. (1974). *Woman hating*. New York: E. P. Dutton.

Dworkin, A. (1979). *Pornography: Men possessing women*. New York: Perigee Books (G.P. Putnam's Sons).

Eisnitz, A. J. (1980). The organization of the self-representation and its influence on pathology. *Psychoanalytic Quarterly, 49*, 361–392.

Feeling fat in a thin society. (1984, February). *Glamour Magazine*, pp. 198–201, 251–252.

Frick, R. (1982). The ego and the vestibulocerebellar system: Some theoretical perspectives. *Psychoanalytic Quarterly, 51*, 93–122.

Garner, D. M., Garfinkel, P. E., & Moldofsky, H. (1978). Perceptual experiences in anorexia nervosa and obesity. *Canadian Psychiatric Association Journal, 38*, 227–236.

Garner, D. M., Garfinkel, P. E., Schwartz, D., & Thompson, M. (1980). Cultural expectations of thinness in women. *Psychological Reports, 47*, 483–491.

Garner, D. M. Olmsted, M. P., & Polivy, J. (1983). Development and validation of a multidimensional eating disorder inventory for anorexia nervosa and bulimia. *International Journal of Eating Disorders, 2*, 15–34.

Gilbert, M., & Gubar, S. (1979). *The madwoman in the attic: The woman writer and the nineteenth-century literary imagination*. New Haven: Yale University Press.

Griffin, S. (1981). *Pornography and silence: Culture's revenge against nature*. New York: Harper & Row.

Hall, A. (1982). Deciding to stay an anorectic. *Postgraduate Medical Journal, 58*, 641–647.

Halpern, S. (1965). Body-image symbols of repression. *International Journal of Clinical and Experimental Hypnosis, 13*, 83–91.

Heusner, A. P. (1965). Phantom genitalia. *Transactions of the American Neurological Association, 75*, 128–131.

Hoffman, J. (1954). Phantom limb syndrome. *Journal of Nervous and Mental Disease, 119*, 261–270.

Hoffman, J. (1955). Facial phantom phenomenon. *Journal of Nervous and Mental Disease, 122*, 143–151.

Horowitz, L. (1966). Body image. *Archives of General Psychiatry, 14*, 456–460.

Hsu, L. K. G. (1982). Is there a disturbance in body image in anorexia nervosa? *Journal of Nervous and Mental Disease, 170*, 305–307.

Jarvis, J. H. (1967). Post-mastectomy breast phantoms. *Journal of Nervous and Mental Disease, 144*, 266–272.

Jessner, J., & Abse, D. W. (1960). Regressive forces in anorexia nervosa. *British Journal of Medical Psychology, 33*, 301–312.

Kaywin, L. (1955). Notes on the concept of self-representation. *Journal of the American Psychoanalytic Association*, 293–301.

Keys, A., Brozek, J., Henschel, A., Mickelsen, O., & Taylor, H. L. (1950). *The biology of human starvation* (2 vols.). Minneapolis: University of Minnesota Press.

Kolb, L. C. (1975). Disturbances of the body-image. In M. F. Reiser (Ed.), *American handbook of psychiatry* (Vol. 4, pp. 810–837). New York: Basic Books.

Kubie, L. S. (1934). Body symbolization and the development of language. *Psychoanalytic Quarterly, 3*, 430–444.

LeMagnen, J. (1971). Advances in studies on the physiological control and regulation of food intake. In E. Stellar & J. M. Sprayne (Eds.), *Progress in physiological psychology* (Vol. 4, pp. 203–261). New York: Academic Press.

Lukianowicz, N. (1967). "Body image" disturbances in psychiatric disorders. *British Journal of Psychiatry, 113*, 31–47.

Lussier, A. (1980). The physical handicap and the body ego. *International Journal of Psychoanalysis, 61*, 179–185.

Mazur, A. (1983). *American trends in feminine beauty, and overadaptation*. Unpublished manuscript.

McCrea, C. W., Summerfield, A. B., & Rosen, B. (1982). Body image: A selective review of existing measurement techniques. *British Journal of Medical Psychology, 55*, 225–233.

Melzack, R., & Bromage, P. R. (1973). Experimental phantom limbs. *Experimental Neurology, 39*, 261–269.

Metropolitan Life Insurance Company. (1959). New weight standards for men and women. *Statistical Bulletin, 40*, 1–4.

Money, J. (1969). Phantom orgasm in the dreams of paraplegic men and women. *Archives of General Psychiatry, 3*, 65–74.

Murphy, W. F. (1957). Some clinical aspects of the body ego. *Psychoanalytic Review, 44*, 462–477.

Nylander, I. (1971). The feeling of being fat and dieting in a school population. *Acta Socio-Medica Scandinavica, 1*, 17–26.

Olsen, T. (1965). *Silences*. New York: Delta (Dell).

Pankow, G. W. (1974). The body image in hysterical psychosis. *International Journal of Psychoanalysis, 55*, 407–416.

Pearlson, G. D., Flournoy, L. H., Simonson, M., & Slanney, P. R. (1981). Body image in obese adults. *Psychological Medicine, 11*, 147–154.

Peto, A. (1972). Body image and depression. *International Journal of Psychoanalysis, 53*, 259–263.

Riddoch, G. (1941). Phantom limbs and body shape. *Brain, 64*, 197–222.

Riding, J. (1976). Phantom limb: Some theories. *Anaesthesia, 31*, 102–106.

Schilder, P. (1930). The unity of body, sadism, and dizziness. *Psychoanalytic Review, 17*, 114–122.

Schilder, P. (1950). *The image and appearance of the human body*. New York: International Universities Press.

Selvini-Palazzoli, M. (1978). *Self-starvation: From individual to family therapy in the treatment of anorexia nervosa*. New York: Jason Aronson.

Shoenberg, P. J. (1975). The symptom as stigma or communication in hysteria. *International Journal of Psychoanalysis and Psychotherapy, 4*, 507–517.

Shontz, F. C. (1974). Body image and its disorders. *International Journal of Psychiatry in Medicine, 5*, 461–472.

Stevens, J. D. (1971). *Awareness: Exploring, experimenting, experiencing*. New York: Bantom.

Stierlin, H. (1981). *Separating parents and adolescents*. New York: Jason Aronson.

Story, I. (1976). Caricature and impersonating the other: Observations from the psychotherapy of anorexia nervosa. *Psychiatry, 39*, 176–188.

Strunk, W., Jr., & White, E. B. (1979). *The elements of style* (3rd ed.). New York: Macmillan.

Stunkard, A. J., & Burt, V. (1967). Obesity and the body image: II. Age at onset of disturbances in the body image. *American Journal of Psychiatry, 123*, 1443–1447.

Stunkard, A., & Mendelson, M. (1967). Obesity and the body image: I. Characteristics of disturbances in the body image of some obese persons. *American Journal of Psychiatry, 123*, 1296–1300.

Szasz, T. S. (1949). Psychiatric aspects of vagotomy: IV. Phantom ulcer pain. *Archives of Neurology and Psychiatry, 62*, 728–733.

Tepperman, H., & Tepperman, J. (1964). Adaptive hyperlipogenesis. *Federation Proceedings, 23*, 73.

Thompson, M., & Schwartz, D. (1982). Life adjustment of women with anorexia nervosa and anorexic-like behavior. *International Journal of Eating Disorders, 1*, 47–60.

Wangenstein, O. H. & Carlson, A. I. (1931). Hunger sensations in a patient after total gastrectomy. *Proceedings of the Society for Experimental Biology and Medicine, 28*, 545–547.

Weiss, S. A. (1958). The body image as related to phantom sensation: A hypothetical conceptualization of seemingly isolated findings. *Annals of the New York Academy of Sciences, 74*, 25–29.

Wooley, O. W., & Wooley, S. C. (1981). Relationship of salivation in humans to deprivation, inhibition and the encephalization of hunger. *Appetite: Journal for Intake Research, 2*, 331–350.

Yalom, I. D. (1975). *Theory and practice of group psychotherapy* (2nd ed.). New York: Basic Books.

CHAPTER EIGHTEEN

Time-Limited Individual and Group Treatment for Bulimia

J. HUBERT LACEY

THEORY

"Depression" is a term used to describe both a symptom and a syndrome. "Bulimia" is used in a similar way. The clinical treatment of depression has undoubtedly suffered from the confusion; it is necessary to define our terms if a similar fate is not to dog the effective management of bulimia.

The *symptom* of bulimia, or binge eating, is a common behavior. Because of its close association with failed "dieting," it is probably not an uncommon mode of normal eating. Certainly, it is a frequent response to emotional stress and can, by its own presence, cause yet more distress. Even so, it would be wrong to elevate it to the status of a syndrome and prescribe a blanket treatment devised for a more profound disorder. If this were to be done, there would be the danger of creating illness where none existed, or, at the very least, of potentiating the distress we are claiming to alleviate. First, we must recall the maxim, "Do no harm!"

This chapter concerns itself with the treatment of the *syndrome* of bulimia. It does not deal in any detail with bulimia occurring in the massively obese or in anorexics at low body weight. This is not to say that elements of the treatment about to be described are not more widely applicable, but that the treatment has been specifically devised to deal with the psychopathology of the bulimic syndrome.

The bulimic syndrome — or perhaps more accurately, syndromes — is a disorder mainly occurring in women[1] and is manifest by powerful and intractable urges to overeat, particularly with carbohydrate foods. The weight gain, ordinarily the result of binge eating, is thwarted either by psychogenic vomiting, purgation, or intermittent periods of starvation, such that the patient remains within her normal range of weight. The bulimic episodes are associated with great distress, and with feelings of loss of control, self-disgust, anger, and depression.

In recent years, the syndrome has been variously labeled. It has been called "bu-

---

1. Because of this prevalence, the feminine pronoun is used throughout this chapter to refer to bulimic patients.

J. Hubert Lacey. Academic Department of Psychiatry, St. George's Hospital Medical School, London, England.

limarexia" (Boskind-Lodahl, 1976), "hyperexia nervosa" (Ziolko, 1976), "bulimia nervosa" (Russell, 1979), "dysorexia" (Vandereycken & Pierloot, 1980), and the "bulimic syndrome" (Lacey, 1980), as well as the "thin–fat syndrome" (Bruch, 1974), the "dietary chaos syndrome" (Palmer, 1979) and the "abnormal–normal weight control syndrome" (Crisp, 1981). With the diversity of symptoms offered by such patients, it would be surprising if the clinical descriptions were identical; emphasis varies, which perhaps indicates the heterogenous nature of the condition in both its clinical presentation and its etiology.

Two major etiological types are met, and this seems to be important for treatment outcome. The majority—which I designate as Type I—give no history of previous anorexia nervosa, weight phobia, or major weight loss, although weight fluctuation is common. The minority—Type II bulimics, who constitute about 30% of the clinical population—describe having had previous anorexia nervosa, but have now "recovered" to normal body weight. The previous diagnosis can be confirmed against established criteria, such as those set forth by Feighner, Robins, Guze, Woodruff, Winocur, and Muñoz (1972). Recovery is such that they no longer express a phobia of normal body weight, which Crisp (1967) declares to be the pathognomonic feature of anorexia nervosa, nor do they express a *morbid* fear of becoming fat (Russell, 1970), although both types will demonstrate the normal female preoccupation with shape and weight (Nylander, 1971). Perhaps because of the profound experiential effects of anorexia nervosa, Type II bulimics tend to have a slightly poorer prognosis (Lacey, 1983a).

Clinical Presentation

The clinical presentation of the syndrome is diverse, and it is this—rather than the presence or absence of previous anorexia nervosa—that has the most marked effect on treatment outcome. Three clinical groups present in the clinic (Lacey, 1982), and the treatment of each is different.

THE NEUROTIC GROUP

The neurotic group is the largest group. The patients tend to be hard-working and ambitious women with high ethical standards. The predominant clinical symptom, apart from the eating disorder, is anger, although it is often initially denied. More usually the patients declare sadness or depression, which has often previously been diagnosed as "reactive depression." A small number present with anxiety–phobic features. Such patients may describe their eating behavior in depersonalized terms: It is as if they are automatons, observing their bulimic behavior from afar, their bodies being divorced from themselves. Again, there is barely hidden yet undeclared anger; this may be directed toward the patient herself or, more usually, a male partner or even men in general. Superficially, there is little disturbance to the personality: In fact, the patients give every impression to their friends and relatives of being stable and generally able to cope. On deeper examination, they declare low self-esteem and a feeling of being a failure, particularly in relationship terms. Their presentation at the clinic is usually precipitated by emotional distress associated with relationship difficulties.

THE PERSONALITY DISORDER GROUP

In the personality disorder group, which is much smaller, manipulation of food is associated to a varying degree with alcohol and drug abuse. The patients "use" them interchangeably and in similar ways. Thus they binge with alcohol and describe alterations of brief bouts of grossly pathological drinking with long phases of normality, during which they are able to drink socially or to abstain altogether. Phases of drinking, like their bulimia, may commence with explosive suddenness. Similar behavior is shown toward the addictive drugs, with the choice of drug depending more on their current social acquaintances than on personal choice.

In patients whose appetitive behavior is so impulsively out of control, it is not surprising that periods of sexual disinhibition occur. In others, a *fear* of "going out of control" leads them to seek "safe" relationships, which take a number of forms. Thus, the partner may be married and unprepared or unwilling to make a commitment, or he may be held in such low esteem by the patient that the relationship has little intrinsic worth. Sometimes the partner may be homosexual or bisexual, or simply described by the patient as "weak." Occasionally, the partner is female, but the sexual orientation of the relationship is less important than the underlying meaning: The partner is used as protection—a way of seeking sexual release without meaningful commitment or future. Clinically, such patients present as emotionally shallow or histrionic. Overdosing and superficial wrist cutting are not infrequent. The clinical presentation of this group is markedly dissimilar from that of the neurotic group of bulimic patients, described above. Unsurprisingly, the treatment is also different and is certainly more lengthy.

SECONDARY BULIMIA

In a small number of patients, the bulimic syndrome is secondary to a physical illness. Epilepsy and diabetes are the most common primary conditions. In the case of epilepsy, it should be emphasized that fits are not secondary to vomiting or laxative abuse, occurring as a result of electrolyte imbalance, but are primary. Diagnosis needs to be based on a clear history of fits predating the bulimia or psychogenic vomiting, or the presence of epileptiform phenomena following a resolution of the abnormal dietary behavior. A constant feature in the history of these patients is that the first epileptic fit takes place within the context of puberty; the normal insecurities of that time are heightened by the lack of control intrinsic within a fit. Similarly, where diabetes provides the primary focus, the diagnosis and initial treatment of it occurs within the insecurity of puberty. Diabetes, with its emphasis on carbohydrate management, is a disorder where control is vital; the bulimia stems from intrapersonal and family conflict. Asthma and other allergic phenomena may also provide the background for a secondary bulimic syndrome, which can generalize into a psychological food intolerance (Lacey, 1983b).

Pathogenesis

If the clinical features of the various types of bulimia are diverse and the etiological relationships to anorexia nervosa are variable, the pathogeneses show some remarkable consistencies. These consistencies are important for treatment.

Bulimic patients describe a series of factors that, usually in combination, underlie the disorder. While they are different from the factors that maintain the symptoms (to be discussed later), the clinician must delineate them, determine their relevance to the particular patient, and build them into the formal therapy of the treatment. These underlying factors represent long-term and chronic difficulties (Lacey, Coker, & Birtchnell, 1983). They are as follows:

1. Doubts concerning femininity; these involve a major discrepancy, associated with distress, between the patient's concept of herself and her concept of a stereotyped "ideal" woman.

2. A poor relationship with parents as reported by the patient.

3. Parental marital conflicts; this involves long-standing difficulties in the parents' relationship and includes profound argument, violence, infidelity, separation, and/or divorce. Usually the patient finds herself allied with her mother in a way that marks her out from her other siblings. The mother (or occasionally the father) burdens her with anxieties at a time when the patient is unable — usually through immaturity — to handle them. Role reversal occurs, with the daughter acting as mother. A pervading sense of unsureness and poor adult modeling results. Anger is common.

4. Academic striving, in which achievement gained is incompatible with the patient's concept of femininity, or in which the desire for achievement stems from low self-esteem.

5. Poor peer group relationships.

Bulimia is caused by a series of threatening events occurring in the life of a woman already made vulnerable and unsure by the difficulties described above. The disorder is precipitated by the interaction of at least two of three factors:

1. Sexual conflicts, particularly those surrounding the beginning or termination of a major relationship, or a profound uncertainty of a sexual nature within an ongoing or significant relationship.

2. A change in occupation and/or geographical location, such that the patient feels rootless and unsure.

3. "Loss" involving bereavement, estrangement, or separation from a significant family member or close friend.

Whatever the mixture of the factors outlined above, the patient feels wounded, examines herself critically, and feels very low in self-esteem. She feels herself to be a failure as a woman and projects this failure onto her body shape. By dieting and altering her shape, she feels she can alter herself; however, she quickly stumbles into bulimia, a symptom that reinforces her sense of failure. The seeds of the bulimic eating derive from the emotional turmoil of late adolescence, and sometimes from a movement in social class as a result of education. Attempting to identify with a slimmer body shape or lower body weight, the future patient relates social and emotional security with carbohydrate abstention. "Dieting," or, more accurately, carbohydrate avoidance, is seen as a means of bringing control to the chaos she feels in and around her life. She links her body shape (and weight) emotionally and socially to her sexuality, a matter about which these women in general are highly unsure; their body shape and its manipulation become all-preoccupying. Logically, as they see it, the manipulation of shape and weight becomes the answer to any major emotional stress (Lacey, 1982; Lacey, *et al.*, 1983).

The underlying factors and precipitants outlined above are important and need to be examined within the therapy. Because of their remarkable consistency from one patient to the next, the examination can perhaps be profitably done within a group setting. However, the factors that *maintain* the bulimia are different and are usually best dealt with on a one-to-one basis. Individual bulimic attacks are triggered by three conditions:

1. A deficient emotional state. In such a condition, the bulimia acts as a *stimulant* — a means of filling a "need." Thus loneliness, boredom, depression, or unstructured time in the evening can, individually or in combination, generate the compulsion to stuff oneself that will briefly replace the deficient state. Generally, these patients use carbohydrates in excess to calm the sense of loss they feel in and around their lives. The carbohydrates can develop an addictive quality.

2. An aroused emotional state. In this state, the bulimia acts as a *sedative* — "an always available tranquilizer," as one patient put it. It may be used to reduce — or, perhaps more accurately, to avoid — anger or guilt. Gorging oneself to the point of sedation may lower heightened sexual drive or may be used as a means of avoiding sexual pressure; similarly, anxiety — say, about a proposed visit to the parental home — can be made manageable.

3. Food as physical stimulus. The bulimic is fascinated and haunted by food, and small amounts of carbohydrate, illicitly taken at a time when she is starving herself, can precipitate a binge. As a patient graphically told me, "The dam was breached and the flood water just poured over." Alcohol or other drugs may also provide the stimulus for bulimia, mainly by lowering cerebral control. Alternatively, structure and order can prevent attacks, as can, interestingly, intercourse or masturbation (Lacey, *et al.*, 1983).

The *epidemiology* of the bulimic syndrome also has implications for treatment. The condition occurs overwhelmingly in women, and the possible reasons for this have been discussed elsewhere (Lacey, 1983b). The prevalence in the general population is unknown but symptoms associated with bulimia are common (Crisp, 1981; Crisp, Palmer, & Kalucy, 1976; Fairburn & Cooper, 1982; Lacey, Chadbund, Crisp, Whitehead, & Stordy, 1978). Reports from clinics (Lacey, 1982; Pyle, Mitchell, & Eckert, 1981) and surveys of groups at risk (Halmi, Falk, & Schwartz, 1981) suggest that the condition is reaching an "epidemic" prevalence. Certainly established treatment centers are overwhelmed with referrals, and referral letters suggest that there are many previously undetected patients who are judged by both their general doctors and themselves to be ill and who have no locally available treatment.

Conclusion

The clinical and research findings outlined in the pages above lead naturally to certain general decisions about the treatment required:

1. The clinical population is not homogeneous. The treatment needs of the neurotic group are different from the needs of the personality disorder group. Two treatment programs thus appear to be needed.

2. Large numbers of patients are afflicted. The treatment should therefore be not only effective, but also cost-effective. It is probably best for it to be short and capable of being conducted in the outpatient department, perhaps as a part of a general psychiatric service.

3. The treatment should be eclectic. The treatment must be capable of handling the underlying and precipitating factors of the bulimic syndrome, and the similarity among patients suggests that an insight-directed group component may be helpful. Alternatively, different skills are needed to control and replace the maintenance factors of bulimia.

4. For a disorder marked by such chaos, control and structure appear to be vital. Yet this must not detract from an effective engagement in treatment, particularly since the illness is so humiliating.

THERAPY

Initial Consultation

The initial assessment is crucial. Not only must the diagnosis be made, but the patient must be firmly engaged in a therapeutic relationship to a degree that will assure her future commitment and enhance her motivation. Assessment is a two-way affair, and the patient must be provided with a structure within the assessment that will clarify her needs and determine the relevance to herself of any offered treatment.

The assessment should be preceded by a physical examination. There are advantages in the physical and psychiatric examinations' being conducted by the same person; the doctor–patient relationship and the professionalism and eclectic nature of the assessment itself are thereby established. In addition, the efficacy of the psychiatric assessment is probably enhanced, because the bulimic patient tends to value and judge herself in terms of her body. If she benefits from an open relationship with her physician when discussing her physical health worries, she will equate this with the advisability of quickly establishing an open relationship during the psychiatric assessment.

The physician should particularly note the patient's teeth and mouth (Hurst, Lacey, & Crisp, 1977), should examine her abdomen (and include auscultation in the examination), and should look for signs of edema and tetany. Positive findings, such as eroded palatial surfaces of the premolars, painless swelling of the salivary glands, or menstrual irregularity, should be discussed — both in their incidence and their probable etiology — with the patient immediately. Body weight and height should also be measured by the physician rather than by the nurse. The reasons for this are discussed later.

The psychiatric assessment is a lengthy procedure, and at least 3 hours should be set aside for it. Within this sort of time, a patient should fully respond to the accepting atmosphere of the assessment. Some patients, on the other hand, "vomit" out personal information, and the interviewer needs to impose structure if the clinical picture is to be clarified. The eating symptoms themselves, paradoxically, are of relatively minor importance; rather, it is their temporal relationship to the social and emotional factors precipitating them that is of primary concern in this interview. In addition to the precipitants, the underlying and associated family and interpersonal dynamics should be exposed, so that the physician can understand not only the symptoms, but also *why* the patient "chose" them and *why* they occurred when they did. Particular emphasis needs to be placed on the relationship between patient and mother, and her judgment of and involvement in her parents' own relationship. The patient's involvement with men and her feeling about her own femininity also tend to be important points in the pathogenesis (see above). Such an interview, with its emphasis not only on the psychiatric but also on the psychodynamic aspects fueling the disorder, is in itself therapeutic. The result should be a forging of links between therapist and patient, which can be profitably used in the forthcoming treatment session.

The Outpatient Treatment Program

INTRODUCTION

This program was devised to provide an effective and cost-effective short-term outpatient treatment of eclectic orientation. It can be conducted by nonspecialist staff members acting under medical supervision, and involves both individual and group psychotherapy. The cardinal features include a contract, through which the patient agrees to maintain a stabilized weight and a prescribed diet, while being held in therapeutic control and given supportive yet insight-directed psychotherapy.

This program is aimed at the vast majority of bulimic patients. It should be emphasized that it is only suitable for patients who are within a normal range of weight. It has been devised particularly to meet the needs of the neurotic group of bulimics. Such patients are usually working and so cannot contemplate either lengthy treatment or inpatient care; nor would such treatment seem to be appropriate for them. Experience has shown that gross personality disorder, particularly when associated with alcohol or drug abuse and perhaps sexual disinhibition, indicates the need for longer and more intense treatment than given in this program. The suitability of this program for a patient who is actively suicidal needs to be carefully assessed, like any outpatient work.

The *aim* of this treatment is to remove all symptoms of pathological eating without allowing the development of a weight disorder. It has been devised to give enough psychiatric help to allow the patient to deal herself with emotional and relationship problems that may be exposed during treatment, or, at worst, to allow her to seek help from the general psychiatric services without being encumbered by an eating disorder.

THE SETTING FOR TREATMENT

The treatment program takes place on one half-day a week for 10 consecutive weeks. Five patients are treated in each group. During the half-day, each patient has an individual session with her therapist, and then all five patients meet in a group session. There are two therapists in our clinic, and so one therapist sees three patients in individual therapy and the other only two. Both therapists attend the group. There is nothing magical, of course, about treating five patients at a time. However, fewer than five patients appear more a crowd than a therapy group, while more than five patients are difficult to deal with in a single afternoon. Consideration was obviously given to making the group a standard eight-patient group. However, eight patients would get little "therapeutic time" in only 10 sessions (we tried a six-patient group in one program, and we found it necessary to extend the length of treatment to 12 sessions). In general, therefore, a five-patient program seems to provide the right balance of adequate time, individual attention, and efficiency.

Two points are worth noting: First, the group session should take place on the same afternoon as the individual sessions; and second, the group session should occur after the individual sessions. The patients are encouraged to see the individual and group sessions as linked, being the two halves of a whole. In practice, the individual sessions fuel the group session, and this is partly why it is possible for such brief therapy to be so effective.

Communication between the two therapists is important. They should meet together at the end of the individual sessions to compare notes and prepare for the group. This exchange should not be limited to emotional or social information, but the patients' dietary and weight data should be shared. It may be necessary to pick up this information in the group.

STYLE OF TREATMENT

The treatment is eclectic. The balance and orientation were determined by a series of pilot studies. It was noted that psychodynamic treatment undoubtedly led to an increase in well-being and was appreciated by the patients as being relevant, but, unfortunately, had comparatively little impact on the overt eating symptoms. Behavioral treatment, on the other hand, reduced or temporarily stopped the symptoms, but led to major unresolved tensions and seemed to deny the obvious transference development. Further, all patients asked so many questions about their symptoms that some form of counseling was clearly needed. Also, cognitive therapies, such as cognitive rehearsal or the testing out of alternative behaviors to bulimia, were very helpful. In my hands at least, drug treatment seemed irrelevant for the vast majority of patients, although it does have a role in secondary bulimia (cf. Pope & Hudson, 1982; Sabine, Yonace, Farrington, Barratt, & Wakeling, 1983; Walsh, Stewart, Wright, Harrison, Roose, & Glassman, 1982).

The patients themselves were polled to determine what aspects of the various types of treatment seemed most relevant and effective, and, just as important, what seemed to them to be missing from their treatment. A close supportive relationship with the therapist was felt to be essential; also deemed very important was a formal structure of disciplined help aimed at symptom removal; finally, they required a forum in which they could, with sensitivity and insight, examine the anger and sadness released when eating is brought under control. It is interesting that such a view reflected the broad consensus not only of the patients, but also the various cotherapists working with them.

There was more variation of opinion as to the mechanics of the therapy. How were the various components to be built into the structure? Should the individual sessions be behavioral throughout? (No.) Should the eclectic approach occur in the group session, or just in the individual sessions? (Individual sessions only.) Should what is declared to an individual therapist be common property to the group? (Difficult, but, considering the brevity of treatment, the answer — with qualifications — is probably yes.)

The final pattern devised was that each individual session would last for 30 minutes, prior to a group session of 1½ hours in length. The individual sessions initially use simple behavioral and cognitive techniques before moving on to insight-directed therapy. The move in the individual sessions from behavioral to psycho-dynamically oriented therapy is led by the patient herself, as she realizes that the quicker she brings her symptoms under control, the more time is available for insight-directed therapy. Strictly speaking, it is not the point of symptom reduction that marks this shift, but rather the point of symptom control. With this control, the patient feels a new but often distressing intensity of emotion. Conversely, she can now perceive a future that is not hamstrung by dietary disorder. The ensuing confidence allows her to push the therapy in its new direction.

It must be re-emphasized that this movement must come from the patient herself; the therapist can only guide. Those patients who do not achieve this movement find help increasingly hard to accept, and the long-term prognosis is much poorer. The psychodynamically oriented therapy—the now combined individual and group therapy—handles and controls the pronounced tension, anger, and depression that follow giving up the symptoms of bulimia. This approach also mitigates against symptom substitution and provides an adequate forum for coping with major interpersonal problems. The relationship between patient and therapist is not confrontative or authoritarian, but it does put responsibility for change—that is, getting better—on the patient herself. It cultivates the patient's undoubted motivation. In analytic terms, an alliance is forged between the therapist and the rational self of the patient against the dietary and emotional chaos.

THE PROCESSES INVOLVED IN TREATMENT

The program consists of a series of controls, a graduated contract, and formal opportunities for therapy.

Controls. For a disorder that is marked by behavioral chaos, control is essential. Dietary chaos is the presenting complaint, and the bulimic patient craves order. However, her wish is ambivalent: Vigorous attempts to impose outside control will lead to anger, aggression, and avoidance. The high dropout rate of some treatments stems from such therapeutic zeal. Rather, control has to be exerted through the patient—yet the patient herself has usually made repeated efforts in vain to achieve just such discipline. The program must therefore provide a structure that will enable the patient to bring order to her eating. She may later rationalize, for whatever reason, that control has been imposed on her; this is not so, for manifestly, it never can be.

Five controls are built into the program. First, the patient uses the rigid structure of the treatment program itself; second, she uses the relationship (and its transference) between herself and her therapist. The structure of the treatment is important. The patient sees the same therapist at the same time in the same room, and meets with the same fellow patients in the group. The weighing ritual always precedes the therapy. Generally, there is order; nothing is hidden from her, and she learns to trust and believe in the system. However, in addition, three other strategems of control are used.

The first of these other stratagems is that the patient is weighed on the same scales and by the therapist at approximately the same time each week. It seems to be important that this is done by the therapist and not, say, by the clinic nurse. It is done just prior to the individual interview. Such a regular procedure emphasizes and underlines the commitment made by the therapist that the patient's weight will not be allowed to get out of control. Getting on the scales symbolically "reveals all" and will release the main anxieties of the week even before the interview has formally begun.

Second, the patient is given a dietary diary by the therapist. The diary is a 16-page booklet with written instructions on the cover, together with a section in which to write down the contract of the week. The diary is given by the therapist to the patient at the end of the individual session and handed back to the therapist at the beginning of the next session. The act of handing over the diary thus immediately follows the weighing, and these two exchanges between therapist and patient set the scene and tone of the interview.

The dietary diary becomes an intensely personal document symbolizing the relationship between therapist and patient; it can, perhaps, be described as a transitional object. Certainly, it is not unusual for the therapist to figure strongly in it. The diary provides control and discipline throughout the week and an outlet for emotions, and is perhaps the single most important stratagem that mitigates against the need for hospital admission.

The written instructions on the diary state that the patient is to carry it on her person everywhere throughout the week, including the lavatory. It is necessary to reinforce this instruction verbally; this alone has a tremendous impact on the disorder — a discovery that is quickly appreciated by the patient.

Each double page of the diary is divided into columns, in which the patient is instructed to record the quantity and description of all food and drink consumed, the time when eaten, and the incidence of bulimia, vomiting, and laxative abuse. She also records her feelings and thoughts in temporal sequence to the details of food consumed or eating symptoms displayed. Initially, the patient concentrates on emotions encountered with eating, bingeing, and vomiting. Later, she is encouraged to expand to other feelings, trying particularly to explain *why* she was bingeing or vomiting at that particular moment.

The last stratagem of control is the diet sheet, which outlines a prescribed diet structured into meals. The diet sheet emphasizes that bulimia can be thwarted by adequate carbohydrates when these are taken regularly. The quantity of bread, potatoes, and other carbohydrate foods that the patient contracts to eat is clearly marked. The patient has a choice, however, in both the variety and quantity of other foods. The giving of this choice reduces the battles of authority between therapist and patient. The diet sheet informs the patient of the amount of food needed to maintain her weight — a matter about which she often has little knowledge. The aim is to control her carbohydrate intake (that is the problem, rather than the energy value of all the food eaten). The patient agrees that she will not change her diet without reference to her therapist.

The Contract. The contract is made between patient and therapist. It is developed and agreed upon during each individual session, and written down by the patient herself in her dietary diary in the place provided. A copy is made by the therapist in his or her notes. Before the onset of treatment, the patient contracts to do the following:

1. To attend the 10 sessions and their related groups. The reasons for this are explained: first, that if she drops out of therapy, she has needlessly taken a place that could have been of benefit to another; second, that if she does not attend, her presence will be missed, and this will have an effect on the other four members of her group.

2. To maintain her presenting weight throughout the 10 weeks of the program. This is a crucial point. Most patients wish to lose a small amount of weight. However, the therapist must insist that weight be neither gained nor lost during the time of the program. This insistence temporarily removes the drive to diet and thereby allows the bulimia to stop, under the impact of the treatment.

3. To eat the prescribed diet mentioned above. This means eating three meals a day at set times, with the times taking prearranged social events into account. The patient chooses the times, not the therapist; however, once she commits herself, the meals become a part of the contract. One hour is set aside for breakfast and lunch, and up to 2 hours are set aside for dinner.

From the beginning of the treatment program, the patient is encouraged to stop eating in binges and vomiting. Though this is rarely possible, the patient is encouraged to reduce and then to stop the bulimia, each stage being marked by its incorporation into the contract. If bulimia occurs, she is encouraged, and then contracted, not to vomit. Most importantly, she contracts to eat the next prescribed meal, irrespective of the proximity of the previous binge. Thus if the patient binges at 6 P.M. but is contracted to dine at 7 P.M., then she must follow her contract through (or else she may binge at 9 P.M.). The decision to eat at 7 P.M. is thus more than a decision about dinner: it is really a decision about whether or not the patient has decided to remain ill (Greenberg & Marks, 1982; Long & Cordle, 1982; Loro & Orleans, 1981).

Therapy. Three treatments are built into the program: first, the diary, which is "available" throughout the day; second, the individual sessions; and third, the group.

Details of the therapy used in the individual sessions are described in various sections of this chapter. The group component of the treatment is particularly valued. Because of the brevity of the program, an information sheet about the group should be provided. The purposes of the group are as follows:

1. To provide mutual support to enable the group members to change their eating habits and to examine the difficulties and consequences of giving up their symptoms.

2. To provide group members with a safe place to explore their problems and their feelings, and perhaps to experiment with new ways of dealing with them.

No issues are forbidden in group discussion, although confidentiality is emphasized. The group is encouraged to concentrate on the "here and now," and in particular on the relationships and feelings established among members of the group and between them and the therapist. Group members should be encouraged to redefine their eating problems in terms of relationships and interpersonal difficulties. Patients should be told *not* to meet or talk to each other outside the group sessions (at least until the end of the treatment program); if members accidentally meet each other, the incident should be mentioned in the group.

It is noteworthy that each group forms a marked and noticeable *esprit de corps*, which helps individual patients over difficult patches. This tends to continue after the formal ending of the treatment, as the patients meet together to form a self-help group, thereby maintaining peer pressure and consolidating their improvement.

Full details of group content are outside the scope of this chapter. However, the groups tend to be fast-moving and very open, and to have much expressed affect, sometimes to the extent that the therapist needs to prevent the group members from "bingeing" with emotions and thereby preventing meaningful work.

The first group meeting of each program mainly concerns itself with aims of the group. In addition, members discuss individual experiences of fatness, weight control, shape, vomiting, and laxative abuse. Thereafter, the topics of fatness and shape tend to recur only when an interaction becomes too intense. Therapist intervention is necessary in early groups; in later ones, the other group members tend to deal with such problems.

It is noteworthy that the relationship between a patient and her mother tends to be as prominent a topic as the relationship between a group member and her partner. Knowledge of our view of the pathogenesis of the disorder (see above) explains this. However, group content is wide-ranging, and typical areas of interaction include parental conflict; parental emotional abuse; identification with the mother in parental conflict; female rivalry; sibling rivalry; women's role in society and feminism; anger directed at a male therapist, generalizing to men in general; improving communications; supporting other members; determining whether therapists (or parents) care; shortness of group experience; need to keep in touch; and the future.

STAGES OF TREATMENT

Treatment naturally falls into four stages: the assessment interview, the initial treatment session, subsequent treatment sessions, and follow-ups. The assessment interview has been described above.

Before treatment begins, the patient should complete — say, over a 2-week period — a simple dietary schedule of daily food intake and eating behavior. The therapist can then refer to it during the first treatment session.

First Treatment Interview. After weighing the patient and concluding the initial pleasantries, the therapist needs to restate the aims of treatment. These aims have already been outlined at the end of the assessment interview and also set down in a handout. Few problems can be expected at this point; the patient will readily concur, although she may seek some reassurance that treatment is likely to be effective. The therapist will need to reemphasize the points that treatment is only likely to be effective if the patient really wants to get better, and that responsibility for change must rest with the patient herself. Having firmly said this, the therapist can usually defuse the patient's understandable anxiety by suggesting that he or she appreciates the patient's ambivalence about change — that she must be concerned about what to put in the place of the bulimia, and, in particular, how to cope with life without using food for its sedative or stimulant qualities. With this cue, the patient will amplify her concerns.

The therapist must end this introduction with a warning: The giving up of symptoms is likely to lead to clinical sadness (see Figure 18-1). This should be seen by the patient as a natural consequence of the emotions' being redirected away from the disordered eating. The affective change will give impetus to the patient's exploration of the underlying factors that have generated her behavior; adequate provision has been made for this exploration in the treatment program.

The therapist will need to explain again the importance of regular attendance; after getting the patient's commitment, any practical difficulties should be ironed out, and the timing of her regular appointments should be fixed. "Emergency" telephone numbers can then be given. Already, the structure of the program, the concern and warmth of the therapist, and the clear direction of the treatment will be having the desired effect: The patient will be relaxed but highly motivated. This time, she feels, there really will be a change.

A basic tenet of the program is that body weight must remain stable. The therapist should emphasize that this applies only for the 10 weeks of the program and that the patient's eventual weight is entirely up to her. The impossibility of giving up bulimia while attempting to lose weight should be understandable to the patient: It is illogical to burden the patient with carbohydrate craving while she is attempting to give up the bulimia.

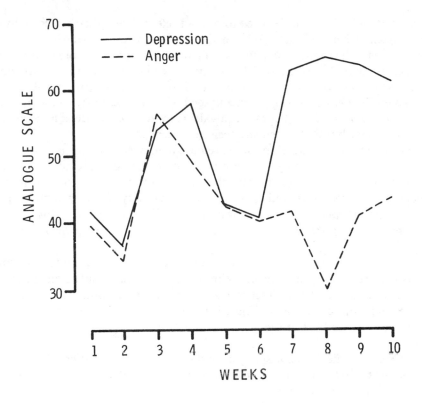

Figure 18-1. Mean analogue scale scores for depression and anger during each week of treatment.

No target weight should be given, for two reasons. First, the patient's weight is within a normal range, and, therefore, there is no medical need for it to be altered. Second, to do so would collude with the patient's psychopathology, for although the bulimic does not possess a weight phobia, she does cling to the view that a slight downward change in weight would improve her emotional state or capacity to achieve satisfaction within her relationships. It is worth re-emphasizing that the therapist should assume that the patient has as much right to alter her weight for cosmetic reasons as any other person, but that this is only likely to be effective when she is not suffering from an eating disorder.

The patient should then be given the diet booklet. The patient is only required to eat the foods that are underlined on the sheet and that form the basic "carbohydrate" components. The patient usually claims that it would be impossible for her—or, for that matter, anyone else—to eat the amount prescribed. This is, of course, simply not true; the therapist will need to make reference to the dietary schedule that the patient has just completed to emphasize to her that, because of her binge eating and vomiting, she has little idea of a normal dietary intake. The patient will be partially reassured when the therapist points out that he or she will personally weigh her, and together they will make sure that no weight increases occur. The realization (usually in about the third week of treatment) that a "normal" diet does not lead to obesity is a crucial and very personal discovery: No amount of handouts or discussions will really convince the patient until it happens.

Practical aspects of the diet need to be made clear. The prescribed carbohydrates must be eaten; other foods are optional. Thus, whether the patient prefers a cheese or a meat sandwich is immaterial, but two standard slices of precut bread are essential. The lunch is composed of sandwiches so that it can easily fit into a busy working woman's schedule, while dinner is more traditional; however, the meals are interchangeable. The patient should be encouraged to stick religiously to the diet for the first week or so, using carbohydrate equivalents (note, *not* calorie equivalents) from the list provided, but only when she feels confident in doing so.

Agreement is then reached on some reduction in overt symptoms — for example, no binge eating in the evening. The contract should then be concluded: The patient must maintain stable weight; eat prescribed carbohydrates in the form of meals; eat at predetermined mealtimes; and complete the dietary diary and carry it on her person.

The therapist can then end the session by spending a little time going beyond the symptoms, thereby giving the patient an introduction to the range of possibilities of therapy.

Subsequent Sessions. The disordered eating can be brought under control with a regimen of regular food at regular times and in amounts sufficient to maintain weight. The section of the contract restricting these overt symptoms, and the rate of its implementation, are variable. There is no set order for the following points, but they can be slowly added to the graduated contract.

1. Cease bulimia for some specified part of the day. Most patients find the morning to be the easiest time for control, followed by, in order, the afternoon, the late evening, and the early evening.
2. Eat the next prescribed meal even if a binge occurs.
3. Do not vomit even if a "binge" occurs.
4. Contract not to binge at all.
5. Do not buy or take laxatives.

The therapist and patient find the pace of the disorder together, and the symptoms will begin to remit. All improvement should be reinforced by warmth and congratulations. The reinforcement must never, however, be patronizing: A "schoolteacher" approach invariably undermines improvement.

Pattern of Improvement. Most patients stop their bulimia and vomiting between the third and sixth week of treatment. In a controlled study (Lacey, 1983a), in which 30 patients were treated in six groups of five patients to each group, the impact of this program on symptomatology was examined. During the treatment, all patients reduced the frequency of their bulimia and the associated vomiting attacks. The mean weekly incidence of both symptoms progressively declined after each treatment session, except for the eighth session (this seemed to be due to anxiety at the prospect of treatment's end; see Table 18-1). Figure 18-2 shows this pattern graphically and also shows the tendency of symptoms to exacerbate in the latter part of the week as the impact of each treatment session wanes.

The treatment had a significant impact on the incidence of both bulimia and vomiting (see Table 18-2). A mean of 47 bulimic attacks were reported during the 14 days before the treatment program began. This fell to a mean of just over two attacks during the 2 weeks after assessment ($p < .01$, Mann–Whitney). The incidence of vomiting fell from a mean of 53 episodes to a mean of just over two episodes during

Table 18-1. Mean Weekly Incidence of Bulimia and Vomiting Attacks in 30 Patients during the Week after Each Treatment Session

BULIMIA	SESSION	VOMITING
18.5	1	27.1
14.4	2	20.1
10.3	3	11.4
6.2	4	7.1
4.5	5	3.2
3.2	6	1.8
2.0	7	0.4
3.3	8	1.1
0.9	9	0.2
1.5	10	1.1

Figure 18-2. Mean daily incidence of bulimia in 30 patients before, during, and after treatment.

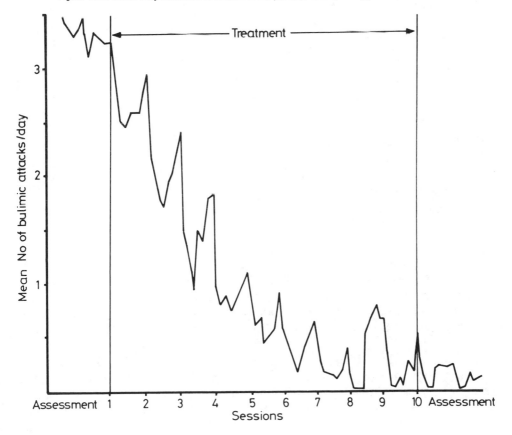

Table 18-2. Incidence of Bulimia and Vomiting over 14-Day Assessment Periods

PATIENT	BULIMIA		VOMITING	
	PRE-TREATMENT	POST-TREATMENT	PRE-TREATMENT	POST-TREATMENT
1	120	28	136	36
2	45	0	54	0
3	31	0	39	0
4	34	0	41	0
5	27	0	35	0
6	50	0	52	0
7	48	0	55	0
8	22	0	31	0
9	50	13	52	13
10	73	0	94	0
11	56	0	56	0
12	50	0	51	0
13	29	0	31	0
14	67	0	82	0
15	15	0	24	0
16	99	26	92	15
17	42	0	52	0
18	29	0	34	0
19	49	1	56	0
20	25	0	29	0
21	41	0	46	0
22	43	0	55	0
23	45	0	52	0
24	59	0	51	0
25	48	0	48	0
26	38	1	47	1
27	56	2	60	0
28	31	0	37	0
29	43	0	52	0
30	38	0	46	0
Mean	46.6	2.36	53	2.17

the 2-week posttreatment assessment period ($p < .01$). These results include those for two patients (Cases 1 and 16) who, although reducing the severity of their symptoms, remained severely afflicted. In fact, 24 patients (80%) had stopped binge eating and vomiting completely by the end of the 10th session, and a further four patients stopped within 4 weeks of the end of treatment. This brought the overall initial rate of success to 93%.

Bulimia is a fluctuating symptom occurring often in suggestible patients. It was thus important to determine whether improvement resulted from the treatment program or from any other factors, such as the intensive assessment, the monitoring procedures, the knowledge of impending treatment, or the simple passage of time. This was achieved by allocating patients alternatively to the treatment program or to a non-treatment control program of similar length. Those who were initially placed in the control program entered treatment after assessment. Table 18-3 shows that the control program had no demonstrable effect on the incidents of bulimia or vomiting. Though individual fluctuations occurred, the patients reported a mean of 45 bulimic episodes during the 2-week assessment period before the control program began and just under a mean of 47 episodes afterwards. Similarly, the incidence of vomiting did not significantly change over the 10-week control period (see also Cohen, 1978).

Mood Changes. At the beginning of treatment, patients are depressed and angry, as judged clinically and as measured on self-rated analogue scales (see Figure 18-1). Initial control of the eating disorder is associated with profound mood fluctuation and a feeling of being "disturbed." The last third of the treatment program is usually associated with a reduction in anger, unmasking a now-declared depression.

Follow-Up. Follow-up is an essential part of treatment. The patients find the "lifeline" of regular attendance reassuring; however, frequent attendance after the program ends is quite unnecessary. Patients should be seen 1 month and 3 months after treatment's end, and thereafter at 3-month intervals. The pattern of improvement takes three forms:

1. The majority of patients—usually about two-thirds—have no bulimic or vomiting episodes at all. Most will feel an impulse to binge, but are able to resist the compulsion. All describe feeling intermittently emotionally "disturbed," and in some the intensity is such that they consider further psychotherapy—therapy that is undisturbed by dietary disorder. In the study described above, 20 of the 30 patients had

Table 18-3. Incidence of Dietary Abuse in Patients Acting as Their Own Controls, before and after Control and Treatment Programs

	BULIMIA			VOMITING		
PATIENT	PRE-CONTROL	PRE-TREATMENT, POSTCONTROL	POST-TREATMENT	PRE-CONTROL	PRE-TREATMENT, POSTCONTROL	POST-TREATMENT
1	129	120	28	141	136	36
3	34	31	0	42	39	0
5	18	27	0	26	35	0
7	43	48	0	51	55	0
9	43	50	13	53	52	13
11	57	56	0	59	56	0
13	32	29	0	34	31	0
15	17	15	0	25	24	0
17	29	42	0	40	52	0
19	50	49	1	57	56	0
21	49	41	0	55	46	0
23	29	45	0	41	52	0
25	50	48	0	52	48	0
27	57	56	0	57	60	0
29	39	43	0	49	52	0
Mean	45.07	46.67	2.8	52.1	52.93	3.26

no dietary symptoms during 2 years of formal follow-up. Six considered further psychotherapy, but only one pursued it.

 2. A smaller group—about 25%—have occasional bulimic episodes. In my study, this was the outcome in eight patients. Before treatment, these patients were vomiting (on average) more than four times a day, and judged their diet to be in daily "chaos." After treatment, these chaotic periods were reduced to a mean of three times a year. The patients themselves judged this to be a satisfactory outcome. Three of these patients requested further psychotherapy, but only two began treatment during the follow-up period. No other patients received treatment, and the overall need for additional psychotherapy is about 10%. Such a patient should be advised that if she begins to binge again, she should immediately recommence her dietary diary in the knowledge that she will hand it to her therapist. She should put herself back onto her structured diet and make an appointment to see her therapist. Control is established within 2 days or so—usually before the patient is seen by her therapist.

 3. A small number—about 5%—need to be considered for inpatient treatment; this is discussed later.

Complications of Treatment

MARITAL STATUS

Married patients tend to experience difficulties during or shortly after the treatment program. These difficulties spring from the changes brought by the treatment, for it is noteworthy that in my study similar problems did not occur at the end of the control program. In most cases, a shift in the relationship is generated by anger when the patient gives up her eating symptom, and this leads to the marriage's being questioned. Generally, the husband complains of depression, gastrointestinal problems, or "stress." In one case, a husband was admitted to a psychiatric hospital. The difficulties described tend to occur if the marriage itself has taken place within the context of the patient's illness (and hence psychopathology). In those cases where the marriage predates the onset of the bulimia, adaptation to change appears to be easier.

Patients who present when married or who have stable unions with partners should be warned of the possible impact on their relationships of giving up the bulimia. The problem is best dealt with in two ways. First, a patient should be encouraged to tell her symptoms to her spouse or partner and to involve him in treatment. The spouse should not be confining, for that is likely to precipitate conflict; but he should provide a background of support, agreement, and understanding, thereby substantially bolstering the patient's self-control and self-esteem. Second, both should be offered short-term family therapy, timed to begin at the end of the program, with the aim being to work toward a renegotiation of the relationship in the light of the changed circumstances. Such an approach makes illness in the spouse an inappropriate adaptation and helps both partners toward health.

PREGNANCY

Conception may occur at or soon after the end of treatment. Some 8% of the patients seen in my clinic seek help because they wish to become pregnant but are fearful that the bulimia and vomiting may damage the developing fetus. It would be reasonable advice to suggest that patients wait and become more used to their changed emotional and physiological state before embarking on a family. However, this advice is rarely heeded. In support of their view, it should be said that none of my patients have developed hyperemesis and all have had normal deliveries. Dietary abuse does not return after the puerperium. However, one baby developed projectile vomiting at 10 days and was operated on successfully for proven pyloric stenosis. Patients apparently cope without difficulty to the increased caloric demands of lactation.

Prognostic Indicators

Poorer outcome is associated with the abuse of alcohol and, to a lesser extent, with previous anorexia nervosa (Type II bulimics). This is confirmed in Table 18-4, which shows the incidence of these indicators in each outcome group in my study. However, it should be emphasized that all Type II bulimics improved during treatment; Four of the six were satisfied with the outcome; either stopping or having only mild bulimic episodes; a further patient (Case 1) felt that the outpatient program allowed her to face inpatient treatment, something that she had avoided for 16 years and that eventually proved successful. Generally, we find that the longer the patient has been in low-body-weight anorexia nervosa, the poorer the prognosis. However, if patients have been anorexic for less than a year, there is little outcome difference between Type I and Type II bulimics.

Severity and chronicity of bulimia are also related to outcome. The longer the patient has been ill, the more difficult it is for her to recover, and the less likely it is that she will do so. The more closely the patient compares to the clinical description of the *neurotic group*, the better the prognosis, probably because of the underlying personality potential of that group. Certainly patients in the *personality disorder group*, particularly when their disorder is associated with alcohol and drug abuse and perhaps with sexual disinhibition, need longer treatment than is given in this program and seem to benefit more from the *inpatient treatment program* (see below). The presence of alcoholism in the parents, profound eating disorders in other family members, and parental psychiatric illness are all associated with treatment difficulties. Last, and perhaps most important, lack of motivation to change makes outpatient work almost impossible. However, the therapist should remember that it is a part of his or her function to facilitate motivation, and only to judge its absence after careful inquiry in optimum conditions.

Table 18-4. Alcohol Abuse and Previous Anorexia Nervosa as Prognosticators of Outcome

OUTCOME GROUP	n	ALCOHOL ABUSE	PREVIOUS ANOREXIA NERVOSA
No bulimic episodes	20	1	1
Mild occasional episodes	8	4	3
Needed further treatment	1	—	1
Refused follow-up	1	1	1
Total	30	6	6

Status and Sex of Therapists

The program described above was devised to be run by a paramedical staff. Adequate supervision is important; sometimes shifts of mood occur to a degree that briefly require a psychiatrist's observation (but rarely intervention). In addition, there is a distinct physical morbidity of which the nonmedically trained therapist needs to be aware: The significance of a swollen neck, shaking hands, and other such symptoms should be understood. With proper supervision, the therapist can gain confidence to bring about quite profound mental changes in therapy, and the need for precipitate re-referral to a psychiatrist or to inpatient care can be minimized. The advantage to the patient of working through the program with the same therapist cannot be overemphasized; the result is that longer-term follow-up can be achieved with only occasional contact, because both patient and therapist are sure of each other.

It is necessary that therapists be appropriately qualified. They should have knowledge of psychiatric methods and experience of psychiatric patients. In particular, they need to acquaint themselves fully with the practicalities of managing eating disorders and the psychopathology associated with them. It is usually more expedient to gain this experience on the inpatient ward before working in the outpatient program. Therapists should also have experience of group process and techniques. However, it is not necessary for therapists to have had formal group training or analytic training.

For a disorder marked by sexual uncertainty and conflict, it would be reasonable to expect that the sex of the therapist would be important. We have found that there are no differences in outcome, as measured by overt symptoms, between patients treated by two female therapists and patients treated by a man and a woman working together. However, patients prefer two women therapists; they significantly consider them to be more relevant and helpful to their needs than mixed-sex therapists (see Figure 18-3). The reader needs to recall the pathogenesis (see above) of the disorder to understand this view, although, as stated above, the impact of it is on the process of treatment rather than the result.

The female therapist is seen by the bulimic as a healthy woman; it is noteworthy that the patient often checks this by questioning her about her eating habits — something she would never do with a male therapist. She is also aware that her therapist is both a caring person and a woman who has achieved something professionally. The emotional investment is such that the therapist tends to be seen as an "ideal woman," someone who has successfully combined the many disparate and often conflicting attitudes to womanhood expressed by our society. The therapy should allow the discrepancy the patient expresses between her own concept of herself and her concept of a stereotype "ideal" woman to be displayed, often with consequent envy, anger, and admiration. The female therapist faces two possibilities: On the one hand, the discrepancy in the patient's mind may be so great that her self-esteem becomes further lowered and her sense of failure is confirmed. On the other hand, the therapist can provide a concrete affirmation that the conflicts experienced by the patient can be resolved.

The sex of the therapist seems to have a greater effect on the group component of treatment than on the individual sessions. Transference toward a male therapist tends to draw out the interpersonal difficulties that lead a patient to seek treatment, or to expose the uncertainties experienced by the patient within an ongoing sexual relationship. Some patients will attempt to ally themselves to a male therapist against other

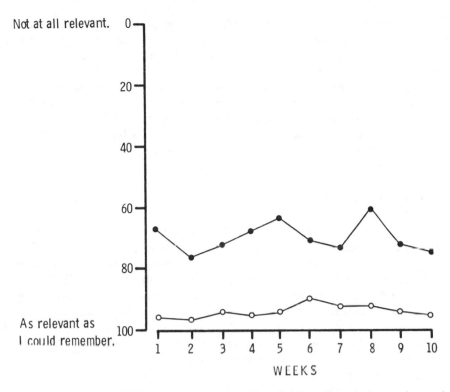

Figure 18-3. Mean analog scores of patients reporting the relevance of their weekly group therapy when conducted by a man and a woman therapist (●——●) and when conducted by two women therapists (O——— O).

group members (siblings) or the female therapist (mother). Such behavior can be very destructive to the group, as well as distressing to the patients, and great skill needs to be exercised if these emotions are to be held within therapeutic controls.

While groups with mixed-sex therapists seem to concentrate more on parental marital conflict, all-women groups tend to concentrate on relationships with mothers in a way that the presence of a man precludes. Similarly, the exploration of poor peer relationships tends not to occur when a man is present, the matter being submerged by (sexual) competition. Difficulties surrounding the beginning or ending of major relationships, and particularly the association of these difficulties with the onset of bulimia, appear to be discussed irrespective of the sex of the therapists. One is left with the impression that although men are just as effective as women in dealing with bulimia, the patients are more comfortable and less tense when their condition is dealt with in an all-female environment. The choice of the appropriate sex of therapist will thus depend on the individual needs of the patients and the areas of conflict that are to be aired.

The status of the therapist has little impact on outcome. Psychiatrists, psychiatrists in training, psychoanalysts, social workers, and occupational therapists achieve similar results. The therapist's personality and knowledge of the bulimic's psyche would seem to be more important than the type of professional training.

I approach this point with some trepidation, but clearly the psychopathology of the therapist must be important for patient outcome. Women therapists may find themselves drawn to treating eating disorders by difficulties of a similar nature within themselves. Such therapists do badly: In simple terms, they tend to relate to the patient's problem rather than to form an alliance with that part of the patient's mind that wishes to get better. Male therapists, on the other hand, can get into difficulties when they misunderstand the psychopathology of the disorder. The bulimic is a woman "out of control," and the sexuality of this can be vicariously enjoyed by the poorly trained or inadequate male therapist.

The Individual Outpatient Treatment Program

The outpatient treatment program is flexible. The group component can be replaced by therapy based solely on individual sessions; the treatment, however, remains eclectic. It goes through the same stages, has the same process, and manifests the same style.

The patient attends on 12 occasions to consult the same therapist. Each individual session is lengthened to just less than an hour. The average time the therapist spends with a patient remains the same (11 hours), as in the standard program described above (see Table 18-5). However, each patient's "notional" therapy time — the amount of therapy time equally apportioned — is increased (from 8 to 11 hours), while exposure to available therapy is reduced (from 20 hours).

It should be borne in mind that although service costs are based on a therapist's time, efficacy of treatment is more related to available therapy time than to notional therapy time. Perhaps it is for this reason that outcome without the group component is not as good. The *esprit de corps* is not as high: The sense of being "in the same boat" and pulling together to conquer the disorder is more muted. The poorer outcome appears to be due solely to a higher dropout rate (although this still remains small). For those who complete treatment, outcome is broadly similar to that enjoyed by the standard program. It appears that the self-help effect of the groups is lost; certainly, the longer-term support provided by fellow group members is missed by pa-

Table 18-5. Cost of Therapy (in Hours)

TYPE OF TIME MEASURED		STANDARD PROGRAM	MODIFIED PROGRAM
Therapy "exposure" time	Group	15	—
	Individual	5	11
	Total	20	11
Notional "available" therapy	Group	3	—
	Individual	5	11
		8	11
Therapist time	Group[a]	30	—
	Individual	25	11
	(5 patients)	55	
	Each patient	11	11

[a]Group conducted by two therapists.

tients. It should be remembered that in the controlled study four patients stopped their symptoms *after* the formal end of therapy; this was, in part, the result of pressure from other group members. The more diffident patients and those lacking in motivation get a substantial "charge" from the group. In addition, the structure of individual sessions gives less opportunity to deal with such issues as peer relationships and family conflict, and they give no opportunity to share practical problems.

However, there is tremendous value in having a solely individual program. First, it is effective, although less so than the standard program; second, it has the advantage of flexibility; and third, it is preferred by certain patients. It is, thus, a useful option for our clinic, and it is best for it to run concurrently with the standard program.

On what basis does the clinician advise the patient as to the most suitable program for her needs? Sometimes it is practical: A patient may be unable to meet with a group at the required time, or the therapist may find that there are insufficient patients to make up a balanced group. More usually, though, the decision is made on clinical grounds. Thus, the modified program is advised for the following groups of patients:

1. The personality disorder group. In such cases, the treatment is aimed not only at removing the symptoms, but also at preparing the patient for inpatient admission.

2. Patients with secondary bulimia. Here, because treatment is conducted in association with a physician, the flexibility of the *individual program* is preferred.

3. The very young. An overwhelming age difference between one patient and the other group members will prejudice group cohesiveness.

4. The very reserved or shy. Such patients are unlikely to make use of short-term group treatment. However, when the eating disorder is in control, *long-term* group therapy should be considered.

5. The immature. For the patient who appears clinically immature, in the sense that her life experiences are *markedly different* from other group members, short-term group therapy is likely to expose these differences unreasonably and potentiate her loneliness.

Some additional comments on secondary bulimia are in order. The precipitation of secondary bulimia depends not only on the psychosocial and operant factors described earlier, but also (and always) on the physiological cues inherent in the primary disorder. Hypoglycemia can contribute to the craving for carbohydrates; similarly, tricyclics and phenothiazines can have pronounced effects on energy intake, and the interplay of epilepsy and bulimia has been discussed above. Such cues become so entwined with the more general diet-related and emotional triggers of bulimia that disentangling them can be clinically taxing, particularly as the patient may rationalize and manipulate not only her reports of symptoms, but also her medication.

Patients with secondary bulimia tend to be younger than those in the neurotic or personality disorder groups. This, coupled with a consequent lack of life experiences and a need for concurrent management of the primary disorder, makes these patients less suited for the group outpatient program. The individual outpatient program is to be preferred.

Successful management depends on a close relationship between the therapist and the physician managing the patient's physical care. There are advantages in maintaining a separation of responsibility. It limits the patient's ability to manipulate therapy through her physical illness. In fact, it is best that therapy be made contingent on the patient's maintaining her physical well-being. Before treatment begins, both patient and therapist need to agree that manipulation of, say, insulin or anticonvulsant medication represents an "escape" from the emotional intensity of therapy, and by implication means that the patient is unready to start treatment. In such a circumstance, the patient is maintained on therapeutic "hold," instead of engaging in treatment aimed at a curative result. Such a contract tends to mobilize motivation and provide the right background for the individual treatment program to be effective (but see Greenway, Dahms, & Bray, 1977; Wermuth, Davis, Hollister, & Stunkard, 1977).

The Inpatient Treatment Program

The inpatient program is relevant to a minority of bulimic patients. It is devised particularly to meet the needs of the personality disorder group, or those who are actively suicidal. Despite the poorer prognosis of the personality disorder group, treatment can help. However, there is no point in offering it unless such a patient is genuinely desirous of change. Rather than damage the patient's self-esteem by an abortive admission, the therapist should attempt to engage the patient in a holding therapy. It may be years before the patient can make the decision to request admission, but the "lifeline" of occasional outpatient appointments will tend to facilitate the decision.

Patients, in my view, should not be admitted to an inpatient unit to deal with the disordered eating itself, but rather to deal with the underlying emotional difficulties by intensive psychotherapy in a structured setting. In other words, the reason for admission is the personality disorder, not the bulimia. Prior to admission, the patient should take part in the individual outpatient program so that eating is in control or nearly so. Binge eating or vomiting is not "allowed" on our unit. If abuse of food does occur, the patient's future as an inpatient is reconsidered. The patient should clearly understand, prior to her admission, that if she channels her emotions into food rather than into therapy, she is, in a sense, stating that she is unready for treatment, since the therapy is the reason for her admission.

The patient agrees not to change her body weight during admission. Weekly weighings help her exercise her own control. She chooses her own food and eats it in the company of other patients. Sometimes a patient may need a firmer structure than this for the first few days of her admission, but the aim should be to establish quickly a self-controlled structure of dietary continence, weight stability, and motivation to change. Sometimes, a patient may specifically request greater supervision during a period of great emotional stress. This should be dealt with sympathetically, but should not be provided for more than a few days.

On admission, the bulimic, free of her overt symptoms, has the opportunity to reflect on herself and consider alternative ways of relating to others and alternative attitudes. Clearly, the ongoing relationship with nurses and other staff members is very important. The nurses need to respond thoughtfully and nonjudgmentally, and with care and firmness when relevant (Crisp, 1980). Transference problems invariably arise and, in my opinion, apply to a larger number of staff members than is the case with other neurotic patients. This is probably because there is a tendency to "binge" on staff relationships to an unusual extent. It may be necessary to remind the patient that her relationship with staff members is a professional one, and that she should be wary of investing them with feelings more appropriate to her private relationships. Such simple interpretations free communication and allow the patient to make the best use of her available time.

Small-group psychotherapy is particularly relevant. The hospitalized bulimic tends to do better in general small groups than in groups composed solely of anorexic or bulimic patients. Within them, the patient begins to share her problems with fellow patients in a formal and supervised way and to assume some responsibility for beginning to help others with their problems.

Inpatients also benefit by joining a closed "trust" group. These groups are time-limited and conducted by a constant therapist. Patients are encouraged to "sculpt" their families or important relationships within supervised and interpreted psychodrama. Complementing these activities, the patient may experiment with feelings through dance, exercise, or touching others. This can help to develop a more realistic appreciation of her individuality and autonomy, and the relationship of these to shape and weight. Concurrent art therapy is helpful, particularly with those bulimics who have difficulty in acknowledging and revealing their feelings to others. They can be encouraged to paint their feelings, their families, or themselves. It is best that the art therapy group work on a common theme and have consistent therapist input. The therapist should suggest topics that allow the patient to paint change or fantasy. Such paintings can be incorporated into formal individual psychotherapy, and can also be open to group interpretation within the art therapy sessions.

For those patients who are still closely enmeshed with their parents or who live within a stable union, family therapy is essential. The initial aim must be for the therapists to gain information from the family, and for the family or spouse to meet the therapists and to understand the therapeutic process. Later, the meetings allow a wider sharing of feelings and, for that matter, experiences. Habitual patterns, such as argument, blame, or smothered anger, should be examined. The development of the symptoms, often within the context of the relationships being studied, is a sensitive area. However, individuals can learn, and, by testing each other within the structure of therapy, can grow.

If clinical depression is not present on admission, it is highly likely to arise during treatment. Antidepressant drugs should be avoided, and the patient should be encouraged to explore the origins of her despair. As the depression declines, the patient will be strongly tempted to return to her eating disorder. She should enlist the support of fellow patients and staff. The mechanics of this are easier if the unit operates on milieu therapy lines.

CONCLUSION

Bulimia is eminently treatable; however, the prognosis is not uniform over the whole population. It is necessary to diagnose the bulimic subgroup into which each patient falls, for each needs a different approach. This chapter describes the clinical features and psychopathology of the subgroups, as well as practical details of three treatment programs. The approach should be eclectic: Behavior therapy or insight-directed therapy alone gives a poorer result than when the essential elements of both are combined.

The overwhelming majority of patients can be treated in brief outpatient programs, which are effective and cost-effective. The cardinal features of each program — a contract through which the patient agrees to maintain a stabilized weight on a prescribed carbohydrate intake, while being held in therapeutic control and given supportive, yet insight-directed psychotherapy — are appreciated by patients and are successful. Most importantly, the results seem to be maintained over time.

The treatments described here have the advantage that they can be conducted by a paramedical staff under medical supervision. No claim is made that these programs represent the only possible treatment for bulimics, but they can be set up as a part of a general psychiatric service. Therefore, they provide perhaps the best opportunity for the large number of patients at present asking for help.

REFERENCES

Boskind-Lodahl, M. (1976). Cinderella's stepsisters: A feminist perspective on anorexia nervosa and bulimia. *Signs, 2*, 342–356

Bruch, H. (1974). *Eating disorders.* London: Routledge & Kegan Paul.

Cohen, S. (1978). Hostile interaction in a general hospital ward leading to disturbed behavior and bulimia in anorexia nervosa. *Postgraduate Medical Journal, 54*, 361–364.

Crisp, A. H. (1967). Anorexia nervosa. *Hospital Medicine, 1*, 713–718.

Crisp, A. H. (1980). *Anorexia nervosa: Let me be.* London: Academic Press.

Crisp, A. H. (1981). Anorexia nervosa at normal body weight: The abnormal weight control syndrome. *International Journal of Psychiatry in Medicine, 11*, 203–233.

Crisp, A. H., Palmer, R. L., & Kalucy, R. S. (1976). How common is anorexia nervosa?: A prevalence study. *British Journal of Psychiatry, 128*, 549–554.

Fairburn, C. G., & Cooper, P. J. (1982). Self-induced vomiting and bulimia nervosa: An undetected problem. *British Medical Journal, 284*, 1153–1155.

Feighner, J. P., Robins, E., Guze, S. B., Woodruff, R. A., Winocur, G., & Muñoz, R. (1972). Diagnostic criteria for use in psychiatric research. *Archives of General Psychiatry, 26*, 57–63.

Greenberg, D., & Marks, I. (1982). Behavioural therapy of uncommon referrals. *British Journal of Psychiatry, 141*, 148–153.

Greenway, F. L., Dahms, W. T., & Bray, G. A. (1977). *Phenytoin as a treatment of obesity associated with compulsive eating.* Therapeutic Research Press.

Halmi, K. A., Falk, J. R., & Schwartz, E. (1981). Binge-eating and vomiting: A survey of a college population. *Psychological Medicine, 11*, 697–706.

Hurst, P. S., Lacey, J. H., & Crisp, A. H. (1977). Teeth, vomiting, and diet: A study of the dental characteristics of seventeen anorexia nervosa patients. *Postgraduate Medical Journal, 53*, 298–305.

Lacey, J. H. (1980, September). *The bulimic syndrome.* Paper presented at the 13th European Conference on Psychosomatic Research, Istanbul.

Lacey, J. H. (1982). The bulimic syndrome at normal body weight: Reflections on pathogenesis and clinical features. *International Journal of Eating Disorders, 2*, 59–66.

Lacey, J. H. (1983a). Bulimia nervosa, binge-eating and psychogenic vomiting: A controlled treatment study and long-term outcome. *British Medical Journal, 286*, 1597–1678.

Lacey, J. H. (1983b). The patient's attitude to food. In M. H. Lessof (Ed.), *Clinical reactions to food* (pp. 35–58). London: Wiley.

Lacey, J. H., Coker, S., & Birtchnell, S. (1983). *Bulimia nervosa: Its aetiology and maintenance.* Manuscript in preparation.

Lacey, J. H., Chadbund, C., Crisp, A. H., Whitehead, J., & Stordy, J. (1978). Variation in energy intake of adolescent girls. *Journal of Human Nutrition, 32*, 419–426.

Long, G. C., & Cordle, C. J. (1982). Psychological treatment of binge-eating and self-induced vomiting. *British Journal of Medical Psychology, 55*, 139–145.

Loro, A. D., & Orleans, C. S. (1981). Binge-eating in obesity: Preliminary findings and guidelines for behavioral analysis and treatment. *Addictive Behaviors, 6*, 155–166.

Nylander, I. (1971). The feeling of being fat and dieting in a school population: An epidemiologic interview investigation. *Acta Socio-Medica Scandinavica, 3*, 17–26.

Palmer, R. L. (1979). The dietary chaos syndrome: A useful new term? *British Journal of Medical Psychology, 52,* 187–190.

Pope, H. G., & Hudson, J. I. (1982). Treatment of bulimia with antidepressants. *Psychopharmacology, 78,* 176–179.

Pyle, R. L., Mitchell, J. E., & Eckert, E. D. (1981). Bulimia: A report of 34 cases. *Journal of Clinical Psychiatry, 42,* 60–64.

Russell, G. F. M. (1970). Anorexia nervosa: Its identity as an illness and its treatment. In J. H. Price (Ed.), *Modern trends in psychological medicine* (Vol. 2, pp. 131–164). London: Butterworths.

Russell, G. F. M. (1979). Bulimia nervosa: An ominous variant of anorexia nervosa. *Psychological Medicine, 9,* 429–448.

Sabine, E. J., Yonace, A., Farrington, A., Barratt, A., & Wakeling, A. (1983). Bulimia nervosa: A placebo controlled double-blind therapeutic trial of mianserin. *British Journal of Clinical Pharmacology, 15,* 1955–2025.

Vandereycken, W., & Pierloot, R. (1980, September). *Dysorexia: Bulimia and anorexia nervosa.* Paper presented at the 13th European Conference on Psychosomatic Research, Istanbul.

Walsh, T., Stewart, J. W., Wright, L., Harrison, W., Roose, S. P., & Glassman, A. H. (1982). Treatment of bulimia with monoamine oxidase inhibitors. *American Journal of Psychiatry, 139,* 1629–1630.

Wermuth, B. M., Davis, K. L., Hollister, L., & Stunkard, A. J., (1977). Phenytoin treatment of the binge-eating syndrome. *American Journal of Psychiatry, 134,* 1249–1253.

Ziolko, H. U. (1976). Hyperexia nervosa. *Psychotherapie Medizinische Psychologie, 26,* 10–12.

CHAPTER NINETEEN

The Evolution of a Multitherapy Orientation

ROSS S. KALUCY / PETER N. GILCHRIST /
CATHERINE M. McFARLANE / ALEXANDER C. McFARLANE

INTRODUCTION

In 1977, an anorexia nervosa treatment unit was opened in Adelaide, South Australia, within the Department of Psychiatry at Flinders Medical Centre. Adelaide is the capital of South Australia, a large Australian state of about 1¾ million square miles. Many towns receive medical specialist services by air, and patients may travel hundreds of miles for assessment and management. Adelaide has a population of about 1 million, and the state as a whole has a population of about 1.3 million. The Flinders Medical Centre is a teaching hospital on the campus of The Flinders University of South Australia.

Prior to the establishment of the unit, there was no specialized treatment unit for people with anorexia nervosa. It was at about this time that there was a rapid escalation in the apparent prevalence of the disorder. The unit provides a specialist state-wide service. While the full range of patients with anorexia nervosa is seen by the unit, there is a tendency for the more problematical patients to be referred. We remain in contact with large numbers of anorexia nervosa sufferers over extended periods of time.

The program initially used by the unit was based on that of Crisp (1965) and Kalucy (1978). This program evolved to cater to the habitual clientele of these authors — anorexia nervosa patients whose predominant method of maintaining low weight and avoiding weight gain was by abstaining from food, particularly carbohydrates. These patients were mostly in their middle to late teens, had been ill for 3 to 5 years, and had had treatment from a number of other therapists. The original approach emphasized long-term inpatient care, with a focus on weight gain to normal levels. The principles underlying our approach and understanding of the disorder have been discussed in detail elsewhere (Kalucy, 1978) and are outlined below.

This model continues to guide our approach, but new conceptions and practices have emerged because of the following issues:

1. Only a minority of our patients (about 35%) fit the description of the "typical patient." Both considerably younger and older patients, and patients with durations

Ross S. Kalucy. Department of Psychiatry, The Flinders University of South Australia, Bedford Park, South Australia.

Peter N. Gilchrist and Catherine M. McFarlane. Flinders Medical Centre, Bedford Park, South Australia.

Alexander C. McFarlane. The Flinders University of South Australia, Bedford Park, South Australia.

of illness of less than 1 year and more than 10 years, have become more common. We have become much more aware of the wide variety of weight-losing strategies employed by these patients, including bingeing–vomiting; laxative, emetic, diuretic, and thyroid hormone abuse; and heavy exercise programs.

2. We found that our facilities, particularly inpatient beds, were inadequate to cope with the large number of patients who presented for care, even within the traditional abstaining population.

3. Experience has led to a change in our philosophy and level of optimism. The original program concentrated on the patients' return to normal body weight and the accompanying psychobiological maturity (Kalucy, 1978; Kalucy, Crisp, Chard, McNeilly, Chen, & Lacey, 1976), the latter being an essential prerequisite of the patients' ability to deal with the psychosocial tasks of their stage of development. We came to realize that the patients' long-term social and psychological well-being were not being adequately considered. Psychopathology within individual patients and their interpersonal relationships had been underestimated by us, in terms of its severity, its resistance to treatment, and the amount of dysphoria and disordered behavior it causes. We have become increasingly impressed by the complexities of the treatments needed to deal with these issues. The importance of long-term follow-up and management have been highlighted by our experience with these patients, a significant number of whom remain in a tenuous physical state for many years.

4. We have become more aware that a reasonable number of patients can be adequately managed as outpatients. It is difficult to tell which patients will cope in an outpatient setting and which will require inpatient care. Young, relatively acute patients seem to be more amenable to outpatient programs. Two further reasons for continuing our outpatient programs are considerations of cost, particularly in the current climate of economic recession, and the potential benefits of maintaining patients within their social networks.

5. We have found that it is not possible to refer a substantial number of outpatients into other treatment settings. Our resources for long-term follow-up have become exhausted, despite an availability of psychotherapy in the private sector. Many private psychotherapists find these patients difficult or beyond their expertise; furthermore, they require us to work in collaboration with them as resource people, and as a backup service if the patients deteriorate.

All of these considerations led us to a growing awareness of the heterogeneity of the anorexia nervosa population. We recognize that each patient is an individual with individual needs, and that each family requires a unique management approach. This heterogeneity is not infinite; it is possible to recognize subgroups.

We do not wish to propose a new classification of anorexia nervosa. However, we recognize that there are subgroups that differ phenomenologically. Based on our experience with 230 patients in the last 7 years, we see the following as having some logic, and describe them in detail later, together with the differing treatment requirements.

1. Anorexia nervosa (abstinence syndrome) of less than 2 years duration (18% of our population).

2. Anorexia nervosa (abstinence syndrome) of greater than 2 years but less than 10 years duration (32%).

3. Chronic normal-weight anorexia nervosa (6%). These are patients who are at a normal weight and often menstruating, but who remain preoccupied with issues of control, diet, and weight, which permeate all aspects of their existence.

4. Anorexia nervosa with bulimia, vomiting, and laxative abuse (22%). Of this group, approximately 80% are within ± 10% of a normal weight; most of the remainder are remarkably underweight.

5. Male anorexia nervosa patients (6%).

6. Chronic anorexia nervosa sufferers, who have been intractably ill for more than 10 years (16%).

It became increasingly apparent to us that the aims and tasks of treatment were different, both for different types of patients and for different stages of treatment. It was also clear that the range of motivations of our patients for help, and the range of objectives that they were willing to entertain for themselves, were very diverse.

We found ourselves evolving treatment programs that consisted of admixtures of insight-oriented individual psychotherapy, behavior therapies, family therapies, dietetic advice, community support, and inpatient and outpatient care. Again, the various groupings of this admixture are not infinite, and are described later in relation to a more detailed consideration of the subtypes that we have outlined above.

The fundamental decision that the unit made was that it would attempt to provide a comprehensive service for anorexia nervosa patients. We have had to experiment with our range of services and our styles of treatment. This article describes the evolution of these experiments, the range of patients, and the management strategies that we have brought to bear on the problems that they face.

MANAGEMENT ISSUES: GUIDING PRINCIPLES

Our management efforts are guided by the following principles:

1. With the exception of our chronic patients, mechanisms that guarantee a restoration of weight to normal levels need to be defined on a contractual basis. This should be achieved inside or outside the hospital by a diet that guarantees an orderly and slow weight gain of approximately 1 kg (2.2 lb) per week. The diet should contain no high-calorie supplements; it consists of three meals per day, the weight gain being achieved by including morning and afternoon snacks and a midevening supper.

The guiding principle is that biological maturity is necessary to achieve psychological and social maturity, and that interventions aimed at the latter two variables — psychotherapy, behavior therapy, and family therapy — cannot be carried out optimally if the patient is biologically prepubertal (Kalucy, 1978). The achievement of a postpubertal biological status is weight-dependent and requires that the subjects be above certain readily definable weights. It is very unusual for patients under 45 kg (99 lb) to be biologically mature. Patients need to learn to eat normally and should have the experience of being in control of food, rather than of food controlling them. Furthermore, large uncontrolled diets containing food supplements predispose the patients to bulimia and vomiting.

2. Gaining weight and being at a normal weight are central fears for the anorexic. The emphasis on these in our programs confronts that terror. The basis of this terror is diverse and includes fears of normal sexuality, fears of loss of control, and fears relating to separation and individuation. Difficulties in the control of anger and rage are important. Such fears are not confined to intrapsychic experience; adolescent growth may be experienced by anorexics as destructive to their families. This treatment approach begins to undo the patients' use of weight and food-related issues as a magical solution to their life difficulties.

3. We have a commitment to an eclectic frame of reference in the management of anorexia nervosa patients. We can see no special advantage, and considerable dangers, in clinical approaches (often framed as trials) that are linked to one single approach or theoretical stance. Our attitudes toward and reservations about the various treatment modes available are discussed below.

4. Although we take the view that anorexia nervosa can arise within and be supported by pathological family systems, we also believe that all patients carry within them severe psychopathology, which may or may not require treatment.

Anorexia nervosa patients often seem to us to display some of the features of so-called "borderline" personality organization (Kernberg, 1975; Masterson, 1972). These are mainly disturbances of ego functioning and the regulation of affect. Their sense of self is uncertain; they have trouble recognizing their own needs, beliefs, and feelings; and they often report a sense of "inner emptiness" related to their pervasive identity confusion. Impaired reality testing is evident in their body image disturbances and their magical beliefs about the effects of food on their bodies. Primitive defenses, such as projection, splitting, and denial, are often used. The patients tend to split relationships into "good" and "bad" ones, either idealizing or devaluing others. Their weight-losing behavior often reaches self-destructive proportions. The issue of self-control is paramount in anorexia nervosa patients because of their overriding fear of complete loss of control. Most anorexics, particularly abstainers, keep their affect and impulses under very rigid control to counter this fear, a characteristic that distinguishes them from patients with borderline personality disorders (as defined by the third edition of the *Diagnostic and Statistical Manual of Mental Disorders*, or DSM-III). Some bulimics, in whom self-control mechanisms fail, behave as "borderline" patients.

Obsessionality has been noted by others as a poor prognostic sign (Dally & Gomez, 1979). We are particularly concerned when there has been evidence of obsessional traits and symptoms for years preceding the anorexia nervosa. There is a small group of patients who have such symptoms, seemingly from their very earliest years. Their families seem unable to generate a sense of order and predictability for these individuals.

We also regard a lifelong history of separation anxiety, perhaps reflecting symbiotic pathology, as a particularly poor prognostic sign, and one requiring prolonged and difficult psychotherapy. Many of our patients appear to deal with this issue, if they are doing well, by distancing themselves physically from their families of origin and developing an apparently independent life style. They note, however, that when they are in contact with their families, there is a return to anorexic styles of thinking and pathological forms of behavior.

TREATMENT ISSUES

In this section we discuss our views about the various modes of treatment available for anorexia nervosa sufferers. This discussion forms the basis for understanding the eclectic approach that we adopt and the management strategies we have evolved for the various subtypes of disorder that we meet. We discuss separately hospitalization, family therapy, behavior therapy, individual psychotherapy, the use of medication, and outpatient support.

Hospitalization

In recent times we have been forced to reconsider the use of hospitalization as the central thrust of our treatment. We have moved cautiously, as our results in the past have been comparatively quite good (Kalucy, Crisp, & Harding, 1977).

Recently some of our patients have had a trial of outpatient therapy as the initial intervention. This involves a contract that commits the patient to inpatient care if adequate weight gain and psychological and social objectives are not being met. The major problem we face is that we have been unable to evolve guidelines as to who will do well in an outpatient versus an inpatient setting.

Our reading of current trends is that younger patients who have been ill for less than 2 years are being treated in a more flexible and less intense fashion; they are often, for example, not admitted to the hospital. Such patients are characteristic of those described by family therapists such as Minuchin, about whose results we remain skeptical, for reasons stated below.

A critical dimension of successful treatment is the establishment of a therapeutic alliance with both the patients and their families. We suspect that the decision as to whether to try outpatient or inpatient therapy as our first step depends on this rather nebulous concept. If we believe that we have a reasonable working relationship (and this is only possible to judge over a period of a month or two), we will continue and intensify a trial of outpatient management. One important function of the inpatient phase of treatment is the establishment of a therapeutic alliance in a population of patients who are often grossly ambivalent about treatment and the treatment team. In general terms, if a patient has not been ill for too long, if the family system is reasonably supportive, if the patient has initiated some part of the referral, if he or she demonstrates a degree of psychological-mindedness, and if his or her physical well-being is reasonable, the chances of a successful outpatient program are enhanced.

Although we think these things are important for a good prognosis (Kalucy, Crisp, Lacey & Harding, 1977), we remain skeptical. We have seen a significant number of patients who seem to fulfill all these criteria, but who nonetheless evolve into some of our most difficult therapeutic challenges. One possible explanation for this is the difficulty of obtaining a reliable history from both the patients and their families in the assessment phase.

We see no relationship between the weights at which patients present and their ultimate "therapeutic potential." The relationship between the degree of starvation and the need for hospitalization is a complex one. On one hand, the most emaciated patients are also those who are the most damaged in terms of their ability to assess their situation, and therefore those for whom a more authoritative or directive input needs to be made, sometimes because they are cognitively impaired. It is obviously necessary to admit the severely starved patients, simply for their own survival. On the other hand, hospitalization may be just as necessary for patients with severe psychopathology who may, nonetheless, not show signs of severe starvation and weight loss.

At present, we operate four hospitalization programs. The first involves a short-term admission for those who are in an extreme state of emaciation. This is basically a life-saving procedure and one aimed at getting the patient into a state of psychological and physical well-being in which full assessment can be made.

The second program also involves a short-term admission, used for patients whose eating is substantially out of control. In our experience, such patients are also psychologically and socially in a state of chaos. The aim here is to stabilize their present situation and to restore physical and metabolic well-being. They may be, for example, hypokalemic.

The third program involves a short admission of about 1 month, which is aimed at establishing a good therapeutic alliance and completing our assessment of the potential of patients and their families to work on an outpatient basis. This allows us to establish a reasonable, predictable set of rules about eating and diet. By the end of such a short admission, a patient should have a clear notion of what can and cannot be eaten, as well as of the relationship of this to orderly weight gain. Simultaneously, the family members are often better integrated and more able confidently to approach an outpatient program than they were when the patient first presented.

Our final program is the one described previously (Kalucy, 1978). This is a protracted inpatient stay, where patients remain on strict bed rest with a clearly defined normal-constituent weight-gaining diet until they reach target weight. They are then mobilized over a period of 4 to 6 weeks, and during this time much psychological work is done in terms of their ability to control and manage their own diet, weight, and such skills as shopping and clothing themselves. Freedom of visiting, freedom to enjoy recreational activities, and relaxation of controls are not solely contingent on weight gain; greater emphasis is placed on the quality of the therapeutic alliance with a patient.

In summary, the pattern of care that has evolved is tailored to each patient. At one extreme is a trial of outpatient therapy, and at the other is a moderately long-term, intense inpatient treatment program. The choice of programs seems to us to depend partly on the patient's personal resources, partly on the family's resources, and partly on the severity of the psychopathology. Perhaps the most critical factor is the persistence of a good therapeutic alliance. These are judgments that can only be made over time. We emphasize to the patients that hospitalization is not a punishment for failure in a more flexible and moderate program.

Family Therapy

The role of a family therapy approach to the problem of anorexia nervosa has recently been emphasized, partly because of the recent book by Minuchin, Rosman, and Baker (1978). The family of origin makes an important contribution both to the difficulties that our patients experience in adolescence in general, and to the genesis and maintenance of anorexia nervosa in particular. These contributions include the following:

1. There may be specific pathologies within family members that contribute in a direct fashion to the development of the child's problems. We have noted particularly the effect that a severely phobic, obsessional, or depressed parent can have in altering the system within which the future patient grows up, and in generating within the vulnerable child urgent needs to care for the sick parent (Kalucy, Crisp, & Harding, 1977).

2. There are specific "systems pathologies" that mitigate against separation, individuation, autonomy, and identity formation. The characteristics described by Minuchin *et al.* (1978) of rigidity, overprotectiveness, excessive enmeshment, and lack of conflict resolution have validity. A lack of functioning in appropriate roles is also important, and we are increasingly aware of the failure of fathers to take an active emotional part in the development of the future patients.

3. These families often have excessive and overdetermined interests in food, weight, dietary habits, and shape, which take on special family meanings in the realm of self-control, self-esteem, emotional expression, and development (Kalucy, Crisp, & Harding, 1977).

4. Many parents of patients with anorexia nervosa seem unusually inexperienced with the adolescent phase of development. In some general way they seem to be good at raising children, but not adolescents. This phase of development can be a threatening one to them; the parents often report inhibited and highly controlled experiences during their own adolescence.

5. The changes in the family system during the course of treatment of the anorexic child may precipitate or unmask psychopathology in other family members. For example, we have seen families in which a parent has developed a severe depressive episode or a phobic anxiety disorder during the course of therapy, often as the anorexic member is improving. We think this has an important influence on the well-being of all family members and the outcome for the patient.

There has been a trend in recent times toward seeing family therapy as an exclusive mode of treatment. Perhaps because of the enthusiasm of Minuchin *et al.*'s writing, and the high percentage of claimed good results, the approach has attracted many adherents in Australia. We have many reservations about the Minuchin *et al.* systems approach to family therapy as the treatment of choice, however; some of them are as follows:

1. Although Minuchin *et al.* have treated a large number of patients, they have presented results on outcome in only a very small number of these (Minuchin, Baker, Rosman, Liebman, Milman, & Todd, 1975). The weights of the patients presented in this follow-up work are remarkably low for the patients' ages. Many are in the 25th percentile or below in terms of weight for age. There are only three possibilities here:

    a. They are a very abnormal sample.

    b. They are a normal weight for height, which means they are remarkably stunted for their age.

    c. They still have anorexia nervosa.

Since there is no doubt that Minuchin's approach has induced substantial weight gain in his patients, and since they and their families appear to report significant improvements, it is possible that this approach has produced a stabilized system within which a physically stable anorexic is not threatened. If this is true, considerably more study of the approach is required.

2. The systems approach to family therapy is, by definition, not oriented toward dealing with illness in the patient as an individual. There are at least two problems here:

    a. The patients are overlooked, and their long-term follow-up may therefore not include a careful assessment of either their weight or their developmental status. If the patients are stunted, it may be that they are below a weight at which normal growth could occur.

    b. It is our experience that many anorexia nervosa patients will strive very hard to put on a good front to avoid the recognition of serious intrapsychic pathology.

We have, on many occasions, only discovered such problems after knowing the patient for several years. This psychopathology can remain undetected during the course of family therapy. Similarly, individual members of the family may be ignored. It is our experience that there is more psychiatric pathology within the family than other writers have stressed. This psychopathology — for example, major depressive disorder, agoraphobia, severe obsessive–compulsive disorder, and alcoholism (Kalucy, Crisp, & Harding, 1977) — may have an important bearing on the understanding of the case, the family's functioning, and the final outcome. Our impression is that the family will often unite to deny such psychopathology in the interests of one of its members.

While we value the systems approach in helping us to understand the family's contribution to the generation and maintenance of anorexia nervosa, we place just as much emphasis on trying to understand the impact of the sick member on the family, and the family's attempts to come to terms with a serious and life-threatening illness.

Distortions of communication, attitude, and experience are common in the families of our patients. Many adolescent patients appear to have incorporated these distortions and are seemingly unaware of the nature of normal relationships. Individual psychotherapy is one way of overcoming this problem.

In short, while there can be no doubt that family therapy in its own right has much to offer and can remove some of the obstructions to progress — for example, by changing the maintenance factors of the disorder — it is not always or even often the case, in our experience, that such therapy removes the internalized intrapsychic elements that impede progress and understanding.

Behavior Therapy

Behavior therapy has been taken up enthusiastically by some in our country. The therapists are often characterized by a lack of tolerance for (or even antipathy toward) other theoretical models, such as psychoanalysis or family therapy.

The least thoughtful of such behavior therapists apply such simplistic formulations to the complex problem of anorexia nervosa that sensible communication is well-nigh impossible. The more sophisticated therapists have gone down the path of the so-called cognitive therapies. We find a meeting ground here with our own constructions and with those of the psychodynamically inclined.

Our own views in this area of controversy are as follows:

1. Patients do not fit theories of treatment. We thus attempt to pick our way through the various approaches, using what is useful and omitting what we regard as harmful.

2. The notion of exclusive treatment approaches is simplistic. It is not possible to conduct a program that does not include some cognizance of the family dimension. For example, those programs that extract children from their families and place them in the hospital have already made a very powerful family intervention. Similarly, it is not possible to design a program that has no behavioral impact. If this is accepted, the only consideration is how thoughtfully one wishes to study all aspects of the interactions of patients, families, and therapists, and to capitalize on the insights that each theoretical model provides.

3. Our approach does not easily lend itself to scientific appraisal, and low standards can prevail in such a setting if care is not taken.

The usual behavior therapy program in our country is similar to that described by Halmi, Powers, and Cunningham (1975), who reported no advantage for the approach over conventional support and bed rest. The mainstay of behavioral programs is the granting of privileges for satisfactory weight gain. There are a number of grave limitations to this approach, and these include the following:

1. One runs out of rewards before an adequate weight is reached. The anorexic is thus discharged at a weight of about 40–45 kg (88–99 lb). This is compatible with reasonable physical health, but incompatible with good psychological and social health. The patient is still obviously anorexic.

2. Some of these programs allow food to be made freely available. Patients are thus seduced into eating as much as they can in order to gain their freedom. We have seen a number of patients who have developed the habit of bingeing as a function of this practice.

3. This technique does not allow for the detection of serious psychopathology, either within the individual or the family.

4. Such approaches often emphasize rewards in the nature of congratulations and encouragement. This does not allow for the fact that many anorexics have severe personality defects that generate feelings of guilt for being congratulated or having done something well.

5. A final problem with behavior therapy is that the very act of concentrating on specific goals and objectives, and attempting to tie the team and the patient to these goals and objectives via a contract, can produce major disruptions. The anorexic can manipulate the whole team into seriously arguing about the meaning of half a kilogram or a potato.

Behavior therapy undoubtedly has a role to play in a number of systematic behaviors that are overrepresented in the anorexia nervosa syndrome — for example, social phobic behavior or obsessive–compulsive disorder. We have found such interventions to be an important component of our treatment strategies following mobilization after the achievement of target weight, and also during outpatient care. Behavioral theories also help us to understand the nuances of some aspects of our inpatient care program. The notion of repeatedly facing a phobic situation, such as eating, has parallels with desensitization therapies.

Individual Psychotherapy

Most, if not all, our patients have had severe intrapsychic pathology prior to their illness, which has played an important part in the generation and maintenance of their disorder. The illness both expresses and defends against this psychopathology. This becomes most evident during the phase of maintenance of a normal weight. This psychopathology is often magnified and worsened by pathological interactions within a patient's family of origin. Such pathological interactions are also internalized and incorporated, and are often re-experienced during psychotherapy.

Some patients appear to do useful psychological work of a reparative and growth-promoting kind without prolonged or intensive psychotherapeutic contact. These patients always require some kind of supportive system, which is available at times of crisis, despair, or anxiety.

Approximately 30% of patients in our series receive intensive individual psychotherapy for periods of 6 to 24 months. A few patients, perhaps 10% of the series, receive longer and more intensive therapy than this.

We believe that the outcome of anorexia nervosa bears a relationship to the severity and intensity of individual psychopathology. Our general model is to apply an intensive inpatient psychotherapeutic milieu with good supportive follow-up and availability for crisis intervention, and to assess the patient's progress without intensive psychotherapeutic care before embarking on protracted individual psychotherapy.

As a general rule, the patients whom we take on for protracted or intensive individual psychotherapy have many of the qualities of moderate to severe borderline personality organization as described by Kernberg (1975) and others. They are difficult to treat, require advanced experience in psychotherapy, and have the same kinds of outcomes as borderline patients in general.

We have no skill in detecting which patients require such care and which patients will do reparative work on their own. As with our general approach to therapy, whereby we apply an outpatient model prior to inpatient treatment, we here provide a supportive model prior to intensive individual therapy. There are pragmatic as well as philosophical reasons for this. Pragmatically, we have a limited number of skilled psychotherapists available; in any event, we would be reluctant to take into therapy patients who would have otherwise done well. At a philosophical level, we presume that patients who "work things out for themselves" might find this an added bonus in terms of self-esteem and self-confidence.

Medication

Severe dysphoria and disorganizing experiences are common in anorexia nervosa patients. These are often seen as a gross and pathological exaggeration of normal adolescent experiences. Within a predictable, supportive, and well-controlled environment, most patients can work through these experiences without medication. This working through can result in a growing sense of mastery and self-esteem, with the development of new coping mechanisms for dealing with both personal and interpersonal experiences. As a general rule, the more informed and trained the nursing staff is, the less one needs to use medication.

Some of our patients, however, have the features of major depressive disorder or psychosis at presentation. These require treatment with either tricyclic antidepressants or antipsychotic drugs.

Against this background, the following points can be made:

1. There are a number of patients who develop the features of severe affective disorder later in their treatment. This compromises their capacity to work within a psychotherapeutic environment. In such circumstances, we use antidepressants in the usual dose ranges.

2. There are a small number of patients who become psychotic for brief periods of time, and a slightly larger number who become so intolerably aroused by anxiety that neuroleptics are required to stabilize them during the period within which one is attempting to create a therapeutic alliance. The dose of neuroleptics required varies considerably; interestingly, some patients can tolerate doses as high as the equivalent of 600–1200 mg of chlorpromazine without major side effects.

3. We avoid the use of benzodiazepines, barbiturates, and other sedative-hypnotics wherever possible, because anorexia nervosa patients seem to have a greater capacity for developing dependence on these drugs than the population in general.

THE DESCRIPTION AND MANAGEMENT OF SUBTYPES

As mentioned earlier, we believe that different populations can be identified within the heterogeneous group of anorexics that present to our unit. These populations differ phenomenologically, in terms of their psychological and social adjustment, and in terms of their management needs. This section focuses on these issues.

Anorexia Nervosa (Abstinence Syndrome) of Less than 2 Years Duration

There are two groups of patients in this subpopulation: a young population aged 10–14, which constitutes some 5% of the total anorexia nervosa population, and a group aged 15–25 (mean 18.5 years), who make up 13% of the total. These two groups are discussed separately.

The younger patients have all been more than 25% under ideal body weight. They have had primary amenorrhea, and all have been remarkably physically underdeveloped for their age. All have shown some signs of the beginnings of puberty. They have all been treated previously. All have been very emotionally upset and defensive at initial interview. The families have been remarkable for multiple pathological syndromes, which include evidence of anorexia nervosa in other family members and first-degree relatives.

Unlike other clinicians (Minuchin et al., 1978), we have found this population very difficult to treat. There are three possible explanations for this. The first may be a selection factor: We may be seeing only the most difficult cases, while others may have been treated more easily elsewhere. Secondly, our program may not be suited to this young population—a view supported by child psychiatrists with whom we work, who recommend a more rigid program.

The third possible explanation has to do with the nature of our weight-gaining schedule. When the young patients reach an optimal weight for their height and age, they are physically underdeveloped. Our contract must, therefore, provide for ongoing biological development. We therefore set a target weight that is at the 50th percentile for the patient's height and age. As growth begins to occur, the target weight is progressively changed for her height. This means, in patients for whom the program is going satisfactorily, that normal height and secondary sexual characteristics emerge. As we have mentioned previously, we suspect that many other units, including Minuchin's group, do not take this biological dimension into account, and thus produce children who have gained weight but are not of sufficient weight to allow normal growth to occur.

We became aware of this problem during the treatment of a 12-year-old girl weighing 26 kg (57 lb), height 147 cm (4 ft 10 in), who showed some early pubertal development. She came from an Italian family in which at least five first-degree relatives had had anorexia nervosa. The father had had anorexia nervosa as a teenager, and probably still had some symptoms of the disorder. In attempting to treat her in our unit, we were faced with chaos. She literally wailed for the first 3 weeks and was overwhelmed with terror about eating and gaining weight. The child psychiatrists advised us to operate a much more behaviorally oriented program, with very strictly defined privileges for weight gain. With this regimen, she reached a weight of 42 kg (92 lb), but was virtually unchanged in terms of her attitudes to eating and weight. She stuck rigidly to 42 kg for the next 3 years. Members of her family reported that they were much more at ease with one another and with her, and they did not report any signs of anorexia nervosa in the patient. However, by the age of 15, she was 152 cm (5 ft) tall, remarkably underdeveloped, and as anorexic as she had ever been. During subsequent treatment to achieve a progressive weight gain according to height, she was as terrified on each occasion as she was during her first admission. The treatment of this patient continues.

We find that the families of these patients are difficult to work with and often create situations that either lead to our refusing treatment, or force us to adopt quite unconventional strategies. For example, a 13-year-old patient, weighing 22 kg (48 lb), height 129.5 cm (4 ft 3 in), was a ballet dancer. She had maintained gross underdevelopment and supported this by a social ruse: She took child roles in her dancing, whereas her peers were beginning to move into adolescent roles and training. The parents of this patient were extremely rigid and controlling and very overinvolved with their child. They were aghast at the notion that they and their child would have to investigate their psychological world and the workings of their family. They took the child home, refusing treatment after the first interview. Some 2 weeks later the mother reported that her daughter was depressed and suicidal, and requested a further appointment. The mother attended on her own and produced a series of observations about the child's inability to separate from her. She asked advice about this. We had a long conversation about attachment behavior, during which time the mother pieced together its relevance to her view of the child's development. She went away with a copy of Bowlby's *Attachment and Loss* (1971). Two weeks later she returned to say that she had spent some hours discussing these issues with her daughter, and that there had been an improvement in her daughter's anxiety about separation. The subsequent six interviews over a 3-month period were carried out by Kalucy with the mother, who subsequently discussed the material with her daughter. The child has gained weight steadily and has begun to grow. She is now able to adjust her eating and weight to the pace of her own growth. Her mother continues to be the primary therapist. This unconventional intervention clearly contains pathological elements, such as the mother's need to remain in control. On the other hand, it may, in some curious way, be a mutually beneficial experience for both mother and child.

The second and larger group of patients, aged 15–25, who have presented in this category are quite different. They have lost between 15 and 40% of their body weight (mean 25%). Three have had primary amenorrhea. The remainder have all had amenorrhea that developed after they began dieting. None has been engaged in any substantial bingeing, vomiting, or laxative taking, although many of them have been obviously overactive. Most of them were somewhat overweight prior to the onset of their illness. Unlike our experience with patients who have had anorexia nervosa (abstinence syndrome) for more than 2 but less than 10 years, these patients have reported precipitating circumstances to their illnesses. These usually relate to some family crisis—for example, a threatened separation between mother and father, or a sibling's acting out (e.g., a sister's becoming sexually active). Sometimes the patient has reported a feeling that the family and her peers are demanding more independence of her than she feels she can cope with. There is a tendency for the family members to be isolated, overinvolved with one another, and somewhat threatened by "outsiders."

Initial assessment interviews and family interviews are different from those we experience with more established anorexics, in that both the patients and the families are more open, communication is more honest, and the patients and their families are much more aware of the price they are paying for this illness. The patients do not show the same degree of denial as more established anorexics and are aware of much more dysphoria. They are often more aware of the physical limitations imposed by their weight loss and dieting, such as an inability to play sports because of easy fatiguability. They are unusually willing to acknowledge problems.

The patients tend to be successful, outgoing adolescents with good school performances. Premorbidly, they have shown an excessive eagerness to please others, a great deal of sensitivity to moods and problems of others, and a conscious wish to maintain peace and stability within their families. They are all aware of their inability to identify and acknowledge their own needs or wishes. Overinvolvement between and among family members is not so striking as in our other patients. The fathers tend to show more involvement with their daughters and to accept a degree of responsibility for their care, which is unusual for the fathers of anorexic patients. All the patients display more personal assertiveness than our typical anorexia nervosa patients. We presume that all these factors are important to the good prognosis that these patients, in general, show.

Almost all these patients have been treated as outpatients, with weekly psychotherapy and regular advice about appropriate behavior. All patients have been on a contract to follow a diet in a predictable fashion and to gain weight regularly (about 1 kg, or 2.2 lb, per week) to a specified target weight, which is the average ideal weight for their height and age at the onset of the illness. Each week they have seen our community nurse, who has developed some unusual maneuvers, such as having lunch with these patients in town.

These patients seem to do very well. About 75% of them are now at normal weight and menstruating, and their psychological adjustment is better than we have seen in patients with more established forms of the disorder. Their psychotherapy has been marked by periods of very severe depression and anxiety, as well as outbursts of anger, particularly aimed at the therapists' controlling behavior. We see this anger as healthy, reflecting an unusual capacity for separation and self-assertion.

Some family interviews have been conducted with this group of patients. The patient and her parents usually attend once every 6 weeks. Other members of the family have been invited and have attended from time to time, but we have not insisted on their presence. The families have many problems, but they appear to be able to express these, often with considerable feeling. They actively seek answers to their problems. Some part of these sessions has been given over to providing advice and information.

It is our practice to provide our patients and their families with books about anorexia nervosa. Hilde Bruch's *The Golden Cage* (1978) seems to be the most informative one as far as the "consumer" is concerned. These patients and their parents read these books avidly and ask many questions about the contents.

Anorexia Nervosa (Abstinence Syndrome) of Greater than 2 Years and Less than 10 Years Duration

This is our largest group of patients, comprising 33% of our total population. The mean length of illness has been 4.5 years, with a range from 2.5 to 10 years. Their mean age has been 18.5 years, and at presentation they have been a mean of 30% under their ideal weight. These patients have all maintained low weight primarily by abstaining from food, particularly carbohydrates. Many have reported episodes of overeating, but vomiting has been unusual. Laxative abuse has been common, but intermittent, and overactivity has been marked.

The most common reason for presentation has been a mixture of symptoms, including those secondary to advanced starvation (e.g., coldness and faintness), some depression and anxiety, and pressure from families and friends. It has not been uncommon for schoolteachers or school peers to have generated the first assessment. All patients have been treated more than once previously.

The characteristics of these patients and the management procedures have been described in detail elsewhere (Kalucy, 1978).

The premorbid personalities of these patients have been those characteristically described in the literature. They are generally intelligent and sensitive people who are eager to please. They have anticipated other people's problems and unhappinesses. They have been sensitive to family stresses and strains, hard-working, perfectionistic, and high-achieving. They have shown the usual lack of childhood neurotic traits and eating disorders. Their families have varied in their degree of pathology, both as systems and as groups of individuals. Overprotectiveness by both mothers and fathers, a certain rigidity of outlook, and a low level of contact with nonfamily members are common. The fathers have been characterized by a degree of emotional distance and have often been perplexing figures to their anorexic daughters. There is a strong tendency to overvalue loyalty to each other and to deny problems. Some families are clearly quite ill or have very ill members, with disorders such as agoraphobia, major depressive disorder, obsessive–compulsive disorder, and alcoholism, as has been previously described (Kalucy, Crisp, & Harding, 1977). It has not been difficult to get these patients to acknowledge their anorexia nervosa, although in Australia the publicity that the disorder received was relatively limited prior to 1980. There were some patients who actually did not know what was wrong with them. In general terms, the parents were cooperative.

The assessment procedure has routinely included an extended interview by Kalucy, the aim of which is to get the patient and her family to acknowledge the presence of the disorder and the need for treatment. This has been successful in over 90% of this group. All patients have been introduced to other anorexics currently in the unit prior to their admission, and family members have frequently had a chance to talk with one another about the milieu and the inpatient regimen. We believe this facilitates admission, as well as being a valuable experience for the patients who are actually in the hospital. Our impression is that when an inpatient is invited to explain the regimen and her reactions to it to somebody who is terrified of the prospects that lie ahead, the experience often heightens her own awareness of her disorder and the problems it creates. These patients are also given books to read on anorexia nervosa. There is no doubt that they facilitate conversation in the early phases of individual and family treatment. All patients have a family assessment (or conjoint interview, for married patients) prior to admission.

We have not changed the basic elements of our treatment program for this group in the past 10 years. The possible exception is that we tend to begin individual psychotherapy a little later than we used to, because of our feelings about the importance of psychobiological maturity. We also concentrate more on an admixture of psychodynamic and behavioral psychotherapy. We pay more attention to the borderline components of intrapsychic psychopathology and the implications of these in our therapeutic relationship.

Our results with this regimen have been reported elsewhere (Kalucy, Crisp, & Harding, 1977). Over 90% of the patients that we admit to the hospital complete the full inpatient program and are discharged at a normal weight. Varying degrees of relapse are common, and rehospitalization is necessary in a minority for a failure to maintain target weight. Most of our patients continue for long periods of time to be very conscious about weight and food issues, and most of them display degrees of neurotic symptomatology, such as depression, phobias, or compulsive behavior, which in its own right may require treatment. Many of them notice a return to anorexia-nervosa-like styles of thinking, which may be associated with weight loss, especially when under stress. Maintaining the patient's motivation to get well becomes a central issue at this stage.

The return of menstruation is delayed in over half of our patients. The reasons for this are discussed below. Resumption of menstruation is taken by us to be a good sign not only of biological but also of psychological recovery.

It is our impression that our results with this population cannot be reported as favorably as those of some other authors. About 70% of them are doing reasonably well. They have normal weight and adult female endocrinological status. Most are working and living independent existences, or doing well at school, and show a reasonable range of friendships. However, only four of this group are totally free of symptoms of anorexia nervosa and can be described as both psychologically and socially symptom-free. This may be seen as a very harsh measure to apply in assessing the effectiveness of treatment. On the other hand, we would regard the rest as at least vulnerable to psychiatric disorder or to a relapse in their anorexia nervosa, and we attempt to continue follow-up for many years with all of them.

Three of the patients in this group have been treated as outpatients. The reasons for this were partly intentional and partly accidental. In the first case, the patient had had an overwhelmingly terrifying experience with a previous hospitalization and refused any consideration of admission. She requested that she and her family be allowed to attempt to reduplicate our inpatient program within their own home; we decided to go along with this idea. Over a period of 6 months, we saw the parents every 2 weeks and advised them on points of nursing technique and psychotherapy. Both the mother and the father took a very active part in this program. The patient reached 47 kg (103 lb) (from 33 kg, or 73 lb) by this method; she was mobilized and then managed by regular visits to the outpatient clinic. She reached her target weight of 52 kg (114 lb) and had a period of some 18 months of apparently excellent health. In recent times she has undergone a partial remission, perhaps illustrating the chronicity of her problem.

In the other two cases, the patients could not be admitted because there were no beds available for an extended period of time. Both of them initiated, with their parents, their own home programs while awaiting admission, and they made good progress under these circumstances. The unit delayed their admission to see whether progress would continue in this manner. One of the patients is now at target weight after a 3- or 4-month period of relapse, and the other is a few kilograms from target weight, having gained weight steadily for some 7 months. The only things that distinguished these two patients in any obvious manner from the remainder of the group were that they both had extremely traumatic first assessments. For example, one of the patients discussed the death of her mother, which had occurred when she was aged 10, at the interview. She appeared not to have explored her feelings about this for 8 years. She spent the best part of an hour in a state that can only be described as extreme despair. It may be that the first interview caused a very significant shift in the psychological position of these girls.

It is of some interest that the parents of these three outpatients were not remarkable for their good mental health; indeed, one of them was as disabled as any that we have seen. Two sets of parents, nonetheless, put an enormous amount of personal effort into the therapy in two cases. The third family, the most pathological one, responded by more or less ignoring the therapeutic needs of their daughter. This, paradoxically, appeared ultimately to help the patient recover.

The relative success with these three patients is one of the factors that has led us to review our approach to inpatient care. As mentioned earlier, we are moving toward a position of longer trials of outpatient therapy and shorter periods of hospitalization as a means of dealing with this population. As with any other innovation, there are prices to be paid: The dropout rate would seem to us likely to become a problem; staff work is not decreased by having patients mainly cared for as outpatients; there is a lot of guidance, interviewing, and crisis management involved; the amount of time taken per patient on a one-to-one basis is greater; and the stress for staff members is magnified.

Chronic Normal-Weight Anorexia Nervosa

This group has constituted about 6% of our patients. They have had the following characteristics: At presentation, they have all been within 5% of their target weight. They have reported a past history of classical anorexia nervosa, with amenorrhea of a duration of 3 to 5 years. The primary mechanism of weight control has been abstinence from food. All have shown both mild hysterical and more obvious obsessional features. Their main reasons for presenting have been continuing fears of their eating getting out of control, concerns about weight and appearance, and intermittent return to anorexia-nervosa-like thinking under stress. They have reported few dysphoric or neurotic symptoms at presentation, except on visits to their families of origin. These symptoms have become much more obvious during treatment.

The social adjustment of these women has been superficially good. They have all held down good jobs and had stable marriages, which they have professed to be happy. On closer examination, all have tended to be very controlling and to have fears of loss of control in general. These fears, as well as their need to avoid social eating situations, have led to their restricting their own social lives and those of their families. They have tended to remain secretive about their anorexia-nervosa-like thoughts and to exclude their husbands from this realm of their experiences. Their husbands have tended to be somewhat passive and isolated men, who have not attempted to intrude into their wives' psychological world and who have acquiesced readily to their wives' need to keep things under control.

The families of origin of these patients have been stable, although they have shown many of the features of families who produce anorexia nervosa patients. The patients have all had obsessional mothers who placed great emphasis on cleanliness, high standards, emotional control, and the suppression of conflict within their families. The mothers often attempted to be overinvolved in their daughters' lives. The daughters have continued to be seriously influenced by their mothers' views, although they are no longer in close contact. All have shown a considerable amount of anger with their mothers and with themselves because of the continuing pathological influence that their mothers have had on them. The fathers tended to be passive and emotionally absent men who found their wives difficult to influence. They have been described as men who "sought the quiet life."

Separations and changes are perceived as particularly difficult by these patients. They cope best with very busy, highly structured, and predictable lives, tending to feel empty and dysphoric whenever they have nothing to do, or when faced with novel circumstances.

In each of these cases, we have attempted to set up a therapeutic situation where we would work with both husband and wife. All patients have refused this concept and have sought individual psychotherapy. The style of psychotherapy used has been an admixture of psychodynamic psychotherapy and behavioral psychotherapy. One aim of this therapy has been to bring each patient to a point where her need to control her symptoms and to be secretive would diminish so that conjoint therapy could be undertaken. This has only been very partially realized as a treatment objective.

Two illustrative cases involved patients who were a little underweight and were admitted to the hospital because they could not gain the last few kilograms as outpatients. They were admitted for 2 weeks to achieve this end and to stabilize their eating patterns. Although the hospital-based interventions were brief, they served two useful functions. First, their families were brought into the therapy situation, and second, the admission acted as a public declaration of the difficulties they were having. The patients experienced some sense of relief and some upsurge of self-esteem when they realized they no longer needed to appear as strong and resourceful as before, and when they realized that they could give up some of their secretive behavior. On the other hand, they also experienced considerable fear and depression when they saw that their anorexia-nervosa-like behavior was no longer available to them as a solution to interpersonal difficulties. The admissions thus had several very positive effects, although they were invariably associated with unhappiness.

Such admissions as these have allowed some opportunities for conjoint work. The husbands do not enter into this aspect of therapy with enthusiasm, and it can readily be seen that they are, beneath an agreeable facade, men who experience considerable anxiety and depression. There have been some increases in communication between the partners and some increases in the husbands' assertiveness within these marriages. Two of these patients became pregnant during the course of therapy. The pregnancies were noteworthy because the patients experienced a decrease of anorexia-nervosa-like symptoms during their pregnancy. The pregnancies themselves were unremarkable and were experienced in a positive manner by the patients. Normal, healthy sons were delivered. There were no postpartum problems, and the mothers breast-fed without conscious ambivalence. One patient, however, had a great deal of trouble in giving up breast feeding, continuing it until the child was 3, in a way that suggested that she had difficulty in letting the child separate from her. It is also of some interest that when the children reached the age of approximately 9 months, the mothers became depressed in a manner that required antidepressant therapy. It seemed to us that the children's growing independence was experienced as a loss by these mothers, and also that they may have had difficulty in coping with the loss of such easy control over their babies.

Our dietitian and community nurse have assisted in the management of these patients. They weigh the patients weekly and provide advice about diet and weight control. In the course of doing this, they act as practical, warm support figures. The amount of psychological pain experienced by the patients and their husbands during the therapy has been striking.

The outcome for these patients at this stage appears to be good. One patient still experiences occasional anxiety about food when she is under severe stress and when her mother visits; however, she appears to be able to cope with this without any change in weight. All patients report being somewhat closer to their fathers and having a greater understanding of their fathers' lives. They appear to have separated somewhat more in a psychological sense from their mothers, although the relationships are characterized more by tolerance and resignation than by warmth.

No other members of the families of origin or of the immediate families have fallen ill during the course of therapy. We have had relatively little contact with the families of origin in any therapeutic sense, although we have met them as part of our initial assessment. It seems important that we accept the social reality of a patient's having separated from her family of origin and having established an independent lifestyle. Over the period of treatment, the couples and/or patients have never been seen more frequently than once a week, and quite often contact is monthly for therapeutic interviews and weekly for weighing and dietary advice sessions.

Anorexia Nervosa Associated with Bulimia, Vomiting, and Laxative Abuse

Some 22% of our patients have had overeating and vomiting associated with anorexia nervosa. These patients are older and have been ill longer than our abstaining anorexics. Only a minority of them at presentation have been remarkably thin, the others being at ± 10% of their target weight. They thus may not be seen as currently having anorexia nervosa by strict diagnostic criteria. All had anorexia nervosa prior to the onset of bulimia, the mean duration of which has been over 5 years. The patients in this group have eventually moved into gross overeating and vomiting after a period of abstaining anorexia nervosa with intermittent inability to control their eating. A few patients developed bulimia very soon after the onset of their anorexia nervosa.

As a population, these patients have been more physically ill, have shown more psychopathology, have had more disorganized personal lives, and have had more overtly disturbed family backgrounds than our abstaining anorexics. They are often very secretive and isolated people. They have been much more sexually experienced than the abstaining anorexics.

When the treatment unit was first established, we did not accept these patients into treatment, because it was thought that our treatment model was inadequate to cope with their needs. However, a few years ago the number of referrals of bulimic patients had increased to such an extent that we were forced to take some of them into treatment. Our initial approach mirrored our programs for abstaining anorexia nervosa; it emphasized hospitalization, family therapy, and personal psychotherapy, together with behaviorally based maneuvers. Our general aim was to stabilize weight and eating patterns. We saw this as a necessary precursor to being able to work with the chaotic intrapsychic and interpersonal life of these patients. Our results were singularly disappointing. Only 30% of our bulimics showed an acceptable reduction in concerns about shape, weight, and eating, and a reasonable improvement in psychological and social functioning.

More recently, we have been experimenting with a predominantly outpatient-based program, with hospitalization reserved for those patients whose eating and vomiting are grossly out of control, and for those who are acutely suicidal. We have also evolved a strategy that attempts to deal with the propensity of these patients to separate their behavior from their affect. They are given permission to binge and vomit, provided they make a conscious decision to do so and carefully record not only their thoughts, but their feelings, prior to the act. This has the paradoxical effect of decreasing the number of bingeing–vomiting episodes, and makes it possible to deal with the underlying emotional conflicts. This technique also allows the patient to get in touch with her dysphoria and to begin to identify a range of unpleasant feelings that seem to be connected with the need to overeat and vomit.

Our program also emphasizes the physical aspects of this disorder, and we closely monitor the patients' electrolytes, calcium, and hormonal status. A number of our patients need potassium supplements for long periods of time.

It is too early to comment on the success or failure of this program, but some patients have done reasonably well, managing to reduce or eliminate their bingeing–vomiting behavior. These patients have a sense of despair and helplessness, and have great difficulty in taking responsibility for themselves. They tend to drop out of therapy more often than patients with other forms of anorexia nervosa.

Male Anorexia Nervosa Patients

Only 6% of the 230 patients seen in the last 7 years have been male. Only four of these patients have been over the age of 16 years. Abstinence from food and compulsive exercise have been the principal methods of weight control.

Two of these patients agreed fairly readily to come into the hospital. They gained weight easily, seemed to declare very few psychopathological issues during treatment, and have remained well after hospitalization without intensive follow-up. The remainder have been very difficult to manage. All have displayed extreme resistance to weight gain, come from very disturbed families, and have shown major psychopathology in the area of gender identity. They have been locked into extremely hostile relationships with their families. Food refusal and avoidance of eating with their parents are major methods of expressing this hostility.

A number of these patients have shown significant growth retardation and have required a regimen where progressive elevation of target weight with growth is indicated. This has complicated treatment enormously. These patients are ambivalent about growing up; they are terrified of being dwarfed, and yet are simultaneously terrified of weight gain.

Our experience is that male anorexia nervosa is a much more difficult problem to manage than the female equivalent of abstaining anorexia nervosa.

Chronic Anorexia Nervosa

About 20% of our patients have had their condition for more than 10 years (a range of 10–35 years, mean 15 years) and are judged by us to have a chronic disorder. About half of these patients are married and locked into pathological relationships. All demonstrate gross disturbances in their relationships with their mothers. They have all had innumerable treatments, and none presents with the hope of "a cure." Nor do they express any real desire to gain weight. They maintain very low weights (30–35 kg or 66–77 lb) mainly by abstinence from food. All have had periods of bingeing and laxative abuse, but vomiting has not been a major feature of their disorder.

All are chronically preoccupied with food and weight. They tend to be socially isolated people who lead eccentric lives. Most are working. Almost all have marked obsessional traits and symptoms, as well as very low self-esteem. They exude a pervasive feeling of helplessness.

These chronic patients usually present with the following problems:

1. They have been through a period of stress, leading to an exacerbation of their anorexia nervosa and a further fall in weight from an already very vulnerable position.

2. They have complications of chronicity, such as osteoporosis associated with multiple fractures, or hypokalemia associated with generalized weakness.

3. They often present with depression, associated with some kind of wish to get out of their disordered life style.

The majority of chronic anorexia nervosa patients will not consider a program that involves significant weight gain. Many of them, if forced to gain weight, deteriorate psychologically to a severe degree. We know of three chronic patients placed in this situation who have committed suicide. It seems that forced weight gain may precipitate not only severe psychiatric disorders, but also a very painful awareness of all that has been missed in life (Crisp & Kalucy, 1973).

It would obviously be easy to decide not to take on these patients, since any decision involves a lifetime of effort. Kalucy decided to evolve a "chronic program." This program attempts to deal with the following issues:

1. A weight compatible with physical survival must be achieved. This weight is often 25–35% below the ideal body weight. It is surprising how many of these patients can be maintained over very long periods of time in a state of relatively reasonable health, compared with their position prior to starting a program. However, they all remain very disabled, physically, socially, and psychologically.

2. We have discovered, by talking to these patients for many hours, that the more successful ones maintain an extremely boring, predictable, and often eccentric diet from which they do not deviate in any manner. With some reluctance, we have moved to the viewpoint that it is best to help these patients create and live with such diets. We usually begin with a diet that will allow a very small amount of weight gain, often only 2–3 kg (4–7 lb), and then help them evolve a program of a predictable nature. To manage these patients, one often has to adopt quite eccentric positions. For example, one patient, who is 28 years old, has been anorexic for 11 years, and weighs

32 kg (70 lb), has the following as her routine diet: nothing for breakfast; chocolate milk for "morning tea" (the Australian equivalent of a coffee break); a sandwich for lunch; chocolate milk for afternoon tea; and boiled vegetables with a small amount of cheese sauce, a bowl of stewed fruit, and a bowl of bran for dinner. She can maintain this intake by a range of psychological tricks, such as denying that she is eating. The price, however, is that she can never go any place where it is likely that she will have to eat in an unexpected fashion. It is this sort of dilemma as much as anything else that contributes to the chronic patient's social isolation.

3. The care of these patients' physical status requires a great deal of attention to detail. When osteoporosis is present, we supplement the diet with calcium and manage to get some patients to take estrogens. Most, however, will not tolerate that form of therapy. They seem frightened both of the return of menstruation and of the feeling of femaleness and sexuality that they attribute to estrogen medication. We have done some preliminary studies, which suggest that the absorption of calcium in these artificially menopausal women is a little abnormal. They often require potassium and sodium supplements. The potassium is necessary to reverse the hypokalemia of chronic laxative abuse. The sodium supplements are mainly used in summer. Adelaide has very hot summers, and because these patients do not adjust their food and fluid intake, they may become relatively dehydrated and lose an excess of salt, which they usually avoid in their diet. A good number have developed organic brain syndromes and hypotension during the high summer.

These patients initially resist taking medication because of their need to deny illness and difficulties of any kind. A compromise can be reached whereby one agrees to go along with their eccentric position in regard to weight and diet if they accept essential medication, physical treatment, and a minimum safe weight. Most patients will become cooperative over a period of several years, because they feel much less weak and lethargic than formerly.

These patients require an unusual style of psychosocial care. They are all extremely anxious to please, insecure, indecisive, and frightened of the world in every sense of the term. Over a long period of time, it is possible to coax such patients gently into increasing their social activities and experimenting with meeting and talking to people outside their own families and marriages. No particular style of therapy matches our experience with these patients. It seems to require a combination of social skills training, advice, and elaborate congratulations for progress. This part of the therapy is the most difficult by far, and often the most hazardous. In particular, any change in the anorexics' life style is likely to produce unfavorable and sometimes disastrous responses from members of their immediate families.

Two cases dramatically illustrate these hazards. The first, that of a schoolteacher who had been anorexic for 14 years and weighed 36 kg (79 lb), began on this program 3 years ago. She remained in relatively good physical health and gradually widened her circle of friends, took up a number of new hobbies, and eventually left home to live in an apartment by herself. She was extremely anxious about this move. At this point, her mother developed a major depressive disorder, but the only symptom she would discuss was her chest pain. The patient became extremely guilty about this problem and was on the verge of returning home. We construed the mother's depression as being secondary to the daughter's newly found independence. We also believed that her mother's complaints about chest pain and fears of dying were an attempt to bring the daughter back home. With some encouragement, the patient decided that she would urge her mother to see a cardiologist rather than return home. The mother's response to this advice was to commit suicide the following day by pouring gasoline over herself and setting herself on fire.

In a second case, the patient, a woman aged 29, managed to leave home and set up a relatively independent existence. Her background was marked by an intense and probably incestuous relationship of very long duration with her wealthy father. After several years of living alone, the patient decided to marry. This occurred after a very long period of counseling and support. The relationship had its eccentricities, as one might expect, but nonetheless appeared happy. The husband was a rather schizoid man, extremely quiet but a lover of good food. This appeared to unite the couple. Within a week of the patient's marrying and after what was a relatively unremarkable wedding ceremony, the father committed suicide by hanging himself.

We cannot emphasize too strongly the need for moving very slowly with these patients.

COMMON PROBLEMS ENCOUNTERED IN THE MANAGEMENT OF ANOREXIA NERVOSA PATIENTS

This final section deals briefly with a range of common problems encountered in our management programs. It is not meant to be exhaustive.

Problems with Admission to the Hospital

Our general management policy aims to avoid responding inappropriately to crises. Great emphasis is placed on a complete and orderly assessment of the illness, the family, and the physical and mental status of the patient, as well as on preparation for management. As indicated earlier, such preparation includes meeting other patients and families who are involved in our program, reading a range of books about the disorder, and meeting other members of the staff. This assessment process may take place over several weeks.

There are several situations that bring great pressure to bear on this orderly procedure. They are best construed as cases of patients presenting in crisis.

The most common of these crises is associated with the collapse of the patient's support structure. Patients with anorexia nervosa have an unusual capacity for generating despair. They are, in general, young people who have been pleasant and sensitive, eager to help others, successful in school and home life, and, in every sense of the term, "nice people." Even at presentation they look like helpless children. In contrast to this, their pervasive denial, evasiveness, tendency to minimize problems, and deceitfulness frequently reduce their family support system to a state of rage, despair, and impotence. Other sources of support, such as general practitioners, often reach a point where they feel that they have nothing more to offer. It is also not uncommon for schools, peers, and teachers to escalate a sense of crisis.

In this situation there is always the temptation to respond immediately by admitting the patient to the hospital. Our experience has been that this kind of response is, in the long term, often inappropriate. It is not difficult to get such patients to agree to hospitalization and to get them into inpatient programs that involve weight gain. However, once the crisis has settled, we often find that questions of motivation on the part of the patient or the family have not been adequately assessed, and the long-term management of the patient is thus jeopardized.

It is usually possible to dissipate this kind of crisis and to create some sense of order and calm by outlining our normal procedures for assessment, and by discussing our expectations for the patient over a period of several years. This process creates a perspective on both the severity of the illness and its course. It is common for us to put the patient's name on a waiting list at the first assessment interview, even if we strongly believe that the patient may be best served by entering an outpatient program. This symbolic gesture often serves to calm the family and to orient the patient toward the future.

In a similar vein, it is not uncommon for patients whose history is characterized by periods of anorexia nervosa, interspersed with periods of bulimia and vomiting, to present in a state of crisis when their bulimia and vomiting are out of control. These patients are terrified of the potential for becoming fat, and are overwhelmed with feelings of helplessness. Such patients will often agree to anything in order to escape the immediate situation. Where the patient has been chronically ill and resistant to treatment for a very long time, there is a temptation to respond to this present willingness. In practice, we see that this is a mistake. When we have admitted such patients, they have very quickly become extremely manipulative. They see themselves as needing control in order to lose weight, rather than a stabilizing process aimed at reassessment of their future needs. Compliance with any program that we evolve is usally poor, and it is usual for these patients to discharge themselves prematurely.

There are several groups of patients whose presenting situation is as critical as those described above, but where the crisis is of a different nature and requires more urgent attention.

The first of this group are patients who present in extreme states of physical disorder. They are usually, but not invariably, very low in weight; they are often severely dehydrated, may be hypokalemic (although more usually they have low body potassium, which in the presence of dehydration does not show up as low serum potassium), and are usually hypotensive and faint. On mental state examination, these patients may show some of the features of an acute brain syndrome. On the surface they appear well integrated, and if one only talks about anorexia nervosa and related experiences, it is possible to miss this aspect of the presentation. When one enters less well-rehearsed areas of the patient's life, however, one finds degrees of confusion, disorientation and memory disturbance.

We regard this kind of presentation as a very sinister situation. It is our experience that this physical and mental status may precede death in anorexia nervosa. Furthermore, we take the view that the presence of an acute brain syndrome means that such patients can no longer be seen as people who can make rational decisions about their own well-being or their treatment needs.

With these patients, we take a more authoritarian approach. They are not invited into the program, but rather are admitted as acutely ill patients with an organic brain syndrome that requires management in its own right. The general components of this management are restoration of physical well-being by rehydration, electrolyte replacement, and restoration of weight to levels that are compatible with reasonable physical health (e.g., between 34 and 36 kg, or 75 and 79 lb). Initial weight gain is often quite considerable (e.g., 3–5 kg or 7–11 lb) in the first week, reflecting their previous dehydration. Once the patients are out of danger, they are assessed in a routine manner for ongoing therapy. It is quite likely that they may be discharged at this stage and enter an outpatient program.

A very small number of anorexia nervosa patients present with physical disorders requiring immediate admission that differ from those described above. We have had patients who have had both anorexia nervosa and the complications of vomiting, such as hematemesis or pancreatitis, and others who simultaneously have had ulcerative colitis or Crohn's disease. These disorders are obviously treated on their own merits.

Finally, there is a group of patients who present with anorexia nervosa and also have another major psychiatric disorder. By far the most common of this otherwise small group are those who have anorexia nervosa and a major depressive disorder. These patients are usually in an advanced state of despair and hopelessness, and may be psychotic. There is often a considerable suicide risk; a family history of major depressive disorder and suicide is not rare. Most importantly, these patients have "given up." They are no longer able to maintain any kind of stance about their anorexia nervosa, and it is not uncommon for them to have given up eating and drinking altogether. They are often in an advanced state of physical debilitation.

Such patients are routinely admitted on an emergency basis. The initial objectives are the management of their depression and the restoration of their physical status. The management involves bed rest with a reduction of general stimulation, strong nursing support, and the use of antidepressant medication or electroconvulsive therapy. The restoration of their general physical status follows the principles outlined for our physically ill patients. We very rarely need to use intravenous or nasogastric feeding in either these severely ill or the depressed patients.

With this approach, it is usual for depressed anorexics to show a good response over a period of 2 to 3 weeks. They normally gain weight and comply reasonably with the program. At this time, we reassess the situation in order to decide whether or not the patient will continue with the full anorexia nervosa program, or will be discharged and assessed along routine lines. In the past we have favored the former approach, but more recently have considered that discharge and readmission is the better strategy. The reason for this is that such patients will acknowledge that they have reached a point where they could no longer cope, but they will not acknowledge either that they have anorexia nervosa or that they need help for it. We thus find that as their depression lifts there are many resentful feelings among the patients, their parents, and the staff; these are not easily dealt with, because the patients were not in a position to make a judgment about what lay ahead of them at the time of their admission.

Major depressive disorder at presentation is not common. It usually emerges later in treatment, when the patient is beginning to face the full impact of a return to life at a normal weight.

There is a very small group of patients who present with both anorexia nervosa and schizophrenia. Over a 10-year period we have had three such patients. It seems to us that such patients are not in a position to assess their own needs or to make an informed general statement of consent about the management of their anorexia nervosa. We have admitted these patients, in the first instance, for the management of their schizophrenia. When this is under reasonable control, they are reassessed for the treatment of their anorexia nervosa. It is of some interest that the management of these two disorders is quite separate. An improvement in one does not necessarily lead to an improvement in the other.

Structure and Maintenance of the Management Team

The management of anorexia nervosa depends upon a strong, knowledgeable, and experienced team. Our own team consists of a group of four consultants, registrars training in psychiatry, general nursing staff, a community health nurse, and a dietitian.

We regard the high quality of our nursing staff as essential to the success of our treatment programs. Our nurses are required to be competent, confident of their roles, and willing to be involved in endless discussions about food and weight, growing up, families, friends, and sexuality. They are, in fact, practicing a type of informal psychotherapy. When the morale of the nursing staff is high, the need for medication in the treatment programs is low. Furthermore, cheating and failure to gain weight are much less common, and premature discharge from the hospital is rare.

Anorexic patients are difficult to look after. We routinely have between three and six in the ward at any one time. It is no surprise, therefore, that from time to time the nurses' morale drops or they become tired — perhaps "burned out" might be an appropriate phrase. It is also noteworthy that if the nurses' morale is low for some other reason — for example, the untimely death of a patient, or lack of support or unfair criticism from the administration — things can go wrong for the anorexia nervosa patients. The anorexics appear to be unusually "useful" objects for projection of the nurses' feelings. At such times it is common for the nurses to see themselves not as essential therapists, but rather more in the role of servants who simply deliver meals. It can also become difficult for the senior nursing staff to see our intelligent, attractive, and personable patients as sick and requiring protracted inpatient care.

One very good index of the morale and quality of the nurses caring for patients with anorexia nervosa is their manner of dealing with "cheating." Since all our patients are on a contract that specifically prohibits such behavior, and since our treatment unit is designed in such a way that it is very difficult for patients to dispose of food by subterfuge, cheating should be relatively easily picked up by the staff. Experienced nurses can usually detect cheating by the way that patients talk to them. For example, whenever a patient questions the size of her meals, or complains that the kitchen staff has not gotten the diet right, one can be almost certain that she is cheating. It is clear that almost all our patients, at some time or another, do cheat to some extent. When the nurses are feeling confident, they see this as an expected phase of treatment, a testing of the staff. It is detected and handled quickly, without humiliation or embarrassment. When the staff is not confident and morale is low, cheating often continues for a considerable period of time and is seen as "breaking the contract."

Maintaining morale is difficult when one is dealing with a chronic illness that has a high relapse rate. Some 40% of our total population of anorexic patients require readmission at one time or another. It is a tribute to the professionalism of the nursing staff that we have only rarely had to make the decision not to readmit a patient because of the threat that it constitutes to morale.

Choosing staff members for a unit that specializes in the treatment of anorexia nervosa is a delicate matter. Anorexia nervosa is a common disorder among nurses, dietitians, social workers, and female doctors. Such professionals are attracted to a unit that specializes in the treatment of the condition for conflicting reasons: Perhaps on the one hand, they wish to be treated vicariously or by default, and on the other hand, they wish to undermine a program. Despite elaborate selection procedures, we have been in a position about once every 3 years of employing someone who ultimately turns out to have the condition. Anorexia nervosa patients seem to be able to detect these people almost immediately. In these circumstances, the patients invariably suffer. There is a loss of confidence in the program by both patients and staff.

The occurrence of sexual seduction of the male nursing staff by patients with anorexia nervosa, particularly those who overeat and vomit, is a rare but unpleasant issue that needs to be discussed. Kalucy has seen this happen on three occasions in the past 15 years. The male nurses were, on at least two occasions, fairly inexperienced. Obviously, this was a disaster both for the patients and for the nurses' careers.

The Community Nurse

All our outpatient programs are supervised by our community nurse. She is responsible for weighing the patients and for supportive psychotherapy, and she is usually the first person to know when things are going wrong. The community nurse has had to evolve unusual strategies, some of which have been mentioned previously in this chapter. These include dining in town with working patients during their lunch hours, and inviting other patients to the unit for breakfast. This is a way of both supervising eating and assessing the patients' progress.

The community nurse is often a rich source of social and psychological data. As an example of this, one of us was telephoned by a patient whom he was seeing for psychotherapy. The patient was in tears and talked of feeling suicidal. She told the therapist that she was lonely and was finding she could not control her diet or eating. The patient's parents had both died some years ago. On contacting the community nurse, the therapist learned that one of the patient's friends, who had an extremely severe case of anorexia nervosa, had taken to cutting her wrists and had been re-admitted to the unit. Both of these patients had previously been told that they could not again be admitted and would only be managed as outpatients. The community nurse said that the first patient was feeling very jealous of the second because she had been allowed to come into the hospital. The patient had also told the community nurse about some problems she was having in her relationship with a young man. She had not been able to deal with this or tell the therapist about it. It is this kind of "domestic" information that characterizes the community nurse's store of wisdom.

There seem to be parallels between a patient's relationship with our unit and the functioning of an ordinary family. For whatever reason, however, we do not seem to encounter difficulties very often with a patient's family. There appears to be little rivalry or jealousy between, for example, the mothers of patients and our community nurse. The job of the community nurse is an extremely demanding one. Our patients are clearly using their relationship with her to think through many of the developmental issues of adolescence. She supports the patients through innumerable small crises, such as the weekly confrontation of weight gain.

The Dietitian's Role

The dietitian's role in an anorexia nervosa treatment unit is, for us, a problematical one that we have not been able to resolve until the past 4 years. The dietetic or nutritionist profession is, by its nature, concerned with the "good" qualities of foods and their relationship to health, growth, and general well-being. In broad terms, the philosophical milieu of the profession, at least in Australia, would tend to emphasize the "badness" of refined carbohydrates and the "goodness" of bran, fruit, and fresh vegetables. The deleterious effects of being overweight are also emphasized; health is equated with fitness and, to a degree, with thinness and good nutrition.

Several consequences that flow from this professional philosophy have particular significance for anorexia nervosa sufferers and their management team. The first of these is the possibility that the dietitian, if inexperienced, can be easily persuaded by an anorexia nervosa patient into agreeing that her diet is nutritious, sensible, and rational because it contains large amounts of vegetables and fruit and very few carbohydrates. A dietitian can unwittingly agree with an anorexic life style by virtue of the patient's manipulations and denials, and may find himself or herself becoming an ally of the patient against parents, doctors, schoolteachers, and friends. A dietitian must evolve new skills if he or she wishes to take part in a treatment program for anorexia nervosa. He or she needs to develop some psychotherapeutic skills, and to some extent must ignore the traditional philosophies of the profession.

The dietetic profession attracts an unusual number of adherents who have anorexia nervosa, anorexic attitudes, or, at a minimum, unusually overdetermined value systems about food, weight, and fitness. In selecting a dietitian for a unit that specializes in the management of anorexia nervosa, great care must be taken to avoid employing someone with anorexia nervosa.

Over the past 15 years, Kalucy has gone through several phases of excluding dietitians from the management of anorexia nervosa patients. More recent experiences, however, have been happier ones. We have been privileged over this time to have three dietitians, all of whom have been able to grow into the role and to become powerful allies of the treatment team as a whole and the patients in particular. In our own unit, the dietitian and the community nurse can be likened to "front-line troops" in the day-to-day management of anorexia nervosa patients.

Problems Related to the Female Patient's Reproductive System

THE RETURN OF MENSTRUATION

Menstrual functioning in anorexia nervosa is complex and not well understood. Some aspects of the hormonal basis of the changes in menstrual functioning have been well described (Kalucy et al., 1976), but many puzzles remain. While it is clear that dieting, in its own right, can affect the menstrual functioning of most women, it seems undeniable that the amenorrhea of anorexia nervosa can develop very early in the phase of weight loss, much earlier than in women who lose weight for other reasons. Similarly, the return of menstruation can be delayed. About one-third of our female patients resume menstruating at the time they return to normal weight or very shortly thereafter. In another third, periods return within about 6 months if the patients maintain their target weight and eat relatively normally. The remaining third present a management problem.

Many girls who remain amenorrheic for longer than 6 months become quite distressed. Probably quite correctly, they see menstruation as some kind of mark of "being better." Many are also anxious to have normal periods so that they are reassured that they have normal female bodies. They often conceptualize this as some kind of ability eventually to become pregnant.

Factors commonly associated with delayed return of menstruation are the following:

1. Continuing preoccupation with weight and abnormal eating patterns, particularly the continued avoidance of carbohydrates.
2. Continuing high levels of arousal, tension, or depression.
3. The fact that the patient, although at a normal weight, is still well below her usual premorbid weight. These patients have been obese prior to developing anorexia nervosa.

Menstrual periods may return following the resolution of some critical conflict within the patient's life. For example, a patient who had severe abstaining anorexia nervosa, and who had become engaged during the course of her illness, found upon regaining her normal weight and solving some of her intrapsychic problems that she was no longer attracted to her fiancé. As is usual in anorexia nervosa, she did not like to hurt people, and she took a whole year to break off her engagement. Within a month of her doing this, her periods returned.

When a patient has been premorbidly obese, and her amenorrhea is related to her failure to regain her premorbid weight, we do not recommend further weight gain. While this may be a biologically sound idea, it is psychologically and socially unacceptable.

We have not evolved a routine policy for dealing with continuing amenorrhea; we tend to treat each case on its merits. A few patients have been so distressed by their amenorrhea that they have been given the oral contraceptive pill to induce monthly bleeding, but we are not convinced that this is a wise maneuver, as it masks the patient's true biological status. Another two patients were given clomiphene in an attempt to induce ovulation. This was successful in one of them, but she was unable to sustain a menstrual cycle without medication. If possible, we prefer to wait until the patient's cycle returns naturally.

THE MANAGEMENT OF PREGNANCY IN ANOREXIA NERVOSA

We have examined a small series of patients who have become pregnant during the course of their anorexia nervosa, either with or without the help of hormonal therapy. Interestingly, one of these patients became pregnant naturally, despite remaining amenorrheic. There are several important management issues relating to these patients:

1. We do not encourage patients with established anorexia nervosa to attempt to become pregnant if they are markedly underweight and amenorrheic, although this

is now possible with hormonal intervention. We aim to have the patient become as biologically normal as possible before embarking on a pregnancy.

2. Patients who have recovered biologically from the effects of the illness with regard to weight and menstruation are often still concerned about their weight and shape. Although they may desire pregnancy strongly, they may become very anxious as their pregnancies progress, because it is no longer easy for them to gauge whether they are eating too much or too little to maintain their weight. They are aware that many women become overweight during pregnancy. We provided one such patient with a chart showing the average expected weight gain $\pm$ 2 kg (4–5 lb) for each month of pregnancy, and helped her to organize her diet to stay within that range. This proved to be a relatively successful endeavor. Perhaps surprisingly, most of the patients who have been pregnant claim to have been unconcerned about the change in their weight and shape during pregnancy. They are able to see the "fatness" of pregnancy as being different from ordinary obesity.

3. In the patients we have seen, there has tended to be a marked lessening of anorexic symptoms during their pregnancies, and all the women have been perhaps too positive about their feelings toward their growing babies. They have not admitted to the ambivalent feelings that have been documented in normal pregnant women. Child rearing, on the other hand, seems to have posed certain problems for these women. Several of them have had fears or anxieties about their ability to feed their babies adequately, and they have had some difficulties in allowing their babies to individuate and separate. Two of the women have become depressed at about the time when their children were becoming more mobile, and another two at the time when they finally and with some reluctance decided to wean their children from the breast. Another prominent aspect of these women's mothering behavior has been their attempt to resist their identifications with their own mothers. They have made a particular point of trying to raise their own children quite differently from the way that they were raised themselves. It has been evident that they have not managed to separate emotionally from their own mothers. They have noticed, however, that despite their best attempts, they have found themselves behaving toward their children as they remember their mothers behaving with them.

CONCLUSION

For the clinician, anorexia nervosa is a complex and heterogeneous disorder. Subgroups can be identified as functions of premorbid personality, personal and family psychopathology, stage of illness, and motivation. Different treatment strategies have been evolved for each of these subgroups. Simultaneous attention to the physical, psychological, and family needs of these patients is always required. A competent and well-supported team structure is the core of any program. We would emphasize that an eclectic and nondoctrinaire approach is important.

We find that treatment is always prolonged. The most vexing aspect of management is the problem of relating to a patient who is constantly struggling with the wish to be simultaneously well and anorexic. An effective treatment regimen must contain an unambiguous setting that allows the patient to confront this dilemma.

REFERENCES

Bowlby, J. (1971). *Attachment and loss* (Vol. 1). Harmondsworth, England: Pelican Books.

Bruch, H. (1978). *The golden cage: The enigma of anorexia nervosa*. London: Open Books.

Crisp, A. H. (1965). A treatment regime for anorexia nervosa. *British Journal of Psychiatry, 112*, 505–512.

Crisp, A. H., & Kalucy, R. S. (1973). The effect of leucotomy in intractable adolescent weight phobia (primary anorexia nervosa). *Postgraduate Medical Journal, 49*, 883–893.

Dally, P., & Gomez, J., with Isaacs, A. J. (1979). *Anorexia nervosa*. London: Heinemann Medical Books.

Halmi, K. A., Powers, P., & Cunningham, S. (1975). The treatment of anorexia nervosa with behavior modification. *Archives of General Psychiatry, 32*, 93–96.

Kalucy, R. S. (1978). An approach to the therapy of anorexia nervosa. *Journal of Adolescence, 1*, 197–228.

Kalucy, R. S., Crisp, A. H., Chard, T., McNeilly, A., Chen, C. N., & Lacey, J. H. (1976). Nocturnal hormonal profiles in massive obesity, anorexia nervosa and normal females. *Journal of Psychosomatic Research, 20*, 595–604.

Kalucy, R. S., Crisp, A. H., & Harding, B. (1977). A study of 56 families with anorexia nervosa. *British Journal of Medical Psychology, 50*, 381–395.

Kalucy, R. S., Crisp, A. H., Lacey, J. H., & Harding, B. (1977). Prevalence and prognosis in anorexia nervosa. *Australian and New Zealand Journal of Psychiatry, 11*, 251–257.

Kernberg, O. (1975). *Borderline conditions and pathological narcissism*. New York: Jason Aronson.

Masterson, J. F. (1972). *Treatment of the borderline adolescent: A developmental approach*. New York: Wiley.

Minuchin, S., Baker, L., Rosman, B. L., Liebman, R., Milman, L., & Todd, T. (1975). A conceptual model of psychosomatic illness in children. *Archives of General Psychiatry, 32*, 1031–1038.

Minuchin, S., Rosman, B. L., & Baker, L. (1978). *Psychosomatic families: Anorexia nervosa in context*. Cambridge, MA: Harvard University Press.

PART EIGHT

Support and Educative Methods

CHAPTER TWENTY

Self-Help and Support Groups in the Management of Eating Disorders

AMY BAKER ENRIGHT / PAULA BUTTERFIELD /
BELINDA BERKOWITZ

INTRODUCTION

Since the early 1970s, support and self-help groups have been gaining rapidly in popularity. There are now over half a million such groups in this country, serving nearly 15 million people (Gartner & Riessman, 1982) and addressing a myriad of problems. There are groups for single parents, parents who have suffered the loss of a child, child abusers, drug abusers, smokers, drinkers, overeaters, widowed persons, and divorced persons. Groups have emerged for persons suffering from physical diseases, such as cancer and ostomies, and persons with psychological problems, such as depression, schizophrenia, and bipolar disorders.

Many of these groups were developed by persons who felt that their particular needs were not being satisfied by the professional community (Hatfield, 1981; Silverman, 1978). Frustrated by a lack of effective treatment approaches and often by a lack of professional understanding, they began turning to one another for mutual assistance in overcoming a shared problem; Alcoholics Anonymous (AA) is a prime example of such a group. Other groups, such as Parents Without Partners, La Leche League, and Widow-to-Widow, developed in response to the deterioration of the extended family and other natural support networks or in reaction to rapid social change (Gartner & Riessman, 1982; Silverman, 1978); again, they rely on the notion of peers helping one another through difficult life changes. These two features — a common problem and reliance on peer help — are the consistent threads running through various support and self-help group philosophies. But, as Pearson (1983) has discussed, there is a great deal of confusion about what support groups actually do, how they differ from traditional counseling and psychotherapy groups, and, more basically, what the concept of "support" actually means.

In our own survey of support networks and organizations available for persons with eating disorders, there were nearly as many variations on the theme of self-help and support as there were respondents to our questionnaire. This not only underscored the range of options available to persons wanting to form or join self-help networks, but it also illustrated the confusion that Pearson (1983) has observed. Part of the am-

Amy Baker Enright, Paula Butterfield, and Belinda Berkowitz. The Bridge Counseling Center; Center for the Treatment of Eating Disorders; and The National Anorexic Aid Society, Columbus, Ohio.

biguity stems from what Pearson identifies as "a very undifferentiated understanding of the concept 'support'" or the lack of a clear and consistent operational model. It can also be traced to the disparate forces that led to the initiation of the self-help/support movement. Our aim in this chapter is twofold. First, we attempt to synthesize the current theory and application related to self-help/support groups. Secondly, we will attempt to distill the salient factors requisite for the effective use of self-help/support networks as adjuncts to the treatment of eating disorders.

Terminology

Before examining the antecedent factors contributing to the development of the self-help/support movement, it is important to make some distinctions in terminology. The terms "support," "self-help," "mutual help," and "mutual aid" or "exchange" have all been used to refer to groups that rely on peer networks as a means of coping with specific problems. Gartner and Riessman (1982) define "self-help" groups as small networks "usually formed by peers . . . for mutual assistance in satisfying a common need . . . and bringing about desired social and/or personal change" (p. 631). Silverman (1978) claims that when a "mutual help" network is "formalized in a systematic organization and program," then it is called a "self-help organization," which she contrasts with the professional helping system, which has "no room . . . to integrate the experience people gain from living and successfully dealing with their problems" (p. 5). Gottlieb (1976) uses the term "mutual help" groups in reference to groups that may not share a common problem but do emphasize peer help. And Pearson (1983) uses the term "support" to refer to groups characterized by two features, peer help and a common problem. Following Pearson (1983), we use the term "self-help/support" throughout this chapter to refer to peer networks addressing a common problem, with the understanding that support groups, unlike self-help groups, often involve affiliation with professionals. The specific role of the professional is discussed in more detail later.

Origins of the Self-Help/Support Movement

The support or self-help group movement began with the notion that people who have coped successfully with a problem can provide a valuable resource for others struggling with similar problems. What characterizes the exchange is the commonality of experience shared by the helper and the person in need. As suggested earlier, many groups developed in response to the failure of professionals to provide adequately for client needs. When members of the lay community, whether clients or relatives of clients, discovered solutions on their own, they often shared their expertise with others, thus filling the professional void with peer help. Many of the self-help organizations for anorexics and bulimics and their families were formed at a time when professional expertise was scant and public awareness of the problem was minimal. A mother who developed one of the early support groups for parents with anorexic adolescents has summed up the dilemma:

The disease [anorexia nervosa] is not very well known. Unless one has lived with an anorexic or bulimic child they cannot possibly understand the sheer hell that this condition creates. Even sympathetic relatives and friends can't understand how parents can "allow" their child to starve to death. Many doctors have little or no knowledge or are actually misinformed about the disease so that the usual source of help where severe physical symptoms are present, frequently is of no avail. It is in dealing with problems such as these and confronting the terrible sense of isolation among families, that family support groups can be of tremendous value. ("Families Learn to Cope," 1980, p. 4)

Not only do group members find a place to discuss their mutual problems, but they can provide solace, encouragement, and a sense of universality to others. In more structural terms, these group members provide one another with elements identified by Hirsch (1980) in a study of natural support systems: cognitive guidance, tangible assistance, socializing, emotional support, and social reinforcement.

According to Silverman (1978), self-help/support groups (which she terms "mutual," "since the help invariably goes both ways") also developed in response to professional success. She cites a variety of medical conditions that, with technological developments, have either extended the life expectancy of individuals (e.g., cystic fibrosis) or have allowed persons to survive a previously terminal condition (e.g., severe burns). These people were facing disabilities that required them to adjust to unanticipated situations, and, in taking up the challenge to improve the quality of their lives, they began working with one another in a supportive effort. As Silverman points out, these groups do not replace professional care; rather, they augment both medical and mental health services in a collaborative way.

A third factor that Silverman associates with the development of the self-help/support group movement is rapid social change and its impact on the effectiveness of traditional support networks. She contends that advancements occur so rapidly that "a time lag exists between the new knowledge as public information and the individual's ability to integrate and use this knowledge" (Silverman, 1978, p. 7). Families used to provide individuals with a set of values and a behavioral repertoire to cope with the world, but they increasingly have not been able to keep up with rapid social changes and concomitant changes in the needs of family members. As a result, Silverman claims that "role vacuums" develop as individuals move through "normal transitions in the natural life cycle so that people do not know how to behave as they go from one experience to another" (pp. 7–8). In particular, she cites the changes in such normal life stages as birth, with "a marked breakdown" of traditional supports for expectant parents, and death, with changing mores about grief and bereavement that often leave the individual feeling isolated and estranged. In between is the remarkable incidence of divorce and marital disruption, which again leaves individuals in need of help in overcoming feelings of failure and isolation within the context of forming new lives without their former spouses. From our perspective, the recent changing roles and expectations of women in this society have contributed to some of the conflicts underlying women's emphasis on weight and body image, and hence are relevant issues to be addressed by support networks.

Structure and Function of Self-Help/Support Groups

Although these antecedent factors help explain the development of the self-help/support movement, they do not address the structural or functional nature of support networks. Our survey suggested three structural categories (affiliates of national organizations, independent organizations, and organizations with professional affiliates). These correspond roughly to the three categories identified in a survey by Hatfield (1981) of self-help groups for families of the mentally ill (independents, affiliates of mental health organizations, and "Huxley" groups affiliated with the American Schizophrenia Association). These are discussed at length later.

Powell (1982) has conducted a fairly detailed analysis of structural factors influencing the provision of support services offered by self-help organizations (SHOs) as compared to agency-sponsored support groups (ASGs). In general, he claims that SHOs are "relatively permanent and autonomous," often affiliated with national organizations that provide stability and a complex structure, as opposed to ASGs, which he sees as structurally simpler and more temporary, since there are often fewer tasks in which members become involved. He examines several properties of networks (e.g., size, density, frequency, content, and intensity) that influence the provision of support, and analyzes each in both SHOs and ASGs, concluding that the former generally have richer programs and more opportunity to provide ongoing support services than the latter. He reports that his purpose is primarily "to highlight the benefits of the SHO which may be systematically overlooked by professionals," but he provides no data to support his analysis and conclusions. However, there are virtually no controlled comparison data available about the effects of self-help participation on outcome (Estroff, 1982).

Pearson (1983) has attempted to delineate the functions of support groups more clearly. According to his observations, the most common view of support, especially in the context of helping groups, is what he calls the "deficiency amelioration" view, in which support serves a remedial role — either in alleviating dysfunctional behavior, or in preventing individuals from becoming more dysfunctional by providing such things as comfort, acceptance, encouragement, and help. The majority of self-help/support groups are founded on and function according to this model. But Pearson argues, logically, that this model is really only adequate for people who are in crisis or experiencing adjustment reactions. He proposes the alternative notion of support as "[more] than an extraordinary intervention to remove deficiency." According to this view, "effectiveness, maintenance and enhancement" are most appropriate in providing continual resources for individuals in the process of developing and maintaining personal effectiveness. Elements characteristic of this type of support include love and companionship, honesty and knowledge, encouragement and altruism (Pearson, 1983). In both ameliorative and enhancement situations, he defines support groups as "surrogate support systems" for people who have lost their support networks or whose support systems do not adequately meet their needs.

From Pearson's (1983) perspective, a combined approach recognizing both the ameliorative and enhancing functions of support is often in order. He recommends that the counselor who is working with clients in need of support networks identify deficiencies in the client's existing support system and then specify particular goals and formats that would be most effective in meeting those deficiencies. He also advocates that as the needs of group members change, the group format and goals need to be adapted accordingly. This may lead to a shift of focus in groups from meeting ameliorative needs to serving enhancement/effectiveness needs.

Self-help/support groups may also be distinguished from traditional counseling or therapy groups. Pearson (1983) has differentiated the two by categorizing "behavioral and/or intrapsychic barriers" to support resources as the domain of therapy groups, and the provision of surrogate support for persons without natural support resources as the domain of support groups. Although he does recognize that support groups may help alleviate intrapsychic problems, his distinction seems quite theoretical.

Larocca (1983) views self-help as a most important but often neglected part of the treatment program for persons with anorexia nervosa and bulimia. In distinguishing those qualities and characteristics that differentiate support groups from therapy groups, Larocca focuses on the evolving role of the therapist. Over time, as self-help group members assume increasing responsibility for the group interaction, Larocca suggests that the role of the therapist changes from "expert" to "facilitator" to "being little more than a time-keeper and occasional interpreter."

There are some clear structural differences between self-help/support groups and therapy groups. The former are often free of charge, with meetings being held in a nontherapy setting, such as a community center, church, or educational facility. By contrast, therapy groups usually have a set fee and meet in a clinic or professional office. Self-help/support group facilitators are not typically trained professionals; therapy groups are led by professional therapists. Attendance is not mandatory for self-help/support groups, but is expected with therapy groups. The key issues that distinguish between support and therapeutic approaches include member stability, group cohesiveness, the functions of the groups, and the goals of the group leaders.

Support groups are often an individual's first contact with someone else suffering from an eating disorder. Bulimic women in particular are often so ashamed of and embarrassed by their behavior that it may take weeks or months between the time of their first contact and the time they attend their first support group meeting. They often experience a tremendous sense of relief when they discover that they are not alone and that their condition is not hopeless. For these women, the groups primarily provide support and feedback, as well as information about eating disorders and available treatment. Yalom (1975) has stressed that "stability of membership seems to be a *sine qua non* of successful therapy" and that group cohesiveness is a critical factor in therapeutic outcome. Most therapy groups are carefully composed in order to attain a balance between homogeneous and heterogeneous patient variables that can affect the group's cohesiveness. But support groups frequently lack this stability of membership; members often attend on an as-needed basis, and group size and composition can vary dramatically from meeting to meeting. Since support groups rarely can achieve the cohesiveness optimal for therapeutic change, concurrent professional treatment in addition to support services is advisable.

Frequent member turnover and changes in group composition also influence the facilitator's tasks. One important difference between self-help/support groups and therapy groups has been identified by Yalom (1975): Therapy groups that seek to effect enduring change occur mainly in the here and now; they focus on illuminating the process of member interactions. Thus, the therapist attempts to direct members away from personal history and events occurring outside the group; they are encouraged to focus on their relationships with one another. In contrast, the self-help/support group facilitator often encourages members to talk about their personal history and current living circumstances. In addition, information about eating disorders is also discussed, as, at times, are treatment referrals.

Although self-help/support groups may lack the stability and cohesiveness requisite for structural personality change, we do see them as a potentially valuable therapeutic tool, especially in the treatment of bulimia. Since they offer a nonauthoritarian interaction with other women who have faced similar struggles, they can help reduce the defensive barriers presented by many women with eating disorders. Along with comfort and support, group members who have "been there" can challenge certain ideas in a way that may seem less judgmental than similar challenges posed by therapists and family members. The diversity within the support group also allows the individual to understand the range of individual differences and experiences better.

In summary, it is not our opinion that self-help/support groups can replace therapy as an effective means of treating eating disorders. Rather, we believe that self-help/support groups can augment and enhance the treatment process by providing an additional source of group "curative factors" (Yalom, 1975), such as universality, interpersonal learning, altruism, the imparting of information, the instilling of hope, and catharsis.

SURVEY METHOD

With the significant increase in the number of persons seeking treatment for eating disorders in the past 6 or 7 years, it is not surprising that self-help and support groups for persons with anorexia nervosa and bulimia, as well as groups for their family members, have begun to appear. There are no current reports on how many such self-help/support groups actually exist, what populations they purport to serve, the structure and format of the group meetings, or the role of the professional in such groups.

This section of the chapter represents an attempt to survey a range of settings to determine the format and structure of self-help/support groups currently operating in North America. No attempt was made to evaluate the effectiveness or the impact these organizations have on the treatment or recovery process. The first step of this research was locating contact persons and addresses for as many groups as possible. The Support Group Registry was obtained from the National Anorexic Aid Society (NAAS), and a list was provided by the National Self-Help Clearinghouse. Other persons and organizations were contacted to request names and addresses of self-help or support groups for anorexics, bulimics, or their family members.

A total of 102 survey questionnaires were mailed. Twelve questionnaires were returned for incorrect or insufficient addresses. A total of 52 questionnaires were returned. Of these, nine were eliminated from the survey because they were strictly therapy groups. Therefore, only those respondents providing self-help or support services have been included in this report. Several of the groups included in the survey stated that they provided psychoeducational or therapy groups in addition to self-help/support groups.

Thus, 43 usable surveys from 23 different states comprise the sample. Respondents fell into three basic categories that form a continuum, reflecting degrees of professional involvement in the groups.

Self-Help Groups

At one end of the continuum are "self-help groups," which are organized and facilitated by persons who have previously been afflicted with an eating disorder. The primary characteristics of these groups are that members share a common problem;

they rely on one another for empathic understanding; and they assist one another in working toward recovery from their eating disorder. By definition, "self-help" implies that peer interaction is the primary curative factor. Professionals are not included in a leadership role in these groups unless they have also suffered from an eating disorder. Initially, these groups may have been designed to fill a professional void, and may have been considered an alternative to professional care. However, many of the self-help groups responding to this survey now encourage members to seek professional care in addition to attending the self-help group.

A total of 14 survey participants (32.5%) fell into this category.

Professionally Led Support Groups

On the other end of the continuum are those groups facilitated strictly by trained professionals. They are closely related to therapy groups and may employ the name "support group" to attract individuals for whom participation in therapy carries too great a stigma. They may also have been developed to reduce the cost of providing support services to clients. An example of this type of group has been reported by Rose and Garfinkel (1980), who designed a family support group as an alternative for parents refusing family therapy while their daughters were hospitalized for the treatment of anorexia nervosa and bulimia. The group was facilitated by a psychiatric social worker. While social support was available through the group, group members assumed no ongoing responsibility for group maintenance functions.

Twelve groups in the current sample (27.9%) were defined as "professionally led support groups."

Support Groups

The third category, "support groups," comprised 39.5% of the survey sample. This category falls between the two ends of the spectrum. Support groups allow both lay and professional facilitators and are designed to provide support for individuals whose natural support systems are inadequate or deficient. Excluded from this category are groups that prohibit professional leadership and groups that exclude lay persons in leadership roles. Unlike the situation in self-help groups, there is no implied concept of "cure" when attending support groups.

SURVEY FINDINGS AND STRUCTURAL OPTIONS

The survey consisted of 20 questions divided into three sections: Section I, Group Affiliation and Group Population; Section II, Group Format and Structure; Section III, Group Facilitation and the Role of the Professional.

A number of structural options were identified in the survey. While little evaluative research has been performed, we can assume that some thought has gone into designing the groups and that, by virtue of their continued existence, they must meet certain needs of the participants. We identify the range of options and discuss factors to be considered in referring to or creating a self-help or support group.

Group Affiliation

Table 20-1 lists the three principal types of group affiliations: national, independent, and professional.

NATIONAL ORGANIZATIONS

One-third (32.4%) of the groups responding to the survey reported that they were affiliated with or a chapter of a national organization. Four national organizations were identified, including the NAAS, Columbus, Ohio (founded 1977); Anorexia Nervosa and Related Eating Disorders, Eugene, Oregon (founded 1980); American Anorexia and Bulimia Association, Teaneck, New Jersey (founded 1978); and Anorexia Nervosa and Associated Disorders, Chicago, Illinois (founded 1976).

These four national organizations are very similar in origin, mission, the nature of the services they provide, and the way in which they conduct their self-help/support groups. All four organizations were founded by women. Two of the founders are parents of daughters who suffered from an eating disorder, and the other two had themselves recovered from an eating disorder. These organizations were created to provide information and support to family members and to persons with anorexia nervosa and bulimia. Each organization provides a national telephone hotline; printed information on eating disorders; periodic newsletters; referral resources for professional treatment and self-help/support groups; workshops, seminars, and conferences for the lay and professional communities; and consultation to parents, professionals, and the media.

These national organizations are subsidized in part by membership fees and donations. Several programs receive a substantial amount of their funding from conferences and workshops, while others receive funds from foundations and corporations. The major differences among these organizations are in the area of self-help/support group development and affiliation. For instance, one national organization provides information, consultation, and training to persons interested in starting support groups,

Table 20-1. Group Affiliation and Group Population by Group Type

	SELF-HELP GROUPS ($n = 14$)	SUPPORT GROUPS ($n = 17$)	PROFESSIONAL GROUPS ($n = 12$)	TOTAL SAMPLE ($n = 43$)
Group affiliation (%)				
National	57.1	23.5	16.7	32.4
Independent	35.7	41.2	16.7	32.4
Professional	7.2	35.3	66.6	35.2
Group population (%)				
Parent groups only	21.4	0.0	16.7	12.7
Spouse groups only	0.0	7.1	8.3	5.1
Groups for families and friends	71.4	82.4	66.7	73.5
Separate groups for anorexics and bulimics	9.1	41.2	70.0	40.1
Combined eating disorder groups	90.9	58.8	20.0	56.6
Combined family and eating disorder groups	7.1	11.8	25.0	14.6

but does not formally affiliate chapters, because the process of affiliation brings with it a myriad of quality control and legal issues. However, other organizations assist in the development of new groups and recruit existing groups to become affiliates.

Most survey participants in this category conduct either self-help or support groups (85.7%). Only two of the groups affiliated with a national organization report that their groups are run by professionals who have not previously been afflicted with the disorder.

In general, these groups have open attendance policies, do not require members to be prescreened before joining the group, meet once a week or twice monthly, and do not charge for meetings. They also do not require group members to be involved in professional treatment or under a physician's care as a prerequisite to participation, although they do encourage group members to seek professional help. Most groups have a nonstructured meeting format, with occasional guest speakers.

National chapters or affiliates, in most instances, run one combined group for both anorexics and bulimics. They also provide a separate group for family members and friends of persons with eating disorders.

Surprisingly, 66.7% of the groups for persons with eating disorders utilize professionals as primary facilitators or cofacilitators. However, most often professionals have either recovered from the disorder themselves or are paired with persons who have recovered. Professionals facilitate 45% of the groups for families and friends alone; another 18% are paired with parents who have children with an eating disorder. Almost 35% of the national affiliates do not involve professionals in any capacity.

INDEPENDENT ORGANIZATIONS

"Independent organizations" are defined as groups with local impact that are not chapters or affiliates of a national organization and are not part of a hospital, mental health, or university program. One-third of the groups responding to the survey defined themselves as independent organizations.

As may be expected, these groups vary widely in their format, structure, and use of facilitators. Out of the 14 independent groups, five are self-help groups, seven are support groups, and two are professionally led support groups. Most independent organizations run groups for families and friends and combine anorexics and bulimics into another group.

A majority of the organizations run free, weekly, open-ended groups that do not require regular attendance. The content of these groups is normally structured: Either a speaker presents a lecture on a topic, or a specific issue is addressed by group members. Fewer than half of the independent groups require prescreening, and very few require an individual to be in counseling or under a physician's care before attending the group meetings.

Although only 42% of the organizations require their facilitators to have special training before leading a group, 90% require their facilitators to participate in at least periodic supervision with a mental health or health professional. Professionals are utilized as primary facilitators or cofacilitators in approximately 70% of the groups for persons with eating disorders and 38% of the groups for families and friends.

Most of the independents also provide community awareness programs, printed information on eating disorders, and local telephone hotlines. Funds for these additional services come primarily from individual donations, fees from group meetings, foundations, and corporate gifts.

PROFESSIONAL AFFILIATES

Respondents identifying their group as being affiliated with a hospital, mental health or counseling center, or university counseling service comprised approximately one-third (34.9%) of the survey sample and were categorized as "professional affiliates." These organizations derive their funding from a variety of sources, including (but not limited to) group fees, third-party payments, individual donations, fees from professional training seminars and workshops, and revenue from their parent organizations.

Of the survey participants in this category, 67% run professionally led support groups. Only one group is run by a recovered anorexic, and six are cofacilitated by professionals and recovered individuals. All but one of the professional affiliates run groups for persons with eating disorders; over half of these place anorexics and bulimics in separate groups. Separate groups for parents, family members, and friends are run by 72%.

Format and group structure vary within this category. However, a majority of these organizations run open groups where regular attendance is not required. Individuals or family members interested in joining the groups may be required to complete a telephone or face-to-face screening interview before attending. In addition, a fee may be assessed for the group services. Meetings are weekly or bimonthly; they are most likely to last from 1 to 3 hours and to have a structured format.

Almost 60% of the groups have cofacilitators. Mental health or health professionals are involved in facilitating 92% of the groups for persons with eating disorders and 91% of the groups for family members, parents, and friends. Most of the group facilitators in this category receive compensation for running the meetings. In addition, most facilitators receive specialized training before leading a group and are required to participate in regular supervision sessions while facilitating the group.

Group Population

Table 20-1 also lists different types of groups according to population. A number of groups, for example, were originally started for parents. While some remain for parents only (or, in some cases, for spouses only), most have expanded to include other family members and friends of persons with eating disorders. Thirty-two (73.5%) of the respondents reported providing groups for parents, family members, or friends. Of these groups, only 12.5% combine family members and anorexic and bulimic individuals into the same group.

Thirty-nine respondents (90.7%) indicated that they conduct groups for individuals with anorexia nervosa and bulimia. Almost all (90.9%) of the self-help groups combine persons with anorexia nervosa and bulimia into one group. In contrast, only 30% of the professionally led support groups run groups that mix anorexic and bulimic persons.

In deciding among these options when forming a particular group, the crucial determinants are the overall size of the self-help/support group program and the extent to which facilitators are trained in group process. If individuals and their families are included in the same group, the outcome is inevitably a variant of family therapy and is not appropriate in a support group model. Combined groups should only be considered a viable option when the program is large enough to permit members of the same family to be in separate groups. To be successful, the group format must be well structured, with trained facilitators who can identify and intervene when members begin playing out family conflicts within the group.

Whether to combine anorexic and bulimic individuals in the same group is also partly determined by the capacity of the program. A small program may not be able to provide enough facilitators to offer separate groups. If only a few (two to four) members participate in each group, the support function may be met more effectively by combining groups. On the other hand, many bulimic individuals have reported feeling intimidated by ultrathin anorexics, who are envied because of their ability to hold their weight at a low level. Instead of providing support, this kind of group interaction serves only to magnify the bulimic individual's self-disgust. Group facilitators must remain sensitive to this issue if they choose to combine the two populations.

Separate groups require some definition of who belongs in which group. While rigid diagnostic systems may clearly distinguish between anorexia nervosa and bulimia, it is our clinical experience that many individuals do not clearly fit into one category or the other. We have generally encouraged persons who are uncertain about their disorder to participate in both groups to determine which most clearly addresses their personal needs.

Group Format

Table 20-2 lists a number of variables having to do with group format and structure.

STRUCTURE

Our survey defined structure as either "open" or "closed." An open group is one that permits members to attend as needed, with no commitment or attendance requirements. Closed groups normally require prescreening of members and regular attendance, and do not allow interested persons or potential members to sit in on group meetings. Closed groups more closely approximate therapy groups in this respect. Most of the groups responding to this survey conduct open meetings (72.1%) that do not require regular attendance (73.5%).

A self-help or support group program requires some degree of openness in order to be a resource to individuals identifying their problem for the first time. Often these individuals first need to obtain information and recognize that they are not alone in their problem before they are willing to make a commitment to a group.

CONTENT

Content reflects the extent to which meetings are guided by a predetermined format. Our survey revealed that half the groups have speakers and limited discussion sessions. The other half are loosely defined, incorporating a few basic rules (such as a provision for confidentiality, which may be read at the beginning of the meeting), but otherwise they rely entirely on the group participants to determine the content. Some groups incorporate both, having occasional speakers as well as open discussion.

Table 20-2. Group Format and Structure by Group Type

	SELF-HELP GROUPS (n = 14)	SUPPORT GROUPS (n = 17)	PROFESSIONAL GROUPS (n = 12)	TOTAL SAMPLE (n = 43)
Group structure (%)				
Open	92.9	64.7	58.3	72.1
Closed	0.0	35.3	33.3	23.2
Semiclosed	7.1	0.0	8.4	4.7
Attendance (%)				
Is not required	85.7	76.5	58.3	73.5
Is required	14.3	23.5	41.7	26.5
Meeting content (%)				
No defined meeting content	57.1	29.4	50.0	45.5
Speaker or defined issue	42.9	70.6	50.0	54.5
Frequency (%)				
Weekly	37.4	35.7	62.5	45.2
Every 2 weeks	18.8	0.0	12.5	10.4
Twice a month	25.0	35.7	12.5	24.4
Monthly	18.8	28.6	12.5	20.0
Duration (%)				
1–1½ hours per meeting	41.7	41.7	100.0	61.1
1½–3 hours per meeting	58.3	58.3	0.0	38.9
Screening (%)				
Telephone or face to face	9.1	50.0	55.6	38.2
No screening required	90.9	50.0	44.4	61.8
Professional care (%)				
Required to be under professional care	0.0	14.3	0.0	4.8
Encouraged but not required	81.8	71.4	75.0	76.1
Not an issue	18.2	14.3	25.0	19.1
Group fees (%)				
Meetings are free	100.0	52.9	41.7	64.9
A fee is charged	0.0	35.3	58.3	31.2
Membership fee is required	0.0	11.8	0.0	3.9

Groups in which the content is less well defined require facilitators with more training in group process or with clearly specified guidelines for group interaction.

FREQUENCY AND DURATION

Of the groups in our survey, 45.2% meet on a weekly basis. Some (10.4%) meet every 2 weeks (i.e., 26 times a year); others (24.4%) meet twice a month (i.e., 24 times a year), and a few (20.0%) meet only once a month. The availability of resources, such as meeting space and facilitators, may determine the frequency and duration of meetings. Most meetings (61.1%) last from 1 to 1½ hours.

When weekly meetings are not possible, one option is to establish an informal "buddy system," where group members agree to contact one another on a regular basis between group meetings.

SCREENING PROCEDURE

While most of the self-help groups (90.9%) do not require prescreening, half of the support groups and professionally led support groups require either telephone or face-to-face contact prior to attending a group meeting for the first time. A screening procedure allows new members to obtain information about the group and to identify whether the group is appropriate for their needs. Such a procedure can also prepare group facilitators for new additions to the group.

REQUIREMENTS FOR PROFESSIONAL TREATMENT

Very few of the groups surveyed (4.8%) require that members seek professional care; however, most (76.1%) encourage involvement with therapy in addition to attending a self-help/support group. For some self-help/support organizations, such as Parents Without Partners, the issue of treatment is less critical than in the field of eating disorders. Since both anorexia nervosa and bulimia are potentially life-threatening, an attitude of working cooperatively with treatment providers is essential. Many groups maintain a referral registry of professionals who are particularly well qualified to treat eating disorders.

Group facilitators must retain the option of requiring treatment for some members in order for them to continue attending support groups. This is imperative for group members who are in medical danger due to bulimic or anorexic behaviors, and who are refusing to get medical care. Ethically, a program cannot knowingly participate in this type of serious denial. Facilitators must also retain the option of referring individuals with other major diagnoses to alternative resources. For instance, individuals with borderline or histrionic personality disorders have occasionally sought the support of our groups, but have not been found appropriate for the programs. In these cases, the facilitator often needs to recommend professional treatment rather than participation in a support group.

FEES

The majority of groups surveyed (64.9%) do not require fees in order for persons to attend meetings. However, several groups require or strongly encourage donations or annual membership fees.

The question of whether to charge a fee for a support group may be determined by the status of funding available for the support group program or by the values of facilitators and group members. Self-help/support groups may ascribe to the belief that a financial investment encourages more commitment. But to avoid the possibility of excluding potential members because they are unable to pay, the fee should be kept at a reasonable level. Groups may want to ask for an investment of time from their members in the form of administrative tasks, fundraising, and other activities that contribute to group maintenance.

Use of Facilitators

Table 20-3 lists a number of variables having to do with the use of facilitators.

NUMBER OF FACILITATORS

Support groups are most likely to utilize cofacilitators to run the groups (88.2%). Usually the cofacilitators are professionals teamed with recovered individuals. Professionally led support groups most often have one facilitator (66.7%).

Table 20-3. Use of Facilitators by Group Type

	SELF-HELP GROUPS ($n = 14$)	SUPPORT GROUPS ($n = 17$)	PROFESSIONAL GROUPS ($n = 12$)	TOTAL SAMPLE ($n = 43$)
Group facilitators (%)				
No facilitator	7.1	0.0	0.0	2.3
One facilitator	42.9	11.8	66.7	40.5
Cofacilitators	50.0	88.2	33.3	57.2
Facilitator compensation (%)				
Compensation	15.4	41.2	66.7	41.1
Facilitator training (%)				
Special training to run group	15.4	68.7	58.3	47.5
Facilitator supervision (%)				
No supervision required	10.0	7.7	28.6	15.4
Supervision provided as needed by mental health or health professional	60.0	53.8	14.3	42.7
Regular supervision required by mental health or health professional	30.0	38.5	57.1	41.9

The use of cofacilitators allows for continuity in the group, should one leader be absent or choose to end his or her role as facilitator. It also provides practical training for new facilitators, who can be paired with someone more experienced in the role. We would not recommend using more than one facilitator, however, when the number of group members is very small. In that case, the members could feel overwhelmed by facilitators, and the emphasis on peer support may be lost.

FACILITATOR COMPENSATION

Facilitators do not receive compensation in 84.6% of the self-help groups; however, in 66.7% of the professionally led support groups, leaders are compensated. In some cases, the ability to pay group facilitators is a matter of funding; however, in others it is a matter of group philosophy. One advantage of paid facilitators is that they are more likely to remain involved with the group for a longer period of time.

FACILITATOR TRAINING AND SUPERVISION

Most self-help group facilitators are not required to participate in any formal training program before leading a group (84.6%). However, almost 70% of the facilitators in support groups and 60% of the facilitators in professionally led support groups are required to participate in formal training before they are permitted to lead a group. One group in our survey uses no group facilitator at all.

The role of the facilitator in self-help/support groups is the focus of considerable controversy. Some groups believe that a professionally trained facilitator is requisite, even though that person may share the role with a recovered anorexic or bulimic or with a family member. For other groups, personal experience with eating disorders is viewed as the only significant qualification.

The issue of facilitator qualifications is directly linked to the need for and the extent of training and supervision provided to group facilitators. It cannot be assumed that a person with an advanced degree will be knowledgeable about eating disorders or able to develop a good rapport with group members. Nevertheless, a thorough training and supervision program is crucial when new facilitators have little or no background in communication skills, group process, and/or the medical and psychological aspects of anorexia nervosa and bulimia. Most self-help and support groups solve the problem of supervision by having a mental health or health professional available as needed; the majority of professionally led support groups (57.1%) require regular supervision by a mental health or health professional.

Role of the Professional

Tables 20-4 and 20-5 list variables having to do with the role of the professional.

GROUPS FOR FAMILIES AND FRIENDS

Professionals are involved in 64.6% of the groups for parents, families, and friends. Most self-help groups involve a parent of an anorexic or bulimic in the role of either primary facilitator or cofacilitator (70.0%). Of the support groups, 31% utilize parents as primary facilitators, and 38.4% couple a parent with a professional. Only 38.8% of the groups are led by professionals alone, and half of these groups are led by parents who have recovering children and are also trained professionals.

GROUPS FOR PERSONS WITH EATING DISORDERS

Mental health or health professionals are involved in facilitating 62.7% of the groups for persons with eating disorders. None of the self-help groups responding to the survey involve professionals who have not also had an eating disorder. Of the support groups, 88% involve professionals as cofacilitators with persons who are recovering from an eating disorder.

A MODEL FOR SUPPORT GROUP PROGRAMS

A review of the diverse structural characteristics of groups around the country indicates that many models are being used. We prefer a model emphasizing professional leadership of support groups for eating disorders, and we propose that five essential factors

Table 20-4. Type of Facilitator Running Groups for Families/Friends/Parents by Group Type

	SELF-HELP GROUPS (n = 14)	SUPPORT GROUPS (n = 17)	PROFESSIONAL GROUPS (n = 12)	TOTAL SAMPLE (n = 43)
Type of facilitator (%)				
Parent of an anorexic or bulimic	60.0	30.8	0.0	30.3
Mental health or health professional	30.0	15.4	100.0	48.5
Professional with parent	10.0	38.4	0.0	16.1
Parent who is also a professional	0.0	15.4	0.0	5.1

Table 20-5. Type of Facilitator Running Groups for Persons with Eating Disorders by Group Type

	SELF-HELP GROUPS ($n = 14$)	SUPPORT GROUPS ($n = 17$)	PROFESSIONAL GROUPS ($n = 12$)	TOTAL SAMPLE ($n = 43$)
Type of facilitator (%)				
Recovered anorexic or bulimic	75.0	0.0	0.0	25.0
Mental health or health professional	0.0	0.0	100.0	33.3
Professional with recovered anorexic or bulimic	0.0	88.2	0.0	29.4
Professional who is recovered from eating disorder	25.0	11.8	0.0	12.3

be incorporated into every support group program: broad-spectrum goals, peer support, accessibility, confidentiality, and trained facilitators.

Broad-Spectrum Goals

"Broad-spectrum goals" refers to Pearson's (1982) formulation of support groups as providing maintenance and enhancement of effectiveness, as well as amelioration of deficiency. In working with bulimic individuals, we have found that nearly all perceive recovery as being free of bingeing and purging. It has been our experience, however, that once bulimic behavior is under control, individuals find themselves faced with emotional needs and experiences that have previously been masked by the binge–purge behavior. Support groups can be valuable in (1) managing eating behavior, (2) identifying and expressing feelings, (3) learning how to reach out to other people, and (4) developing realistic expectations for self and others.

Support groups are often an opportunity for members to share techniques of behavior management that have been effective in their recovery. The role of the facilitator is to remind members that suggestions are not magic formulas for success and that what is effective for one person may be ineffective for another. Group members are often seeking solutions and would like a "right answer" that will make recovery easy. Members can support one another by recognizing that recovery may be a slower process than anticipated and by providing encouragement to keep working when enthusiasm wanes.

Bulimic individuals often have difficulty identifying and expressing feelings, especially disappointment, loneliness, boredom, and anger. Support groups can provide an arena for members to test these "negative" feelings and to recognize that others experience similar emotions. The facilitator's role is to assure that everyone has the opportunity to express feelings and to receive nonjudgmental feedback. It is especially important that the facilitator not impart judgments; if he or she has an opinion, it should be given as feedback on a level equal to the responses of every other group member. Our experience is that support group members often look to the facilitator as an authority figure and seek advice rather than peer support. Thus, another function of the facilitator is to direct requests for information, feedback, and support to other group members as much as possible, emphasizing the value of everyone's knowledge and experience.

Most support group members have felt socially isolated because of their eating disorders. They have avoided or lacked opportunities to give and to receive support. Facilitators can encourage members to identify their own needs for encouragement and to offer support in return. While facilitators can be helpful in modeling this behavior, the emphasis remains on sharing mutual support among peers.

Finally, group members may be helpful to one another in establishing realistic rather than perfectionistic goals. Individuals with eating disorders tend to have highly perfectionistic standards both for themselves and for others. Learning to accept oneself as less than perfect, yet still valuable and cared about, can be accomplished through experiencing the acceptance and support of others within the group. Families of bulimic individuals tend to be highly achievement-oriented, so that even recreational activities are perceived within a competitive framework. It is difficult to relax and to enjoy family interaction when expectations for perfection and excellence dominate. Family support groups can offer members an opportunity to receive support and acceptance for being human rather than for being perfect.

Peer Support

Peer support is an essential function of support groups. This does not exclude professional involvement in groups, but reflects our belief that the emphasis needs to be on nonauthoritative peer interaction. However, we recommend that mental health and health professionals be actively involved in support groups, for several reasons. First, their knowledge and experience are necessary in a program that deals with potentially life-threatening disorders. Second, facilitators faced with a difficult or disruptive group participant need to have a competent resource person to consult with or refer to for assessment. Finally, support group involvement may provide a learning experience for professionals who have had limited contact with bulimic or anorexic individuals and their families.

It is unfortunate that frustrations with a few poorly trained or insensitive individuals have soured the attitudes of many people who could benefit from professional care. A support group is not intended to be an alternative to professional treatment, but rather a complement to it. We suggest that support group facilitators encourage, whenever possible, the appropriate use of counseling and medical care. The role of the support group is to provide a support system to those individuals and their friends and families who do not have the necessary information, understanding, or emotional resources to deal with an eating disorder in a positive way. While therapeutic, this role is quite different from the expectations of behavior change that are implicit in psychotherapy.

The groups included in our survey were differentiated according to the extent of professionals' involvement in them. Of the facilitators in the professional groups, 100% were mental health treatment providers. Support groups, which are viewed as an extension of the treatment process, had both lay and professional facilitators. Self-help groups were led only by individuals who had recovered from an eating disorder and defined their goals as providing an option for recovery with or without professional help.

Overeaters Anonymous (OA), based on the AA model, has become a popular self-help/support group for anorexia nervosa and bulimia. It is our opinion, however, that there are some significant limitations to the analogy between abuse of alcohol and the "abuse" of food. Complete abstinence may be achieved for alcohol but not for food. Also, there is greater support for physical addiction to alcohol (Goodwin, 1979) than there is for addiction to particular types of food. Finally, the model of strict abstinence, when applied to self-induced vomiting, may create guilt or shame in the bulimic patient who relapses under stress. It may be unrealistic to expect the AA structure, which has been successful in the treatment of alcoholism, to meet the varied psychological and educational needs of the bulimic or anorexic patient. Since one of the goals of OA is interrupting "binge eating by avoiding sugars," it may reinforce the bulimic's food fads and not encourage normalization of eating as well as weight gain. These are essential aspects of recovery (Fairburn, 1983; Garner & Bemis, 1982; Garner, Rockert, Olmsted, Johnson, & Coscina, Chapter 21, this volume).

The self-help approach often fails to identify physiological problems related to eating disorders. This includes not only the medical problems that may have developed as a result of starving or purging, but also the physiological imbalances that may result in cravings. Bulimic individuals often condemn themselves for being weak-willed and unable to control obsessive thoughts about food. Rather than being evidence of deficient character, these symptoms often point to nutritional deficiencies (Garner & Bemis, 1982). When self-help groups focus only on developing will power and overcoming unacceptable urges, the nutritional issues remain unaddressed, and the problems continue.

Currently, there is little treatment outcome research for anorexia nervosa or bulimia, and none examining the efficacy of self-help or support groups. This is not to say that self-help is ineffective; however, until there is systematic evaluation of this approach, we would recommend a conservative philosophy, which involves a liaison with experienced therapists plus the development of a well-structured program meeting the identified needs of this population. Once a history of success has been established, mental health counselors and therapists may be able to work confidently with self-help organizations in providing support to their anorexic and bulimic members.

Our position is that peer support is not an alternative to professional treatment, but, rather, an adjunctive part of the treatment process. The self-help approach alone is inadequate for dealing with the complex issues related to eating disorders, and we believe that those who discredit the value of competent medical and psychological treatment may inadvertently collude with some emaciated patients' wish to recover without gaining weight (Garner & Bemis, Chapter 6, this volume).

Accessibility

"Accessibility" relates to having the support program available on a regular basis to new and ongoing members. This requires a continual effort toward increasing community awareness of eating disorders and of the availability of local support programs. A liaison person should be identified to keep schools, churches, and the local media informed of meeting times, dates, and locations. It is important to have a clear procedure for referring individuals and families to the support program, preferably by having some type of telephone linkage regularly available. This may be accomplished by having an individual trained to handle referrals to support groups available at the facility where groups are held, or by utilizing a local information hotline service. Many metropolitan areas have established these hotlines as a resource for residents to obtain information about various social services. Use of a community hotline requires that the staff members have regular training about eating disorders and current information regarding the support program. Members of the support group may volunteer to be available to hotline staff to answer questions that may arise.

We recommend that support groups meet at least bi-monthly, or weekly whenever possible. Members may need support between meetings, as problems rarely occur "on schedule." One solution to this is to formalize personal contact among group members through telephone calls or personal visits.

Finally, we recommend that no fees be charged for open meetings, so as not to exclude individuals for whom finances may be a problem.

Confidentiality

Confidentiality is of critical importance to the success of support groups. As a consistent reminder of this, we recommend that groups develop a simple written statement of their own confidentiality policy, to be read at the beginning of every meeting. While family members may share with one another their personal experience following a meeting, other members' experiences or comments should not be discussed. Likewise, facilitators may seek supervision concerning the group meetings, but should be cautious about sharing information with anyone other than the supervisor. When a student or professional person asks to visit a group meeting, we generally discuss the request with the group in advance, and then invite the visitor to the next meeting. Group members have never refused such a request, but have appreciated the consideration of being consulted.

Confidentiality also extends to communication with a group member's therapist. When a group member is in treatment, and information is discussed in a support group that may be significant in therapy, we ask the person to make an agreement to share the information at the next treatment session. Facilitators do not contact therapists directly.

Trained Facilitators

Trained facilitators are central to the success of the support program. Individuals trained in the medical and health professions should receive the same training and supervision as lay facilitators. It is a mistake to assume that an academic training program will be sufficient to prepare a person to work in a support group program for eating disorders. Equally insufficient are the credentials of having simply recovered from an eating disorder or having a friend or family member who is an anorexic or bulimic.

Recruiting, training, and supervision are ongoing activities in a support program. We have successfully recruited treatment providers and graduate students as support group facilitators. To insure continuity, a 1-year commitment should be required from individuals requesting facilitator training.

A training program should include medical and psychological information about eating disorders, information about locally available treatment resources, and specific training and communication skills in group facilitation. We advocate developing co-facilitator teams that combine an experienced facilitator with someone in training.

The opportunity to discuss group interactions and problems offers an excellent learning experience and helps facilitators prevent burnout. We recommend that all facilitators meet regularly for ongoing group supervision, with a medical consultant available as needed.

MAKING REFERRALS

The two major considerations for mental health and health professionals in making referrals to a support group are the nature of the groups available in the community and the specific needs of each client.

Persons treating individuals with eating disorders may benefit by receiving newsletters or other printed information about local groups. Visiting an open support group can be useful to the professional, since it allows first-hand learning about the group's operation. Making the first contact may be difficult for the client, and clear, accurate information from the referring professional can be helpful in initiating that contact. While the therapist may provide information about meeting dates and times, the client should assume responsibility for making the initial contact.

In addressing the specific needs of the client, the primary concern is whether the client is psychologically able to benefit from a support system. In their work on social support, Procidano, Heller, and Swindle (1980) found that when research subjects were more depressed, their ability to perceive existing social support declined. This does not suggest that depressed individuals cannot benefit from support groups, but, rather, that additional effort may be required to engage them in the support network. Therapists may encourage prospective clients to telephone for information during or following a counseling session, or have the clients contact someone who will agree to accompany them to the support group meeting.

Berkowitz (1983) found that families of bulimic women were higher in self-rated depression and lower in perceived social support than families in a comparison group. Thus, support groups may be an important resource not only for the clients but for their family members as well. Parents often express feelings of frustration and helplessness in dealing with bulimic or anorexic children, and can benefit from sharing these concerns with other parents. Siblings of anorexics may need objective information, plus the opportunity to express feelings ranging from fear of having the anorexic die, to anger over the attention they are receiving. When family members are experiencing depression, assistance may be required for them to learn how to provide support to one another. The support group can be an effective tool for enhancing the natural support system within the family. In making a referral to a support group, the therapist should consider the benefit of involvement of the whole family.

Support groups are appropriate for those individuals with anorexia nervosa or bulimia who do not suffer from severe characterological disorders. Those who have disordered thought processes of psychotic proportions are more appropriately referred to a therapy group or to a support program that focuses on their primary problem. Depressed individuals expressing suicidal thoughts or individuals with borderline personality disorders often are not appropriate for support groups, since their intense needs can easily result in exclusive interaction with the facilitator while other group members become bystanders—a situation that defeats the supportive purpose of the group.

CONCLUSION

Self-help/support groups for individuals with eating disorders evolved because of the absence of adequate as well as competent professional resources. Many alternative approaches to self-help/support are being utilized in providing these services; however, there is currently little research to evaluate the comparative effectiveness of these groups.

Since support groups may be quite complementary to traditional treatment, it is advisable for mental health and health professionals to become aware of the availability of support resources in their communities. The support group movement has had a growing impact on professional treatment services. Historically, one function of support groups has been consumer advocacy. In a field in which the consequences of inadequate treatment can be severe, the support group movement is becoming increasingly powerful in demanding high-quality care. Poorly trained and inexperienced therapists are likely to be identified and excluded as a referral source by the support community as groups become more sophisticated in their expectations of professional services.

As the support group movement gains in popularity and power, the effectiveness of various treatment approaches is likely to be challenged. Rather than being a threat, this challenge has the potential for stimulating carefully controlled research on the outcome of therapeutic interventions. Similarly, the impact of support groups on treatment and recovery needs to be explored, as well as the comparative effectiveness of the different approaches to organized support. Cooperation among treatment professionals and support group organizers and facilitators not only will open the door to more comprehensive services, but will probably hasten the development of workable solutions to the growing problem of eating disorders.

REFERENCES

Berkowitz, B. (1983). *The implications of family characteristics in the classification and treatment of anorexia nervosa and bulimia.* Unpublished doctoral dissertation, Ohio State University.

Estroff, S. E. (1982). The next step: Self help. *Hospital and Community Psychiatry, 33*, 609.

Fairburn, C. G. (1983). Bulimia: Its epidemiology and management. In A. J. Stunkard & E. Stellar (Eds.), *Eating and its disorders* (pp. 235–258). New York: Raven Press.

Families learn to cope. (1980, October). *NAAS Newsletter*, p. 4.

Garner, D. M., & Bemis, K. M. (1982). A cognitive-behavioral approach to anorexia nervosa. *Cognitive Therapy and Research, 6*, 123–150.

Gartner, A. J., & Riessman, F. (1982). Self help and mental health. *Hospital and Community Psychiatry, 33*, 631–635.

Goodwin, D. W. (1979). Alcoholism and heredity: A review and hypothesis. *Archives of General Psychiatry, 36*, 57–61.

Gottlieb, B. H. (1976). Lay influences on the utilization and provision of health services: A review. *Canadian Psychological Review, 17*, 126–136.

Hatfield, A. B. (1981). Self help groups for families of the mentally ill. *Social Work, 26*, 408–413.

Hirsch, B. J. (1980). Natural support systems and coping with major life changes. *American Journal of Community Psychology, 8*, 159–172.

Larocca, F. E. F. (1983, June). The relevance of self-help in the management of anorexia and bulimia. *Res Medica* (St. John's Mercy Medical Center, St. Louis, MO), pp. 16–19.

Pearson, R. E. (1982). Support: Exploration of a basic concept in counseling and informal help. *Personnel and Guidance Journal, 61*, 83–87.

Pearson, R. E. (1983). Support groups: A conceptualization. *Personnel and Guidance Journal, 61*, 361–364.

Powell, T. J. (1982). *The organizational and social network benefits of the self-help organization versus the agency support group.* Paper presented at the annual conference of the National Council of Community Mental Health Centers, New York.

Procidano, M., Heller, K., & Swindle, R. (1980). *Experimental studies of the nature and effects of social support.* Paper presented at the 88th Annual Meeting of the American Psychological Association, Montreal.

Rose, J., & Garfinkel, P. E. (1980). A parents' group in the management of anorexia nervosa. *Canadian Journal of Psychiatry, 25*, 228–237.

Silverman, P. R. (1978). *Mutual help groups: A guide for mental health workers.* Rockville, MD: National Institute of Mental Health.

Yalom, I. D. (1975). *The theory and practice of group psychotherapy* (2nd ed.). New York: Basic Books.

CHAPTER TWENTY-ONE

Psychoeducational Principles in the Treatment of Bulimia and Anorexia Nervosa

DAVID M. GARNER / WENDI ROCKERT /
MARION P. OLMSTED / CRAIG JOHNSON /
DONALD V. COSCINA

INTRODUCTION

Bulimia is a serious disorder involving periodic episodes of overeating in which the person feels out of control. Such episodes are often followed by self-induced vomiting or purgative abuse aimed at reducing the caloric consequences of overconsumption. Depression and self-critical thoughts related to losing control of eating are common. Finally, bulimia almost always occurs within the context of strenuous efforts to diet, due to extraordinary dissatisfaction with body shape. Bulimia has also been referred to as "binge eating," "bulimia nervosa," "dietary chaos," "bulimarexia," and "the binge–purge syndrome," among a host of other names. There is some controversy regarding the classification of the syndrome, although it has been observed in approximately 50% of anorexia nervosa patients (see Garfinkel & Garner, 1982) and obese patients (Edeleman, 1981; Gormally, Black, Daston, & Rardin, 1982; Loro & Orleans, 1981), as well as in growing numbers of women[1] who are at a normal weight (Garner, Garfinkel, & O'Shaughnessy, in press; Halmi, Falk, & Schwartz, 1981; Pyle, Mitchell, & Eckert, 1981; Strangler & Printz, 1980). Its occurrence in both college and high-school women has been estimated to be approximately 4% (Pyle *et al.*, 1983) and it has been reported as common in community-based samples (Cooper & Fairburn, 1983; Fairburn & Cooper, 1982).

In the last several years, bulimia has received widespread attention in the media and has been the subject of intensified research efforts by psychologists and psychiatrists. It is a complex disorder, which, in many instances, appears to be caused and

1. Because bulimia and anorexia nervosa patients are primarily women, such patients are referred to as female throughout this chapter.

David M. Garner. Department of Psychiatry, Toronto General Hospital; and the University of Toronto, Toronto, Ontario, Canada.

Wendi Rockert and Marion P. Olmsted. Department of Psychiatry, Toronto General Hospital, Toronto, Ontario, Canada.

Craig Johnson. Institute of Psychiatry, Eating Disorders Program, Northwestern University Medical School, Northwestern Memorial Hospital, Chicago, Illinois.

Donald V. Coscina. Section of Biopsychology, Clarke Institute of Psychiatry; and Departments of Psychiatry and Psychology, University of Toronto, Toronto, Ontario, Canada.

then maintained by an interaction of social, psychological, and biological factors. Although much still remains unknown, recent research has begun to clarify the probable contribution of many of these factors. It has been our experience that most bulimic patients begin treatment with a variety of misconceptions about dieting, weight regulation, nutrition, and the social context of their disorder. We have found that many bulimic patients benefit from, and that some actually recover because of, an improved understanding of complications and factors perpetuating the disorder. Psychoeducational material has become an integral component of a growing number of individual and group approaches to bulimia and anorexia nervosa (Fairburn, 1981; Garner & Bemis, 1982; C. Johnson, Connors, & Stuckey, 1983; Long & Cordle, 1982; Mitchell *et al.*, Chapter 11, this volume; S. C. Wooley & Wooley, Chapter 17, this volume).

The purpose of this chapter is to provide information and specific recommendations derived from our interpretation of the scientific literature pertaining to various aspects of these disorders. Selected research findings related to weight regulation, dieting, obesity, cultural factors, and physical complications of bulimia are presented. Finally, specific recommendations are made on the basis of research and clinical experience. The reader should be cautioned that the information presented in this chapter should not be considered as a replacement for psychotherapy, but rather as a supplement to it. The information is intended to be used by individuals suffering from these disorders, as well as by practitioners who are not familiar with the psychological and physiological mechanisms that play a role in anorexia nervosa and bulimia.

It has been our impression that many conventional treatment programs have placed a disproportionate or exclusive emphasis on either the emotional or the physical aspects of these disorders. Moreover, many popular theories of their development have been couched almost entirely in physical or psychological terms. The exclusively physical explanations are not consistent with conventional wisdom and may result in a patient's giving up any hope of being able to affect her condition. She may feel that if it is all "physical" (i.e., related to some neurological or chemical deficiency), then there is nothing that she can really do about it. The exclusively psychological theories ignore much of the physiological literature on the effects of dieting and starvation. Even worse, they may result in the patient's concluding that many psychological *by-products* of the disorder are actually *causes*. She may subject herself to protracted self- and professional analysis in search of emotional causes when many of her symptoms actually have biological roots. For example, it has been concluded by some theorists that bulimia is caused exclusively by sexual or relationship conflicts, stress, repressed anger, or masochistic wishes. While this may be true for some, these purely psychological interpretations of bulimia fail to rule out more basic physiological underpinnings first. Many cases of binge eating may be directly linked to efforts to restrict dietary intake. Dieting, in turn, is largely determined by the social context in which women live. Therefore, treatment for bulimia must emphasize the interdependence between mental and physical aspects of experience. Failure to integrate these aspects only further reinforces the split or conflict between mind and body that is so often experienced by anorexic and bulimic patients. This interdependence forms the basis for discussion in the current chapter. We review evidence that substantiates the validity of the following points:

1. In the past several decades, women have been victims of a tragic set of standards for physical appearance, which have placed them under intense pressure to diet to meet the social expectations for thinness.

2. Generally speaking, body weight resists change. Weight appears to be physiologically regulated around a "set point," or a weight that one's body tries to "defend." Significant deviations from this weight result in a myriad of physiological compensations aimed at returning the organism to "set point."

3. Dieting is a relatively ineffective method of weight control, because it usually goes against these biological determinants of weight.

4. There are marked interpersonal differences in "set point"; some people are naturally heavier and some naturally thinner. Most women's "natural weight" is well above the current ideal for feminine beauty.

5. Bulimia, as well as certain distressing biological and social changes, may be linked to chronic dietary restriction.

6. Bulimia and vomiting become an escalating or vicious cycle, since vomiting allows the dieter to give in to her desire to eat without the fear of the caloric consequences.

7. The gradual return to the weight that one's body "prefers" leads to the gradual reduction of these symptoms, including the tendency toward binge eating.

The scientific literature bearing on these points is reviewed in some detail; these reviews are followed by specific practical recommendations for overcoming bulimia and related disorders.

THE CULTURAL CONTEXT

"Thin Is Beautiful"

It has been postulated that one factor responsible for the epidemic increase in anorexia nervosa and bulimia is the intense pressure on women to diet in order to conform to an unrealistic standard for feminine beauty (cf. Garner, Garfinkel, & Olmsted, 1983). In the last two decades, the preoccupation with thinness for women has taken on almost fetish-like quality. From every quarter, women are barraged with the message from the media that beauty, success, personal happiness, and self-worth are based on a thin shape. Bruch (1978) has speculated that the fashion industry, movies, magazines, and television are all responsible for promoting the view that "one can be loved and respected only when slender" (p. viii). Studies of prime-time television support the view that programming is dominated by thin body types and that, for women, thinness is associated with favorable personality traits (Kurman, 1978). This bias is apparently shared by most women, who view slenderness as the most salient aspect of physical attractiveness (S. B. Beck, Ward-Hull, & McLear, 1976; Berscheid, Walster, & Bohrnstedt, 1973; Horvath, 1979, 1981; T. Miller, Coffman, & Linke, 1980).

The aim of this section is to convince the reader that the enormous pressures on women to diet in pursuit of a thinner shape have become more and more unrealistic and destructive. There is a natural reluctance to accept the argument that the unprecedented emphasis on thinness and dieting may have negative consequences, since the presumed virtues of these ideals are deeply woven into the fabric of our health-conscious culture. However, the health benefits of slenderness have been profoundly overemphasized, with little attention to the harmful effects of dieting. As we document later, bulimia may become a problem in psychologically normal individuals after a period of intense caloric restriction. The gradual recognition of the unreasonable stresses on women to conform to the contemporary "gaunt look" provides the basis for urging those suffering from eating disorders to understand that what they have assumed to be their "wish" to control weight is actually founded in distorted social norms and expectations. Thus, shape dissatisfaction, dieting, and even bulimia, which selectively affect women, may be in large part attributed to our culture. The moral and political implications of this contention are extraordinary. We have found that helping those with eating disorders to develop an awareness of these issues, as well as of the physical obstacles to weight loss, enables them to begin to question and resist the oppressive values that may have contributed to their severe personal suffering.

Several years ago, it was our impression that not only were women being confronted more aggressively by the media's lean images of feminine beauty, but also that these models were thinner than they had been in the past. Evidence for this gradual shift toward more slender shape preferences comes from our survey of *Playboy* centerfolds and Miss America Pageant contestants (Garner, Garfinkel, Schwartz, & Thompson, 1980). Both the centerfolds and the pageant contestants have become significantly thinner over the last 20 years. With smaller bust, larger waist, and smaller hip measurements, the *Playboy* centerfolds have "changed shape" and are more "tubular" than their predecessors. The trend toward thinner shapes in *Playboy* centerfolds is even more remarkable, since it is in direct opposition to actual changes in young women's bodies over the last 25 years. An update of the Metropolitan Life Insurance weight tables indicates that the expected weight for women under 30 years of age has actually *increased* at about the same rate as the average weight of the centerfolds has *decreased* (Garner *et al.*, 1980). Figure 21-1 illustrates this growing disparity between actual and "ideal" standards. The fact is that very few women actually possess bodies as slim as those of the models with whom the media continually confronts them. It is worth noting that just over 5% of female life insurance policy holders between the ages of 20 and 29 are as thin as the average Miss America Pageant *winner* between 1970 and 1978.[2] Considering that *Playboy* centerfolds and Miss America contestants hardly represent the bony-thin body frame that is typically promoted by the fashion and advertising industries, it is obvious that the prevailing shape standards do not even remotely resemble the actual body shape of the average woman consumer.

Exercise for Weight Control

The intense pressure on women to be slender is embedded in other currently popular cultural values. The growing emphasis on fitness is laudable; however, it bears a different message for women than it does for men. For women, it seems to be inextricably intertwined with achieving a sleek and curveless body shape, rather than, for example, attaining cardiovascular or other health benefits. According to the recent *Glamour* magazine survey ("Feeling Fat in a Thin Society," 1984), 95% of the 33,000 female respondents had used exercise explicitly for weight control. It is our impression that

2. We are grateful to the Society of Actuaries and Association of Life Insurance Medical Directors of America for providing the distribution of weights for 50,107 female insurance policy holders between the ages of 20 and 29.

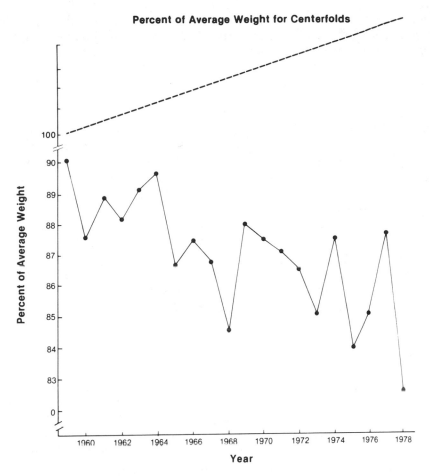

Percent of Average Weight for Centerfolds

Figure 21-1. Changes in the percent of average weight of centerfolds over 20 years. Average weight is based upon the Society of Actuaries' 1959 norms. The broken line represents prorated changes in the average weights for women over the same 20-year period, based upon the revised Society of Actuaries' 1979 norms. (Adapted from "Cultural Expectations of Thinness in Women" by D. M. Garner, P. E. Garfinkel, D. Schwartz, and M. Thompson, 1980, *Psychological Reports, 47*, 483 491. Reprinted by permission.)

fitness for men usually occurs within the context of sports, with more emphasis on competence than on physique. In contrast, shape change is the acknowledged priority in women's pursuit of fitness through solitary "workout" programs or "fitness" classes. The admired and even worshipped proponents of the popular women's "fitness" movement are invariably thin and attractive, while the truly fit female athletes receive far less recognition. For many women, exercise simply may have become another weapon in the arsenal dedicated to rigid weight control. When most women are able to step back and attend to how much "locker room energy" is expended in talking, thinking, and fantasizing about food, weight, and dieting, they are shocked. While men's locker room conversation is generally no less banal, it rarely involves weight or dieting. Women must individually and collectively examine the implications of the fitness trend, in order to determine the extent to which it is motivated by the joys intrinsic to physical activity or propelled by the dread of weight gain. For many, fitness has become a "thinly" veiled recapitulation of the old theme of beautifying the body; recently this has involved a desperate striving to achieve ultrathinness. This shape standard is physically and psychologically destructive for most women.

Glorification of Youth

Postadolescent women are also encouraged to diet because of the premium our culture places on youth as a sign of beauty and sensuality. Men ostensibly become more "distinguished" with age, while women maintain their attractiveness only if they inhibit any signs of aging. Although the preference for young, nubile women has been virtually universal across societies, desirability has historically been connoted by roundness rather than by angularity. The current ideal seems to push previous standards further toward those of the prepubescent girl, with her wrinkle-free, taut, and immature body. In order to achieve this youthful shape through dieting, most mature women would have to reduce their level of body fat to a degree that would compromise normal reproductive hormones and menstrual functioning (Frisch, 1983). It is truly ironic that the current image of sexual attractiveness in women is a shape associated with both loss of reproductive functioning and sexual appetite.

Impact of Pressures to Be Thin

Although women have indicated remarkable dissatisfaction with their shape for decades (Jourard & Secord, 1955), the broadening gulf between actual and preferred shapes can only amplify the self-disparagement. The inevitable identification with the media's unrealistic role models provides the seedbed for women's growing insecurity about their bodies. There is even considerable confusion among many women about what actually constitutes overweight. Many women of statistically normal weight label themselves as overweight (Halmi *et al.*, 1981) and many statistically underweight women fail to recognize that they are underweight (Gray, 1977). It has been repeatedly documented that "feeling too fat" and dieting are conditions that selectively affect women even when their weight is within normal limits (Dwyer, Feldman, & Mayer, 1970; Hampton, Huenemann, Shapiro, Mitchell, & Behnke, 1966; Huenemann, Shapiro, Hampton, & Mitchell, 1966; Nylander, 1971). In contrast, males seldom feel fat and usually want to gain rather than to lose weight.

In the face of mounting pressures on women to lose weight, dieting efforts have intensified to an incredible degree. This is reflected in the increase in the number of diet articles appearing in women's magazines in recent years. Garner *et al.* (1980) found over 70% more diet articles in six women's magazines in the years 1969 to 1978 than in the preceding 10-year period. The weight loss industry is thriving, as evidenced by the steady stream of best-selling diet books, diet aids, appetite suppressants, weight spas, Calorie-sparing TV dinners, "light" beers, and even dietary products for pets. The desperation behind efforts at weight control is poignantly illustrated by the apparent lapse in critical analysis applied to dieting merchandise. In a society in which there is a growing concern with truth in advertising and legal settlement of false claims, there is exceptional tolerance of obviously fatuous and occasionally dangerous dieting products that make gratuitous claims for success. Probably the most ridiculous, but sadly one of the most popular, deceptions is Mazel's (1981) Beverly Hills Diet. The long list of scientifically inaccurate and hazardous principles espoused in this absurd dieting philosophy have been well documented (Mirkin & Shore, 1981; O. W. Wooley & Wooley, 1982). Mazel recommends seriously disturbed eating patterns, food myths, self-starvation, and binge eating, and proudly advocates self-induced diarrhea as part of her weight control regimen. In a penetrating critique, O. W. Wooley and Wooley (1982) point out that it is an alarming testimonial to our weight-obsessed culture that symptoms of anorexia nervosa are offered as a solution to obesity.

Glamorizing of Anorexia Nervosa

The mass acceptance of Mazel's book may be simply a more perverse manifestation of a widespread public misperception of anorexia nervosa. We have argued that the preoccupation with weight control, the current "thin image" of beauty, and the association of anorexia nervosa with positive attributes (i.e., upper-class affiliation, intelligence, perfectionism, self-discipline, exercise, etc.) are probably responsible for the tragic, yet favorable stereotype being applied to the disorder (Garner, Garfinkel, & Olmsted, 1983). Anorexia nervosa has been glamorized in the media, beginning with its identification as the "Golden Girl's Disease" (*Playgirl*, 1975) and extending to a full range of popular novels, television dramas, and accounts of heroic battles waged against it by media personalities. The public's fascination with anorexia nervosa as mirrored (and promoted) by the press is one consequence of the positive connotation that the disorder has acquired. Another may be the actual development of the disorder in certain women who admire the qualities of anorexics. Bruch (Chapter 2, this volume) has referred to this new generation of "me-too" cases of anorexia nervosa as resulting from social contagion: In some individuals, there may not be simply a "drive for thinness," but also a drive for anorexia nervosa itself. Some patients report beginning self-induced vomiting as a weight-control method following exposure to media articles describing the practice (Chiodo & Latimer, 1983).

Despite the inordinate demands on women to become slim and the increased pervasiveness of dieting, the fact that young women's weights have increased in the past 20 years deserves further discussion. What accounts for this paradoxical change, particularly given the frequent assertion by the health professionals and the diet industry that weight can be easily modified with a little self-discipline and proper eating habits? Several explanations may be marshaled. It may be that women react perversely to the pressure to lose weight by eating more. Alternatively, it could be argued that women are simply weak-willed and are unable to lose weight to meet the prevailing standard. Many have suggested that fatness is a reflection of psychological disturbances: The increase in women's weights may indicate their declining mental health. All of these speculations are insulting to women and are inconsistent with the wealth of evidence that women have displayed skill, strength, and ingenuity in winning extensive social change during the last 20 years. It is much more logical to assume that the increased weights among women are a reflection of improved nutrition. This is supported by large population studies, which have indicated upward trends in body weights during periods free from war and famine (Brundtland, Liestol, & Walloe, 1980). Moreover, as we explain later, these "natural weights" may be relatively resistant to change through dieting.

Prejudice against Obesity

Women are encouraged to diet not only because of the virtues associated with slender-ness, but also because of the unparalleled social stigma against obesity. It has been suggested that "public derision and condemnation of fat people is one of the few re-maining sanctioned social prejudices . . . allowed against any group based solely on appearance" (Fitzgerald, 1981, p. 223). There is evidence that obese individuals are denied educational opportunities, jobs, promotion and housing because of their weight (Bray, 1976; Canning & Mayer, 1966; Karris, 1977). However, disdain toward obesity begins much earlier. Several studies have documented that grade-school children con-sistently attribute negative qualities to larger body shapes (Lerner, 1969, 1973; Lerner & Gelbert, 1969; Lerner & Korn, 1972; Staffieri, 1967, 1972). Both normal-weight and overweight children describe obese silhouettes as "stupid," "dirty," "lazy," "slop-py," "mean," "ugly," and "sad," among other pejorative labels (Allon, 1975; Staffieri, 1967, 1972). Earlier studies reported that drawings of obese children were evaluated less favorably than drawings of children who were physically handicapped or dis-figured (Goodman, Dornbusch, Richardson, & Hastorf, 1963; Richardson, Goodman, Hastorf, & Dornbusch, 1961). Even more incredible is the finding that professionals, including psychiatrists, psychologists, and social workers, also ranked the obese figures as less desirable. In a comprehensive review of these and other studies, O. W. Wooley, Wooley, and Dyrenforth (1979) suggest that these prejudices "learned in childhood no doubt become the basis for self-hatred among those who become overweight at later ages, and a source of anxiety and self-doubt for anyone fearful of becoming overweight" (p. 83).

Two justifications frequently offered for the determined efforts to combat obesity are that it represents a major health risk and that it is an indication of psychological disturbance. During the last decade, several studies and reviews have challenged the assumption that obesity is a significant health problem and have concluded that the fervor of treatment efforts reflects our prejudice rather than a realistic response to the risks inherent to the condition (Bennett & Gurin, 1982; Bradley, 1982; Fitzgerald, 1981; Mann, 1974; O. W. Wooley et al., 1979; S. C. Wooley & Wooley, 1979; S. C. Wooley, Wooley, & Dyrenforth, 1979). For example, Mann (1974) has indicated that there is little support for the often-cited relationship between obesity and high blood pressure, heart disease, and cholesterol levels. However, if obesity occurs with hyper-tension or hypercholesterolemia, the risks are magnified (Keys et al., 1972). Neverthe-less, it is an error to conclude that an association between obesity and illness necessarily implicates obesity as the cause. Obesity and illness may both be caused by a third fac-tor. For example, predispositions toward obesity and diabetes mellitus may originate from the same genetic deviation. Moreover, the psychological stress associated with being obese in our culture, rather than obesity per se, could contribute to increased risk of illness (Fitzgerald, 1981). It is well known that stress has a fundamental role in the development of cardiovascular disease, cancer, and many other disorders. A study of a community in which the incidence of obesity was high, but in which obesity was considered a socially acceptable condition, found lower-than-average frequencies of heart disease and diabetes (Stout, Morrow, Brandt, & Wolf, 1964). In this regard, it has been argued that frequent weight fluctuations, probably in connection with repeated but failed attempts to lose weight, may pose a greater health risk than obesity *per se* (Fitzgerald, 1981; S. C. Wooley & Wooley, 1979; S. C. Wooley *et al.*, 1979). Finally, there is some evidence to suggest that obesity is actually associated with *reduced* risk of illness and mortality! In some age categories, obese individuals live as long or longer and survive illness better than their lean counterparts (Andres, 1980; Bray, 1976; Gubner, 1973; Noppa, Bengtsson, Wedel, & Wilhelmsen, 1980; Sorlie, Gordon, & Kannel, 1980).

Results from a large epidemiological study indicate that for both men and women within the middle 60% of the weight distribution, there is absolutely no relationship between weight and mortality (Sorlie *et al.*, 1980). This means that for women of average height (160 to 168 cm or 5 ft 3 in to 5 ft 6 in), risk of death is virtually the same for those between 52 and 88 kg (115 and 194 lb)! Women in *both* the highest and lowest 20% of the weight distribution have a higher risk of death, but this is still considerably lower than the mortality rate for thin and average-weight men. Yet, as O. W. Wooley and Wooley (1982) point out, "90% of the victims of the diet/obesity industry are women" (p. 67).

In spite of the contentions made above, there is adequate evidence to suggest that extreme obesity does carry certain health risks (Fitzgerald, 1981; Hubert, Feinleib, McNamara, & Castelli, 1983). However, virtually no data indicate that mild to moderate overweight has the same detrimental consequences.

Even if there were a strong association between overweight and health risk, it would not imply that dieting is necessarily a solution. Given the wealth of scientific information indicating the unmitigated failure of dieting in achieving permanent weight loss (cf. Bennett & Gurin, 1982; Fitzgerald, 1981; S. C. Wooley & Wooley, 1979), there is little justification for offering it as a cure for obesity. The failure of current treatment makes it virtually impossible even to assess the impact of weight loss on health. The legitimacy of offering such treatment to a patient when the available success rates are so poor has to be seriously questioned, particularly considering the self-reproach and humiliation experienced by the vast majority who fail to maintain their weight loss. Hirsch (1978) has concluded that subjecting the obese to available treatment is "the modern day equivalent of beating the insane to keep them quiet" (p. 2). Certainly the prescription of dieting is unwarranted for those who are not suffering from illnesses that are clearly complicated by obesity. What is so deceptive is that most treatment approaches succeed to some degree in the short run. This, in conjunction with the social incentives for believing that a remedy is possible, is probably responsible for the unprecedented prosperity of the multibillion-dollar weight loss industry (Bray, 1976).

It is almost invariably assumed that obese individuals bring on their condition through gluttony. This is a fundamental assumption of most treatment approaches to overweight. When an obese person consumes a dessert in public, most people believe that it reflects overindulgence. On the other hand, if eating is restrained in public, it is assumed that the obese must be "closet" eaters who consume vast quantities when alone. However, the facts do not support the contention that the obese eat more than their leaner counterparts (S. C. Wooley & Wooley, 1979).

As we indicate later, there is considerable evidence that overweight for many may be a natural condition. Nevertheless, the health care profession has persisted in attributing obesity to psychological disturbance. It has been interpreted as the expression of sexual fears or cravings, sadistic or aggressive impulses, unconscious conflicts, or masked depression or anxiety, as well as numerous personality disturbances (for excellent summaries, see Bennett & Gurin, 1982; McReynolds, 1982). The implication that obese individuals bring their condition on themselves for psychological reasons is often subtle. For example, Orbach (1978) claims that women use their fat to protect themselves from being accepted purely as sexual objects. This thesis apparently assumes that women passively choose their obesity to cope with certain relationships and that obese women are frightened of being seen in sexual terms.

While psychological factors may be responsible for overweight in some individuals, most controlled studies do not find the obese to be more neurotic, sexually inadequate, or emotionally disturbed than individuals of normal weight (Bennett & Gurin, 1982; McReynolds, 1982; Rand, 1979; Stunkard, 1976; Weinberg, Mendelson, & Stunkard, 1961). In fact, some studies have found obese individuals to be less anxious, less depressed, and less prone to suicide than those of normal weight (Bray, 1976; Crisp & McGuiness, 1976; McReynolds, 1982). Nevertheless, the obdurate preconception that obesity must reflect psychological aberration has led to the paradoxical interpretation of negative findings. Simon (1963) asserted that there is an "undeniable connection" between overweight and *underlying* depression, based on the finding of a relative absence of *overt* depression in a group of military personnel. Gottesfeld (1962) found that obese subjects were less satisfied with their bodies but more satisfied with their personality traits than "neurotic" patients, and concluded that the obese "tend to deny that there is anything wrong with their personalities [with a] facade of satisfaction" (p. 182).

Based upon these and other observations, O. W. Wooley and Wooley (1982) have concluded that:

> Except for a minority of extreme cases, there is no such "disease" as obesity; treatments have failed because there is nothing to "cure"; they are dangerous because they are bred out of desperation and ignorance.
>
> Some people are naturally fatter than others, and until we can learn to live comfortably with our differences, we will be [needlessly] expanding the psychiatric nomenclature of eating disorders for years to come. (p. 68)

To summarize, more recent investigations of obesity suggest that (1) the health risks it poses have been dramatically overemphasized; (2) it generally does not reflect an emotional disturbance; (3) it may represent a natural state for some individuals; and (4) it is a target for glaring social prejudice. If those conclusions are true, then social reform may be a far more reasonable response to its occurrence than currently available treatments. It is important for both professionals and the general public to recognize the serious damage resulting from the past oversimplifications about obesity.

Some may question the relevance of a lengthy treatise on obesity in a chapter of a treatment manual for anorexia nervosa and bulimia. However, we believe that it is appropriate, for several reasons: (1) Many bulimic women are battling against obesity or overweight; (2) many obese women are bulimic (Edeleman, 1981; Loro & Orleans, 1981); and (3) many of the points outlined above apply to those who are of normal weight but feel compelled to diet because they perceive themselves to be overweight.

EFFECTS OF STARVATION ON BEHAVIOR

There is a remarkable parallel between many of the experiences observed in victims of semistarvation and those found in individuals with bulimia or anorexia nervosa. Probably the most systematic study of the effects of starvation was conducted over 30 years ago by Ancel Keys and his colleagues at the University of Minnesota (Keys, Brozek, Henschel, Mickelsen, & Taylor, 1950). The experiment involved restricting the caloric intake of 36 young, healthy, psychologically normal men who had volunteered for the study as an alternative to military service. During the first three months of the experiment, they ate normally while their behavior, personality, and eating patterns were studied in detail. During the subsequent 6 months, the men were restricted to approximately half of their former food intake and lost, on the average, 25% of their original body weight. This was followed by 3 months of rehabilitation, during which the men were gradually refed. Although their individual responses varied considerably, the men experienced dramatic physical, psychological, and social changes as a result of the starvation. In most cases, these changes persisted during the rehabilitation or renourishment phase.

Attitudes and Behavior Related to Eating

An inevitable result of starvation was a dramatic increase in preoccupation with food. The men found concentration on their usual activities increasingly difficult, since they were plagued by persistent thoughts of food and eating. In fact, food became a principal topic of conversation, reading, and daydreams. Many of the men began reading cookbooks and collecting recipes. Some developed a sudden interest in collecting coffeepots, hot plates, and other kitchen utensils. This hoarding even extended to non-food-related items:

> [Some of the men collected] old books, unnecessary second-hand clothes, knick knacks, and other "junk." Often after making such purchases, which could be afforded only with sacrifice, the men would be puzzled as to why they had bought such more or less useless articles. (Keys et al., 1950, p. 837)

One man even began rummaging through garbage cans with the hope of finding something that he might need. This general tendency to hoard has been observed in starved anorexic patients (Crisp, Hsu, & Harding, 1980) and even in rats deprived of food (Fantino & Cabanac, 1980). Despite little interest in culinary matters prior to the experiment, almost 40% of the men mentioned cooking as part of their postexperiment plans. For some, the fascination was so great that they actually changed occupations after the experiment: Three became chefs, and one went into agriculture.

During starvation, the volunteers' eating habits underwent remarkable changes. The men spent much of the day planning how they would eat their allotment of food. Much of their behavior served the purpose of prolonging the ingestion and hedonic appeal or saliency of food. The men often ate in silence and devoted total attention to consumption.

The Minnesota subjects were often caught between conflicting desires to gulp their food down ravenously and consume it slowly so that the taste and odor of each morsel would be fully appreciated. Toward the end of starvation some of the men would dawdle for almost two hours over a meal which previously they would have consumed in a matter of minutes. (Keys *et al.*, 1950, p. 833)

The men demanded that their food be served hot, and they made unusual concoctions by mixing foods together. There was a tremendous increase in the use of salt and spices. The consumption of coffee and tea increased so dramatically that the men had to be limited to 9 cups per day; similarly, gum chewing became excessive and had to be limited after it was discovered that one man was chewing as many as 40 packages a day.

During the 12-week rehabilitation phase, most of these attitudes and behaviors persisted. For a small number of men these became even *more* marked during the first 6 weeks of refeeding:

In many cases the men were not content to eat "normal" menus but persevered in their habits of making fantastic concoctions and combinations. The free choice of ingredients, moreover, stimulated "creative" and "experimental" playing with food . . . licking of plates and neglect of table manners persisted. (Keys *et al.*, 1950, p. 843)

Bulimia

During the starvation regimen, all of the volunteers reported increased hunger; some appeared able to tolerate the experience fairly well, but for others it created intense concern or even became intolerable. Several men failed to adhere to their diets and reported episodes of bulimia followed by self-reproach. While working in a grocery store,

[one subject] suffered a complete loss of will power and ate several cookies, a sack of popcorn, and two overripe bananas before he could "regain control" of himself. He immediately suffered a severe emotional upset, with nausea, and upon returning to the laboratory he vomited. . . . He was self-deprecatory, expressing disgust and self-criticism. (Keys *et al.*, 1950, p. 887)

During the eighth week of starvation, another subject "flagrantly broke the dietary rules, eating several sundaes and malted milks; he even stole some penny candies. He promptly confessed the whole episode, [and] became self-deprecatory" (Keys *et al.*, 1950, p. 884).

When presented with greater amounts of food during rehabilitation, many of the men lost control of their appetites and "ate more or less continuously" (Keys *et al.*, 1950, p. 843). Even after 12 weeks of rehabilitation, the men frequently complained that they experienced an *increase* in hunger immediately *following* a large meal:

[One of the volunteers] ate immense meals (a daily estimate of 5,000–6,000 cal.) and yet started "snacking" an hour after he finished a meal. [Another] ate as much as he could hold during the three regular meals and ate snacks in the morning, afternoon and evening. (Keys *et al.*, 1950, p. 846)

The investigators reported:

This gluttony resulted in a high incidence of headaches, gastrointestinal distress and unusual sleepiness. Several men had spells of nausea and vomiting. One man required aspiration and hospitalization for several days. (Keys *et al.*, 1950, p. 843)

There were weekend "splurges" in which intake commonly ranged between 8,000 and 10,000 Calories. The men frequently found it difficult to stop eating:

Subject no. 20 stuffs himself until he is bursting at the seams, to the point of being nearly sick and still feels hungry; no. 120 reported that he had to discipline himself to keep from eating so much as to become ill; no. 1 ate until he was uncomfortably full; and subject no. 30 had so little control over the mechanics of "piling it in" that he simply had to stay away from food because he could not find a point of satiation even when he was "full to the gills." . . . Subject no. 26 would just as soon have eaten six meals instead of three. (Keys *et al.*, 1950, p. 847)

After about 5 months of rehabilitation, the majority of the men reported some normalization of their eating patterns; however, for some the extreme overconsumption persisted: "No. 108 would eat and eat until he could hardly swallow any more and then he felt like eating half an hour later" (Keys *et al.*, 1950, p. 847). More than *8 months* after renourishment a few men were still eating abnormal amounts, and one man still reported consuming "about 25 per cent more than his pre-starvation amount; once he started to reduce but got so hungry he could not stand it" (Keys *et al.*, 1950, p. 847).

Factors that distinguished men who rapidly normalized their eating from those who continued to eat prodigious amounts were not identified. However, the important point here is that there were tremendous differences among volunteers in their responses to the starvation experience, and that a subset of these men developed bulimia, which persisted many months after they were permitted free access to food.

Emotional Changes

The strict procedures used to select subjects for the experiment led the experimenters to conclude that the "psychobiological 'stamina' of the subjects was unquestionably superior to that likely to be found in any random or more generally representative sample of the population" (Keys *et al.*, 1950, p. 916). Although the subjects were psychologically healthy prior to the experiment, most experienced significant emotional changes as a result of semistarvation. Some reported transitory and others protracted periods of depression, with an overall lowering of the threshold for depression. Occasionally elation was observed, but this was inevitably followed by "low periods." Although the men had quite tolerant dispositions prior to starvation, tolerance was replaced by irritability and frequent outbursts of anger. For most subjects, anxiety became more evident. As the experiment progressed, many of the formerly even-tempered men began biting their nails or smoking because they felt nervous. Apathy became common, and some men who had been quite fastidious neglected various aspects of personal hygiene. Most of the subjects experienced periods during which their emotional distress was quite severe, and all exhibited the symptoms of "semistarvation neurosis" described above. Almost 20% of the group experienced extreme emotional deterioration that markedly interfered with their functioning. Standardized personality testing with the Minnesota Multiphasic Personality Inventory (MMPI) revealed that semistarvation resulted in significant increases in depression, hysteria, and hypochondriasis for the group. This profile has been referred to as the "neurotic triad" and is observed among different groups of neurotically disturbed individuals (Greene, 1980). These emotional aberrations did not vanish immediately during rehabilitation, but persisted for several weeks, with some men actually becoming more depressed, irritable, argumentative, and negativistic than they had been during semistarvation. During semistarvation two subjects developed disturbances of "psychotic" proportions. One of these was unable to adhere to the diet and developed alarming symptoms:

[He exhibited] a compulsive attraction to refuse and a strong, almost compelling, desire to root in garbage cans [for food to eat]. . . . He repeatedly went through the cycle of eating tremendous quantities of food, becoming sick, and then starting all over again . . . [and] became emotionally disturbed enough to seek admission voluntarily to the psychiatric ward of the University Hospitals. (Keys *et al.*, 1950, p. 890)

After 9 weeks of starvation, another subject exhibited signs of disturbance:

[He went on a] spree of shoplifting, stealing trinkets that had little or no intrinsic value. . . . He developed a violent emotional outburst with flight of ideas, weeping, talk of suicide and threats of violence. Because of the alarming nature of his symptoms, he was released from the experiment and admitted to the psychiatric ward of the University Hospitals. (Keys *et al.*, 1950, p. 885)

Another man chopped off three fingers of one hand in response to stress. For a few volunteers, mood swings were extreme:

[One subject] experienced a number of periods in which his spirits were definitely high. . . . These elated periods alternated with times in which he suffered "a deep dark depression." [He] felt that he had reached the end of his rope [and] expressed the fear that he was going crazy . . . [and] losing his inhibitions. (Keys *et al.*, 1950, p. 903)

Personality testing (with the MMPI) of a small minority of subjects confirmed the clinical impression of incredible deterioration as a result of semistarvation. Figure 21-2 illustrates one man's personality profile: Initially it was well within normal limits, but after 10 weeks of semistarvation and a weight loss of only about 4.5 kg (10 lb, or approximately 7% of his original body weight), gross personality disturbances were evident. On the second testing, all of the MMPI scales were elevated, with severe personality disturbance on the scales for neurosis as well as those for psychosis. Depression and general disorganization were particularly striking consequences of starvation for several of the men who became the most emotionally disturbed.

It may be concluded from clinical observation as well as standardized personality testing that the individual emotional response to semistarvation conditions varies considerably. Some of the volunteers in Keys *et al.*'s experiment seemed to cope relatively well, and others displayed extraordinary disturbance following weight loss. The type of disturbance was quite similar to that described in obese individuals exposed to "therapeutic" semistarvation (Glucksman & Hirsch, 1969; Rowland, 1970). In the Minnesota experiment, prestarvation personality adjustment did not predict the emotional response to caloric restriction. Some of the men who appeared to be the most stable reacted with severe disturbance. The fact that people respond so differently and un-

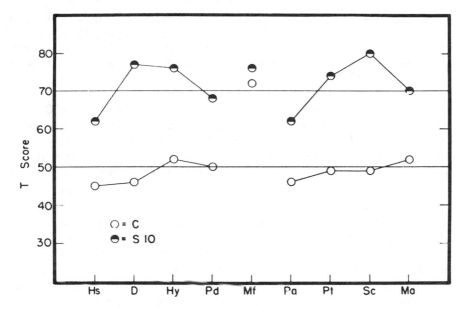

Figure 21-2. Scores on the MMPI for one subject in the Minnesota semistarvation experiment during the control period (C) and after 10 weeks of semistarvation (S10). *T* scores between 50 and 70 are in the normal range. (From A. Keys, J. Brozek, A. Henschel, O. Mickelsen, and H. L. Taylor, *The Biology of Human Starvation.* Copyright © 1950 by the University of Minnesota, University of Minnesota Press, Minneapolis.)

predictably to weight loss is clearly relevant to an assessment of those who have dieted below their optimal weight. Since the emotional difficulties in the Minnesota volunteers did not immediately reverse themselves during rehabilitation, it may be assumed that the abnormalities were related more to body weight than to short-term caloric intake. It may be concluded that many of the psychological disturbances found in anorexia nervosa and bulimia may be the result of the semistarvation process.

Social and Sexual Changes

The extraordinary impact of semistarvation is reflected in the social changes experienced by most of the volunteers. Although originally quite gregarious, the men became progressively more withdrawn and isolated. Humor and the sense of comradeship diminished markedly amidst growing feelings of social inadequacy:

Social initiative especially, and sociability in general, underwent a remarkable change. The men became reluctant to plan activities, to make decisions, and to participate in group activities. . . . They spent more and more time alone. It became "too much trouble" or "too tiring" to have contact with other people. (Keys *et al.*, 1950, pp. 836–837)

The volunteers' social contacts with women also declined sharply during semistarvation. Those who continued to see women socially found that the relationships became strained. These changes are illustrated in the description from one man's diary:

I am one of about three or four who still go out with girls. I fell in love with a girl during the control period but I see her only occasionally now. It's almost too much trouble to see her even when she visits me in the lab. It requires effort to hold her hand. Entertainment must be tame. If we see a show, the most interesting part of it is contained in scenes where people are eating. (Keys *et al.*, 1950, p. 853)

Sexual interests were likewise drastically reduced. Masturbation, sexual fantasies, and sexual impulses either ceased or became much less common. One subject graphically stated that he had "no more sexual feeling than a sick oyster." (Even this peculiar metaphor made reference to food.) The investigators observed that "many of the men welcomed the freedom from sexual tensions and frustrations normally present in young adult men" (Keys *et al.*, 1950, p. 840). The fact that starvation perceptibly altered sexual urges and associated conflicts is of particular interest, since it has been hypothesized that this process is the driving force behind the dieting of many anorexia nervosa patients. According to Crisp (1980), anorexia nervosa is an adaptive disorder in the sense that it curtails sexual concerns for which the adolescent feels unprepared.

During rehabilitation, sexual interest was slow to return. Even after 3 months, the men judged themselves to be far from normal in this area. However, after 8 months of renourishment, virtually all of the men had recovered their interest in sex.

Cognitive Changes

The volunteers reported impaired concentration, alertness, comprehension, and judgment during semistarvation; however, formal intellectual testing revealed no signs of diminished intellectual abilities.

Physical Changes

As the 6 months of semistarvation progressed, the volunteers exhibited many physical changes, including the following: gastrointestinal discomfort, decreased need for sleep, dizziness, headaches, hypersensitivity to noise and light, reduced strength, poor motor control, edema (an excess of fluid causing swelling), hair loss, decreased tolerance for cold temperatures (cold hands and feet), visual disturbances (i.e., inability to focus, eye aches, "spots" in the visual fields), auditory disturbances (i.e., ringing noise in the ears), and paresthesia (i.e., abnormal tingling or prickling sensations, especially in the hands or feet).

Various changes reflected an overall slowing of the body's physiological processes. There were decreases in body temperature, heart rate, and respiration, as well as in basal metabolic rate (BMR). BMR is the amount of energy (Calories) that the body requires at rest (i.e., no physical activity) in order to carry out normal physiological processes. It accounts for about two-thirds of the body's total energy needs, with the remainder being used during physical activity. At the end of semistarvation, the men's BMRs had dropped by about 40% from normal. This drop, as well as other physical changes, reflects the body's extraordinary ability to adapt to low caloric intake by reducing its need for energy. One volunteer described that it was as if his "body flame

[were] burning as low as possible to conserve precious fuel and still maintain life process" (Keys *et al.*, 1950, p. 852). During rehabilitation, metabolism again speeded up, with those consuming the greatest number of Calories experiencing the largest rise in BMR. The group of volunteers who received a relatively small increment in Calories during rehabilitation (400 Calories more than during semistarvation) had no rise in BMR for the first 3 weeks. *Consuming larger amounts of food caused a sharp increase in the energy burned through metabolic processes.*

The changes in body fat and muscle in relation to overall body weight during semistarvation and rehabilitation are of considerable interest (see Figure 21-3). While weight declined about 25%, the percentage of body fat fell almost 70%, and muscle decreased about 40%. Upon refeeding, a greater proportion of the "new weight" was fat; in the eighth month of rehabilitation, the volunteers were at about 110% of their original body weight, but had approximately 140% of their original body fat! How did the men feel about their weight gain during rehabilitation?

Those subjects who gained the most weight became concerned about their increased sluggishness, general flabbiness, and the tendency of fat to accumulate in the abdomen and buttocks. (Keys *et al.*, 1950, p. 828)

These complaints are similar to those of many bulimic and anorexic patients as they gain weight. Besides their typical fear of weight gain, they often report "feeling fat" and are worried about acquiring distended stomachs. However, as indicated in Figure 21-3, the body weight and relative body fat of the Minnesota volunteers had begun to approach the preexperiment levels after just over a year.

Figure 21-3. Body weight and body fat expressed as percentages of the control values for the volunteers in the Minnesota semistarvation experiment. C—control period; S—weeks of semistarvation; R—weeks of rehabilitation. (From A. Keys, J. Brozek, A. Henschel, O. Mickelsen, and H. L. Taylor, *The Biology of Human Starvation.* Copyright © 1950 by the University of Minnesota, University of Minnesota Press, Minneapolis.)

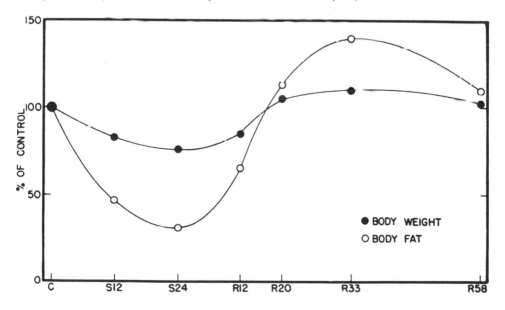

Physical Activity

In general, the men responded to semistarvation with reduced physical activity. They became tired, weak, listless, and apathetic, and complained of lack of energy. Voluntary movements became noticeably slower. However, according to the original report,

some men exercised deliberately at times. Some of them attempted to lose weight by driving themselves through periods of excessive expenditure of energy in order either to obtain increased bread rations . . . or to avoid reduction in rations. (Keys *et al.*, 1950, p. 828)

This is similar to the practice of some anorexic and bulimic patients, who feel that if they exercise strenuously, they can allow themselves a bit more to eat. The difference is that for the patients the caloric limitations are self-imposed.

Significance of the Starvation Study

As is readily apparent from the preceding description of the Minnesota experiment, many of the symptoms that might have been thought to be specific to anorexia nervosa or bulimia are actually the result of starvation. These are not limited to food and weight, but extend to virtually all areas of psychological and social functioning. Since many of the symptoms that have been postulated to *cause* these disorders may actually *result* from undernutrition, it is absolutely essential that weight be returned to "normal" levels in order that emotional disturbances may be accurately assessed.

The profound effects of starvation also illustrate the tremendous adaptive capacity of the human body and the intense biological pressure on the organism to maintain a relatively consistent body weight. This makes complete evolutionary sense. Over the hundreds of thousands of years of human evolution, a major threat to the survival of the organism was starvation. If weight had not been carefully modulated and controlled internally, animals most certainly would simply have died when food was scarce, or when their interest was captured by countless other aspects of living. The starvation study illustrates how the human being becomes more oriented toward food when starved and how other pursuits important to the survival of the species (e.g., social and sexual functioning) become subordinate to the primary drive toward food.

One of the most notable implications of the starvation experiment is that it provides compelling evidence against the popular notion that body weight is easily altered if one simply exercises a bit of "will power." It also demonstrates that the body is not simply "reprogrammed" to adjust to a lower weight once it has been achieved. The volunteers' experimental diet was unsuccessful in overriding their bodies' strong propensity to defend a particular weight level. One might argue that this is fine as long as a person is not obese to start with; as we point out later, however, these same principles seem to apply just as much to those who are naturally heavy as to those who have always been lean. It should be emphasized that following the months of rehabilitation, the Minnesota volunteers did not skyrocket into obesity. On the average, they gained back their original weight plus about 10%; then, over the next 6 months, their weight gradually declined. By the end of the follow-up period, they were approaching their preexperiment weight levels.

If this process implies a mechanism operating to maintain the organism's weight around a preferred or predetermined point, then it could be expected that deviations *above* this point would be met by equally staunch resistance. Sims and his colleagues put this notion to the experimental test in a study designed to produce obesity in a group of normal-weight male prison inmates (Sims *et al.*, 1968). The volunteers were dedicated to the task of gaining between 20 and 25% of their original body weight over the 6 months of the experiment. They all consumed about twice their usual daily allotment of Calories. Most of the men gained the initial few pounds with relative ease, and two prisoners with a family history of obesity showed the least resistance to weight gain. However, the remainder of the group found it increasingly difficult to accumulate extra weight, despite the consumption of vast numbers of Calories. One man was able to tolerate close to 10,000 Calories per day with only a modest increase in weight!

Just as the Minnesota volunteers conserved energy through a metabolic adaptation to undernutrition, the prisoners burned up much of the excess energy through increased metabolic activity. They perspired profusely and complained of oppressive body heat. The amount of weight gained only accounted for about 25% of the excess Calories ingested. Moreover, the hypermetabolic state created by overeating meant that the men required 50% more Calories to maintain their experimental obesity. The overindulgence became increasingly unpleasant; many of the men contemplated withdrawing from the experiment. Some became physically ill after meals, and their psychological state deteriorated. As soon as overeating was no longer required, the men rapidly began losing weight and ultimately stabilized at almost exactly their preexperiment weight levels. The only exceptions were the two men who initially gained weight rapidly, as well as two others with a family history of obesity or diabetes. The marked differences among individuals in the *rate* of weight loss and resistance to weight gain suggests differences in the biological propensity to overweight.

More recently, Brunner *et al.* (1979) overfed 26 agricultural workers 4553 Calories each daily for 7 months, which resulted in an average weight gain of less than 3.2 kg (7 lb). This accounts for only about 5% of the excess energy ingested! The fact that the agricultural workers "burned off" even more of the extra Calories may be accounted for by their physical activity, their high-fat diet, or their genetic predisposition for leanness (Brunner *et al.*, 1979).

In other studies where normal-weight individuals are experimentally overfed, they gain far less weight than they should, considering the vast excess of Calories that they consume (Ashworth, Creedy, Hunt, Mahon, & Newland, 1962; D. S. Miller & Mumford, 1966; D. S. Miller, Mumford, & Stock, 1967; Sims *et al.*, 1968). Even when eating several thousand Calories per day, there is a remarkable propensity for the body to "waste away" the surplus Calories. Although these overfed volunteers do gain weight, they certainly do not become obese.

Metabolic rate appears to adapt to increased caloric intake by producing excess heat, a process termed "diet-induced thermogenesis." Although this phenomenon was first described over 80 years ago, its importance in the regulation of energy balance has only recently been acknowledged. In a now classic study, Neuman (1902) set out to determine the effect of overeating over a prolonged period of time. During the first year of his experiment, he increased his intake by 430 Calories per day, and during the second year, by an additional 300 Calories per day. A little arithmetic shows that he should have gained about 18 kg (40 lb) the first year and an additional 27 kg (60 lb) the second, since the surplus amounts were well beyond the number of Calories he needed to maintain his initial body weight. Surprisingly, Neuman described only a modest weight increase during the 2-year period. He realized that his body was somehow able to dispose of the surplus Calories, and he called this ability *Luxoskonsumption* ("extra burning"). Gulick (1922) also reported a 10-month period during which he systematically overate; he, too, gained less weight than could be predicted from the number of Calories he was ingesting. He could not account for an estimated 27–37% of his Calories.

Later studies have not been successful in replicating these surprising findings. There is still some controversy as to the significance of diet-induced thermogenesis in humans, although it is known to play an important role in animals. In a variety of animals, including rats, there appear to be two kinds of fat stores. The "brown" fat cells house the mechanism for wasting Calories through thermogenesis, whereas the "white" fat cells are responsible for the deposition of Calories. Brown fat also helps to maintain body temperature in response to environmental cold (Himms-Hagen, 1981). When rats are overfed, their brown fat cells either become larger or increase in function (Rothwell & Stock, 1979; Trayhurn, Thurlby, & James, 1977).

Whether or not the site for caloric wasting in humans is truly brown adipose tissue, there is some evidence to suggest that diet-induced thermogenesis can raise metabolic rate by about 10% (Sims, 1976). Moreover, a highly fattening diet has been shown to enhance the thermic effect of a meal (Goldman *et al.*, 1976; D. S. Miller, 1973) and of activity (D. S. Miller, 1973; D. S. Miller *et al.*, 1967). Diet-induced thermogenesis appears to be triggered by a cumulative surplus of 20,000 Calories and begins working after about 2 weeks of overeating (Bennett & Gurin, 1982).

The propensity of the body to burn off "excess" Calories is more pronounced in lean individuals than in the obese (Kaplan & Leveille, 1974; Pittet, Chappuis, Acheson, DeTechtermann, & Jequier, 1976). This may relate to the fact that most obese people diet to some extent, but it may also be due to a more basic impairment in the mechanism of diet-induced thermogenesis (DeLuise, Blackburn, & Flier, 1980; Trayhurn *et al.*, 1977). Genetically obese animals show this reduced thermogenic capacity (Himms-Hagen, 1981; James & Trayhurn, 1981; Romsos, 1983). They are able to acquire excess fat without overeating in part because of this diminution in caloric expenditure.

REGULATED WEIGHT OR "SET POINT"

The experiments by Keys *et al.*, Sims *et al.*, and others illustrate the exceptional resistance of most normal individuals to weight gain or loss. Changes in volunteers' weight were countered by metabolic adaptation designed to restore the state of body weight equilibrium. Weight loss is accompanied by hypometabolism, designed to facilitate weight gain by using Calories more efficiently; weight gain produces hypermetabolism, in which excess Calories are wasted. Changes in mood and appetite also promote return to the status quo. The precise mechanism by which this defense of body weight operates is a matter of speculation and controversy; however, there is a wealth of compelling scientific evidence indicating that our bodies try to "defend" an apparently physiologically programmed weight level (cf. Keesey, 1980; Mrosovsky & Powley, 1977) and that this phenomenon obviously has absolutely nothing to do with our aesthetic preferences, which may change from time to time.

Beyond the underfeeding and overfeeding experiments, support for the concept of set point comes from the observations of relative long-term stability of body weight, as well as the incredible resistance of the obese to permanent weight loss. As Hollifield (1968) proclaimed, the "active man who remains the same weight over a period of 20 years must have balanced his food intake against energy expenditure to the nearest crumb" (p. 1471). In recent years, there has been a growing recognition that, despite substantial variations in caloric intake, body weight remains remarkably stable over time. Many people are able to maintain a relatively constant weight without monitoring food intake against energy output. Fox (1973) reported a personal weight range of between 71 and 77 kg (156 and 170 lb) over 20 years, although he gave no conscious attention to the amount eaten or amount of exercise taken.

A fact attesting to the degree of precision dictated by the mechanisms responsible for weight regulation is that a gain of 4.5 kg (10 lb) in one year would require a consistent error of only about 100 Calories daily. It has been shown that over a 6- to 10-week period, body weight varies by only .5% around an average weight (Adam, Best, & Edholm, 1961; Durnin, 1961; Khosha & Billewicz, 1964; Robinson & Watson, 1965). This is a deviation of less than 280 g (10 oz) for a 55-kg (120-lb) woman, despite the fact that most adolescent women have as much as a fourfold variation in daily caloric intake (Lacey, Chadbund, Crisp, & Whitehead, 1978). Again, these assumptions rest on the unlikely possibility that the woman is not consciously attempting to alter her body weight by dieting. As we indicate later, dieting usually causes large but temporary fluctuations in body weight. However, large-scale nutrition surveys have found that the average weight of men aged 60 is within 2.3 kg (5 lb) of men 30 years of age (Keescy, 1980).

Probably the most profound implications of the set point concept is that it challenges most of the previous interpretations of obesity as a reflection of disease or pathology. Nisbett (1972) originally marshaled considerable evidence for the argument that, like all biological parameters, body fat and the baselines for set point vary from one individual to another in the population. The absolute level of body fat determined by the set point mechanisms may differ markedly in individuals of the same height and bone structure, depending on heredity and feeding experiences in childhood, when set point appears to be more malleable. According to this view, obesity for some individuals represents a "normal" or even an "ideal" body weight.

Moreover, Nisbett (1972) observed many behavioral parallels between obese humans and hungry or starving individuals. It was concluded that many obese people are genuinely hungry and in a chronic state of energy deficit because they are desperately trying to hold their weight below their physiologically determined set point in response to social pressures to be thinner. Thus, many statistically *overweight* individuals who have responded by reducing their weight may actually be biologically *underweight*! A 9-kg (20-lb) weight loss in a 55-kg (120-lb) and a 73-kg (160-lb) woman may have the same biological impact; however, we have been culturally programmed not to expect the heavier woman to experience the same degree of hunger. Weight reduction in those who are naturally obese, or failure to allow natural obesity to develop by restricting food intake, may have grave biological consequences.

There is recent evidence from the animal literature that restricting the food intake of genetically obese rats throughout life to that eaten by their lean littermates normalizes body weight, but does so at the expense of vital organs rather than body fat (Cleary & Vasselli, 1981; Cleary, Vasselli, & Greenwood, 1980). These studies found that the weights of brain, kidneys, liver, and muscle were significantly reduced in the food-restricted obese rats. Cleary *et al.* (1980) also found that restricting the food intake in the young obese animals actually aggravated their obese condition later. In a similar experiment, Greenwood, Maggio, Koopmans, and Sclafani (1982) found that intestinal bypass surgery reduced the body weights of naturally obese rats to nearly those of their genetically lean littermates, but did so again at the expense of vital organ mass. The preservation of adipose tissue in preference to brain, liver, kidneys, and muscle suggests a powerful biological defense of fat.

Another compelling argument for the operation of such a mechanism is the miserable failure of obesity "treatment" programs to achieve lasting weight reduction, despite the previously mentioned stigma against overweight. One of the few long-term studies of the impact of "therapeutic fasting" found that virtually all of the 121 patients lost weight initially and that the majority maintained the loss for 1 year, but that 50% of the group returned to their original weight within 2 years (D. Johnson & Drenick, 1977). Nine years later, only 5.8% weighed less than they did originally, while 42% of the child-onset and 26% of the adult-onset obese weighed *more* than they did before fasting. Other outcome studies register equally dismal results. In general, only 5% of obese individuals maintain a weight loss of at least 9 kg (20 lb) for 2 years or more (Bray, 1979; Foreyt, Goodrick, & Otto, 1981; Jeffrey & Coates, 1978; Stunkard, 1978; Stunkard & Penick, 1979; Wing & Jeffrey, 1979). Therefore, the obese appear to defend their higher-than-average weights with the same tenacity as that displayed by the Minnesota volunteers.

Furthermore, contrary to popular belief, the obese usually maintain their larger reserves of body fat on the same number of Calories as, or fewer Calories than, the non-obese. A review of 20 studies on the topic revealed that all but one found that the obese consume equal amounts or less food than the non-obese (S. C. Wooley & Wooley, 1979). In one well-known study, the investigators monitored the eating of customers at ice-cream parlors, fast-food restaurants, and snack bars. Since each serving was standardized, it was possible to record the caloric content of each patron's meal. The results confirmed those of earlier studies, indicating that in naturalistic settings, overweight and normal-weight individuals consumed remarkably similar amounts of food. Other studies of infants and children support the conclusion that the obese do not eat more than the non-obese (Bradley, 1982). Despite the fact that many of these studies are plagued with methodological flaws, S. C. Wooley *et al.* (1979) conclude that "the congruence of the results is so striking that the burden of proof must be said to rest with those who contend that there is a difference" (p. 5). The observation that the obese use their Calories efficiently has been extended to some nonhuman species. For example, McCGraham (1969) reported that obese sheep consumed one half as much fodder as lean sheep.

Similar findings have been reported for rats and mice specifically bred to be fat. The "Zucker fatty," affectionately named after the woman who discovered it, is a genetically obese rat with a large number of large-sized fat cells (Zucker & Zucker, 1961). This strain does eat more than its leaner counterparts; however, when the amount eaten is calculated as a proportion of their greater body mass, their consumption is similar to that of the lean animals (Bray, 1970). Zucker fatties need the same number of Calories as do normal-weight rats (Deb, Martin, & Herschberger, 1976). Furthermore, if their weight drops, they will work hard to regain the lost weight. Zucker fatties demonstrate vigorous regulation of their body weight, albeit at an elevated level (Greenwood, Quartermain, Johnson, Cruce, & Hirsch, 1974).

Cabanac, Duclaux, and Spector (1971) proposed the term "ponderstat" for the mechanism responsible for detecting when the organism is above or below set point and providing feedback to restore it to this weight level. According to this view, the ponderstat functions as a biological thermostat, much like a thermostat that stabilizes the heat level in a room. If the heat controls are set at a certain number, the system operates to maintain that temperature. If a window is opened and the room temperature drops, the thermostat automatically goes to work to increase the heat level. The machinery starts to churn and begins to pump out heat. If the room gets too hot, the furnace shuts off temporarily until the temperature returns to normal. This bidirectional sensing mechanism is alerted automatically; it is extremely responsive to changes that displace the heat level from the temperature level that has been set. Our bodies apparently work in much the same way, responding to deviations from set point by turning the metabolic "furnace" up or down.

Although much is still unknown, it appears that the set point mechanism is not located in any particular part of the body or brain (Bennett & Gurin, 1982). Some assume that what is regulated by set point is the *quantity* of fat stored in adipose tissue (Faust, Johnson, & Hirsch, 1977; Sjostrom, 1980). The number of fat cells that an individual has is largely determined by a combination of genetic factors and early nutritional experience; however, the degree to which each of these factors contributes is currently a matter of debate. Although earlier studies concluded that the number of fat cells remained constant throughout the lifespan, more recent work indicates that the number of fat cells may change even in adulthood if an animal becomes obese (Faust, 1981). At present, there appears to be no means of reducing the number of fat cells in the body (Sjostrom, 1980). Dieting reduces the size of fat stores but not their number; thus, the potential for *weighing* the set amount by refilling the increased number of fat cells is never lost.

Research is currently focusing on the means by which fat cells give and receive feedback about defending set point. Some have speculated that certain enzymes or chemicals released from adipose tissue may be responsible for this signaling function. One such enzyme may be adipose tissue lipoprotein lipase (AT-LPL), which is elevated following weight loss (Schwartz & Brunzell, 1978, 1981), during refeeding (Bjorntorp, Yang, & Greenwood, 1983), and in genetically obese rats (Cleary et al., 1980). It has been speculated that inherited or acquired enhancement of AT-LPL activity renders white fat cells more efficient in storing nutrients as fat.

Whatever the mechanism may be, it has long been known that impairing the function of certain brain areas in experimental animals has dramatic effects on set point. When tissue is surgically damaged in the lateral hypothalamus (LH), the level at which rats regulate their weight is permanently lowered. These animals quickly lose weight and chronically maintain their new weight. However, what is most interesting is that regulation of the lowered set point is as precise as its regulation in normal rats and is defended in the same way when the animal is starved or overfed (Keesey, 1980, 1983).

It was once believed that damage to a nearby brain structure, the ventromedial hypothalamus (VMH), caused the "lipostat" (as it was then called) to be reset at a higher level (Kennedy, 1953). Animals with lesions of the VMH eat enormous amounts of food and eventually get fat. Their weight eventually stabilizes at an obese level. This observation led many researchers to conclude (wrongly) that damage to this part of the brain destroys a satiety center, an area that, when intact, lets the rat know that it has had enough to eat. It was later discovered that the VMH-damaged rat gets fat even when consuming normal amounts of food (Cox & Powley, 1981).

The degree of obesity shown by the VMH-damaged rat is dependent on the type of diet it is fed. These animals are known for being extremely finicky about the food they eat. If given highly palatable, good-tasting food, they consume great quantities and become very obese. If the food is bad-tasting, these rats gain much less excess fat and regulate their weights at a reduced level. Thus the set point for body weight can be determined by a number of factors. It is altered by certain brain dysfunctions, as well as the palatability of the food to which the organism has been exposed.

In summary, being overweight is usually no more a sign of psychological or metabolic aberration than is underweight. Just as some individuals are naturally lean, others have no choice but to be statistically overweight, by virtue of the physiological settings in their bodies that control weight maintenance.

FACTORS INFLUENCING SET POINT

A number of factors appear to govern the "setting" of the set point mechanism. Under their influence, body weight is defended at somewhat higher or lower levels. Much of the information regarding these factors has been derived from experiments with laboratory rats. Although extrapolations to human beings must be made with extreme caution, the highly controlled conditions in the laboratory are ideally suited for systematic study of the factors influencing body weight.

Food Palatability

It is well known that rats are rather precise regulators of body weight when fed bland and monotonous laboratory chow. However, when exposed to more palatable high-sugar or high-fat diets, they will maintain their weight at significantly higher levels; the opposite effect is observed when they are forced to consume unpalatable rations (Peck, 1978; Sclafani, 1980). When given a choice, rats strongly prefer high-fat diets to chow; the more fat in the diet, the stronger the preference (Sclafani, 1980). Obesity resulting from a highly palatable diet occurs for two reasons. The animals not only ingest more Calories, but also convert a larger proportion of Calories consumed into body fat (Sclafani, 1980). The degree of obesity produced by highly palatable food depends on other factors, such as the age, genetic background, and activity level of the animal. Rats fed a high-fat diet from the time of weaning usually attain a higher weight than those given the diet in adulthood (Sclafani, 1980). Weight gain is exaggerated in animals with preexisting genetic obesity due either to heredity or to a hypothalamic lesion (Sclafani, 1980). Although obesity resulting from a highly palatable diet is largely reversible with a return to less palatable food, it can lead to permanent elevations in adipose cells and higher body weight (Faust, 1981).

Some have argued that the prevalence of human obesity may be partially attributable to the rather sudden change, in evolutionary terms, in our diet (Bennett & Gurin, 1982). Compared with that of our ancestors, the modern Western diet is laden with highly accessible, rich, and good-tasting foods.

Exercise

It has been noted that many individuals experience weight gain during periods of inactivity following injury (Brownell & Stunkard, 1980). Various studies of the human and the rat have shown that moderate physical activity reduces both body weight and food consumption (Brownell & Stunkard, 1980; Epling, Pierce, & Stefan, 1983; Woo, Garrow, & Pi-Sunyer, 1982). More vigorous exercise may lead to increased consumption, but the organism still maintains a lower body weight (Bennett & Gurin, 1982). As mentioned earlier, there is evidence to suggest that exercise enhances diet-induced thermogenesis (Brunner *et al.*, 1979); in the rat, exercise augments the thermogenic function of brown fat tissue (Hirata, 1982). Regular physical activity is probably the most sensible and effective method of keeping weight at the low end of one's weight range. However, there are limits to the amount of weight that may be comfortably lost through exercise. Brownell and Stunkard (1980) cite numerous studies indicating that fat loss in obese and normal-weight persons rarely exceeds 5%.

Stress

Weight gain in humans is frequently associated with stress and emotional upset. Reports of precipitous weight gain during the first year of college or following various traumas are common indeed. As explained earlier, we believe that the role of these factors has been overstated in the unrelenting search for a psychogenic cause for obesity. As we indicate later, overeating in response to stress is less common in nondieters than in dieters whose weight is being suppressed through caloric restriction. Nevertheless, there is evidence indicating that nondieting rats may overeat when exposed to stress from a mild tail pinch, especially in the presence of familiar, palatable, and readily available food (Rowland & Antelman, 1976).

Age

Besides the observation that average weight, according to most norms tables, increases with age, there is evidence suggesting that body weight in rats drifts upward with age and that this drift is exacerbated by high-fat diets (Sclafani, 1980). The mechanism by which this drift occurs is not known, but it makes evolutionary sense that set point would be more inclined to gravitate up than down. There are advantages to having increased fat stores as one becomes older and less able to compete for resources. On the other hand, storing a little extra energy when the opportunity arises may be the difference between life and death for the animal when food is scarce.

Smoking Cigarettes

A study by Jacobs and Gottenborg (1981) suggests that smoking may *not* reduce appetite, since smokers were observed to consume about 200 Calories a day more than nonsmokers and yet weighed less. Smoking may account for this difference by increasing metabolic rate. Alternatively, smokers may differ on some other dimension, such as anxiety or activity, which may be responsible for their increased caloric expenditure. In any event, the radical reduction in life expectancy associated with cigarette smoking makes it a deadly alternative to several unwanted pounds.

METABOLIC ADAPTATIONS TO DIETING

At the beginning of embarking on a diet, it may be relatively simple to lose a few pounds as a result of water loss. But after that, the dieter frequently reaches a "plateau" where further weight loss is difficult, even at markedly reduced levels of intake. "The body reacts to stringent dieting as if famine had set in" (Bennett & Gurin, 1982, p. 84). It adapts to the shortage of food by slowing the metabolic rate and conserving Calories, using the limited available energy with increased efficiency. Dieting reduces the metabolic rate by an astounding 15–30% and reduces the number of Calories expended during activity (Apfelbaum, Bostsarron, & Lacatis, 1971; Bray, 1969; Burskirk, Thompson, Lutwak, & Whedon, 1963; Drenick & Dennin, 1973; Sims, 1976). This compensation is found in both normal-weight (Keys et al., 1950) and overweight (Bray, 1969) dieters.

In one study, obese patients were placed on a highly restricted 220-Calorie "protein" diet for 15 days. Even at this extraordinary level of deprivation, the patients only lost, on the average, 170 g (6 oz) of fat per day. Significant metabolic changes occurred even after such a relatively short period of semistarvation. Metabolic rate slowed by almost 1% per day, with a total reduction in energy expenditure at the end of the 2 weeks that ranged from 12% to 17% (Apfelbaum et al., 1971). There is some evidence to suggest that this increased food efficiency may not be just an initial response to a cutback in Calories. In rats, metabolic rate slows further as the length of starvation progresses (Kleiber, 1961). Thus, on a fixed reducing diet where caloric intake is reduced from 2000 to 1500 Calories per day, the amount of weight lost is cut in half each month (Apfelbaum et al., 1971).

In an attempt to explain differences in the rate at which people lose weight, D. S. Miller and Parsonage (1975) looked at women from diet clinics who had already lost a substantial amount of weight, but who were having difficulty reducing further. There was some question as to why these women were unable to shed more weight: Had they experienced some form of metabolic adaptation, or were they inaccurately reporting the number of Calories they were eating? The women were placed on a "well-supervised" 1500-Calorie diet for 3 weeks, at the end of which two-thirds were able to lose more weight. Those women who did not lose more weight were found to have very low metabolic rates, were thinner, had lower percentages of body fat, and had lengthy dieting histories. This association between chronicity of dieting and suppression of metabolism suggests that the longer one diets, the more the body will fight against further weight loss.

There is some evidence to suggest that it is not only the length of dieting that alters fuel efficiency, but also the cycling between dieting and nondieting that has profound effects. With each new diet, weight appears to be lost more slowly and later to be regained more readily. With repeated attempts to restrict food intake, it apparently takes longer for metabolic rate to recover. Moreover, metabolic rate drops more easily when there is a return to dieting (Garrow, 1974). The body becomes adept at responding to marked fluctuations in intake by compensating more quickly for the next cycle of deprivation.

This observation has important implications for understanding the effects of the bulimic's eating cycles. It suggests that weight loss becomes increasingly difficult each time the bulimic embarks on a new diet, and that the Calories ingested during the inevitable binge are less likely to be burned as fuel and are stored more readily by the body as fat. Metabolic rate may remain suppressed because it has no real opportunity to recover.

The impact of these adaptations to reduced intake becomes clear when one considers what happens to weight and metabolic rate during refeeding after dieting. When rats are starved, their weight increases rapidly when they are later fed normal amounts of food. It is well documented that starved animals gain weight at a rate many times that of animals of normal weight fed the same amount (Levitsky, Faust, & Glassman, 1976). In one study, rats that were starved 20% below their normal weight gained 29.6 g during refeeding, while nonstarved animals gained only 1.6 g, even though the starved rats were eating somewhat less. This represents an astounding 18-fold increase in metabolic efficiency following weight loss (Boyle, Storlien, & Keesey, 1978). A more recent investigation reported a 6-fold increase in food efficiency following deprivation in rats (Bjorntorp & Yang, 1982).

This tendency to restore weight rapidly after a period of food restriction followed by a resumption of a normal level of intake has also been demonstrated in hospitalized anorexia nervosa patients. Many patients gain weight at a rate much higher than would be predicted by the number of Calories consumed during refeeding (Pertschuk, Crosby, & Mullen, 1981; Stordy, Marks, Kalucy, & Crisp, 1977). The fact that there is so little correspondence between the level of intake and the amount of weight gained in the weight recovery of women with anorexia nervosa suggests that the body conserves whatever Calories it can get in an attempt to return the starved individual to a more biologically appropriate and stable weight.

The mechanism for this adaptation is not yet well understood, although it is clear that some form of feedback process operates to slow metabolic processes in response to dieting. The net effect of this compensation contradicts the intent of dieting; it predisposes the system to weight gain and excess storage of fat. S. C. Wooley and Wooley (1979) speculate that "in at least some individuals, over-reaction to mild obesity—to a body weight which is within the normal distribution typical of all physical traits—may predispose to further weight gain" (p. 73). They argue that "it seems possible that the loss of 5 pounds may virtually ensure the later gain of 6 so that dieting—the major treatment for obesity—may also be a major cause of obesity" (p. 73). It has been our clinical impression that some women presenting with bulimia have achieved a weight level from bingeing and dieting that is much higher than their premorbid highest weight. Once they have begun to eat "normally" and to minimize the frequency of bulimic episodes, they are often able to maintain a somewhat lower weight without dieting.

EATING BEHAVIOR AND DIETING

The logic of Nisbett's (1972) argument—that the majority of obese resemble starved organisms because of their attempt to suppress their weight below natural levels—may be extended to all chronic dieters, regardless of their weight. Following this reasoning, Herman and Mack (1975) found that dieters displayed eating patterns similar to those previously identified in the obese (Schachter, Goldman, & Gordon, 1968). Herman and Mack divided subjects into habitual dieters (they used the term "restrained eaters") and nondieters ("unrestrained eaters"). Under the guise of a "taste experiment," subjects consumed either one milkshake, two milkshakes, or no milkshakes and then were asked to "taste and rate" several flavors of ice cream. The real purpose of the experiment was to determine the effect of the different preloads on subsequent ice cream consumption. The results were surprising in that the dieters ate *more* following a preload than they did after no milkshake. Nondieters, on the other hand, ate the most when they were not given a preload, less after one milkshake, and still less after two milkshakes. Nondieters seemed to regulate their intake well in these circumstances, while dieters "counterregulated" by eating more if they had already eaten and less if they had not (Herman & Mack, 1975; Hibscher, 1974).

Herman and Polivy (1980) propose that the dieter eats more following a preload because she has already exceeded the number of Calories prescribed by her diet; since she has already "blown it," she feels that she might as well continue eating. Similarly, Mahoney and Mahoney (1976) have described the tendency of perfectionistic dieters to overeat in response to breaking their diet by eating a "forbidden fruit." To test whether it is simply the dieter's *belief* that she has broken her diet that leads to this counterregulation, Polivy (1976) varied the actual caloric content of the preload and the information (or misinformation) that subjects received about its caloric value. Results indicated that dieters ate more when they *believed* that the preload was high in Calories, regardless of the real caloric content. Moreover, it is interesting that when dieters were told that the preload was high in Calories, they substantially overestimated its caloric value. These findings imply that it is not simply the amount of food initially eaten but the belief about the caloric value of the food that "disinhibits" subsequent eating in dieters.

In another series of studies, Herman and Polivy (1980) have found that alcohol, anxiety, and depression also tend to augment the eating of dieters. They reason that these manipulations have a "disinhibitory" effect on eating because they serve to disrupt cognitively mediated self-control processes related to dieting. Although Herman and Polivy tend to emphasize the cognitive component of their model, it would seem that their explanations are most compelling within the larger context of the caloric deprivation experienced by dieters. It requires considerable mental effort to maintain inexorable self-control in the face of mounting biological pressure to eat. Either competing cognitions (e.g., "I have blown it") or potential emotional arousal may lead to the breakdown of the resolve to diet. Any stimulus that impinges on the extremely difficult task of warding off hunger could be capable of "disinhibiting" eating.

DIETING AS A CAUSE OF BINGEING

Several authors have suggested that dieting causes binge eating. The suggestion is based on parallels between the counterregulation displayed by dieters following a preload of food and the clinical syndrome of bulimia (Polivy, 1976; Spencer & Fremouw, 1979; Wardle, 1980). Wardle (1980) found that the incidence of binge eating was much higher among dieting than among nondieting medical students.

In a postal survey of university students, Clarke and Palmer (1983) found a positive relationship between bingeing and dieting on a self-report measure. Although it is not justified to compare the binge eating identified in nonclinical samples of college students with the debilitating episodes of overeating typical of the patient with bulimia, both types of individuals may bring on their conditions by actively restricting their food intake to below the level required for optimal functioning. The more intense or drastic the dieting, the greater the potential for ravenous overconsumption if the cognitive controls begin to break down.

Probably the most compelling evidence that severe dietary restriction causes binge eating comes from the Minnesota semistarvation experiment described earlier (Keys *et al.*, 1950). Many of the men experienced uncomfortable bouts of overeating, which persisted many months after they were given free access to food. Although more overpowering, the Minnesota volunteers' responses to food resembled the "counterregulatory" behavior observed in the dieting experiments just described. However, it is important to note that the volunteers' voracious appetites during rehabilitation occurred in the absence of the cognitive self-control or restraint characteristic of college dieters. Weight suppression is critical in setting the occasion for binge eating, since presumably none of the men engaged in binge eating prior to the semistarvation experiment. Since not all of them succumbed to overconsumption, there are probably individual differences in both biological cravings and cognitive resolves to hold these urges in check.

Further clinical evidence that dieting primes the individual for bingeing may be derived from patients with anorexia nervosa, in which self-imposed starvation is a primary feature. Recent studies have found that between 30–50% of patients referred for anorexia nervosa also have bulimia (Beumont, George, & Smart, 1976; Garfinkel, Moldofsky, & Garner, 1980; Hsu, Crisp, & Harding, 1979). Moreover, the proportion of anorexic patients with bulimia seems to have been increasing steadily in recent years (Casper, 1983a). What is most striking about these bulimic anorexic patients is the sequence of symptom development. Garfinkel *et al.* (1980) found that dieting preceded bingeing, on the average, by more than 1½ years in their sample of bulimic anorexia nervosa patients. Dally and Gomez (1979) found that the gradual breakdown of self-control with the emergence of binge eating typically occurs about 9 months after the initiation of dieting. Crisp (1967) indicates that bulimia is related to chronicity in anorexia nervosa; that is, the longer that the patient has been starved, the more likely it is that she will show bouts of overeating. Similar observations have been made about bulimic patients who have not lost sufficient weight to meet the formal diagnosis of anorexia nervosa. Pyle *et al.* (1981) observed that 88% of their sample of bulimic patients began dieting prior to the onset of binge eating. Fairburn and Cooper (1982) found that over 80% of their sample of bulimic women reported that they were attempting to lose weight when their bingeing began. This pattern has been described in other samples of bulimic women as well (Boskind-Lodahl, 1976). Finally, bingeing is common among obese dieters. In a study of 102 obese individuals seeking treatment for overweight, Gormally, Rardin, and Black (1980) found that 78% were judged as having moderate to severe problems with bingeing.

THE INEFFECTIVENESS OF VOMITING, LAXATIVES, AND DIURETICS IN CONTROLLING WEIGHT

As illustrated in Figure 21-4, the dieting–bingeing–purging cycle is self-perpetuating, since purging effectively eliminates the feedback loop whereby eating would normally cause a reduction in appetite. While vomiting "solves" the short-term problem of

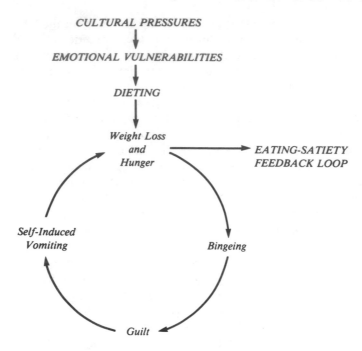

Figure 21-4. The vicious cycle whereby emotional disturbances may both lead to and be perpetuated by the starvation state.

evacuating unwanted food, it does not resolve the mounting hunger. Moreover, vomiting and purgative abuse initially begin as methods of regaining control after overeating; however, these practices soon result in even greater breakdown in controls, since they "legitimize" bingeing. The bingeing–vomiting cycle usually escalates, and the patient eventually loses control in the sense that she feels that she must vomit after every meal. It is not uncommon for patients to become depressed at the realization that bingeing and vomiting are consuming many hours each evening. The expense of food becomes a financial burden, and the dangers of electrolyte disturbances become a significant risk to health. Moreover, vomiting often fails to remove all Calories from the stomach, so frequent bingeing and vomiting may actually lead to weight gain.

Besides being extremely dangerous, laxatives are a completely ineffective method of trying to prevent the absorption of Calories. Laxatives primarily affect the emptying of the large intestine, which occurs *after* Calories from foodstuffs have already been absorbed in the small bowel. A recent study of both bulimic and normal women documented that even extremely large dosages of laxatives do little to impair caloric absorption (Bo-Lynn, Santa-Ana, Morawski, & Fordtran, 1983). One patient consumed 50 Correctol tablets after her meals; although it produced tremendous diarrhea (over 6 L or 6.3 qt), the caloric absorption only decreased by 12%. This amounts to less than 200 Calories, which is the equivalent of one small candy bar! As Bo-Lynn *et al.* (1983) point out, this is a small reward, considering the life-threatening effects of diarrhea plus the effort and expense involved. They reported that both of their bulimic patients discontinued laxative abuse, partly in reaction to the results of the study.

Nevertheless, the misconceptions about the effects of laxatives are widespread among pseudohealth groups. In an informal survey of 10 Dallas area health food stores, Bo-Lynn and his colleagues (1983) found that 9 of the stores represented laxatives as helpful in weight control. It is not clear whether this type of nonsensical advice reflects ignorance or malicious deception aimed at the weight-conscious consumer. However, it is easy to see how patients could be deceived into believing that the laxatives "work," in that they do produce an acute weight loss, which is comprised almost entirely of fluid. This is followed by rebound water retention, which may result in a weight even higher than the original weight.

Similarly, it is not uncommon for women to believe that body fat can be reduced with diuretics. This mistaken belief was shared by 25% of female physical education students in one study (Cho & Fryer, 1974). Diuretics have absolutely no effect on Calories or body fat. Regular use may lead to transient (MacGregor, Markandu, Roulston, Jones, & deWardener, 1979) or persistent water retention (Edwards & Dent, 1979) upon drug withdrawal.

HOW TO DETERMINE AN APPROPRIATE BODY WEIGHT

Those suffering from bulimia, anorexia nervosa, and related disorders are often uncertain about how to determine their proper weight. Until recently, we and other professionals have adopted the convention of determining recommended weight by consulting average weight tables provided by insurance companies. There are several problems with this practice, however. It does not take into consideration that insurance company norms are statistical *averages* (based upon height and age), which reveal nothing about the natural variability in weights around these midpoints. As suggested earlier, weight, like most other physical attributes, naturally varies among all individuals in a population. Deriving desirable weights from an average weight table is as inappropriate as calculating expected heights from average height tables! Figure 21-5 represents the theoretical normal distribution of body weights in the entire population of women, based on the data reported by Sorlic et al. (1980). For each age and height category, the "average weight" represented by the vertical line in the middle of the distribution is the one that is recorded on the tables found in most doctors' offices. Some tables of "desirable weights" are even more unrealistic, since they recommend that people weigh 90% of average weight. It is obvious from Figure 21-5 that there is a natural range in body weights, and that to conclude that there is one "ideal" weight is a gross misinterpretation of insurance company weight tables. This argument, as well as our clinical experience with bulimic patients, has led to a modification of our previous guideline of establishing a treatment goal weight of 90% of average weight (Garfinkel & Garner, 1982). Many bulimic patients have a personal and family history of overweight, and 90% of average or even "average" weight is not realistic. They must settle at a higher weight than they would prefer in order to reduce the biological pressure to overeat.

Our general recommendation is to establish a "goal weight range" of about 2.3 kg (5 lb) that is about 10% below the patient's highest weight prior to the onset of her eating disorder. This is simply a guideline and may have to be modified, based on the patient's weight and eating history. For example, some patients have had brief periods of rapid weight gain prior to the onset of their disorder, and 90% of the highest weight may be unrealistically inflated. Others may have always dieted, so that they

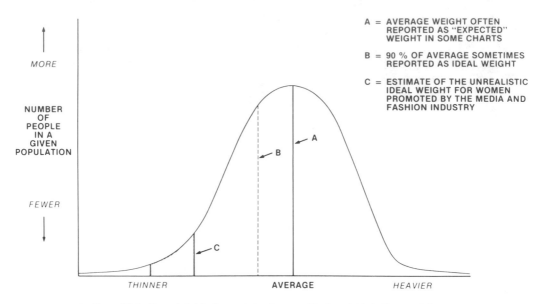

Figure 21-5. Normal distribution or natural range of body weights in the population.

never have experienced a healthy or natural weight. However, consistent with our recommendation, Abraham and Beumont (1982) indicate that the "previous stable weight" for a group of bulimic patients is almost precisely 90% of their "highest weight ever attained." Moreover, we have found that one of the most powerful predictors of disturbed eating in ballet dancers is a weight below 90% of highest adult weight.

Rather than establishing an exact weight expectation for some patients, it is far preferable to help them to allow their weight to settle at a level that does not require chronic dieting to maintain. This involves their consuming appropriate quantities of food, as well as gaining control of bingeing and vomiting; weight will probably drift upward and then settle at a level that their bodies find comfortable. Very often, this corresponds to about 90% of highest weight. Initially, most patients react negatively to these recommendations, since it usually means accepting a weight higher than that which is preferred. Most patients with bulimia would prefer to be between 3 and 7 kg (6.6 and 15.4 lb) thinner than their current weight. If they are satisfied with their current weight, it is almost invariably lower than their biologically natural or "healthy weight" (Russell, 1979).

Galvanizing patients into making a commitment to a higher weight, despite prevailing social pressures and "diet specialists" who offer promises of happiness at a lower weight, is difficult indeed; however, it is one of the most important ingredients in overcoming bulimia. It is our impression that the bulimic's ultimate success is in large part related to her willingness gradually to compromise on the issue of body weight. A staunch refusal to compromise, despite the recognition that it may lead to a reduction of bingeing, purging, and other symptoms, is an ominous sign. It must be pointed out that this does not mean that all patients are irrevocably destined to remain at a weight that they find unacceptable. In many instances, we have found that once the patient truly accepts the *possibility* that her weight may have to be higher, and once she resolves that she is no longer willing to sacrifice her personal health or comfort for a lower weight, an important battle has been won. Many patients actually lose weight once the bingeing ceases and normal eating begins.

WATER BALANCE AND THE SCALE

For many women, the scale has become a daily emotional barometer, in the sense that their morning weight significantly influences their mood or self-confidence for the rest of the day. The 1984 *Glamour* survey found that 63% of the female respondents answered "often" and 33% "sometimes" to the question "Does your weight affect how you feel about yourself?" For many women, losing several pounds is followed by elation, pride, and self-assurance; gaining results in depression, self-loathing, and curtailing of social plans. This practice of ascribing surplus meaning to "feedback" from the scale is exaggerated by those with bulimia, anorexia nervosa, and related disorders.

Not only is using weight to infer self-worth a gross oversimplification but weight is also an extremely unreliable measure of body fat. No less than 50% of the total body weight for females is water. Much of the weight lost during the initial phase of dieting is due to dehydration, particularly for diets involving extreme reductions in overall Calories or carbohydrates (Apfelbaum, 1976; Van Itallie & Yang, 1977). This is the key to the fantastic claims of most fad diets. They result in immediate "success"; however, the bulk of weight lost is due to loss of water rather than fat. After the first week or so, there is a remarkable slowing of weight loss; sometimes there is even weight gain, despite rigid adherence to the diet. Unfortunately, most dieters interpret this failure as somehow related to a lapse in will power.

In bulimic patients, fluctuations in water balance are further magnified by vomiting and purgative abuse. As explained earlier, this occurs because these behaviors lead to temporary dehydration, followed by "rebound" water retention. To the degree that the bulimic's feelings about herself are tied to the scale, she is destined to an endless ride on an emotional roller coaster. When patients begin treament for bulimia, we usually recommend that they discontinue weighing themselves at home, but that they be weighed on a weekly basis by their therapist or someone else whom they trust. This helps to reduce the panic resulting from transient or small increases in weight. Many of our patients report being relieved of the burden of weighing themselves every day; some have commemorated their resolve to avoid these daily weighings by donating their scales to our rather impressive "scale museum." Emphasis instead is placed upon normalizing food intake and discontinuing vomiting or purgative abuse.

Some patients prefer to be informed of their weight each week, so that potential distress may be addressed in therapy. Others who tend to become preoccupied with minute shifts in weight prefer to be "blind" to the weighings and to be informed only if there is a consistent trend up or down over several weeks.

In summary, the following principles may serve as general guidelines for establishing and monitoring body weight:

1. It is preferable to avoid choosing a specific goal weight and simply to concentrate on normal eating, as well as on discontinuing bingeing and purging.

2. Weight often varies, due to daily fluctuations in water balance and the contents of the digestive tract; thus, a realistic weight range rather than a specific weight should be determined.

3. The goal weight range should take into consideration a personal or family history of obesity.

4. A goal weight range that is 10% below one's highest weight prior to the onset of eating problems often serves as a good estimate of the weight that can be maintained without extreme dieting.

5. Weight should be monitored once a week, preferably by a trusted therapist.

RECOMMENDATIONS FOR CONTROLLING BINGEING AND VOMITING

Russell (1979) has indicated that the bulimic's "cravings for food are the result of her starved body rebelling and demanding to be fed" (p. 447). As mentioned earlier, tremendous mental effort is required to hold these urges in check. Most bulimic patients begin vomiting and laxative abuse because they appear to be solutions to the dilemma posed by their appetite on the one hand and their terror of weight gain on the other. Prior to the discovery of vomiting, overeating is avoided for the most part because of the anxiety and guilt that it elicits. In this sense, vomiting actually comes to "reinforce" or legitimize overeating by reducing anxiety and guilt. Not having to pay the caloric consequences of eating usually leads to an escalation in the frequency, duration, and amount eaten during bulimic episodes.

If vomiting is prohibited for some reason, bingeing usually subsides, even though the urge to overeat persists. We have seen many patients who have attempted but quickly given up self-induced vomiting because they were unable to elicit the gag reflex or because they found the process of vomiting repulsive. This provides support for the contention that in most cases bingeing is maintained by vomiting (Garner, Garfinkel, & Bemis, 1982; W. G. Johnson & Brief, 1983; Rosen & Leitenberg, 1982; Russell, 1979). In these instances, it also explains why initial attempts to resist vomiting are so difficult: They involve contending with tremendous anxiety following the consumption of certain foods that have come to be seen as "fattening." Unfortunately, the avoidance of these foods eliminates the opportunity to dispel the irrational fear that they will inevitably lead to obesity.

Rosen and Leitenberg (see Chapter 9, this volume) have suggested that, in addition to the anxiety reduction model described above, binge eating may be explained by the eating-habit control and interpersonal stress models. According to the eating habit control model, binge eating is precipitated by drastic dieting and vomiting, which develop as a method of controlling weight (Wardle, 1980; Wardle & Beinart, 1981). According to the interpersonal stress model, binge eating is triggered by negative feelings, such as depression, anxiety, or anger resulting from relationship problems (Abraham & Beumont, 1982; Clement & Hawkins, 1980; Lacey, 1982 and Chapter 18, this volume). Binge eating is maintained because it temporarily reduces the stress that results from negative feelings and interpersonal events. The development of more adequate coping strategies is advocated as a solution to binge eating and vomiting.

In our experience, many interpersonal, emotional, or situational factors may trigger bingeing and vomiting, but all these must be understood within the context of drastic dieting. It must be remembered that bingeing is an unlikely response in those who are depressed, anxious, or stressed unless they have been dieting. Moreover, binge eating and self-induced vomiting may be motivated by a combination of the factors or even by different factors from those described above. For example, self-induced vomiting is occasionally maintained by positive contingencies rather than anxiety avoidance. One patient claimed that vomiting even after small meals was appealing because it made her feel virtuous by allowing her to meet her stringent dieting objectives. Self-induced vomiting, as well as many of the other symptoms exhibited by the anorexic or bulimic patient, may be activated by self-administered positive reinforcement (Garner & Bemis, 1982 and Chapter 6, this volume; Slade, 1982). Other patients describe vomiting as an indirect means of punishing others or even themselves for perceived wrongdoings. One patient openly admitted that her vomiting had become an act of defiance against her controlling mother. It was preferred over more conventional forms of adolescent rebellion because it could be defined as an "involuntary symptom" of illness.

Despite the variety of possible explanations for bingeing and vomiting, not all of which have been presented here, there are a number of clear therapeutic guidelines that may be followed in attempting to interrupt the process. For most patients, self-induced vomiting is connected to the fear of weight gain and the specific belief that the wrong type or quantity of food has been consumed. As stated before, rigid dieting has resulted in avoidance of any foods that may be construed as "fattening." The majority of bulimic patients experience tremendous anxiety at the suggestion that they give up dieting. They firmly believe that once they allow themselves to eat the foods they crave, they will lose all self-control and continue to gain weight indefinitely. One of the ultimate goals of recovery is the *freedom from dieting* that results from the recognition that virtually every type of food may be consumed in moderation without dramatic weight gain. For most patients with severely disturbed eating patterns, relearning "nondieting" food preferences and allowing food intake to be determined ultimately by internal signals of hunger and satiety is a long and frustrating struggle. Initial attempts to deviate from highly structured rules for dieting may result in panic or confusion. Some patients have dieted for so many years that they simply do not know any other system of eating. They are continually plagued with the temptation to restrict intake when they feel fat, insecure, or otherwise uncomfortable. For some, the virtuous feeling of self-control at oral self-restraint has been the only reliable source of pleasure they have experienced for years.

The first step on the road to recovery is an understanding of the biological and cultural factors contributing to disturbed eating patterns, as outlined earlier. Next, it is necessary to dispel several common myths that pervade the thinking of most eating-disordered patients. These faulty beliefs, as well as methods for their correction, have been presented elsewhere (Fairburn, 1982; Garner & Bemis, 1982 and Chapter 6, this volume; Garner *et al.*, 1982; Guidano and Liotti, 1983); however, one myth that repeatedly emerges during the course of recovery is some variant of the following: *It is possible to recover while still dieting and occasionally vomiting.*

We have found that many patients seek treatment because of the distress elicited by bingeing, but they balk at the suggestion that dieting and vomiting must be attacked with equal vigor. Throughout treatment, the fact that dieting and vomiting are inconsistent with recovery must be pointed out. There may be many obstacles and backslidings on the road to recovery, but the commitment to all of the principles of recovery must be frequently reemphasized. In our opinion, this must be done without creating excessive guilt for relapses. Abstinence from dieting and vomiting should be *strongly encouraged*, because they are inconsistent with ultimate recovery; however, we disagree with those who *insist* upon abstinence as a prerequisite for treatment (Mitchell *et al.*, Chapter 11, this volume), for several reasons.

First, in our experience, some patients who appear initially unable to eliminate bingeing and vomiting are subsequently able to discontinue these behaviors. Later in treatment, with the development of a trusting therapeutic relationship and the integration of the principles of recovery, the strong encouragement to abstain is more consistent with the patient's capacity for change.

Second, we are concerned about the negative psychological impact of the practice of dividing patients into "abstinent" or "nonabstinent" groups or of requesting that patients leave treatment because of symptomatic behavior (Mitchell *et al.*, Chapter 11, this volume). This may generate even further guilt and despair in a person already suffering from abysmally low self-esteem. For those who relapse often, we prefer to emphasize repeatedly the contradiction between their apparent values—the wish to recover on the one hand, and their persistent vomiting on the other. If symptoms continue despite a strong wish to recover, hospitalization may be offered as the only realistic alternative. The sincerity of the motivation to recover must be questioned in those who refuse hospitalization at this point. For these patients, the "secondary gain" from symptoms may be playing an instrumental role in the maintenance of the disorder. This should be discussed openly within therapy; it may lead to the patient's withdrawal from treatment because of a recognition that she is really unwilling to part with her symptoms at this point. The invitation for return to treatment is always left open should her feelings change.

Once bingeing and vomiting have been interrupted, it often takes many months for psychological and possibly physical cravings for particular foods to subside. During this time, patients are constantly battling with the decision whether or not to eat. Therefore, one of the fundamental principles on the road to recovery is that eating must become "mechanical" in the sense that it is determined by a definite and predetermined plan. Early in treatment, the patient should make every attempt to avoid decisions about eating, since making such decisions will lead to drifting back into dieting or eating more than prescribed. The meal plan should be discussed at weekly meetings, and adjustments should not be made prior to consultation with the therapist. This type of structure is relatively easy to impose in an inpatient setting and usually leads to rapid compliance with normal eating patterns. The difference for outpatients is that the structure must depend on cognitive rather than behavioral controls.

Prevention of Bingeing and Vomiting

A number of authors have recommended meal-planning techniques in the treatment of bulimia (Fairburn, Chapter 8, this volume; Lacey, 1983 and Chapter 18, this volume; Mitchell *et al.*, Chapter 11, this volume; S. C. Wooley & Wooley, Chapter 17, this volume). The details of different meal-planning methods vary somewhat; however, the structure they impose appears to be very helpful.

MEALS: QUANTITY

The number of Calories prescribed will vary, depending on the patient's weight, metabolic condition, current eating patterns, and tolerance for change. The general rule is that the amount eaten should be consistent (i.e., mechanical) and sufficient ultimately to reduce hunger. As illustrated in the Minnesota study of semistarvation (Keys *et al.*, 1950), urges to overeat may take considerable time to normalize. Emaciated patients may actually become *more* hungry once they begin to increase their food intake. Most patients who gradually gain weight through consistent and planned overconsumption experience a marked reduction in hunger once their weight reaches a normal level. The number of Calories should be adjusted weekly to promote gain at the rate of 0.5–1 kg (1.1 to 2.2 lb) a week. As the patient shifts from a hypometabolic to a hypermetabolic state, daily consumption may be as high as 3500 Calories. If the patient has a personal or family history of obesity, it will usually take fewer Calories to accomplish the desired rate of weight gain. Nonemaciated bulimic patients should be encouraged to maintain or gain weight gradually by consuming no fewer than 1800 to 2400 Calories every day. It is totally inappropriate to replace bingeing and vomiting with a weight-reducing diet. The intense urges to binge will decrease only after a prolonged period during which the caloric intake is biologically and psychologically satisfying. Bingeing becomes much less attractive if plenty of food may be legitimately consumed every day. Many patients find that consuming substantially more Calories than they did while "dieting" leads to little or no weight gain. This may be related to the fact that once they cease absorbing unnecessary Calories through bingeing and vomiting (some Calories are usually retained in the stomach after vomiting), they have more Calories available at mealtime. Also, increases in eating may result in increases in metabolic rate, which make it possible to ingest more food without gaining weight. Studies described earlier have demonstrated that virtually the same weight can be maintained with consistent differences in caloric intake because of adaptive shifts in metabolic rate.

MEALS: QUALITY

Most patients begin treatment with a variety of misconceptions about food and eating. Many of these are absolutistic interpretations of sensible guidelines for eating. These include the following: broiling and baking rather than frying; consumption of unlimited vegetables without butter; salads with little or no dressing, and sugar substitutes only; obsessive avoidance of red meat, sweets, "junk food," "empty Calories," and carbohydrates. The only foods that do not elicit guilt are those that may be considered Calorie-sparing. The result is a rather unappealing but "safe" dietary program. It is the strength and the rigidity of the patient's convictions that distinguish between the "hard-core dieter" and the person with a formal eating disorder. For the latter, these strict rules are applied to everything consumed, with transgressions being followed by unbearable guilt, anxiety, and attempts to undo the damage by purging.

Most patients begin treatment with considerable confusion about what constitutes "normal" eating. They must slowly learn how to feel more relaxed eating a wide range of foods. The weekly meal plan should gradually incorporate small amounts of previously avoided foods, even if the patient assumes that the reason for her avoidance is legitimately related to "healthy" preferences. Food preferences prior to the onset of the eating disorder may serve as a guideline in establishing an appropriate menu. Patients must be encouraged to challenge their tendency to divide food into "good" and "bad" categories by recognizing that the Calories of those foods previously considered "bad" have no greater impact on weight than the most Calorie-sparing items. Bulimic patients should consume small amounts of the food typically reserved for bingeing episodes. These foods should be redefined as "medication" that will help inoculate them against bingeing by reducing psychological cravings and by establishing new response tendencies to food that previously only denoted a "blown" diet (Fairburn, 1982; Garner *et al.*, 1982; Mahoney & Mahoney, 1976; Russell, 1979).

Challenging specific irrational beliefs about food may require some specialized knowledge of nutritional issues. We often recommend that therapists engage in selective reading in order to develop the necessary background to help patients combat food myths. Finally, persistent patterns of distorted thinking about food may reflect a more basic tendency toward faulty reasoning. Using principles derived from A. T. Beck's (1976) cognitive approach, we have identified misconceptions that are very common with eating-disordered patients (Garner & Bemis, 1982 and Chapter 6, this volume; Garner *et al.*, 1982). Resistance to experimenting with different types of foods may require the application of these more powerful cognitive–behavioral methods.

MEALS: SPACING

Many anorexic and bulimic patients tend to "save" their Calories for later in the day, with the hope that they may be able to avoid eating altogether. Others save their meager allotment of food with the hope that a substantial evening meal will pacify their voracious appetites.

In many cases, however, the mounting hunger during a day of starvation leads to overconsumption in the evening. On occasion, this oscillation between starving and overconsumption has resulted in patients' gaining weight to well above their highest weight prior to the onset of bulimia. One of our patients developed a pattern in which she avoided eating until 10:00 P.M. each evening and then ravenously ate approximately 3000 Calories of food before bedtime. She felt bloated and uncomfortable throughout the next morning, but began to experience gnawing hunger early in the afternoon. The next 8–10 hours of starvation were followed by another bout of overeating. Although a strict interpretation of set point theory might argue against this consistent pattern's leading to obesity, it appears that in at least some instances, the periods of vast overconsumption override the adaptive mechanisms that normally control body weight.

Thus, proper spacing of meals should be strongly encouraged; three or four meals daily are preferable to the same number of Calories ingested in one large feast. Eating may have to be rigidly tied to specific times during the day in order to reduce the unwitting tendency to delay eating. The rationale for proper spacing of meals goes beyond the obvious goal of reducing hunger. Frequent eating takes advantage of diet-induced thermogenesis (Goldman *et al.*, 1976; D. S. Miller, 1973). More Calories are burned (more to enjoy) by frequent "stoking of the furnace" with fuel. Probably the most compelling argument for proper spacing of meals through more frequent eating is that consuming the same number of Calories in fewer meals appears to lead to a greater accumulation of body fat. In a now classic experiment, Cohn and Joseph (1959) allowed one group of rats to "nibble" food freely throughout the day, which is natural for this species. A second group was "pair-fed" the same number of Calories per day, but in the form of large meals only twice daily. Although the two groups weighed the same amount after 2 weeks, the meal-fed animals had accumulated more than *three times* as much body fat as the rats that spread their Calories over more frequent meals.

Finally, short-term fasting (i.e., skipping breakfast) has been found to affect problem-solving ability adversely in children (Pollitt, Lewis, Garza, & Shulman, 1983). There is no reason to assume that the impact of fasting on cognitive functioning is any less dramatic for adults.

RECORD KEEPING

Many patients find record keeping helpful in establishing a more appropriate eating routine, as well as in monitoring the circumstances and feelings associated with bingeing, vomiting, or laxative abuse. The recommendation that patients complete a structured daily diary has been popular (Fairburn, 1982; Lacey, 1983 and Chapter 18, this volume; Long & Cordle, 1982; Loro & Orleans, 1981; Mitchell, Pyle, & Eckert, 1981; Mitchell et al., Chapter 11, this volume; Mizes & Lohr, 1983; Welch, 1979). We have encouraged self-monitoring with the form illustrated in Figure 21-6. These forms may be voluntarily shared with the therapist on a regular basis, so that recommendations may be made to help patients achieve greater understanding and control over their disturbed eating. Such sharing presupposes a collaborative therapeutic relationship based upon mutual trust.

At least in the short term, the process of self-monitoring apparently leads to a reduction in the frequency of bingeing and vomiting. Bulimic patients who are requested to engage in self-monitoring prior to treatment experience a 25–30% decrease in symptoms (C. Johnson, Connors, & Stuckey, 1983). The reasons for this decline are probably complex; however, its occurrence indicates that many patients may be able to exert at least temporary control over their symptomatic behavior.

The structure imposed by self-monitoring allows most patients to depart from their rigid rules about food, with the security that they will not be allowed to go too far in the direction of over- or underconsuming. This structure also may facilitate the identification of recurrent situations or mood states that seem to lead to disturbed eating patterns. The records often allow the discovery of temporal connections between binge eating and particular events, moods, or behavior. Moreover, beliefs and assumptions pertaining to these circumstances may be explored in greater detail in an effort to develop more realistic methods of coping.

Interruption at the Prebinge Stage

As a result of self-monitoring, most bulimic patients learn to identify situations that increase their vulnerability to binge eating. Nonetheless, they will continue to experience periodic pressure to binge. Specific stategies may be implemented to control the impulse to engage in bingeing and purging.

DAILY RECORD

DATE	FOOD & LIQUID CONSUMED	CALORIES (OPTIONAL)	URGE TO BINGE OR PURGE: RATE DEGREE, 1-100 %	INCIDENCE (CHECK)	1) THOUGHTS, EMOTIONS 2) METHODS USED TO AVOID DYSFUNCTIONAL BEHAVIOR

Figure 21-6. Form for self-monitoring daily eating routines.

552

DISTRACTION

The impulse to binge may be interrupted by the simple "palliative technique" of distraction (Garner & Bemis, Chapter 6, this volume). In general, the distractions must involve an activity that is salient enough, at least for the moment, to override anxiety and maladaptive thoughts that lead to bingeing. Going for a walk, making a telephone call to a friend, listening to loud music, watching television, or engaging in vigorous activity may provide potent enough distraction to reduce the impact of intrusive thoughts or strong urges to vomit.

DELAY

Similarly, by delaying bingeing or vomiting, many patients find that the strong urge to engage in these behaviors subsides. Such delay may be facilitated by constructing a short list of alternative behaviors that must be performed prior to bingeing or vomiting. This predetermined repertoire of behaviors should be as enjoyable and self-enhancing as possible. One patient decided to listen to a favorite song and read one page of poetry before she would consider vomiting. This procedure seemed to break the familiar chain of events surrounding bingeing and vomiting, and it led to a reduction in symptoms. With some patients, it is helpful for the list of prebinge behaviors to be written on a "mnemonic card," which may be consulted when thinking becomes confused because of overwhelming postmeal anxiety. Delaying strategies are particularly valuable for those who find it too threatening to make a commitment to eliminate vomiting.

PARROTING

In the presence of overwhelming anxiety related to eating, patients are often unable to employ more sophisticated methods of challenging their irrational thoughts about eating. We have encouraged patients to evoke certain predetermined "coping phrases" aimed at the avoidance of destructive behaviors that could sabotage weeks of therapeutic progress (Garner & Bemis, Chapter 6, this volume). In difficult situations, this may involve covert rehearsal of such phrases as these: "These foods will not lead to radical weight gain," "Vomiting now will only increase its likelihood later," "Eating is part of getting better; I must take food like medication," "Regardless of what I feel, I am at an appropriate weight." "Palliative techniques" such as those mentioned above are most useful in early stages of therapy, when reasoning capacity may be diminished, or in later stages, when the patient is already committed to abstaining from vomiting but is temporarily overwhelmed by anxiety in a particularly difficult situation. Essentially, these methods "involve forcefully 'changing the cognitive channel' rather than attempting to modify beliefs" through the more systematic application of cognitive techniques (Garner & Bemis, Chapter 6, p. 122). They are useful in overcoming a temporary lapse in motivation, but are ineffective if the patient is in complete disagreement with the parroted phrase or the purpose behind delaying maladaptive behavior.

Postbinge Sequence: Breaking the Cycle

The primary aim of the postrelapse sequence is to challenge the beliefs or assumptions following an episode of bingeing and purging, which, if unchecked, tend to perpetuate the escalating cycle. Most patients construe a failure in a way that makes them more vulnerable to further episodes. Some errors in thinking reflect more general cognitive distortions (e.g., dichotomous reasoning, overgeneralization) that have been described in patients with eating disorders (Fairburn, Chapter 8, this volume; Garner & Bemis, 1982, and Chapter 6, this volume; Garner *et al.*, 1982). Erroneous beliefs that predispose bulimic patients to further relapses include the following:

- My binge has spoiled all of my progress to date — now I must start over from square one.
- Now that I have "blown it," I might as well give up.
- Since I binged this morning, the rest of the day is ruined, so I might as well binge again.
- My binge this afternoon is evidence that I fail at everything.
- Since I could not stop bingeing today, I will never be able to recover.

Magnifying the significance of failure to control bingeing and vomiting undermines self-esteem. The spurious conclusion that "it doesn't matter any more" leads to a sense of hopelessness and despair, which may promote further symptomatic behavior. Moreover, further bingeing may be elicited, because it provides temporary distraction from unpleasant feelings. With practice, patients usually improve in their ability to interrupt a vicious spiral downward by monitoring and challenging self-defeating beliefs.

It must be recognized that bulimia has evolved as a response to complex biological, social, and psychological forces; there will inevitably be periodic relapses. Progress is rarely linear in nature; more commonly, it follows an erratic pattern in which ultimate success can only be measured amidst intermittent failures. Since recovery is a gradual process, there must be preparation for relapse. Bingeing and vomiting should not be taken casually; however, patients should be discouraged from overinterpreting the significance of either success or failure. These are not always reliable indices of one's psychological status. Instead, the task is to recover immediately from each relapse by reinstituting all of the behaviors described in the preceding sections. One of the most common reactions to an episode of bingeing and vomiting is to make compensatory adjustments in subsequent meal plans. Patients frequently will feel compelled to skip the next meal or to abandon eating for the entire day after binge eating. Such punitive measures initiate the oscillating pattern of over- and undereating and virtually guarantee a repetition of the self-defeating sequence of behaviors. Relapse must be followed by the commitment to begin at the first step of prevention — consuming the entire next meal without avoiding any of the foods outlined in the meal plan.

COMPLICATIONS OF BULIMIA

In addition to the physiological factors that may contribute to the development and maintenance of bulimia, there are serious physical complications that should be considered. It is our belief that the understanding of these risks play a major role in solidifying many patients' commitment to abstain from or drastically reduce bingeing and purging. Moreover, a thorough understanding of these dangers is essential for the clinician treating bulimia.

Electrolyte Disturbances

Probably the most dangerous complication of vomiting and purgative abuse is the depletion of the electrolytes potassium, chloride, and sodium. These elements, among others, are called electrolytes because they have the property of carrying electrical charges when they are dissolved in solution. They are essential to the organism for metabolic processes, as well as for the normal functioning of nerve and muscle cells. Frequent vomiting, laxative abuse, and diuretic abuse can lead to the depletion of sodium, potassium, and chloride. Alkaline intoxication may result from the loss of sodium (hypoatremic alkalosis), chloride (hypochloremic alkalosis), or potassium (hypokalemic alkalosis). The mechanisms responsible for these changes are complex, the medical consequences are extremely dangerous (Mitchell, Pyle, Eckert, Hatsukami, & Lentz, 1983). Electrolyte abnormalities may cause weakness, tiredness, constipation, and depression (Webb & Gehi, 1981). Moreover, as described below, they may result in cardiac arrhythmias and sudden death. Mitchell *et al.* (1983) have found electrolyte disturbances in almost 49% of their nonanorexic patients with bulimia. These abnormalities were clearly related to frequency of self-induced vomiting.

Cardiac Irregularities

Undoubtedly many of the deaths in anorexia nervosa and bulimia are the consequences of cardiac abnormalities (see Garfinkel & Garner, 1982). Starvation seriously compromises cardiac functioning in many cases, and this, compounded by electrolyte disturbances, may result in serious irregularities in the heartbeat. Profound heart abnormalities have been observed during exercise and these may be associated with sudden death. In a postmortem study of three women who died with anorexia nervosa, Isner, Roberts, Yager, and Heymsfield (1984) identified a potentially fatal slowdown in the electrical impulses that signal the heart to contract and relax. This particular electrical disturbance, called "QT internal prolongation," may result in one of the most lethal forms of irregular heartbeat, malignant cardiac arrhythmias. If not treated within several minutes, such arrhythmias can result in sudden death. Occasionally patients attempt to induce vomiting by ingesting an emetic such as ipecac. This may have fatal consequences. Adler, Walinsky, Krall, and Cho (1980) have described a bulimic patient who died of cardiac arrest following repeated use of an emetic. Brotman, Forbath, Garfinkel, and Humphrey (1981) have also described a bulimic patient who developed progressive muscle weakness and cardiac abnormalities following ipecac abuse.

Another case report describes a 23-year-old university student who died of cardiac arrest while participating in a drug study at the National Institutes of Health (Kolata, 1980). The woman failed to reveal her history of self-induced vomiting to the investigators and volunteered to take the mood-stabilizing drug lithium, as well as another experimental drug. It was concluded that the cardiac arrest was the direct result of hypokalemia from both vomiting and lithium (which also tends to deplete the body of potassium). Aside from demonstrating our point, this tragic case should also serve as a caution, since some investigators have recently recommended lithium as a treatment for bulimia.

Kidney Dysfunction

Kidney disturbances occur in some patients and are probably related to chronic hypokalemia. Russell (1979) has described three patients who required treatment for urinary tract infections. Kidney damage has been reported in patients with potassium deficiencies (Russell, 1979; Wigley 1960; Wolff *et al.*, 1968). After 8 years of self-induced vomiting, one of Russell's patients developed kidney failure and ultimately required a kidney transplant. Even after recovering from the operation, she still engaged in occasional episodes of self-induced vomiting.

Neurological Abnormalities

Abnormal electrical discharges in the brain are common in some patients with bulimia. They are usually associated with electrolyte disturbances (Mitchell & Pyle, 1982). Epileptic seizures have been reported in 4 of 30 cases described by Russell (1979). Muscular spasms (tetany) and tingling sensations in the extremities (peripheral paraesthesias) have also been described (Fairburn, 1982; Russell, 1979).

Swollen Salivary Glands

A painless swelling of the salivary glands and accompanying facial swelling have been reported in patients with bulimia (Levin, Falko, Dixon, Gallup, & Saunders, 1980; Pyle *et al.*, 1981; Russell, 1979; B. T. Walsh *et al.*, 1981). Salivary glands tend to return to normal with the discontinuation of bulimia and vomiting, although in some cases the swelling may persist (B. T. Walsh *et al.*, 1981). The mechanisms for this abnormality are not known, although it has been speculated that it may be related to electrolyte disturbances, physical irritation of the glands through vomiting, endocrine dysfunction, or nutritional deficiencies (B. T. Walsh *et al.*, 1981).

Gastrointestinal Disturbances

Frequently patients complain of abdominal pain due to the physical trauma of vomiting. Repeated self-induced vomiting occasionally results in the development of spontaneous regurgitation of food, which may perpetuate the disorder. Episodes of extreme bulimia may lead to severe abdominal discomfort. There have been numerous case reports of extreme expansion of the stomach (gastric dilatation) due to binge eating (e.g., Mitchell, Pyle, & Miner, 1982; Russell, 1966); such expansion has led to stomach rupture and death in some instances (Matikainen, 1979; Saul, Dekker, & Watson, 1981). Russell (1979) has commented on the possibility of permanent loss of bowel reactivity with chronic abuse of laxatives. Some patients who have become dependent on laxatives for bowel functioning experience constipation once they discontinue the medication; however, in most instances bowel functioning returns with normal eating. Self-induced vomiting may also lead to serious tearing of tissue in the mouth and throat. Patients may choke on instruments that they have been using to attempt to induce vomiting, as well as on the vomitus itself.

Dental Deterioration

Many chronic bulimic patients begin to notice the deterioration of their teeth. Tooth color changes from white to brown or grey, and complications may require extensive dental work or removal of the teeth. The gastric acid from self-induced vomiting is reponsible for general dental erosion and loss of enamel. This erosion results in caries and periodontal disease (Brady, 1980; Stege, Visco-Dangler, & Rye, 1982).

Finger Clubbing or Swelling

Finger clubbing or swelling has been observed in several cases as a consequence of chronic laxative abuse (Malmquist, Ericsson, Hulten-Nosslin, Jeppsson, & Ljungberg, 1980; Prior & White, 1978; Silk, Gibson, & Murray, 1975). This condition gradually reverses itself once laxatives are discontinued.

Edema and Dehydration

Dieting, vomiting, and laxative or diuretic abuse often lead to alternating periods of dehydration and "rebound" excessive water retention (Fairburn, 1982). The dehydration is indicated by tremendous thirst and reduced urinary output. Many patients notice swelling or "puffiness" in their fingers, ankles, and faces as a result of edema. Edema is usually at its worst immediately after vomiting and laxative abuse have *ceased*. Some bulimic patients will gain between 2.3 and 4.5 kg (5 and 10 lb) of water once they refrain from these abnormal weight control practices. Normalization of intake and discontinuation of vomiting and purgatives will gradually reduce the wide swings in water balance; however, patience is essential. Many bulimic patients become so alarmed at the sudden weight gain or swelling that they return to vomiting or laxatives before their bodies have had a chance to achieve balance; this starts the cycle all over again.

Emotions

There have been no systematic studies of the effects of electrolyte disturbances on emotions; however, it is our impression that depression, anxiety, and general malaise are either created or aggravated by the metabolic abnormalities. Most bulimic patients not only feel badly about their behavior, but also experience a general lack of psychological well-being, which they can link to episodes of vomiting and purgative abuse.

Menstruation

Finally, menstrual irregularities and amenorrhea are common among bulimia patients, even if their weight is within normal limits. In a self-report survey of 50 cases of bulimia, C. Johnson, Stuckey, Lewis, and Schwartz (1983) found that 20% of the sample had experienced amenorrhea following the onset of eating problems and that over 50% were experiencing menstrual irregularity at the time of the survey.

PSYCHOLOGICAL FACTORS IN EATING DISORDERS

The purpose of this chapter has been to review specific biological and social factors that play a role in the genesis and perpetuation of bulimia and anorexia nervosa. We have proposed that disturbed eating patterns may be viewed as a tragic yet logical consequence of the conflict between current social norms and biological realities; this explanation does not necessarily imply the presence of fundamental psychopathology.

While it is undeniable that social factors have contributed to the recent increase in eating disorders, anorexia nervosa has been described in cultures and at times in history where the values have been very different from those operating today. We have attempted to present a more balanced view:

Cultural influences do not in a precise sense *cause* serious eating disorders like bulimia and anorexia nervosa. Culture is mediated by the psychology of the individual as well as the more immediate social context of the family. Both individual and family characteristics may be either predisposing or protecting for any particular disorder. (Garner, Garfinkel, & Olmsted, 1983, p. 79)

Extensive clinical and empirical evidence indicates that psychological disturbance is central to the development of anorexia nervosa and bulimia in many individuals. Despite the selective focus of this chapter, it would be a serious misrepresentation not to highlight some of the psychological characteristics that have been linked to eating disorders. The following is hardly an exhaustive review, but it may be useful in directing the reader to relevant source material.

Body Image

Body disparagement may be culturally determined, but the magnitude of self-loathing observed in eating-disordered patients is exceptional (Casper, Offer, & Ostrov, 1981; Garner & Garfinkel, 1981; Garner, Olmsted, & Polivy, 1983). The tendency for anorexia nervosa patients to overestimate the size of their own bodies was originally observed clinically by Bruch (1962) and since then has been well documented (Casper, Halmi, Goldberg, Eckert, & Davis, 1979; Crisp & Kalucy, 1974; Freeman, Thomas, Solyom, & Miles, 1983; Garfinkel, Moldofsky, & Garner, 1977; Garner, Garfinkel, Stancer, & Moldofsky, 1976; Goldberg, Halmi, Casper, Eckert, & Davis, 1977; Pierloot & Houben, 1978; Slade & Russell, 1973; Strober, 1981a; Strober, Goldenberg, Green, & Saxon, 1979; Wingate & Christie, 1978; for a review, see Garner & Garfinkel, 1981). Although Hsu (1980) has recently questioned the validity of the evidence for body image distortion in anorexia nervosa, the finding that self-overestimation is highly predictive of poor prognosis at a 1-year follow-up (Garfinkel *et al.*, 1977) argues for the utility of the concept in the study of eating disorders.

Internal Perceptions

Bruch (1962) hypothesized that anorexic patients suffer from an inability to identify accurately and to respond to emotions, as well as internal cues such as those denoting hunger and satiety. Confusion and mistrust related to bodily functioning has been clinically observed by many writers (Bruch, 1973; Frazier, 1965; Garfinkel & Garner, 1982; Garner & Bemis, Chapter 6, this volume; Goodsitt, 1977 and Chapter 4, this volume; Selvini-Palazzoli, 1978). Selvini-Palazzoli (1978) has labeled the anorexic patient's profound mistrust of her own impulses and body "intrapsychic paranoia." Although the empirical confirmation of these areas of disturbed functioning is not compelling, a number of studies have suggested that anorexic patients have poor perceptions of their internal states (for a review, see Garfinkel & Garner, 1982).

Self-Concept Deficits

Again, Bruch (1962, 1970, 1973, 1977, 1982) has repeatedly noted that the primary deficit in anorexia nervosa is an "overwhelming sense of ineffectiveness," in which self-starvation is the manifestation of a struggle for autonomy, competence, control, and self-respect. According to this view, the parents' failure to recognize and confirm their daughter's independent needs leads to serious psychological deficits. The disorder involves the misinterpretation of thinness as specialness and of starvation as self-control. Others have observed similar themes in anorexia nervosa and have offered a range of developmental theories to support their views (Casper, 1982, 1983b; Goodsitt, 1969, 1977, and Chapter 4, this volume; Masterson, 1977; Rampling, 1978; Selvini-Palazzoli, 1974; Sours, 1969, 1980). From the perspective of cognitive psychology, we have described principles for modifying self-concept deficits common in anorexia nervosa and bulimia (Garner & Bemis, Chapter 6, this volume; Garner *et al.*, 1982).

Fears of Psychobiological Maturity

Crisp and others have contended that the central psychopathology in anorexia nervosa is rooted in the biological and psychological experiences associated with an adult weight (Crisp, 1967, 1980; Kalucy, 1978; Palmer, 1979). Starvation becomes the mechanism for avoiding psychobiological maturity, because it results in a return to prepubertal appearance, hormonal status, and experience (Crisp, 1980). This regression is reinforced by the relief it provides from adolescent turmoil and related conflicts within the family. Crisp (1981) views the causes of bulimia as similar to those precipitating anorexia nervosa, the major difference being that the nonemaciated bulimia patient has failed to achieve the much-coveted prepubescent shape.

Family Conflicts

Some of the earliest descriptions of anorexia nervosa emphasized the role of the family in the development of the disorder (Charcot, 1889; Gull, 1874; Lasegue, 1873/1964). More recently, Bruch (1973) has suggested family features that are usually associated with anorexia nervosa. These involve a failure by the parents to verify the child's competence in functioning as an independent person. There is often a facade of "super togetherness" and stability that covers deep discontentment on the part of one or both parents. Selvini-Palazzoli (1974) has observed similar themes and has commented on the ambiguous communication patterns within the family. The theme of faulty family interaction has been more fully elaborated by the group at the Philadelphia Child Guidance Clinic (Liebman, Minuchin, & Baker, 1974; Minuchin, Rosman, & Baker, 1978; Rosman, Minuchin, Liebman, & Baker, 1976; Sargent, Liebman, & Silver, Chapter 12, this volume). They have described the interactional patterns of enmeshment, overprotectiveness, conflict avoidance, and rigidity as characteristic of anorexic families. Empirical attempts to identify prototypical parental personality profiles or family interactional patterns have generally failed to support the clinical observations (Crisp *et al.*, 1980; Garfinkel *et al.*, 1983; Hall & Brown, 1983; Kalucy, Crisp, & Harding, 1977); however, this may be due to the extraordinary methodological problems inherent in family studies. For example, several authors have commented on the serious problem of separating preexisting factors from the disturbed family functioning that could be expected to result from having a serious illness in the family (Garfinkel *et al.*, 1983; Yager, 1982).

Several recent studies have found that bulimic patients experience a more chaotic family life, or at least perceive it to be more distressing than restricting anorexia nervosa patients (Garner, Garfinkel, & O'Shaughnessy, in press; Strober, 1981b, 1984; Strober, Salkin, Burroughs, & Morrell, 1982).

Relationship to Depression

It has recently been postulated that anorexia nervosa and bulimia actually may represent variants of depression (Cantwell, Sterzenberger, Burroughs, Salkin, & Green, 1977; Hudson, Laffer, & Pope, 1982; Hudson, Pope, Jonas, & Yurgelun-Todd, 1983; Winocur, March, & Mendels, 1980). The rationale for this contention rests on several observations. First, many individuals with eating disorders experience the symptoms of depression (Eckert, Goldberg, Halmi, Casper, & Davis, 1982; C. Johnson & Larson, 1982; Lacey, 1983; Palmer, 1979; Russell, 1979; Strober, 1981b). Second, several studies have found higher-than-expected incidences of primary affective disorder and alcoholism among first-degree relatives of anorexic or bulimic patients (Hudson *et al.*, 1983; Strober *et al.*, 1982). Third, while some recent studies have suggested that eating disorders share some neuroendocrine abnormalities with depression that are not an artifact of low weight (Gwirtsman, Roy-Byrne, Yager, & Gerner, 1983), most studies are more equivocal in their results and interpretations (see T. Walsh, 1982, for a review). Finally, some have reported symptom improvement following the administration of antidepressant medications (Pope, Hudson, Jonas, & Yurgelun-Todd, 1983).

As Cooper and Fairburn (1983) have argued, it may be premature to conclude that anorexia nervosa and bulimia have the same etiology as depression. Depressed mood is a by-product of starvation and electrolyte disturbances. Moreover, it is important to note that the co-occurrence of bulimia and a family history of depression does not indicate a causal link between these disorders or their determinants (Cooper & Fairburn, 1983; Strober et al., 1982; T. Walsh, 1982).

Other Personality Features

A review of the extensive literature on personality features associated with anorexia nervosa and bulimia is well beyond the scope of this chapter; however, several observations have emerged repeatedly. Anorexic patients have been found to be obsessional, introverted, socially anxious, conscientious, perfectionistic, competitive, overcontrolled, socially dependent, shy, and "neurotic" (see Garfinkel & Garner, 1982; Garner, Olmsted, & Polivy, 1983; King, 1963; Solyom, Freeman, Thomas, & Miles, 1983; Strober, 1980). However, Morgan and Russell (1975) have observed normal personality development in some patients.

Recently, much attention has been focused on differentiating bulimic patients from those with the "restricting" subtype of anorexia nervosa. Most studies have found the bulimics to be impulsive, prone to addictive behaviors, emotionally turbulent, and depressed (Casper, Eckert, Halmi, Goldberg, & Davis, 1980; Garfinkel et al., 1980; Lacey, 1982; Strober, 1981b; Strober et al., 1982). Recent studies have found similarities between anorexic bulimics and patients with bulimia who have never been emaciated (Garner, Garfinkel, & O'Shaughnessy, in press; Norman & Herzog, 1983). Nevertheless, there appears to be a growing consensus that there is no one personality structure characteristic of either anorexia nervosa or bulimia. Psychological typologies have been empirically derived; these differ in qualitative terms, as well as in the degree to which they reflect impairment (e.g., Garner, Olmsted, & Garfinkel, 1983; Garner, Olmsted, Polivy, & Garfinkel, 1984; Strober, 1983). Growing evidence supports the view that anorexia nervosa and bulimia are multidetermined and multidimensional syndromes; they develop in different people at different times for different reasons. In some instances, bulimia may occur in the absence of primary psychological disturbance. However, the emotional consequences of chaotic eating patterns and the often dangerous attempts to compensate for the loss of control have a profound impact on the individual.

CAVEATS AND CONCLUSIONS

Bulimia and anorexia nervosa are complex disorders that are caused and then maintained by various social, psychological, and biological factors. The current chapter selectively reviews research findings related to semistarvation, weight regulation, dieting, obesity, and the cultural milieu that appear to bear upon the development and perpetuation of these disorders. However, we believe that it is important to emphasize several points.

First, *we have not attempted a comprehensive review of all of the scientific literature related to each of the points of emphasis*. Each of the areas surveyed (e.g., weight regulation, dieting, etc.) is enormous; each has inspired countless books, monographs, and scientific articles. We have no pretensions that our selective review of studies and viewpoints is complete. Evidence has been presented that relates specifically to issues of therapeutic relevance. Moreover, we recognize that many areas are filled with far more controversy than is apparent from our presentation. Thus, while the preceding material does not represent an arbitrary point of view, it does not impartially present all of the contradictory evidence related to every issue.

Second, *we do not suggest that psychoeducational material should be a substitute for psychotherapy.* As noted earlier, our selective focus is not meant to disavow the importance of psychological mediators in eating disorders. There is adequate evidence indicating that food and the body can become the battleground for a variety of psychological and interpersonal conflicts. Although some patients improve simply through understanding more about the social and biological contradictions with which they have been struggling, the majority find some type of therapeutic intervention necessary.

In conclusion, it has been our intention in the current chapter to emphasize the social and biological factors that play a role in anorexia nervosa and bulimia; it has been our experience that many patients and psychotherapists are less familiar with these areas. Many patients appear to benefit from a limited understanding of the scientific basis for our recommendations that they alter their eating patterns and attitudes toward food, weight, and their bodies.

ACKNOWLEDGMENTS

We are very grateful to Victoria Mitchell, Vanessa Boratto, and Mary Deacon for their valuable assistance in the preparation of this manuscript. This work was supported by grants from Health and Welfare Canada, the Ontario Mental Health Foundation, and the Medical Research Council of Canada (Scholarship to David M. Garner).

REFERENCES

Abraham, S. F., & Beumont, P. J. V. (1982). How patients describe bulimia or binge eating. *Psychological Medicine, 12,* 628–635.

Adam, J. M., Best, T. W., & Edholm, O. B. (1961). Weight changes in young men. *Journal of Physiology* (London), *156,* 38.

Adler, A. G., Walinsky, P., Krall, R. A., & Cho, S. Y. (1980). Death resulting from ipecac syrup poisoning. *Journal of the American Medical Association, 243,* 1927–1928.

Allon, N. (1975). Latent social services in group dieting. *Social Problems, 32,* 59–69.

Andres, R. (1980). Effect of obesity on total mortality. *International Journal of Obesity, 4,* 381.

Apfelbaum, M. (1976). The effects of very restrictive high protein diets. *Clinics in Endocrinology and Metabolism, 5,* 417–430.

Apfelbaum, M., Bostsarron, J., & Lacatis, D. (1971). Effect of caloric restriction and excessive caloric intake on energy expenditure. *American Journal of Clinical Nutrition, 24,* 1405–1409.

Ashworth, N., Creedy, S., Hunt, J., Mahon, S., & Newland, P. (1962). Effects of nightly supplements on food intake in man. *Lancet, ii,* 685.

Beck, A. T. (1976). *Cognitive therapy and the emotional disorders.* New York: International Universities Press.

Beck, S. B., Ward-Hull, C. I., & McLear, P. M. (1976). Variables related to women's somatic preferences of the male and female body. *Journal of Personality and Social Psychology, 34,* 1200–1210.

Bennett, W. B., & Gurin, J. (1982). *The dieter's dilemma: Eating less and weighing more.* New York: Basic Books.

Berscheid, E., Walster, E., & Bohrnstedt, G. (1973, November). The happy American body: A survey report. *Psychology Today,* pp. 119–131.

Beumont, P. J. V., George, G. C. W., & Smart, D. E. (1976). "Dieters" and "vomiters and purgers" in anorexia nervosa. *Psychological Medicine, 6,* 617-622.

Bjorntorp, P., & Yang, M. U. (1982). Refeeding after fasting in the rat: Effects on body composition and food efficiency. *American Journal of Clinical Nutrition, 36,* 444-449.

Bjorntorp, P., Yang, M. U., & Greenwood, M. R. C. (1983). Refeeding after fasting in the rat: Effects of carbohydrate. *American Journal of Clinical Nutrition, 37,* 396-402.

Bo-Lynn, G., Santa-Ana, C. A., Morawski, S. G., & Fordtran, J. S. (1983). Purging and calorie absorption in bulimic patients and normal women. *Annals of Internal Medicine, 99,* 14-17.

Boskind-Lodahl, M. (1976). Cinderella's step-sisters: A feminist perspective on anorexia nervosa and bulimia. *Signs: Journal of Women in Culture and Society, 2,* 342-356.

Boyle, P. C., Storlien, H., & Keesey, R. E. (1978). Increased efficiency of food utilization following weight loss. *Physiology and Behavior, 21,* 261.

Bradley, P. J. (1982). Is obesity an advantageous adaptation? *International Journal of Obesity, 6,* 43-52.

Brady, W. F. (1980). The anorexia nervosa syndrome. *Oral Surgery, 50,* 509-516.

Bray, G. A. (1969). Effect of caloric restriction on energy expenditures in obese patients. Lancet, *ii,* 397.

Bray, G. A. (1970). Metabolic and regulatory obesity in rats and man. *Hormones, Metabolism and Research, 2,* 175-180.

Bray, G. A. (1976). The risks and disadvantages of obesity. *Major Problems in Internal Medicine, 9,* 215-251.

Bray, G. A. (1979). Obesity in America: An overview of the Second Fogarty International Centre Conference on obesity. *International Journal of Obesity, 3,* 363-375.

Brotman, M. C., Forbath, N., Garfinkel, P. E., & Humphrey, J. (1981). Ipecac syrup poisoning in anorexia nervosa. *Canadian Medical Association Journal, 125,* 453-454.

Brownell, K. D., & Stunkard, A. J. (1980). Physical activity in the development and control of obesity. In A. J. Stunkard (Ed.), *Obesity* (pp. 300-324). Philadelphia: W. B. Saunders.

Bruch, H. (1962). Perceptual and conceptual disturbances in anorexia nervosa. *Psychosomatic Medicine, 24,* 187-194.

Bruch, H. (1970). Instinct and interpersonal experience. *Comprehensive Psychiatry, 11,* 495-506.

Bruch, H. (1973). *Eating disorders: Obesity, anorexia nervosa and the person within.* New York: Basic Books.

Bruch, H. (1977). Psychological antecedents of anorexia nervosa. In R. A. Vigersky (Ed.), *Anorexia nervosa* (pp. 1-10). New York: Raven Press.

Bruch, H. (1978). *The golden cage: The enigma of anorexia nervosa.* Cambridge, MA: Harvard University Press.

Bruch, H. (1982). Anorexia nervosa: Therapy and theory. *American Journal of Psychiatry, 139,* 1531-1538.

Brundtland, G. H., Liestol, K., & Walloe, L. (1980). Height, weight and menarcheal age of Oslo schoolchildren during the last 60 years. *Annals of Human Biology, 7,* 307-322.

Brunner, D., Weissbort, J., Fischer, M., Bearman, J. E., Leoble, K., Schwartz, S., & Levis, S. (1979). Serum lipid response to a high caloric high fat diet in agricultural workers during 12 months. *American Journal of Clinical Nutrition, 32,* 1342.

Burskirk, E., Thompson, R., Lutwak, L., & Whedon, G. (1963). Energy balance of obese patients during weight loss reduction: Influence of diet restriction and exercise. *Annals of the New York Academy of Science, 110,* 918.

Cabanac, M., Duclaux, R., & Spector, N. H. (1971). Sensory feedback regulation of body weight: Is there a ponderstat? *Nature, 229,* 125-127.

Canning, H., & Mayer, J. (1966). Obesity: Its possible effect on college acceptance. *New England Journal of Medicine, 275,* 1172-1174.

Cantwell, D. P., Sturzenberger, S., Burroughs, J., Salkin, B., & Green, J. K. (1977). Anorexia nervosa: An affective disorder? *Archives of General Psychiatry, 34,* 1087-1093.

Casper, R. C. (1982). Treatment principles in anorexia nervosa. *Adolescent Psychiatry, 10,* 86-100.

Casper, R. C. (1983a). On the emergence of bulimia nervosa as a syndrome: A historical view. *International Journal of Eating Disorders, 2,* 3-16.

Casper, R. C. (1983b). Some provisional ideas concerning the psychologic structure in anorexia nervosa and bulimia. In P. L. Darby, P. E. Garfinkel, D. M. Garner, & D. V. Coscina (Eds.), *Anorexia nervosa: Recent developments* (pp. 387-392). New York: Alan R. Liss.

Casper, R. C., Eckert, E. D., Halmi, K. A., Goldberg, S. C., & Davis, J. M. (1980). Bulimia. *Archives of General Psychiatry, 37,* 1030-1035.

Casper, R. C., Halmi, K. A., Goldberg, S. C., Eckert, E. D., & Davis, J. M. (1979). Disturbances in body image estimation as related to other characteristics and outcome in anorexia nervosa. *British Journal of Psychiatry, 134*, 60–66.

Casper, R. C., Offer, D., & Ostrov, E. (1981). The self-image of adolescents with acute anorexia nervosa. *Journal of Pediatrics, 98*, 656–661.

Charcot, J. M. (1889). *Diseases of the nervous system*. London: New Sydenham Society.

Cho, M., & Fryer, B. A. (1974). Nutritional knowledge of collegiate physical education majors. *Journal of the American Dietetic Association, 65*, 30–34.

Chiodo, J., & Latimer, P. R. (1983). Vomiting as a learned weight-control technique in bulimia. *Journal of Behavior Therapy and Experimental Psychiatry, 14*, 131–135.

Clarke, M. G., & Palmer, R. L. (1983). Eating attitudes and neurotic symptoms in university students. *British Journal of Psychiatry, 142*, 299–304.

Cleary, M. P., & Vasselli, J. R. (1981). Reduced organ growth when hyperphagia is prevented in genetically obese (fa/fa) Zucker rats. *Proceedings of the Society of Experimental Biology and Medicine, 167*, 616–623.

Cleary, M. P., Vasselli, J. R., & Greenwood, M. R. C. (1980). Development of obesity in Zucker obese (fafa) rat in absence of hyperphagia. *American Journal of Physiology, 238*, E284–E292.

Clement, P. F., & Hawkins, R. C. (1980). *Pathways to bulimia: Personality correlates, prevalence and a conceptual model*. Paper presented at the meeting of the Association for the Advancement of Behavior Therapy.

Cohn, C., & Joseph, D. (1959). Changes in body composition attendant on force feeding. *American Journal of Physiology, 196*, 965.

Cooper, P. J., & Fairburn, C. G. (1983). Binge-eating and self-induced vomiting in the community: A preliminary study. *British Journal of Psychiatry, 142*, 139–144

Cox, J. E., & Powley, T. L. (1981). Intragastric pair feeding fails to prevent VMH obesity or hyperinsulinemia. *American Journal of Physiology, 240*, E566–E572.

Crisp, A. H. (1967). The possible significance of some behavioral correlates of weight and carbohydrate intake. *Journal of Psychosomatic Research, 11*, 117–131.

Crisp, A. H. (1980). *Anorexia nervosa: Let me be*. New York: Grune & Stratton.

Crisp, A. H. (1981). Anorexia nervosa at a normal weight!: The abnormal–normal weight control syndrome. *International Journal of Psychiatry in Medicine, 11*, 203–233.

Crisp, A. H., Hsu, L. K. G., & Harding, B. (1980). The starving hoarder and voracious spender: Stealing in anorexia nervosa. *Journal of Psychosomatic Research, 24*, 225–231.

Crisp, A. H., & Kalucy, R. S. (1974). Aspects of the perceptual disorder in anorexia nervosa. *British Journal of Medical Psychology, 47*, 349–361.

Crisp, A. H., & McGuiness, B. (1976). Jolly fat: Relation between obesity and psychoneurosis in a general population. *British Medical Journal, 1*, 7–9.

Dally, P. J., & Gomez, J. (1979). *Anorexia nervosa*. London: Heinemann.

Deb, S., Martin, R. J., & Herschberger, T. V. (1976). Maintenance requirement and energetic efficiency of lean and obese Zucker rats. *Journal of Nutrition, 106*, 191–197.

DeLuise, M., Blackburn, G. L., & Flier, J. S. (1980). Reduced activity of the red-cell sodium–potassium pump in human obesity. *New England Journal of Medicine, 303*, 1017–1022.

Drenick, E. J., & Dennin, H. F. (1973). Energy expenditure in fasting obese man. *Journal of Laboratory and Clinical Medicine, 81*, 421–430.

Durnin, J. V. G. A. (1961). "Appetite" and the relationships between expenditure and intake of calories in man. *Journal of Physiology* (London), *156*, 294–306.

Dwyer, J. T., Feldman, J. J., & Mayer, J. (1970). The social psychology of dieting. *Journal of Health and Social Behavior, 11*, 269–287.

Eckert, E. D., Goldberg, S. C., Halmi, K. A., Casper, R. C., & Davis, J. M. (1982). Depression in anorexia nervosa. *Psychological Medicine, 12*, 115–122.

Edeleman, B. (1981). Binge eating in normal weight and overweight individuals. *Psychological Reports, 49*, 739–746.

Edwards, O. M., & Dent, R. G. (1979). Idiopathic oedema. *Lancet, i*, 670.

Epling, W. F., Pierce, W. D., & Stefan, L. (1983). A theory of activity-based anorexia. *International Journal of Eating Disorders, 3*, 27–46.

Fairburn, C. G. (1981). A cognitive–behavioral approach to the management of bulimia. *Psychological Medicine, 141*, 631–633.

Fairburn, C. G. (1982). *Binge-eating and bulimia nervosa*. London: Smith, Kline & French.

Fairburn, C. G., & Cooper, P. J. (1982). Self-induced vomiting and bulimia nervosa: An undetected problem. *British Medical Journal*, *284*, 1153-1155.

Fantino, M., & Cabanac, M. (1980). Body weight regulation with a proportional hoarding response in the
rat. *Physiology and Behavior*, *24*, 939-942.

Faust, I. M. (1981). Factors which affect adipocyte formation in the rat. In P. Bjorntorp, M. Cairella,
& A. N. Howard (Eds.), *Recent advances in obesity research* (pp. 52-57). London: John Libbey.

Faust, I. M., Johnson, P. R., & Hirsch, J. (1977). Surgical removal of adipose tissue alters feeding behavior
and the development of obesity in rats. *Science*, *197*, 393-396.

Feeling fat in a thin society. (1984, February). *Glamour Magazine*, pp. 198-201, 251-252.

Fitzgerald, F. T. (1981). The problem of obesity. *Annual Review of Medicine*, *32*, 221-231.

Foreyt, J. P., Goodrick, G. K., & Otto, A. M. (1981). Limitations of behavioral treatment of obesity:
Review and analysis. *Journal of Behavioral Medicine*, *4*, 159-174.

Fox, F. W. (1973). The enigma of obesity. *Lancet*, *2*, 1487-1488.

Frazier, S. H. (1965). Anorexia nervosa. *Diseases of the Nervous System*, *26*, 155-159.

Freeman, R. J., Thomas, C. D., Solyom, L., & Miles, J. E. (1983). Body image disturbance in anorexia
nervosa: A reexamination and a new technique. In P. L. Darby, P. E. Garfinkel, D. M. Garner, & D.
V. Coscina (Eds.), *Anorexia nervosa: Recent developments* (pp. 117-128). New York: Alan R. Liss.

Frisch, R. E. (1983). Fatness and reproduction: Delayed menarche and amenorrhea of ballet dancers and
college athletes. In P. L. Darby, P. E. Garfinkel, D. M. Garner, & D. V. Coscina (Eds.), *Anorexia
nervosa: Recent developments* (pp. 343-364). New York: Alan R. Liss.

Garfinkel, P. E., & Garner, D. M. (1982). *Anorexia nervosa: A multidimensional perspective*. New York:
Brunner/Mazel.

Garfinkel, P. E., Garner, D. M., Rose, J., Darby, P. L., Brandes, J., O'Hanlon, J., & Walsh, N. (1983).
A comparison of characteristics in the families of patients with anorexia nervosa and normal controls. *Psychological Medicine*, *13*, 821-828.

Garfinkel, P. E., Moldofsky, H., & Garner, D. M. (1977). Prognosis in anorexia nervosa as influenced
by clinical features, treatment and self-perception. *Canadian Medical Association Journal*, *117*,
1041-1045.

Garfinkel, P. E., Moldofsky, H., & Garner, D. M. (1980). The heterogeneity of anorexia nervosa. *Archives of General Psychiatry*, *37*, 1036-1040.

Garner, D. M., & Bemis, K. M. (1982). A cognitive-behavioral approach to anorexia nervosa. *Cognitive
Therapy and Research*, *6*, 123-150.

Garner, D. M., & Garfinkel, P. E. (1981). Body image in anorexia nervosa: Measurement, theory and clinical
implications. *International Journal of Psychiatry in Medicine*, *11*, 263-284.

Garner, D. M., Garfinkel, P. E., & Bemis, K. M. (1982). A multidimensional psychotherapy for anorexia
nervosa. *International Journal of Eating Disorders*, *1*, 3-46.

Garner, D. M., Garfinkel, P. E., & Olmsted, M. P. (1983). An overview of the socio-cultural factors
in the development of anorexia nervosa. In P. L. Darby, P. E. Garfinkel, D. M. Garner, & D. V.
Coscina (Eds.), *Anorexia nervosa: Recent developments* (pp. 65-82). New York: Alan R. Liss.

Garner, D. M., Garfinkel, P. E., & O'Shaughnessy, M. (in press). The validity of the distinction between
bulimia with and without anorexia nervosa. *American Journal of Psychiatry*.

Garner, D. M., Garfinkel, P. E., Schwartz, D., & Thompson, M. (1980). Cultural expectations of thinness in women. *Psychological Reports*, *47*, 483-491.

Garner, D. M., Garfinkel, P. E., Stancer, H. C., & Moldofsky, H. (1976). Body image disturbance in
anorexia nervosa and obesity. *Psychosomatic Medicine*, *38*, 329-336.

Garner, D. M., Olmsted, M. P., & Garfinkel, P. E. (1983). Does anorexia nervosa occur on a continuum?
Subgroups of weight-preoccupied women and their relationship to anorexia nervosa. *International
Journal of Eating Disorders*, *2*, 11-20.

Garner, D. M., Olmsted, M. P., & Polivy, J. (1983). Development and validation of a multidimensional
eating disorder inventory for anorexia nervosa and bulimia. *International Journal of Eating Disorders*,
2, 15-34.

Garner, D. M., Olmsted, M. P., Polivy, J., & Garfinkel, P. E. (1984). Comparison between weight-
preoccupied women and anorexia nervosa. *Psychosomatic Medicine*.

Garrow, J. S. (1974). *Energy balance and obesity in man*. New York: Elsevier.

Glucksman, M. L., & Hirsch, J. (1969). The response of obese patients to weight reduction. *Psychosomatic
Medicine*, *31*, 1-7.

Goldberg, S. C., Halmi, K. A., Casper, R. C., Eckert, E. D., & Davis, J. M. (1977). Pretreatment predictors of weight change in anorexia nervosa. In R. Vigersky (Ed.), *Anorexia nervosa* (pp. 31–42). New York: Raven Press.

Goldman, R. F., Haisman, M. F., Bynum, G., Horton, E. S., & Sims, E. A. H. (1976). Experimental obesity in man: VII. Metabolic rate in relation to dietary intake. In G. A. Bray (Ed.), *Obesity in perspective* (pp. 165–186) (DHEW Publication No. NIH 75-708). Washington, DC: U.S. Government Printing Office.

Goodman, N., Dornbusch, S. M., Richardson, S. A., & Hastorf, A. H. (1963). Variant reactions to physical disabilities. *American Sociological Review, 28,* 429–435.

Goodsitt, A. (1969). Anorexia nervosa. *British Journal of Medical Psychology, 42,* 109–118.

Goodsitt, A. (1977). Narcissistic disturbances in anorexia nervosa. In S. C. Feinstein and P. L. Giovacchini (Eds.), *Adolescent psychiatry* (Vol. 5, pp. 304–312). New York: Jason Aronson.

Gormally, J., Black, S., Daston, S., & Rardin, D. (1982). Assessment of binge eating severity among obese persons. *Addictive Behaviors, 7,* 47–55.

Gormally, J., Rardin, D., & Black, S. (1980). Correlates of successful response to a behavioral weight control clinic. *Journal of Counseling Psychology, 27,* 179–191.

Gottesfeld, H. (1962). Body and self-cathexis of super-obese patients. *Journal of Psychosomatic Research, 6,* 177.

Gray, S. H. (1977). Social aspects of body image: Perception of normalcy of weight and affect of college undergraduates. *Perceptual and Motor Skills, 45,* 1035–1040.

Greene, R. L. (1980). *The MMPI: An interpretive manual.* New York: Grune & Stratton.

Greenwood, M. R. C., Maggio, C. A., Koopmans, H. S., & Sclafani, A. (1982). Zucker fafa rats maintain their obese body composition ten months after jejunoileal bypass surgery. *International Journal of Obesity, 6,* 513–525.

Greenwood, M. R. C., Quartermain, D., Johnson, P. R., Cruce, J. A. F., & Hirsch, J. (1974). Food motivated behavior in genetically obese and hypothalamic–hyperphagic rats and mice. *Physiology and Behavior, 13,* 687–692.

Gubner, R. S. (1973). Overweight: Some facts, foibles and fallacies. *South African Medical Journal, 47,* 868.

Guidano, V. F. and Liotti, G. (1983). *Cognitive processes and emotional disorders: A structural approach to psychotherapy.* New York: Guilford Press.

Gulick, A. (1922). A study of weight regulation of the adult human body during overnutrition. *American Journal of Physiology, 60,* 371–395.

Gull, W. W. (1874). Apepsia hysterica: Anorexia nervosa. *Transcripts of the Clinical Society of London, 7,* 22–28.

Gwirtsman, H. E., Roy-Byrne, P., Yager, J., & Gerner, R. H. (1983). Neuroendocrine abnormalities in bulimia. *American Journal of Psychiatry, 140,* 559–563.

Hall, A., & Brown, L. B. (1983). A comparison of the attitudes of young anorexia nervosa patients and non-patients with those of their mothers. *British Journal of Medical Psychology, 56,* 39–48.

Halmi, K. A., Falk, J. R., & Schwartz, E. (1981). Binge-eating and vomiting: A survey of a college population. *Psychological Medicine, 11,* 697–706.

Hampton, M. C., Huenemann, R. L., Shapiro, L. R., Mitchell, B. W., & Behnke, A. R. (1966). A longitudinal study of gross body composition and body conformation and their association with food and activity in a teenage population: Anthropometric evaluation of a body build. *American Journal of Clinical Nutrition, 19,* 422–435.

Herman, C. P., & Mack, D. (1975). Restrained and unrestrained eating. *Journal of Personality, 43,* 647–660.

Herman, C. P., & Polivy, J. (1980). Restrained eating. In A. J. Stunkard (Ed.), *Obesity* (pp. 208–225). Philadelphia: W. B. Saunders.

Hibscher, J. (1974). *The effect of free fatty acid and preload level on the subsequent eating behavior of normal weight and obese subjects.* Unpublished doctoral dissertation, Northwestern University.

Himms-Hagen, J. (1981). Nonshivering thermogenesis, brown adipose tissue and obesity. In R. F. Beers, Jr. & E. G. Basset (Eds.), *Nutrition factors: Modulating effects on metabolic processes* (pp. 85–99). New York: Raven Press.

Hirata, K. (1982). Enhanced calorigenesis in brown adipose tissue in physically trained rats. *Japanese Journal of Physiology, 32,* 647–653.

Hirsch, J. (1978). Obesity: A perspective. In G. A. Bray (Ed.), *Recent advances in obesity research* (pp. 1–5). London: Newman.

Hollifield, G. (1968). Glucocorticoid-induced obesity: A model and a challenge. *American Journal of Clinical Nutrition, 21,* 1471.

Horvath, T. (1979). Correlates of physical beauty in men and women. *Social Behavior and Personality*, 7, 145–151.

Horvath, T. (1981). Physical attractiveness: The influence of selected torso parameters. *Archives of Sexual Behavior, 10*, 21–24.

Hsu, L. K. G. (1980). Outcome of anorexia nervosa: A review of the literature (1954–1978). *Archives of General Psychiatry, 37*, 1041–1046.

Hsu, L. K. G., Crisp, A. H., & Harding, B. (1979). Outcome of anorexia nervosa. *Lancet, i*, 61–65.

Hubert, H. B., Feinleib, M., McNamara, P. M., & Castelli, W. P. (1983). Obesity as an independent risk factor for cardiovascular disease: A 26-year follow-up of participants in the Framingham Heart Study. *Circulation, 67*, 968–977.

Hudson, J. I., Laffer, P. S., & Pope, H. G. (1982). Bulimia related to affective disorder by family and response to dexamethasone suppression test. *American Journal of Psychiatry, 139*, 685–687.

Hudson, J. I., Pope, H. G., Jr., Jonas, J. M., & Yurgelun-Todd, D. (1983). Family history study of anorexia nervosa and bulimia. *British Journal of Psychiatry, 142*, 133–138.

Huenemann, R. L., Shapiro, L.R., Hampton, M. C., & Mitchell, B. W. (1966). A longitudinal study of gross body composition and body conformation and their association with food and activity in a teenage population. *American Journal of Clinical Nutrition, 18*, 325–338.

Isner, J., Roberts, W. C., Yager, J., & Heymsfield, S. (1984). QT interval prolongation in anorexia nervosa. Report to the 56th session of the American Heart Association.

Jacobs, D. R., Jr., & Gottenborg, S. (1981). Smoking and weight: The Minnesota Lipid Research Clinic. *American Journal of Public Health, 71*, 391–396.

James, W. P. T., & Trayhurn, P. (1981). Thermogenesis and obesity. *British Medical Bulletin, 1981, 37*, 43–48.

Jeffrey, R. W., & Coates, J. J. (1978). Why aren't they losing weight? *Behavior Therapy, 9*, 856–860.

Johnson, C., Connors, M., & Stuckey, M. (1983). Short-term group treatment for bulimia. *International Journal of Eating Disorders, 2*, 199–208.

Johnson, C., & Larson, R. (1982). Bulimia: An analysis of moods and behavior. *Psychosomatic Medicine, 44*, 333–345.

Johnson, C., Stuckey, M., Lewis, L. D., & Schwartz, D. (1983). Bulimia: A descriptive survey of 509 cases. In P. L. Darby, P. E. Garfinkel, D. M. Garner, & D. V. Coscina (Eds.), *Anorexia nervosa: Recent developments* (pp. 159–172). New York: Alan R. Liss.

Johnson, D., & Drenick, E. J. (1977). Therapeutic fasting in morbid obesity: Long-term follow-up. *Archives of Internal Medicine, 137*, 1381–1382.

Johnson, W. G., & Brief, D. (1983). Bulimia. *Behavioral Medicine Update, 4*, 16–21.

Jourard, S. M., & Secord, P. F. (1955). Body cathexis and the ideal female figure. *Journal of Abnormal and Social Psychology, 50*, 243–246.

Kalucy, R. S. (1978). An approach to the therapy of anorexia nervosa. *Journal of Adolescence, 10*, 197–228.

Kalucy, R. S., Crisp, A. H., & Harding, B. (1977). A study of 56 families with anorexia nervosa. *British Journal of Medical Psychology, 50*, 381–395.

Kaplan, M. L., & Leveille, G. A. (1974). Calorigenic effect of a high protein meal in obese and nonobese subjects. *Federation Proceedings, 33*, 701.

Karris, L. (1977). Prejudice against obese renters. *Journal of Social Psychology, 101*, 159–169.

Keesey, R. E. (1980). A set point analysis of the regulation of body weight. In A. J. Stunkard (Ed.), *Obesity* (pp. 144–165). Philadelphia: W. B. Saunders.

Keesey, R. E. (1983). A hypothalamic syndrome of body weight regulation at reduced levels. In *Understanding anorexia nervosa and bulimia: Report of the Fourth Ross Conference on Medical Research* (pp. 60–66). Columbus, Ohio: Ross Laboratories.

Kennedy, G. C. (1953). The role of depot fat in the hypothalamic control of food intake in the rat. *Proceedings of the Royal Society* (Series B), *140*, 578–592.

Keys, A., Brozek, J., Henschel, A., Mickelsen, O., & Taylor, H. L. (1950). *The biology of human starvation*. Minneapolis: University of Minnesota Press.

Keys, A., Aravanis, G., Blackburn, H., van Buchem, F. S. P., Buzina, R., Djorfevic, B. S., Fidanza, E., Karvonen, M. J., Menotti, A., Puddu, V., & Taylor, H. L. (1972). Coronary heart disease: Overweight and obesity as risk factors. *Annals of Internal Medicine, 77*, 15–27.

Khosha, T., & Billewicz, W. Z. (1964). Measurement of changes in body weight. *British Journal of Nutrition, 18*, 227–239.

King, A. (1963). Primary and secondary anorexia nervosa syndromes. *British Journal of Psychiatry, 109*, 470–479.

Kolata, G. (1980). NIH shaken by death of research volunteer. *Science, 209*, 475–479.

Kleiber, M. (1961). *The fire of life: An introduction to animal energetics.* New York: Wiley.

Kurman, L. (1978). An analysis of messages concerning food, eating behaviors and ideal body image on prime-time American network television. *Dissertation Abstracts International, A*, 1907–1908.

Lacey, J. H. (1982). The bulimic syndrome at normal body weight: Reflections on pathogenesis and clinical features. *International Journal of Eating Disorders, 2*, 59–62.

Lacey, J.H. (1983). Bulimia nervosa, binge eating and psychogenic vomiting: A controlled treatment study and long-term outcome. *British Medical Journal, 286*, 1611–1613.

Lacey, J.H. Chadbund, C., Crisp, A. H., & Whitehead, J. (1978). Dietary patterns in normal schoolgirls. *British Journal of Human Nutrition, 32*, 419.

Lasegue, C. (1964). De l'anorexie hysterique. In R. M. Kaufman and M. Heiman (Eds.), *Evolution of psychosomatic concepts. Anorexia nervosa: A paradigm* (pp. 141–155). New York: International Universities Press. (Original work published 1873).

Lerner, R. M. (1969). The development of stereotyped expectancies of body build–behavior relations. *Child Development, 40*, 137–141.

Lerner, R. M. (1973). The development of personal space schema toward body build. *Journal of Psychology, 84*, 229–235.

Lerner, R. M., & Gelbert, E. (1969). Body build identification, preference and aversion in children. *Developmental Psychology, 5*, 256–262.

Lerner, R. M., & Korn, S. J. (1972). The development of body build stereotypes in males. *Child Development, 43*, 908–920.

Levin, P. A., Falko, J. M., Dixon, K., Gallup, E. M., & Saunders, W. (1980). Benign parotid enlargement in bulimia. *Annals of Internal Medicine, 93*, 827–829.

Levitsky, D. A., Faust, I. M., & Glassman, M. (1976). The ingestion of food and the recovery of body weight following fasting in the naive rat. *Physiology and Behavior, 17*, 575–580.

Liebman, R., Minuchin, S., & Baker, L. (1974). An integrated treatment program for anorexia nervosa. *American Journal of Psychiatry, 131*, 432–436.

Long, G. C., & Cordle, C. J. (1982). Psychological treatment of binge eating and self-induced vomiting. *British Journal of Medical Psychology, 55*, 139–145.

Loro, A. D., & Orleans, C. S. (1981). Binge-eating in obesity: Preliminary findings and guidelines for behavioral analysis and treatment. *Addictive Behaviors, 6*, 155–166.

MacGregor, G. A., Markandu, N. D., Roulston, J. E., Jones, J. C., & deWardener, H. E. (1979). Is "idiopathic oedema idiopathic?". *Lancet, i*, 397–400.

Mahoney, M. J., & Mahoney, K.. (1976). *Permanent weight control.* New York: Norton.

Malmquist, J., Ericsson, B., Hulten-Nosslin, M. B., Jeppsson, J. O., & Ljungberg, O. (1980). Finger-clubbing and aspartylglucosamine excretion in a laxative abusing patient. *Postgraduate Medicine, 56*, 862–864.

Mann, G. V. (1974). The influence of obesity on health. *New England Journal of Medicine, 291*, 178–185.

Masterson, J. F. (1977). Primary anorexia nervosa in the borderline adolescent: An object-relations view. In P. Hartocollis (Ed.), *Borderline personality disorders* (pp. 475–494). New York: International Universities Press.

Matikainen, M. (1979). Spontaneous rupture of the stomach. *American Journal of Surgery, 138*, 451–452.

Mazel, J. (1981). *The Beverly Hills diet.* New York: Macmillan.

McCGraham, N. (1969). The influence of body weight (fatness) on the energetic efficiency of adult sheep. *Australian Journal of Agricultural Research, 20*, 375.

McReynolds, W. T. (1982). Toward a psychology of obesity: Review of research on the role of personality and level of adjustment. *International Journal of Eating Disorders, 2*, 37–57.

Miller, D. S. (1973). *Thermogenesis in everyday life.* Paper presented at the XXVI International Congress of Physiological Sciences, New Delhi.

Miller, D. S., & Mumford, P. (1966). Obesity: Physical activity and nutrition. *Proceedings of the Nutrition Society, 25*, 100.

Miller, D. S., Mumford, P., & Stock, M. (1967). Gluttony: Thermogenesis in overeating man. *American Journal of Clinical Nutrition, 20*, 1123–1229.

Miller, D. S., & Parsonage, S. (1975). Resistance to slimming. *Lancet, i*, 773–775.

Miller, T., Coffman, J., & Linke, R. (1980). Survey on body image, weight and diet of college students.

Journal of the American Dietetic Association, 77, 561–566.

Minuchin, S., Rosman, B. L., & Baker, L. (1978). *Psychosomatic families: Anorexia nervosa in context.* Cambridge, MA: Harvard University Press.

Mirkin, G. B., & Shore, R. N. (1981). The Beverly Hills diet: Dangers of the newest weight loss fad. *Journal of the American Medical Association, 246,* 2235–2237.

Mitchell, J. E., & Pyle, R. L. (1982). The bulimic syndrome in normal weight individuals: A review. *International Journal of Eating Disorders, 1,* 61–73.

Mitchell, J. E., Pyle, R. L., & Eckert, E. D. (1981). Binge eating behavior in patients with bulimia. *American Journal of Psychiatry, 138,* 835–836.

Mitchell, J. E., Pyle, R. L., Eckert, E. D., Hatsukami, D., & Lentz, R. (1983). Electrolyte and other physiological abnormalities in patients with bulimia. *Psychological Medicine, 13,* 273–278.

Mitchell, J. E., Pyle, R. L., & Miner, R. A. (1982). Gastric dilatation as a complication of bulimia. *Psychosomatics, 23,* 96–99.

Mizes, J. S., & Lohr, J. M. (1983). The treatment of bulimia (binge-eating and self-induced vomiting): A quasi-experimental investigation of the effects of stimulus narrowing, self-reinforcement and self-control relaxation. *International Journal of Eating Disorders, 2,* 59–65.

Morgan, H. G., & Russell, G. F. M. (1975). Value of family background and clinical features as predictors of long-term outcome in anorexia nervosa: Four year follow-up of 41 patients. *Psychological Medicine, 5,* 355–371.

Mrosovsky, N., & Powley, T. L. (1977). Set points for body weight and fat. *Behavioral Biology, 20,* 205–223.

Neuman, R. O. (1902). Experimentelle Beitrage zur Lehre von dem Taglichen Nahrungsbedarf des Menschen unter besonderer Berucksichtigung der notwendigen Eiweissmenge. *Archiv. fur Hygiene, 45,* 1–87.

Nisbett, R. E. (1972). Eating behavior and obesity in men and animals. *Advances in Psychosomatic Medicine, 7,* 173–193.

Noppa, H., Bengtsson, C., Wedel, H., & Wilhelmsen, L. (1980). Obesity in relation to morbidity and mortality from cardiovascular disease. *American Journal of Epidemiology, 111,* 682–692.

Norman, D. K., & Herzog, D. B. (1983). Bulimia, anorexia nervosa and anorexia nervosa with bulimia: A comparative analysis of MMPI profiles. *International Journal of Eating Disorders, 2,* 43–52.

Nylander, I. (1971). The feeling of being fat and dieting in a school population: Epidemiologic interview investigation. *Acta Sociomedica Scandinavia, 3,* 17–26.

Orbach, S. (1978). *Fat is a feminist issue.* London: Paddington.

Palmer, R. L. (1979). Dietary chaos syndrome: A useful new term? *British Journal of Medical Psychology, 52,* 187–190.

Peck, J. W. (1978). Rats defend different body weights depending on palatability and accessibility of their food. *Journal of Comparative and Physiological Psychology, 92,* 555–570.

Pertschuk, M. J., Crosby, L. O., & Mullen, J. L. (1981). *Non-linearity of weight gain and nutrition intake in anorexia nervosa.* Paper presented at the Anorexia Nervosa International Conference, Toronto.

Pierloot, R. A., & Houben, M. E. (1978). Estimation of body dimensions in anorexia nervosa. *Psychological Medicine, 8,* 317–324.

Pittet, P., Chappuis, P., Acheson, K., DeTechtermann, F., & Jequier, E. (1976). Thermic effect of glucose in obese subjects studied by direct and indirect calometry. *British Journal of Nutrition, 35,* 281.

Playgirl, June 1975.

Polivy, J. (1976). Perception of calories and regulation of intake in restrained and unrestrained subjects. *Addictive Behaviors, 1,* 237–243.

Pollitt, E., Lewis, N. L., Garza, C., & Shulman, R. J. (1983). Fasting and cognitive functioning. *Journal of Psychiatric Research, 17,* 169–174.

Pope, H. G., Hudson, J. I., Jonas, J. M., & Yurgelun-Todd, D. (1983). Bulimia treated with imipramine: A placebo-controlled, double-blind study. *American Journal of Psychiatry, 140,* 554–558.

Prior, J., & White, I. (1978). Tetany and clubbing in a patient who ingested large quantities of senna. *Lancet, ii,* 947.

Pyle, R. L., Mitchell, J. E., & Eckert, E. D. (1981). Bulimia: A report of 34 cases. *Journal of Clinical Psychiatry, 42,* 60–64.

Pyle, R., Mitchell, J. E., Eckert, E. D., Halverson, P., Neuman, P., & Goff, G. (1983). The incidence of bulimia in freshman college students. *International Journal of Eating Disorders, 2,* 75–85.

Rampling, D. (1978). Anorexia nervosa: Reflections on theory and practice. *Psychiatry, 41,* 296–301.

Rand, C. (1979). Obesity and human sexuality. *Medical Aspects of Human Sexuality, 13,* 140–152.

Richardson, S. A., Goodman, N., Hastorf, A. H., & Dornbusch, S. M. (1961). Cultural uniformity in relation to physical disabilities. *American Sociological Review, 26,* 241–247.

Robinson, M. D., & Watson, P. E. (1965). Day to day variations in body weight of young women. *British Journal of Nutrition, 19,* 225–235.

Romsos, D. R. (1983). Low sympathetic nervous system activity in the brown adipose tissue of obese (ob/ob) mice. In B. C. Hansen (Ed.), *Controversies in obesity* (pp. 122–129). New York: Praeger.

Rosen, J. C., & Leitenberg, H. (1982). Bulimia nervosa: Treatment with exposure and response prevention. *Behavior Therapy, 13,* 117–124.

Rosman, B. L., Minuchin, S., Liebman, R., & Baker, L. (1976). Input and outcome of family therapy in anorexia nervosa. In J. Claghorn (Ed.), *Successful psychotherapy* (pp. 128–139). New York: Brunner/Mazel.

Rothwell, N., & Stock, M. (1979). A role for brown adipose tissue in diet-induced thermogenesis. *Nature, 281,* 31–35.

Rowland, C. V., Jr. (1970). Anorexia nervosa: A survey of the literature and review of 30 cases. *International Psychiatry Clinics, 7,* 37–137.

Rowland, N. E., & Antelman, S. M. (1976). Stress-induced hyperphagia and obesity in rats: A possible model for understanding human obesity. *Science, 191,* 310.

Russell, G. F. M. (1966). Acute dilatation of the stomach in a patient with anorexia nervosa. *British Journal of Psychiatry, 112,* 203–207.

Russell, G. F. M. (1979). Bulimia nervosa: An ominous variant of anorexia nervosa? *Psychological Medicine, 9,* 429–448.

Saul, S. H., Dekker, A., & Watson, C. G. (1981). Acute gastric dilatation with infarction and perforation: Report of fatal outcome in a patient with anorexia nervosa. *Gut, 22,* 978.

Schachter, S., Goldman, R., & Gordon, A. (1968). Effects of fear, food deprivation and obesity on eating. *Journal of Personality and Social Psychology, 10,* 91–97.

Schwartz, R., & Brunzell, J. (1978). Increased adipose tissue lipoprotein lipase activity in moderately obese men after weight reduction. *Lancet, i,* 1230–1231.

Schwartz, R., & Brunzell, J. (1981). Increase of adipose tissue lipoprotein lipsase activity with weight loss. *American Journal of Clinical Investigation, 67,* 1425–1430.

Sclafani, A. (1980). Dietary obesity. In A. J. Stunkard (Ed.), *Obesity* (pp. 166–181). Philadelphia: W. B. Saunders.

Selvini-Palazzoli, M. (1974). *Anorexia nervosa.* London: Chaucer.

Selvini-Palazzoli, M. (1978). *Self-starvation: From individual to family therapy in the treatment of anorexia nervosa.* New York: Jason Aronson.

Silk, D. B. A., Gibson, J. A., & Murray, C. R. H. (1975). Reversible finger clubbing in a case of purgative abuse. *Gastroenterology, 68,* 790–794.

Simon, R. (1963). Obesity as a depressive equivalent. *Journal of the American Medical Association, 183,* 208–210.

Sims, E. A. H. (1976). Experimental obesity, diet-induced thermogenesis and their clinical implications. *Clinics in Endocrinology and Metabolism, 5,* 377–395.

Sims, E. A. H., Goldman, R., Gluck, C., Horton, E. S., Kelleher, P., & Rowe, D. (1968). Experimental obesity in man. *Transcript of the Association of American Physicians, 81,* 153.

Sjostrom, L. (1980). Fat cells and body weight. In A. J. Stunkard (Ed.), *Obesity* (pp. 72–100). Philadelphia: W. B. Saunders.

Slade, P. D. (1982). Towards a functional analysis of anorexia nervosa and bulimia nervosa. *British Journal of Clinical Psychology, 21,* 167–179.

Slade, P. D., & Russell, G. F. M. (1973). Awareness of body dimension in anorexia nervosa: Cross-sectional and longitudinal studies. *Psychological Medicine, 3,* 188–199.

Solyom, L., Freeman, R. J., Thomas, C. D., & Miles, J. E. (1983). The comparative psychopathology of anorexia nervosa: Obsessive–compulsive disorder or phobia? *International Journal of Eating Disorders, 3,* 3–14.

Sorlie, P., Gordon, T., & Kannel, W. B. (1980). Body build and mortality: The Framingham study. *Journal of the American Medical Association, 243,* 1828–1831.

Sours, J. A. (1969). Anorexia nervosa: Nosology, diagnosis, developmental patterns and power-control dynamics. In G. Caplan & S. Lebovici (Eds.), *Adolescence: Psychological perspectives* (pp. 185–212). New York: Basic Books.

Sours, J. A. (1980). *Starving to death in a sea of objects: The anorexia nervosa syndrome.* New York: Jason Aronson.

Spencer, J. A., & Fremouw, W. J. (1979). Binge eating as a function of restraint and weight classification. *Journal of Abnormal Psychology, 88*, 262-267.

Staffieri, J. R. (1967). A study of social stereotype of body image in children. *Journal of Personality and Social Psychology, 7*, 101-104.

Staffieri, J. R. (1972). Body build and behavior expectancies in young females. *Developmental Psychology, 6*, 125-127.

Stege, P., Visco-Dangler, L., & Rye, L. (1982). Anorexia nervosa: Review including oral and dental manifestations. *Journal of the American Dental Association, 104*, 648-652.

Stordy, B. J., Marks, V., Kalucy, R. S., & Crisp, A. H. (1977). Weight gain, thermic effect of glucose and resting metabolic rate during recovery from anorexia nervosa. *American Journal of Clinical Nutrition, 30*, 138-146.

Stout, C., Morrow, T., Brandt, E., & Wolf, S. (1964). Unusually low incidence of death from myocardial infarction in an Italian-American community in Pennsylvania. *Journal of the American Medical Association, 188*, 845.

Strangler, R. S., & Printz, A. M. (1980). DSM-III: Psychiatric diagnosis in a university population. *American Journal of Psychiatry, 137*, 937-940.

Strober, M. (1980). Personality and symptomatological features in young, non-chronic anorexia nervosa patients. *Journal of Psychosomatic Research, 24*, 353-359.

Strober, M. (1981a). The relation of personality characteristics to body image disturbance in juvenile anorexia nervosa: A multivariate analysis. *Psychosomatic Medicine, 43*, 323-330.

Strober, M. (1981b). The significance of bulimia in anorexia nervosa: An exploration of possible etiological factors. *International Journal of Eating Disorders, 1*, 28-43.

Strober, M. (1983). An empirically derived typology of anorexia nervosa. In P. L. Darby, P. E. Garfinkel, D. M. Garner, & D. V. Coscina (Eds.), *Anorexia nervosa: Recent developments* (pp. 185-196). New York: Alan R. Liss.

Strober, M. (1984). Stressful life events associated with bulimia in anorexia nervosa: Empirical findings and theoretical speculations. *International Journal of Eating Disorders, 3*, 3-16.

Strober, M., Goldenberg, I., Green, J. K., & Saxon, J. (1979). Body image disturbance in anorexia nervosa during the acute and recuperative phase. *Psychological Medicine, 9*, 695-701.

Strober, M., Salkin, B., Burroughs, J., & Morrell, W. (1982). Validity of the bulimia-restricter distinction in anorexia nervosa. *Journal of Nervous and Mental Disease, 170*, 345-351.

Stunkard, A. J. (1976). *The pain of obesity*. Palo Alto, CA: Bull.

Stunkard, A. J. (1978). Behavioral treatment of obesity: The current status. *International Journal of Obesity, 2*, 237-248.

Stunkard, A. J., & Penick, S. B. (1979). Behavior modification in the treatment of obesity: The problem of maintaining weight loss. *Archives of General Psychiatry, 36*, 801-806.

Trayhurn, P., Thurlby, P. L., & James, W. P. T. (1977). Thermogenic defect in pre-obese ob/ob mice. *Nature, 266*, 60-61.

Van Itallie, T. B., & Yang, M. U. (1977). Current concepts in nutrition: Diet and weight loss. *New England Journal of Medicine, 297*, 1158.

Walsh, B. T., Katz, J. L., Levin, J., Kream, J., Fukushimo, D. K., Weiner, H., & Zumoff, B. (1981). The production rate of cortisol declines during recovery from anorexia nervosa (Technical note). *Journal of Clinical Endocrinology and Metabolism, 53*, 203-205.

Walsh, T. (1982). Endocrine disturbances in anorexia nervosa and depression. *Psychosomatic Medicine, 44*, 85-91.

Wardle, J. (1980). Dietary restraint and binge eating. *Behavior Analysis and Modification, 4*, 201-209.

Wardle, J., & Beinart, H. (1981). Binge eating: A theoretical review. *British Journal of Clinical Psychology, 20*, 97-109.

Webb, W. L., & Gehi, M. (1981). Electrolyte and fluid imbalance: Neuropsychiatric manifestations. *Psychosomatics, 22*, 199-202.

Weinberg, N., Mendelson, M., & Stunkard, A. J. (1961). A failure to find distinctive personality features in a group of obese men. *American Journal of Psychiatry, 117*, 1035-1037.

Welch, G. J. (1979). The treatment of compulsive vomiting and obsessive thoughts through graduated response delay, response prevention and cognitive correction. *Journal of Behavioral Therapy and Experimental Psychiatry, 10*, 77-82.

Wigley, R. D. (1960). Potassium deficiency in anorexia nervosa, with reference to renal tubular vacuolation. *British Medical Journal, 2*, 110-113.

Wing, R. R., & Jeffrey, R. W. (1979). Outpatient treatments of obesity: A comparison of methodology and clinical results. *International Journal of Obesity, 3,* 261–272.

Wingate, B. A., & Christie, M. J. (1978). Ego-strength and body image in anorexia nervosa. *Journal of Psychosomatic Research, 22,* 201–204.

Winocur, A., March, V., & Mendels, J. (1980). Primary affective disorder in relatives of patients with anorexia nervosa. *American Journal of Psychiatry, 137,* 695–698.

Wolff, H. P., Vecsei, P., Kruck, F., Roscher, S., Brown, J. J., Dusterdieck, G. O., Lever, A. F., & Robertson, J. I. S. (1968). Psychiatric disturbance leading to potassium depletion, sodium depletion, raised plasma-renin concentration and secondary hyperaldosteronism. *Lancet, i,* 257–261.

Woo, R., Garrow, J. S., & Pi-Sunyer, F. X. (1982). Voluntary food intake during prolonged exercise in obese women. *American Journal of Clinical Nutrition, 36,* 478–484.

Wooley, O. W., & Wooley, S. C. (1982). The Beverly Hills eating disorder: The mass marketing of anorexia nervosa (editorial). *International Journal of Eating Disorders, 1,* 57–69.

Wooley, O. W., Wooley, S. C., & Dyrenforth, S. R. (1979). Obesity and women. II. A neglected feminist topic. *Women's Studies International Quarterly, 2,* 81–92.

Wooley, S. C., & Wooley, O. W. (1979). Obesity and women: I. A closer look at the facts. *Women's Studies International Quarterly, 2,* 67–79.

Wooley, S. C., Wooley, O. W., & Dyrenforth, S. R. (1979). Theoretical, practical and social issues in behavioral treatments of obesity. *Journal of Applied Behavioral Analysis, 12,* 3–25.

Yager, J. (1982). Family in the pathogenesis of anorexia nervosa. *Psychosomatic Medicine, 44,* 43–60.

Zucker, L. M., & Zucker, T. F. (1961). Fatty: A new mutation in the rat. *Journal of Heredity, 52,* 275–278.

Author Index

Holland, A. J., 215, 238*n.*
Hollifield, G., 533, 566*n.*
Hollister, L. E., 355, 359*n.*, 454, 457*n.*
Hollon, S. D., 142, 145*n.*
Holt, S., 350, 358*n.*
Hood, J., 130, 145*n.*
Horney, K., 119, 145*n.*
Horowitz, L., 397, 398, 429*n.*
Horton, E. S., 531, 532, 550, 566*n.*, 570*n.*
Horvath, T., 515, 567*n.*
Houben, M. E., 558, 569*n.*
Houts, P. S., 219, 224, 239*n.*
Hsu, L. K. G., 107, 142, 145*n.*, 193, 208*n.*,
    398, 429*n.*, 523, 541, 559, 564*n.*, 567*n.*
Hubbard, F. A., 217, 223, 233, 238*n.*, 317,
    326, 333, 343*n.*
Hubert, H. B., 521, 567*n.*
Hudson, J. I., 26, 51*n.*, 166, 192*n.*, 243,
    248, 252*n.*, 253*n.*, 325, 343*n.*, 355,
    358*n.*, 438, 457*n.*, 560, 567*n.*, 569*n.*
Hueneman, R. L., 518, 566*n.*, 567*n.*
Hulten-Nosslin, M. B., 557, 568*n.*
Humphrey, J., 349, 357*n.*, 555, 563*n.*
Hunt, J., 531, 562*n.*
Hunter, M., 129, 143*n.*
Hurst, P. S., 436, 456*n.*

Isner, J., 555, 567*n.*

Jacob, R. A., 110, 143*n.*
Jacobs, D. R., Jr., 537, 567*n.*
Jacobson, E., 365, 389*n.*
James, W. P. T., 532, 567*n.*, 571*n.*
Jarvis, J. H., 398, 429*n.*
Jazwinski, C., 161, 176, 192*n.*, 193, 209*n.*
Jeejeebhoy, K. N., 350, 358*n.*
Jeffrey, D., 244, 252*n.*
Jeffrey, R. W., 534, 567*n.*, 571*n.*
Jeppsson, J. O., 557, 568*n.*
Jequier, E., 532, 569*n.*
Jessner, J., 398, 399, 429*n.*
Jessner, L., 60, 81*n.*, 134, 145*n.*
Johnson, C., 24–26, 28, 29, 50*n.*, 55, 82*n.*,
    82*n.*, 193, 195, 196, 208*n.*, 209*n.*, 245,
    252*n.*, 514, 551, 555, 558, 560, 567*n.*
Johnson, D., 534, 567*n.*
Johnson, P. R., 534, 535, 565*n.*, 566*n.*
Johnson, V. E., 244, 252*n.*
Johnson, W. G., 194, 208*n.*, 546, 567*n.*
Jonas, J. M., 26, 51*n.*, 243, 253*n.*, 325,
    343*n.*, 355, 358*n.*, 560, 567*n.*, 569*n.*
Jonas, M. D., 166, 192*n.*
Jones, J. C., 543, 568*n.*

Joseph, D., 551, 564*n.*
Jourard, S. M., 518, 567*n.*
Judas, I., 77, 81*n.*

Kalucy, R. S., 23, 50*n.*, 109, 115, 145*n.*,
    368, 389*n.*, 398, 428*n.*, 435, 456*n.*,
    458–460, 462–465, 471, 472, 477, 487*n.*,
    539, 558, 559, 560, 564*n.*, 567*n.*, 571*n.*
Kannel, W. B., 521, 543, 570*n.*
Kaplan, A. S., 355, 358*n.*
Kaplan, M. L., 532, 567*n.*
Karris, L., 520, 567*n.*
Karvonen, M. J., 520, 567*n.*
Katz, J. L., 556, 571*n.*
Katz, R. C., 244, 252*n.*
Katzman, M. A., 194, 208*n.*
Kaufman, M. R., 57, 82*n.*
Kay, D. W. K., 355, 358*n.*
Kaye, W., 327, 343*n.*
Kaywin, L., 397, 429*n.*
Keesey, R. E., 532, 533, 535, 539, 563*n.*,
    567*n.*
Kehrer, H. E, 149, 158*n.*
Kelleher, P., 531, 570*n.*
Kennedy, G. C., 535, 567*n.*
Kennedy, S., 355, 356, 358*n.*
Kernberg, O., 461, 467, 487*n.*
Kestenberg, J., 365, 389*n.*
Keys, A., 27, 50*n.*, 72, 81*n.*, 113, 128,
    145*n.*, 152, 158*n.*, 319, 327, 343*n.*,
    394, 429*n.*, 520, 523–530, 538, 541,
    549, 567*n.*
Khantzian, E., 65, 81*n.*
Khosha, T., 533, 567*n.*
Kiecolt-Glaser, J., 245, 252*n.*
King, A., 110, 145*n.*, 327, 343*n.*, 561, 568*n.*
Kirker, W. S., 129, 146*n.*
Kirschner, B., 110, 143*n.*
Kleiber, M., 538, 568*n.*
Kohut, H., 56, 59, 61, 64, 65, 81*n.*
Kolata, G., 555, 568*n.*
Kolb, J. E., 383, 389*n.*
Kolb, L. C., 398, 399, 429*n.*
Koopmans, H. S., 534, 566*n.*
Korn, S. J., 520, 568*n.*
Krall, R. A., 555, 562*n.*
Kream, J., 556, 571*n.*
Krongrad, E., 350, 359*n.*
Kruck, F., 556, 572*n.*
Krystal, H., 65, 81*n.*
Kubie, L. S., 397, 429*n.*
Kuiper, N. A., 129, 146*n.*
Kurash, C., 61, 82*n.*

Subject Index